28.50
80 R

A+I-3
Sec.1

Reader Series
in Library and Information Science

Published *Readers* in the series are:

Reader in Library Administration. 1969.
Paul Wasserman and Mary Lee Bundy.

Reader in Research Methods of Librarianship. 1970.
Mary Lee Bundy and Paul Wasserman.

Reader in the Academic Library. 1970.
Michael M. Reynolds.

Reader in Library Services and the Computer. 1971.
Louis Kaplan.

Reader in American Library History. 1971.
Michael H. Harris.

Reader in Classification and Descriptive Cataloging. 1972.
Ann F. Painter.

Reader in Library Cooperation. 1972.
Michael M. Reynolds

Reader in Technical Services. 1973.
Edward L. Applebaum.

Reader in Medical Librarianship. 1973.
Winifred Sewell.

Reader in Government Documents. 1973.
Fredric J. O'Hara.

Reader in Documents of International Organizations

edited by

Robert D. Stevens

and

Helen C. Stevens

1973

Microcard Editions Books

An Indian Head Company

A Division of Information Handling Services

Foreword

Unlike many other academic disciplines, librarianship has not yet begun to exploit the contributions of the several disciplines toward the study of its own issues. Yet the literature abounds with material germane to its concerns. Too frequently the task of identifying, correlating, and bringing together material from innumerable sources is burdensome, time consuming or simply impossible. For a field whose stock in trade is organizing knowledge, it is clear that the job of synthesizing the most essential contributions from the elusive sources in which they are contained is overdue. This then is the rationale for the series, *Readers in Library and Information Science.*

The Readers in Library and Information Science will include books concerned with various broad aspects of the field's interests. Each volume will be prepared by a recognized student of the topic covered, and the content will embrace material from the many different sources from the traditional literature of librarianship as well as from outside the field in which the most salient contributions have appeared. The objectives of the series will be to bring together in convenient form the key elements required for a current and comprehensive view of the subject matter. In this way it is hoped that the core of knowledge, essential as the intellectual basis for study and understanding, will be drawn into focus and thereby contribute to the furtherance of professional education and professional practice in the field.

Paul Wasserman
Series Editor

Contents

V
THE UNITED NATIONS

VI
THE SPECIALIZED AGENCIES OF THE UNITED NATIONS

VII

NON-GOVERNMENTAL AND REGIONAL ORGANIZATIONS

Introduction

The purpose of this volume is to give an insight into the nature and scope of the documents of international organizations and to provide information about the work of documentalists and librarians in making the mass of information available in these documents available to readers. All too many librarians regard government documents and in particular, the documents of international agencies as esoteric, unlike the usual library materials in format and publication pattern, and as presenting problems of acquisitions, control and service so complex and so frustrating that they are best left to the specialist in documents. The result is that international documents are a puzzlement to the general librarian, and a source of frustration to the ill informed administrator; a situation exacerbated by the present general tendency of library school curricula to ignore the question of international documents except for cursory mention in one or at most two sessions of a general course in government documents to which relatively few students are exposed. The information in this volume will allay the fears of the generalist librarian. It also provides the data on which to base additional emphasis on international documents in the library school curriculum.

The documents and work of bi-national international organizations is considered as outside the scope of this volume. The documents of such organizations are normally printed as the documents of one or both of the governments party to the agreement. A partial list of the bi-national organizations in which the U.S. participates appears in the current issue of the *U. S. Government Organization Manual.*

An international organization is defined as a body formed by three or more member states. No reliable count of the number of such international organizations is available. Amos J. Peaslee in his compendium of constitutional documents identifies about a hundred inter-governmental organizations.[1] The earliest such organization extant is the Central Commission for the Navigation of the Rhine founded in the nineteenth century. The majority of such organizations, however, sixty-five of the hundred, were founded after 1944. Unofficial international organizations follow roughly the same pattern of proliferation in the years following World War II. They are far more numerous than the international governmental organizations and have received surprisingly little attention from librarians and documentalists. An exception to the general rule is the article by Katherine O. Murra about the work of the Library of Congress International Organizations Section which appears in the final section of this book.

The documents of international organizations constitute a sizeable proportion of the world's printing production. From its founding in 1920 to its dissolution in 1945 the League of Nations issued an estimated 150,000 documents. The United Nations issues an estimated 6,000 to 7,000 documents a year or about 150,000 documents since the date of its founding. While no figure for the total publication of the Specialized Agencies of

---

[1] Amos J. Peaslee, *International Governmental Organizations; Constitutional Documents,* The Hague, Nijhoff, 1956.

the United Nations or for the other non-governmental and governmental international agencies is available, their annual output undoubtedly exceeds that of the United Nations proper.

The scope of the documents of international organizations embraces all fields of human knowledge. For the political scientist and the historian they constitute a body of primary sources. The demographer or economist finds in these documents statistical data in a world-wide basis. The subjects covered range from art to atomic energy with particular strength in the social sciences.

The readings in this book have been drawn from a variety of sources. Where possible the official documents of the organizations themselves have been used as the most authoritative sources for describing their functions or documents. The emphasis in this book is on the twentieth century and in particular on the years following 1945.

We wish to express our sincere thanks to Mr. Daitsu Satake, Associate Librarian of Tokyo University Library who provided a study room and whose staff provided cheerful assistance during the initial stages of preparing this work.

Honolulu, Hawaii   Robert D. Stevens
July 1, 1973   Helen C. Stevens

Reader in Documents of International Organizations

I

CHARACTERISTICS OF INTERNATIONAL DOCUMENTS

Apart from the sheer volume of publications the documents of international organizations share certain common characteristics that affect the work of librarians. A large percentage of international documents are issued in series. An even larger percentage are issued in mimeographed rather than printed form. They are not generally available through the normal commercial book-trade. For the most part these documents are ignored by the various national bibliographies and to make matters worse they are not completely recorded by the issuing organizations themselves. Only a fraction of the documents of international organizations are included in the commercially produced indexing and abstracting services. The guides and indexes produced by the international organizations themselves are for the most part incomplete and inadequate in their subject approach. This section presents some of the reasons for these inadequacies and gives an overview of the documents of international organizations.

The Documents and Publications of International Organizations

A. D. Roberts

The nature and importance of international documents is discussed. Proposals for indexing controls by the issuing organizations and for a collective approach to bibliographic control are presented. Recommendations are also made for maintenance of an archival set of the documents of each organization and for improved practices for distribution of documents. This article was originally written by A. D. Roberts, Librarian at the United Nations, as a working paper for UNESCO.

1. INTRODUCTION

1.1 Kinds of Organizations

The organizations from which these documents and publications originate can be divided into the following groups: (a) the United Nations and its Specialized Agencies, (b) other inter-governmental organizations, and (c) non-governmental organizations. Some of these bodies are not restricted to one part of the world, while others are regional in character. When reading this paper one must always bear in mind the differences between international organizations (they are mostly non-governmental) whose documents and publications are concerned with the "scientific" literature of a special subject field and those organizations which are of a diplomatic or administrative character.

1.2 Size of the Problem

The United Nations and its 13 Specialized Agencies are responsible for an increasingly large and important amount of material. A United Nations document (E/818 Rev 1), lists 67 other inter-governmental organizations and there are certainly other associations of states not recorded. Some inter-governmental organizations operate for a limited time only and are then disbanded, while there are also inter-governmental conferences which meet only once and which have no continuing secretariat.

International conferences arranged by inter-governmental organizations produce much material of importance. The October 1 1948 issue of the *List of International Conferences and Meetings* published by the United States Department of State, records 16 of these conferences in progress, 59 scheduled to take place between October 1 1948 and December 1 1949, and 32 tentatively scheduled between those dates. Some conferences are listed which may not produce much documentation of interest to social scientists; however other conferences of importance not recorded in this publication will undoubtedly take place.

The non-governmental organizations are even more numerous. The Department of Public Information of the United Nations assists some 300 of them, while 83 have consultative status with the United Nations. Many others exist, some of which are recorded in the *Annuaire des Organisations Internationales*. Many of these bodies hold regular conferences.

The United States Department of State estimated that there would be approximately 450 international gatherings during 1948 and that most of these would be official meetings at which governmental understandings would be reached.

SOURCE: Reprinted from A. D. Roberts, "The Documents and Publications of International Organizations, "*Revue de la Documentation,* 17 (1950) pp. 3–17.

1.3 Importance of What They Issue

The great majority of the organizations and conferences covered by the figures quoted above are concerned with social science matters, though some of the bodies, in particular some of the non-governmental ones, do not issue much material of interest. Many organizations do, however, publish the results of research of the first importance, as well as secondary compilations of statistics, laws, etc. which are very valuable indeed. What is likely to be of even greater interest to many scholars is the quantity of source material which exists in the papers of most of these organizations. It should also be noted that international organizations primarily concerned with scientific and technical matters have also claims for consideration. They may include economic and legal matters on the agendas of their conferences, they may conclude international agreements, and the operations of these bodies themselves may be the subject of studies made by social scientists.

The extensive scientific study of "the problems involved in international organization and collaboration" called for by resolutions 4.42 of the Unesco Beirut Conference (14) would be greatly assisted by improved bibliographical records.

1.4 Peculiarities of Form of Publication

Some of the material under discussion is published in book, pamphlet or periodical form and in this respect is similar in character to publications issued by commercial publishing houses. International organizations, however, often issue their works in more than one language and they usually distribute, and may publish, in more than one country. National bibliographies, especially those compiled by commercial publishing houses, may be less active in recording works issued by international organizations than they are in entering commercially published books. Few of the publications of the type we are considering, have individual authors and this may make them less easy to trace in bibliographies and catalogues.

International organizations do, however, produce much mimeographed and printed material in other forms. Some of them issue large series of documents which may or may not be in numbered sequences. Sometimes material is produced during the conduct of official business, with no thought of general or even restricted distribution to outside libraries and research workers. Even the archival aspect of preserving copies of these documents is sometimes neglected. Nevertheless they are not infrequently required by persons doing research and it is a serious matter that few libraries have them and that the bibliographies which record them are, on the whole, most inadequate.

It will be necessary to consider directories of international organizations which pay little or no attention to the publications of the organizations they record, for such directories often have to be consulted at the beginning of a search for publications.

During the twentieth century international conferences have been increasingly associated with international organizations; it will be necessary to consider the bibliographies and directories of conferences separately. The best account of the growth of the problem presented by conferences is probably that of Gjelsness (6).

For the purpose of this paper the term "congress" will be considered synonymous with "conference."

Inter-governmental documents and publications may be printed or reprinted by national governments, and useful directories are also published by national governments. Some of the latter are cited later in this report. Where the only source of an international document or publication is in a work issued by a national government, such a work should, of course, be entered in the bibliographies and indexes of the international organization concerned. Where the work issued by the national government is a secondary source, the desirability and feasibility of its entry in such bibliographies and indexes will vary. The problems mentioned in this paragraph are not referred to this paper.

Treaties and other international agreements are sometimes the results of meetings of international organizations, perhaps of organizations which have a temporary existence for the purpose of framing such an agreement. There are bibliographical lacunae in the general field of treaties, but they are not dealt with in this paper.

Many references are made in this paper to the publications of the United Nations. It is hoped that each of these references is helpful in its place; it should, however, be remembered that what is desirable for the documents and publications of the United Nations may not be desirable or feasible for other international organizations. The author has not found it practicable to examine and report on other international organizations with such fullness.

This paper is primarily concerned with making material more accessible to persons doing study and research; it is less concerned with the dissemination of popularized information to the general public.

Although the author of this paper is an employee of the United Nations, the opinions expressed are his own and this paper has no official status.

2. EXISTING BIBLIOGRAPHIES, INDEXES AND DIRECTORIES

2.1 Bibliographies and Indexes

There are few bibliographies and indexes which record the documents and publications of more than one international organization. More use has to be made of the lists of and indexes to their own material issued by individual organizations. With the exception of the United Nations, however, no bibliographies or indexes to items issued by individual international organizations are recorded below. Publications which are not primarily bibliographical have been placed in the directory section.

2.11 Current or Recent Bibliographies and Indexes Covering the Publications of more than one Agency.

Checklist: publications of Specialized Agencies. June 1947- .

Compiled by the Specialized Agencies Section of the Department of Public Information, United Nations, and issued at irregular intervals. Is not exhaustive, but includes the names of pamphlets, etc. issued by the public information departments of the agencies concerned; these latter may not be included in other bibliographies. Latest issue no. 4, December 1948, with Add. 1, 1949.

Documents of international organizations: a selected bibliography. Boston, World Peace Foundation, December 1947- .

Published quarterly; a three-year cumulation is contemplated which will take note of documents originally listed as mimeographed and which have later appeared in printed form. Supported

by a three year grant totalling $12,000 and given jointly by the Rockefeller Foundation, the Carnegie Endowment for International Peace and the Carnegie Corporation. Each issue costs $700 to print (apart from editorial costs); there are 510 paid annual subscriptions at $2.50 each and some 150 copies are distributed free. These figures of costs were given verbally by Mr. Raymond Dennett of the World Peace Foundation.

Goodrich, L. M. Charter of the United Nations: commentary and documents, by L. M. Goodrich and E. Hambro. 2nd ed. Boston, World Peace Foundation, 1949.

Select bibliography, pp. 659-681. An example of an unofficial book with a bibliography which includes a number of the documents and publications of international organizations.

International book news, Boston, World Peace Foundation, 1928-1932.

Was irregular. It recorded the output of intergovernmental organizations with which the World Peace Foundation had made contracts. Some issues listed the publications of more than one agency, others were bibliographies of a single agency or subject.

International organization. Boston, World Peace Foundation, 1947- .

Quarterly; includes a bibliography.

International reporter. New York, Columbia University Press, 1937- .

Monthly, now listing items of the United Nations, the Specialized Agencies and other intergovernmental organizations, which the press has for sale. Some 3,000 copies of each issue are distributed free.

Myers, D. P. Manual of collections of treaties and of collections relating to treaties. Cambridge, Harvard University Press, 1922.

The section "International administration," pp. 426-575, records the publications of several inter-governmental agencies. More recent information about some agencies can be found in *International Agencies in which the United States participates,* which is recorded later as a directory.

Stümke, H. Bibliographie der internationalen Kongresse und Verbände in der preussischen Staatsbibliothek. 1939- .

The first volume deals with medicine; eleven others were planned which would have included volumes dealing with subjects of more interest to social scientists. This first volume does contain some relevant material.

United Nations. Selected bibliography of the Spe-

cialized Agencies related to the United Nations.
1949.

United Nations. Yearbook. 1946-47- . 1947- .
Each issue includes a bibliography listing a
selection of the documents and publications of
the United Nations and its Specialized Agencies.
A French translation of the first volume is
available.

Weekly index to documents and publications of
the United Nations and the Specialized Agencies. 1949- . Lake Success, United Nations.
A subject index, followed by a check list.
Three experimental issues were published early
in 1949. At the time writing it has not been decided whether the work shall be continued or
not. If it is established it will, to some extent,
supersede *Documents of International
Organizations.*

The reading list and digest now included in the
United Nations Bulletin records a selection of the
documents of the United Nations and the Specialized Agencies. Other periodicals, such as the
United States quarterly *Foreign Affairs,* have bibliographies which include a selection of recent items
issued by international organizations. The International Documents Service of the Columbia University Press also prepares from time to time check
lists of sales items issued by individual international organizations with which the press has
contracts.

Some useful information about the publications
of international organizations in pre-20th century
times can be found in the footnotes in *Der Ge-
danke der internationalen Organisation in seiner
Entwicklung,* by J. ter Meulen. The Hague,
Nijhoff, 1917-1940 (3 vols.).

2.12 United Nations

The list below is selective only and it excludes
items issued by the Specialized Agencies. At the
time of writing a fuller, but also incomplete, bibliography of the bibliographies and indexes issued
by both the United Nations and its Specialized
Agencies is being prepared in the United Nations.

United Nations Conference on International
Organization.

1. Cumulative list of documents issued. 1945.
   Document number 1184, G/125.
2. List of documents arranged by symbols.
   Document number 1216, G/134.

Archives References Guides.

1. Index to the documents of the United Nations Preparatory Commission, 1945-1946,
   1947.
2. Index to the documents of the Executive
   Committee of the United Nations Preparatory Commission, 1945. 1948.
6. Subject guide to United Nations documents
   symbols, August 1945-April 1948. 1949.

These three documents have not received general distribution.

Preliminary cumulative list of documents in un-
restricted series issued by the General Assembly,
Security Council, Atomic Energy Commission,
Economic and Social Council and its commis-
sions, International Health Conference to 31
July 1946.

Check list of United Nations documents. 1949- .
Issued in parts, each part being devoted to the
documentation of a particular ogran. The first
number of any part will be retrospective to the
beginning of the organ concerned and subsequent numbers will be issued currently after
each session. The principal bibliographical features of these volumes are the check lists themselves (arranged in document symbol order) and
the subject indexes to these check lists. They
are exhaustive of both sales publications and
documents. Information about unpublished
records of meetings, sound recordings deposited
in the archives of the United Nations, press releases, etc. is also included.

The following numbers have been published
to date:

4, no. 1. Trusteeship Council 1947/48.
First and second sessions. 1949.

4, no. 2. Trusteeship Council 1948. Third
session. 1949.

5, no. 1. Economic and Social Council
1946-1947. First to fifth session.
1949.

6H, no. 1. Fiscal Commission 1947-1948.
First session. 1949.

Documents distributed. Documents IC/Docs/1 to
IC/Docs/487.
Published between 27 May 1946 and 19 July
1948. It should also be noted that a section
"Documents distributed" is included in the
Journal of the General Assembly, a publication
which appears when that body is sitting.

Bibliographies and indexes are also included in
the different "Information Series" of documents

which various organs of the United Nations issue. Other special bibliographies are included, on occasion, in other document series, and there is a separate series which is almost entirely bibliographical in character and which is called "Index Notes." Items included in the latter series are, for the most part, bibliographies or indexes to the documents of more than one organ. The "Index Notes," the *Check List* quoted above, and a number of the other special bibliographies are prepared by the Documents Index Unit, Library Services, United Nations. Some of these works index parts of documents as well as the documents as individual entities.

United Nations publications. Catalogue no. [with Supplement no. 1.] 1947.
Prepared by the Sales Section of the United Nations and restricted to sales documents. A revised and expanded edition will appear as soon as possible during 1949, and it is hoped to follow it by annual supplements with new editions over longer periods.
New United Nations publications placed on sale, Aug. 1947- .
Monthly, mimeographed. Has limited distribution to sales agents, other international organizations, etc.

Various other organizations away from Lake Success have prepared indexes to the documents and publications of the United Nations, primarily for their own use. Sales publications of the United Nations are entered in some national bibliographies, e.g. the *Cumulative Book Index* and *Whitaker's Cumulative Book List,* and His Majesty's Stationery Office in Great Britain issues a separate catalogue of them. Sales publications, together with a selection of documents are recorded in the *Cumulative Catalog of Library of Congress printed cards.*
Bibliographical introductions to United Nations documents and publications in essay form are included in the general bibliography appended to this paper.

2.13 International Conferences

Including some which deal only with natural science and technology.

Doré, E. Essai d'une bibliographie des congrès internationaux. Paris, Edouard Champion, 1923.
Reprinted from *Revue des bibliothèques,* vol. 32, 1922. pp. 388-444. Includes only those conferences which have held at least one session in a French speaking country. Does not give bibliographical information about some conferences.

Gregory, W. International congresses and conferences, 1840-1937: a union list of their publications available in libraries of the United States and Canada. New York. H. W. Wilson, 1938.
Excludes diplomatic congresses and conferences, and those held under the auspices of the League of Nations. Issued with the support and sponsorship of three societies and with a $5,000 grant from the Carnegie Corporation. 894 copies were printed, of which about 40 remain unsold (Jan. 1949); the work will soon be out-of-print.

Grombach, H. Bibliographie des publications des principaux organismes et congrès internationaux dans le domaine des sciences appliquées. Zürich, Ecole Polytechnique Fédérale, 1945.
Excludes inter-American organizations, but includes inter-European ones. Arranged by the Universal Decimal Classification, with a subject index.

Index-catalogue of the Library of the Surgeon General's Office, United States Army (Army Medical Library). 4th series, vol. 3. Washington, Government Printing Office, 1938.
Includes an extensive list of national and international conferences, arranged under subject headings, with an index of names and subjects. Does include many conferences of interest to social scientists. A first additional list is prefixed to 4th series, vol. 4 (1939) of this work.

International conferences. *In* A world list of scientific periodicals published in the years 1900-1933. 2nd ed. London. Oxford University Press, 1934, pp. 769-780.

Proceedings and reports of congresses and conferences. *In* Serials of an international character: tentative list. *Institute of International Education, Bulletin,* 2nd series, no. 3, 1921, pp. 19-60.

Synopses of technical Pan American conferences and congresses. *In* The International conferences of American States: first supplement, 1933-1940, Washington, Carnegie Endowment for International Peace, 1940, pp. 381-452.
Includes bibliographical notes. These synopses have been expanded and extended in time in a work entitled "Conferencias internacionales Americanas, primer supplemento, 1938-1942," Washington, Carnegie Endowment for International Peace, 1943.

The documents of international conferences, particularly those of a diplomatic and legal character, can often be traced through the references in the "Chronicle of international events" which is included in each quarterly issue of the *American Journal of International Law.* Certain of the catalogues published by the firm of Nijhoff at The Hague contain information not easily found elsewhere.

2.2   Directories

Unless otherwise stated, no bibliographical information is given in the works listed in this section. Directories concerned only with natural science and technology are not included.

2.21   Directories of Organizations: (pre-World War II).

International Institute of Administrative Sciences. A directory of international organizations in the field of public administration. Brussels, 1936.
Includes bibliographical information.
League of Nations. Handbook of international organizations (associations, bureaux, committees, etc.). Geneva, 1938.
Includes a small amount of bibliographical information. The edition listed above was the latest published. It was intended to make this annual from 1939 onwards and to incorporate into it the publication listed immediately below.
League of Nations. Section of International Bureaux. Quarterly bulletin (afterwards *Bulletin*) of information on the work of international organizations. Geneva, 1922-1938.
Included bibliographical information in the first few issues only. Excluded labour organizations since these were recorded in *Industrial Labour Information* published by the International Labour Office. This latter periodical has recently been revived, but has, as yet, included no information about conferences.
Schmeckebier, L. F. International organizations in which the United States participates. Washington, Brookings Institution, 1935.
Includes bibliographical information.
Synopses of Pan American commission and other bodies. *In* The International conferences of American states: first supplement, 1933-1940. Washington, Carnegie Endowment for International Peace, 1940, pp. 453-494.

See also the Spanish counterpart of this work, "Conferencias internationales Americanas: primer supplemento, 1938-1942," Washington, Carnegie Endowment for International Peace, 1942, pp. 357-468. Both works include bibliographical references.
Union des Associations Internationales. Annuaire de la vie internationale. Vols. 1-3, 1905-1907; 2e sér. vols. 1-2, 1908/09-1910/11. Monaco and Brussels. [1905-1912.]
Some entries include bibliographical information.
Union des Associations Internationales. Liste des associations internationales. Brussels, 1912.

Directories of Organizations: (post World War II)

Annuaire des organisations internationales. Geneva, Societé de l'Annuaire des Organisations Internationales, 1948-   .
Includes some bibliographical information.
Great Britain. Central Office of Information. International economic organizations: the transition from war to peace. London, His Majesty's Stationery Office, 1947.
Great Britain. Ministry of Information. Short guide to some agencies of international cooperation. London, 1945.
Masters, R. D. Handbook of international organizations in the Americas, by R. D. Masters and others. Washington, Carnegie Endowment for International Peace, 1945.
"Those which have their headquarters in the Western Hemisphere." Includes some bibliographical information about most of the organizations listed.
Peace year book. London, National Peace Council.
Each issue includes lists of governmental and nongovernmental international organizations, and also the names of co-ordinating bodies.
United Nations. Handbook of non-governmental organizations with consultative status.
In preparation.
United Nations. International organizations in contact with the section for non-governmental organizations. [1948].
Mimeographed; distribution limited.
United Nations. Implementation of Economic and Social Council resolution 131 (VI) on the coordination of cartographic services of Specialized Agencies and international organizations: information received from international organiza-

tions. 1949. Working paper of the Meeting of Experts on Cartography, no. 4.

Includes bibliographical information.

United Nations. List of inter-governmental organizations. 1948. United Nations document E/818/Rev. 1.

United Nations. List of non-governmental organizations granted consultative status by the Economic and Social Council. 1948. United Nations document E/C.2/87; also included as annex B to document E/INF/23 and as an annex to Background Paper 45 of the Department of Public Information, United Nations. A revised edition of E/INF/23 is in preparation.

United Nations Educational, Scientific and Cultural Organization. First list of international non-governmental and semi-governmental organizations proposed for consultative arrangements. 1948. Annex 1 to Unesco document EX/3CO/2, and Annex 1 to Unesco document 3C/OXR/15.

United Nations Educational, Scientific and Cultural Organization. General information concerning international non-governmental organizations. 1947. Unesco document Com. ONG/1st session/3.

United Nations Educational, Scientific and Cultural Organization. Liste des organisations internationales non-gouvernementales et semi-gouvernementales avec lesquelles l'Unesco maintient des relations officiels. 1948. Unesco document Unesco/XR/NGO/3.

United Nations Information Office. Guide to United Nations and allied agencies. New York, The Office, 1945.

Includes bibliographical references.

United States. Department of State. International agencies in which the United States participates. Washington, Government Printing Office, 1946.

Includes bibliographical information.

2.22 Directories of Conferences: (pre-World War II.)

Aperçu des réunions internationales, 1919-1939. *In Bulletin of the Institut Intermédiaire [afterwards Juridique] International.* 1919-1940.

Includes some bibliographical information.

Baldwin, S. E. List of memorable international conferences, congresses or associations of official representatives of governments, exclusive of those mainly concerned in dealing with the re-

sults of a particular war. *American Journal of International Law,* vol. 1, 1907, pp. 808-829.

Internationale Kongresse und Konferenzen im Jahre 1929-34.

Printed each year *in Weltwirtschaftliches Archiv;* for some conferences bibliographical information is given in footnotes.

Kelchner, W. Inter-American conferences, 1826-1933: chronological and classified list. Washington, Government Printing Office, 1933.

(United States. Department of State. Conference Series, 16.)

Liste chronologique des réunions internationales. *In Annuaire de la Vie Internationale* 1908-1909; 1910-1911. Brussels, Union des Associations Internationales [1910-1912].

A "Calendrier des réunions internationales" was also included periodically in *La Vie Internationale* published by the same union; the latest issue was that for Nov. 1921. The earlier volumes of this *Annuaire* have not been examined.

Permanent Centre of International Information in Geneva. Congresses, courses and conferences in Geneva, 1931- .

Geneva, A. Kundig. 1931- .

Each issue also included a list of institutions. The 1938 volume is the last traced by the present writer.

United States. Department of State. American Delegations to international conferences, congresses and expositions, and American representation on international institutions and commissions, with relevant data. Washington, Government Printing Office, 1933- .

Published annually until June 30, 1941; for the period since 1941 called "Participation of the United States in international conferences;" published annually again since June 30, 1946.

Directories of Conferences: post-World War II

(a) Calendar of future congresses; (b) Calendar of the congresses held in 1948. *Both in the Bulletin mensuel* of the Union des Associations Internationales, no. 1 1949, pp. 11-14.

Calendrier des conférences et congrès internationaux.

Issued as nos. 649 and 837 of *Notes documentaires et études,* 1947-48. Presumably later editions will appear.

Pan American Union. Forthcoming inter-American conferences and meetings: list. 1948- .

Separate editions in English, Spanish and Portuguese. From no. 2 onwards, indicates, where known, the sponsoring agency or other source from which more information can be obtained.
United Nations. Bulletin.
Includes a "Monthly calendar of international meetings."
United Nations. Conference Division weekly information sheet. May 5 1947- .
United Nations Educational Scientific and Cultural Organization. Timetable of conferences, meetings and seminars for 1949. Unesco document/CPS/2.
United States. Department of State. Division of International Conferences. List of international conferences and meetings, including expositions, exhibitions, trade fairs and celebrations. 1946-
The Department of State also includes lists of international conferences in its *Bulletin* and until recently, in *Documents and state papers*.

In addition there are specialized lists such as that appearing in the *Transport and Communications Review* published by the United Nations.

3. THE PRINCIPAL LIBRARIES AND DOCUMENTATION CENTRES

There are few research libraries in the world which have as their whole province most sections of the social sciences. In some countries and areas international social science publications will have to be sought in the larger general libraries. On the other hand some national libraries pay less attention to material of the kind under discussion than they do to works in the humanities.

The number of libraries and centres which have good collections in the separate subjects of economics and law is much larger; it is not possible to enumerate more than a few of them here. The parliamentary libraries and the libraries of the ministries of foreign affairs in individual countries often have good collections of inter-governmental materials, though these libraries are not recorded below. Some centres for the study of international affairs have been listed. There are many other organizations of this kind which are of recent origin and which have good collections of current materials, but which are less well stocked with older works.

In the *United Nations Bulletin,* vol. 6 (1949) pp. 274-275 there is a list of "Depository libraries for United Nations documents." Additional information will also be found in the "Handbook of reference centres for international affairs" (1931) and the "Handbook of institutions for the scientific study of international relations" (1929) both compiled by the International Institute of Intellectual Co-operation, and, of course, in more up-to-date directories of the libraries and centres of individual countries.

Belgium
Office International de Bibliographie et de Documentation, Brussels.

France
Bibliothèque de Documentation Internationale Contemporaine, 102 rue de Bac, Paris, 7e.
Bibliothèque Nationale, Paris.
Centre d'Etudes de Politique Etrangères, 54 rue de Varenne, Paris, 7e.
Chambre de Commerce de Paris. Service de la Bibliothèque et des Archives, 16 rue de Chateaubriand, Paris 8e.
Dotation Carnegie pour la Paix Internationale, 173 Boulevard St. Germain, Paris, 6e.
Faculté de Droit, Université de Paris.

Germany
Information uncertain.
Hamburgisches Welt-Wirtschafts Archiv, Hamburg.
Institut für internationales Recht, Kiel.

Italy
Author has no information.

Netherlands
The Peace Palace Library, The Hague.

Norway
Nobel Institutet, Drammensvej 19, Oslo.

Switzerland
Institut Universitaire de Hautes Etudes Internationales, Geneva.
International Labour Office Library, Geneva.
United Nations Library, Geneva.

USSR
Information uncertain.
Lenin State Library, Moscow.
Standard Library of Social Sciences, Academy of Sciences, Moscow.
Marx-Engels Institute, Moscow.

United Kingdom
British Museum Library, London.
British Library of Political and Economic Science, Houghton Street, Aldwych, London, W.C.2.

Royal Institute of International Affairs, Chatham House, St. James Square, London.

United States

Carnegie Endowment for International Peace Library, 700 Jackson Place, Washington, D.C.

Columbia University Library, New York.

Columbus Memorial Library, Pan American Union, Washington, D.C.

Council of Foreign Relations, Inc., Library, 58 East 68th Street, New York, 21.

Edwin Ginn Library. Fletcher School of Law and Diplomacy, Medford, Massachusetts.

Hoover Institute and Library on War, Revolution and Peace, Stanford, California.

The Library of Congress, Washington, D.C.

The New York Public Library, 42nd Street and Fifth Avenue, New York.

United Nations Library, Lake Success, New York.

Woodrow Wilson Memorial Library, 45 East 65th Street, New York.

World Peace Foundation Library, 40 Mount Vernon Street, Boston, 8.

4. COMMENT, WITH SOME SUGGESTIONS ON THE DOCUMENTATION PROBLEMS

4.1 Archive Problem

It is hoped that all inter-governmental and non-governmental organizations are keeping together a complete collection of at least one copy of all their own publications and documents. These bodies should also take active steps to preserve in their own archives, or to place elsewhere in a suitable repository, other material, such as correspondence, internal papers, etc., which is likely to be of use to scholars.

Nothing should be destroyed until it has been examined and its destruction approved by a competent person. If the forthcoming conference makes other recommendations to international organizations, it might include one embodying the points just discussed and suggesting that appropriate instructions be embodied in the statutes or rules of operation of the organizations concerned. If the steps suggested are taken, they would ensure that, when other possibilities fail, scholars will most likely be able to find what they need at the source.

International organizations should be encouraged to microfilm their documents for archival reasons

and to publicize the possibility of supplying positive copies of the film. The present writer does not think that microfilm or microcard are suitable media for distributing most of the current documents produced by international organizations, though they are useful methods of obtaining back files of documents or otherwise filling gaps. It may be that it will be economical to film very bulky material which has to be dispatched by air.

The whole series of United Nations documents is being transfered to film by the United Nations archives and it is possible for outside libraries to secure copies. The work is, however, six months to a year behind current output at present and difficulties can arise because the confidential documentation is also on the films. It is possible, too, that United Nations documents will be reproduced on microcards and be available at an approximate cost of $1,000 for the output of one year.

4.2 Bibliographies and Indexes

4.21 What is Desirable for Each Individual International Organization?

Each international organization should adopt the practices and produce the bibliographies and indexes recommended below:

(1) The department(s) of an international organization responsible for the production of documents and printed publications should adopt consistent publishing practices and they should not change these without good reasons. These practices should also apply where printing and other reproduction are done away from the organization by different contractors.

Each item issued should have a distinctive title and an imprint which includes a date. It may be helpful, especially if the number of items issued is large, to give each item a number or symbol. If symbols are given, they should be applied consistently.

As a small example of some of the difficulties caused by not adhering to these advices, the publications and documents of the United Nations which have neither sales numbers nor document symbols, may be cited. They include a number of works reproduced from varitype and it is usually difficult to trace them bibliographically.

(2) An organization should see that there is central control and direction of the production of

bibliographies of, and indexes to, its documents and publications. This is most important in organizations with a large output of material.

Although the present writer is employed by the United Nations at its headquarters, there was, at the time this paper was begun, no bibliography of the bibliographies and indexes produced to its own documents and publications by this organization. The task of beginning to construct one was time consuming. The United Nations is an extreme case and with it improvements in these matters are likely. However, other medium sized and large organizations should be warned of the danger of dispersal of effort.

(3) Wherever possible the work of compiling bibliographies and indexes should be done by trained persons. When this is not possible, expert supervision should be sought.

The following bibliographies and indexes should be prepared:

(4) A complete bibliography, kept reasonably up-to-date at regular intervals by supplements or new editions. The use of such a work to the scholar is obvious and it will not be elaborated here.

Librarians need them because few libraries, if any, have resources adequate enough to enable them to attempt to catalogue in detail the documents issued by international organizations. Although the publication of a separate printed or mimeographed bibliography does not necessarily absolve a library from all further cataloguing treatment of the material covered, in most cases it is a very great help. It also nearly always permits a librarian to check his holdings and to claim or purchase material he needs.

It was the opinion of the private organizations represented at the first conference on the distribution of documents called by the World Peace Foundation in the United States in March 1947, that the production of complete records of its documents were "ultimately the responsibility of the individual public body itself" and with this the present writer concurs.

Complete records were not made currently of the output of the League of Nations, apart from its somewhat bare *Monthly list of documents distributed,* which was not cumulated. It has taken a grant of $53,000 from the Rockefeller Foundation and nearly four years work at the library of the Woodrow Wilson Foundation in New York to remedy this. Other international organizations should take note, and should attempt the work currently, both for their own immediate benefit

and for the use of scholars and librarians both currently and later.

(5) Subject indexes to documents and publications. It may be convenient to include these in (4) above, particularly if the total output to be recorded is small. It is desirable that subject indexes should be as thorough as possible; if the number of documents to be indexed and the staff available permits, indexes which include entries for parts of individual documents are very valuable. This has been done, for example, in the *Library index of PICAO documents August 1945–April 1947* prepared by the International Civil Aviation Organization.

(6) Separate bibliographies, with any necessary subject indexes, to printed publications placed on sale. It is assumed that these publications will also be included in (4) and (5) above. It is believed, however, that these printed publications will receive wider distribution and that they will be obtained by many individuals, libraries and other organizations not interested in the complete documentation. Organizations whose total output is small should be able to combine (4), (5) and (6).

(7) When an organization has been established for some time and has published a number of sales items, some of which have gone out of print, it should prepare either (a) a separate catalogue of those of its publications which are in print and revise it from time to time, or (b) a complete catalogue of sales items, showing which items are out-of-print. In doing this it would be following the practices of most commercial publishers.

(8) "Promotional material" in the form of prospectuses, advance notices and advertising is desirable for sales items.

(9) It is desirable that all sales items and also other suitable material should be entered in the national bibliographies of the country or countries of publication, and also in other bibliographies aiming to give complete coverage of all material in a particular language. These entries should be bibliographically adequate.

(10) It is desirable, too, that sales items and the more important documents should be recorded in the *Cumulative Catalog of Library of Congress printed cards* which is the most extensive "author" catalogue of current publications in the world today.

(11) International organizations should supply abstracting journals, analytical indexes, and journals carrying reviews of repute, with appropriate publications for entry or review. In some cases it may be possible for international organizations

to obtain partial or even complete recording of their documents and publications in analytical indexes or abstracting journals.

(12) The serial publications of international organizations should be recorded in appropriate directories of serials.

(13) When the literature produced by an organization reaches considerable proportions, descriptive guides explaining methods of publication and distribution, bibliographical aids, etc., should be produced. By the time the conference meets it will be apposite to recommend that such a work be produced to deal with the output of the United Nations and its Specialized Agencies. Guides of this kind exist for the documents and publications of the League of Nations, (18, 19) and for the publications of some national governments. Such works are among the basic works of reference a librarian uses and they are very useful to social scientists themselves. They deserve to be widely used in courses of instruction in the use of the literature of the social sciences.

(14) An international organization should compile, keep current and publish from time to time bibliographies of the writings *about* itself. The United Nations and the International Court of Justice do this in their yearbooks; those organizations which have not contemplated doing it should be encouraged to do so. Inter-governmental organizations should decide whether to include the relevant publications of national governments alongside their own publications in bibliographies suggested in (4) above or whether to include them with "about" material.

(15) It is desirable that information about research in progress in international organizations should be published. The United Nations has issued a *Directory of economic and statistical projects, No. 1* (1948), a revised enlarged edition of which is in preparation. These works include projects organized by the Specialized Agencies. National lists of this kind (11) and lists of the work in progress in specific sections of the social sciences (5) have also been published. These record, for the most part, the activities of national research organizations. Research in progress in inter-governmental and non-governmental international organizations should be recorded in any appropriate collective work and the organizations in question should be encouraged to make this kind of information available regularly in their own publications.

(16) Organizations which maintain card files which index and/or abstract their documents and

publications should consider whether it is possible to reproduce these cards for distribution. If microcards are produced (see 4.1), this will not, of course, be necessary.

It is assumed that international organizations will want to make both their publications and bibliographical information about them available in as many languages as possible and that some of the records requested above would be either bi- or multi-lingual or would be available in separate editions in different languages.

It is realized that the sixteen points enumerated above may not be applicable to every organization. An organization whose output consists largely of propaganda and news information and which itself does little or no research will not need to produce all the records requested.

There should be a recognized periodical source or sources where one could look for news of bibliographies and indexes to the documents and publications of international organizations.

International Organization has included a short list of this kind in its recent issues and presumably the *Bibliographic Index* is also interested. *Unesco Bulletin for Libraries* and the *Review of Documentation* might be other possibilities. It is desirable that this list should be so complete as possible and that it should be in a journal with a wide international distribution. If it is felt that entry in a journal which is primarily for librarians would not reach the persons doing study or research with the documents and publications concerned, it might be wise to repeat it elsewhere.

It is suggested that recommendations on the lines of those given above should be distributed to appropriate international organizations in social science fields and that Unesco itself should take any appropriate action necessary to further these aims, particularly when it is giving grants for publication purposes. These recommendations should include a section about conference publications, as proposed later in this report.

4.22 What is Desirable Collectively, Including a Discussion of Existing Bibliographies and Indexes

The present writer does not think a serial bibliography or index to the publications of all international organizations in the social sciences desirable or feasible. It is possible to produce collective serial records of certain kinds for the United Nations and its Specialized Agencies (see below); and it would be useful if a collective serial record of the publications of inter-governmental organizations outside the United Nations group could be produced. For this latter work, however, a permanent staff would be needed and the expense involved would be considerable. *Documents of International Organizations* and *International Organization* do include some information, but they survey only a small number of such organizations. *International Book News* did, and the *International Reporter* now does, include some items of this kind, but only for a few organizations and for them with no attempt at completeness. The *International Reporter* is a sales catalogue and is mainly for use in the United States; it cannot be considered as filling the gap discussed here.

A retrospective bibliography of the publications of inter-governmental organizations outside the League of Nations, the United Nations and the Specialized Agencies would also be useful, though it might have to refer in certain cases to other bibliographies instead of giving full listings, if the amount of material to be recorded proved too great: works like Myers' *Manual of Treaties* . . . include much relevant material. A grant in aid to some person or body would be necessary. The International Law Library in Columbia University has abstracted its holdings of material of this kind on a special set of cards; these would be useful to anyone undertaking such a task. The field would have to be carefully defined before the work was commenced; if necessary it could be delimited by the exclusion of regional international organizations.

4.221 United Nations and Specialized Agencies

The International Advisory Committee of Library Experts which met at Lake Success in August 1948 recommended on p. 13 of its report (40) that "a consolidated check list of the documents and publications of all United Nations organizations be published . . . ." This aim would best be accomplished if the Specialized Agencies produced check lists similar to those being issued for the documents and publications of the United Nations itself. Further consolidation would hardly be practicable. The desirability of issuing such check lists should be drawn to the attention of the Specialized Agencies and especially to those which have, as yet, no programme for a check list of any kind.

The United Nations *Check List* . . . is, at the time of writing very much behind in publication. If this is still the case when the conference meets, the latter body might consider recommending that immediate steps be taken to bring it up-to-date and that, if necessary, a special grant be sought from an outside agency for this purpose. Such a grant was received during 1948; it helped considerably at that time.

It is highly desirable that the *Weekly Index* . . . should be published regularly and cumulated, though, in the present writer's view, it might not be necessary to include in it the documents of the Specialized Agencies, if these agencies themselves will produce regular and complete lists of and indexes to their own material. If and when the *Weekly Index* . . . is established, the sponsors of *Documents of International Organizations* should consider the future of that publication. If they are willing to undertake a more difficult task than that being done at present they might either (a) list only the documents of inter-governmental organizations outside the United Nations group, but with some fullness, or (b) attempt a regular listing of the publications of international conferences, in accordance with suggestions made later in this paper.

The conference convened by the Carnegie Endowment for International Peace in Paris in November 1948 recommended that French editions of all United Nations bibliographies and indexes be prepared. The present writer agrees that this is desirable, but he is aware of the considerable effort and expense that would be involved. The International Advisory Committee of Library Experts recommended on p. 12 of their report (40) that polyglot dictionaries of the headings used might be an economical substitute. The Paris conference also recommended that classification symbols from an accepted scheme be added to all documents. The present writer thinks that the cost of doing this out of proportion to any advantages which might ensue.

In a document stating its publication policy, (39) Unesco has said that efforts should be made to promote the establishment of a central publishing house or organization for the United Nations and the Specialized Agencies. The Sales and Circulation Section of the United Nations agrees with this opinion; if no action has been taken in this direction by the time the conference meets, it should consider whether it should urge such action. In any case, the present writer feels that a monthly bibliography, with monthly and annual subject indexes, of the sales publications, and possibly public information items, of the United Nations and the Specialized Agencies is immediately desirable and feasible. If necessary this publication could itself be placed on sale. At the time of this writing co-ordination activities between the United Nations and its Specialized Agencies have been planned which *may* make these suggestions absolute.

4.23 Directories of International Organizations, with Bibliographical Information

The present writer thinks it desirable that there be published a general directory of the international organizations of the world, and that revised editions of it be produced at regular intervals. If the amount of material in it should prove too extensive for one volume, it should be split into parts and the social sciences should be dealt with separately.

The directory should include bibliographical information in each entry. It may be feasible to record all the publications of organizations whose output is very small. If the output is not small, retrospective and current bibliographies should have priority. Vague statements, such as "issues a journal," should be avoided. The total entry for each organization, including the bibliographical information, might average less than a page. The proposed work would, then, be less detailed than the old *Annuaire de la Vie Internationale.* The League of Nations produced several editions of its *Handbook of International Organizations* and the United Nations or Unesco should edit the work now proposed. That is unless the *Annuaire des Organisations Internationales,* which now partly covers the field, can be improved and extended. Alternatively, the proposed work could be purely bibliographical.

4.24 International Conferences

The bibliographical tools available in this field are most inadequate. Advanced notices of the venues of many conferences can be found fairly easily through the published lists mentioned under 2.22 and by diligently reading other periodicals. It is often less easy to find an address to which one can write enquiring about publications.

Information as to the way in which papers, proceedings, journals, etc. will be published is usually not found. It may be that the proceedings of the conference will be issued in volume form when the meetings are over and that, if this should be the case, many libraries would be satisfied with the opportunity of securing those proceedings when ready. If it is not known, however, whether the proceedings will be issued in volume form, those libraries may request the working documentation because they are afraid that nothing else will be published. Other libraries may need both the working documentation and the final volumes. For some conferences, the documentation may be available only to participating governments or organizations; if this be the case, librarians would like to be informed. Preprints of the papers to be presented at "technical" conferences may be available and it may be a long time before they are finally incorporated in volume form. Many libraries will need the preprints.

From the librarian's point of view it would be ideal if there were a truly world wide serial list of forthcoming conferences which would include, amongst other information, the addresses of the secretariats preparing for the conferences and brief details of what publications are contemplated before, during and after them, with a note as to their probable availability to non-participants. The entries for each conference could still be quite short. It is true that governmental libraries usually have an opportunity of securing the papers of an inter-governmental conference and that unofficial libraries can also sometimes secure documents of this kind through their own governments. This does not help with non-governmental conferences. It is, in all cases, most desirable that direct access to the organizations in question be possible. The number of libraries making requests would not be large enough to embarrass most conferences.

As far as coverage is concerned, there is much to be said for not restricting the work suggested to the social sciences, if the material is not too bulky for one publication. In social science fields themselves, political, legal and/or administrative conferences present particular problems of their own, for the production of many of their documents is often incidental to negotiations in progress and they thus differ from the proceedings of many "technical" conferences which add discussions to papers prepared beforehand, but which do not, in general, supersede those papers. The projected work could be produced by the United Nations in collaboration with Unesco, for these two bodies already collect much of the necessary information.

The need for a record of this kind is widespread and it has been expressed in print at least once before—by Mrs. E. Cunningham. 3, 4.

This list of forthcoming conferences might well be followed each year by a retrospective annual list and bibliography of them. The record for the social sciences which appeared in *Weltwirtschaftliches Archiv* for the conferences of 1929-1934, (recorded in 2.22) could well be used, with the inclusion of fuller bibliographical information. Alternatively, for inter-governmental conferences, their publications could be included in the suggested current bibliography of inter-governmental organizations (see p. 24).

A record of the work of conferences over a number of years which might be entirely bibliographical in character is also needed. This might be similar to the bibliography edited for the period until 1937 by Miss W. Gregory (see 2.13), though the latter work is not exhaustive. It would be feasible and useful to produce a continuation for the years 1938-1950; a grant would be needed. This continuation might well discard the listing of the holdings of American libraries, but it should consider, with a reservation noted below, extending its coverage to diplomatic conferences and to those held under the auspices of the United Nations and its Specialized Agencies. It should be possible to incorporate into the supplement of the valuable work already done by Grombach (see 2.13); apparently this latter work has not had the wide circulation it deserves. The present writer knows nothing of the fate of the unpublished parts of the work edited by Stümke (see 2.11).

Any retrospective bibliographies of international conferences which are produced for annual or longer periods must take into consideration the recording of conference material in the indexes and check lists of the United Nations and its Specialized Agencies and also any collective recording of the documents and publications of other inter-governmental organizations which might be started. In compiling retrospective records, use should be made of materials available at such regional centres as the Pan American Union. The proposal made above for a retrospective bibliography of international conferences, 1936-1950, clashes to some extent with a previous suggestion (see 4.22) that a collective retrospective bibliography of items issued by inter-governmental organizations be prepared.

It is also desirable that special bibliographical guides be prepared to the documents of conferences which have a very large number of such items before them; good examples of works of this kind already exist. 21, 22. Conferences with a smaller documentation could well produce guides on a more modest scale.

If an international organization or organizations is formed to promote co-operation in the social sciences, as suggested by resolution 4.11 of Unesco at its Beirut conference, 14 questions of bibliography and publication should be among the subjects it or they should study. If it is not thought feasible or desirable to produce lists of future conferences and retrospective bibliographies of them which are not limited by subject or which deal with all the social sciences, it may be possible to produce new or improved records for special subject fields and regions of the world. Such records need not necessarily be separate publications; they could be parts of other serials. This same comment also applies to the recording of the other documents and publications of inter-governmental and other international organizations.

The Fédération Mondiale des Organisations Juridiques Internationales Non-gouvernementales, for example, includes in its statutes a clause about the exchange of publications; a body such as this might well promote bibliographical records. Other central or co-ordinating international organizations might do likewise. The present writer believes, however, that there are advantages in having records for organizations and conferences which are not so closely limited by subject.

4.3 Coverage in Indexing and Abstracting Services

The suggestions made previously in this paper have largely been concerned with specially prepared lists and indexes to items issued by international organizations; the coverage of these items by indexing and abstracting services not wholly concerned with the activities of international organizations will now be considered.

As far as regular periodicals are concerned, there is no reason to suppose that journals published and made generally available by international organizations fare worse or better than other journals. They are, presumably, considered on their merits and a general improvement in the coverage of indexing and abstracting would make the contents of periodicals issued by international organizations better known.

As far as documents, reports and pamphlets, irregular serials and sometimes books are concerned, the recording is very poor in the field of economics. Some of the best services in this subject confine themselves to periodical articles. There is good coverage for French language editions of works issued by some international organizations in the annual *Bibliographie générale des sciences juridiques, politiques, économiques et sociales,* by A. Grandin. *Public affairs information service* is also an exception, but it is confined to works in English and it is not found in many libraries outside the United States because of its cost.

The reader approaching the literature of economics in search of information on a specific subject is quite likely to miss important items issued by international organizations if he relies on indexes and abstracts.

In the field of political science and international law the situation is somewhat better. The selective coverage in journals like the *American Journal of International Law* is helpful and workers in these fields are more likely to use the check lists of the United Nations and *Documents of International Organizations* to advantage. It is, however, much easier to trace English language material in these fields than it is to find works in other tongues.

If fresh developments are planned (as, for example, the abstracting which may be done by the International Political Science Association) the problem of the documents and publications issued by international organizations should be borne in mind and the question of incorporating them or dealing with them separately should be considered. Existing indexing and abstracting services which at present record periodical articles only, and which might be considering extending their coverage to books, should also remember the documents and publications of international organizations.

4.4 Bibliographical Contents of Individual Volumes

In the instructions received for preparing this paper this subject was not mentioned. It is, however, relevant, and it will be dealt with briefly here. If a pamphlet of suggestions be prepared for distribution to international organizations, as suggested in 4.21, some of the points noted below should be included.

The publications of international organizations often fall below the standards of the best commercial book publishers. Substantial monographs and important works of reference often appear without indexes. It is realized that it is an expensive matter to index publications which appear in more than one language, and it is known that, in the United Nations at least, publications have headlines which are difficult to meet even when the works in question are not provided with indexes. Nevertheless works of substance should have adequate indexes of their own—as should volumes of periodicals and the proceedings of conferences.

The debates of councils and assemblies should have author and subject indexes (combined or separate) to their volumes, as is done for the proceedings in a number of national parliaments. Attempts might be made within individual international organizations, and within the United Nations and Specialized Agencies group, to see that variations in the subject headings chosen for use in their indexes were kept to a minimum.

An international organization should see that its name appears in a consistent form on the title-pages of its publications. If a series of international conferences are held in several different countries and if the proceedings are published separately in those countries, it is very desirable that a standard form of name in some one language be included on the title-page of each. Mrs. E. Cunningham has suggested that "the word 'Internationale' or 'International' be used as the initial key word for the title of published proceedings in order to facilitate uniformity in cataloguing and filing." (4)

A guide might be drawn up describing satisfactory methods of producing and distributing the documents of international conferences. Unesco and other organizations making grants for the publication of conference proceedings should stipulate that certain bibliographical standards should be met in them. It might be possible to stimulate commercial publishers to specialize in this field and to co-operate from the beginning with the conveners of "technical" international conferences in the social sciences, as is being planned in the scientific field by the British journal *Research.* Alternatively, an independent publishing house could be established for this purpose, if adequate support was forthcoming.

4.5 Distribution

4.51 Availability of Working Documentation

The conference might consider the attitudes of various international bodies towards requests from outside for documents produced primarily for internal use by the body itself and its members. Confidential and secret documents are separate groups which are to be considered later.

As far as the United Nations is concerned, though there are some internal reports and other material which do not reach member nations, depository libraries and other recipients, a high percentage of the great mass of documents produced by this organization, including some relatively ephemeral material, is distributed. This practice is also followed by certain other international bodies. It may be added that the International Advisory Committee of Library Experts recommended on p. 10 of their report (40) that the internal papers of the Secretariat of the United Nations should also be distributed to its depository libraries.

On the other hand, a different view is sometimes taken. The Editorial and Publications Division of the International Labour Organization, for example, does not consider it necessary for libraries to have some of the documents of its organization, since changes made by I.L.O. conferences are duly recorded in its *Provisional Record*. The present writer feels that international organizations should be encouraged to make their unrestricted working documentation available to libraries which request it, if the receiving libraries give undertakings that this material will be serviced and made available. If such documents cannot be sent free they should be offered for a fee. The present writer is uncertain what the total demand on any one organization for material of this kind is likely to be; scholars are, however, often voluble about its inaccessibility. If an intergovernmental organization refuses to distribute its working documents, it may, of course, be possible for a private library to obtain them from the government department of its country concerned with the activities of the organization in question. Government departments and their libraries bear responsibilities for the preservation of material of this kind and for making it available, especially if international organizations are not arranging for distribution within their member states.

In this connection it should be noted that the possibility of microfilming or recording on microcards the set of the documents of the League of Nations in the possession of the United States State Department is, at the time this report is being written, under consideration. A full catalogue of the League's items will shortly be available on Library of Congress cards. The conference might care to express itself on the desirability of this filming. It may be that extra purchasers will be needed to enable the project to go through.

4.52 Confidential and Secret Documents

Many international organizations, especially political ones of an inter-governmental character, have a great deal of material of this kind. Access to most of it cannot be expected currently. In many cases it should, however, prove possible to have these items examined regularly and to "declassify" and distribute some of them later. This suggestion applies to international organizations of all kinds.

The United Nations prepares fewer copies of its restricted documents than it does of its unrestricted ones; this effects economies in paper, reproduction and storage. "Declassification" followed by general distribution, which is most desirable, is not, therefore, feasible at present. The International Advisory Committee of Library Experts recommended on p. 10 of their report (40) that distribution of such documents be made at the time of issue, with safeguards at the receiving end.

4.53 Deposit

Appendix 3 shows that only a small percentage of the documents distributed by the United Nations goes to the 148 depository libraries which that organization has chosen in various parts of the world. The majority of these libraries receive both documents and sales publications, though a few have asked for and receive sales publications only. Some of the other distribution, however, to member governments, to non-governmental organizations and to other bodies does, in fact, reach libraries where it will be cared for and made available.

Other international organizations should be encouraged, within the limits of their budgets, to deposit their documents and publications in suitable libraries in different parts of the world. Regional inter-governmental organizations are included in this category and these bodies should be urged to make judicious selections of depositories in libraries outside their respective regions. Where, for example, can the documents and publications of the Pan American Union be found outside the Americas?

International organizations publishing material in different parts of the world should see that the items being issued from these different centers reach libraries and other institutions recorded as depositories.

Non-governmental international organizations should endeavor to place their documents and publications in the principal research libraries on their subject and, in many cases, also in some larger general research libraries. It is feared that though some organizations of this kind have a generous distribution, it may not be reaching libraries where it can be consulted by a wider public and be kept and recorded for the use of scholars in future years.

4.54 Sale

If an international organization cannot distribute its documents free it might make them available at an inclusive subscription price. If the documents are numerous and on different subjects, separate subscription rates are also desirable for each section. The need for publicity for publications placed on sale has already been mentioned. Other international organizations might follow the practice of the United Nations and some of its Specialized Agencies and arrange with booksellers in various parts of the world to act as their sales agents. It is to be hoped that no library will be prevented from buying research materials of this kind because of currency restrictions. It should be noted that the best collective accounts of the sales and other practices of the United Nations and its Specialized Agencies available at present are to be found in the mimeographed reports of four conferences, (30) though they are far from adequate and they are already out-of-date.

4.55 Surplus Stocks

The organizers of international conferences should not destroy surplus copies of the working papers of a conference after it is over without having obtained advice from a competent person that it is not feasible to transport all or some of the material to a place or places where research workers can use it.

It is difficult to give general advice to the non-governmental international organizations about their deposit and sales practices, for these organizations are a heterogenous group. They should consider deposit, exchange and sales as possible ways of distributing their material. If the cost of postage is the only barrier to free deposit, it should be possible to pass on this expense to the recipient.

4.56 Distribution and Sale to Individuals

There is no uniform policy, either in the United Nations group or outside it, regarding requests for documents (as distinct from sales publications) from outside persons. The practice of the United Nations is conservative.

Nevertheless copies are needed—sometimes multiple copies—by such persons as teachers of international law and political science. International organizations should be prepared to satisfy these requests, if necessary by charging a fee.

5. SUMMARY OF PRINCIPAL RECOMMENDATIONS

5.1 General Recommendations

5.11 International organizations should be urged to produce more and better bibliographies of their documents and publications. [4.21]

5.12 It is desirable that these records be in more than one language. [4.221]

5.13 There should be a recognized source or sources for information about new bibliographies of international organizations. [4.21]

5.14 These organizations should preserve suitable material in their archives and record it on microfilm or microcard if possible. [4.1]

5.15 The bibliographical content of the individual items produced should reach higher standards. [4.4]

5.16 Recommendations are made about the deposit and sale of documents and publications, the distribution of working documentation, and the distribution of confidential and secret documents. [4.5]

5.17 National governments have a responsibility to make available in their countries the documents and publications of the inter-governmental organizations of which they are members, if this task is not undertaken by the organizations in question. [4.51]

5.18 To achieve the results desired a report might be drawn up on these matters suitable for approval by Unesco. Afterwards it could be circulated to the bodies concerned. The report would not attempt to standardize practices too rigidly, it would record suitable alternatives. Any grants made by Unesco, and possibly by other international organizations or national foundations, for publication purposes, could be made contingent on adherence to these bibliographical methods. A separable section might deal with methods of documenting conferences. Special guides to the documents of individual conferences can also be useful. [4.24]

5.19 The desirability of stimulating commercial publishing houses to pay special attention to handling the documents of international conferences should be discussed, as should the possibility of establishing an independent publishing house for this purpose. [4.4]

5.2 Recommendations for the United Nations and Specialized Agencies.

5.21 Most of the suggestions above apply to these bodies. The following works are also recommended: (a) a bibliographical guide to their documents and publications, (b) a periodic bibliography, with subject indexes, of all sales and, possibly, public information material; the United Nations *Check list* should be brought up-to-date, by a grant for more personnel if necessary. The Specialized Agencies should be encouraged to produce, if they have not already provided satisfactory alternative works, similar check lists. The proposed *Weekly Index* . . . should be established and cumulated. A central publishing house for all these organizations could be recommended. [4.21]

5.3 Possible New Publications

The possibility of producing one or more of the following new publications should be considered:

a. A directory of international organizations, with some bibliographical information about the organizations included. If the material is too large, the work should be issued in sections. Alternatively, this work could be purely bibliographical. [4.221]

b. Assuming the *Weekly Index* . . . of the United Nations to be established, a current bibliography of the intergovernmental organizations outside the United Nations group. [4.22]

c. A retrospective bibliography of the publications of inter-governmental organizations outside the United Nations group, possibly in part a bibliography of bibliographies, possibly excluding regional inter-governmental organizations, and bearing in mind duplication with (f) below. [4,22]

d. A periodical giving advance listing of inter-governmental and non-governmental international conferences, universal in scope and including both the addresses of secretariats and notes on publication programmes. This might not be restricted to social science fields. [4.24]

e. An annual bibliography of international conferences, which might or might not include other information about them. [4.24]

f. A retrospective bibliography for longer periods which might in the future be a cumulation of (e); in the meantime a work of this kind could be commissioned for the period 1938-1950. Duplication with (c) above should be borne in mind. [4.24]

These are the present writers own suggestions; other advices should be sought. The order in which the suggestions are given is not an order of priority.

6. ANNEXES

6.1 Some of the Channels through which the Activities of International Organizations are Co-ordinated at Present

(Note: Some of the bodies mentioned have been established for specific objectives which do not include the consideration of bibliographical problems).

1. For the United Nations and its Specialized Agencies there is an Administrative Committee on Co-ordination. This committee has specialized advisory committees and working parties, including two dealing with the subjects of (a) the sale

and distribution of publications, and (b) the libraries of the organizations concerned.

2. The United Nations, Unesco and other Specialized Agencies themselves are concerned with co-ordination in their respective fields.

3. An Interim Committee of Consultative Non-Governmental Organizations has been formed by those organizations which have consultative status with the Economic and Social Council of the United Nations.

4. The Department of Public Information of the United Nations convenes a Conference of Non-governmental Organizations from time to time. It will meet next in April 1949.

5. A Union of International Associations has its headquarters in Brussels, Palais d'Egmont, 8 Place du Petit Sablon, Bruxelles.

6. Joint Committee of the Major International Associations, 5 rue Gay Lussac, Paris. 5e. Unesco itself has information about the status of this organization; during 1948 another organization was formed linking international organizations with their headquarters in Paris.

7. Federation of Private and Semi-Official International Organizations established at Geneva, 37 Quai Wilson. Geneva.

8. World Union of Peace Organizations, 37 Quai Wilson, Geneva. Among its aims is "the effective exchange of documents and information through a jointly supported service."

9. Regional co-operation is effected through such bodies as the Organization of the American States.

6.2 Some Financial Implications

Few, if any, of the bibliographical publications specified as desirable in this paper could be expected to pay for themselves if they were placed on sale; the majority would have to be produced at a loss. As far as the bibliographies of and indexes to the documents and publications of a single organization are concerned, it is the responsibility of each organization to produce adequate records of these kinds. Only when there are special difficulties, such as a large backlog, coupled with proven inability to bear the cost, should aid from an outside body be necessary.

Some of the collective records of organizations and conferences specified as desirable in 4.22-4.24 might, it is hoped, be undertaken by either Unesco or the United Nations. It is assumed that the organization concerned would bear the cost.

The production of retrospective bibliographies of inter-governmental organizations (see 4.22), and of conferences for the period 1938-50 would mean subsidies for compilation and publication. A foundation might well be asked to support these projects.

The following foundations have made grants in recent years for projects connected with the bibliographies and indexes to the documents and publications of international organizations:

Carnegie Corporation
Carnegie Endowment for International Peace
Rockefeller Foundation
Woodrow Wilson Foundation
World Peace Foundation

6.3 Statistics Illustrating the Distribution of the Documents and Publications of the United Nations, etc., as of February, 1949.

Percentage distribution
a. To the United Nations Secretariat 42%
b. To member governments 32%
c. Distributed on behalf of United Nations Library to:
   depository libraries
   exchange libraries
   centres for the study of international affairs
   By the Non-governmental Organizations Section to organizations in consultative status with the Economic and Social Council
   By the Department of Public Information to U.N.
   Information Centres and others, including adult education agencies } 8%
d. Stock 13%

Some of the 32% received by member governments is reaching certain of the libraries of those governments; it is not known how many governments distribute United Nations documents and publications to non-governmental libraries. It may be noted that two-thirds of all the documents of the League of Nations were consumed in distribution to its secretariat and its member nations.

Numbers of libraries and organizations receiving documents and publications.

a. Depository libraries 148
(The majority receive both documents
and sales publications. Some receive only
sales publications. A few receive material
in certain categories only.)
b. Libraries purchasing documents 20
(Mostly in the United States. 1949 subscription price $225.00.)
c. Libraries purchasing all sales publications
in the United States. (Figures for other
countries not obtained.) 225
d. United Nations associations
"All" documents 36
Printed material only 17
Mimeographed items only 3   56
e. Non-governmental organizations
(Some in consultative status with
the Economic and Social Council,
others not.)
Mimeographed items only 80
Selected printed items only 21
All printed items in English 52
All printed items in French 32
All printed items in Spanish........... 24
Mimeographed and printed items
(some selective) 131   340

Numbers of subscriptions to the *Monthly Bulletin of Statistics* approx. 2,700.

(As of December 1948; before World War II the
number of subscriptions to the equivalent publications of the League of Nations was between 1,400
and 1,500.)

6.4 Other comments on some of the matters under discussion

a. Professor Manley O. Hudson:

"We lack adequate facilities particularly for
studying the work of international conferences resulting in the making of this legislation [the making of treaties] . . . I am frequently embarrassed
because I am unable to get, even through writing
to friends all over the world, the records of international conferences that are held."

*(Proceedings of the Fifth Conference of Teach-
ers of International Law and Related Subjects,
Washington, April 1933*. Washington Carnegie
Endowment for International Peace, 1933, p. 39.)
b. F. C. Macken:

"Though documentary and other source materials were adequate for the purpose in many instances, in others data could be obtained only
from secondary sources, or occasionally only from
the recollections of individuals. In a few cases . . .
no records of any kind were found."
*(The International Conferences of American
States. First supplement, 1933-1940. Washington, Carnegie Endowment for International Peace,
1940, p. 380.)*
c. Editorial in *Research*, vol. 1, Dec. 1948,
p. 673.

[Conferences.] "Publication . . . is apt to be
left to a committee after the event, resulting in
considerable and unnecessary delay before a
hotch-potch of disjointed papers finally appears
"in print." Under these working conditions poor
results are unavoidable and it is no good blaming
publisher or printer; a high standard of editing
and production is not economically feasible for a
specialized volume, the distribution and usefulness
of which is diminished by delay."
d. Teachers of international law expressed their
concern about the difficulties they experienced in
obtaining the documents of the United Nations
and in using the bibliographical records of them.
*(Proceedings of the Eighth Conference of Teach-
ers of International Law and Related Subjects,
1946*. Washington, Carnegie Endowment for
International Peace, 1946.)
e. H. Grombach:

"On trouvera bien des notices bibliographique-
ment incomplètes, car, en dépit de recherches
laborieuses, il n'a pas toujours été possible, là où
la publication originale ne pouvait être consultée,
d'avoir tous les reseignements bibliographiques."
(Introduction, p.v., to *Bibliographie des publications des principaux organismes et congrès internationaux dans le domaine des sciences appliquées.*
Zürich, Ecole Polytechnique Fédérale, 1945.)

BIBLIOGRAPHY

General

1. *Bittner, L.* Die Lehre von den völkerrechtlichen Vertragsurkunden. Struttgart, Deutsche Verlags-Anstalt, 1924.
2. *Breycha-Vauthier, A. C. de.* Le rôle des publications gouvernementales et des publications d'organisations internationales: essai sur une politique de publication. *In* Mélanges offerts à M. Marcel Godet. Neuchâtel, Impr. Paul Attinger, 1937.
3. *Cunningham, E. R.* [Publications of international congresses.] Acts du Comité International des Bibliothèques, 13me session, Oslo, 20-22 Mai, 1947, pp. 102-103.
4. *Cunningham, E. R.* [Publications of international congresses.] Actes du Comité International des Bibliothèques, 11me session, Bruxelles, 4-5 juillet, 1938, pp. 83-84.
5. Current research in international affairs. *In* International conciliation, published by the Carnegie Endowment for International Peace. Has appeared in the January and December 1948 issues.
6. *Gjelsness, R.* International congresses. Library quarterly, vol. 9, 1939, pp. 334-341. A review article of the work edited by Gregory, recorded in 2.13.
7. *League of Nations. Committee of Experts for the Progressive Codification of International Law.* Questionnaire No. 5. Procedure for the conclusion and drafting of treaties, 1926. League of Nations document. C.47.M.24. 1926.V.
8. *League of Nations.* Educational activities and the coordination of intellectual work accomplished by the Union of International Associations. 1921. League of Nations document A.42(B). 1921.
9. *Otlet, P.* Les associations internationales et la documentation. Congrès mondial de la documentation universelle. Paris, 1937, texte des communications, pp. 259-265.
10. *Pastuhov, V. D.* A guide to the practice of international conferences. Washington. Carnegie Endowment for International Peace, 1944.
11. Register of research in the social sciences in progress and in plan. London, National Institute of Economic and Social Research, Annually.
12. *Shenton, H. N.* Cosmopolitan conversation: the language problems of international conferences. New York, Columbia University Press, 1933.
13. *Unesco.* International organizations in the social sciences. 1948. Unesco document 3C/PRG/6.2.
14. *Unesco.* Resolutions adopted on the report of the programme and budget commission. 1948. Unesco document 3C/105.
15. *Union des Associations Internationales.* Bulletin mensuel. janvier 1949-
16. *United Nations. Secretariat.* Past experience and present efforts in inter-organizational relationships: working paper no. 6 for the exploratory conference of non-governmental organizations granted consultative status by the Economic and Social Council of the United Nations, to be held in Geneva, May 1948.
17. *White, L. C.* The structure of private international organizations. Philadelphia. George I. Ferguson Company, 1933.

League of Nations

With one exception (see below), the bibliographies issued by the League itself of its own documents and publications are not listed below, though they have been consulted.
18. *Bouglé, C.* Le guide de l'étudiant en matière de Société des Nations: livres, revues, écoles. Paris, Marcel Rivière, 1933.
19. *Breycha-Vauthier, A. C. de.* Sources of information: a handbook on the publications of the League of Nations. London. Allen & Unwin; New York, Columbia University Press, 1939.
 (German ed., 1934; Czech ed., 1936; abridged Russian version, 1937; French ed., 1937.)
20. *Carroll, M. J.* Key to League of Nations documents placed on public sale. 5 vols. Boston, World Peace Foundation, 1930-38.
21. *League of Nations.* International Economic Conference, Geneva, May 1927. Guide to the documents of the conference. 1927.
22. *L'Hote, A.* Renseignements documentaires sur la Conference pour la Réduction et la Limitation des Armaments. 1936. Paris, Charles Lavauzelle, 1936.
23. *Myers, D. P.* League of Nations documents. Proceedings of the Fifth Conference of Teachers of International Law and Related Subjects, Washington, 1933, pp. 148-155.
24. *Wendelin, E. C.* Subject index to the economic and financial documents of the League of Nations, 1927-1930. Boston, World Peace Foundation, 1932.

United Nations and its Specialized Agencies

25. *Bates, M. L.* and *Turner, R. K.* International documentation, an introduction. International organization, vol. 1, 1947, pp. 607-618.
26. *Bruce, W. J.* The San Francisco Unesco documents. American archivist, vol. 9, 1946, pp. 6-16.
27. *Buck, S. J.* The archivist's "one world." American archivist, vol. 10, 1947, pp. 9-24.
28. *Claus, R.* The archives program of the United Nations. American archivist, vol. 11, 1948, pp. 195-202.
29. *Claus, R.* The United Nations archives. American archivist, vol. 10, 1947, pp. 129-132.
30. [Conferences on the distribution of documents, organized by the World Peace Foundation and the Carnegie Endowment for International Peace. Mimeographed reports.]

1st. March 1947.
2nd. June 1947.
3rd. December 1947
4th. November 1948 [Paris].

31. *Dougall, R.* The archives and documents of the Preparatory Commission of the United Nations. American archivist, vol. 10, 1947, pp. 25-34.
32. Draft classification for United Nations official publications in the library of the Carnegie Endowment for International Peace. [1948].
33. *Lloyd, G.* Are you stymied by United Nations documents? Library Journal, vol. 72, 1948, pp. 1337, 1350-1351, 1453, 1460-1461, 1529-1585, 1603.
34. *Meyer, J.* Publications of the United Nations. College and research libraries, vol. 7, 1946, pp. 311-318.
35. *Meyer, J.* Significant early documents of the Specialized Agencies related to the United Nations, College and research libraries, vol. 8, 1947, pp. 142-146.
36. *Rounds, J. B.* Research facilities of the International Labour Organization available to American libraries. Chicago, American Library Association, 1939.
37. *Russell, F. H.* United Nations source material. Proceedings of the Eighth Conference of Teachers of International Law and Related Subjects, Washington, 1946, pp. 102-118.
38. *Signor, N.* The San Francisco Conference—its structure and documentation. Special Libraries, vol. 37, 1946, pp. 3-6.
39. *Unesco.* Publications policy. 1948. Unesco document 3C/PRG/O.2.
40. *United Nations. International Advisory Committee of Library Experts.* Report of session held at Lake Success, New York, 2-9 August 1948. United Nations document A/C.5/222, also published later in pamphlet form as "Library services of the United Nations," [1949]. References in the text of this paper are to the original document.
41. *United Nations. International Advisory Committee of Library Experts.* Working paper 2. Distribution and use of United Nations documents and departmental publications. 1948.
42. *United Nations. Publications Board.* Papers and minutes including Report attached to Publication Board Paper 243, 1948, on the distribution of United Nations documents to member and non-member states, and Paper 244, 1948, on the "Weekly index to documents and publication."
43. *Winton, H. M.* Documents and publications of the United Nations. College and research Libraries, vol. 9. 1948, pp. 6-14.
44. *Yale University. Library.* United Nations classification scheme, Nov. 18, 1948.

Current Bibliographical Control of International Intergovernmental Publications

James B. Childs

James B. Childs, the Dean of documents librarians has had a long and distinguished career at the Library of Congress where he continues to work daily on documents problems despite his official retirement some years ago. In this article Childs notes the publishing activities of a variety and number of international organizations and points out the serious gaps in bibliographic control.

"A step backwards in the long-range effort to provide complete bibliography control of documentation within the United Nations family"[1] is an official mention of the action that apparently had to be taken at the beginning of 1963 by eliminating from the monthly *United Nations Documents Index* the fifteen specialized agencies.[2] This comment may well serve as the basis on which to review the possibility of attaining more-nearly comprehensive current bibliographical control of the documents of the international intergovernmental bodies, during the period when the member states of the United Nations have increased from 51 to 114 and the intergovernmental agencies outside the UN have likewise increased.

To get a view of the extent and implications of international intergovernmental organizations, even beyond the participation of the United States, it is desirable to keep in mind three works.

The first, those intergovernmental agencies having some relationship to science have been included in the LC Guide,[3] which was compiled and published under a grant from the National Science Foundation, with Robert W. Schaaf making considerable contributions. Several quotations from the Introduction seem pertinent. First, "the cataloging and bibliography of the official documents of national governments have always presented complex problems of differentiation and description." In some countries the library cataloging pattern is still similar to that of the Prussian Instructions. Hence there is no provision for corporate entry under the name of the jurisdiction or under the name of the intergovern-

mental agency. The entry is under an individual author or under the first substantive, or the first word, of the title other than an article. Next, "with the exception of such tools as the *United Nations Documents Index*, there are very few bibliographical works which serve for any sizable group of [international] organizations." And, as mentioned above, even the *UNDI* has had to divest itself of the documents of the specialized agencies. In the *Guide*, also, there is no ready differentiation of the intergovernmental agencies. For instance, the COMECON, the international intergovernmental agency of the People's Democracies for economic development, is listed with no mention of its publications beyond one of the Standing Committee on Agriculture.

The second significant publication is the revised second edition of the two-volume *International Governmental Organizations: Constitutional Documents* (The Hague, 1961), by the international lawyer, Amos J. Peaselee. Arranged alphabetically by the English form of name of the agencies, it includes, as his title indicates, only "international organizations created by governments and themselves of governmental nature," and only "multilateral bodies (i.e. with three or more members)." Thirty-five entirely new organizations have appeared since the first edition in 1956. Peaselee makes the seemingly overoptimistic statement that "the bibliographies do not in the main include the publications of the organizations themselves since this information is readily obtainable at source." The work is dedicated "to better international organization."

SOURCE: Reprinted from: James B. Childs, "Current Bibliographic Control of International Intergovernmental Publications," *Library Resources and Technical Services*, 10, (Summer 1966) pp. 319–331.

My pleas for better current bibliographical control of the documents and publications of international intergovernmental agencies represent one facet of better international organization; the importance of this is not always too well esteemed.

The third publication to be mentioned is the *Yearbook of International Organizations: Annuaire des Organisations Internationales,* published at Brussels by the Union of International Associations; in the 10th edition (1964-65) the first three parts (nearly 300 pages of a total of 1702 pages) are devoted to (I.) the United Nations family, (II.) the European community, and (III.) other intergovernmental organizations. Here the distinction between the governmental organizations or agencies is maintained. Brief notices of publications, particularly serial publications of the organizations, seem to be given wherever possible.

Now let us turn to the United States. In the introduction to the *12th Report on the Extent and Disposition of U. S. Contributions to International Organizations for the Fiscal Year 1963* (House Document 313, 88th Congress, 2d session, 1964), the Department of State makes the following explanatory statement that would seem essential for understanding the problem and the importance of the fullest coverage from the point of view of one of the 114 member-states[4] of the United Nations:

> For practical reasons of enlightened self-interest, the United States has, by virtue of a treaty, convention, special act of Congress, or executive agreement, joined with many other nations in various programs of international cooperation to work *against* situations known to be wrong and to work *for* situations believed to be right.
>
> The range of subject matter dealt with is encyclopedic: atomic energy, children's welfare, civil aviation, coffee, cotton, cultural affairs, economic development, education, fish, furs, geography, history, health, malaria, medical research, navigation, postal matters, radio frequencies, refugees, rubber, seed testing, sugar, telecommunications, travel, weights and measures, whales, wheat, yellow fever, zinc.
>
> No matter how large or how small, each of these international [intergovernmental] activities is of value to the United States—or we would not contribute. The concept of multilateral cooperation and action has long been actively supported by the United States as a means of achieving a better world in which to live.
>
> United States participation in the Universal Postal Union (for example) dates back to 1875, while as recently as six months ago the Congress authorized United States participation in three "new" undertakings, the Hague Conference on Private International Law, the International Institute for the Unification of Private International Law, and the International Agreement regarding the Maintenance of Certain Lights in the Red Sea.

The number of countries collaborating in these organizations ranges from three or four countries (in the case of organizations dealing with a specific problem or with problems in a certain locality) to well over one-hundred (in the case of the United Nations and some of the specialized agencies).

Currently the organizations and programs to which the United States contributes carry out activities which support one or both of two basic aims of U. S. foreign policy: First, the promotion of peace and security, Second, the promotion of economic and social growth, which may well be one of the best ways to achieve peace and security in the long run. Some of these international programs are similar in character to activities, which we also help finance bilaterally. In any given case, the United States may choose between bilateral or multilateral actions since one may be more feasible or desirable than the other, or a combination of both may be more effective.

The report deals with contributions to multilateral organizations, i.e., *intergovernmental* bodies having three or more members. Bilateral organizations are not covered in the text or in the total figures, nor are the Inter-American Development Bank, the International Bank for Reconstruction and Development, International Monetary Fund, International Finance Corporation, and International Development Association; since these are the subject of a report to the Congress by the Secretary of the Treasury.

As chairman of the National Advisory Council on International Monetary and Financial Problems, the Secretary of the Treasury presents to the Congress a semi-annual report, and a special report at less frequent intervals, on United States participation in international financial institutions.

Thus, in addition to the United Nations and its special programs, the United States contributes, according to the reports, to

1. Specialized agencies of the UN   (15)
2. Inter-American organizations   (10)
3. Other regional organizations   (12)
4. Other international intergovernmental
   organizations   (25)
   In all   (62)

Even beyond this number, there may be at least twice as many more in which the United States government has not been participating for one reason or another.

While the above-mentioned United States reports scarcely touch upon the matter of publications, probably for the lack of space, the 18th *Report by the President to the Congress for the Year 1963*[5] on U. S. participation in the UN includes at its conclusion an eight-page appendix on publications and documents with lists both for the "sale of publications and visual materials of the

United Nations and the specialized agencies" and for "depository libraries in the United States designated by the United Nations and the specialized agencies."[6] As to the change mentioned at the beginning of this paper, nothing is said beyond the true but limited statement, "Current UN publications and documents are described in the monthly *Index to United Nations Documents,"* without reference to the "step backwards."

That action, UN *Library Report* for 1963 explains as follows:

> However, the projected French version of the *Index* made this curtailment necessary, since it is not feasible to produce at one central point indexes in both English and French to the entire documentation of the United Nations and the specialized agencies. The volume and complexity of the documentation and the fact that those specialized agencies which hitherto had submitted indexing copy in English could not do so in French as well make the task inordinately expensive in terms of manpower.
>
> 26. In any case, there was a certain amount of overlapping of effort, since several agencies produce and publish their own indexes. It is felt that if these indexes were distributed more widely and if the specialized agencies which do not now produce their own indexes would do so, a decentralized system following a uniform overall pattern but pliable enough to suit the special needs of each agency would be more useful than an imperfect combined effort.

No indication has been given other than possibly in the two working papers of quite limited circulation that a precise survey has been made of the situation, specialized agency by specialized agency, to determine what is being done to continue the "imperfect combined effort" represented in the *United Nations Documents Index,* volumes 1-13, for the years 1950 to 1962, or what representation of these there might be made in various national bibliographies.

In the 1962 UN *Library Report,* the change had been foreshadowed, as follows:

> 17. The principal preoccupation with bibliographical services concerned the problems of coping with the rising tide of United Nations documents and planning for the production of some indexes in French as well as in English.
>
> 18. The sheer volume of documentation was startingly greater than in any previous year, an increase which appears not in the number of the documents indexed, but in the bulk of the individual documents and the many more index entries required properly to record the interventions of a Membership which has doubled over the last decade. Thus, whereas the number of documents indexed has remained fairly

constant at about 10,000 per year, the number of index entries established for publication in the Library's principal indexes totalled 124,000 as against about 80,000 entries required in 1959 to index approximately the same number of documents.

> 19. This subterranean swelling required the full attention of the Index Section staff, increased somewhat over previous years, but precluded any new indexing commitments. Nevertheless, plans were made for the eventual publication of a French version of the *United Nations Documents Index.* Towards that end the scope of UNDI was restudied and two working papers in which were proposed certain drastic changes were circulated among the specialized agencies' librarians and others for comment.

Indeed it might be well to look at a few instances.

The Food and Agriculture Organization at Rome has been issuing a *Catalogue of FAO Publications* every two years in each of the three official languages (English, French, and Spanish), cumulated from 1945, with supplements between editions. The emphasis here is placed on publications for sale, without mention of those for limited distribution. Since 1961, there has been a processed checklist of working papers under the title: *FAO Documentation, a Quarterly List of Documents and ETAP* [Expanded Program of Technical Assistance] *Final Reports*, distributed only to authorized recipients as determined by the FAO National Committees. Whether there is anything like a full coverage currently of FAO publications in the Italian National Bibliography *(Bibliografia nazionale italiana)* has not been determined.

With the location of certain of the specialized agencies in Switzerland, mainly at Geneva, various questions may be asked. For instance, does the Swiss current national bibliography (*Schweizer Buch*), edited by the National Library (Landesbibliothek) at Berne, attempt to record in its two series (A in the booktrade, B not in the booktrade) all of the publications of the specialized agencies in Switzerland? Even the Swiss National Library has been issuing, beginning with 1946, an annual bibliography of Swiss official publications.[7]

For the International Telecommunication Union, Geneva, a four-page comprehensive list of publications, revised from time to time, seems to include only publications for sale and is kept up to date in the numbers of the *Telecommunication Journal.* Publications of both the attached International Telegraph and Telephone Consultative Committee and the International Radio Consultative Committee are also recorded. At the beginning of the comprehensive list is the statement: "As the General Secretariat of the Union sells its publications on a non-profit and nondiscount basis no reduction can be made to booksellers." Thus, it would seem that there is no depository system for these. All of the documents are published in French, also, as required, in English, Spanish, Russian, and Chinese.

The World Health Organization, Geneva, occasionally issues a comprehensive catalog of its publications, cumulative from 1947, and has also published a *Bibliography of WHO Publications* for 1947–1957 and for 1958–1962. In May, 1965, at the annual assembly of the Organization, a resolution was presented to institute an international agency for research in cancer. If and when such an agency may be instituted, there is even more need to have coordination and indexing of the various actions of the specialized agencies.

Each of the other UN specialized agencies in Switzerland,[8] has a similar more-or-less formal catalog or list of its publications. Such small bibliographical books are often thrown away when superseded or when the immediate use ceases, despite the fact that certain of the older editions may be the only clues to the existence of some publications no longer in print but which may be needed for some important purpose.

For all international organizations at Geneva, whether intergovernmental or not, occasional directories have been published by the Association des Intérêts de Genève under the title *Annuaire International de Genève: Geneva International Year-book. Edité par le Centre Permanent d' Informations Internationales*.

The Bureau International de l'Union Postale Universelle is located at Berne; all of its publications except the monthly *Union postale,* are issued in French, the official language of the UPU. The publications are furnished free only to postal services and then on a quota.

The only specialized agency in France is the United Nations Educational, Scientific, and Cultural Organization (UNESCO), Paris. A quarterly processed *List of UNESCO Documents and Publications* (UNESCO/ARC/List/), issued in both English and French, has appeared regularly at least since 1951. It includes the processed working documents for limited circulation of the General Conference, the Executive Board, and the Secretariat, as well as the UNESCO periodicals, the UNESCO non-periodical publications, and further publications issued by other publishers. The second part of each number is a combined

subject-author index, and a cumulative index is contained in the last quarter for each year. Thus, it will be noted that this quarterly *List* seems to be the only one thus far mentioned as following more nearly the pattern of the *United Nations Documents Index.*

The UNESCO documents noted above are not included in the *General Catalogue of UNESCO Publications and UNESCO Sponsored Publications, 1946–1959* (UNESCO, 1962) nor in the much briefer *Check List,* the *Annual Current List of UNESCO Publications,* nor in the various subject lists.

UNESCO, through unanimous vote of its General Conference in December, 1962, approved the charter of the International Institute for Educational Planning at Paris, with facilities provided by the French Government and with its first budget assembled by UNESCO, the World Bank, and the Ford Foundation. The Institute is an autonomous body within the broad legal framework of UNESCO, serving all of the member states, but especially assisting the developing countries of Africa, Asia, and the Middle East; it has thus far issued three publications of more than a hundred pages each.

The occasional supplement of the *Bibliographie de la France*, devoted to official publications, has a section for those international intergovernmental bodies centered in France. This international section apparently records all UNESCO publications deposited in the Bibliothèque Nationale.

It may be noted that the Intergovernmental Maritime Consultative Organization, which is at Chancery House, Chancery Lane, London, W.C.2, and is the only specialized agency of UN in the United Kingdom, has issued as of 24 May 1965 a two-page foolscap folio list of its publications appearing in English and French and also, to a certain necessary extent, in Russian and Spanish.

Thus, the information about the documents and publications of all the specialized agencies of the UN, which ceased to appear after 1962, needs badly to be kept updated, even if only for the users in one or more of the member states.

The Pan American Union at Washington, D.C., which serves as Secretariat for the Organization of American states, adopted in 1960 an organizational classification scheme for the official documents of the OAS. Spanish is the principal working language of the Organization (Spanish: Organización de los Estados Americanos, abbreviated OEA), and the sixty-eight page combined guide, scheme, and tables, issued in April 1961 is in Spanish: *Serie de los documentos oficiales de la Organización de los Estados Americanos: Gúia, esquama y cuadros explicativos de categorias.*

The first annual list and index of the official documents of the Organization under the new classification scheme appeared as a volume of almost 500 pages, entitled: *Documentos oficiales de la Organización de los Estados Americanos: Indice y lista general,* volumen I, Enero-Diciembre 1960, having the reference numbers OEA/Ser. Z/I. 1 (español) vol. I. In all, 3,900 documents, extending to 42,000 pages, appeared in the classified list. The compact index to the more important documents prepared in the Columbus Memorial Library of the Union is on colored paper—about 140 pages at the end of the volume. Each listing gives the classification and the language (Spanish, English, French, or Portuguese), whether the item is for limited distribution or for sale, price, and in a few instances whether the numbers have been cancelled or not used. The classification is by organization, and the volume includes only the acts and documents of the Organization, the Inter-American Conferences, its Council, the Inter-American Economic and Social Council, the Meetings of Ministers of Foreign Relations, specialized Inter-American Conferences, and other central councils, commissions, and agencies. The informational and technical publications of the Pan American Union, of which separate lists are issued regularly, are not included; nor are the publications of the specialized agencies for public health, child welfare, geography and history, agriculture, and Indian affairs. Deposit for these publications may be subject to official representation through the appropriate national representative to OAS.

Turning next to the *Central American Organization of States,* we find the ten agreements and treaties tending to integrate the economies of the Central American Organization of States (or ODECA as it is often referred to) have been collected in a volume of 251 pages, and have appeared as series 2, number 26, of its *Boletin informativo,* published by the Secretaría General at San Salvador, Republic of El Salvador. These documents cover the period November 8, 1956, to December 13, 1960, and seem to represent the striving towards a Central American common market. In 1965 Costa Rica completed ratification of the Charter signed at Panama in 1962, and the Charter is now in effect. The Secretariat continues to be at San Salvador.

The Inter-American specialized agencies include one linked with Spain, the Postal Union of the Americas and Spain, with the permanent bureau at Montevideo, Uruguay. Such an agency tends to limit its contacts to the postal services of the various member countries.

Spain, through its official Instituto de Cultura Hispánica, has been able to set up Ibero-American organizations in the fields of education, social security, and the official language academies. In these the United States has not participated. And since 1948, Spain apparently has been a member of the European Insurance Supervising Authorities Conference, and also a member of the International Congress of State Lotteries.

By 1940 in Spain, the great number of government publications existing in state-supported libraries was in contrast to the situation at the time of the approval of the first edition of the cataloging instructions in 1902. The obvious convenience for users of the catalogs in bringing the titles together under the name of the jurisdiction and agency motivated the drawing up and inclusion of fifteen additional rules for corporate entries in the second revised edition of the official cataloging rules of 1941.[9]

By 1959, the need for some revision of the *Instrucciones* had become apparent. The printing of unit catalog cards by the Biblioteca Nacional at Madrid pointed up some need for clarification and expansion. The International Conference on the Principles of Cataloging at Paris in October 1961 furnished impetus to the work of revision. Now twenty-two rules devoted to government publications appear in the third revised edition of 1964.[10]

Turning now to the special grouping of Western European intergovernmental agencies it may be helpful to quote from the introduction to vol. X (1962) of the *European Yearbook*[11] by L. Benvenuti, the Secretary-General of the Council of Europe.

During the ten years which have elapsed, the scope of European activities has expanded enormously. The first volume reported on the constitutions and activities of eight organisations; in the intervening period, the number has doubled. Two of the oldest have been transformed: The Brussels Treaty Organisation into the Western European Union and O.E.E.C. into the Organisation for Economic Co-operation and Development. The principal newcomers are, of course, the Economic Community, Euratom, and the European Free Trade Association. The oldest international organisation in existence, the General Commission for the Navigation on the Rhine, is now among the contributors, as are the newer technical organisations such as the Customs Co-operation Council, the Commission for Civil Status, the European Civil Aviation Conference, "Eurocontrol," the Conference on Posts and Tele-communications, and the two newest members of the European family: the European Space Research Organisation (ESRO) and the European Launcher Development Organisation (ELDO).

The number of these bodies and the variety of subjects with which they deal show that consciousness of the need for European co-operation is not limited to politicians and economists but extends to almost every branch of public activity.

Neither the European regional agencies of UN nor the specialized agencies with headquarters in Europe are treated in the *European Yearbook.* Summary lists of the official publications of the various Western European agencies accompany the appropriate section from year to year, thus forming, so far as can be ascertained, the most comprehensive record extant. The Council of Europe came into being in 1949 at Strasbourg, France, as a forum for the development of public opinion, and has stimulated and fostered the growth of various specialized agencies. A 28-page *Catalogue of the Publications of the Council of Europe* for 1964 represents a remarkable impact. By the Treaty of 18 April 1951, signed by the German Federal Republic, Belgium, France, Luxembourg, and the Netherlands, the European Coal and Steel Community was created with seat in the Grand Duchy of Luxembourg. By Treaty at Rome, 25 March 1957, between the same powers, the European Economic Community came into being at Brussels, Belgium, with close and inter-weaving ties with the European Coal and Steel Community. The 56-page *Publications of the European Communities: Catalogue, March, 1964,* Luxembourg-Brussels, has been followed by a 49-page *Bibliographical Supplement,* also issued at Luxembourg-Brussels, and by a 39-page catalog, *European Economic Community Publications,* 1965, now issued only at Brussels.[12] All of the Community publications are in Dutch, French, German, and Italian. The Library of the Community in its *Bulletin des acquisitions* mentions that official publications of the Community are not included since it has complete periodical sets. As to current bibliographical coverage in the Belgian national bibliography, it must be remembered that the *Bibliographie de Belgique* only records books and pamphlets actually published and placed on sale in Belgium and that the publication activities of the Communities had been spread over various western European countries, with the main publication, sales, and distribution

activity at 2 Place de Metz, Luxembourg, Grand Duchy of Luxembourg.

It may be helpful to note in the European Economic Community 1965 catalog the following: "Publications marked 'limited distribution' are reserved for specialists in the field concerned, and for libraries, universities, etc. *Working papers* (unprinted drafts) emanating from the various services of the E.E.C. Commission and not intended for distribution outside the organization are not listed in this catalogue." It is quite likely that many of the European Community publications are recorded currently in the monthly classified accessions list of the Central Library of the Belgian Ministry of Economic Affairs and Power.[13]

The very useful device of considering the establishment of a certain number of depository libraries for Community publications might well benefit by experience in one of the member states (German Federal Republic). By a Supplementary Order of March 17, 1961, printed in the *Gemein-sames Ministerialblatt,* 1961, no. 11, p. 235, the Bundesministerium des Innern designated the Bayerische Staatsbibliothek at Munich as the fourth national depository library for German Federal Republic Documents. Under the Reich, that institution had for some years been designated as one of the national depositories for Reich official documents. The three national depositories established for German Federal Republic Documents by the Bundesministerium des Innern through its order of May 12, 1958, are as follows:

1. Deutsche Bibliothek, Frankfurt am Main.
2. Westdeutsche Bibliothek, Marburg.
3. Bibliothek des Deutschen Bundestages, Bonn.

A similar standard order to provide in each Land (State) for systematic deposit for the official publications of each jurisdiction has been proposed by the Kommission für Amtsdrucksachen of the Verein Deutscher Bibliothekare.

As a counterbalance to the "Common Market" in the European Economic Community, the European Free Trade Association (EFTA) was instituted by Convention in 1960, between Great Britain, Sweden, Norway, Denmark, Austria, Portugal, and Switzerland (Finland later an associate member), with headquarters in Geneva.

The Organization for Economic Cooperation and Development (mentioned earlier), the European Economic Community, and EFTA all maintain information offices in the United States in Washington, D.C.

Two instances of peculiarity of distribution in a closely-related subject field may be explained. At Brussels, Belgium, there is the Bureau International de Tarifs Douaniers (International Union for the Publication of Customs Tariffs), established by Convention of 5 July 1890, the United States being a member. The Bureau translates customs tariffs into five languages (German, English, French, Spanish, and Italian) and publishes these in the *Bulletin international des douanes* which is furnished only to the pertinent official agency of the contracting governments for distribution or subscription in the country. In the United States, this agency is the Office of International Regional Economics, Bureau of International Commerce, U. S. Department of Commerce, Washington, D. C. 20320. The other is the Customs Co-operation Council in Brussels, established late in 1954, under the Convention of 15 December 1950, in which 26 countries are members, not including the United States. As of 1 January 1964, the Council has a four-page list of publications available for sale, ordinarily in both French and English. One of these is the three-volume *Explanatory Notes to the Brussels Convention,* which was, for instance, translated into Spanish, adopted officially, and printed by the Spanish Government for use in Spain.

For the People's Democracies in Eastern Europe, there is a COMECON (Council for Mutual Economic Aid),[14] which dates from January 1949, and which has headquarters in Moscow, the Soviet Union. Despite the occasional lengthy news dispatches concerning COMECON and its activities, the only substantial publication which apparently can be cited is the *Agricultural Review,* edited by the Standing Committee for Agriculture at Sofia, Bulgaria, and also published in German at Berlin in the German Democratic Republic under the title *Internationale Zeitschrift für Landwirtschaft.* What the Central Secretariat, as well as the various other standing committees, may have issued has not yet been determined beyond the fact that any and all such documents have apparently been for official use only. My recent discussion of official publications in a People's Democracy may even have some pertinence.[15]

Next, the Warsaw Treaty Organization for defense purposes was set up in 1955. Here again, no documents have been cited. Further, the Organization for the Collaboration of Railways (OSShD) was also established at Warsaw in a decision of the first Conference of Ministers of Transport of the Socialist Countries in 1956. A bimonthly *OSShD Journal* is published at Warsaw in German and reportedly also in Chinese and Russian. Mention of other OSShD publications is occasionally made in the *Journal.*

For the Arab countries of North Africa and the Middle East, the League of Arab States was set up with headquarters at Cairo in 1945, the official language being Arabic. The Arab Postal Union was set up in 1954 with Arabic again as the official language. There have probably been various other Arab states intergovernmental agencies.

For Africa the picture of intergovernmental agencies is not entirely clear. The Organization of African Unity was founded at Addis Ababa, Ethiopia, in May, 1963. This and other related agencies have been described as of 1965.[16] There is also the Organisation Commune Africaine et Malgache at Yaoundé, Cameroons, of February 1965. Apparently there has not been sufficient time yet to determine whether any systematic plan for the issuance of documents and other publications is evolving.

In conclusion, the rather hasty picture sketched herein of current bibliographical control (or lack of control) of international documents seems to be one for the most part of continuing change of both agencies and publications as well as increasing members. Several possible points of approach might be recommended, such as:

1. For the agencies of which the United States is a member, to endeavor to have the needs of libraries and library users included regularly in the instructions to the missions and representatives, with, wherever necessary, mention of the utility of a library depository system.
2. For the agencies of which the United States is not a member, to seek to interest pertinent foreign library associations and institutions in having such needs presented to the agencies.
3. To stress along the same lines the desirability of striving for the fullest possible bibliographical coverage or control.

To ensure the coverage desired, even with conventional means of approach, constant alertness and adaptation to the realities of the situation are required, and may tend to stimulate better international organization.*

---

*Note. At Geneva on 24–25 February 1966, an Inter-Agency Working Party on the Indexing of Agency Documents was convened, and any tangible results of this or subsequent sessions would be awaited with much interest.

REFERENCES

1. *Report of the Headquarters Library and the Geneva Library 1963.* United Nations, 1964, p. 6, par. 25.
2. Food and Agriculture Organization, Rome.
   General Agreement on Tariffs and Trade, Geneva.
   Intergovernmental Maritime Consultative Organization, London.
   International Atomic Energy Agency, Vienna.
   International Bank for Reconstruction and Development (World Bank), Washington, D. C.
   International Civil Aviation Organization, Montreal.
   International Development Association, Washington, D. C.
   International Finance Corporation, Washington, D. C.
   International Labor Organization, Geneva.
   International Monetary Fund, Washington, D. C.
   International Telecommunication Union, Geneva.
   United Nations Educational, Scientific and Cultural Organization, Paris.
   Universal Postal Union, Berne.
   World Health Organization, Geneva.
   World Meteorological Organization, Geneva.
3. *International Scientific Organizations, a Guide to their Library, Documentation and Information Services.* Prepared under the Direction of Katherine O. Murra. Washington, D. C. Superintendent of Documents, 1962, 794p.
4. One hundred seventeen, as of late September, 1965, with the addition of Gambia, Singapore, and the Maldive Islands.
5. Washington, D. C., U. S. Govt. Print. Off., 1964; also as 88th Congress, *House Document* 188.
6. Only International Court of Justice, Food and Agriculture Organization, International Civil Aviation Organization, UNESCO, and World Health Organization.
7. *Bibliographie der schweizerischen Amtsdruckschriften. Bibliografie des publications officielles suisses.*
8. International Labor Organization, World Meteorological Organization. General Agreement on Tariffs and Trade, and the Universal Postal Union.
9. Spain. Junta Técnica de Archivos, Bibliotecas y Museos. Instrucciones para la redacción del catálogo alfabético de autores y obras anónimas en las bibliotecas públicas del Estado, dirigidas por el Cuerpo Facultativo de Archiveros, Bibliotecarios y Arqueólogos, Segunda edición, reformada, aprobado y autorizada su publicación por Orden Ministerial de 24 Enero 1941. Madrid, 1941. 210p.
10. Spain. Junta Técnica de Archivos, Bibliotecas y Museos. Instrucciones para la redacción del catálogo alfabético de autores y obras anónimas en las bibliotecas públicas del Estado, dirigidas por el Cuerpo Faculativo de Archiveros, Bibliotecarios y Arqueólogos, Tercera edición reformada. Madrid, 1964. 264p. (Anejos del Boletin de la Dirección General de Archivos y Bibliotecas. 62)
11. *Annuaire Européen. European Yearbook.* Published under the auspices of the Council of Europe. The Hague, Martinus Nijhoff. General editor is Professor B. Landheer, Library of the Peace Palace, The Hague. French and English text, these being the official languages of the Council of Europe.
12. Weil, Gordon Lee, ed. *A Handbook on the European Economic Community.* New York, Praeger. Published in cooperation with the European Community Information Service, Washington, D. C., 1965. 479p. *(Praeger Special Studies in International Economics)* A compilation of the basic documents in English. The bibliography, p. 465–479, includes "a complete listing of official documents of the EEC which are available to the public." Does not include mimeographed documents.
    Beginning with January 1965, the Publications Division, Press and Information Service, Brussels, has been issuing a processed monthly listing of the new official publications, entitled *Relevé bibliographique mensuel, Monatliches Veröffentlichungsverzeichnis.*
13. Belgium *Ministere des Affaires Economiques et de l'Energie.* Accroissements de la Bibliothèque Centrale (Fonds Quetelet). Liste mensuelle.
14. Russian: Sovet ekonomicheskoi vzaimopomoshchi. German: Rat fur gegenseitige Wirtschaftshilfe.
15. "Government and Official Publications in a People's Democracy" [German Democratic Republic] in *Library Science Today* (Ranganathan Festschrift) v. I, p. 163–170, and also as a reprint, 8 p.
16. *The Department of State Bulletin,* Washington, D. C., 3 May 1965, v. 52, p. 469–477. Also in reprint form.

II

THE LEAGUE OF NATIONS

The League of Nations was founded in 1920 in the optimism following World War I. The objectives of the League were to achieve and preserve peace and security. The successes and ultimate failure of the League are recorded by history. The successes and failures of the League's documentation program and of the librarians who tried to cope with the publications of the League are recorded here. An organization with a broad representation of nations and with a multiplicity of subsidiary social and economic purposes related to the main objective of keeping the peace, the League was by far the largest and most complex international organization up to its time. Much of the organizational structure and the patterns of operation of the League were adopted later by the UN; hence an understanding of the League and its publications is important for an understanding of the work and publications of its successor. The publications of the League are no longer available in their original form. A commercial microfilming project now in progress aims at providing a comprehensive set of League publications. The availability of the information in microform will make accessible to libraries a mass of information in the fields of social science, and the humanities for the period 1920-1945.

The League of Nations; Its Constitution and Organization

League of Nations Information Section

This basic document outlines the provisions of the League's constitutional document, the Covenant, which sets forth conditions of membership, the organization of the League, and its functions. The auxiliary organizations and their functions are also explained.

INTRODUCTION

The League of Nations is an association of self-governing States organised on permanent lines in an effort to broaden the basis of peace and to lessen the chances of war. Its constitution is contained in the Covenant, which forms Part I of the Treaties of Versailles, Saint-Germain, Neuilly, and Trianon, and it came into force on January 10th, 1920, the date on which the instrument of ratification of the Treaty of Versailles was deposited by the representatives of Germany.

The general principles are simply stated in the Preamble, by which the Members of the League agree to its terms as a means of promoting international co-operation and achieving international peace and security:

By the acceptance of obligations not to resort to war;

By the prescription of open, just and honourable relations between nations;

By the firm establishment of the understandings of international law as the actual rule of conduct among Governments; and

By the maintenance of justice and scrupulous respect for all treaty obligations in the dealings of organised peoples with one another.

The means of applying these principles are described in the subsequent twenty-six articles, which govern the actual work of the League.

It is essential for a clear understanding of this new organisation to realise that it is an inter-State society explicitly retaining the principle of national sovereignty. It is not a separate organisation existing apart from and above the States of which it is composed. It is international, not super-national. It does not impose settlements; its chief weapons are the publicity of facts and such force of persuasion as is inherent in all work of mediation. It seeks agreement, in which it may or may not be successful, but failure to accept its decisions or recommendations involves no penalty. The League's penalties may be applied only to a breach of faith by resort to war before following lines of procedure designed in the hope of securing settlement without war, or by resort to war against a unanimous decision of the League. The League is, in fact, a body of States working together on a common basis, seeking to promote their common interest in peace and progress, and for this purpose they have voluntarily agreed beforehand to observe certain rules of conduct, and, in the mutual interest, to limit their freedom of action in certain directions.

As the Members of the League are States, the business of the League is conducted by representatives of Governments which are the State executives. There can be no League initiative except on the proposal of one or more Governments, and no League work can be accomplished except through the Governments. The Governments, collectively and individually, are the responsible League authorities. It is their instrument to do what they decide it shall do. Whatever the League achieves is a result of inter-Governmental agreement.

SOURCE: Reprinted from *The League of Nations; Its Constitution and Organization*, Geneva, League of Nations Information Section 1926, pp. 5–40.

It has no magic power to dispel rapidly and easily all the necessarily complicated issues of the world. States, on entering the League, do not by this step relinquish their national aims and interests, and these aims and interests may just as easily clash with those of other States when problems are dealt with through the League as when they are dealt with outside it. The League is a method of facilitating settlements, and where it differs from what has hitherto existed is that, by the Covenant, inter-State dealings are organised under a written constitution, with permanent machinery, with settled though not rigid rules of procedure for various eventualities, and with definite obligations. This gives order, regularity and continuity to the study and solution of international problems and makes collaboration easier and more customary. The League system, with its complete set of organs for political, judicial, economic and other questions, and its wide responsibilities, is rooted in the life of the world to-day.

THE MEMBERS OF THE LEAGUE

The States qualified as original Members were the Allied and Associated Powers, signatories to the Treaties of Peace, and invitations to accede (also as original Members) to the Covenant were extended to the thirteen States which remained neutral during the war. Of the signatories of the Versailles Treaty of other treaties including the Covenant, all entitled to original membership, with the exception of the United States of America, Ecuador and the Hedjaz, became Members by the ratification of one or other of these treaties. The thirteen neutral States invited to join all accepted, and by March, 10th, 1920, the membership was forty-two. Since then, fourteen additional States have been admitted including Germany, Austria, and Hungary. The total number of States in the League is now fifty-six[1], though for various reasons the Argentine Republic and one or two Central and South American States have not regularly participated in League work. At the same time, they retain their membership.

On January 1st, 1925, Costa Rica gave notice of intention to withdraw. Brazil and Spain also gave notice on June 12th, 1926, and September 8th, 1926, respectively. In accordance with the Covenant, such withdrawal takes effect two years after the date of notification.

The League has frequently invited and secured the collaboration of non-Members.

THE COVENANT CONSIDERED

I. Conditions of Admission and Withdrawal

The consideration of the terms of the Covenant may be taken under one or two broad divisions. First of all, membership is open to any fully self-governing State, Dominion or Colony, provided it gives effective guarantees of its sincere intention to observe its international obligations, accepts such regulations as may be prescribed by the League in regard to its armed forces, and secures the consent of two-thirds of the Members: that is to say, there is no restriction concerning the political character of any State, provided it is self-governing. The political tendencies of this or any other international body naturally follow the direction of the prevailing political tendencies of the Members, and as national Governments reflect the political and economic ideas of the majority of electors, so the League will reflect the political and economic ideas of the majority of States.

A State wishing to join lodges an application with the Secretary-General, who automatically places it on the agenda of the next Assembly.

Any Member of the League may, after two years' notice of its intention to do so, withdraw from the League, provided that all its international obligations and all its obligations under the Covenant have been fulfilled at the time of its withdrawal. A State may be expelled from the League for breach of the Covenant.

2. The Organs of the League.

The main constitutional organs of the League are:

The Assembly;
The Council;
The Permanent Secretariat.

It has two essential wings in:

The Permanent Court of International Justice;
and the International Labour Organisation.

The Covenant also implies the establishment of auxiliary bodies for various questions of a more or less technical kind.

The relations between the Assembly and the Council are not explicitly defined, and their competence, with a few exceptions, is much the same. Each body may deal with any matter within the sphere of action of the League or affecting the peace of the world. Particular questions or tasks may be referred either to the Council or to the Assembly, and reference may be passed on from one body to the other. The framers of the Covenant left the relations purposely elastic for reasons of convenience, and each body possesses a large degree of independent authority. At the same time, they are not precisely separate or independent bodies, as all the Members of the Council are also Members of the Assembly, and the Secretariat is a further link between the two. The First Assembly, which had some of these points under review, adopted one or two guiding principles. It declared that neither body had jurisdiction to render a decision in a matter which had been expressly committed to the other organ of the League, but either body might discuss and investigate any matters within the general competence of the League. It also decided that each year the Council should present to the Assembly an account of its work.

Unanimity Rule and Exceptions—Decisions of the Assembly and the Council, except in matters of procedure and in some other specific cases, such as the admission of new Members, must be unanimous. Important facts in this connection are the provision that in cases of dispute the consent of the parties to the dispute is not required for unanimity, and that where reference of a dispute is made to the Assembly a decision requires the consent of the majority only of the Assembly, but including all the Members of the Council. This general regulation concerning unanimity is, of course, the recognition of national sovereignty. The League seeks solution by consent and not by dictation. Sovereign States are not ready to be bound by majority decisions of other States and successful international action, whether in League meetings or in non-League Conferences, requires general consent. So many conflicting customs and tendencies of a legitimate kind have to be taken account of that, with or without the unanimity rule, the practical necessity for unanimity would in a general way still exist. Otherwise State action as part of some general international plan could scarcely be secured. It is, in fact, the expression of the necessity for agreement as distinct from the delivery of judgments, but it is

modified by two facts: first, in disputes the votes of the contesting parties do not count; second, a resolution carried by majority, and not unanimously, becomes a recommendation upon which any States Members are severally entitled to act. It is however, a fundamental consideration that, apart from the power of collective persuasion exercised by mediation, publicity and delay, no penal action can be taken, even in the case of unanimity, against States refusing to agree to a decision, unless one or other of them goes to war against the terms of a decision taken unanimously. In matters not arising from disputes, the votes of the interested parties are included and these comprise also the votes of any non-Member of the Council sitting temporarily for the discussion of a particular question in which it is interested, so that the interests of Powers not ordinarily represented on the Council are constitutionally safeguarded. Resort to war in certain circumstances is a penal offence; failure to accept a solution is not.

The Assembly—The Assembly consists of representatives of all the Members of the League and meets annually in September. It may also meet at such times as the Assembly at a previous meeting, or the Council, by a majority vote, decides. A special session of the Assembly may be summoned at the request of a Member, provided a majority of the Members concur. Each delegation is composed of not more than three members, but commands one vote only. The special functions of the Assembly include the admission of new Members, the periodical election of non-permanent Members of the Council, the election with the Council of the judges of the Permanent Court, and the control of the budget. It may also, from time to time, advise the reconsideration by Members of the League of treaties which have become inapplicable, or the consideration of international conditions whose continuance might endanger the peace of the world. In practice, the Assembly has become the general directing force of League activities; it reviews the work of the past and indicates the lines of progress in the future. So large a body is not a practical one for ordinary detailed international work or for special emergencies. It is partly for this reason, and partly to give a certain balance of representation in relation to the organised political power of the world, that the Covenant provides for the Council, which does most of the detailed work.

Assembly Procedure—The sessions of the

Assembly are summoned by the President *ad interim* of the Council acting through the Secretary-General, and the summons is addressed to Members not less than four months before the opening of the session, except in special circumstances, where the Council, by a majority, may sanction a shorter period. The agenda of a general session includes a report on the work of the Council since the last session of the Assembly, on the work of the Secretariat, and on the measures taken to execute the decisions of the preceding Assembly; all items whose inclusion has been ordered by the Assembly at a previous session; any items proposed by the Council or by a Member of the League; and the budget. There are arrangements for placing additional items on the agenda by the Assembly itself. The delegations may include substitute representatives who may take the place of representatives in case of need, and the same applies to technical advisers at Assembly Committees.

The Assembly opens under the temporary presidency of the acting President of the Council. Its first business is the election of its President and six Vice-Presidents. They, with the Chairmen of the main Committees of the Assembly, who become *ex-officio* Vice-Presidents of the Assembly, form the General Committee for the conduct of the business of the Assembly. These elections, as far as possible, have regard to the main groupings of international life, so that the various forms of civilisation and the various political interests may have their representation.

The actual work of the session begins with the discussion of the report on the work of the Council and the action taken on the decisions of the preceding Assembly, and after this general debate the Assembly divides its work amongst six general Committees, which in themselves are small Assemblies, as every State has one representative on each of them. These Committees deal with different groups of subjects, as follows:

1. Constitutional and Legal Questions.
2. Work of the Technical Organisations.
3. Disarmament.
4. Budget and Questions of Internal Administration.
5. Social Questions.
6. Political Questions.

The Committees consider all the reports presented to the Assembly by various League bodies and make final recommendations to the Assembly, a general account of the discussions and conclusions being made to the Assembly by a Rapporteur appointed by each Committee. The plenary Assembly affords an opportunity for a final debate on any point still at issue, and it takes the final vote.

The official languages are English and French, and speeches delivered in one are interpreted into the other. Another language may be used, but in this case the speaker is responsible for providing the interpretation into English or French.

The whole of the work of the Assembly, both in the Committees and in the plenary sessions, is open to the Press and to as many of the general public as can be accommodated. The Assembly may decide that particular meetings shall be private, but this right has never been exercised.

The Council—The Council which consists to-day of five permanent members, including Germany, and nine non-permanent members, was originally to consist of five permanent Members, namely the Principal Allied and Associated Powers (British Empire, France, Italy, Japan, and the United States of America), and four non-permanent Members elected from time to time by the Assembly. The failure of the United States of America to ratify the Versailles Treaty reduced the number of original permanent Members to four. The Covenant also provides that the number of Council seats, either permanent or non-permanent, may be increased by unanimous decision of the Council with the approval of a majority of the Assembly. The first step in this direction was taken when in 1922 the number of non-permanent Members of the Council was increased from four to six.

The Council took its present form in September, 1926, as the result of the admission of Germany and of the adoption of a scheme of reorganisation governing the method of election, term of office, and conditions of re-eligibility of non-permanent Members. Germany was elected to a permanent seat, and the number of non-permanent Members was increased from six to nine. Under the new scheme the Assembly, at its ordinary session each year, elects three non-permanent Members for three years, and they take office immediately on election. A retiring Member is not eligible for re-election during the three years following the expiration of its term of office, unless the Assembly, on the expiration of a Member's term of office or during the course of the three years subsequent to its period of office, decides by a two-thirds majority of the votes cast that such a Member is re-eligible. A vote on re-eligibility is taken only at the request of a Member itself. The number of Members re-elected in consequence of having been previously declared re-eligible is restricted so as to prevent the Council from containing at the same time more than three re-elected Members. Notwithstanding these provisions, the Assembly may at any time by two-thirds majority, decide to proceed, in application of Article 4 of the Covenant, to a new election of all the non-permanent Members of the Council.

Several temporary provisions were made to meet the special situation of 1926. Amongst them was one which gave power to the Assembly to declare immediately, at the beginning of their terms of office, a maximum of three States, re-eligible on the expiry of their terms instead of leaving such a declaration, as provided for in the general and normal rules, until after the expiration of the term of office. One State only, Poland, submitted a request for re-eligibility under this temporary provision and was declared re-eligible. In order to enable the scheme to be brought into effect, three Members were elected for three years, three for two years, and three for one year.

The Committee which drew up the main lines of the reorganisation report which was ultimately adopted considered that the increase of the non-permanent seats on the Council would permit the Assembly to take account in a more comprehensive and equitable measure of the principle of the geographical distribution of seats.

Each Power has one representative on the Council and one vote. Any Member of the League not represented on the Council is invited to sit as a full Member during the consideration of any matters especially affecting its interests. The Council is to meet as occasion may require and at least once a year. In practice, it meets normally four times a year—March, June, September and December—, and it is summoned immediately in cases of emergency. In the latter event, it is the Secretary-General who is charged with the duty of summoning a meeting forthwith at the request of any Member of the League.

Certain special functions are attributed to the Council, such as the supervision of the mandates system, and the preparation of plans for the limitation of armaments; the Peace Treaties entrusted it with other duties concerning the government of the Saar Territory and of the Free City of Danzig, and minorities. All the

work of the Council in these and any other connections is subject to discussion by the Assembly.

Council Procedure—The Council is convened by the President acting through the Secretary-General and appoints a Rapporteur for each subject on the agenda. The Presidency changes at each session according to alphabetical rotation, the names of the States in French being taken for this purpose. The Council meets either in private or in public according to circumstances, but wherever possible public meetings have been the order of the day. A representative of the Council acts as Rapporteur on each subject; that is to say, he pays particular attention to the subject and is responsible for the reports explaining to the Council the circumstances, suggesting possible means of settlement, and giving public account of decisions reached by the Council. All the minutes of Council proceedings, whether taken in private or in public, are subsequently printed and published.

The Permanent Secretariat—The Permanent Secretariat, established at the seat of the League at Geneva, comprises a body of experts in various spheres under the direction of Sir Eric Drummond, whose name is included in the Annex to the Covenant as the first Secretary-General. The members of the Secretariat are appointed by the Secretary-General with the approval of the Council and at present include representatives of over forty different nationalities. There is a Deputy Secretary-General and there are two Under Secretaries-General; the rest of the Secretariat is divided into Sections according to subjects, not according to nationality, and each section forms the secretariat of organisations dealing with its particular subject. The principal Sections are under the control of a Director, and there are some others under the control of a *chef de service*. Under these officials are the members of the Secretariat, who are divided into two classes according to seniority and responsibility, and the rest of the Secretariat is composed mainly of the subordinate staff for typing, shorthand, and other cognate duties. The total staff, including all the clerical services, comprises about 500 persons, including the London, Paris, and Rome Offices.

The Secretariat is in the common service of all the Members of the League and undertake, for the purposes of League work, services similar to those undertaken by Civil servants in national administrations, though all comparisons between the organisations of the League and those of national institutions can be made only in rough terms. The principal Sections of the Secretariat are:

Political;
Financial and Economic;
Transit;
Minorities and Administrative (Saar Territory and Danzig);
Mandates;
Disarmament;
Health;
Social (Opium and Protection of Children and Young People);
Intellectual Co-operation and International Bureaux;
Legal; and
Information.

There are other services, such as the financial administration of the League itself, internal administration, translation and interpretation, précis-writing, publications, registry, library, distribution, central typing and shorthand services, etc.

Each Section is responsible for all the official secretarial work connected with its particular subject and prepares and organises all meetings and conferences held in that connection. The general Secretariat is responsible for the organisation of all Council and Assembly meetings, and its duties involve the preparation and publication of all League documents in the two official languages, and the preparation and issue of all League proceedings and all data and statistics, according to instructions.

The higher officials hold office for seven years; members of both classes are appointed for twenty-one years subject to review of their appointments at the end of each period of seven years; the subordinate staff holds office for twenty-eight years, also subject to review at the end of each seven years. The financial administration is subject to rigid control set up by the Assembly.

The Permanent Court of International Justice—The Permanent Court of International Justice was provided for by the Covenant but not established by it. Its constitution was the work of the Council and the Assembly, its judges are elected by the Council and the Assembly, and its budget is provided by the Assembly. Roughly, it possesses internationally the same kind of relation to the League as courts of law bear nationally to State legislatures. The Council first of all

appointed a committee of eminent jurists to prepare a draft scheme which, after close examination and some modification by the Council and Assembly, was finally adopted as the Court Statute. The judges were elected in September 1921, and the Court began its work in June 1922.

The Court is competent to hear and to determine any dispute of an international character which the parties concerned submit to it, and it may give an advisory opinion upon any dispute or question referred to it by the Council or the Assembly. The Council or the Assembly may also, with the consent of the parties concerned, refer disputes to it for judicial decision.

Questions of fact as well as questions of law may be submitted. The Court is open to all the nations of the world under certain broad conditions. For the reference of a case for judicial decision, the consent of the parties concerned is essential. One State cannot cite another State before the Court except: (1) under treaty terms by which the signatory Powers have agreed to automatic reference of certain kinds of differences to the Court; and (2) under what is known as the optional clause in the Protocol of Signature of the Statute. By this clause, any States which sign it recognise as compulsory, *ipso facto* and without special agreement in relation to any other State accepting the same obligation, the jurisdiction of the Court in any legal disputes concerning:

1. The interpretation of a treaty;
2. Any question of international law;
3. The existence of any fact which, if established, would constitute a breach of international obligations;
4. The nature or extent of the reparation to be made for the breach of an international obligation.

The treaties and conventions affecting the compulsory jurisdiction of the Court extend over a wide field.

The Court is composed of eleven judges and four deputy-judges, elected for nine years. The nominations are made by the national groups of the Permanent Court of Arbitration, or in the case of Members of the League which are not represented in the Court of Arbitration, by similar groups formed for that purpose. The Council and the Assembly vote separately, and those candidates who secure an absolute majority in both the Council and the Assembly are declared elected. Further elections follow to fill any remaining vacancies on the same conditions, and various provisions are made to avoid a deadlock, including finally the power of the already elected judges to co-opt.

This system overcomes the obstacles which have hitherto prevented the creation of such a permanent international Bench.

The law to be applied by the Court is:

1. International Conventions establishing rules expressly recognised by the contesting States;
2. International custom as evidence of a general practice accepted as law;
3. The general principles of law recognised by civilised States;
4. Subject to certain provisions, judicial decisions and the teachings of the most highly qualified publicists of international law.

The Court, whose seat is at The Hague, appoints its own Registrar and staff.

The International Labour Organisation—Although the Members of the League accept by Article 23 of the Covenant an obligation to endeavour to secure and to maintain fair and humane conditions of labour, the Labour Organisation, which comes within the general scheme of the League, is based, not on the Covenant, but on Part XIII of the Treaty of Versailles, which lays down a series of principles governing labour conditions. The International Labour Organisation, although all the States Members of the League are members of it and although the budget is subject to the control of the League Assembly, is an autonomous organisation with its own Governing Body, its own General Conference, and its own Secretariat, and its constitution is somewhat different from that of the League, representation being accorded not only to Governments but to representatives of employers and workers' organisations. According to the Constitution of the Organisation, the Governments undertake to place before their Parliaments all conventions passed.

3. Provisions for Preservation of Peace.

The provisions of the Covenant aimed at the preservation of peace include:

Limitation of armaments, etc.
Guarantees against aggression.

Recognition that any threat to peace is of international concern.

Agreement not to resort to war before settlement has been tried by peaceful procedure.

Methods of securing peaceful settlement.

Penalites for resort to war in specified circumstances, etc.

They may be taken under the following heads:

Limitation of Armaments—An obligation is imposed upon the Council to formulate plans for the limitation of armaments to the lowest point consistent with national safety and to submit them to the consideration of the Governments. Once having accepted any such plan, States agree not to exceed them without the concurrence of the Council. There are also obligations to deal with various effects arising from the private manufacture of munitions, trade and traffic in munitions, etc., and members agree to interchange information on the scale of their armaments.

Guarantees against Aggression—These are contained in Article 10, by which Members undertake to respect and to preserve against external aggression in territorial integrity and existing political independence of all Members of the League. It is for the Council to advise how this obligation shall be fulfilled when the occasion arises.

Article 10 must be considered in conjunction with Articles 11 and 19. Article 11 declares war or threat of war to be the concern of the whole League and every Member has the friendly right to call the attention of the League to any circumstance threatening peace or the good understanding of nations. Article 19 provides the Assembly with the possibility of advising the consideration of treaties that have become inapplicable, and the consideration of international conditions whose continuance might endanger peace. Taken together, these three Articles show that Article 10 is not necessarily meant to perpetuate existing territorial conditions for all time, as the Covenant provides means for considering peacefully new conditions as they may arise. There has been considerable discussion at all Assembly meetings about the exact interpretation of Article 10. At the Fourth Assembly, as a result of points raised by Canada, an effort was made to obtain an interpretative resolution which stated:

"It is in conformity with the spirit of Article 10 that, in the event of the Council considering it to be its duty to recommend the application of military measures in consequence of an aggression or danger or threat of aggression, the Council shall be bound to take account, more particularly, of the geographical situation and of the special conditions of each State.

"It is for the constitutional authorities of each Member to decide, in reference to the obligation of observing the independence and the integrity of the territory of Members, in what degree the Member is bound to assure the execution of this obligation by employment of its military forces.

"The recommendation made by the Council shall be regarded as being of the highest importance, and shall be taken into consideration by all the Members of the League with the desire to execute their engagements in good faith."

One State—Persia—voted against it and thirteen States abstained from voting. Abstentions do not prevent unanimity, but the resolution was not adopted on account of Persia's vote. The President announced, however, that, in accordance with precedent, he would not declare the motion rejected, as it could not be argued that the Assembly in voting as it had done had pronounced in favour of the converse interpretation. It may therefore be assumed that, in any question arising under Article 10, the Council and the Members of the League generally will have in mind the terms of this discussion.

Machinery of Peaceful Settlement—The Members of the League agree not to go to war before submission of disputes to arbitration, to judicial settlement, or to the mediation of the Council or Assembly. They agree in no case to resort to war until three months after the award, decision, or report by the Council. When cases are submitted to arbitration or judicial settlement, the States agree to carry out the awards in full good faith. If any dispute likely to lead to rupture is not submitted to arbitration or judicial settlement, it must be submitted to the Council, whose first duty is to endeavour to effect a settlement. If it fails to do so, it issues a report either unanimously (not counting the votes of the parties), or by majority vote, giving what it considers to be appropriate terms of settlement. If its decision is unanimous, any State going to war in defiance of the decision commits an act of war against all the Members of the League, which undertake in such circumstances to break off relations with the offending State and to subject it to blockade. It is the duty of the Council in such case to recommend to the several governments concerned what armed forces shall be contributed for the protection of the Covenant. If the decision is not unanimous, the Members of the League

"reserve to themselves the right to take such action as they shall consider necessary for the maintenance of right and justice." War is therefore only contemplated as possible when unanimity is lacking, or, if the matter is referred to the Assembly, when the necessary majority of the States in the Assembly (including all the Members of the Council) is not obtained. There is no definite provision for giving practical effect to a unanimous decision. Penalties apply only to breaches of the Covenant involving resort to war and not to failure to accept decisions. Any State violating the Covenant may be expelled from the League.

The sequence of procedure for disputes is:

1. Direct negotiations by ordinary diplomatic channels;
2. Arbitration or judicial settlement;
3. Reference to the Council or the Assembly.

The Council may on its own account obtain from the Permanent Court of International Justice advisory opinions on legal points, or may, with the consent of the parties, refer the case to the Court for settlement. The Council may also refer a dispute to the Assembly.

Disputes with Non-Members—In a dispute between a Member and a non-Member, the latter is invited to become a Member for the purposes of the dispute on conditions laid down by the Council. If it refuses, the Council takes such action as seems most effectual. If it refuses and also goes to war against a Member, the League penalties become applicable. When a dispute arising between non-Members is brought before the League, the parties are invited in the same way to accept membership, and if they refuse, the Council does what it thinks best to prevent war.

Domestic Jurisdiction—The League is excluded from any intervention in a dispute if one of the parties claims, and the Council decides, that the dispute arises out of a matter which by international law is solely within the domestic jurisdiction of that party.

Treaties and Understanding—Other Articles provide for the registration and publication of treaties (which, without such registration and publication, are not binding), and Members engage themselves not to enter into any obligations inconsistent with the terms of the Covenant and to abrogate any such existing obligations. The validity of regional understandings for the maintenance of peace is acknowledged.

With regard to the registration and publication of treaties, a register is kept at the Secretariat in which all treaties so communicated are entered, and they are then printed in a *Treaty Series* in the two official languages as well as in the original languages of the treaties themselves. Over 1,200 treaties have been registered by Members and Non-Members of the League.

4. Other Peace Functions.

The League supervises, with the assistance of a Permanent Commission, the operation of the new system whereby certain States exercise Mandates on behalf of the League and in its name over former German and Turkish possessions whose peoples are not yet able to govern themselves. These Mandates are exercised as "a sacred trust of civilisation," Annual reports are rendered to the League by the mandatory Powers, the original terms of the Mandates, containing a variety of safeguards, having been first approved by the Council.

The Members of the League undertake to endeavour to secure and to maintain fair and humane conditions of labour, just treatment of native inhabitants in territories under their control, freedom of communications and transit, and equitable treatment of commerce; to take steps in matters of international concern for the prevention and control of disease; and to entrust the League with the general supervision over the execution of agreements in regard to the traffic in women and children, the traffic in opium and other dangerous drugs, and the trade in arms and munitions in which the control of this traffic is necessary in the common interest. International bureaux already established by general treaties may, if desired by the parties, be placed under the League, and all such bureaux constituted in the future are to come under the direction of the League.

5. Special Duties Under Treaties.

The Saar Basin–The Peace Treaty conferred upon the Council of the League various duties. It is the trustee for the Government of the Saar Basin and appoints the Governing Commission which is responsible to the League. A plebiscite is to be taken in 1935 as to the future status of the territory. The members of the Commission, including one citizen of France, one native inhabitant of the Saar, and three members belonging to three countries other than France or Germany, are elected annually by the Council. They present official quarterly reports, which are made public, and occasionally send reports on matters of particular interest. These are considered by the Council, which also deals with matters that may be brought before it by the inhabitants of the territory, by the German Government, by the Commission itself, or by the members of the Council. According to the terms of the Treaty, the Council's decisions on all Saar questions may be taken by a majority vote.

Free City of Danzig–The Council appoints a High Commissioner of the League of Nations in the Free City of Danzig, which is placed under the protection of the League, with a constitution guaranteed by the League. Any differences of opinion arising between the Free City and Poland (which has wide treaty rights in connection with Danzig) that cannot be settled with the good offices of the High Commissioner are brought before the Council, with whom the decision rests.

Minorities–The League also has responsibilities in regard to various treaties concluded after the war for the protection of racial, religious and linguistic minorities. Any violation or danger of violation of the Minorities Treaties may be brought to the attention of the Council of the League, by any Member of the Council. Petitions by the minorities themselves may be addressed to the League, and, if so, are forwarded to the interested Government for any comments. The petitions, with the Government's comments, are then sent to the Members of the Council, and the President and the representatives of two Members of the Council form a committee to examine such appeals. If any member of this committee, or any other member of the Council, finds that the matter deserves serious attention, it is then placed on the agenda. Arrangements of a somewhat similar kind are in force with regard to petitions concerning mandated territories.

6. Amendments to the Covenant.

The Covenant provides for the possibility of amendments. Such amendments, if adopted by the Assembly, come into force when they have been ratified by all the States Members of the Council and by a majority of the States in the Assembly. A number of amendments have been adopted, five of which have received the necessary number of ratifications. These are confined in the main to simplifying the procedure where the Covenant has left conditions to some extent unprovided for, and though several of them are of considerable importance, they make no really fundamental change.

The amendments ratified concern Articles 4, 6, 12, 13 and 15. The amendment to Article 4 provides that the Assembly shall fix by a two-thirds majority the rules for election of the non-permanent Members of the Council. The amendment to Article 6 provides that the expenses of the League shall be borne by Members in the proportion decided by the Assembly, instead of as provided for in the original text, which declared that they should be borne in accordance with the apportionment of the expenses of the International Bureau of the Universal Postal Union.

Roughly speaking, the amendments to Articles 12, 13 and 15 provide for the possibility of referring disputes to arbitration, judicial settlement or enquiry by the Council. According to the original text, Members of the League were under an obligation to refer disputes likely to lead to a rupture either to arbitration or to enquiry by the Council. As a result of the creation of the Permanent Court of International Justice, a third choice of action has now been added within the terms of this obligation by the inclusion of reference to judicial settlement.

ORGANISATIONS ARISING FROM THE COVENANT

The Covenant left a wide discretion to the Council and the Assembly in constituting the Permanent Court of International Justice and the auxiliary organs foreshadowed in general terms. The establishment of these organisations has been a considerable creative effort marking an important stage in the evolution of inter-State association. In its operations the League uses all possible representative international agencies and frequently invites the co-operation of representative unofficial agencies. In such circumstances, the final decisions and the final action rest always with the Governments.

The many tasks devolving upon the League necessitated the creation of various auxiliary bodies, which are of two kinds, namely:

Technical organisations, dealing with finance and economics, transit, and health; and
Advisory committees dealing with armaments

questions, mandates, Protection and welfare of Children and Young People, opium, and intellectual co-operation.

The technical organisations have been provided with enough independence and flexibility to make them effectively useful, yet they remain under the general control of the Council and the Assembly. They are modelled in principle on the League as a whole; that is to say, they consist of a standing committee, loosely corresponding to the Council, a general conference of Government representatives, corresponding to the Assembly, and a secretariat, which forms a section of the Secretariat-General of the League under the control of the Secretary-General.

Of the three technical organisations, those of Transit and Health are complete, but the Financial and Economic Organisation, which has been associated with some of the most important features of League work, is still somewhat provisional in character.

The advisory committees are composed of members sometimes elected by the Council for their individual competence on any given subject and sometimes by the Governments officially, as expert bodies to assist the Council and the Assembly in particular directions.

In addition to these two kinds of auxiliary bodies, there has been a great variety of special committees and commissions appointed for particular tasks in which the Council has required assistance. Included within this class are the commissions of enquiry in connection with political disputes, commissions to watch over the execution of frontier decisions, and others of a more or less temporary nature. Two of the most important are the Preparatory Committee for the International Economic Conference and the Preparatory Commission for the Disarmament Conference, which, because of their immediate interest, are included in the description given in the following pages of the technical and advisory bodies.

THE TECHNICAL ORGANISATIONS.

The Financial and Economic Organisation.

This was set up as a result of the Brussels Financial Conference summoned by the Council in 1920. It is divided into two sections, the Financial Committee and the Economic Committee. Each section operates independently, but they meet together frequently in plenary session in order to consider matters which are of interest to both. The members are not official representatives of their Governments but are chosen by the Council as experts, and include high treasury officials, directors of great private banks, banking associations or banks of issue, heads of departments or directors in ministries of commerce in various States, the president of an important co-operative society, a statistician and so on. They all hold commanding positions in their own countries and are competent to reflect currents of opinion in qualified circles. All their recommendations or resolutions are sent to the Council, which takes the final decisions.

The duties of this Organisation cover the whole range of financial and economic matters entrusted to the League, and include problems such as the equitable treatment of commerce, financial reconstruction schemes, etc.

The Preparatory Commission of the International Economic Conference, which completed its work this month, was a temporary commission only.

Its task was to prepare for the Economic Conference a programme of carefully defined questions admitting of practical solutions, and to submit to the Council a report on this programme as well as on the composition, rules of procedure, and date of meeting of the Conference.

The secretariat of the Organisation is the Financial and Economic Section of the General Secretariat of the League.

The Transit Organisation.

The Transit Organisation, which, at the request of the First Assembly, was constituted by the General Conference on Freedom of Communications and Transit convoked by the League at Barcelona in March 1921, comprises:

1. An Advisory Committee,
2. A General Conference, and
3. A Secretariat forming the Transit Section of the General Secretariat of the League.

1. *The Advisory Committee*—The Advisory Committee consists of one member nominated by each of the Members of the League permanently represented on the Council and of other members nominated by States Members of the League not so represented on the Council, chosen by the General Conference. This selection has regard, as far as possible, to technical interest and geographical representation. The members of the Committee are not to exceed one-third of the number of Members in the League and they hold office for not less than two years.

Its duties are to consider and to prepare measures to ensure freedom of communications and transit, to assist the League in discharging the functions entrusted to it by the Versailles and other Treaties in the investigation of any disputes, or to endeavour to adjust such disputes by conciliation. Another of its duties, in addition to preparing the work of the General Conference, is to report on the working of general conventions in practice. The Committee is convened by the Chairman, who is elected by the Committee itself.

2. *The General Conference*—The General Conference consists of representatives of States Members of the League, each State having one representative, accompanied, if necessary, by deputies and experts. Non-Members may be invited by the League to participate, and the Conference itself, by a two-thirds majority, may admit non-Members in an advisory capacity for specific questions. It meets when summoned by the Council, and a two-thirds majority is required for the adoption of proposals on the agenda. These proposals may take the form—subject to Council and Assembly control—of international conventions, recommendations to Governments, or resolutions for submission to the Assembly. The members of the Advisory Committee may attend but may not vote. Limited conferences may be summoned by the Council on the advice of the Advisory Committee for questions of interest only to certain States. The ordinary procedure of the Conference follows much the same lines as the procedure of the Assembly and any subject may be included on the agenda at the request of a Member.

3. Its secretariat is the Transit Section of the General Secretariat.

The Health Organisation.

The constitution of the League Health Organisation was drawn up in close co-operation with the Office international d'hygiène publique, a previously existing governmental organisation. The Health Organisation comprises:

1. An Advisory Council,
2. A Health Committee, and

3. A secretariat forming the Health Section of the General Secretariat of the League.

1. *The Advisory Council*—The Committee of the Office international d'hygiène publique, whose seat is at Paris, and which retains all its powers, acts as the Advisory Council. Its duty is to consider and to discuss any questions which the Health Committee may think fit to submit to it either on its own initiative or at the request of the Council. The Office international, which is a body of Government representatives meeting every six months, is by its constitution, especially charged with such tasks as framing international health conventions.

2. *The Health Committee*—The Health Committee, whose seat is at Geneva, is composed of sixteen members, namely, the Chairman of the Advisory Council, nine members chosen by the Advisory Council, and six members appointed by the Council of the League. The Council may, in addition, appoint four extra health assessors, who would be regarded as active members of the Committee. The appointments extend over a period of three years. The Health Committee acts as the advisory body on health questions to the Council and Assembly of the League; holds itself at the disposal of the Council of the League to consider all questions within its competence; and directs the technical work of the Health Section of the League Secretariat. It may carry out enquiries, appoint special sub-committees and attach to them any qualified persons whose assistance it desires.

The Health Committee presents to the Advisory Council an annual report on the work of the League Health Organisation, which is submitted to the Assembly.

3. *The Secretariat*—The Health Section of the General Secretariat of the League acts as the secretariat of the Health Organisation.

THE ADVISORY BODIES.

Armaments

There are two advisory organs on armaments, namely,

The Permanent Advisory Commission on Military, Naval and Air Questions, and

The Preparatory Commission for the Disarmament Conference.

There was previously in existence a body known as the Temporary Mixed Commission on Armaments, appointed in February 1921, and composed of persons of recognised competence in political, economic and military matters. It worked during several years on various aspects of the armaments problem and produced a general scheme which was the preliminary basis of a good deal of the League's discussion on the subject. Its place has now been taken by the Preparatory Commission, which is organised on a more authoritative scale.

1. The Permanent Advisory Commission, was, under Article 9 of the Covenant, appointed by the Council in May 1920. It gives expert advice to the Council on military affairs which may arise on questions submitted to the League, and advises the Council on the armaments provisions of the Covenant. It is composed of a naval, a military and an air representative of each of the States represented on the Council and appointed by the Governments, but each State has only one vote. Each of the three branches of the Commission forms a Sub-Committee, and the secretariat consists of three technical officers, who act severally as secretaries for the respective Sub-Committees; these officers form part of the Disarmament Section of the General Secretariat, under a *chef de service,* whose Section is also responsible for the secretarial work of the Preparatory Commission.

2. The Preparatory Commission for the Disarmament Conference was set up in its present form by a Council decision of December 1925, its purpose being, as the title indicates, to organise work which is to culminate in a General Conference for the Reduction and Limitation of Armaments. It consists of representatives of States Members of the new Council, representatives of other countries chosen from amongst those which, by reason of their geographical situation, occupy a special position as regards the problem of disarmament and which are not otherwise represented on the Commission, namely, Bulgaria, Finland, the Kingdom of the Serbs, Croats and Slovenes, and representatives of the United States of America (the Union of Socialist Soviet Republics was invited but declined the invitation). The retiring Members of the Council, originally members of the Commission, were invited by the Council to continue to serve; Spain and Sweden accepted, and Brazil declined the invitation. Any State not represented on the Commission is entitled to submit memoranda on matters in which its is specially interested and to be heard in support of these memoranda. The Commission is to decide on the proposals for the

Conference to be submitted to the Council and is to assure the control and co-ordination of the work preparatory to the Conference. It is empowered to obtain the co-operation and advice of the competent organisations of the League and this co-operation is effected in two ways:

1. In the case of any questions relating to the military, naval or air aspect of the question under consideration, with the Permanent Advisory Commission;
2. In respect of the economic aspect of these questions, with a Joint Commission composed of two members each of the Economic, Financial and Transit Organisations of the League and two members each of the Employers' Group and Workers' Group of the Governing Body of the International Labour Office.

Mandates

The Permanent Mandates Commission is constituted under Article 22 of the Covenant to receive and to examine the annual reports required from the Mandatories, and to advise the Council on all matters relating to the observance of Mandates. It was appointed by the Council in February 1921 and held its first meeting on October of the same year. It consists of nine members, the majority of whom are nationals of non-mandatory Powers. They were appointed individually by the Council and while members of the Commission they may not hold any office which puts them in a position of direct dependence on their Governments. An expert from the International Labour Office attends in an advisory capacity when labour questions are discussed and any other expert assistance may be obtained when necessary. During the consideration of the reports, representatives of the Powers concerned are invited to offer any supplementary explanations or information which the Commission may desire. The Commission, to which these reports are forwarded, ultimately transmits them to the Council together with its observations and those of the representatives of the Mandatories. Provision is also made for the consideration of petitions.

The Mandates Section of the General Secretariat acts as the secretariat of the Commission.

Opium and Other Dangerous Drugs.

The Opium Advisory Committee was set up in accordance with a resolution of the First Assembly in 1920. It is composed of one Government representative from Bolivia, China, France, Germany, Great Britain, India, Japan, the Netherlands, Portugal, Kingdom of the Servs, Croats and Slovenes, Siam, Switzerland and the United States of America respectively, as countries chiefly concerned; and three assessors are appointed by the Council, one of these being an American. A special delegation from the United States, headed by Senator Porter, attended the meeting of the Committee preceding the 1923 Assembly, the discussions which took place in the Assembly Committee on the proposals presented to the plenary Assembly and one of the Opium Conferences in 1924. Three months before the beginning of every session of the Assembly, the Committee presents to the Council, for automatic submission to the Assembly, a report on all matters relating to the execution of arrangements in connection with the traffic in opium and other dangerous drugs.

The Social Section of the General Secretariat acts as the secretariat of this Committee.

Protection of Children And Young People.

What was originally known as the Advisory Committed on the Traffic in Women and Children was organised as the result of a recommendation by a General Conference summoned by the League in June 1921, for the purpose of securing a common understanding between various Governments with a view to future united action. The Governments of Denmark, France, Great Britain, Italy, Poland, Roumania, Spain and Uruguay appointed their representatives, and the Council appointed as assessors—with all rights of delegates except the right to vote—representatives of:

(a) The International Bureau for the Suppression of the Traffic in Women and Children;
(b) The Women's International Organisations;
(c) The Federation of National Unions for the Protection of Girls;
(d) The International Catholic Association for the Protection of Girls;
(e) The Jewish Association for the Protection of Girls.

On the invitation of the Council, the Government of the United States of America nominated a representative to sit in an advisory capacity.

In December 1924, this Committee was reorganised in accordance with a resolution of the

Fifth Assembly, which had decided to entrust it with the work done by the International Association for the Protection of Children, whose seat was at Brussels. The Committee is now entitled *The Advisory Commission for the Protection of Children and Young People*, and includes the same members as before, with the addition of a representative of the Belgian Government. It is divided into two parts, one dealing with the Prevention of the Traffic in Women and Children and the other with Child Welfare, each Committee having a different group of assessors nominated by important organisations. These groups include the National Conference of Social Work, the Bureau of the Pan-American Union, the Social Service Council of Canada, the Canadian Council for the Protection of Children and the International Federation of Trade Unions of Amsterdam. The two Committees may meet together in plenary session for the discussion of any question of interest to both.

The Social Section of the General Secretariat acts as the secretariat of this Commission.

Intellectual Co-operation.

The International Committee on Intellectual Co-operation arose out of a resolution submitted by the Council and adopted by the Second Assembly in 1921. Its function is to examine international questions relating to intellectual co-operation and to develop intellectual contacts. It was appointed by the Council in May 1922, and includes twelve members of distinction in intellectual life.

It has established a series of national committees as an intermediary between the International Committee and the intellectual centres of various countries.

Through the generosity of the French Government, the International Institute of Intellectual Co-operation was established in Paris in 1924, and this has permitted an extension of the Committee's activities. The Intellectual Co-operation Committee acts as the Governing Body, draws up the budget, and fixes the programme of the Institute. It appoints the Committee of Directors, which consists of five members of different nationalities, including the Chairman of the Governing Body, and it also appoints the director and other officials of the Institute. The work of the Institute is distributed amongst several divisions which correspond to the several spheres of action of the Committee, comprising a University Section, a Section for Bibliography and Scientific Research, a Legal Section, a Section for Artistic Relations, a Section for Literary Relations, a Section for General Business, and an Information Section.

The Secretariat of the International Committee forms part of the General Secretariat of the League.

Brief Guide to League of Nations Publications

League of Nations Library

This article identifies and describes briefly the major periodicals and series issued by the League. It also describes the establishment of a category of sales publications of interest to the general public as distinct from an official set of publications for use by League personnel. The rationale for establishing the sales category and the numbering system used is explained. This pattern of categorization and distribution has been continued by the UN and some of its specialized agencies.

DESCRIPTION OF LEAGUE PUBLICATIONS.

All documents issued by the League of Nations are accessible to the public in their final form. They are published by the League Secretariat and may be divided into two main classes:

I. Periodical publications.
II. Non-periodical publications.

I. PERIODICAL PUBLICATIONS.

These may be divided into three groups:

A. Publications appearing several times a year at regular intervals.
B. Publications appearing continuously, but not at fixed intervals.
C. Year-books.

A. Publications appearing Several Times a Year at Regular Intervals.

1. *Official Journal.* – The *Official Journal* has appeared since 1920. During its first year, only eight numbers were published, but since then it has appeared regularly every month. During 1920-21, it was published in a bilingual edition; since January 1922, two editions have been published, one in French, the other in English. Some of the numbers from 1920 to 1923 are out of print, but will be reprinted in 1931.

From the sixteenth session[1] (January 1922), all the Council Minutes have appeared in the *Official Journal,* together with the texts of the reports and resolutions adopted by the Council. (At the end of the record of each session there is an index of contents.) The numbers of the *Official Journal* which do not contain Council Minutes comprise a selection of the chief official documents circulated by the League Secretariat, including the budget.

Indexes to the *Official Journal* have hitherto been published in the form of special supplements, but from 1929 the annual index will form part of the annual volume. The special supplements from 1920 to 1922 contain documents relating to particular questions, such as the Polish-Lithuanian dispute, the question of the Aland Islands, etc. From 1923 to 1929, the Records of the Assemblies (Plenary and Committee meetings), including the resolutions and recommendations adopted, have also been included. From 1929 onwards, the Assembly Records (including recommendations, resolutions and indexes) will form a separate collection.

2. *Publication of Treaties and International Engagements registered with the Secretariat of the League.* – The *Treaty Series* contains the texts of international engagements of all kinds: treaties of peace, commercial treaties, prolongations of treaties of commerce and navigation, denunciations of treaties, etc. It constitutes the most complete collection published on the subject and is absolutely authentic.

The treaties are published in their original text, followed by an English and French translation when they are not drawn up in either of these languages.

Up to the end of 1928, 72 volumes of this series,

SOURCE: Reprinted from: *Brief Guide to League of Nations Publications,* Geneva, League of Nations Library, 1930. pp. 16–28.

containing 1,700 treaties, had appeared. An index to the first thousand treaties registered (Volumes 1/39–Treaties Nos. 1 to 1,000) was published in 1926. Since then a new index has been published for each further group of 500 treaties.

3. *Monthly Summary.*–The *Monthly Summary* gives a general survey of the League's work during the previous month. It appears in six languages: Czech, English, French, German, Italian and Spanish. It contains a summary of all the meetings of the League and a special chapter on the work of the Permanent Court of International Justice. The principal documents relating to disarmament, the full text of the Locarno Agreements, the documents concerning the financial restoration of Austria, Hungary, Greece, and other subjects, have appeared *in extenso* in special supplements or annexes to the *Monthly Summary*. The number which appears immediately after the annual session of the Assembly contains the text of all the resolutions adopted thereat. From 1928 (Vol. VIII) onwards, a separate index has been added for each year.

4. *Monthly Bulletin of Statistics.*–This bulletin is a synopsis of the economic position of fifty-six countries; it contains information on the production of coal, iron and steel, the export trade, price fluctuations, cost of living, unemployment, monetary questions, etc., based on official information specially supplied each month.

5. *Quarterly Bulletin of Information on the Work of International Organisations.*–This bulletin gives a summary of the discussions at the meetings of over four hundred international organisations established either under general conventions concluded between Governments or by private initiative. It also contains a report of all international congresses or conferences, together with the text of the most important resolutions; the date and place of forthcoming meetings are also given.

6. *Educational survey.*–Since July 1928 the Educational survey is issued twice a year in January and July. It contains reports, notes and articles by educational specialists dealing with various aspects of the question "How to make the League of Nations known and to develop a spirit of international co-operation."

7. *Monthly Epidemiological Report.*–The Service of Epidemiological Intelligence and Public Health Statistics of the Health Section of the Secretariat receives periodical official reports on the prevalence of diseases–with special reference to compulsorily notifiable diseases–from a large number of countries. This information is classified and published monthly in the *Monthly Epidemiological Report.* This *Report* has appeared regularly every month since January 1924; before that date, it was published at irregular intervals. Nos. 1–61 are out of print.

8. *Weekly Epidemiological Report.*–The Health Section also publishes a *Weekly Epidemiological Report* which gives information on the prevalence of plague, cholera, yellow fever, smallpox, typhus, and any other disease, such as influenza, which for the moment constitutes an international danger. Until 1929, this *Report* was intended for official use only, but from then onwards it has been put on sale.

9. *Assembly Journal.*–During the sessions of the Assembly, a *Journal* containing the programme of meetings, the agenda, a record of the meetings held, etc., etc., is issued every morning. This *Journal* is published solely for the convenience of the delegates and the public and should therefore not be used for purposes of official record or reference. It is, however, very useful as a source of information pending the final publication of the full records of the Assembly meetings, which do not appear until several months later.

10*a*. *Monthly List of Selected Articles.*–From January 1929, the League of Nations Library has published a selection of articles on the work of the various sections of the Secretariat. Abstracts of about 900 periodicals are regularly made for this purpose. The subjects are: the general work of the League; political, legal, social, educational, economic and financial questions and problems of communications and transit.

10*b*. A supplement entitled *"International Treaties and Legislative Measures"* gives information on the latest treaties and conventions concluded as well as on the most recent legislative measures of the different States which may have any connection with the various activities of the League of Nations. This publication indexes from the official journals and collections of laws of nearly all countries throughout the world.

These lists are also published on thin paper so that they can be cut up and pasted on to catalogue cards.

11. *Monthly List of Books Catalogued.*–This list includes all books received and catalogued by the League Library during the month preceding publication, with the exception of new periodicals, year-books and Government documents published in serial form. It has appeared since January 1928.

B. Publications appearing continuously but not at fixed Intervals.

1. *Memorandum on Balance of Payments and Foreign Trade Balances.* – This memorandum contains a general study of world trade, tables showing separately the total imports and exports of sixty-three countries, general trade tables showing the trade by values and by weight of all countries in the world, a trade table showing trade at 1913 prices, and a trade table showing imports and exports by countries.

It further contains estimates of the balance of international payments of some twenty-five countries for the last few years.

It was first published in 1923 and covered the period between 1910 and 1923. The latest volume covers the period from 1913 to 1927.

2. *Memorandum on Production and Trade.* – This memorandum gives the changes since 1913 in the world's population, the production of raw materials, world trade and prices.

It appeared in 1926, 1927 and 1928.

3. *Memorandum on Public Finance.* – This memorandum deals with the movement of the national budgets and the national debts of twenty-six countries, and gives the figures of total taxation and details of the assets and liabilities of States. The chapter relating to each country is preceded by notes which explain its budgetary system and give information on technical details which are frequently confusing to those who desire to study the financial situation of other countries.

Four volumes have so far been published relating to the years 1920, 1921 and 1922-1926.

4. *Information Section Pamphlets.* – In order to make known to all the organisation and multifarious activities of the League of Nations, the Information Section has undertaken the publication of a series of pamphlets (see page 25) on the work of the League and its various organs.

C. Year-Books.

1. *International Statistical Year-Book.* – This book, which has been published since 1926, gives in concise form the most important statistics relating to area and population, production, foreign trade, movement of shipping, ocean freights, railways, motor-cars, public finance, currency statistics, exchange rates, wholesale and retail prices, etc.

2. *International Health Year-Book.* – This has appeared since 1924. It gives an account of the progress achieved by the different countries in the field of public health. It reports changes in the working of the various health administrations, contains the latest vital and health statistics, and also gives an outline of the work of the principal international organisations dealing with public health.

3. *Armaments Year-Book.* – This Year-Book contains general and statistical information on the military, naval and air armaments of sixty countries. In the case of countries with a colonial army, the Year-Book also gives detailed information on the organisation and composition of that army.

4. *Statistical Year-Book of the Trade in Arms, Ammunition and Implements of War.* – This has appeared since 1924 and contains information on the import and export of arms, ammunition and implements of war of fifty-six countries and forty-three colonies. Until 1928, it appeared under the title of *Statistical Information on the Trade in Arms, Ammunition and Implements of War.*

II. NON-PERIODICAL PUBLICATIONS.

Non-periodical publications include all documents circulated separately to the Assembly, the Council, Committees, or to Conferences.

These publications are not classified according to subject, but according to the body for whom they are intended – Council, Assembly, a League Committee, etc. This classification can best be understood if these documents are divided into four chronological periods:

1. From the Origin of the League to May 1921.

Documents published during this period of the organisation of the League's work were classified according to an internal administrative system; only a small number were distributed and most of them are out of print.

2. From May 1921 to End of 1925.

During this period documents were classified according to the body for whom they were intended:

1. A.–Assembly.
2. C.–Council.
3. C.M.–Council and Member States.
4. C.L.–Circular Letters.
5. Various Committees–in this series documents bear the initials of the French title of the particular Committee, *e.g.,* C.I.C.I. (Commission internationale de coopération intellectuelle); C.H. (Comité d'Hygiène), etc.

In order to make it easy to consult series 1, 2, 3 and 4 a *Subject List* of documents has been published monthly, a cumulative list being issued at the end of the year. This system of numbering met the needs of Government Offices, but not the needs of the general public, since there was nothing to indicate which of these documents were available to the public and placed on sale and which were not. Libraries and other institutions therefore found great difficulty in knowing whether their collections were complete.

3. From 1926 to End of 1928.

In order to remedy these drawbacks, special numbers, known as sales numbers, were introduced on January 1st, 1926; the new figure (sales number) was given at the foot of documents intended for sale, while the official number continued to appear at the head of the document.

This special numbering is quite distinct from the official numbering; documents are classified according to the Sections by which they are published. This practically constitutes classification by subjects:

IA. Administrative Commissions.
IB. Minorities.
II. Economic and Financial Questions.
III. Health.
IV. Social Questions.
V. Legal Questions.
VIA. Mandates.
VIB. Slavery.
VII. Political Questions.
VIII. Communications and Transit.
IX. Disarmament.
X. Financial Administration.
XI. Opium Traffic.
XIIA. Intellectual Co-operation.
XIIB. International Bureaux.
XIII. Refugees.
Q.G. General Questions.

This system enabled series to be classified methodically and in the right order. Difficulties were still encountered, however, owing to the fact that the sales number was not sufficiently prominent on the documents, and because documents were always referred to by the official number.

4. From January 1929.

A radical revision of the system was therefore necessary, and the present system was introduced on January 1st, 1929. This system is based on a clear distinction between two categories of readers of League publications: (1) official readers (Governments, etc.), for whom the official numbering is intended; and (2) independent students of the League's work, for whom sales numbers were introduced.

The official letters (C. for Council, A. for Assembly, etc.) continue to appear at the head of the document, but it is preceded by the words: *Official No.* The sales number (according to subject) is now placed at the foot on the righthand side, preceded by the words: Series of League of Nations Publications. The number "Series of League of Nations Publications V. Legal Questions 1930.V.2." indicates for example the *second* document placed on sale during 1930 by Section V, i.e. the *Legal Section.* Both numbers are mentioned whenever a document is referred to or annexed to the *Official Journal* or to any other periodical publication. The catalogue of publications on sale quotes both sales and official numbers but the two numbers are clearly separated and the sales number is always preceded by "Series of League of Nations Publications." This catalogue also contains a list of the documents included in the *Official Journal* which are not on sale separately.

SUGGESTIONS TO READERS OF LEAGUE PUBLICATIONS.

Readers of League documents may be roughly divided into three main groups:

1. The general public, which wishes to follow the work of the League in a general way, and demands mainly nontechnical publications.

To meet their needs, the Information Section

has issued

A. Descriptive pamphlets, entitled *The League of Nations, its Constitution and Organisation,* which is intended to give broad elementary ideas; *The League of Nations, A Survey (January* 1920 *to December* 1926*),* since 1927 regularly supplemented by a pamphlet called *The League of Nations from Year to Year.* Further pamphlets, periodically revised, are devoted to the various aspects of the League's work, for example, *The Economic and Financial Organisation of the League of Nations, The Social and Humanitarian Work of the League of Nations,* etc.
  Several of these pamphlets have appeared in other than the official languages.
B. The *Monthly Summary,* which gives a short account of the chief events of the month (see page 17).

2. Persons who, without specialising, desire to follow the work of the League more closely.—The main publications recommended for this class of reader are:

1. The *Official Journal,* which may be regarded as the official gazette of the League of Nations, and contains the Council Minutes, reports of Committees, the records of the Assembly and the principal published documents.
2. The report on the work of the League, submitted to the Assembly each year by the Secretary-General.[2]

These may be supplemented by separately published documents, such as the Minutes of certain Committees (Mandates, Transit, Health, etc.).

3. Specialists.—It should be mentioned that every question dealt with by the League is submitted to the Assembly, the Council, a Conference, or one of the Committees (advisory or technical).
  In order to ascertain whether a problem has been submitted to one of these bodies, and, if so, with what result, specialists have two sources of information:

1. The *Official Journal* (including the Council Minutes and the *Records of the Assembly*), with a detailed index published at regular intervals;
2. The catalogue of publications on sale, classified by subjects.

SUGGESTIONS FOR CLASSIFYING LEAGUE PUBLICATIONS.[3]

In classifying League documents, the two following principles should be observed by libraries and institutions desirous of possessing a complete and up-to-date collection of all publications accessible to the public:

(*a*) Periodical publications should be grouped together, the indexes and tables edited by the Secretariat being attached as and when they appear. The Libraries should keep the collection of the *Official Journal* in the following way:
  1. A set of Council Minutes;
  2. A set of Assembly Records;
  3. A set of issues of the *Official Journal* not containing Minutes; and
  4. A set of Supplements to the *Official Journal* dealing with special subjects.
(*b*) Non-periodical publications should be classified by subjects, all non-periodical documents dealing with the same questions being grouped together. As regards publications issued since 1926, this result will be automatically achieved by merely arranging them according to their sales number, this numbering having been allotted according to subject (see page 23). In collecting documents issued before 1926, the official number should be taken into account only for the purpose of arranging them in chronological order.

From 1930 onwards, the Secretariat will publish a covering page and an index for each category of documents on sale, which will greatly facilitate the classification of documents.

HOW TO OBTAIN LEAGUE PUBLICATIONS.

Any League publication which is not out of print may be obtained from the authorised agents for the publications of the League of Nations, whose addresses are given below (see pages 29 and 30).

Customers desirous of obtaining all publications issued or those on some particular topic, e.g., Economic and Financial, Health, and Social questions, Mandates, Disarmament, etc., may take out an all-inclusive subscription, against which all such publications will be sent as they appear. (Particulars regarding all-inclusive subscriptions are sent free on application.)

If preferred, a notification of all new documents issued on a particular subject will be sent to anyone who communicates his interest in them to the Publications Department of the League of Nations, Villa St. Victor, Geneva (Switzerland). The latter, or any of its authorised agents also supplies free of charge a periodical list of publications recently issued, which contains particulars of all new documents placed on sale during a period of two months.

NOTES

[1] The Minutes of the first fifteen Council sessions were published separately.

[2] This report, which can be obtained separately, also forms part of the *Assembly Records*.

[3] Since January 1928 the Library of the League of Nations issues for each document put on sale a catalogue card prepared according to the rules of the Library of Congress at Washington:

Numbering Systems and Cataloging

Marie J. Carroll

To facilitate reference service and processing at the World Peace Foundation where she was Chief of Reference Service on International Affairs, Miss Carroll compiled a guide to the official numbering system. This introduction to her guide explains the numbering system and describes briefly the arrangement of League documents in several libraries including her own.

League of Nations documents are produced primarily to facilitate the conduct of the international business which the organization forwards on behalf of the Member states. Placing documents on sale for the public is but a secondary object of publication. It follows that forms of enumeration employed on League documents must serve first of all the requirements of official business. Since the use of the documents by students and research workers has become widespread, efforts have been made by the League, during the last few years, to aid librarians in classifying the varied types of publications issued.

Two systems of *official* enumeration have been employed on League documents. The first system was used from the establishment of the League in 1920 up to April, 1921. For example, the Minutes of the first meeting of the Council bore the number 20/29/1. In that official number the "20" represented the year, 1920; and "29" represented an arbitrary number for that division of the League—the Council as a body producing Minutes—and the "1" indicated the order of the document published under Council auspices. Again, under this first system, the publications of the Assembly were indicated by the number "48." Thus, Assembly documents for the year 1920 bore numbers as follows: 20/48/1, 20/48/2, etc. Based upon the theory of filing in an official registry, this system was discontinued because it was not sufficiently elastic for the requirements of publication and official distribution.

OFFICIAL NUMBERS

The new system of *official* numbering in force from April 22, 1921, utilizes numbers assigned to documents for the Distribution of Documents Service, one of the divisions of the Secretariat of the League of Nations. The official numbers in most frequent use are those appearing on documents distributed to the Assembly, the Council, and the Council and Member states. For instance, A.1. 1921 indicates Assembly document No. 1, distributed to the Second Assembly of the League in 1921; C.1. 1921 designates Council document No. 1, distributed to Members of the Council only; and a document numbered C. 15.M.10.1921 means that it was the fifteenth document distributed to the Council in that year and the tenth to the Member states of the League.

Another series—Circular letters sent by the Secretary-General to Members of the League—designated as C. L.—is not available for sales separately. Occasionally, however, Circular Letters are printed in connection with other related documents placed on sale.[1]

Due to the fact that the Secretariat is charged with the task of preparing documents for official circulation and for publication, Roman numerals from I-XIII, (a list of which is printed at p. 13 of this Key), appear on the documents as a part of the official number. These Roman numerals indicate the particular Section of the Secretariat of the League from which these documents have emanated. From the librarian's point of view, this Roman numeral may be regarded both as an author and a key to the general subject matter of the document. For instance, II is used on all Economic and Financial documents. A number such as C.92.M.47.1922.II means a document issued by the Economic and Financial Section of the League in 1922, being the 92d document in order of distribution to the Council and the 47th document furnished to Member states.

SOURCE: Reprinted from: Marie J. Carroll, *Key to League of Nations Documents Placed on Public Sale*, 1920-1929. Boston, World Peace Foundation, 1930. pp. 7-12. Reprinted with permission of the World Peace Foundation.

The words "Official No." have preceded the number in the upper right-hand corner of League documents since 1929.

LEAGUE OF NATIONS PUBLICATIONS NUMBERS

A small number of librarians have attempted to classify documentation by "A," "C" and "C.M." numbers, but as a large proportion of the documents are not printed separately, but are included in the *Official Journal,* Records of Assemblies, etc., this proved to be a very complicated task of cross-reference. In order to help classification, the League of Nations, beginning with the calendar year 1926 added to the lower right-hand corner of all documents placed on sale a box containing the *Publications Sales Number.* It was felt that this enumeration would aid librarians in determining the number of documents issued for sale each year under each Roman numeral. It is known as "Series of League of Nations Publications" number (Ser. L. o. N. P.). It consists of two identifying lines: The Roman numeral for the Section, the name of the Section written out in full, and on the bottom line the year of publication, the Roman numeral symbolizing the Section of origin, and an Arabic numeral indicating that it is the 10th or 15th, whatever the case may be, publication of that particular Section for that year. For example

---

SERIES OF LEAGUE OF NATIONS PUBLICATIONS
II. ECONOMIC AND FINANCIAL
1929.II.47

Interpreted, this means that the document was the 47th issued for sale from the Economic and Financial Section in the year 1929.

In addition to the list of Roman numerals used in *Series of League of Nations Publications,* there are a few documents which fall into a category denominated as "General Questions" or "General." This division is almost wholly confined to such publications as the *Report to the ... Ordinary Session of the Assembly of the League on the Work of the Council, on the Work of the Secretariat ...* the agenda of the Assembly, papers relating to League buildings, and other miscellaneous matters.

COMMITTEE AND CONFERENCE NUMBERS

The development of League activities made it necessary to create a system for identifying documents circulated to committees or to conferences, either as a whole or for the special attention of their committees. In devising a scheme for recording such distribution, the initials of the French names for the committees, conferences, etc., were adopted. A list of these abbreviations with the French text and English equivalents is printed at p. 227. The documents are frequently reissued to the Council and Member states and placed on sale. In such instances, librarians will find them indicated in this Key, for example, as follows:

C. 351. M. 112. 1925. XII.
(C. I. C. I. 141)

The parenthesized number indicates Commission Internationale de Coopération Intellectuelle (International Committee on Intellectual Cooperation), 141 signifying the 141st document distributed to that committee. It is important to recognize that these subsidiary committees and conference numbers do not run by the year, but are continuous for the life of the body to which they are distributed. Committee and conference numbers are carried under the *official numbers,* as noted in the example given above.

Not infrequently, such documents are printed in the *Official Journal,* annexes to Minutes of the Council, annexes to minutes of meetings of various Committees, Commissions, etc., or in the Records of the Assemblies.

The Secretariat's policy of making public substantially all documents results in the occasional publication for sale of documents bearing these committee or conference numbers only. While such instances are infrequent, they create bibliographic difficulties, and the list of all initials used up to 1930 for the identification of League of Nations documents has been added to this Key for the purpose of solving this difficulty.

REGISTRY NUMBERS

It has been emphasized that League documents are prepared primarily for the use of Governments Members of the League. It will be apparent to all that the keeping of archives of the Secretariat is a matter distinct from distribution. In the internal administrative services of the Secretariat, the Registrar is intrusted with keeping the archives, a task similar to any official docket service, and the registry number relates solely to this service. Identification of incoming papers is effected by registry numbers[2] which not infrequently appear upon documents published in numbers of the *Official Journal* and sometimes elsewhere.

EDITIONS AND SUPPLEMENTS

The following information will be of assistance in checking: In an *official number* a parenthesized Arabic figure indicates an edition. Thus, C. 190(1). M. 93. 1929. V. indicates that the document was originally issued to the Council as C. 190. 1929. V. It was subsequently issued a second time in a revised form to the Council and simultaneously to the Member states for the first time. In this form it was issued to the public and the *official number* it then bore shows the foregoing to have been its previous history.

An official number containing a parenthesized lower case letter indicates a supplement to a previous document. Thus, C. 73(a). M. 38(a). 1929. V. indicates that the document contains information strictly supplementary to that contained in C. 73. M. 38. 1929. V. It is apparent that the plain number is the original document, that the (a) document is a first supplement, etc. This notation is frequently required in cases where Member states make replies to inquiries by the Secretary-General and exigencies of time are involved in the preparation for publication of material in hand or where delays occur in receipt or replies. Collation of material in such cases sometimes offers difficulties but cross references to supplementary documents should be added to the catalog card for the primary document. A case in point is: C. 73. M. 38. 1929. V. which has the *Ser. L. o. N. P.* number 1929. V. 1, and C. 73(a). M. 38(a). 1929. V. has 1929. V. 8., while C. 73(b). M. 38(b). 1929. V. has 1927. V. 12. These documents should be bound with their respective years under Section V, if binding is being done under Series of League of Nations numbers.

LANGUAGE OF DOCUMENTS

French and English are the official languages of the League of Nations, and League publications are issued in both languages. Ordinarily, only the English version is handled by this Foundation. The permanent exception is certified copies of treaties, which are always published with the text of both languages in parallel. Occasionally a document is issued in a single language. French documents supplied on the global subscription services offered by World Peace Foundation are customarily technical studies prepared for the use of committees which are made available to the public on account of their scientific value. (A number of Health Committee publications are printed in French only.)

STRUCTURE OF ORGANIZATION

The structural organization of the League is graphically indicated on the chart facing page 233, with particular reference to sources of documentation. A full development of activity on subjects handled by the League of Nations involves three parts: A section of the Secretariat, an advisory or technical committee made up of governmental or private experts, and a series of conferences in which the Governments of the world give definite form and force to recommendations found by the committees to be ripe for international agreement in treaty form. The Roman numeral classification denoting the Section of origin can be applied to all three. For instance, Communications and Transit, VIII, will cover the section of the Secretariat, the Advisory Committee and the General Conferences, with subsidiary shelf number indications for each division, if desired. In the case of a conference, special documents for its use are likely to be issued, but may also be assimilated under the Roman numeral.

Three such groupings, known as Technical Organizations, existed at the beginning of 1930 as follows:

Economic and Financial Organization, with the former fully developed in itself as the Economic Organization;
Organization for Communications and Transit;
Health Organization.

These organizations are only the full development of a series of cognate activities and their structure corresponds to the normal progress of a problem through the League of Nations machinery. Consequently, it is advisable to handle all similar material on the basis indicated above and with a view to its subject taking eventually the form of a treaty negotiated in a League conference.

LIST OF LEAGUE MEETINGS
AND CONFERENCES

In order to provide a ready means for finding or identifying specific meetings or conferences held under the auspices of the League of Nations, a compilation of the sessions of the Assembly, Council, committees of the League, conferences, etc., is attached to this Key at page 233. The arrangement followed is identical with that used throughout the Key; the section of origin is the determining factor.

The purpose, for which the various organs of the League, as well as the committees, sub-committees and conferences were established is given under each committee or conference.

HANDLING OF THE COLLECTION

The problem of shelf listing can be approached from two angles: Shall the publications be kept together or shall they be distributed on the shelves by subject? The choice of method will naturally depend upon the library and the needs of its users. Most libraries file the documents as a whole under a single shelf number. The World Peace Foundation recommends this treatment. To that number in the case of the Records of the Assembly, and the Minutes of the Council (up to the 16th sess.) and the *Treaty Series* initial letters denoting the series are added. The Roman numerals of the *Official Numbers* are the best practical criterion for classification of all other documents.

The Foundation has found it convenient to give the publications of the Information Section of the Secretariat the major shelf number, plus the additional classification of news. The Information Section serves the entire League Secretariat and its publications do not bear Roman numerals. Publications of the Library, such as the *Books on the Work of the League of Nations catalogued in the Library of the Secretariat,* will require a special treatment.

The record of matters handled as international business is so complex that too close shelf listing involves the necessity of multiplying folio pamphlet files or temporary binders to hold the documents of the many subjects simultaneously under consideration. It is, in our judgment, better to assemble material broadly by subject and to depend upon added entries on catalog cards for detailed analysis.

Another reason that too close shelf listing is impractical is that every subject explored and worked up to a practical form in sections of the Secretariat or in League commissions or committees is given its final form and effect by the Council in the first instance, and perhaps, by the Assembly in the second instance. It follows that the Minutes of Council and the Records of the Assembly are necessary complements of the publications of any section of the Secretariat. This is not, however, the case with conferences, which are made up of delegates accredited by Governments and the action of which consequently is independent of either the Assembly or Council, except as they may provide in resolutions for the convocation and physical arrangements of a conference.

Many libraries have bound the publications by Section designation. For instance, the Minutes of the Sessions of the Health Committee may be bound together. Whether Reports to the Assembly and Council on such sessions should be intercollated with the Minutes of the Committee will depend upon individual preference, but we should advise against such a practice.

Pending binding, there will remain a quantity of documents of varying bulk to be shelved. We advise carrying these, appropriately shelf numbered, in folio pamphlet boxes or in folio spring binders.

The arrangement used in this Key may serve as a binding guide for libraries which have not yet selected a permanent binding scheme for the publications of the League. A complete list of all documents placed on sale from 1920-1929 is herewith provided. Libraries may check their publications for binding in annual volumes, using the lists of documents as Tables of Contents, or they may bind each Roman numeral section separately for each year, or in convenient volumes covering the period 1920-1929. The practical advantages of the first method have been described by Mr. Thomas Franklin Currier, Assistant Librarian, Harvard College Library in the March 15, 1930, issue of the Library Journal. Beginning with the year 1930 title and contents pages are to be supplied from Geneva for "each category of documents placed on sale."[3]

Various binding schemes in use in the libraries subscribing to annual global service offered by the World Peace Foundation have been studied by Mr.

Charles E. Walton, Chief of the Acquisition Department, Washington Square Library, New York University, New York City. Mr. Walton has worked out for his own collection a comprehensive binding scheme for form treatment of League publications, which he presented to the Catalog Section of the American Library Association at the Washington Conference, May, 1929.[4] His survey of binding practice in the 37 university libraries reporting, out of a total of 55, shows that "16, or 43%, have adopted permanent methods of treatment," dividing almost equally between the use of Roman numeral classification on League documents, represented by *Series of League of Nations* numbers since 1926, and various individual methods of classification.

Subject classifications are in use in the libraries of Johns Hopkins, Princeton and Southern Methodist Universities. The classification methods used are set forth in considerable detail in "Classifying, Cataloging and Binding League of Nations Publications"[5] by C. E. Walton (Library Journal, February 15, 1930). Reprints of the articles by Mr. Currier and Mr. Walton are available from the World Peace Foundation.

It is assumed as a matter of course that every student of League of Nations documentation is now familiar with the League of Nations Library publication "Brief Guide to League of Nations Publications," available without charge from the World Peace Foundation.

Marie J. Carroll

Boston, Massachusetts.
March 31, 1930.

NOTES

[1] *Cf.* Replies from Governments to requests for information, *Official Journal,* X, p. 477.

[2] For comparing these numbers with those of bibliographic value, reference is made to the "Official Journal," Vol. X, No. 9, p. 1322, 1323, 1365, and 1366, where the registry numbers are as follows:

3D/12002/12002
IA/12507/8450
5B/13362/948
13C/46569/29880
5B/13503/823

[3] League of Nations Library. *Brief Guide to League of Nations Publications,* Geneva, 1929, p. 27.

[4] American Library Association. *Proceedings of the Catalog Section, including annexes and a directory of Catalog Section members:* Washington, D. C. Conference, May 13-18, 1929. Chicago, Catalog Section, A. L. A., 1929, p. 70-86.

[5] Paper read before the Seventeenth Annual Conference of Eastern College Librarians, Columbia University, Saturday, November 30, 1929.

The Classification of the Documents of the League of Nations

C. E. Walton

The rapid proliferation of sub-bodies of the League and practice of issuing sub-series present complications in numbering that mar the basic logical simplicity of the system. C. E. Walton, then Chief, Acquisitions Department, New York University Library, describes here the problems of arranging League documents in an order most useful to a university community.

Only the most general aspects of the classification of League publications can be touched on this evening. Probably the most significant factor in the whole question of classification and treatment is the publishing procedure which, at various times and under different circumstances, the League has pursued. The more important conclusions on this question are represented in the synopsis of the plan in use at the Washington Square Library of New York University which is available in mimeographed form; and I propose tonight to tell you from what point of view the question was opened and how those conclusions were reached.

The question of the document notation in the publications of the League was first opened, so far as I know, by Mr. Denys Myers, Director of Research of the World Peace Foundation of Boston. On the basis of Mr. Myers' discussion in an article on International Documentation in Mar. 1927 *Libraries*,[1] the following document terminology has been adopted:

Official distribution registry series: example C. 124. M. 120. 1927. IX. C. P. M. 431; C. O. P. 45, etc. Upper right corner.

Public distribution registry series: example 1927. IX. 14, etc. Lower right corner, sometimes on title-page, or on back cover.

Archives registry series: example 12/636/5996, etc. Early notation (1920); now used only on material in Official Journal.

The present study of the League of Nations publications has been undertaken from the point of view of a university library serving both undergraduate and graduate and faculty investigators. It has been based more particularly upon the publications themselves, and upon such works about the League as might contain matters of interest: notably the recent volume by Howard-Ellis, and the Annuaire de la Société des Nations edited by Ottlik.[2] The collection of official League publications which formed the basis of the study was fairly complete from 1920 to the present time.

The purpose of the investigation was to determine upon some suitable scheme for a permanent routine which would see the material through the various departments of the Library to the shelves, providing thereby for binding, for cataloging, and for classification. It was thought especially desirable, if possible, to achieve a grouping which would not emphasize such eccentric characteristics as would make the publications temporarily available in whole or in part to special groups or from special subject viewpoints. Rather, an important point was to secure such an arrangement as would satisfy the demands of our University public, whether usual or special, after those methods of procedure common in such libraries as ours, and moreover usual in the treatment of the more complicated serial collections. It was understood at the outset that many possibilities in other directions were at hand. Some of them seemed alluring. One could, for example, have arranged everything by subject, thus presenting all pieces on any given topic in one place. Or everything could have been arranged by document number, thus providing

SOURCE: Reprinted from: C. E. Walton, "The Classification of the Documents of the League of Nations," *Proceedings of the Catalog Section American Library Association*. Chicago, American Library Association, 1929 (Catalogers' and Classifiers' Yearbook No. 1)

quick access to a large class of citations. In this latter connection the question arose: by which document number? The difficulties in the way of passing sensible judgment on this made obvious the necessity for further study.

The conclusions presented here can in few senses be either definitive or final. The study is far from concluded, and from present indications must be pursued for some time to come. We are still embarrassed by such questions as these: When is a set of League publications complete? How far is the publication of documents in the Official Journal to be recognized, in view of their frequent duplication elsewhere? How many document series are there, and how many have ceased publication? Enough has been learned, however, to aid us in building up a general working method which seems to give promise of meeting successfully those demands upon material of this kind usual in a university library.

It is important at this point to make clear that no criticism of the League is intended at any point. The difficulties we have encountered are, I should say, very largely unavoidable in publications of this kind and arise naturally from a close tieup of more than one hundred and fifty serials in a single set, about which on the whole comparatively little information has been easily obtainable. As Sir Eric Drummond has said:[3]

Nothing has been more characteristic in the history of the first years of the League than the freedom with which it has formed new organisms or modified those already existing in order to meet the changing tasks with which it has been faced.

Its freedom in this respect has contributed largely to their successful solution and to the general readiness which has been shown to submit difficult questions to the consideration of the League . . . unless [the reader] has been in the habit of following closely the records of the League's work, probably [he will] be surprised at the number and variety of the bodies which function or have functioned under its auspices.[4]

Little difficulty has been encountered in respect to those more general titles such as the Official Journal, the Treaty Series, The Monthly Summary and such others as appear under the authority of the League as a whole. These we have thrown together at the head of the collection; and to them we have added the minutes of the first fifteen sessions of the Council and the Records of the first three Assemblies, in order that they might be shelved near their respective continuations in the Official Journal and its Supplements. Here have

been placed also such material as bore the authority of no section, the whole being divided into two main groups: serials, and publications other than serials.

There remained for consideration the material officially issued through the Secretariat as indicated either by the appearance of a section name on the title page, or by some official document notation. In working out the details for treatment here, we wished particularly to avoid undue emphasis on individual pieces such as the Records of any one Conference at the expense of others bibliographically more obscure but nevertheless of equal importance. Another need for caution lay in our desire to avoid large or obscure collections which, for want of more appropriate nomenclature, would have to be called "miscellaneous." In passing, it is of some importance perhaps to remark that we have been able to assign every publication to a definite sub-division.

In arriving at a decision to group the material being discussed in that arrangement laid down in the structure of the Secretariat, the following facts were considered: In the material were found more than one hundred and fifty serials issued under various conditions by various agencies, and tied together only in so far as the sections of the Secretariat are tied together. They differed widely as to subject, form, size, and rate of issue. They were complicated by extensive duplication both in the Official Journal where each piece was treated as a complete entity in itself, and by republication in whole or in part in subsequent reports of bodies higher in authority or more inclusive in makeup. The Health Committee, for example, publishes its minutes in one serial; and then reports them to the Council in another.

These serials, furthermore, were characterized by wide gaps where, for unknown reasons, material was not offered for sale. They were complicated by questions of author authority which, not infrequently, ran to three stages in subdivisions of corporate entries. Reports, begun in one publication, jumped without warning to another. The early minutes of the Council and records of the Assembly, first published separately, were later transferred to the Official Journal and its Supplements. Certain other reports began their existence with an issue not the first. The Child Welfare Committee minutes begin with the second session, the first being contained as Annex 13 to the minutes of the fourth session of the Committee on Traffic in Women and Children which is a Council document. The Child Welfare Committee reports begin also with number two, number one being contained in A.22.1925.IV, an Assembly document. Other serials changed their names with a success in hiding their relationships which seemed often unfathomable. The Epidemiological Intelligence Monographs, for example, run in one size for seven numbers. With number eight the size changes, but the title and numbering continue through ten. This makes three of the new size. With number 11, the title and numbering are represented only by a small (E.I.11) in the upper right hand corner. The new title is now Fourth Epidemiological Report.

Certain bodies, once provisional: that is, appointed by the Council: were replaced by other bodies now permanent: that is, ratified by the Assembly: and these permanent bodies then proceeded to divide, maintaining still, however, the old series of publications to take care of their joint sessions. This process, once known, was found to be accompanied by a concomitant overlapping in the publication series concerned. The Provisional Economic and Financial Committee reports ran from 1921-1922. At that time they seem to have been taken over by the Economic and Financial Organization Annual reports, which appear to end in 1925. Meantime the Economic and Financial Organization is found to have divided into two committees, the Economic and the Financial, each of which publishes a series.

Or, for another variety, committees born within the League were, usually at an inconvenient point in their publication series, left to pursue their activities under other auspices. The International University Information Office Bulletin, begun under the authority of the Committee on Intellectual Co-operation, was transferred with the beginning of its third volume to the International Institute of Intellectual Co-operation at Paris, where from volume three it was known as the Bulletin for University Relations. This Bulletin, once a League publication, joins three publications of the Institute: The Bibliographical Bulletin on International Affairs, The Bulletin for Scientific Relations, and the Information Section Bulletin to become in 1929 La Coopération intellectuelle, a monthly periodical published only in French.[5] Often the reverse of this occurred, and authorities outside the League lent their names to publications within it. Many of the early documents were published in London during the time the Secretariat was located there; and the first eighteen numbers (v.1-v.2, no. 6) of the Monthly Bulletin of Statistics were published there by the Supreme Economic Council.

Finally, all these complications taken together constituted a fact to be considered in itself.

We found many points of helpfulness in the practices of other institutions none of which, however, gave us precisely what we wanted.[6]

Probably the best known of all ways by which the series issued by the Secretariat are referred to, both among the library profession and the public, is as Assembly and Council documents. It is, therefore, worth while to consider briefly whether any possible arrangement by document number would be practical. Surprisingly enough, what we have come to regard as Assembly and Council documents of the League break up, upon examination, into more than sixty series, each to be identified by its own combined alphabetical and numerical document notation scheme. In considering the Secretariat material by official distribution registry series numbering, important points include the following: The Assembly and Council series are annual, reverting to number one at the beginning of the publishing year which apparently varies for each year and for each series. Numbers of each are frequently issued also as numbers of the other. Each is the inclusive series through which run subseries, in the Assembly 2 and in the Council 8, partly published independently. Both include subseries, for the Assembly 6 and for the Council 19, not found elsewhere. Both include 4 series which run in both; and both include 4 other series which appear independently. Finally, 11 other sub-series appear only independently. And, whereas the Assembly and Council series are annual, all the others have apparently been running consecutively since their beginnings. Furthermore, about 20 per cent of the Assembly series, and about 70 per cent of the Council series appear also in the Official Journal, where many are duplicates, and where some others evidently are not. From this picture, it is perhaps easy to imagine to what confusion any attempt to handle this material by document numbers would seem to lead. It was decided that this whole question of document notation in the official distribution registry series was too vast in scope to be well handled by any means other than comprehensive document indexes more carefully worked out than any yet issued. The sections of the Secretariat are now working on such indexes I understand. The situation with regard to document notation was interestingly forecast in 1921 when in the course of a report on the Secretariat, a Commission of Experts declared:[7]

> We are glad to observe that a Central Registry, which is universally admitted to be the most economical and satisfactory system, has been set up for the Secretariat. We have observed, however, a tendency on the part of certain sections to keep their own records of documents which concern their sections. The tendency for such records to develop into Sub-Registries, involving duplication of work, loss of efficiency, increase of personnel, must be carefully guarded against. The only sound principle is to rely on Central Registry for all registration work, and the sections are enjoined that it is only if they trust to the Registry and to the Registry alone, that it can function to the complete satisfaction of the whole office.

In deciding upon the structure of the Secretariat as a key to the grouping of its publications, we spent some time on factors other than those found in the nature of the publications themselves. In 1922 the general services of the Secretariat cost 5,227,135 gold francs; in 1926, this expense had increased to 6,055,954. And for 1928 the estimate in the budget was placed at 7,611,876.[8] These figures indicate a growth in importance and activity well worth attention. But for the fact that the Secretariat's organization was initially planned somewhat larger than the work actually called for, this comparison would have been even more significant. Since the Assembly and Council are maintained as laid down in the Covenant, it is natural that the responsibilities of increasing activity should fall upon the Secretariat. In this connection, Dr. Gonsiorowski says:[9]

> It would be a mistake to think that the Secretariat of the League is a simple organ of information. Its importance is much greater. Certain authors even say that the true authorities for action in the League are the Council and the Secretariat, or even the Secretariat first, then the Council.

Of course, no perfect plan can be found. The technical limits in the treatment of printed matter prevent it. Our problem remained, then, one of building up one which would do least violence to the material it should profess to encompass. Here again, the emphasis laid upon the organization of the Secretariat seems not unwise, since most of the difficulties which have arisen seem to be traceable to lack of adequate attention to that very point; and, furthermore, changes easily imagined for the future will be likely to be within the structure of the Secretariat itself. A final and convincing point, however, was the introduction in 1926 of a public distribution registry series mechanism in addition to the official distribution registry series, under the terms of the former of which the documents of each section are numbered in annual consecutive order as they are released for sale.

The arrangement by section having been decided upon, it was found that the documents in each formed a document series by public distribution registry numbering. It was therefore possible to collate by annual public distribution registry series, with the assurance that such a plan would emphasize that subject value of the material usually set forth as of major importance in those schemes which arrange by subject to the exclusion of all else. The establishment by series, moreover, gave us a valuable check upon the completeness of our collection since 1926, and provides for a guide against future obscurities.

It was also found that the more than sixty serials by title did not override the section walls. The Child Welfare Committee, whatever its publishing vagaries, always confined them to the social section. This led to the question: Why would it not be possible to emphasize important commissions and conferences by handling them as sub-series within the public distribution registry series, in each case under their own titles? This procedure was followed. Documents issued as conference reports, committee minutes, and so on, were removed from the registry series and handled under title, the resulting situation being exactly like that in our own Bureau of Education Bulletin which customarily runs about six sub-series of its own. In this way, two kinds of citation, by registry series number and by name of commission, are provided for in the binder's title. Documents published before 1926 without the public distribution registry series numbering are arranged by section in annual volumes by date of issue.

When we stop to consider that there are eighteen sections of the Secretariat this procedure seems complicated, but in practice it has not proved so. The eighteen sections, after all, merely duplicate a publishing condition not at all unusual in our own country. We find it being followed by such bodies as Ohio State University which maintains an Ohio State Educational Conference Proceedings series within its Bulletin; by the National Education Association which issues an annual Yearbook within its Department of Elementary School Principals Bulletin; and, in fact, by the American Library Association itself which runs a Yearbook, an Annual Reports, and a Proceedings within its Bulletin.

In conclusion, it may be well to outline briefly certain features of the check record to be employed on material issued in the future. For the general publications a simple entry, one for each title, in the customary way will be adequate. Each section, however, will be represented by a check card with the notation LN, with the section name, Documents. On this all documents from that section will be checked by public distribution registry series number. This card will be followed by others with titles indented, listing the sub-series officially established for that section. If the serial assistant comes to the 40th Periodical Report of the Saar Basin, say, as she checks it in by registry series[10] as 1929. I. 4., she glances below to see if Saar Basin—Periodical Report has a check card. It will have; so she checks it on that card as 40th, and the job is done.

LEAGUE OF NATIONS PUBLICATIONS

(To accompany preceding paper)

Details of the groupings, the titles of the series treated under title, and the clues to arrangement on the shelves, to binding, and to classification follow in the outline given below:

League of Nations General Official Publications

(JX1975: Cutter by title). Serials.
   Assembly—journal, 1st-date. (Complete for each Assembly; no index).
   Assembly—procès-verbaux of committees, 1st, 2nd. (Not published after 2nd Assembly).
   Assembly—provisional verbatim record, 1st-date. (Complete for each Assembly).
   Assembly—records, 1st-3rd. (Published in Official Journal Supplement series, 4th—date. 2 v. to each Assembly).
   Council—Minutes, sessions 1-15. (Yearly index; session 16-date published in Official Journal). (Bound 1-8, 9-10, 11-15).
   List of delegates and members of delegations, 1st Assembly-date. (Each yearly issue contains 2 numbers, a provisional (no. 1) and a revised (no. 2). Bound 2 nos. in 1 v. for each Assembly).

Monthly bulletin of statistics, v. 1-date. (Index in last no. usually two: one English-French, one French-English. v. 1-v. 2, no. 6 published in London by the Supreme Economic Council. Bound 1 v. yearly).
   Monthly list of books catalogued in the Library of the League of Nations, v. 1-date. (Very complete index supplied loose soon after the completion of the annual volume. Bound 1 v. yearly).
   Monthly summary of the League of Nations, v. 1-date. (With index loose in early number of next volume. Infrequent supplements, discontinued in 1927 arranged at end of v. Three of these supplements serve as the forerunner of the Monthly list of books . . . Bound 1 v. yearly).
   Official journal, v. 1-date. (Bound 2 v. yearly Jan.-June, and July-Dec. Indexes, contained in the Special Supplement series, bound separately).
   Official journal—Special supplements, nos. 1-date. (Bound 1 v. yearly; contains Assembly resolutions and records, 1923-date).
   Press opinions, 1st Assembly-date. (Mostly out of print. Complete for each Assembly).
   Quarterly bulletin of information on the work of the international organizations, nos. 1-date. (Published 4 times yearly; index issued to each 4 as supplement to early subsequent numbers, except for nos. 22-25 whose index is paged into no. 26 (unnumbered; published as v. 2, no. 1). Bind nos. 1-25 as 1 v.).
   Treaty series, v. 1–date. (2 general indexes).

(JX1975.1: Cutter by author or title). General publications other than serials.
   Permanent Court of International Justice, 3 v. 1920-1921. (Organization documents published by the League).

(JX1975.2). League of Nations Secretariat official publications.
   (A1). Serials. (General).
   (A3). Publications other than serials. (General).
   (A5). General questions: serials.
   Report to the Assembly on the work of the Council, 1st-date. (Bound 1-4, 5-6, 7-8, etc.).
   Subject list of documents, 1925–date.
   (Bound in annual volumes).
   (A7). General questions: documents series.
   Arranged by year and registry series. Stubbed for numbers withdrawn to form parts of series listed above.
   (B1). I.A. Administrative commissions: serials.
   Free city of Danzig—general report, Sept. 1922-Mar. 1925. (Bound in 1v.).

Saar basin–periodical report, 1st-date. (To terminate in 1935. Bound 1-20, 21-32, etc.).

Saar basin–general report, Sept. 1922-Mar. 1925. (Bound in 1 v.).

(B3). I.A. Administrative commissions: document series.

Arranged by year and registry series. Stubbed for numbers withdrawn to form parts of series listed above.

(B5). I.B. Protection of minorities: serials.

(B7). I.B. Protection of minorities: document series.

Arranged by year and registry series.

(C1). II. Economic and financial section: serials.

Commissioner for the settlement of Bulgarian refugees–report, 1st-date. (Bound nos. 1-8, etc.).

Commissioner-general for Austria–monthly report, nos. 1-42. (With index). (Bound in 1 v.).

Commissioner-general for Hungary–monthly report, nos. 1-date. (Bound nos. 1-25).

Economic and financial organization–annual reports, 1922-1925.

Economic committee–report to the council, nos. 1-date. (Nos. 1-11 were not published separately, and no. 17 was not offered for sale).

Financial committee–report to the council, nos. 1-date. (Nos. 1-16 were not published separately; index covers nos. 1-25 with notes on nos. 1-16. Index bound with nos. 17-25).

Greek refugee settlement commission–quarterly report, nos. 1-date. (Bound nos. 1-17, etc.).

International economic conference–journal, 1927. (Complete for the conference).

International economic conference–reports and proceedings, 1927. (Complete for conference).

International statistical yearbook, 1926-date. (Bound annually).

Memorandum on balance of payments and foreign trade balances, 1910-1923 to date. (2 v. bound in 2).

Memorandum on currency and central banks, 1913-1924 to date. (Formerly two series: Memorandum on currency, 1913-1921 to 1913-1923; and Memorandum on central banks, 1913-1923. Bound by issue).

Memorandum on production and trade, 1913, 1923-1926 to date. (Presented by a report on the subject as a preliminary undated document: C. E. I. 3. 1926. II. 52. Bound by issue).

Memorandum on public finance, 1921-date. (Bound by issue).

Provisional economic and financial committee –report, 1921-1922.

(C3). II. Economic and financial section: document series.

Arranged by year and registry series. Stubbed for numbers withdrawn to form parts of series listed above.

(D1). III. Health section: serials.

Epidemic commission–annual report, nos. 1, 2. (Bound in 2 v.).

Epidemiological reports, 4th-date. (Preceded by Epidemiological intelligence, nos. 1-10. No. 11 marked E. I. 11. and titled 4th Epidemiological report. Bound nos. 1-7, 8-11).

Health committee–annual reports, 1925-date. (Bound 1925-1927, etc.).

Health committee–minutes of sessions, 1st-date. (Bound sessions 1-12).

Health committee–report to the council, 1st-date. (Bound sessions 1-12).

International health yearbook, 1924-date. (Each issue bound).

Monthly epidemiological report, nos. 1-date. (Nos. 1-61 not placed on sale). (Bound by year; no index).

Provisional health committee–minutes of sessions, 1st-6th. (Bound in 1 v.).

Statistical handbook series, nos. 1-date. (Bound in fives).

(D3). III. Health section: document series.

Arranged by year and registry series. Stubbed for numbers withdrawn to form part of series listed above.

(E1). IV. Social questions: serials.

Annual reports from governments relating to traffic in women and children, 1922-date.

Child welfare committee–minutes of sessions, 2nd-date. (1st not published separately; contained in Committee on traffic in women and children–minutes of 4th session, 1925, p. 99, Annex 13). (Bound 1-4).

Child welfare committee–report to the council, 2nd-date. (1st not published separately; contained in document A. 22. 1925. IV). (Bound 1-4).

Commission for the protection of women and children in the Near East–report, 1925-1926 to date.

Committee on traffic in women and children– minutes of sessions, 1st to date. (Bound sessions 1-7).

Committee on the traffic in women and children–report, 1st-date. (Bound no. 1-7).

(E3). IV. Social questions: document series.

Arranged by year and registry series. Stubbed for numbers withdrawn to form parts of series listed above.

(F1). V. Leg 1 section: serials.

Committee of experts for the progressive codification of international law—questionnaire, no. 1-date. (Bound nos. 1-11).

Review of reviews of international law, nos. 1-4. (1 v.).

(F3). V. Legal section: document series.

Arranged by year and registry series. Stubbed for numbers withdrawn to form parts of series listed above.

(G1). VI. A. Mandates: serials.

Permanent mandates commission—minutes of sessions, 1st-date. (Index published for 1-5, 6-10, etc.). (Bound by indexes).

Permanent mandates commission—report to the council, 1st-date. (Bound 1-10).

Reports of mandatory powers. Grouped here by country and bound annually.

(G3). VI. A. Mandates: document series.

Arranged by year and registry series. Stubbed for numbers withdrawn to form parts of series listed above.

(G5). VI. B. Slavery: serials.

Slavery convention—annual report by the council, 1927-date. (Usually with supplement). (Bound by twos).

Temporary slavery commission—minutes of sessions, 1st-2nd. (Never on sale).

(G7). VI. B. Document series: arranged by year and registry series. Stubbed.

(H1). VII. Political section: serials.

Committee on the composition of the council —report of sessions, nos. 1, 2. (Bound in 1 v.).

(H3). VII. Political section: document series.

Arranged by year and registry series. Stubbed for numbers withdrawn to form part of series listed above.

(K1). VIII. Communications and transit: serials.

Advisory and technical committee for communications and transit—report to the council, between 2nd and 3rd Assemblies-date.

General conference on communications and transit—preparatory documents and records and texts, 2nd-date. (First conference as Barcelona Conference, 1921. 2nd-date, 2 v. each).

Technical committee for buoyage and the lighting of coasts—minutes of sessions, nos. 1-3. (Bound in 1 v.).

(K3). VIII. Communications and transit: document series.

Arranged by year and registry series. Stubbed

for numbers withdrawn to form parts of series listed above.

(M1). IX. Disarmament: serials.

Armaments yearbook, 1st-date. (Supplied bound).

Preparatory commission for the disarmament conference—documents, series 1-7. (Bound in 1v.).

Preparatory commission for the disarmament conference—sub-commission B, reports, nos. 1-3. (Bound in 1 v.).

Satistical information on the trade in arms, 1st year-date. (Bound each issue).

Temporary mixed commission on armaments— report, 1921-1924. (Bound in 1 v.).

(M3). IX. Disarmament: document series.

Arranged by year and registry series. Stubbed for numbers withdrawn to form parts of series listed above.

(N1). X. Financial administration: serials.

Allocation of expenses, 1st financial period-date. (For periods 1-5 in Assembly records). (Bound 6-10, etc.).

Audited accounts, 1st financial period-date. (For periods 1-5 in records of 7th Assembly). (Bound 6-10).

Budget, 1st financial period-date. (For periods 1-5 in Assembly records; 11th period- to appear in November number of Official Journal). (Bound 6-10).

Supervisory commission—report, 1st session-date. (Early numbers obscure).

(N3). X. Financial administration: document series.

Arranged by year and registry series. Stubbed for numbers withdrawn to form parts of series listed above).

(P1). XI. Traffic in opium: serials.

Advisory committee on traffic in opium— minutes of sessions, 1st-date. (Bound by threes).

Advisory committee on traffic in opium—summary of annual reports, 1924-date.

Advisory committee on traffic in opium—report to the council, 1st-date. (Bound every three).

Opium conferences—preparatory documents and records, 1st-date. (2 v. for each conference, one for preparatory document; one for records).

List of seizures, 1921-date. (Bound 1921-1926).

(P3). XI. Traffic in opium: document series.

Arranged by year and registry series. Stubbed for numbers withdrawn to form parts of series listed above.

(R1). XII. A. Intellectual coöperation: serials.

Committee on intellectual coöperation—brochures, 1st ser. nos. 1-5; 2nd ser. nos. 6-?
(Bound 1st ser. nos. 1-5; 2nd ser. 6-10, etc.).

International committee on intellectual coöperation—minutes of sessions, 1st-date. (Index: 1-4, 5-7, etc.).

International committee on intellectual coöperation—report to the council, 1st-date. (Bound 1-4, 5-7, etc.).

(R3). XII. A. Intellectual coöperation: document series.

Arranged by year and registry series. Stubbed for numbers withdrawn to form parts of series listed above.

(R5). XII. B. International bureaux: serials.

Handbook of international organizations, 1921-date. (Bound each issue).

(R7). XII. B. International bureaux: document series.

Arranged by year and registry series. Stubbed for numbers withdrawn to form parts of series listed above.

(S1). XIII. Refugees: serials.

(S3). XIII. Refugees: document series.

Arranged by year and registry series. Stubbed for numbers withdrawn to form parts of series listed above.

(T1). Information section: serials.

Pamphlet series. (Unnumbered).

(T3). Information section: official publications not serials.

(JX1975.4). League of Nations: works about.

(JX1975.5). Autonomous organizations in order of founding.

(A1). International Labour Office.

(A9). Works about.

(B1). Permanent Court of International Justice.

(B9). Works about.

(C1). International Institute of Intellectual Co-operation.

(C9). Works about.

(Z). Miscellaneous works about international organizations.

Note: Within the sections of the Secretariat, serials may be Cuttered by title. The document series may be marked by year. An especial point in this classification is the very large amount of room left at all important points for change, growth, or expansion from the addition of new groups or sections. The General Questions material is put first, since it contains the Subject list of documents used with material in JX1975. The information Section is put last, since its material is more informal in character. This position, therefore, serves to bridge over to JX1975.4.

Dewey Classification: Since 341.1 must serve for all International Congresses, it is possible to adapt the LC scheme to Dewey by replacing JX1975 in all cases by 341.1L, giving 341.1L, 341.1L1, 341.1L2, 341.1L4, and 341.1L5 for the principal classes.

NOTES

[1] *Libraries*, v. 32, no. 3, Mar., 1927.

[2] Short bibliographies are frequently published on the League. Few contain information about the publications. Following are of some value:

Annuaire de la Société des Nations, 1920-1927; préparé sous la direction de Georges Ottlik. Lausanne et Genève, Librairie Payot et Cie, n.d. 1005 p.

Butler, Sir Geoffrey. *A Handbook to the League of Nations, brought down to the end of the fifth Assembly . . . with an introduction by the Right Hon. Viscount Cecil of Chelwood.* London, Longmans Green, 1925. 239 p.

Fry, C. B. *Key-book of the League of Nations.* London, Hodder and Stoughton, n. d. 183 p.

Gonsiorowski, Dr. Miroslas. *Société des Nations et problème de la paix.* Paris, Rousseau, 1927. 2 v.

Howard-Ellis, C. *The Origin, Structure, and Working of the League of Nations.* Boston, Houghton, 1928. 528 p.

Jones, Robert, and Sherman, S. S. *The League of Nations.* London, Pitman, 1927. 213 p. Bibliography, p. 206.

Rask-Orstedfonden. *Les Origines et l'Oeuvre de la Société des Nations.* Copenhagen, Gyldendalske Boghandel, 1924. 2 v.

Library of Congress. Division of Bibliography. *League of Nations: Short list of recent writings . . .* 1920-1922, with supplement, 1928.

[3] *Annuaire de la Société des Nations: 1920-1927.* Avant propos de Sir Eric Drummond, p. xi. (Free translation in French text.)

[4] Estimated roughly, such bodies would probably number about four hundred and fifty.

[5] As this is written, new information comes that the Bibliographical Bulletin . . . is being continued by another publisher as new series, no. 1.

[6] It is not possible, within the limits of this paper, to discuss the methods of treatment in other libraries.

[7] Organization of the Secretariat . . . Report of the Commission of Experts . . . A. 3, 1921.

[8] Figures for 1922 from Budget for the sixth financial period . . . C.668.M.268. 1923.X; for other years from Budget for the tenth financial period . . . C.520.M.178.1927.X.

[9] Gonsiorowski, Dr. Miroslas. *Société des Nations* . . . p. 274.

[10] Registry series as used in this classification scheme means always the public distribution registry series. Subject List of Documents, 1921-1924 not offered for sale.

The League of Nations Cataloging Project: General Overall Review October 1, 1945–February 28, 1950

Harriet Van Wyck

During the lifetime of the League there was no complete bibliographic record of its publications. The Library of the League of Nations in Geneva issued printed cards for sales publications starting in 1928. An effort was made to reach a shared cataloging agreement between the League Library and the Library of Congress but this attempt failed because the League Library insisted on following its own rules for author entry rather than Anglo-American practice. It was only in 1945 that a grant from the Rockefeller Foundation made possible the shared cataloging project between the Woodrow Wilson Memorial Library and LC described in this report.

I. BACKGROUND SUMMARY

When in 1945, the Woodrow Wilson Foundation appealed to the Rockefeller Foundation for funds to catalogue its League of Nations collection there existed only a limited catalogue covering documents offered for sale. The appeal was based largely on the realization that the Woodrow Wilson Memorial Library contained the only comparatively complete States' Member service of League of Nations documentation publicly available in the United States. This League collection was known to be one of a handful throughout the world accessible to the public outside of the collections in foreign offices of the member states. The League's published, or printed, material on public sale at one time reached some 160 libraries in the United States through global subscription arrangements. This material, catalogued by the Library of Congress and in part by the League's Library, comprised but a small part of the total documentation issued during the 1920–1946 period.

Some contend that no *complete* set of League documents, in chronological and numerical order, exists. If so, this fact may explain the difficulty of arriving at comprehensive estimates of total non-sale documentation. From the Geneva Library it was learned that from 100,000 to 125,000 individual documents were issued by the League during its twenty-six year history. Of that figure about ten per cent were printed documents and of that ten per cent about one-half were placed on sale. This non-sale, States' Member documentation, is composed of both public and restricted material essential for an understanding of the evolution of this first attempt at international organization, and equally essential if established precedents are to serve in the formulation of new efforts following World War II.

The Woodrow Wilson Foundation's Directors felt, and opinions have been justified by events, that the Library's exceptional collection could be used as a form of text, and a completed catalogue, or index, to this first world effort would serve the purposes both of officials working within the new agency and the scholars analyzing the previous one.

During the course of this four and one-half year project some 39,242 non-sale documents have been examined, and 9,463 new entries prepared for the catalogue. The 1945 catalogue of sales material has been expanded by the addition of 12,137 new entries, or can be so counted when the last printed cards are received from the Library of Congress. From a catalogue of 20,000 cards in 1945, the total of printed and typed cards now approaches 61,000, which in the Woodrow Wilson

SOURCE: Reprinted from: Harriet Van Wyck "League of Nations Cataloging Project Over-All Review," October 1, 1945–February 28, 1950. N.Y. Woodrow Wilson Memorial Library [1950].

Library covers the League documentation and the publications of the International Institute of Intellectual Cooperation, the International Labor Organization and the Permanent Court of International Justice. As would be expected, long series of sale and non-sale documentation are covered by series or open entries which eliminate thousands of individual entries for series items. Methods of "brief" and "group" cataloguing were employed for collections of preliminary drafts, circular letters and other relatively unimportant material, thus providing a subject rather than a direct approach to groups of similar documents.

Throughout the period of the project every effort was made to fill gaps in the collection. The generous cooperation of the Geneva Library can not be overstated. Through other sources such as the World Health Organization, the International Institute for the Unification of Private Law, Harvard University Library, Hoover Institute and Library, Fletcher School of Law and Diplomacy, the Pan American Union and numerous individuals, some 1,272 missing items were gathered. It is still impossible to estimate amounts of documents which never reached the Library. In some restricted series there are incomplete files; other series, issued in limited quantities for small working committees, are missing altogether in spite of diligent search. It was a bold, new program which the Woodrow Wilson Library undertook, and the project has extended far beyond first expectations.

II. ROCKEFELLER FOUNDATION GRANTS-IN-AID

Through the following grants-in-aid the Rockefeller Foundation enabled the Woodrow Wilson Memorial Library to catalogue its unique collection of non-sale documents of the League of Nations, issued over the period of the League's history from 1920 through 1946. On the following grants the project has functioned:

7/24/45 $5,600
   Oct. 1, 1945-Sept. 30, 1946—12 months
RF 46094   21,000
   Oct. 1, 1946-Dec. 31, 1947— 15 months
RF 47086   31,500
   Jan. 1, 1948-Aug. 31, 1949— 20 months
   (extended to Feb. 15, 1950) $5\frac{1}{2}$ months
                         $\overline{52\frac{1}{2}}$ months

Detailed financial statements, covering expenditures and receipts, have been submitted periodically with the progress reports. An over-all financial statement and duplicates of previous statements are included as Appendix C.

III. PROGRESS REPORTS

In order to acquaint the Rockefeller Foundation with details of progress, as the project developed, the Librarian has submitted reports for the following periods:

1st report—October 1945-March 1946
2nd report—April-September 1946
3rd report—October 1946-March 1947
4th report—April-December 1947
5th report—January-December 1948
6th report—January 1949-February 28, 1950
(enclosed)

During 1949 no progress report was submitted, but two rather extensive letters covering details of the project were forwarded to Mr. Stevens: a letter from Dr. Harry D. Gideonse, on January 17th; and one from the Librarian on July 22nd, 1949.

IV. ADMINISTRATION AND CATALOGUING STAFF

Laura S. Turnbull, Director, October 1945-September 1946.
Elizabeth M. Langer—cataloguer, and later Director when Miss Turnbull returned to Princeton University. October 1945-February 15, 1950.
Ragnhild F. Luhnenschloss, cataloguer and Assistant Director, October 1946-August 1949.
Marie Ponzo—cataloguer—October 1946-December 1947
Phyllis Novack—cataloguer—October 1946-December 1947.
Dora Hesse—cataloguer—March 1947-August 1949
Winifred W. Fremont—cataloguer—January 1948-August 1949.

William T. Perry—cataloguer—May 1948–July 1949.

Dorothy Dodd—typist-assistant—May 1946–January 1950

By the very nature of the project the recruiting of a competent staff presented difficulties. Not only was specialized training important but the search was carried on during a librarian-shortage and resulting increases in salary scales. To have enlisted the services of top-rank librarians is due to the challenge and importance of the work to be accomplished. To this special staff of diligent and resourceful librarians, and their co-workers in the Library of Congress, all credit is gratefully extended.

As we close the books on the actual cataloguing work we are glad to report that the Director moves on to similar work in the United Nations Library at Lake Success. No other one person is better fitted to take over the reference on and cataloguing of the League of Nations material, to which Miss Langer is assigned, than one who, since 1945, has worked exclusively with this documentation. Miss Dodd turned immediately to work which promises to be worthy of the special talents she has demonstrated in the typing and general assistance essential to the project.

V. CONSULTATIONS WITH EXPERTS

The Woodrow Wilson Library's reputation as a primary source for League documentation, and the professional approach of the special staff to the cataloguing project, enabled the Library to draw on the services of experts who gave liberally of their time and ideas. Among the many who have bestowed the blessings of advice and encouragement, Arthur Sweetser—Chairman of the Library Committee, and champion of the League and the United Nations—is top of the list. His abiding interest and inspiration, his time and talents have guided the staff over many hurdles.

The following individuals, and the organizations they represent, receive also deep thanks: A. C. Breycha-Vauthier, Albert Gerould, S. H. Rasmussen, and Carl H. Milam, Librarians of the United Nations, and others of the United Nations Secretariat include Marie J. Carroll, Violet H. Cabeen and Harry Winton; from the Library of Congress,—Herman Henkle, Lucile H. Morsch, Janet Paris and Verner Clapp; from the State Department,—Alice Bartlett and John Ottemiller; from the International Labor Office,—Janet F. Saunders; from UNESCO,—Theodore Besterman; from Carnegie Endowment for International Peace,—Helen L. Scanlon; from Hoover Institute and Library,—Nina Almond and Easton Rothwell; from the Joint Bank-Fund,—Martin Loftus and Hans Aufricht; from Fletcher School of Law and Diplomacy,—Louise Walker, Dorothy Fox and Grace Guillet; from New York Public Library,—Caroline Righter and Ralph Carruthers; from Columbia,—Florence Ferner; from Yale Library,—Anne Monrad and Dorothy Livingston; and from Mount Holyoke College,—Flora Belle Ludington. Each of these interested friends has contributed ideas which have proved useful and expedient.

VI. PRESERVATION OF THE LEAGUE DOCUMENTATION

A significant by-product of the cataloguing project, carried on by the Librarian, is the proposed plan for reproducing, and thereby preserving, the non-sale material which is not available generally and which is fast disintegrating. A long story of consultations and correspondence could be told, but it is enough to recount here that there is the definite interest of the State Department and the Library of Congress in exploring fully the costs involved in so large an enterprise.

The Association of Research Libraries, at a meeting in March 1949, expressed enough interest to warrant extensive calculations on costs of microfilming, or some other method of preservation. Among those consulted, for the library angle, were Julian Boyd of Princeton, Verner Clapp of the Library of Congress, John Ottemiller of the State Department Library, Charles David of the University of Pennsylvania Library, and A. C. Breycha-Vauthier and Carl H. Milam of the United Nations Libraries. To explore the reproduction angle, consultations with Ralph H. Carruthers, Chief of the Photographic Services Division of New York Public Library; Fremont Rider of the Microcard Committee; Eugene B. Powell of Universities Microfilms; and Albert Boni of Readex Microprint Corporation, were held.

It was in this connection, in 1949, that Verner Clapp of the Library of Congress, estimated the quantity of non-sale documentation involved. He reported that if ten libraries would participate in the plan, the cost of film per set would run to something like $3,500. A considerable budget item, but when it is recognized that large portions of the documentation are crumbling to pieces, and most of it is unavailable except in a few centers throughout the world, this new plan takes on far-reaching significance. If some form of reproduction of the non-sale documents could be accomplished the value of the cataloguing work just completed would be greatly increased. This phase of the explorations is included, in this over-all report, only to show the significance and inter-relationship of the two projects.

VII. RESEARCH AND CATALOGUING PROCEDURES

A. General Observations

The statistical analysis contained in Appendix A gives the story in blunt arithmetical terms and conveys little in terms of study and research. When we see a total of 727 volumes, and 39,242 documents, and 9,463 catalogued entries we are looking through a fluoroscope at the skeleton on which the body of the project is constructed. Some grasp of the operations can be gleaned from Miss Turnbull's "Memorandum on Checking League of Nations Documents for Cataloguing" which was submitted to the Rockefeller Foundation with the first progress report. Miss Langer's "Guide to the Card Files of the League of Nations Documents," submitted with the sixth report, (Appendix III), is a description of the steps involved in building up the present catalogue, and is a guide to its use. Throughout the progress reports we have attempted to explain, in lay language, the various methods employed; what material was included and what omitted; and other details which in due course were important to recount. It seems unnecessary to enumerate again the many technical aspects and angles.

B. Outside Research and Analysis of Activities

In March, 1948, members of the staff undertook an accounting, for a one-month period, of the various operations involved in the cataloguing process. Under some twenty-three different categories the time-schedules revealed the extent and variety of operations required before final filing of the last card. In the one item of professional reading and research, in and out of the Woodrow Wilson Library, a total of 132 hours was spent during that one month by the various staff members. Small wonder that the Director found it essential to prepare, for the cataloguers, a rather detailed manual of procedures. It was suggested by the Librarian of the International Labor Office that a manual of this kind should see print, and thus provide a basic tool for future students of document cataloguing.

C. Official Number File

This file, consisting of approximately 10,500 cards is felt to be of value not only as an inventory of holdings, but as a quick reference for those seeking a document by official number. Arranged chronologically, and by symbol series, the file reveals at a glance the whereabouts of a particular document, or the lack of it. Where gaps in the file exist they can be explained either as actually missing, or they may represent documents in a series covered by a series or "group" entry.

D. Shelf List and Volume Numbering

An efficiency measure of great importance eliminated the long "bound-in" notes which previously had been typed on all printed cards to lead the reader to a specific document within a specific volume. Working from the Shelf List, volume by volume, and Section by Section, documents can now be located in a few seconds by the use of the volume number within each Section: i.e. III.v.9, as a call number, indicates that in volume 9 of the Health Section, (III) the particular document can be found.

E. Section-by-Section Problems

The Section, or actually the subject approach, is the method by which the Library's League Collection is bound. Thus, within Section II (Economics and Finance) for instance, all documents bearing the Roman II, as part of the official number,—both sale and non-sale,—are bound in chronological order. Each Section has revealed its own dramatic story of successes and failures, and has required the utmost skill on the part of the staff to emphasize the essential themes in the welter of words.

Working in the Intellectual Cooperation Section

it was soon found that so inter-related were the documents issued by the International Institute of Intellectual Cooperation that although this material was not included in original plans it was impossible to omit examination and cataloguing if the record was to be complete. In recording statistics it will be found that some 800 additional documents were covered by detailed or brief cataloguing methods, an effort well worth the extension of time and costs if only in the service rendered to scholars working on UNESCO background material.

In the Health Section, Section III, it became evident that the Library's holdings fell far short of the items recorded in the *Bulletin of the Health Organization,* no.XI, 1945. This bibliography is a comprehensive listing of publications issued from 1920 through 1945 and contains an excellent subject index. Searches for missing documents began with appeals to the League Library and to the World Health Organization, and on to the Surgeon General's Office, the National Health Institute, the New York Academy of Medicine and the medical libraries of Yale University and Columbia University, but to no avail. Explorations revealed that hundreds of monographs and reports on important health subjects were missing also in these medical centers and were unobtainable from Geneva. As a compromise measure the bibliographical listing in the *Bulletin* is checked to show the Library's catalogued holdings and must be used as a supplement to the catalogue to trace unavailable material.

Yesterday's problems and solutions have thrown indirect lighting on the stage at Lake Success where history-in-the making is presented daily. Rules of procedure were applied and modified to meet specific situations. What appeared routine at long range required special treatment when taken in hand. Only by flexibility and versatility have the seasoned troupers handled their roles, and drawn forth for their public of scholars and students the wealth of original source material. To recount again, even in summary form, the progress through each Section of League documentation would be needless repetition.

VIII. COOPERATION WITH LIBRARY OF CONGRESS

A. Staff Consultations

Beginning with and including the initial visit, when three members of the Descriptive Catalogu-

ing Division of Library of Congress,–Herman Henkle, Lucile H. Morsch and Janet Paris,– journeyed to New York on June 4, 1946, our special reviser, Mrs. Paris, has made nine visits: June and December 1946; January, July and December 1947; May and October 1948; and February and June 1949. These all-day consultations have added up to considerable profit for members of the cataloguing staff and they provided Mrs. Paris with information she could not gain by correspondence. To sit in on one of these conferences is to take a quick refresher in world history and advanced cataloguing in one parcel. For all the differences of opinion and healthy arguments, there grew up a deep respect for and understanding of the operations involved in the two libraries before the printer could turn out the finished product.

B. Cooperation in Action

Although it proved rarely possible for the Library of Congress to meet the promised three-week delivery of printed cards, every effort has been made to speed the processing of copy when submitted. Considering the vast number of entries submitted, some 8,169 since the beginning of the project, and the fact that documents could not be checked at the Library of Congress, it is a tribute to the accuracy of the staff and efficiency at the printing end that errors were kept at a minimum, and delivery as prompt as it was.

Back-log copy at Library of Congress was worrysome, in view of time-schedules, and resulted in the preparation of two long lists of documents in process,–one list in December, 1949, and the second in March, 1949. These lists aided in speeding up clearance of snags in Washington. There still remain some 289 entries for which cards have not yet been received, and as these appear within the next few months they will be handled by the Library staff in accordance with established procedures.

C. Cataloguing Rules Changed in Mid-Stream

In the fourth progress report will be found comments on the "new rules" for descriptive cataloguing. Protests were met with understanding and explanations but little hope that the special project could evade the new regulations. Established to provide short-cuts the new rules tended at first to slow down production until initial hurdles could be mastered.

D. Subject Headings à la Woodrow Wilson Library

For some material of historical importance the staff could not agree on headings established by the Library of Congress. It was, therefore, gratifying when the Library was granted the privilege of submitting its own headings, when deemed essential, and thus it became the seventh so-favored library in the United States. Where the Library of Congress could not agree to change its headings in line with our suggestions it printed our suggested subject headings in brackets, in addition to its own, leaving the choice to the individual librarian when the card was put to use.

E. "Group" Cataloguing

Instituted by Library of Congress for the treatment of like material, this method eliminated detailed cataloguing for collections of relatively unimportant documents, abstracts and press releases, and so on. However, as an example, this short-cut measure did not prove adequate for the hundreds of documents covering the invasion of Manchuria, all bearing the identical heading: "Appeal from the Chinese Government. . . ." Although appearing to be similar the individual documents warranted detailed treatment.

F. The "Chief" Commends Us

Commenting on the work which was drawing to a close, Miss Lucile H. Morsch, Chief of the Descriptive Cataloguing Division of Library of Congress, wrote on September 16, 1949:

". . . I do want to tell you that we have all enjoyed working with you and your staff even when we did not always see eye to eye. You have certainly contributed an important addition to our catalog which would have been quite impossible without your help."

IX. CORPORATE HEADING LISTS

The initial tasks facing the staff of two librarians in the fall of 1945 was the compilation of lists of Committees and Commissions which had functioned during the League's twenty-six year history. A working list of some six hundred of these bodies provided the basis for establishing correct corporate entries as documents were catalogued. Section by Section, as work progressed, the listings were brought into line with actual records. Historical notes and cross references were added. Not previously compiled, even in the League's own Library, these lists provided invaluable reference material for the two United Nations Libraries and the Library of Congress. Perhaps no single exhibit, in the whole cataloguing picture, so graphically reveals the extent of original research accomplished as do these corporate heading lists.

Fifteen individual lists, consisting of a total of 779 Committees and Commissions, with historical references, provide the basis for an over-all alphabetical and indexed listing. On this point, A. C. Breycha-Vauthier, Librarian of the United Nations Library in Geneva, wrote on January 28, 1949:

". . . Please let us know if our collection is complete as we are putting this valuable bibliographical instrument at the disposal of research workers and want to give them all the benefit of your work.

We very much hope that you will succeed in carrying on your project of a complete alphabetical listing with an index; in the meantime we shall carry on with the lists you have been kind enough to send us."

It is the Director's and Librarian's cherished hope that a publisher may be found for the finished product. In answer to an exploratory inquiry, when the Committee list for the Economies Section was submitted for examination, Henry H. Wiggins, Manager of the Columbia University Press Publication Department, wrote on January 20, 1950:

". . . The amount of work that has gone into the preparation of this list is certainly staggering, and I can easily see how a publication such as you have in mind would help to give others the benefit of this work. Largely because of the costs I know would be involved, I cannot, at the moment, see just what we could do. We shall, however, give the matter some study, and I will write you further."

Mr. Wiggins' letter of February 9, 1950, which goes fully into the difficulties involved in the publication of an over-all listing, is enclosed as Appendix D.

X. USE OF THE LEAGUE COLLECTION

A. Survey of Users

At the suggestion of the Chairman of the Library Committee, a recent survey was compiled which covered the months from May through December 20, 1949. It was found that attendance figures had increased and also telephone inquiries. Students, both graduate and under-graduate, from 32 institutions in 13 states and the District of Columbia, comprised the largest single group of users. Other categories, in numerical sequence, were: Non-Governmental organizations; Writers, magazine and press representatives; Delegations to the United Nations and Government agencies; Business organizations; College and High School faculty members; United Nations Secretariat and Specialized Agencies; Law office representatives; and Radio commentators and station personnel. For the student, and largest group, an analysis was made of the types of inquiries. For the other categories the listings showed persons and groups served, and information sought,—with no attempt at breakdowns by subject of inquiry.

In the student group the survey showed top billing to the United Nations and the Specialized Agencies, as would be expected. Next in volume of inquiries was material from and about the League of Nations. Again natural, since the Library's League Collection is unique in the country.

B. Samplings of League of Nations Inquiries

It is impossible to over-state the importance of the League cataloguing project in terms of assistance in handling requests for obscure, as well as obvious items. It is only a reference librarian, whose lot it is to plough through volumes of mimeographed monographs, reports, surveys and memoranda—to satisfy a hurry-up call from the United Nations—who can adequately express appreciation of the expanded League catalogue. She now remains calm when the request is vague; official number unknown; date of document approximate; title given in general terms; and author dubious. The United Nations Library, now better equipped in its holdings of League material, is still a frequent borrower of the non-sale documentation, and often the request specifies the French edition, and quick!

From guest book records and tabulations of telephone inquiries the Library compiles its annual statistics, and those for survey purposes. It is natural, in an open-shelf library, that readers help themselves without staff assistance. The use of League material is therefore observed but data on specific study subjects is unrecorded. The catalogue proved indispensable in handling the following inquiries which are taken at random from recent records:

Coordination of measures under Article 16 of the Covenant.
Switzerland's guaranty of rights as a neutral.
Monographs covering aid to under-developed countries.
Broadcasting in the cause of peace.
Model conventions for prevention of double taxation.
Technical agreements regarding railroads.
Unification of air transport conventions.
Rights of innocent passage.
European Union discussions before the League.
Assistance to indigent foreigners.
Manley Hudson's 1924 memorandum on American collaboration with the League.
Nijhoff's report for the Siamese Government on dredging Bangkok Harbor.
Committee of Thirteen on reorganization of the Secretariat.
Minority rights under League conventions.
Cartels and barter agreements.
Inland waterway conventions.
Pasteurization of milk.
Questionnaires regarding drug addiction.
Housing in rural areas.
Specific monographs of the Int. Institute of Unification of Private Law.
Suppression of traffic in persons.

These are but a few of the many inquiries where speedy access to material immeasurably aided a busy Secretariat, a press representative to meet a dead-line, and the equally avid research workers.

TO CONCLUDE

The Rockefeller Foundation has received copies of various letters, during the course of the work, commenting on the value of the project. It is also gratifying to the Directors of the Woodrow Wilson Foundation and to the staff to read additional comments which the President of the Foundation,

Mr. Cleveland E. Dodge, is now forwarding with these final reports. They include comments from:

A. C. Breycha-Vauthier, Librarian, United Nations, Geneva.
Charles W. David, Executive Secretary, Association of Research Libraries.
Florence K. Ferner, Librarian, International Law Library, Columbia University.
Dorothy Fox, Librarian, Fletcher School of Law and Diplomacy.
Martin L. Loftus, Librarian, Joint Bank-Fund Library.
Carl H. Milam, Director of Library Services, United Nations, Lake Success.
John H. Ottemiller, Acting Chief, Division of Library and Reference Services, U. S. Department of State

Worth recording here is the following excerpt from a document issued by UNESCO (UNESCO/SS/AB/1) entitled "Documents and Publications of International Organizations," by A. D. Roberts, dated June 30, 1949:

" . . . Complete records were not made currently of the output of the League of Nations, apart from its somewhat bare *Monthly List of Documents Distributed,* which was not cumulated. It has taken a grant of $53,000 from the Rockefeller Foundation and nearly four years of work at the Library of the Woodrow Wilson Foundation in New York to remedy this. Other international organizations should take note, and should attempt the work currently, both for their own immediate benefit and for the use of scholars and librarians both currently and later . . . "

Scholars and historians for generations to come will turn to the records of the first great experiment in world organization and will be aided in their search for specific information by the work which has been accomplished. Thanks to the generosity of the Rockefeller Foundation, the active cooperation of the Library of Congress, and this staff of diligent and resourceful librarians, there is now an integrated and uniform key to primary source material of lasting historical value.

The Librarian of the Woodrow Wilson Foundation submits these final reports to the Rockefeller Foundation in gratitude for the confidence placed in the Library and for the privilege of participating in the League of Nations cataloguing project. It is hoped that the information provided on the progress and completion of the work has proved adequate and illuminating.

Harriet Van Wyck
Librarian

League of Nations Publications in the Present Emergency

Nelle Signore

World War II disrupted most of the political activities of the League. Some League offices were closed temporarily or completely with a consequent impairment of publication programs. This article by a specialist in political science and history on the staff of the University of Illinois Library describes the status of League publishing programs three years after the start of the war.

It is important, in the light of present-day affairs, for one to review the achievements of the League of Nations during the past twenty years in order to evaluate again the ideals and principles of international cooperation embodied in all its undertakings. The publications of the League of Nations are important sources of information for study and research because of their international aspect, the wide field of subjects included, and their high standards of accuracy and thoroughness. Many people think of the League of Nations only as a political unit, focusing their attention on its several failures and disregarding its constructive and humanitarian activities.

In spite of the present war and the rapid change of governments, the technical organizations in the League of Nations have been able to carry on a fair amount of research and publication. The Publication Department of the League of Nations recently announced the regular continuance of two periodicals, *Monthly Bulletin of Statistics* and *Weekly Epidemiological Record*. In addition, the Treaty Series will be continued and documents will be issued by the Economic and Financial Section, Social Section, Disarmament Section, and Opium Section.

The chaotic conditions in Europe have made it necessary to distribute the work of the League of Nations among various centers. The Political Section was kept at Geneva; the Economic, Financial, and Transit sections were centered at Princeton University; the Opium Section was transferred to Washington; and the International Labour Office, whose work is closely allied with that of the league, was removed to McGill University, Montreal. Difficulties arose over the transportation of French officials of the International Labour Office to a belligerent country, making it necessary to transfer some of the work of this office to Washington. The publications of the Permanent Court of International Justice have been suspended indefinitely. The offices of the World Court were closed when the Peace Palace at the Hague was bombed. The International Institute of Intellectual Cooperation at Paris is closed and no publications are being issued.

Because of the uncertainty of publication and the limited number of copies being printed, libraries, particularly those binding sets by publication number, would be well advised to scrutinize very carefully global subscriptions to League of Nations' documents to insure receipt of all publications. The *Monthly Bulletin of Statistics* and weekly *Epidemiological Record* subscriptions are invoiced separately from global orders and from other corresponding orders; other publications have been placed on a continuation order basis, whereby documents are supplied as they are published and billed at the end of the year. League of Nations publications may be secured through the International Document Service, Columbia University Press, New York City.

American interest in the wartime activities of the League of Nations was first made evident by the organization of a national committee of eminent Americans to aid and preserve the League of Nations nonpolitical work. This was followed by a joint invitation from Princeton University,

SOURCE: Reprinted from: Nelle Signore, "League of Nations Publications in the Present Emergency," *College and Research Libraries*, 3 (Sept., 1942) pp. 326–332.

the Institute for Advanced Study, and the Rockefeller Institute of Medical Research to the League
of Nations to establish its technical services at
Princeton University for the duration of the emergency. This invitation was accepted on behalf of
the Economic, Financial, and Transit sections, and
in August 1940 the director and part of their staff
were sent to Princeton University. Certain members of the sections were left in Geneva to follow
the economic developments within Europe in
order to supply data for continuing the statistical
publications. Much of the present work of this
department has been made possible by a grant of
fifty thousand dollars from the Rockefeller Foundation, to be used during the years 1941 and 1942.

ECONOMIC AND FINANCIAL SECTION

Economic Intelligence Service—Statistical Documents

The Economic and Financial Section of the
League of Nations has doubtless made its greatest
contribution to research in the field of comparative
statistics. The Economic Intelligence Service
which is connected with the Economic and Financial Section is responsible for some of the most
important statistical data published by this section.
This service was founded as a result of the Brussels
Conference of 1920. Its immediate object was to
coordinate and centralize information made public
by national administrators on subjects of economic importance. It has published regularly so
much economic and financial information that it
has now become one of the most valuable and
highly appreciated sources of financial and economic documentation. Previously it published in
the course of the year three strictly statistical
documents and a series of studies dealing with
different aspects of the world economic situation.
Although economic statistics and financial information have been greatly curtailed, the league is
making every effort to continue the work of the
Economic Intelligence Service owing to the fact
that new economic trends which are becoming
more evident during the war period are likely to
become the bases for formulating postwar economic policies. With this in mind the league has
decided to continue two strictly statistical publications, the *Monthly Bulletin of Statistics* and the
Statistical Yearbook; the *World Economic Survey*

and a number of special studies are also being
published.

The *Monthly Bulletin of Statistics*, which has
been issued at Geneva monthly since July 1919, is
continuing without interruption. This gives the
most recent figures on the economic and financial
development of the countries of the world based
on official information specially supplied each
month. With September 1940 copies were also
printed on thin paper to be sent by airmail for the
league's mission in Princeton.

While the *Monthly Bulletin of Statistics* gives a
current indication of the status of economic conditions throughout the world, the *Statistical Yearbook of the League of Nations* is restricted to an
intensive study of statistical data for a selected
number of subjects of current importance. The
latest issue of the *Statistical Yearbook* gives statistics up to the end of 1939 and in some cases also
for the first half of 1940.

Economic Intelligence Service—Special Studies

While the statistical documents described above
are made up largely of statistical tables from which
one may draw his own conclusions, the *World
Economic Studies* are analyses of world conditions
drawn from information collected from all parts
of the world, which were formerly issued in separate memoranda. Available material on such subjects as world trade, production and prices, banking, and public finance, is no longer complete
enough to justify the publication of the separate
memoranda. Instead, the Economic Intelligence
Service has issued a *World Economic Survey* covering the period from the autumn of 1939 to the
summer of 1941. Previous issues of the *World
Economic Survey* (1932–39) consisted of a general analysis of the organization of industry and
commerce in the world as a whole, based mainly
on the results of the various studies carried on by
the Economic Intelligence Service supplemented
by the information drawn from other sources,
such as the International Labour Office. The
World Economic Survey 1939–41, which was published at Princeton by the university press in 1941,
is a survey of the world at war. It deals with the
problems of war economy in the countries at war
as well as the reverberations of the war throughout
the world. The first chapters deal with the means
by which the change from peace to war economy
was effected in the different countries, while the

later chapters deal with the effect of these changes on various forms of economic activity.

Raw Materials and Foodstuffs was published at Geneva in January 1940. It is a study of the sources of supply of all the more important raw materials and foodstuffs arranged by country for the years 1935 and 1938. The main tables are so arranged that by consulting a single table one may see the countries which produce each commodity and the amount of production for each country. It is an excellent reference source for those desiring exact information on production and trade in raw materials and foodstuffs.

Because of the reduction of national trade statistics it has been impossible to continue the publication, *Review of World Trade*, which appeared annually for the years 1933–38. It has been replaced by a special study, *Europe's Trade*, published in Geneva in the spring of 1941. This is an analysis of the part played by Europe in the trade of the world before the outbreak of the present war and a consideration of how far Europe is dependent upon external markets and to what extent external markets are dependent upon her. It is the plan of the Economic Intelligence Service to follow up this analysis with a companion volume covering the trade of the rest of the world.

Since 1931 the Economic Intelligence Service has published an annual memorandum on commercial banks, under varying titles. In 1937 under the title *Money and Banking* a two-volume series was published: v. I. *Monetary Review*, v. 2. *Commercial Banks*. It was decided with the 1939–40 issue of *Money and Banking* to discontinue the second volume but to continue the *Monetary Review*. The latest number was published in Geneva in 1940 and covers the period September 1939–40. It is a study of the far-reaching measures adopted by various governments for the control and operation of the banking system since the outbreak of the war. A brief introductory note precedes the review, which summarizes the monetary situation— from the appearance of the preceding issue of the *Monetary Review* in the spring of 1939 to September 1939.

The Fiscal Committee

Since its organization in 1929 the Fiscal Committee has had as its main objective the formulation of treaties and conventions to prevent double taxation in the fields of income and property taxes. In spite of the present war situation the Fiscal Committee has held two meetings, one at the Hague in April 1940 and the second at Mexico City, June 1940. The second meeting was particularly significant since it was the outcome of a request made in 1938 to the Fiscal Committee by the Mexican government that a study be made of certain principles of taxation which would be helpful to Latin American countries which were in the process of developing their tax systems. Because war had spread all over Europe at this time, the Mexican government extended an invitation to the conference to convene at Mexico City. Representatives from Argentina, Brazil, Peru, Venezuela, Mexico, Canada, and the United States were present to comment on the preliminary studies submitted. The important result of the meeting was the adoption of a draft for a model convention for the prevention of double taxation in the field of income and property taxes, which brings up to date the model conventions framed by the Conference of Governmental Experts of 1928. It is highly important that the work of the Fiscal Committee be continued since the question of double taxation will undoubtedly be an important problem of the postwar period, especially in its relation to inter-American trade.

HEALTH SECTION

Epidemics

The successful work of the League of Nations in the control of infectious diseases is due largely to the Epidemiological Intelligence Service. The work of this service is so important that at the present time it is receiving support both from neutral countries and from countries at war. Since January 1930 it has published the *Weekly Epidemiological Record* regularly at Geneva. This periodical supplies prompt information on the prevalence of contagious disease which at the time constitute an international danger. Until the time of the Japanese occupation, the most important part of the service was centered at Singapore, to which place more than 180 ports in the surrounding area sent in cable messages weekly or even more frequently concerning the occurrence of epidemic disease. In normal times the information received at the Singapore bureau was analyzed and broadcast by ten wireless stations to every health officer, every captain of a ship, and every airplane pilot in the area from Panama on the East, Suez on the West, and Vladivostok on the North, so that they might know to what extent disease prevailed and what quarantine measures to adopt. Before the fall of Singapore the officers in charge of this service were safely transferred to Sydney, but at the present time it is not known whether it will prove possible to reestablish the bureau in another center. The information assembled at Singapore was published currently under the title: *Weekly Fascicules: Epidemiological Intelligence Received by the Eastern Bureau*. No. 878 of January 8, 1942, is the latest that has been seen. A similar service exists at Geneva for information concerning epidemics in Europe, but so far there has been less need for rapid service than in the Far East. With the migrations of peoples and movements of troops resulting from the war the Epidemiological Service has followed very closely all developments of epidemics of infectious diseases and has taken every precaution to prevent their spread.

Biological Standardization

In 1924 the Health Committee of the League of Nations set up a Permanent Commission on Biological Standardization to establish international standards for the use of sera, glandular preparations, vitamins, and other remedies, the activity of which can be measured only by biological methods. By 1935 the commission had made available international standards and units for most of the important drugs which are biologically tested. Since in wartime the standards of serum content are so important, the Copenhagen Serological Institute together with the London Institute have made a great effort to continue the normal distribution of standards of sera, vitamins, hormones, and certain other medicaments to most countries.

The Bulletin of the Health Organization was issued quarterly from March 1932 to December 1936 and bimonthly from February 1937 to December 1939 at Geneva. It includes material brought together by the Health Organization of the league on such subjects as epidemics, malaria, biological standardization, housing, nutrition, cancer, tuberculosis, and rabies. For the information of those interested in medical subjects it includes articles by leading authorities in the field of health and social medicine.

SOCIAL SECTION

Child Welfare

In 1934 the Assembly of the League of Nations established the Child Welfare Information Center to centralize information relating to child welfare. For the last three years it has collected and classified information concerning child welfare and has issued each year a *Summary of the Legislative and Administrative Series of Documents of the Child Welfare Information Center*. The last issue was published at Geneva in January 1940 and as in previous years it summarizes documents relating to maternal and child welfare and social service. The information center also published an *Annual Report on Child Welfare* which aims to show the progress made in child welfare in the various countries from the legislative and administrative points of view. This includes either a summary or the complete text of important laws which have been put in force for the protection of families and children and to combat prostitution. The latest issue was published at Geneva in March 1940.

The Advisory Committee on Social Questions issues annually a *Summary of Annual Reports on Traffic in Women and Children*. This consists of summaries of reports made by the governments of various countries in reply to questionnaires on social questions issued by the advisory committee. The *Summary* for 1939–40 was published at Geneva in May 1941.

OPIUM SECTION

Drug Traffic

At meetings held in Geneva in May 1940 the three international organizations dealing with the drug traffic, namely, the Advisory Committee on Traffic in Opium and Dangerous Drugs, the Permanent Central Opium Board, and the Drug Supervisory Body, decided to continue their technical work during the war, since past experience had shown that need for drug control increased rather than diminished under war conditions.

The Advisory Committee on Traffic in Opium and Other Dangerous Drugs, which met for its twenty-fifth session on May 13-17, 1940, included delegations from thirteen out of the twenty-three government members. Special emphasis was placed on the importance of cooperation of the governments with the international organizations in order to prevent the extension of illicit drug traffic and increased drug addiction resulting from the war. The *Minutes* of this meeting were published in Geneva, December 1940.

The Permanent Central Opium Board is concerned with the control of trade in narcotic drugs, based on statistics supplied by the various governments. In January 1941 it issued the regular *Annual Report on the Statistics of Narcotics for 1939 and the Work of the Board during 1940*. This report which is based on statistics received from fifty countries and from ninety to one hundred dependencies, is mainly statistical as war conditions have made it necessary to omit analysis and comment.

The Drug Supervisory Body is the organization which determines the lawful amount of drugs that may be manufactured and consumed throughout the world during a given year. It examines the estimates of the narcotic requirements submitted by the various governments and draws up estimates for countries for which estimates have not been submitted. Its most recent statement, *Estimated World Requirements of Dangerous Drugs in 1942*, was published in Geneva, December 1941.

In the spring of 1941, owing to difficulties of communication with certain countries, a branch office of the Permanent Central Opium Board and the Drug Supervisory Body was established in Washington where the control of drug traffic will be centered during the present war.

Refugees

By a resolution passed by the Assembly of the League of Nations in September 1938 the Nansen International Office for Refugees ceased its activities in December 1938 and a high commissioner of the League of Nations was appointed to deal with refugees. The high commissioner issued an *Annual Report* in July 1939, a *Supplementary Report*, October 1939, and an *Intermediate Report*, April 1940. His latest report which is dated January 1941, as in the case of previous ones, deals, not only with the humanitarian aspect of the refugee problem, but with the provisions made for the legal protection of refugees and their emigration and settlement. Much of the information included is based on personal interviews of the high commissioner with representatives of the governments and private organizations assisting in the work.

Treaty Series

About two hundred volumes of this series have been published since September 1920. The series includes treaties of peace, treaties of commerce, international conventions, renewals and denunciation of treaties, and so forth. The texts of the treaties are in their original language with an English and French translation added when the text is not in one of these two languages. It is the intention of the league to continue the publication of this series as long as funds permit.

Library

The *Monthly List of Selected Articles* resumed publication in January 1941, after an interruption from May to December 1940. At present it is not published each month but appears in combined issues at various intervals. It is a selected list of articles on political, legal, economic, financial, and social questions of the day compiled from abstracts made of about eight hundred periodicals appearing in all parts of the world. At the present time there is no other such publication being issued in Europe.

Recent Publications on Present Activities of the League of Nations

The purpose of the foregoing article has been to list and describe the services and publications of the league which have continued during the present World War. The articles in the following bibliography are cited as a useful means of current orientation on the actual work of this vast organization.

BIBLIOGRAPHY

Geneva Research Center. "Geneva as an International Centre." (Its *Information Bulletin* v. 3, no. 1, 1940)

Hambro, C. J. "League Agencies Functioning." *New York Times*, Nov. 3, 1941, p. 6.

Mary E. Woolley Committee. Press Release. New York, June 1, 1940.

Sweetser, Arthur. "Correcting a False Impression about the League." *New York Times,* Nov. 23, 1941, Sec. 4, p. 4.

Sweetser, Arthur. "League Work in America." *Changing World* 12:7, 12, Sept. 1940.

Sweetser, Arthur. "The United States and World Organization in 1940." (Geneva Studies, v. 11, no. 8, Dec. 1940). Reprinted in *International Conciliation*, 1941, p. 603–13.

Woolley, Mary E. "Must These Things Die?" *Changing World* 12:9, June 1940.

NOTES

[1] The information in this article is as of June 1942.

The Woodrow Wilson Memorial Library, 1920–1950

The Woodrow Wilson Foundation

The Woodrow Wilson Memorial Library became what was probably the most nearly complete collection of publications issued by and about the League of Nations. This report summarizes the activities of the library for a thirty-year period.

I. IN REVIEW

For the final report on the Woodrow Wilson Memorial Library's services as an international relations study center covering its twenty-one year history it is appropriate to review the reasons for its establishment in 1929, and to give a summary of the Library's expansion and accomplishments under the administration of the Woodrow Wilson Foundation.

Early records of the Foundation reflect the intent of the original founders to perpetuate the ideas and ideals of Woodrow Wilson through a program which would further the concept of international organization and world cooperation. There appeared to be no evidence that the Directors envisioned the creation of a dynamic library on world organization as a living memorial to the Wilsonian philosophy. It was an event of far-reaching importance, which could not have been anticipated in the early days of program planning, that created a project destined to become the Foundation's one continuing and sustaining endeavor for a period of twenty-one years.

This significant event in 1929 was the acquisition of thousands of official documents and internal working papers issued by the League of Nations and presented to the Foundation by Raymond B. Fosdick, first Under Secretary-General of the League. Finding itself the custodian of documentary treasures, unavailable to the public anywhere else in the country, the Foundation soon recognized its unique opportunity and set about assembling the printed and mimeographed material. Through the good offices of Dr. Fosdick and of Mr. Arthur Sweetser, then a member of the Secretariat in Geneva, it was arranged in 1920 that the Foundation should thenceforth receive currently all sale and nonsale League publications on the same depository basis as that provided to member states. This service was maintained. It included both French and English editions and continued through the period of the second World War and until the United Nations took over the functions and assets of the League in 1946.

During the first years the major task assigned to Miss Helen Wheeler, who became the first Librarian, was the preparation of an appropriate catalogue for those public-sale documents of the League for which the Library of Congress and the Geneva Library had issued printed cards. Sorting, assembling and binding the extensive collection of documents, accumulated since the early 1920's, required judgment, skill and patience and it was due in large measure to Miss Wheeler's twelve years of service that the Library's League of Nations collection retained maximum usefulness and preservation.

Beginnings and Growth

With the League of Nations documentation as a nucleus, the Library began the slow and discriminating accumulation of secondary source materials. Of prime importance, obviously, were the published works about the League and its activities. Books, pamphlets and periodicals were selected for their bearing on the central theme of world organization. Gifts were solicited then as later and were numerous even in the early days of the Library. The various League of Nations societies throughout the world were added to the list of donors and their reports, journals and publications contrib-

SOURCE: Reprinted from "The Woodrow Wilson Memorial Library, 1920-1950." *Woodrow Wilson Foundation Annual Report, 1949-50.* N. Y., Woodrow Wilson Foundation, 1950. pp. 13-25.

uted immeasurably to the awakening of public interest in League affairs. Little by little, and always with the central theme the determining criterion in the acquisition of new material, the study center grew. Records show that inter-library loans were arranged and that there were occasional distributions of descriptive folders,—factors which contributed to enlarging the circle of scholars and students, in and out of New York, who came to recognize the value of the Library's unique source material.

The Library's reports prior to 1941 recounted stories of growth and increasing public interest but it remained for the advent of Pearl Harbor and America's entry into World War II to bring Woodrow Wilson and the League of Nations into direct focus insofar as the general public was concerned. Rare in those war years was the publication of any substantial political or historical significance which did not bring forth, often in Mr. Wilson's own words, ideas of international security through an organization of nations in which America should play a major role. Small wonder, then, that the Library took on new meaning and greater usefulness. No more challenging assignment in the field of library service could be imagined than that provided by this Library dedicated to Woodrow Wilson and his concepts of international security and world unity.

Quarters Change—Service Expands

The journey from 6 East 39th Street to 8 West 40th Street was made by the Foundation and Library in the spring of 1934. In lofty quarters, with an outlook over the Hudson and space for expansion, the Library came into a period of enviable luxury. In this mid-town location with ample light and space for visitors and staff it was to be expected that the Library would become a haven for scholars who, in the pre-war days, sought light on world events in the documents of the League of Nations.

Again moving in 1945 the Foundation and Library spread out further and took on new opportunities for service in the building formerly occupied by the Council on Foreign Relations at 45 East 65th Street. The uptown trend of organizations, Consulates and Delegations to the United Nations brought new faces and new friends, compensating in part for those who found scant time to journey from midtown to the mid-60's. While some names dropped off the visitors' book the

telephone knew no geographic boundaries. The Library's public service features took on new dimensions.

The All-Important Library Committee

Directors of the Foundation and others with special qualifications and interest were chosen from time to time to serve on the Library Committee and assist the staff with book selections and policy problems in general. These Committee members rendered invaluable service, provided inspiration and gave generously of their time to bring detached and seasoned judgment when questions of policy arose. Meetings of the Committee were somewhat infrequent and were called only for matters which required general discussion. In all instances when help was solicited the response was immediate. Mr. Arthur Sweetser as former President of the Foundation and for many years Chairman of the Library Committee merits a special place in Library annals. Without his ever-present interest and cooperation and without the vision and understanding of Mrs. Quincy Wright as President during the years of the Library's maximum efforts, it would be impossible to present this accounting.

Widening Circle of Friends

To many individuals, interested organizations and government agencies the Library is indebted for the gifts—large and small, usual and exceptional—which have added directly to the central theme around which the collection revolved. Of outstanding importance have been the hundreds of documents which the Library has received from Geneva in response to requests for missing League items. Through the good offices and immediate cooperation of Dr. A. C. Breycha-Vauthier, the League's Librarian, many important early documents were supplied without cost to the Library and gaps in the collection were thus filled.

A re-reading of the Library's annual reports brought to light the names of friends from overseas and this country who have contributed many treasures from their own libraries to enrich the Woodrow Wilson Library's collection. Among these names, to single out but a few, were Dr. Manley O. Hudson, Dr. James T. Shotwell, Professors Quincy Wright and Clyde Eagleton, Denys

P. Myers, Philip C. Jessup, Samuel Guy Inman, Miss Frances G. Markham and scores of others who felt disposed to donate rare and often out-of-print items for the benefit of a wider reading public.

Through exchanges of publications in which often the gain was one-sided, the Library became the richer thanks to the contributions of cooperating agencies. In the long list of organizations which from time to time have made gifts to the Library the following were conspicuous: Carnegie Endowment for International Peace, Council on Foreign Relations, Foreign Policy Association, Inter-Parliamentary Union, Institute of International Education, League of Nations Association (which became the American Association for the United Nations), National Peace Conference and World Peace Foundation. Libraries which were generous in supplementing this growing collection included Princeton University Library, Columbia University's International Law Library, Hoover Institute and Library, Fletcher School of Law and Diplomacy, Harvard University Library and the Chicago Library of International Relations.

Governmental, inter-governmental and non-governmental agencies and hundreds of private organizations have made the Woodrow Wilson Library a depository for their current publications, enriching the collection to a degree far beyond the rigid confines of its modest budget. Through the continuing generosity of its interested friends the Library has been enabled to expand and serve the ever-widening needs of students of international affairs. This body of good-will, graphically evidenced by gifts of thousands of reports, books, pamphlets and other publications, represented a priceless asset which the Directors of the Foundation, the Library Committee and the Library staff acknowledged with deep gratitude.

While at no time were there sizable quantities of duplicate materials to offer in exchange, the Library responded where it could and took particular satisfaction in responding to requests from libraries in the devastated areas and to inadequately equipped libraries in the South. Visitors were encouraged to help themselves from stocks of duplicate publications.

Survey of the Woodrow Wilson Library

The Directors of the Woodrow Wilson Foundation engaged Mr. William C. Haygood of the Julius Rosenwald Fund to make an objective survey of the Library's accomplishments and potentialities as a guide for future planning. This survey, undertaken in the fall of 1941, resulted in an eleven-page report dated October 20, 1941, which formed the basis for extensive discussions by the Library Committee and recommendations to the Directors at the annual meeting in May, 1942.

After going briefly into the Library's history, contents, budget and staff Mr. Haygood listed the following five alternatives for future policy:

1. The Library can be disbanded and its collection given to some other institution;
2. The Library can continue in its present form with no increase or decrease in budget or personnel and with no change in program;
3. The Library can continue in its present from, i.e., as a specialized reference library open to the public, but with increased budget and staff and a more vigorous expansion of its present program;
4. The Library can be attached to some organization such as the Foreign Policy Association, as a semi-autonomous agency with some program of its own;
5. The library can be transformed from a relatively static reference collection, catering chiefly to local scholars and specialists, into a dynamic agency for the skillful dissemination of ideas on a nation-wide scale.

Mr. Haygood indicated that a choice seemed to lie between the two extremes. Since the Library represented a considerable investment in money and effort and proved to be the one continuous part of the Foundation's program he thought decisions regarding discontinuance should not be made lightly. At the other extreme would be "to discard the concept of the Library as a reference collection serving the public and develop it as a potentially powerful medium for the dissemination of ideas and intelligence." In a discussion of the latter proposal he envisioned a larger staff, the development of a general program and the creation of a "workshop" responsible for the preparation of appropriate bibliographies; distribution of packets of material for debates and selected books on world organization to colleges and university libraries; preparation of newsletters on books, magazine articles and radio programs; supplying of background material to radio stations, newspapers and magazines. Mr. Haygood felt that such a program, if skillfully managed by qualified personnel, would obviously require substantially increased budget appropriations and that it might well become a major, if not *the* major part of the Foundation's program.

After careful study of the Haygood proposals the Library Committee recommended the adoption of the third suggestion and it was on these directives that the present Librarian took over the development of the Library in the fall of 1941.

Monthly Library Reports

To focus attention on specific activities, colorful as well as routine, an innovation was introduced in December 1941 to bring the Library's problems and successes within the thinking of Foundation Directors, many of whom were too preoccupied to visit the Library regularly. This innovation involved at first weekly reporting by the Librarian on the course of events, the new acquisitions and the amount of work undertaken and accomplished. These reports went to the President and members of the Library Committee. Although time-consuming and perhaps too detailed the reports attempted to convey a picture of the Library in action. Weekly accounts were later changed to monthly coverage. This self-imposed task of reporting provided the staff with periodic checks on progress and a record from which to draw material for the annual reports submitted to the full Board of Directors at each annual meeting. Files of these weekly, monthly and annual reports, along with the statistical tabulations, provide the permanent historical record.

II. WILSONIANA

Of obvious interest and importance was the collection of books, pamphlets and magazine articles by and about Mr. Wilson. From a small nucleus of about one hundred titles in 1942 the Library increased this vitally important section to 434 titles, largely as a result of vigilant combings through bibliographies and appeals to friends and book-dealers. Many of the missing items on the Library's want list were out-of-print and difficult to obtain, and the search has continued.

Laura S. Trunbull's "Woodrow Wilson Bibliography," published in 1948, provided the first one-volume listing of Mr. Wilson's published works and became an invaluable guide in the search for missing items.

Within this Wilsonian collection were included innumerable scrapbooks of clippings covering the first World War and the Wilson period, clipping files, photographs and the usual memorabilia eagerly sought by students of this period. Rare was the day or week when the Library did not undertake a search for a necessary quotation from among Mr. Wilson's writings. The need for an adequate cyclopedia loomed large on the horizon. Aid to authors and students was part of the normal Library service and records of Wilson biographies in preparation helped to steer thesis-writers and budding authors away from duplication of efforts.

The gift of Associated Press card files, noting day-by-day references to Woodrow Wilson in the nation's press, in chronological arrangement from July 1, 1906, to February 3, 1924, provided a vastly important source.

On indefinite loan, and greatly enriching the Library's Wilsonian collection, was one of the few sets of the David Hunter Miller "My Diary of the Conference at Paris." To Columbia University Libraries, and to Dr. Shotwell in particular, the Library was indebted for this much-sought reference treasure.

The generosity of Princeton University Library in supplying from among duplicate holdings many rare Wilson titles accounted for the Library's good fortune in acquiring materials not otherwise available.

III. REFLECTIONS OF THE TIMES

At a Board meeting on January 23, 1942, the Directors of the Foundation authorized the establishment of a Post-War Information Center. Minutes of this meeting stated: "To endeavor to develop the Library as a center for post-war plans, projects, memoranda, etc. The Commission to Study the Organization of Peace has agreed to transfer its large supply of such material to the Library; the Free World Association has offered to provide material from abroad; and Dr. Shotwell has volunteered to turn over the large documentation in his possession. In addition, notices will be sent out as to these plans and requests for current material as issued."

The staff of Foundation and Library went into immediate action to acquire the promised material. A new folder was prepared for general distribution describing the Library's special emphasis on reconstruction and post-war planning, and it was not long before material flowed in from public and private agencies in this country and abroad. Files of publications of governments-in-exile and the various friends of "free" groups became valuable sources of information on plans these countries were then making for the days of liberation. Assistance in handling the volume of this new material was enlisted. Special shelves were provided and also a special catalogue for the post-war material was maintained.

The Library became nationally known as a center concentrating on this phase of history-in-the-making. It was consulted by representatives of large libraries who recognized its unique features. The Librarian of the National Resources Planning Board wrote after a visit: "After talking with you and examining your collection I feel more than ever the need of a similar collection in Washington." The Editor of *Post-War Abstracts* in the Library of Congress wrote: "I wish we had a similar collection here, arranged as conveniently as yours." This phase of the Library's activities became one of the most useful and nationally important contributions to adult education undertaken in its twenty-one year history. It was not until 1949, long after there appeared to be any interest or need for this division of the material, that the last remnants of the special post-war collection were merged with the general holdings.

From League to United Nations

The Dumbarton Oaks and San Francisco Conferences were new milestones along the road to international cooperation. Preparations were made by the Library to continue, without interruption, the documentation of both the old and the new organizations. "By and about the League of Nations" became "by and about the United Nations,"—one and the same theme with but a change of name and date. As new special agencies were created to deal with relief, health problems, food and agriculture, science and education, refugees, civil aviation and all the other interests of the new world organization the Library was gratifyingly accorded depository status by each in turn. The International Labor Organization, an Auxiliary Agency of the League, became a Specialized Agency of the United Nations; the International Institute of Intellectual Cooperation emerged as the United Nations Educational, Scientific and Cultural Organization; and the Permanent Court of International Justice took its new name,—the International Court of Justice. The chain of international documentation continued unbroken.

One of the first of the Specialized Agencies to grant the Library depository status was the International Civil Aviation Organization. Many of its documents proved to be essentially scientific and technical and not within the scope of international administration in which the Library focussed its attention. Mutually satisfactory arrangements were completed in 1949 when the collection of scientific documents were presented to the Library of the Institute of Aeronautical Sciences and the Woodrow Wilson Library retained and continued to receive only those documents which dealt with administrative matters or questions of international law.

Caring for the voluminous documentation of the inter-governmental agencies became a full-time task in itself. To provide the researcher with a specific reference it required the immediate examination, recording the filing of the documents if the Library was to live up to its standard for reader-service. Checklists, bibliographies and memories combined to aid in the search since the Library did not attempt actual cataloguing of the United Nations documents, and only partial cataloguing of the printed monographs and reports of the Specialized Agencies. In April, 1950, after several issues of the *United Nations Documents Index* had appeared to simplify reference problems the Library discontinued the system of recording incoming documents.

Materials published by the Specialized Agencies, printed and mimeographed, proved of particular importance to students of international administration. Through its methods of listing and filing the Library provided quick service for the reader and was able to meet not infrequent requests from other libraries for ideas on unraveling knotty document symbol problems.

Other inter-governmental agencies, the numerous bodies in which the United States participated as well as others in which the United States did not take part, were sources of important material covering a wide range of subject interests. From the International Institute for the Protection of Childhood in Montevideo, the International Penal and Penitentiary Commission in Berne, the International Seed Testing Association in Copenhagen, to the International Fisheries Commission in Seattle was a considerable spread as to subject matter to say nothing of geography. Though at first, for instance, we questioned the wisdom of delving into the life history of the Pacific salmon we found the Commission's reports required reading for an editor intent on checking fishery statistics. If the Library was to provide service in the field of international administration it became increasingly difficult to draw lines of demarcation. Documentary material, and in fact all official publications of the international agencies, were considered primary sources for scholarly research but scholars required supplementary material as well. This collateral, up-to-date secondary source material the Library made every effort to acquire.

World Organization Bibliography

To meet demands for reading lists on the Library's central theme, at irregular intervals since 1942, it issued bibliographies of current available books and pamphlets. At first the bibliographies were compiled by Dr. Hans Aufricht, a research associate of the Commission to Study the Organization of Peace, and later issues were prepared by the Library staff. The last issue of the bibliography prepared under the Library's auspices was the seventh revised edition in December, 1946. Since then, in cooperation with the World Peace Foundation, the Woodrow Wilson Foundation and Library have reprinted and distributed free of charge copies of the bibliographical sections which appeared in the quarterly issues of *International Organization*.

The League of Nations Library

League of Nations Information Section

By 1938 the collections of the League of Nations Library had grown to 280,000 volumes housed in a separate building made possible by a grant from John D. Rockefeller. This piece gives a brief history of the library, describes its building and collections, and provides information about the staff and services developed to meet the information needs of League personnel and visiting scholars.

ROLE AND PURPOSE OF THE LIBRARY

The League Library has a two-fold object and serves a double purpose.

In the first place, it supplies the League with printed matter containing information about the various States and their mutual relations in the recent past and at the present time.

Secondly, it provides facilities for outside readers; who can be sure of finding there valuable material on the subjects in which it specialises.

So far as its main purpose is concerned, the members of the permanent Secretariat are, of course, the chief users of the Library. As the technical activities of the League take shape and expand, the Secretariat is coming to rely even more, if possible, on the abundant material classified and catalogued in the Library, on which the numerous and varied publications of the League are based. For instance, the data given in the *Monthly Bulletin of Statistics* and the *Statistical Yearbook of the League of Nations* are obtained by collating hundreds of publications received by the Library from every country in the world.

Apart from the permanent Secretariat, Government delegations, Committees of experts meeting at Geneva, and even the Governments of Ministries of the various countries also make extensive use of the Library. Not only do a growing number of Governments and national Ministries ask for recent and reliable documentation of an international character for legislative or other purposes, which the Library is best, or alone, able to provide, but some Governments, either through their permanent delegates accredited to the League at Geneva, or by sending officials from their capitals, have studied the organisation of the League Library with a view to possible improvements in their ministerial libraries or in their national centres of economic or financial documentation.

At the same time, the Library is tending to be increasingly used by outside investigators—professors, lawyers, historians, publicists, journalists, financiers, specialists of big industrial firms, advanced students preparing these for their doctor's degrees, members of the permanent bureaux maintained at Geneva by some sixty international institutions, etc.

There can be no doubt that international problems, the burning questions of peace and war, are affecting to an increasing extent, not only big undertakings, but even individuals in every country. Hence, no doubt, the growing volume of private studies on certain international questions which are *par excellence* in the province of the League of Nations.

THE LIBRARY AS AN INFORMATION CENTRE

As a rule, the more important official users of the Library need information immediately. A Committee meeting at Geneva for a few days only has no time to wait.

From the outset, therefore, the League Library

SOURCE: Reprinted from: *The League of Nations Library*, Geneva, League of Nations Information Section, 1938. pp. 5–42.

was intended to be, not merely a storehouse for books and periodicals, but also an information centre—that is to say, an institution which itself looks through the mass of material in its possession and supplies the desired information. Specialised librarians, who are used to documentary and bibliographical work, not only help supply the desired book or periodical, but, if the information required calls for search, also furnish the proper text or statistics or even the right map.

This, of course, saves the user a great deal of time. In that respect, the League Library differs from the majority of European libraries, and is more akin to the American concept of a library—that it should, as it were, "break the back" of the work for its users, instead of leaving them to find out everything for themselves, as they formerly had to do. This conception is gaining ground in Europe as well, chiefly because the growing complexity of documentation now makes the assistance of a specialist with a thorough knowledge of the available material practically essential.

A BRIEF HISTORICAL RETROSPECT

The League Library, which was established at the same time as the League of Nations itself, forms part of its Secretariat.

At first, in 1920, it was housed in London, at 117, Piccadilly; it was transferred to Geneva at the same time as the Secretariat. It was allotted a few offices, the old dining-room, and the cellars, in the famous Hôtel National, on the Quai Wilson, where the life of the League was concentrated for the first fifteen years of its existence.

The Library soon began to play an important part in the work of the League. In 1923, a Committee of Librarians set up by the Council of the League of Nations pointed out the great advantages of setting up a world centre for the study of international affairs at the headquarters of the League.

Shortly after the League had decided to construct its own buildings, it received and accepted (September 1927) a generous offer from Mr. John D. Rockefeller, Jr., of two million dollars for building and endowing a library. It was the donor's intention that the library should serve as an information centre, both for the Secretariat and for students and scholars engaged in research work on questions within the League's province.

As the President of the Council pointed out at the time, not merely was the donation materially a large one, but this gesture on the part of an American citizen was of the first importance from the social and moral points of view.

A Committee of experts, consisting of statesmen and librarians, under the chairmanship of M. Scialoja, representative of Italy on the Council, was shortly afterwards appointed to draw up the main outlines of the scheme.

THE LIBRARY PREMISES

The foundation-stone of the League building was laid at an official ceremony on September 7th, 1929. Seven years later, in the autumn of 1936, the Library was transferred to its new premises.

The League building is situated in the Ariana Park, about a kilometre away from the Lake of Geneva, towards which the ground gently slopes. It consists of four blocks: the Secretariat, the Council, the Assembly, and the Library buildings. The front elevation faces the lake, and is 400 metres long.

The Library forms the exact counterpart of the Council building, from which it is separated by the entire width of the Court of Honour. Its volume is about 60,000 cubic metres. The main façade is 48 metres long, the central part 23 metres high, and the total area covered about 3,000 square metres.

The Library consists of two separate parts, the book stacks and the main building.

The *book stacks,* with their ten floors of shelving, cover an area of 17 metres by 38 metres. On two of the floors—those containing the comprehensive collections of laws, statistics, periodicals, etc.—there are a number of small cubicles, so that work can be done on the spot.

There is a lift in the centre for the conveyance of passengers and book-trucks. An electrical book-conveyer is provided for the rapid transport of the volumes required; the books can be automatically unloaded at each floor. This conveyer makes practically no noise, and is perfectly safe.

The light green colour of the enamelled steel, the linoleum-covered floors, and the special lighting give a pleasant appearance to these spacious storerooms, which have accommodation for a million volumes—about 100,000 on each floor.

At the present time, the Library possesses nearly 280,000 volumes, and the number is increasing at the rate of 15,000 to 20,000 a year. The accommodation will therefore last for thirty or forty years. If necessary, moreover, it could be enlarged without affecting the general layout.

The *main building* is simply planned.

On the ground-floor, there are the offices of the Administrative Services, directly connected with the Secretariat building by a tunnel running under the Court of Honour.

The first floor is set aside for general subjects and contains both the general catalogue and the works of reference most in demand (national encyclopaedias, dictionaries, etc.). The first floor also includes several large rooms, two stories high. One of them, which is decorated with a fresco painted by a Norwegian artist, M. Henrik Sörensen, is to be the Historical Museum of the League.

The third floor contains, in addition to a number of offices for the Library officials, the three so-called "special" reading-rooms.

The first room is for political and legal questions. The shelves contain about 5,500 volumes and the current numbers of 200 periodicals, which can be consulted by readers.

The second is for economic, financial, and transport questions. It contains the current numbers of about 200 periodicals dealing with such questions, a complete collection of the Customs tariffs and statistical yearbooks of all the countries in the world, and a collection of 3,500 volumes including special dictionaries, hand-books, and the most recent works on the various subjects to which the room is devoted.

The third room is for the social and humanitarian questions with which the League is called upon to deal in accordance with the Covenant— child welfare, traffic in women and children, and the campaign against opium and other narcotic drugs. This room contains about 2,000 volumes and the current numbers of 100 periodicals.

Most of the offices and reading-rooms are provided with modern built-in steel shelving. This arrangement protects the books from dust, saves space, and adds to the appearance of the rooms.

The Library is heated from the main furnace under the Assembly Hall. A special regulating plant has been installed.

No artificial ventilation has been provided, as the rooms are lofty, well-lighted, and easy to ventilate. Air-conditioning is unnecessary in such a spacious building, with its bay-windows looking on to the magnificent Ariana Park, the Lake, and the Alps beyond.

A very simple system has been employed to ventilate the book stacks. Openings have been made in the floors, in front of the windows, allowing the air to circulate freely from top to bottom and *vice versa.* The stacks are heated, not by radiators, but by a series of pipes running along the walls and in front of the windows. This system increases the circulation of the air, and the penetrating, characteristic smell of dusty books is nowhere to be found.

In short, the new building has borrowed the best features of American technique and experience in regard to library construction, which have been successfully adapted to the special requirements of the League Library and the site and architectural conception of the buildings as a whole.

THE COLLECTIONS OF THE LIBRARY

Before turning to the interesting question of the subjects covered by the Library's collections, we would explain that these collections are mainly of current interest. The League deals with present-day problems. It needs information about things that have happened quite recently, so as to turn it to account with a view to promoting closer international co-operation and improving living conditions in various countries, especially the more backward.

In the last resort, the nature of these collections is determined by the articles of the League Covenant (1920), which defined the various tasks of the League. The contents of the Library can therefore be deduced from the Covenant.

In the first place, the Library possesses one of the most complete collections of *general reference works* (encyclopaedias, dictionaries, year-books, etc.) in Europe; information is needed quickly on a wide variety of subjects, and that information is to be found in works written in many different languages.

The collection of modern and contemporary *historical and geographical works* is likewise very extensive. It forms the basis of certain studies of general questions undertaken by the League. As a rule, the Library makes no attempt to collect older works. For one thing, it is rarely necessary for the purposes of the League's work to go back to the remote past; and, besides, the Geneva University Library is very rich in such works, and is always willing to lend the necessary books or documents. Moreover, the inter-library loan service is very efficiently organised in Switzerland, so that the chain of libraries in the large towns of the country constitutes to all intents and purposes a single library very well equipped.

The League Library does, however, collect all books, pamphlets, and printed matter of any value relating to the history of international organisations, the problems of war and peace, pacifism, etc.

It comprises a collection of *works* on international, constitutional, administrative, etc., *law,* and of codes in force in the various countries, and commentaries thereon.

The *geographical collection* includes a very large number of maps (more than 25,000 sheets), geographical works and dictionaries, etc. It is frequently consulted by the Secretariat in its work. This collection, which is very complete, includes copies of the most recent maps of all the countries in the world.

The Library's collection dealing with *economic and financial questions* is in every respect the most complete—that is to say, the most truly international—in Europe. Some of the most important technical work entrusted to the League relates to questions of this nature. The collection contains books, pamphlets, periodicals, Customs tariffs, reports, statistics, etc., from all over the world.

Transport questions are an important feature of the League's work. The Library's collections in this field also reflect the various problems studied by the League, such as passports, tonnage-measurement, the unification of river law, large-scale public works, road traffic, air navigation, broadcasting, etc.

Medical works and works dealing with public health also occupy an important place in the Library, which contains abundant material on questions such as malaria, cancer, sleeping-sickness, tuberculosis, rural hygiene, housing, popular nutrition in various countries, etc.

Since the crucial question of *armaments* and their limitation has for many years been one of the League's main political concerns, the Library has collected a vast amount of material on all military and naval questions, considered either from a technical or a political standpoint. Such important League publications as the *Armaments Year-Book* and the *Statistical Year-Book*

of the Trade in Arms and Ammunition are based on that material.

The League's work in regard to *colonial mandates* has naturally led the Library to collect and classify a large amount of material on colonial policy and administration.

For many years past, the League has been endeavouring to promote *intellectual co-operation* between individuals and institutions in different States, and hence the Library also contains a great deal of material on education, intellectual work, etc., in various countries.

In the *social sphere,* the work entrusted to the League by the Covenant has vast ramifications, covering the questions of opium and other dangerous drugs, traffic in women and children, and child welfare in general. Here again, the Library is well equipped with the necessary books and periodicals.

One of the Library's most natural tasks was, of course, to make a complete and up-to-date collection of *publications issued by the League's organs.*[1] From the outset, efforts have been made to collect and arrange the material in such a way as to guide the various libraries and others who subscribe to these publications with a view to the arrangement of their collections.

Each special room contains the group of League publications relating to the subject dealt with. For instance, the League's documents on social questions are to be found on the shelves of the social reading-room.

THE VARIOUS CATEGORIES OF PRINTED MATTER RECEIVED AND SORTED BY THE LIBRARY

The Library is increasing its stock at the rate of some 15,000 volumes a year. About a third of these are books, another third volumes of periodicals,[2] and the remaining third Government publications.

The Library's acquisitions are obtained by purchase, exchange, or gift.

Purchases, though greatly helped by the Rockefeller endowment, represent barely a quarter of the acquisitions.

The greater part is obtained by exchange. It is naturally profitable for the League to print some tens or hundreds of additional copies of its own publications, of which it has an extensive series, in order to procure periodicals that it would otherwise have to buy.

Gifts come from Governments, big national or international associations, banks, etc., and authors who have worked in the Library and are aware of their indebtedness to it. The Library, of course, accepts only gifts which are of real use to it.

In order to make its material more readily accessible to Governments and others who are unable to consult it on the spot, the Library publishes, as and when it acquires new volumes, a *Monthly List of Works catalogued in the League of Nations Library.*[3]

This list summarises the chief works that have recently appeared on various international questions. It is compiled with care and discrimination, and some libraries now use it as a guide for their own purchases.

Books

In comparison with most libraries, books play a relatively small part in the League of Nations Library.

In the case of the Secretariat, the coefficient of utilisation of books is comparatively low. The reason for this is evident. All the questions which the League is called upon to study or deal with—political, legal, economic, financial, etc.—are essentially questions of current world interest; and these are dealt with much more in general or special reviews, in periodical Government publications, or even in some of the principal daily newspapers of various countries, than in books. They will only be embodied in books after some years have elapsed, and then only in a somewhat condensed form.

In order to obtain the best possible coefficient of utilisation of its books, the Library must give the preference, in purchasing books or accepting gifts, to those written in the most widely known languages—English, French, German, Spanish, and Italian. It has not yet been able to acquire many books in such important languages as Russian, Arabic, or Chinese; but all the more important languages are represented, so that a Hungarian, Brazilian, or Japanese visitor, for instance, is sure of finding a nucleus of publications in his own language.

Periodicals

The 2,700 odd ordinary periodicals received by the Secretariat are either independent periodicals for which their own editors are responsible, or the publications of national or international institutions, various organisations, universities, etc.

These periodicals contain a very large number of articles. Most of these have nothing to do with the League's current work, and are therefore of no use to the Secretariat; but some are not merely useful but essential to it. The Library therefore has to go through these periodicals and make a selection, so as to give the reader ready access to this considerable minority of useful articles.

That is why the Library publishes a regular *Monthly List of Selected Articles.*[4] This list makes it easy for readers to find important articles containing fresh data which have appeared in any review on subjects within the League's province. For greater convenience, this list is at once cut up by entries, and each of these is pasted on an index-card. The index-cards are then put in a classified catalogue, which is available to the Secretariat and the public.

This list and catalogue are of importance partly because they are always up to date, and partly because, being based on a very large number of periodicals, they have a wide international foundation.

As the catalogue of selected articles has already been in existence for some ten years, it gives access to a very complete world documentation on such subjects as coal, oil, wheat, minorities, shipping, road, railways, and air traffic, etc.

Government Documents

The Secretariat receives some 5,000 volumes of Government documents each year. These publications appear either occasionally or at annual, quarterly, monthly, weekly, or daily intervals. This latter category includes, in particular, official journals, gazettes, etc.

The current files of the Library contain about 2,500 annual publications, 1,300 monthly or weekly publications and about 125 official journals of States or colonies, territories, etc., forming administrative units.

This category of publications tends to increase regularly from year to year, as Governments are led to intervene in fresh spheres of national life. The gradual hold which State control is gaining over the most liberal economics has now become a universal phenomenon quite independent of the form of government in each State.

In order to intervene, Governments must possess data, facts, statistical material, etc., which they are showing a growing tendency to collect for themselves.

One or two typical facts may be quoted to give an idea of the growing importance of this category of publications.

In 1921, the number of pages of United States Government publications issued at Washington[5] was 1,625,000. In 1937, it had increased to 2,385,000, or by nearly 50%.

The various State administrations now prepare and publish so many documents that certain Governments issue at the end of the year detailed annual catalogues of all their publications. The annual catalogue prepared by the Netherlands Government has over one hundred pages of titles for 1936.

Every week, the Library compiles and classifies, by subjects, in a *List of Additions to the Government Document Collection,* the titles of some eighty or more new acquisitions.

Some of these documents are sent direct, free of charge, by the Government services, who know how useful they are to the League of Nations. The Governments themselves need the synthetic publications on an international basis which the Secretariat compiles from these national documents. Sometimes the Secretariat has to ask for them by letter; sometimes, too, an exchange is arranged.

These documents include publications of national statistical offices, Customs services or Ministries of Commerce, in which the country's foreign trade is classified by imports, exports and re-exports, and by countries of origin or destination; statistics relating to immigration and emigration, taxes, etc.; annual reports on prisons, irrigation, national education, railways, etc.; estimates of Government expenditure and receipts, audited State accounts, etc.

The Library sends its *Weekly List* to those members of the Secretariat who need it. The latter are thus enabled to ask that the Government publications which bear on their work should be sent to them immediately.

This is naturally the category of documents of which the Secretariat makes the largest use. From June 1st, 1937, to June 1st, 1938, it borrowed no fewer than 13,138 Government documents,[6] but only 6,200 books and periodicals.

The greatest user is the Economic Intelligence Service of the Secretariat, whose publications are based on data extracted from a large number of these Government documents.

Having early been obliged to devote special care to this category of printed matter, which constitutes the very foundation of the League's technical work, the Library now possesses by far the largest collection of Government documents in Europe.[7] It is no exaggeration to say that, for certain States, the Ariana collections are an improvement on those to be found in their own capitals, because they are all kept in one and the same building instead of being scattered.

Texts of Laws and Treaties

A large part of the League's work consists in comparing national legislations and drawing attention to those laws which, being more advanced, may serve as models to other countries on certain points. Again, international treaties and agreements, political and commercial, form the essential material of the League's work.

The Library has therefore made a special effort from the outset to form as complete a collection as possible of texts of laws and treaties from every continent as fast as they appear. It has also endeavoured to make this very comprehensive collection easily accessible to students and to sections of the Secretariat that may need to consult it.

While it is comparatively easy to find in printed collections texts which are already fairly old, it is often much more difficult to get hold of more recent texts just when they are wanted. They have to be looked for either in national official journals or in the documentary annexes to certain periodicals, or again in the slip laws which appear during the year. This mass of documents has to be analysed with a view to extracting those treaties and conventions and those legislative acts (laws, decrees, ordinances, etc.) which are of any international interest.

Treaties and legislative texts which the specialised Library staff regards as of sufficient interest and importance are dealt with in the monthly publication entitled *Chronology of International Treaties and Legislative Measures.*[8] This Chronology, too, has been cut up by entries and filed in a catalogue. The data covered by the catalogue are classified first by countries, in alphabetical order, and secondly by subjects, also in alphabetical order, so that it is easy to find the most recent treaties or essential legislation on the most varied subjects.

The *Chronology of International Treaties* is

primarily intended for use at Geneva; but it has been found, in practice, that the Chronology and the *Monthly List of Selected Articles* are of interest, not only to Governments, but also to a large number of research institutions, universities, banks, libraries, etc., and some 800 copies of these publications are sent to addresses outside Geneva (including 200 to Governments).

Newspapers

Apart from official gazettes—which are Government publications, and perhaps the bulkiest of those—the Library keeps for three, six, nine, or twelve months, according to requirements, a certain number of daily newspapers from more than twenty-five countries, naturally selecting those which are most serious and most representative, and which give the most space to national and international politics, economic and financial affairs, etc.

Permanent collections of a dozen particularly important daily newspapers[9] are kept in bound volumes, so that the Library is able to meet requests for information from the Secretariat and to supply the actual number of the newspaper, which may contain, not only the desired information, but also comments or other necessary particulars.

One difficulty that arises, however, is to find the exact date of the event, political speech, official statement, or exchange of notes wanted. Two leading dailies—*The Times* and the *New York Times*—do indeed publish indexes at regular intervals; but other newspapers provide no such help. There are, of course, annuals and other publications giving the dates of recent important political, economic, and other events, or even summarising them, but as the questions the League of Nations Library has to answer are often of a special character, it has been necessary to establish machinery appropriate to research of this kind.

This machinery takes the form of the *Fortnightly Survey of Political Events,*[10] which gives an outline of events in foreign or commercial politics and some important events in home politics in the principal countries (elections, changes of government, etc.). By recording the dates, it enables the reader to find details of these events in the newspapers. It is thus a sort of index of the sources available in the Library. All the events recorded in this survey are classified by countries and chronologically in a catalogue, which also names the paper or papers from which the item was taken.

This system has proved extremely useful during recent years.

CATALOGUES

A passing reference has already been made to certain catalogues in the Library. A complete list will now be given. After all, leaving out of account the wealth of the collection—a factor of primary importance—good catalogues may be said to make a good library.

1. The Library has, of course, a *general catalogue,* covering all the material in its possession. This is to be found on the first floor, in the large catalogue and loan room. It has been drawn up on the American system known as the "dictionary catalogue"—that is to say, the authors' names, book-titles, and subjects dealt with are all classified together in alphabetical order. In other words, the number of a book may be found under either the author's name, the title, or the subject dealt with.
2. This room also contains the *shelf list,* which reproduces the classification and arrangement of the books in the stacks and in the special rooms. As the books are arranged on the shelves by subjects, the shelf list is also a classified catalogue.
3. Each of the special rooms has its own shelf list. The rooms dealing with economic and social questions likewise possess catalogues, arranged by author and by subject, of all the printed matter on those special subjects to be found in the Library.
4. The special rooms possess catalogues of the most useful articles selected from about 1,500 periodicals which are regularly indexed.
5. The legal and political room contains a catalogue, indexed by subjects and also by countries, of laws and treaties regarded as of sufficient importance to be included.
6. The legal and political room contains a card index of recent political events, classified by countries.
7. There is also an alphabetical list of all periodicals received by the League Library up to May 1st, 1938. Needless to say, this list is kept regularly up to date.

THE LIBRARY STAFF

The Library staff consists of about twenty-five persons of fourteen different nationalities. Although the official languages of the League are English and French, an international staff—preferably polyglot—is required for the work of the Library. The proper handling and sorting of the books, periodicals, and official documents, and the receiving of visitors of all nationalities who come to the Library, call for a staff familiar with a large number of languages. Fifteen languages are actually used: English, French, German, Danish, Dutch, Hungarian, Italian, Lettish, Norwegian, Polish, Portuguese, Russian, Serbian, Spanish, and Swedish.

● ● ● ●

Such is, briefly, the work of the League of Nations Library, and such are the facilities it offers to Governments and individuals.

The unanimous opinion of the students of all countries attracted by the wealth of its collections and its efficient organisation is that it is a good place to work in.

It will have been seen what an increasingly important part the Library is playing in collecting and placing at the disposal of users the more and more complex material required to conduct the technical studies jointly undertaken by the Members of the League and also by several non-member States.

ANNEX

Facts About the League of Nations Library

Hours of Opening

The Library is open on week-days from 9 a.m. to 12:30 p.m. and from 2 p.m. to 6 p.m. A reduced service is functioning on Saturday afternoons, except in July and August.

Applications for Admission

The Library is open to members of Government delegations, the Secretariat, and other organs of the League of Nations.

Persons interested in international problems can also secure admission. They should apply in writing to the Librarian, stating for what reason they wish to work in the Library, and enclosing a letter of recommendation—in the case of students, from their professor.

A reader's card, renewable at the beginning of each year, is issued to persons whose applications are accepted. This card entitles the holder to enter the Library premises (from the park and lake side), but not the Secretariat buildings.

Outside readers are requested to sign an attendance register.

Smoking is prohibited on the Library premises.

Loans

Books which are kept in the stacks can be borrowed, but only by members of the Secretariat or other League organs.

Books belonging to the reference collections in the special reading-rooms must not be taken out of the Library.

Access to Collections

Readers have free access to the shelves of the various reading-rooms. They may select the books they need for their work, but are not allowed to put the books back.

Access to the stacks is, in principle, prohibited. In exceptional cases, permission to consult the series of periodicals and the series of laws and Government documents on the third and sixth floors respectively may be granted. In no case is access allowed to the other floors.

Readers wishing to consult works kept in the stacks should fill up the application forms obtainable from the Librarian of each room, specifying the room in which they wish to consult the book or books applied for.

There are no restrictions as to the number of books which a reader may consult. They may be held on reserve for a fortnight and can be renewed for an additional period.

The Library Services

On the first floor of the Library there is a catalogue-room containing the general card catalogues (Dictionary Catalogue and Shelf List) of the Library. Dictionaries, encyclopaedias and other general reference works are also at the disposal of the readers.

The loan desk is also in this room and readers can apply to the assistant in charge for any general information they may require. Should the reader ask for special information which that official is unable to supply, the latter directs the reader to the special librarian.

The Library has several special reading-rooms on the third floor for technical or special enquiries and research.

There is at present:

One room for legal and political questions (Legal and Political Room);
One room for economic, financial, and transport questions (Economic and Financial Room);
One room for humanitarian and educational questions (Social Room);
A geographical service.

Readers are at liberty to consult the special librarian in charge of each room.

These rooms contain and offer to readers:

1. A collection of reference-books, text-books, recent acquisitions, etc.;
2. The current numbers of periodicals on the special branch concerned;
3. A few complete collections of important periodicals;
4. The appropriate publications of the League of Nations;
5. Collections of pamphlets and loose-leaf material, which often contain the most recent information on a given subject;
6. Card-index catalogues on the special branch concerned.

A photostatic service enables photographic copies of any text or document to be rapidly obtained. This service is specially intended for persons who wish to have an accurate reproduction of the texts of laws, statistics, etc.

NOTES

[1] The use of this very varied collection is facilitated by the following works:

(1) *Catalogue of Publications* (1920-1935) issued by the Publications Department, League of Nations (with annual supplements);

(2) Marie J. Carroll: *Key to League of Nations Documents.* World Peace Foundation, Boston (with supplement), 5 vol., 1920-1936;

(3) A. G. Breycha-Vauthier: *La Société des Nations centre d' études et source d'informations.* Paris, Pédone, 1937.

[2] On an average, two bound volumes per annum have to be reckoned for each periodical.

[3] Twelfth year, 1939.

[4] Eleventh year, 1939.

[5] Excluding the *Congressional Record* and the specifications of patents, trade-marks, etc.

[6] Exclusive of the automatic circulation of official journals to officials who have to peruse them regularly.

[7] Its principal rivals are, in Europe, the London School of Economics and, overseas, the Library of Congress at Washington, which early realised the growing importance of this type of publication.

[8] Tenth year, 1939.

[9] Including the *Frankfurter Zeitung, Le Temps, The Times,* the *New York Times,* the *Corriere della Sera,* the *Pester Lloyd,* etc.

[10] Fifth year, 1939.

III

SPECIALIZED AGENCIES OF
THE LEAGUE OF NATIONS

The specialized international organizations presented in this section were established soon after the founding of the League or stem from earlier organizations incorporated into the League. As semi-autonomous bodies each was concerned with a set of problems in a broad area of human concern. These readings show the internal administrative organization, the functions, and the relationships between these agencies and their parent body. The more numerous specialized agencies developed in 1945 and later and the successor agencies to those of the League continue to follow a common internal organizational pattern with a central secretariat, governing body, and annual conference or assembly which determines policy and reviews the work of the agency.

The International Labour Organization

League of Nations Information Section

The constitution and administrative organization of the ILO are summarized in this piece. The agency's activities from 1920 to 1939 are reviewed briefly and a list of draft conventions adopted by the International Labour Conference provided.

Parts XII and XIII of the various Peace Treaties concluded in 1919 were devoted to the International Labour Organisation. The Covenant itself makes the following reference to labour conditions:

Subject to and in accordance with the provisions of international Conventions existing or hereafter to be agreed upon, the Members of the League . . . will endeavour to secure and maintain fair and humane conditions of labour for men, women and children, both in their own countries and in all countries to which their commercial and industrial relations extend, and for that purpose will establish and maintain the necessary international organisations. (Art. 23, para. *(a),* Covenant.)

The Preamble to the part of the Treaties of Peace which forms the charter of the International Labour Organisation lays it down: *(a)* that social justice is recognised as a condition of universal peace; *(b)* that conditions of labour exist involving such injustice, hardship and privation to large numbers of people as to produce unrest so great that the peace and harmony of the world are imperilled; *(c)* that the failure of any nation to adopt humane conditions of labour is an obstacle in the way of other nations which desire to improve conditions in their own countries.

CONSTITUTION AND ORGANISATION

The Members of the Organisation consist of all the Members of the League of Nations, which belong to it *ipso facto,* together with three States— viz., the United States of America, which joined specially, and Brazil and Japan, which remained Members after withdrawal from the League.

The main organs of the International Labour Organisation are the International Labour Conference, the Governing Body of the International Labour Office and the International Labour Office.

The *Conference,* which meets at least once each year, is composed of the representatives of the States Members of the Organisation. Each country is represented by four delegates, two for the Government and two for the employers and the workpeople respectively.

The *Governing Body* consists of thirty-two members; sixteen represent the Governments, eight the employers, and eight the workmen. Of the sixteen Government representatives, eight are appointed by the Members which are of the chief industrial importance, and eight are appointed by the other Government delegations at the Conference, with the exception of those of the eight Members mentioned above. The Governing Body meets approximately every three months.

The *International Labour Office* is a body of international officials similar to the Secretariat of the League of Nations. It is under a Director appointed by the Governing Body, to which he is responsible.

The International Labour Office has (December 1938) branch offices or national correspondents in the following countries: Argentine, Belgium, Brazil, Chile, China, Cuba, Czecho-Slovakia, Ecuador, Estonia, France, Germany, Great Britain, Hungary, India, Japan, Latvia, Lithuania, Mexico, Poland, Roumania, Spain, United States of America, Uruguay, Venezuela and Yugoslavia.

SOURCE: Reprinted from "The International Labour Organization," *Essential Facts About the League of Nations,* Geneva, League of Nations Information Section, 1939, pp. 99–107.

Relations Between the International Labour Organisation and the League

As regards the achievement of the objects assigned to the International Labour Organisation in its charter, the Conference, the Governing Body and the International Labour Office work independently of the Assembly and the Council, although in principle the Organisation is part of the League.

There is a certain legal connection between it and the League.

In the financial sphere, the Labour Organisation's draft budget, which is prepared by the Governing Body, is incorporated in the general budget voted by the Assembly of the League.

In the administrative sphere, certain functions germane to the activities of the Labour Organisation are vested in the Secretary-General of the League of Nations—*e.g.*, the custody of the original texts of the conventions and recommendations adopted by the International Labour Conference and the communication of certified copies to the Members of the Organisation. He also receives ratifications and notifies the Governments of their deposit.

The Labour Organisation co-operates with the organs of the League in investigating certain economic and social problems.

Relations Between the International Labour Organisation and the Permanent Court of International Justice

Any questions or difficulties relating to the interpretation of the charter of the International Labour Organisation and the Conventions ratified under it by the Member States have to be submitted to the Permanent Court of International Justice.

The Permanent Court may also be called upon to pronounce on disputes arising between the Member States with regard to the observance of their obligations (Art. 423).

FUNCTIONS AND ACTIVITIES

The essential object of the International Labour Organisation is to frame and supervise the application of international rules with regard to conditions of labour.

(a) Framing of Conventions and Recommendations

This work is done in two stages:

1. In the first place, it is the duty of the International Labour Office and the Governing Body to study and prepare problems for submission to the Conference and take such steps as may be necessary to guide its activities into the appropriate channels. It is, moreover, the Governing Body which draws up the Conference's agenda. Similarly, the Office is expected to follow closely all developments in the social sphere and to collect full and reliable information as a basis for any future settlement on an international scale.
2. In the second place, the Conference discusses and adopts draft conventions and recommendations. From 1919 to 1938, 63 draft conventions and 56 recommendations were adopted in the course of twenty-three sessions.

The adoption of draft conventions and recommendations requires a majority of two-thirds of all the delegates present (irrespective of whether they represent Governments, workers or employers).

For a draft convention to come into force, it must be ratified by several States (as a rule a minimum of two ratifications is sufficient). By December 1st, 1938, 44 conventions had come into force, the number of ratifications received being 835.

Such ratification is the only act which a State need perform in order to bind itself. In that respect it differs from the usual diplomatic ratification which is subsequent to signature.

States are not obliged to ratify draft conventions even when their own Government delegates have voted for them.

Nevertheless, the various States are required under the Treaties to bring draft conventions or recommendations before their competent national authorities within one year (or, in exceptional cases, eighteen months) of the end of the session of the Conference at which they were adopted.

States bound by a convention are required to bring their laws into harmony with its provisions.

Article 408 of the Treaty of Versailles and the corresponding articles of the other Treaties of Peace stipulate that each of the Members of the International Labour Organisation agrees to make an annual report to the Labour Office on the measures which it has taken to give effect to the provisions of conventions to which it is a party.

(b) Supervision of the Application of Conventions

Any industrial association of employers or of workers is entitled to make *representations* to the International Labour Office if it has good reason to believe that a Member State has failed to secure the effective observance of a convention to which it is a party.

The Governing Body may then get into touch with the Government against which the representations have been made and, where appropriate, publish both the representations and the Government's reply.

All Member States are entitled to file with the International Labour Office a *complaint* regarding the execution of a convention by another Member State.

The Governing Body may adopt the same procedure either of its own motion or on the receipt of a complaint from any delegate (whether representing a Government, the employers or the workers) at the Conference.

Complaints are more far-reaching in their effects than representations. In the case of a complaint, indeed, a Commission of Enquiry, and even the Permanent Court of International Justice, may be called upon to intervene. Should the State complained of fail to comply with the report of the Commission of Enquiry or the decision of the Court within the time specified, the other Members may take action against it by applying the economic measures which may have been indicated as appropriate to the case.

(c) Other Attributes

In addition to the preparation of Conferences, the main functions of the International Labour Office are as follows: *(a)* enquiries into labour conditions (contract of employment, working hours, wages, etc.), unemployment, health and safety, the conditions of agricultural labourers, seamen, etc., technical education, labour statistics, etc.; *(b)* relations with associations and institutions dealing with labour problems; *(c)* the collection of documentary material, information and publications on social and labour problems.

DRAFT CONVENTIONS ADOPTED BY THE INTERNATIONAL LABOUR CONFERENCE[1]

1. Limiting hours of work in industrial undertakings (1919; 23).
2. Unemployment (1919; 31).
3. Employment of women before and after childbirth (1919; 16).
4. Employment of women during the night (1919; 30).
5. Minimum age for admission of children to industrial employment (1919; 28).
6. Nightwork of young persons in industry (1919; 31).
7. Minimum age for admission of children to employment at sea (1920; 32).
8. Unemployment indemnity in case of loss or foundering of the ship (1920; 28).
9. Facilities for finding employment for seamen (1920; 26).
10. Age for admission of children to employment in agriculture (1921; 20).
11. Rights of association and combination of agricultural workers (1921; 31).
12. Workmen's compensation in agriculture (1921; 23).
13. White lead in painting (1921; 25).
14. Weekly rest in industrial undertakings (1921; 31).
15. Minimum age for admission of young persons to employment as trimmers or stokers (1921; 32).
16. Compulsory medical examination of children and young persons employed at sea (1921; 33).
17. Workmen's compensation for accidents (1925; 19).
18. Workmen's compensation for occupational diseases (1925; 30).
19. Equality of treatment for national and foreign workers as regards workmen's compensation for accidents (1925; 35).
20. Nightwork in bakeries (1925; 11).
21. Simplification of inspection of emigrants on board ship (1926; 21).
22. Seamen's articles of agreement (1926; 24).
23. Repatriation of seamen (1926; 17).
24. Sickness insurance for workers in industry and commerce and domestic servants (1927; 16).
25. Sickness insurance for agricultural workers (1927; 11).
26. Creation of minimum wage fixing machinery (1928; 22).

27. Marking of the weight on heavy packages transported by vessels (1929; 35).
28. Protection against accidents of workers employed in loading or unloading ships (1929; 4).
29. Forced or compulsory labour (1930; 19).
30. Regulation of hours of work in commerce and offices (1930; 10).
31. Hours of work in coal mines (1931; 1).
32. Protection against accidents of workers employed in loading or unloading ships (revised 1932; 9).
33. Age for admission of children to non-industrial employment (1932; 6).
34. Fee-charging employment agencies (1933; 5).
35. Compulsory old-age insurance for persons employed in industrial or commercial undertakings, in the liberal professions, and for outworkers and domestic servants (1933; 2).
36. Compulsory old-age insurance for persons employed in agricultural undertakings (1933; 2).
37. Compulsory invalidity insurance for persons employed in industrial or commercial undertakings, in the liberal professions and for outworkers and domestic servants (1933; 2).
38. Compulsory invalidity insurance for persons employed in agricultural undertakings (1933; 2).
39. Compulsory widows' and orphans' insurance for persons employed in industrial or commercial undertakings, in the liberal professions, and for outworkers and domestic servants (1933; 1).
40. Compulsory widows' and orphans' insurance for persons employed in agricultural undertakings (1933; 1).
41. Partial revision of the Convention concerning the Employment of Women during the Night, as voted in 1919 (1934; 14).
42. Extension of the list of occupational diseases, the victims of which are entitled to workers' compensation embodied in the Convention on Workmen's Compensation for Occupational Diseases, as voted in 1925 (1934; 11).
43. Regulation of rest intervals and the alternation of shifts in automatic sheet-glass works (1934; 6).
44. Institution of an unemployment insurance system (1934; 3).
45. Employment of women underground in mines (1935; 20).
46. Revision of the Hours of Work (Coal Mines) Convention of 1931 (1935; 1).
47. Reduction of the hours of work to forty per week (1935; 1).
48. Establishment of an international scheme for the maintenance of rights under invalidity, old-age and widows' and orphans' assurance (1935; 4).
49. Reduction of the hours of work in glass bottle manufacture (1935; 6).
50. Recruiting of indigenous workers (1936; 2).
51. Reduction of hours of work (public works) (1936; 1).
52. Holidays with pay (1936; 2).
53. Minimum requirement of professional capacity for masters and officers on board merchant ships (1936; 7).
54. Annual holidays with pay for seamen (1936; 2).
55. Liability of the shipowner in case of sickness, injury or death of seamen (1936; 2).
56. Sickness insurance for seamen (1936).
57. Hours of work on board ship and manning (1936; 3).
58. Revision of Convention fixing the minimum age for admission of children to employment at sea (1936; 4).
59. Revision of Convention on minimum age for admission of children to industrial employment (1937; 1).
60. Revision of Convention on age for admission of children to non-industrial employment (1937; —).
61. Reduction of hours of work (textiles) (1937; 1).
62. Safety provisions (building) (1937; —).
63. Statistics of Wages and Hours of Work (1938; —).

NOTE

[1] The figures shown in parentheses after the title of each draft convention indicate the year in which the latter was adopted and the number of ratifications obtained up to December 1st, 1938.

The Permanent Court of International Justice

League of Nations Information Section

The composition and jurisdiction of the Court are explained in this article. A list of cases submitted to the Court for arbitration from 1923 through 1938 is included.

The Permanent Court of International Justice, which was established in accordance with Article 14 of the Covenant, has its seat at the Peace Palace at The Hague (Telegraphic address: Intercourt, La Haye).

STATUTE AND RULES OF THE COURT

The Statute of the Court was adopted by the Assembly in 1920 and, after ratification by the majority of the Members of the League, came into force in 1921. It was amended by virtue of a Protocol dated September 14th, 1929, which came into force on February 1st, 1936. The Court's activities have been governed by the new text of the Statute since that date.

Under the terms of the Statute, the Court has adopted Rules for the performance of its duties.

These Rules were drawn up in 1922 and amended on various subsequent occasions, the last being in 1936, after the entry into force of the revised Statute.

THE JUDGES

The Court consists of fifteen judges.

The judges are elected by the Council and Assembly[1] for nine years, the candidates requiring for election an absolute majority in both bodies. The latter make their choice from a list of persons nominated by the national groups in the Court of Arbitration,[2] each national group putting forward not more than four names. The members of the Court are as follows:

M. Guerrero, *President* (Salvadorian);
Sir Cecil Hurst, *Vice-President* (United Kingdom);
Count Rostworowski (Polish);
M. Fromageot (French);
M. de Bustaniante (Cuban);
M. Altamira (Spanish);
M. Anzilotti (Italian);
M. Urrutia (Colombian);
M. Negulesco (Roumanian);
Jonkheer van Eysinga (Netherlands);
M. Cheng (Chinese);
Mr. Hudson (United States of America);
M. Ch. De Visscher (Belgian);
M. Erich (Finnish).

The present members of the Court vacate their office on December 31st, 1939.

COMPETENCE OF THE COURT

The Court shall be competent to hear and determine any dispute of an international character which the parties thereto submit to it. The Court may also give an advisory opinion upon any dispute or question referred to it by the Council or by the Assembly. (Art. 14, Covenant.)

The Court is thus empowered: (1) to pronounce judgment (*i.e.,* to decide contentious cases); (2) to give advisory opinions. These are both judicial functions.

As regards the first of these, the Court is open, without special conditions, to all States Members of the League of Nations or States mentioned in the Annex to the Covenant.

It is also open to all other States which make a declaration accepting the jurisdiction of the Court and undertaking to carry out its decisions in all good faith (Statute, Article 35, Council resolution of May 17th, 1922).

SOURCE: Reprinted from "The Permanent Court of International Justice," *Essential Facts About the League of Nations,* Geneva, League of Nations Information Section, 1939, pp. 108–114.

In contentious matters, the Court's jurisdiction is always conditional upon the consent of the parties. Such jurisdiction is said to be compulsory when the parties' consent has been given once and for all in a treaty or convention relating either to all or to certain categories of disputes. In cases in which the Court has compulsory jurisdiction, proceedings may be initiated by an application by one of the parties only. In other cases, a matter may only be brought before the Court by means of a *compromis*—a special agreement under which two or more States submit a given case to the Court.

In regard to the second of its functions, the Court is empowered to give advisory opinions to the Assembly or Council at their request. It thus has no power to give opinions directly to other organisations or to individual States. The Council nevertheless frequently acceeds to requests made to it by organisations or States with a view to obtaining the Court's opinion on stated questions.

In the performance of its judicial duties, the Court applies international conventions, together with the rules of law which it deduces from international custom, from the general principles of law recognised by civilised nations and, as a subsidiary means, from judicial decisions and the teachings of the most highly qualified publicists.

COMPULSORY JURISDICTION OF THE COURT

The Court's compulsory jurisdiction applies more especially to those States which have accepted the "optional provision" embodied in the Statute in Article 36, paragraph 2. States having effectively acceded to this clause undertake in advance to submit to the Court all or certain legal disputes concerning the interpretation of a treaty; any question of international law; the existence of any fact which, if established, would constitute a breach of an international obligation; the nature or extent of the reparation to be made for the breach of an international obligation.

On December 31st, 1938, the above-mentioned clause was binding on the following thirty-eight States:

South Africa, Albania, Australia, Belgium, Bolivia, Brazil, the United Kingdom, Bulgaria, Canada, Colombia, Denmark, the Dominican Republic, Estonia, Finland, France, Greece, Haiti, Hungary, India, Iran, Ireland, Latvia, Lithuania, Luxemburg, Monaco,[3] Netherlands, New Zealand, Norway, Panama, Paraguay, Peru, Portugal, Roumania, Salvador, Siam, Sweden, Switzerland and Uruguay.

In addition to the Optional Clause, the General Act of 1928 providing for conciliation, judicial settlement and arbitration, together with a considerable number of bilateral treaties for the pacific settlement of disputes, invests the Court with compulsory jurisdiction in respect of important classes of disputes, more particularly those of a legal nature, while some provide for such jurisdiction in all disputes without exception. Similarly, numerous special bilateral or multilateral conventions provide for the Court's jurisdiction in particular circumstances.

WORK OF THE COURT

The Court, in the period 1922–1935, held, in addition to a preliminary session in 1922, thirty-five sessions—viz., one session in 1922, three in 1923, one in 1924, four in 1925, two in 1926, one in 1927, three in 1928, two in 1929, two in 1930, four in 1931, three in 1932, four in 1933, three in 1934 and two in 1935, together with two sessions of the Chamber of Summary Procedure in 1924 and 1925 respectively. Since 1936, according to the revised Statute, the Court is always in session, except during the judicial vacations, which are fixed as follows (*Rules,* Art. 25): (*a*) From December 18th to January 7th; (*b*) from the Sunday before Easter to the second Sunday after Easter; (*c*) from July 15th to September 15th.

Between 1922 and 1938, seventy-nine cases were brought before the Court, fifty-one of them being contentious cases and twenty-eight requests for an advisory opinion.

In addition to the twenty-eight judgments and twenty-seven advisory opinions given by the Court in dealing with the cases above mentioned, the Court issued a certain number of Orders, some of which were similar in character to the judgments.

Two cases were brought before the Chamber of Summary Procedure, but up to the present the Chambers constituted to deal with labour disputes and disputes relating to communications and transit, as provided in the Statute of the Court, have not been called upon to deal with any cases.

(*a*) Contentious Cases

Eleven cases were brought before the Court as a result of a preliminary agreement between the parties in question.

Twenty-four were introduced upon a unilateral request.

Two cases were concerned with the interpretation of a previous judgment and fourteen had reference to a preliminary objection.

The principal contentious cases dealt with by the Court were the following:

Case of the *Wimbledon* (Great Britain, France, Italy, Japan—Germany; Judgment of August 17th, 1923);

Case of the Mavrommatis Concessions (Greece—Great Britain; Judgments of August 30th, 1924, March 26th, 1925, and October 10th, 1927);

Case relating to the interpretation of paragraph 4 of the Annex to Article 179 of the Treaty of Neuilly (Bulgaria—Greece; Judgments of September 12th, 1924, and March 26th, 1925);

Cases relating to Polish Upper Silesia (Germany—Poland; Judgments of August 25th, 1925, May 25th, 1926, July 26th, 1927, December 16th, 1927, April 26th, 1928 and September 13th, 1928);

Case of the *Lotus* (France—Turkey; Judgment of September 7th, 1927);

Case relating to the Serbian and Brazilian Loans issued in France (France—Yugoslavia; Brazil—France; Judgments of July 12th, 1929);

Case of the Free Zones of *Haute Savoie* and the *Pays de Gex* (France—Switzerland; Orders of August 19th, 1929, and December 6th, 1930; Judgment of June 7th, 1932);

Case relating to the territorial jurisdiction of the International Commission of the Oder (Germany, Denmark, France, Great Britain, Sweden, Czecho-Slovakia—Poland; Judgment of September 10th, 1929);

Case relating to the interpretation of the Statute of Memel (Great Britain, France, Italy, Japan—Lithuania; Judgments of June 24th, 1932, and August 11th, 1932);

Case of Eastern Greenland (Denmark—Norway; Judgment of April 5th, 1933);

Cases relating to certain sentences rendered by the Hungarian-Czecho-Slovak and Hungarian-Yugoslav Mixed Arbitral Tribunals (Czecho-Slovakia—Hungary, Judgment of December 15th, 1933; Hungary—Yugoslavia, Judgment of December 16th, 1936);

Case regarding the Ottoman Empire; Lighthouse Concession (France—Greece; Judgments of March 17th, 1934 and October 8th, 1937);

Case of Oscar Chian (river traffic in the Belgian Congo) (Belgium—United Kingdom; Judgment of December 12th, 1934);

Case of the waters of the Meuse (Netherlands-Belgium); Judgment of June 28th, 1937).

Case of the Moroccan phosphates (Italy-France; Judgment of June 14th, 1938).

On December 31st, 1938, the following contentious cases were pending before the Court:

Case of the Panevezys-Saldutiskis railway (Estonia-Lithuania; Order of June 30th, 1938).

Case of the Sotia and Bulgaria electricity undertaking (Belgium-Bulgaria).

Case of the *Société commerciale de Belgique* (Belgium-Greece).

(*b*) Advisory Opinions

The requests for an advisory opinion submitted to the Court were addressed to it by the Council of the League of Nations, the Assembly not having as yet availed itself of its right under Article 14 of the Convenant.

The principal cases were the following:

Case relating to the International Labour Organisation (opinions of July 31st, 1922, August 12th, 1922, July 23rd, 1926, August 26th, 1930, and November 15th, 1932);

Case relating to nationality decrees in Tunis and Morocco (opinion of February 7th, 1923);

Case relating to the status of Eastern Carelia (opinion of July 23rd, 1923);

Cases relating to Polish Upper Silesia (opinions of September 10th, 1923, September 15th, 1923, and May 15th, 1931);

Cases relating to frontier questions (opinions of December 6th, 1923, September 4th, 1924, and November 21st, 1925);

Cases relating to the exchange of Greek and Turkish and of Greek and Bulgarian populations (opinions of February 21st, 1925, August 28th, 1928, July 31st, 1930, and March 8th, 1932);

Cases relating to the Free City of Danzig (opinions of May 16th, 1925, March 3rd, 1928, December 12th, 1931, February 4th, 1932, and December 4th, 1935);

Case relating to the competence of the European Commission of the Danube (opinions of December 8th, 1927);

Case relating to the Customs regime between Germany and Austria (opinion of September 5th, 1931);

Case relating to the railway traffic between Lithuania and Poland (opinion of October 15th, 1931).

Case relating to the Albanian minority schools (opinion of April 6th, 1935).

NOTES

[1] At any election of members of the Court which may take place before January 1st, 1940, Germany, Brazil and Japan, being States which are not Members of the League but are parties to the Statute of the Court, if they notify their

desire to do so to the Secretary-General, shall, as a provisional measure and without prejudging any question of principle, also be admitted to vote in the Council (Resolution of the Assembly adopted on October 3rd, 1936).

[2] The Permanent Court of Arbitration was established by the two Hague Conferences of 1899 and 1907. Each contracting State nominates four persons (National Group) who together form a panel of persons who may serve as arbitrators. States wishing to submit a difference to the Court of Arbitration may choose the arbitrators from the persons on this panel.

[3] The acceptance of Monaco is given in accordance with paragraph 4 of No. 2 of the Council Resolution of May 17th, 1922 (see page 110), which provides that States not members of the League or mentioned in the Annex to the Covenant may accept the jurisdiction of the Court as compulsory, but that such acceptance may not, without special convention, be relied upon *vis-à-vis* Members of the League or States mentioned in the Annex to the Covenant which have signed or may hereafter sign the Optional Clause.

Bibliography of the Technical Work of the Health Organization of the League of Nations 1920–1945

Health Organization

The bibliography to which this piece is the introduction covers the work of the Health Organization from its founding in 1920 to its transformation into the World Health Organization in 1945. The nature and format of documents issued by the Health Organization are explained as are the functions and purposes of the agency.

PREFACE

Following the publication of the first 10 volumes of the Bulletin of the Health Organization, *it was essential to publish an index.*

It became apparent, however, that such an index, though it would cover the greater part of the reports of the technical Commissions and Conferences of the Health Organization which have met since 1932, would be apt to present a defective and incomplete picture of the work of the Organization during the last 12 years, since it would omit many studies published either separately, or in other Secretariat periodicals or publications, or, again, simply multigraphed.

It was considered that it would be better to prepare a complete index which would cover not only the period since the Bulletin *was first issued, but the whole 25 years of the existence of the Health Organization.*

Although, in the first place, the idea was to exclude from the Bibliography documents of an administrative character, it very soon became apparent that the choice of subjects and the manner in which they were treated would not be readily comprehended by the reader without references to the discussions of the Health Committee which had inspired this choice and method of approach.

Accordingly, the methodical bibliography by subjects has been preceded by a short section devoted to the Health Organization itself.

This Bibliography, which is completed by an index of authors and a geographical index, is designed to enable those interested in public health

questions to find their bearings among the thousands of studies published by the Health Organization and, at the same time, to serve as a memorial to the work of that body and a tribute to its hundreds of collaborators who, dispersed among the health administrations and scientific institutions of the whole world, have each added their contribution to that work.

The Health Section

July 1945

INTRODUCTION

The Bibliography consists of five parts devoted respectively to:

I. The Health Organization of the League of Nations, its origin and constitution, the examination of its work by the organs of the League of Nations, its chief publications, the operation of its Epidemiological Intelligence Service, etc. (pages 13-22);

II. Field work carried out by the Health Organization in various countries: anti-epidemic activities and investigations with a view to the reorganization of national health services (pages 23-25);

III. Technical studies and publications issued by the Health Organization and grouped by subjects in alphabetical order (pages 26-205). This part constitutes the main feature of the bibliography.

SOURCE: Reprinted from "Bibliography of the Technical Work of the Health Organization of the League of Nations, 1920–1945," Bulletin of the Health Organization, 11 (1945), pp. 2–9.

IV. An alphabetical index of authors (pages 206–227);

V. A geographical index (pages 228-235).

• • • •

The following preliminary observations will facilitate the logical and profitable consultation of the Bibliography.

Features of the Bibliography

(1) The Bibliography covers the years 1920 to 1945; it includes the preparatory work prior to the creation of the Health Organization (1920).

In so far as concerns publications to be issued in 1945, references are given as far as possible.

(2) The name of the author has been indicated before the title of each study, note or report.

This rule does not apply to the documents which result from the collective work of a Conference, a Commission or, again, the Health Section. It was only since 1935 that the scientific studies made by its members under their own responsibility ceased to be anonymous. A list of members of the Health Committee and of the Health Section is given in the index of authors (pages 206 and 207).

(3) As a rule, the titles of articles, reports and other documents are given exactly as they appeared at the head of the actual documents. In some cases, however, it has been necessary to supplement such titles in order to render them intelligible when separated from their context.

(4) French and English being the official languages of the League of Nations, official printed documents are, in principle, published separately in both languages.

The titles of the documents which have not been published in English are given in French, German, or Spanish as the case may be.

Some of the older documents and all epidemiological periodicals published at Geneva since 1923 are bilingual, the French and English texts being given side by side. The fact that a document is bilingual is indicated by the abbreviation "bil.".

(5) Except as otherwise indicated, all documents were published at Geneva by the League of Nations' Publications Department.

(6) When a document has not been *printed*, its reference bears an "M" (multigraphed).

(7) Each title is followed by a reference to the series, document or periodical in which it has been published.

The serial numbers given between brackets indicate the distribution of the documents. Thus, the number *C.610.M.238.1926* signifies the 610th document distributed to the Council of the League of Nations in 1926 and the 238th distributed to States Members of the League of Nations in the same year. No. *C.H.914* signifies a document distributed to the Health Committee (Comité d'Hygiène), No. *C.H./C.P.S./38* signifies document No. 38 of the series prepared for distribution to the Permanent Commission on Biological Standardization appointed by the Health Committee.

The significance of the abbreviations corresponding to the technical series that the multiplicity of documents has made it necessary to create is given on page 11.

(8) A number of printed documents have been considered of sufficient general interest to warrant their being placed on sale. Such documents consequently receive a special sale number which follows the official number and includes after the indication of the year the figure III. *e.g.*: (1930. III.5).

This sale number facilitates the purchase of the documents from the agents of the Publications Department of the League of Nations in the various countries.[1]

(9) Whenever a document has been published in several series, the number of each series has been given.

The first usually corresponds to a preliminary multigraphed edition intended for the Health Committee or for one of its commissions or conferences, the second represents a printed edition.

If there is a third number, this generally represents a reprint in a document distributed to the Council and Members of the League.

The reason why all these particulars are given is that one, multigraphed, series may be available in a research laboratory or specialized institute, whereas another, printed, series will be found in a public library or in official archives.

(10) It will be noted that a very small proportion of the documents bear a sale number, this bibliography, however, is *not* a publisher's catalogue. Not only documents placed on sale, but also those reserved for a special official distribution (multigraphed documents) and some confidential documents, or those of which the stock is exhausted, are intentionally included. This has been done because documents of which the stock is exhausted may exist in libraries (more particularly in that of the League of Nations) and in archives, and because the reference to a confidential

document may be of use to some member of a commission or official body to which a document has in the past been communicated.

(11) A list of the abbreviations used in the Bibliography is given on pages 10 and 11.

Outline of the Origin and Constitution of the Health Organization

Though we have no intention of presenting here a detailed constitutional or historical survey of the Health Organization, which would be out of place in a mere bibliography, it seems necessary, at all events, briefly to outline its origin, composition, administrative organization and methods of work, since an acquaintance with these facts is essential for the guidance of a reader in studying the documents here enumerated.

The following, necessarily incomplete, sketch outlines the normal state of affairs between 1923 and 1939, that is to say, before the reductions or suspensions of activity and the suppressions of administrative machinery brought about by the second world war.

Article 23(*j*) of the Covenant of the League of Nations provides that Member States "*will endeavour to take steps in matters of international concern for the prevention and control of disease.*"

In order to meet the grave health situation in Eastern Europe, the Council of the League of Nations, at its second session in February 1920, decided to convene an International Conference of Health Experts to draw up a scheme for the Health Organization. In April 1920, this Conference proceeded to deal with the most pressing matter by recommending the setting up of an Epidemics Commission; this the Council established in the ensuing months. While this Commission was engaged in co-ordinating the fight against epidemics on the borders of Poland and the U.S.S.R., the provisional Health Committee of the League of Nations set to work in Geneva in August 1921.

One of the tasks of this Committee was to frame, in co-operation with delegates of the Office international d'Hygiène publique, a scheme for the Health Organization. Though political difficulties prevented the fusion of the two international health institutions, the scheme adopted in 1923 established at all events an organic link and technical collaboration between them.

The Health Organization of the League of Nations consists primarily of a *Health Committee,* an *Advisory Council* and the *Health Section* of the Secretariat of the League of Nations.

The *Health Committee* is composed of some fifteen members chosen for their scientific or administrative qualifications in the field of public health. It normally meets twice a year. Its primary duty is to lay down the program of work of the Health Section. It has also to give advice on technical questions referred to it by the Council or Assembly of the League of Nations.

For the exhaustive investigation of problems referred to it or which it decides to take up, it appoints technical commissions and sub-committees, or convenes conferences of experts.

The *Advisory Council* is constituted by the Permanent Committee of the Office international d'Hygiène publique,[2,3] consisting of representatives of Governments, which meets twice a year in Paris. It appoints a proportion of the members of the Health Committee and it is asked to advise on certain problems affecting health services—*e.g.,* questions relating to narcotics.

The *Health Section,* which consists of some fifteen public health specialists and epidemiologists assisted by a still larger number of auxiliary staff (secretaries, statisticians, etc.), carries out the program of work decided upon by the Health Committee. It collects the information required for the various commissions and prepares the ground for conferences and study tours. By means of correspondence, publications or translations, it serves as a connecting-link between all engaged in research work on the same problems. Finally, it collects information regarding the health situation in different countries, in large ports and other cities throughout the world; this information is analysed and published by its Epidemiological Intelligence Service at Geneva for the world as a whole and at Singapore for the Far East.

The Eastern Bureau.—In 1925, a Bureau was established at Singapore for the collection and diffusion by cable and wireless of information regarding epidemic diseases in Eastern countries and some 180 ports on the coasts of the Indian Ocean and Western Pacific.

Originally purely an epidemiological station, this Bureau became in fact the branch office of the Health Section for the Far East.

Its activities are under the supervision of an *Advisory Council* consisting of representatives of the Health Services in countries of the Far East who meet every year or two years.

In addition to weekly and daily wireless bulletins broadcast by twelve stations, it publishes, since

1925, a *Weekly Fasciculus* of Epidemiological Intelligence.[4] The annual report of the Director of the Bureau is discussed first by its Advisory Council and subsequently by the Health Committee.

• • • •

The foregoing sketch of the constitution of the Health Organization will enable the reader to appreciate the origin and nature of the various documents enumerated in the Bibliography.

The Director of the Health Section submits to the Health Committee at each of its sessions a detailed report on the work of the Section since the preceding session. Furthermore, the members of a technical commission such as the Permanent Commission on Biological Standardization, when instructed by the Health Committee to study some question, prepare technical memoranda or notes which bear a number in the series C.H./C.P.S./. . .

These memoranda are discussed by the Commission, which embodies its conclusions in a report which is submitted to the Health Committee and bears a number in the C.H. . . . series.

Reports of the Director of the Health Section and reports of Commissions or Conferences are discussed and, if approved, adopted by the Health Committee, which appends them to its Minutes and to the report which it, in its turn, after each of its sessions, presents to the Council. (This report bears a number in the "Council" series: C. . . . 19. ., or C. . .M. . .19. ., as well as a C.H. number.) Being of too technical a nature for the Council, such a report is accompanied by a report explaining and summarizing it, presented to the Council by one of its members—the rapporteur for health questions. The latter report, like the resolutions adopted by the Health Committee, is published in the League of Nations *Official Journal*.

Just as the Director of the Health Section presents administrative reports to the Health Committee, so the Secretary-General of the League of Nations presents annually to the Assembly of the League of Nations a report on the work of the Secretariat, including that of its Health Section (serial No.: A. . .19. .).

The "Health" chapter of the Secretary-General's report is examined and discussed by the Second Committee of the Assembly, which transmits its conclusions to the Assembly in plenary session (this document is published with the serial number A. . .19. . and is later incorporated in a supplement of the *Official Journal*).

Mention should also be made of the series of *Annual Reports* of the Health Organization which are prepared by the Director of the Health Section and published, either separately or in the *Bulletin of the Health Organization*, or, again, in that Organization's *Chronicle*.

Furthermore, since 1932, the chief technical studies of the Health Organization, the reports of experts or of commissions which until then had been published as separate monographs, have been collected in the (*Quarterly*) *Bulletin of the Health Organization*.

From the outset, epidemiological studies and statistical tables have been published in special periodicals: Annual and Monthly *Epidemiological Reports*, Series E.I. (Epidemiological Intelligence) and series R.E. (Rapports Epidémiologiques) respectively since 1922, and the *Weekly Epidemiological Record*—Geneva—(series R.H.) and the *Weekly Fasciculus* of the Eastern Bureau—Singapore—since 1925.

NOTES

[1] Many printed official documents which bear no sale number, and more particularly periodicals, may nevertheless be obtained on payment from the Publications Department of the League of Nations.

[2] In 1937, 1938 and 1939, meetings of the *Advisory Council of the Health Organization of the League of Nations,* comprising the members of the League of Nations Health Committee and those of the Permanent Committee of the Office international d'Hygiène publique, were held in Paris at the seat of the latter institution.

[3] The Office international d'Hygiène publique has its own publications, the chief of which are:

Its *Bulletin mensuel* which has been published since 1909; this reproduces the text of health legislation and contains original articles or summaries of articles on public health and statistics of pestilential diseases;

Minutes of its sessions: *Procès-verbaux* (Imprimerie Nationale, Paris); An *International Quarantine Directory* (1934).

The *communiqués* of the Office, which are prepared on the basis of information transmitted to it by the various countries under the terms of the International Sanitary Conventions, have been published in the League of Nations *Weekly Epidemiological Record* since 1928 and up to 1944.

[4] The Japanese invasion of Singapore in February 1942 suspended the activities of the Health Organization's Eastern Bureau.

Intellectual Cooperation

League of Nations Information Section

The Intellectual Cooperation Organization of the League of Nations was the predecessor of UNESCO. Many of the activities initiated by ICO and summarized here were later taken over by the successor agency.

A. ORGANISATION

As soon as the League was founded, efforts were begun for improving the international organisation of intellectual workers. On December 18th, 1920, the first Assembly requested the Council to associate itself as closely as possible with all such efforts. The Assembly had in view the possible setting-up for this purpose of a technical organisation attached to the League.

This organisation now exists in the "Intellectual Co-operation Organisation of the League of Nations", which forms one of the League's four technical organisations, side by side with the Health, Communications and Transit, and Economic and Financial Organisations.

Its constitution received the formal approval of the Assembly on two occasions, in 1920 and 1931.

It is composed as follows:

1. International Committee on Intellectual Co-operation. An advisory organ of the Council and the Assembly. It consists of nineteen members appointed by the Council. It directs the work of intellectual co-operation. Between its sessions, an Executive Committee, set up in 1930, sees that its decisions are carried out and that the work is progressing satisfactorily.

2. Committees of Experts to answer special questions. Some of these are permanent, while others exist only for a limited period.

The most important permanent committees are the following:

(1) Permanent Committee on Arts and Letters;
(2) Advisory Committee on the Teaching of the Principles and Facts of Intellectual Co-operation;

(3) Committee of Scientific Advisers; (4) Committee of Architectural Experts; (5) Directors' Committee of the International Museums Office; (6) Directors' Committee of the Institutes of Archaeology and of the History of Art; (7) Committee of Directors of Higher Education; (8) Committee of Library Experts; (9) Committee of Expert Archivists; (10) Publication Committee for the Japanese Collection; (11) Publication Committee for the Ibero-American Collection; (12) Committee on Intellectual Rights; (13) International Commission on Historical Monuments; (14) International Committee for Folk Arts.

Other expert committees are appointed according to the needs of the Organisation, most of the questions referred to above being actually studied by groups of experts.

3. The Organisation has three working bodies:

(a) The Intellectual Co-operation Section. This is the administrative Secretariat of the International Committee, in its relations with the Council and the Assembly and for official communications with Governments. It is also the channel of communication with the Institutes of Intellectual Co-operation and the Educational Cinematographic Institute, and acts as the Secretariat of the Advisory Committee on the Teaching of the Principles and Facts of Intellectual Co-operation and of the Permanent Committee on Arts and Letters, of which it prepares the work and meetings.

(b) The International Institute of Intellectual Co-operation (Paris). As an executive organ of the Committee, the Institute carries out its decisions. It prepares for meetings of expert committees, arranges for enquiries that have been ordered, and publishes the results.

The Institute is not divided strictly into departments, but it none the less forms the secretariat of

SOURCE: Reprinted from "Intellectual Cooperation," *Essential Facts About the League of Nations.* Geneva, League of Nations Information Section, 1939, pp. 265–273.

a large number of international centres working under the responsibility of the International Committee—*e.g.,* International Museums Office, University Information Centre, Educational Documentation Centre, Folk Art, Archaeology and History of Art, Exact and Natural Sciences, Literature, Statistics of Intellectual Employment, Intellectual Rights, etc.

4. Forty-four National Committees in the following countries:

Argentine, Australia, Belgium, Bolivia, Brazil, United Kingdom, Bulgaria, Chile, China, Cuba, Czecho-Slovakia, Denmark, Dominican Republic, Ecuador, Egypt, Estonia, Finland, France, Greece, Haiti, Hungary, Iceland, India, Iran, Latvia, Lebanon, Lithuania, Luxemburg, Mexico, Netherlands, Norway, Peru, Poland, Portugal, Roumania, Salvador, Union of South Africa, Spain, Sweden, Switzerland, Syria, United States of America, Uruguay, Yugoslavia, The Catholic Union of International Studies and the Interparliamentary Union have formed Intellectual Co-operation Committees and an Evangelical Intellectual Co-operation Committee of distinguished representatives of the Evangelical and Orthodox Churches is being formed.

These Committees serve as a link between the International Committee on the one hand and the intellectual circles of the different States on the other.

B. WORK

Conversations—Open Letters

The Committee on Arts and Letters organises "conversations" between eminent representatives of world thought on questions of direct interest to the future of human culture in existing world conditions.

Conversations have been held so far at Frankfort-on-Main (1932), Madrid (1933), Paris (1933), Venice (1934), Nice (1935), Budapest (1936), Buenos Aires (1936) and Paris (1937), and have had as subjects: Goethe, The Future of Culture, The Future of European Thought, Art and Reality, Art and the State, The Training of Modern Man, The Humanities in Contemporary Life, The Relations between Europe and Latin America, Literature in the Near Future. Each "conversation" is afterwards published by the International Institute of Intellectual Co-operation.

The Permanent Committee on Arts and Letters met at Nice in October 1938 to consider the results of the "Conversations" and the method to be adopted regarding them in the future.

Scientific Study of International Relations

The Conference of Higher International Studies serves as a permanent means of co-operation between national institutions devoted to the scientific study of international relations. International liaison between Members of the Conference is effected by an administrative machinery of which the principal elements are: the permanent sessions of the Conference held at regular intervals, the Executive Committee and the administrative services of the International Institute of Intellectual Co-operation.

The annual meetings of the Conference have been held since 1928 successively at Berlin, Copenhagen, Milan, Paris, London and Madrid, and have been devoted to the study of such problems as: The Relations between the State and Economic Life (1932/33), the Collective Organisation of Security (1934/35), Peaceful Change (1936/37), Economic Policies and Peace (1938).

An enquiry is now in progress into certain aspects of the world problem of the growth of mechanisation.

Reports on these enquiries are published by the Institute of Intellectual Co-operation.

Exact Sciences

On July 9th, 1937, an agreement was concluded with the International Council of Scientific Unions, by which the Council of these Unions is to be henceforth the advisory organ of the Intellectual Co-operation Organisation which, for its part, is to be consulted by the International Council on all questions concerning the organisation of scientific work.

A programme was also drawn up, including the arrangement of "scientific conversations" and the appointment of committees of specialists.

Libraries and Archives

The Organisation set up a Committee of Library Experts, directors of important central or national libraries, and a Committee of Expert Archivists, to study methods of co-ordinating work in this field.

It has thus been possible to issue an "International Guide to Archivists," and a number of volumes concerning libraries, the work of librarians and the social rôle of popular libraries.

Literary Questions

Ibero-American and Japanese Collections

The purpose of the Institute's Ibero-American collection is to make the masterpieces of Latin-America known to Europe through translations. The following works have already been published in this collection: "Chilian Historians," "Diamonds in Brazil," "Bolivar," "Facundo," "America," "Don Casmurro," "Essays" by Hostos, "My Mountains," etc.

A Publication Committee for the Japanese Collection has been formed and the first volume, the "Haïkaï" of Bashô and his disciples, was published in 1936.

"Index Translationum"

The Institute began in 1932 to publish an international repertory of translations, covering philosophy, religion, law, social science, education, pure and applied science, history, geography, literature and art. The following fifteen countries are dealt with: Great Britain, Czecho-Slovakia, Denmark, France, Germany, Hungary, Italy, the Netherlands, Norway, Poland, Roumania, Spain, Sweden, the Union of Soviet Socialist Republics, and the United States of America.

The Arts

The Organisation's work in connection with the arts is carried out by an *International Museums Office* (attached to the Institute of Intellectual Co-operation), an *International Office of Institutes of Archaeology and History of Art,* an International Commission on Historical Monuments, and an International Committee for Folk Arts.

The International Museums Office makes its periodical publications, *Mouseion* and *Monthly Information*, available to art museums; it holds periodical conferences: Rome (1930), Athens (1931), Madrid (1934), Cairo (1937).

A quarterly review serves to promote the exchange of information and joint investigations by Institutes of Archaeology and History of Art.

The International Commission on Historical Monuments drew up an international statute of excavations and archaeological discoveries at Cairo in 1937.

The International Committee for Folk Arts organises congresses—Prague (1928), Brussels, Liége and Antwerp (1930)—and has made studies of folk art and workers' leisure and of folk music, which have been published by the Institute.

The Organisation's work on behalf of the arts has led to the adoption of several international agreements, especially on the protection of national artistic and historical possessions; the international statute of excavations and archaeological discoveries; international art exhibitions, and the protection of monuments and works of art in times of war or civil disturbances.

Education

In the sphere of education, the work of the Organisation consists chiefly in the development of the instruction and education given with a view to imparting a better knowledge of other countries, of the interdependence of peoples which is a characteristic of the world to-day, and of the necessity for international co-operation which results from that interdependence and which is the work especially of the League of Nations. The Secretariat publishes for this purpose a *Bulletin of League of Nations Teaching (Teaching of the Principles and Facts of International Co-operation).*

The Organisation is studying the question of broadcasting for schools and the methods employed for the exchange and travel of school pupils and for inter-school correspondence.

Under the auspices of the Institute at Paris, it has set up in more than forty countries Centres of Educational Information and Documentation.

The Institute has published a handbook of National Centres of Educational Information and issues annually a selected educational bibliography.

Another branch of this work is the revision of school textbooks with a view to the exclusion from them of inaccuracies or comments un-favourable to foreign countries. A Declaration on the Teaching of History drawn up by the Committee on Intellectual Co-operation came into force on November 24th, 1937, and is still open for the signature of Governments.

Higher Education

Under the auspices of a Committee composed of the Directors of Higher Education in a certain number of countries representing the various great university systems of the world, the Institute is publishing a series of volumes on "The Organisation of Higher Education," the first of which has already appeared.

In 1937, in collaboration with the Society for Higher Education in Paris, the Institute organised a Conference of Higher Education which was attended by representatives of all the great universities of the world. The results of this Conference will be published in book form.

Since 1928, the Organisation has arranged for co-operation between the leading international student associations, in order that university exchanges might be facilitated and a common study made of questions of current importance, such as unemployment among intellectuals.

Intellectual Rights

The Organisation constantly emphasises the need for adequately safeguarding authors' and inventors' rights. It collaborates in all efforts made for protecting artistic and literary property, and for securing the recognition of journalists' copyright. It is studying the possibility of establishing a universal statute of authors' rights by means of a co-ordination of the Berne and Havana Conventions.

Cinematograph Questions

In collaboration with the International Educational Cinematographic Institute of Rome, a Convention was concluded in October 1933 with the object of facilitating the international circulation of films of an educational character. This Convention will serve to make known educational films and to facilitate the transport and showing of such films in educational establishments and in cinema halls. The Institute will publish a catalogue of these films and will distribute it to all countries. Under the provisions of the Convention, the Institute at Rome was the executive body. Following the withdrawal of Italy from the League, however, the Institute was closed on December 31st, 1937, the result being the virtual abolition of the 1933 Convention. On the proposal of the Council of the League, the States which had signed or acceded to the Convention met at Geneva from September 10th to 12th, 1938, and adopted a *procès-verbal* entrusting to the Committee on Intellectual Co-operation the executive functions which had devolved on the Rome Institute under the Convention.

Broadcasting

The Intellectual Co-operation Organisation has also given attention to the intellectual and educational side of broadcasting, and is studying the question of programmes and their national and international co-ordination, the possibilities of broadcasting as a factor in social and artistic education and its influences in helping peoples to understand one another. An international Convention to ensure the use of broadcasting in the interests of peace was signed in October 1936.

In 1936, the Assembly asked the Intellectual Co-operation Organisation to make a study of modern means of disseminating information in the cause of peace. In 1937 and 1938, with this object, the Organisation called a meeting of experts representing the national broadcasting companies. These experts drew up a plan for the collaboration of the Organisation with the national companies, with a view particularly to the preparation of programmes based on the desire to promote mutual understanding between peoples.

IV

THE TRANSITION FROM LEAGUE TO UNITED NATIONS

The League had been founded on peace treaties following World War I. With the advent of World War II and the breakdown of normal diplomatic relations the League ceased to carry out its political functions. The questions of a new all encompassing international organization mooted at the close of the second war opened the question of the fate of the League and the disposition of its responsibilities, assets, and liabilities. This section explains how the transition was made and describes the documentation produced during the transition period. It describes also the continuity between the League and the United Nations as reflected in the continuity of documentation.

Transition From League of Nations to United Nations

Henry Reiff

Since the preparations for the United Nations took place in San Francisco, the United States as host country supplied a large staff of experts to assist. This article, based on the author's experiences as technical expert with the United States delegation explains the transfer of functions and assets from the old to the new organization. The texts of the agreements for transfer included in the original article are here omitted.

Long before the United Nations Conference on International Organization met at San Francisco in the spring of 1945 it was evident that establishment of a new general organization would necessitate the termination of the League of Nations. Aside from obvious political considerations, the presence among the 51 United Nations of 32 League members suggested the desirability of a speedy elimination of dual burdens and of possible conflicting obligations. In the generation since World War I the functions, activities, powers, and duties of the League had proliferated amazingly both under the Covenant[1] and in pursuance of several hundred separate treaties entrusting matters to the League.[2] During World War II the League had ceased to perform most of its political functions, but it still carried on humanitarian and economic work of universal importance at Geneva, London, Washington, and Princeton.[3] The Permanent Court of International Justice, with its seat at The Hague, and the International Labor Organization, functioning at Geneva and Montreal, both dependent upon the League in various ways, were still in being. It was generally felt that on dissolution of the League there should be as little interruption as possible in the performance of the nonpolitical and technical work. Termination of the League also would require severance of the interests of the International Labor Organization, whatever the ultimate disposition of that organization might be. Establishment of the seat of the new International Court of Justice at The Hague[4] indicated the desirability of using the premises occupied by the old Court. This procedure would

involve also some negotiation with the League. To these several ends, therefore, the conference at San Francisco in the Interim Arrangements adopted June 26, 1945[5] directed the Preparatory Commission, among its other tasks, to "formulate recommendations," for presentation to the first General Assembly of the United Nations, "concerning the possible transfer of certain functions, activities, and assets of the League of Nations which it may be considered desirable for the new Organization to take over on terms to be arranged."

THE UNITED NATIONS COMMITTEES

In pursuance of this mandate, and in further execution of the purposes involved, a series of five committees of the United Nations have dealt successively with the problem of transfer, each carrying the process of solution a few steps further:

1. Committee 9 of the Executive Committee, 14 members, whose report was adopted by the Executive Committee October 12, 1945.[6]
2. Committee 7 of the Preparatory Commission, 51 members, whose report was adopted by the Preparatory Commission December 18, 1945.[7]
3. A small special (interim) committee of eight members appointed at the conclusion of the labors of the Preparatory Commission to enter on its behalf into discussion with the League of Nations Supervisory Commission

SOURCE: Reprinted from Henry Reiff, Transition from *League of Nations to United Nations,* Washington, Government Printing Office, 1946. (U. S. Department of State. *United States - United Nations Information Series* No. 5)

for the purpose of establishing a common plan for the transfer of the assets of the League.[8] This committee operated in the interval between the meetings of the Preparatory Commission and the first part of the first General Assembly and also during that first part. It reported on February 1, 1946 to the *ad hoc* Committee on the League of Nations established by the General Assembly.[9]

4. An *ad hoc* Committee on the League of Nations, established by the first part of the first General Assembly,[10] 51 members, whose report, including the Common Plan, was adopted by the General Assembly, February 12, 1946.[11]

5. A small negotiating committee of eight members set up by the General Assembly in pursuance of the report of the *ad hoc* Committee for the purpose of conferring with the League authorities, the Swiss and Netherlands authorities, and the Carnegie Foundation of the Netherlands on matters arising out of the transfer of the properties located at Geneva and The Hague, as envisaged in the Common Plan adopted.[12]

In consequence of the efforts of these several bodies, certain of the non-political and technical functions of the League are already in process of provisional assumption and continuance by the United Nations;[13] others it is expected will be assumed in the months to come; and the legal transfer of the material assets, it is also expected, will be consummated on or about August 1, 1946.[14]

The United States, as an important member of the United Nations, as a party to numerous separate treaties referring to the League or entrusting to it various non-political and technical functions, particularly those dealing with the control of narcotics,[15] and as having displayed as a nonmember of the League considerable interest in its humanitarian and economic work, particularly in the fields of health and women and children,[16] was represented on each of these United Nations committees.[17]

In all cases where a committee or subcommittee contained fewer than the total of 51 members of the United Nations, care was exercised to produce a composition for the body in proper proportion to the interests of states members of the United Nations which were still members of the League, states like the U.S.S.R., which were formerly members, and states like the United States, which

never had been members. Throughout the discussions, however, there was remarkable unity of appreciation of the task to be performed. All the committees felt the need for a clear-cut, speedy solution of the problem of transition.

Various governments still members of the League offered at different stages working papers[18] as bases for discussion, and the secretariats of the Preparatory Commission, the United Nations, and the League of Nations supplied voluminous data essential to the work of the committees. The presence in the United Nations of 32 of the states which are still members of the League enabled the committees at all times to proceed with ample knowledge of what the League planned to do with respect to its own liquidation. This knowledge operated to permit both the United Nations and the League of Nations, within the spheres of their respective competences, to act with a considerable degree of timely concurrence.

DEVELOPMENT OF SOLUTION

These United Nations committees were confronted with the complex problem of devising a means to effect a transition of limited scope between a general international organization about to be liquidated and a general international organization in process of being constituted. No precise precedent existed for solving that problem. The several committees charged with responsibility in the premises felt their way along toward a solution, step by step. These steps can now be set forth seriatim.

THE EXECUTIVE COMMITTEE OF THE PREPARATORY COMMISSION AND ITS COMMITTEE 9

1. At the beginning of the discussion in Committee 9 of the Executive Committee it was agreed that under the terms of reference of the Interim Arrangements the United Nations could not concern itself with the devising of legal and practical modes of dissolving the League of Nations. That was a task outside its competence and devolved squarely upon the League itself.

2. But it was also agreed that, wherever possible, the United Nations should within its competence facilitate a dignified and speedy dissolution of the

League. A result so achieved would be of mutual interest.

3. Furthermore, complete agreement existed at the outset that only non-political and technical functions and activities and the assets of the League should be considered for transfer.[19] Hence such political functions as the League might still possess under the Covenant or in pursuance of separate treaties would presumably cease upon dissolution of the League or be disposed of otherwise by the interested parties.[20] In this connection, three troublesome items may be mentioned:

(a) No recommendation relating to mandates was made by Committee 9 or any of its successors. If any feature of the mandates system survives the termination of the League, it presumably will appear within the scope of the new trusteeship system.

(b) Committee 9 made no recommendation to transfer the activities concerning refugees,[21] nor did the Preparatory Commission. The first part of the first General Assembly dealt afresh with the subject of refugees.[22]

(c) Although Committee 9 recommended transfer of League functions relating to League-supervised loans (of post-World War I significance),[23] Committee 7 of the Preparatory Commission made no recommendation, believing that the subject could "be brought by any interested government before the Economic and Social Council."[24]

4. It was clear also at the beginning of the discussions in Committee 9 that transfer of functions entrusted to the League under separate treaties involved enormously complex problems of a juridical and practical nature. Hence that committee drew up a separate resolution,[25] readopted with only stylistic changes by both the Preparatory Commission[26] and the first part of the first General Assembly,[27] providing (a) for the performance by the United Nations of secretarial functions required under the treaties and (b) for the continued exercise, provisionally, of such technical and non-political functions as the United Nations might wish to select. It is expected that in due course the parties to these two sets of treaties will wish to make the changes, where necessary, in their terms and in some cases, perhaps, to revise them altogether. (c) In the case, however, of treaties entrusting *political* functions to the League, provision was made in the resolution for examination by the United Nations of any request by the parties to such treaties that the United Nations assume the exercise of any of those functions.

THE EN BLOC AND SELECTIVE FORMULAS

5. Early in the deliberations of Committee 9 it also became apparent that transfer of functions, activities, and assets of the League stemming from the Covenant could be achieved feasibly under one or the other of two principal and relatively simple formulas. After excising certain matters[28] from consideration under either formula, it would be possible either (a) to transfer *en bloc* (or *in toto*) all the remaining League functions, activities, and assets (together with certain of their attached liabilities), placing the burden on the United Nations to discontinue any function or activity transferred and to liquidate any of the assets and liabilities transferred; or (b) to authorize the appropriate organs of the United Nations to make a *selection* of functions, activities, and assets to be assumed, leaving to the League the task of liquidating such matters as had not been embraced in this scheme of transfer.

Either formula was felt by most members of Committee 9 to be justifiable under the provisions of the Interim Arrangements. Each also had its advantages and disadvantages. In brief, the *en bloc* formula was thought to facilitate speedy termination of the League. Under it, dates for the consummation of various stages in the process of transition could be fixed with some degree of certainty. It appealed to most of the governments represented on the Executive Committee as permitting a neat, early, and definitive solution. Certain delegations, opposing it, argued that it would operate to place the burden of liquidating the League on the United Nations and that it would imply a form of "succession" which they felt to be undesirable.

On the other hand, the advocates of the *selective* formula felt that it alone could preserve for the United Nations all the freedom in devising new spheres of non-political and technical work which a new organization ought to have; that if any assets were taken over they should not be encumbered with liabilities; that the League could stay in being or operate through some sort of liquidating body until the United Nations had made the selection of functions and activities which it might wish to assume; and that meanwhile the League should bear the cost of maintaining those functions and activities as well as the risk arising out of the possession of valuable properties until their ultimate disposition could be determined. The process of selection of the functions and activities should not, in their judgment, take more than a few months, perhaps a year.

The opponents of the *selective* formula felt, however, that the process, depending as it would on prior constituting of the organs of the United Nations and their going into operation, could easily take some two or more years. Meanwhile, the League itself or some liquidating body authorized by it would have to stay in being until all League affairs had been wound up. States members of the United Nations which were also League members could not view with enthusiasm a solution which would likely entail for them dual financial and other burdens which might run on for several years until the League was terminated in fact and in law.

In the meantime, for reasons of economy or otherwise, services of great value to the international community might have to be discontinued by the League. Various of the technical experts still employed by the League, facing an uncertain future, might find it necessary to seek other employment, leaving important work unperformed. This loss of experienced personnel could hardly be afforded at a time when it was most desirable that there be no interruption in such non-political and technical work.

There could be little question that a going concern like the United Nations could find suitable uses for the plant and equipment of the League at Geneva in the future, even if the headquarters were moved to some other place in Europe or to America. It could be used for a branch office, for some of the periodic meetings, or as the seat of one or more specialized agencies. With this prospect, it was felt by most members of the Committee that it would hardly be equitable to require a moribund organization to bear the risk and expense of maintaining the plant beyond a minimum of time needed for transition.

Underlying these considerations, for and against the two formulas, were others of a political, sentimental, and fiscal character. Resentment toward the League of Nations for having allegedly failed in its mission; opposition to any settlement which might involve a "return to Geneva" even in some tentacular form; fear, perhaps hope, that acquisition of the properties in Geneva might influence the choice of a site for the new headquarters—feelings such as these were implicit in certain of the arguments put forth in the committee. There was, however, a strong current of belief that undignified or inconsiderate treatment of the interests of the League and its members could hardly redound

to the credit of the new Organization to which the loyalties of many governments and individuals were being transferred. Finally it might be observed that, if the United Nations acquired the material assets of the League, those members of the United Nations which had as members of the League contributed to the creation of those assets would, in equity, be entitled to some credit toward their financial obligations under the new Organization—a consideration not without weight in a period of financial retrenchment.

ADOPTION OF SO-CALLED "EN BLOC" TRANSFER FORMULA

In the end, Committee 9 recommended and the Executive Committee adopted, with certain qualifications, the *en bloc* (or *in toto*) formula for transfer of League functions, activities, and assets.[29] Throughout the deliberations in Committee 9 the representatives of the Union of Soviet Socialist Republics reserved their position with respect to the *en bloc* formula, and in the Executive Committee they voted against adoption of the report containing it. They preferred a restricted form of the selective principle.[30] In the Executive Committee the Australian Delegation announced its preference for the selective principle and joined the Soviet Delegation in voting against adoption of the report.[31]

In all discussions of transfer of League assets until a satisfactory arrangement was achieved under the Common Plan the representatives of the United States reserved their position on the valuation of the buildings involved.[32] At all appropriate times also they insisted that the discretion of the Secretary-General of the United Nations in engaging the services of any of the former League technical personnel remain completely unfettered.[33]

The scheme of transfer as it emerged from the Executive Committee is set forth in the three sections and one appendix contained in chapter IX of part III of its Report. Briefly, those documents embrace the following features:

(a) Section 2 disposes of the problem of treaties entrusting functions to the League along the lines indicated above.

(b) Section 3 surveys the functions, activities, and assets involved in the transfer and stipulates certain exceptions and qualifications to the principle of *en bloc* transfer.

These exceptions and qualifications had become so numerous in the course of the deliberations of Committee 9 that the committee felt in its final drafting sessions that the term *in toto* (or *en bloc*), as used in earlier drafts of the recommendations, could no longer be accurately used. Hence the term was stricken out of the recommendations[34] as presented to the Executive Committee. If a single term were desired to describe the quantum of functions, activities, and assets contemplated under these recommendations for transfer, *residual* would have been more nearly accurate.

(c) The appendix contains a brief statement of assets and liabilities of the League of Nations as of December 31, 1944.

(d) Section 1 contains the so-called *en bloc* formula, hedged with the restrictions finally agreed upon, in the following language:

"The Executive Committee,
"Having considered the possibility of transferring certain functions, activities and assets of the League of Nations which it may be considered desirable for the United Nations to take over; and
"Considering, after it had received the report, contained in Section 3, of a committee which had examined this problem, that it would be useful for the United Nations to state certain terms for this transfer;
"Recommends:
"1. that the functions, activities and assets of the League of Nations be transferred to the United Nations with such exceptions and qualifications as are made in the report referred to above, and without prejudice to such action as the United Nations may subsequently take with the understanding that the contemplated transfer does not include the political functions of the League, which have in fact already ceased, but solely the technical and non-political functions."

For the convenience of the Executive Committee, the conclusions of the report in section 3 were summarized in the following language which appears as a footnote to the above paragraph 1:[35]

"The Committee recommends that no political question should be included in the transfer. It makes no recommendation to transfer the activities concerning refugees, mandates or international bureaux. The contemplated transfer will not include transfer of personnel. Transfer of assets and liabilities should imply neither profit nor loss for the United Nations. The problem of separating the finances of the International Labour Organisation from those of the League is left for later consideration.
"The transfer of economic activities is limited to such work in this field as the United Nations might wish to continue; that of the health activities will be subject to any decisions made in the future regarding a new

health organisation; and that of the social activities would take place with the understanding that the question as a whole will have to be referred to the competent organ of the United Nations. The transfer of functions arising from treaties is contemplated only as far as is possible and desirable."

(e) The remainder of section 1 contains, *inter alia*, a recommendation that continuity be maintained in the work done by the League on economic and health questions and in relation to the control of the drug traffic. It recommended also that "the United Nations effectively assume at the earliest possible moment the powers and functions attributed to the League of Nations under international conventions concerning the control of the Drug Traffic." It further recommended that "the League of Nations, prior to the transfer, settle the question of contributions to be paid to the League of Nations by members in arrears, the question of the payment to the judges of the Permanent Court of International Justice of arrears in salaries and other claims." It also contains a suggestion by the Executive Committee:

"that the Preparatory Commission should appoint a small Committee to discuss with the Supervisory Commission of the League of Nations the parallel measures that should be adopted by the League of Nations and the United Nations. This Committee might, where necessary, consult with representatives of the International Labour Office on all matters regarding the liquidation of the League of Nations which are of interest to the International Labour Office and which it was impossible to settle directly with the League."

REVISION BY THE PREPARATORY COMMISSION

Committee 7 of the Preparatory Commission, assisted by a highly competent small drafting committee,[36] refined the product of the Executive Committee. It separated very clearly the question of transfer of functions and activities from the question of transfer of assets. It drew up two separate recommendations on the subjects. The recommendation relating to functions entrusted to the League under separate treaties was sent forward with only stylistic changes.[37]

ASSUMPTION OF FUNCTIONS, POWERS, AND ACTIVITIES OF THE LEAGUE

Early in the deliberation of Committee 7,[38] a sharp distinction was made between the nature of the operation involved in so-called "transfer of functions and activities" and the nature of the operation involved in the transfer of assets. In the latter case, there would be actual handing over by one organization to the other of certain buildings, equipment, furnishings, and other properties. In the former case, it was contended, despite the language of the Interim Arrangements,[39] there could be, in legal contemplation, only the cessation of performance of function or activity by the League when its mandate expired and the taking up or assumption of the performance of the same substantive tasks by the United Nations under its new mandates. The use of the term *assumption,* it was argued, would avoid the implication of a legal continuity which did not exist. Although it was pointed out that no such implication necessarily arose out of the use of the term *transfer* and that use of the term *assumption* made a distinction without a difference in effect, the Committee, to satisfy doubts on the point, adopted the term *assumption* in its final recommendation on the subject.[40] It was also believed, at the outset of the discussion, that such a terminological change would meet in part the objections of the Union of Soviet Socialist Republics to the Executive Committee's Report.

Verbal magic could not, however, meet those objections. After the Committee had quickly agreed in principle to separate out from the problem of transfer the whole question of assets and to deal with it through a special committee authorized to consult with the Supervisory Commission of the League,[41] the Soviet spokesman, Professor Stein, proposed to the Committee the following formula for "assumption" of League functions and activities:

"that the Economic and Social Council should consider which of its organs might exercise certain non-political functions formerly performed by the League of Nations."[42]

This proposal was in effect a revival of the *selective* formula with the added safeguard that, if the Economic and Social Council performed strictly within its Charter mandate, no function or activity previously exercised by the League and assumed by the Council could lawfully partake of a political character.

"In explanation of the proposed amendment Mr. Stein . . . maintained that the difference of opinion which had caused the Soviet Delegation to vote against chapter IX in the Executive Committee was a difference of opinion on substance and not on presentation as had been suggested at the previous meeting. Recommendation 1 of the Report by the Executive Committee was based on the principle that all non-political functions of the League should be transferred to the United Nations. This principle was not acceptable to the Delegation of the Soviet Union on the grounds that no general distinction could be drawn between political and non-political functions. Separate, careful and concrete consideration was necessary of each particular function before any decision on the desirability of the United Nations carrying out such a function could be made. As the majority of the functions concerned would fall within the competence of the Economic and Social Council it was this body which should properly carry out such an examination."[43]

NEW FORMULA OF TRANSFER

The formula proposed by Professor Stein was, of course, open to most of the objections voiced in Committee 9 of the Executive Committee when it discussed the *selective* principle. Committee 7 of the Preparatory Commission was, therefore, not willing to accept it without considerable qualification. In the end, the formula relating to functions and activities was a compromise between the selective principle as restricted in the Soviet proposal and the so-called *en bloc* principle as restricted in the Executive Committee's Report.

The metamorphosis of Professor Stein's proposal can be sketched briefly. An early suggestion that a time limit should be placed on the survey by the Economic and Social Council[45] was dropped when it was agreed that "pending the adoption of the measures decided upon as a result of this examination, the Council should, on the dissolution of the League,[45] assume and continue on a provisional basis, the work hitherto done" by the Economic, Financial, and Transit Department and the Health and Opium Sections of the League. Additional provision was made for "taking over and maintaining in operation" certain functions of the League which could not fall within the orbit of choice exercisable by the Council, namely, the Library, the Archives, and the completion of the League of Nations Treaty Series. It was also suggested that it was "desirable to engage for the above-mentioned work on appropriate terms such members of the experienced personnel by whom it is at present being performed as the Secretary-General" of the United Nations might select. Having said this, Committee 7 added that it believed the foregoing recommendations covered "all the parts of the Report[46] by the Executive Committee relating to the transfer of functions, powers, and activities of the League of Nations, with the exception of paragraph 9 [relating to League-sponsored loans] ."[47] As so elaborated in Committee 7, the formula on assumption of functions and activities was adopted by the Preparatory Commission[48] and, with the necessary stylistic changes, by the General Assembly.[49]

LEAGUE-SPONSORED LOANS

Another troublesome question disposed of at the Preparatory Commission related to League-sponsored loans.[50] The Executive Committee recommended in paragraph 9 of section 3 of chapter IX of its Report that the United Nations should take over from the League its surviving functions under the several loan arrangements, declaring that "these functions are of a technical character and would involve no financial liability on the part of the United Nations."[51] The Soviet and Chinese Delegations in both the Executive Committee and the Preparatory Commission opposed the assumption of such a responsibility by the United Nations. As part of his original proposal dealing with functions and activities, described above, Professor Stein included a suggestion that the item relating to the loan functions be deleted from any new recommendation on the subject of transfer.[52] His proposal, he said, "was based on the view that the public loans issued with the assistance of the League were in fact more or less political loans for which the United Nations should take no responsibility, even if that responsibility amounted to no more than the appointment of trustees."[53] A compromise was thereupon effected, the recommendation of Committee 7, after excepting from the scope of the transfer formula "Paragraph 9," declaring: "The Preparatory Commission makes no recommendation on this subject; it considers that it can be brought by any interested government before the Economic and Social Council."[54] There the matter rested. The Report of the League of Nations Committee to the General Assembly contains no reference to the subject.[55]

COMMITTEE ON TRANSFER OF LEAGUE ASSETS

The Preparatory Commission, in pursuance of a recommendation of Committee 7,[56] on December 18, 1945 "set up a committee to enter, on its behalf, into discussion with the League of Nations Supervisory Commission, . . . for the purpose of establishing a common plan for the transfer of the assets of the League of Nations on such terms as are considered just and convenient."[57] This plan was to be subject, so far as the United Nations was concerned, to approval by the General Assembly. The Committee consisted of one representative each designated by the Delegations of Chile, China, France, Poland, South Africa, the Soviet Union, the United Kingdom, and the United States. The Committee was instructed to consult the duly authorized representatives of the International Labor Organization on questions connected with the transfer which affected that organization; to have regard to the views of the Executive Committee as expressed in certain parts of its Report; and to submit its plan to the General Assembly, if possible during the first part of the first session.

All of these instructions the Committee on Transfer of League Assets carried out. Beginning on January 4, 1946, in a series of seven meetings by itself and of four jointly with the Supervisory Commission, and after informal consultations by the chairman with representatives of the ILO, the Committee performed its task and reported on February 1 to the full *ad hoc* Committee on the League of Nations set up by the General Assembly.[58]

ELABORATION OF THE COMMON PLAN AND ACCOMPANYING REPORT

The Committee, after discussion of principles upon which a transfer of assets could be arranged and which would be consistent with the instructions of the Preparatory Commission, invited the Supervisory Commission to propose a draft plan for joint discussion.[59] Agreement was relatively speedily reached along certain lines consistent with these principles:

1. That the *material* assets, fixed and movable (i.e. buildings, equipment, furnishings, supplies

and stocks on hand, books, archives, etc.), be separated from the *liquid* assets and the corresponding liabilities;

2. That, on transfer of the *material* assets, some form of total credit covering them be placed on the books of the United Nations in favor of those members of the United Nations which were still members of the League of Nations and which had contributed to the creation of those assets, the total credit depending, of course, upon the value which could ultimately be placed upon those assets after their final disposition had been determined;

3. That the League itself bear the responsibility (a) of fixing the percentages of the total credit to be accorded to its own members as well as (b) of satisfying the claims to shares in the material assets of those members of the League which at the time of transfer should not be members of the United Nations; and

4. That the above credit established on the books of the United Nations take a form consistent with the fiscal policies and needs of the new organization.

With respect to the *liquid* assets and corresponding liabilities and related fiscal matters it was agreed:

5. That the League itself should bear exclusively the responsibility for a proper liquidation or settlement of these intricate matters. They would include (a) the discharge of all League obligations as soon as possible, including the claims of the judges of the Permanent Court of International Justice for salary arrears; (b) the settlement of the question of arrears in contributions of its member states; (c) the separation of the interests of the ILO in the assets of the League before transfer of the material assets to the United Nations; (d) the making of provision for the continued administration of the Staff Pensions Fund for League employees; (e) the making of arrangements for the continued administration of the pensions due the judges of the Permanent Court of International Justice; and (f) the making of arrangements for the crediting or distributing of the remaining liquid assets to members of the League under some scheme to be determined by it.

In view of the desire of the members of the ILO to continue that organization and of the United Nations to utilize[60] for the new Court the premises at The Hague occupied by the old Permanent Court of International Justice, it would be necessary for any common plan for the transfer of League assets to make provision with respect to these matters so far as they were affected by the contemplated transfer. This provision was effected in the following manner:

With respect to the Court premises, it was readily agreed that the furniture, fittings, equipment, library, archives, and other similar properties used by the Permanent Court of International Justice at The Hague should go over to the United Nations as part of the transaction relating to the transfer of material assets of the League. Alterations had, however, been made in the Peace Palace at The Hague to house the old Court. Several instalments on two loans obtained from the Carnegie Endowment for the purpose were still due. Since the United Nations would have the advantage of the improved arrangements at the Palace, it was agreed to assume the obligation of the unpaid instalments.[61]

Although it was well known that the burden of severing the interests of the ILO from the assets of the League would fall upon the League, the Preparatory Commission had enjoined the Committee to "consult the duly authorized representatives of the International Labor Organization on questions connected with the transfer which affect that Organization."[62] This was done through the medium of the chairman of the Committee on Transfer of League Assets, M. Moderow (Poland). The Committee could accordingly in its discussions with the Supervisory Commission dispose of certain of the "connected" questions. Thus it was understood that the ILO building at Geneva, in the final settlement of the transition problem, should be transferred to that organization. It was further agreed that the ILO might "use the Assembly Hall [in Geneva], together with the necessary committee rooms, office accommodation and other facilities connected therewith at times and on financial terms to be agreed from time to time between the United Nations and the International Labour Organization;" and that the ILO might "use the library under the same conditions as other official users thereof."[63]

On details to implement a successful transfer of the material assets there was also ready concurrence, for example, fixing a date for the legal transfer of the assets involved (i.e. on or about Aug. 1, 1946, "the precise date to be determined by the administrative authorities of the two Organizations"); providing for the setting up of properly authorized committees or other agents of the United Nations and the League to make the detailed arrangements attendant upon transfer of the assets with the Swiss and Netherlands Governments respectively and with the Carnegie Foundation at The Hague; and providing for mutual use of the plant and equipment involved by the administrations of the two organizations before and after the date of legal transfer until the business in hand should have been consummated.

PROBLEM OF EVALUATION OF THE MATERIAL ASSETS

But the most persistent of the problems facing the Committee and the Supervisory Commission was the value to be placed upon the material assets contemplated for transfer. That problem lay in the background of all the deliberations of Committee 9 of the Executive Committee and Committee 7 of the Preparatory Commission. Upon its solution depended the transfer of those assets—indeed, quite likely, the speedy and satisfactory liquidation of the League itself.

Obviously, value depended upon the use to which the plant and equipment could be put, and use depended upon political decisions of an intricate and subtle character relating to the position of a European center, particularly one located in Geneva, in the plans for the future of the United Nations. The United Nations Committee sought to make the determination of the value contingent upon decisions to be taken by the United Nations with respect to future use. Hence they offered a formula under which the material assets would be transferred at a provisional value subject to an adjusted valuation to be made by the United Nations not later than December 31, 1948.

This formula, however, was unacceptable to the League Supervisory Commission. Aside from placing the power in the hands of the United Nations unilaterally to write down the values to virtually any sum, it would meanwhile place the League in an exceedingly difficult position regarding League members not members of the United Nations. Their claims to moieties could be settled somehow by the League, but the basis of settlement might be widely different from that adopted in determining the credits to be accorded to members of the League who were members of the United Nations. The unpredictable factor of currency fluctuations also had to be considered. A contingent valuation would require at least the Financial Department of the League to stay in being for another two or three years.

Other complications in winding up the affairs of the League could be visualized. The risk involved for the United Nations, particularly for those members which were not also League members, was, however, forcefully presented in and by the Committee. Possibilities of sale or other disposition of the buildings were explored. Reproduction costs as well as appreciation and depreciation in relation to present book values under various conceivable uses of the property were discussed. At all times, however, the Committee bore in mind the instruction of the Preparatory Commission that it should find a value which should "in principle imply neither profit nor loss for the United Nations" and that the transfer should be consummated on such terms as were "considered just and convenient."[64]

In the end, after the Committee and the Supervisory Commission had in several separate and joint sessions discussed the problem further and after representatives on the United Nations Committee had consulted their respective delegations to the General Assembly, agreement was reached on the basis of a formula which the Supervisory Commission had been invited by the Committee to submit.

FORMULA FOR TRANSFER OF MATERIAL ASSETS

In brief the formula agreed upon, subject of course to approval of the General Assembly, as was all the work of the Committee, provided for the taking over by the United Nations of all the material assets of the League at the price they had cost the League. All gifts, many of which have a high artistic and monetary value, would therefore be transferred without any pecuniary consideration. A schedule of fixed and movable assets, together with their valuations, to be appended to the Common Plan, would, with respect to the inventory of the movable assets and their valuations, be subject to revision as of the date of legal transfer. Finally, with respect to the credits to be entered on the books of the United Nations in favor of the members of the United Nations which were also members of the League of Nations at the time of the transfer, it was agreed that the General Assembly of the United Nations should decide upon the purposes, i.e. to which financial account—building fund, administrative expenses, etc.—these credits should be applied, and on which dates they should be so applied, provided, however, that the credits should begin to be available not later than December 31, 1948.

THE GENERAL ASEMBLY *ad hoc* COMMITTEE ON THE LEAGUE OF NATIONS

In addition to the six main committees of the General Assembly two *ad hoc* committees composed of representatives of all the members of the United Nations were set up, one of them for the purpose of considering "the possible transfer of certain functions, activities and assets of the League of Nations."[65] In one meeting, its second,[66] this committee discharged its task:

1. It examined and, after making certain stylistic changes, approved sections 1 and 2 of chapter XI of the Report of the Preparatory Commission, which dealt, respectively, with the assumption of functions and powers entrusted under separate treaties to the League and the assumption of non-political functions and activities of the League other than those mentioned in Section 1.

2. It examined, discussed, and approved without any changes the Report of the Committee on the Transfer of League Assets together with the Common Plan agreed to by the League Supervisory Commission.

In the course of the consideration by the *ad hoc* Committee, various members solicited and received explanations by Mr. Moderow of parts of the two documents. The Delegate of the United States, Frank Walker, for example, "asked whether in connection with the use by the ILO of the League Assembly Hall and committee rooms it was clear that the ILO had no vested or legal right in the buildings other than that of right of user during the time that the United Nations owned them." Mr. Moderow assured him that "this is the case. To emphasize this the words 'entitled to use' in the first draft had been changed to 'may use.' This point of view had been finally accepted by the ILO."[67]

3. Finally, the *ad hoc* Committee agreed to leave to the General Committee and the General Assembly the nomination of the small committee to negotiate with the Swiss Government and the Carnegie Foundation in relation to the assets located in Geneva and at The Hague respectively. In the absence of objection, however, the final report of the rapporteur of the *ad hoc* Committee provided that this Negotiating Committee should "consist of one representative designated by the delegations, if they so desire, of each of the same eight Members as previously constituted the Committee [on the Transfer of League Assets] created by the Preparatory Commission."[68]

APPROVAL BY THE GENERAL ASSEMBLY

Without debate and with no objections the General Assembly on February 12, 1946 adopted the report of its *ad hoc* Committee as presented by the rapporteur, H. T. Andrews of South Africa.[69]

WORK OF THE NEGOTIATING COMMITTEE

The small Negotiating Committee set up by this action of the General Assembly immediately held several informal meetings in London[70] and, after adjournment of the General Assembly, proceeded to The Hague, where it discussed with the representatives of the Dutch Government and the Carnegie Foundation details relating to the transfer of the use of the Court premises.

Subsequently, the Negotiating Committee made the necessary arrangements with the Swiss authorities in relation to the transfer of the material assets located in Geneva.[71]

NOTES

[1] *Essential Facts about the League of Nations* (Information Section, Geneva, 1939, 10th ed., revised); D. P. Myers, *Handbook of the League of Nations* (Boston, 1935).

[2] *Powers and Duties Attributed to the League of Nations by International Treaties* (League of Nations, C.3.M.3.1944. V, Geneva, July 1944); *List of Conventions with Indication of the Relevant Articles Conferring Powers on the Organs of the League of Nations* (League of Nations, C.100.M.100.1945V, Geneva, Sept. 1945).

[3] *Report on the Work of the League During the War,* submitted to the Assembly by the Acting Secretary-General (Geneva, Oct. 1945, A.6.1946).

[4] Statute of the International Court of Justice, art. 22.

[5] Par. 4 (c).

[6] PC/EX/96, Oct. 13, 1945; *Report by the Executive Committee to the Preparatory Commission of the United Na-*

tions, Nov. 12, 1945, part II, sec. IX, and part III, ch. IX. The Executive Committee sat in London, Aug. 16 to Nov. 24, 1945.

[7] PC/11, Dec. 17, 1945, and PC/12, Dec. 15, 1945; *Journal* no. 22, pp. 107-110; *Report of the Preparatory Commission of the United Nations,* Dec. 23, 1945, ch. XI. The Preparatory Commission sat in London, Nov. 24 to Dec. 24, 1945.

[8] *Report of the Preparatory Commission,* ch. XI, sec. 3. The delegations of the following members were represented: Chile, China, France, Poland, South Africa, the Soviet Union, the United Kingdom, and the United States.

[9] A/18, A/18/Add.1, and A/18/Add.2, Jan. 28, 1946; *Journal* no. 22: Supp. no. 7–A/LN/2, p. 3.

[10] *Journal* no. 16, Jan. 26, 1946, p. 316.

[11] A/28, Feb. 4, 1946; *Journal* no. 30.

[12] The delegations represented on this committee were the same as those on the other small committee, footnote 8 above.

[13] Resolution implementing A/28 above adopted as E/19, Feb. 15, 1946, by the Economic and Social Council on Feb. 16, 1946 (*Journal of the Economic and Social Council,* no. 11, p. 110).

[14] The date agreed on in the Common Plan.

[15] See P. M. Burnett, "International Bodies for Narcotics Control," *Department of State Bulletin* of Oct. 14, 1945, p. 570; also statement of United States Delegate in UNCIO, Committee II/3, Doc. 780, II/3/53, June 4, 1945 and the Report of the Rapporteur of Committee II/3, Doc. 861, II/3/55 (1), June 8, 1945.

[16] See annual survey, "The United States and World Organization during 1939," in *International Conciliation,* no. 361 (June 1940), and for previous years, see the same series.

[17] (1) Executive Committee, Committee 9, Henry Reiff; (2) Preparatory Commission, Committee 7, Dr. Reiff and John W. Halderman, Acting Assistant Chief, Division of International Organization Affairs, Department of State; (3) Committee on Transfer of League Assets, Benjamin Gerig, Chief, Division of Dependent Area Affairs, and Associate Chief, Division of International Organization Affairs, Department of State, A. H. Feller, Department of State, and Dr. Reiff; (4) *Ad hoc* Committee on League of Nations, Frank Walker, Alternate Delegate to General Assembly, Dr. Gerig, Dr. Reiff, and William F. Cronin, Assistant to Mr. Walker; (5) Negotiating Committee, Dr. Gerig.

[18] For example, in Committee 9 of the Executive Committee: PC/EX/LN/3, Sept. 6, 1945, Memorandum by the Chinese Delegation on the future of the League of Nations; PC/EX/LN/8, Sept. 13, 1945, Memorandum by the French Delegation on procedure for transferring functions arising out of international agreements from the League of Nations to the United Nations Organization; PC/EX/LN/10, Sept. 18, 1945, Proposal by the United Kingdom Delegation for a report on the transfer to the United Nations of the functions of the League of Nations under various treaties and international instruments; and several other working papers resulting from comprehensive study by United Kingdom experts.

[19] The future of the League of Nations Intellectual Cooperation Organization was left to be disposed of when the contemplated United Nations Educational and Cultural Organization had been set up.

[20] e.g. those related to minorities, and numerous other political matters accumulated since the peace settlements of 1919.

[21] *Report of the Executive Committee,* p. 108 n.

[22] See discussion on *Report of the Third Committee* on Refugees, A/45, Feb. 11, 1946, in General Assembly, Feb. 12 (*Journal* no. 30, p. 535, and *ibid.,* no. 31, p. 544).

[23] *Report of the Executive Committee,* ch. IX, sec. 3, par. 9.

[24] *Report of the Preparatory Commission,* ch, XI, sec. 2.

[25] *Report of the Executive Committee,* ch. IX, sec. 2.

[26] *Report of the Preparatory Commission,* ch. XI, sec. 1.

[27] *Journal* no. 30, p. 526, and *ibid.,* no. 34, p. 706.

[28] e.g. all political matters, activities concerning refugees and international bureaus, and the League Intellectual Cooperation Organization; and certain of the funds and liabilities of the League.

[29] *Report of the Executive Committee,* p. 108.

[30] PC/EX/96, Oct. 12, 1945.

[31] *Ibid.*

[32] e.g. PC/EN/LN/27, Oct. 8, 1945; PC/EX/LN/27/Corr. 1, Oct. 8, 1945; PC/LN/11, Dec. 8, 1945.

[33] Also with respect to engagement of former League personnel by the contemplated new international health organization (PC/LN/10, Dec. 5, 1945).

[34] Sec. 1; but the term was retained with respect to "assets and liabilities" as qualified in paragraph 28 of the accompanying report in sec. 3.

[35] *Report of the Executive Committee,* p. 108.

[36] Consisting of the representatives of Poland (Mr. Moderow, *chairman*), the U.S.S.R. (Professor Stein), the United Kingdom (Mr. McKinnon Wood), and Egypt (Ahmed Saroit Bey).

[37] *Report of the Preparatory Commission,* ch. XI, sec. 1.

[38] PC/LN/2, Nov. 28, 1945, PC/LN/5, Nov. 29, 1945 and PC/LN/7, Nov. 30, 1945.

[39] Par. 4 (c) quoted above.

[40] PC/12, Dec. 15, 1945.

[41] PC/LN/2, Nov. 28, 1945.

[42] PC/LN/4, Nov. 29, 1945.

[43] PC/LN/5, Nov. 29, 1945.

[44] To the effect that the Council "should report to the General Assembly not later than the second part of the General Assembly's first session" (PC/LN/7, Nov. 30, 1945).

[45] Changed in the General Assembly to "on *or before* the dissolution of the League" (A/28, Feb. 4, 1946).

[46] Meaning sec. 3 of ch. IX of part III of the comprehensive Report.

[47] See discussion immediately below.

[48] *Report of the Preparatory Commission,* pp. 117-18.

[49] A/28, Feb. 4, 1946; *Journal* no. 34, p. 708.

[50] For brief description, see *Powers and Duties Attributed to the League of Nations by International Treaties,* pp. 28-35, cited above, footnote 2.

[51] *Report of the Executive Committee,* p. 111.

[52] PC/LN/4, Nov. 29, 1945.

[53] PC/LN/5, Nov. 29, 1945.

[54] PC/12, Dec. 15, 1945; *Report of the Preparatory Commission,* p. 118.

[55] A/28, Feb. 4, 1946.

[56] PC/11, Dec. 17, 1945.

[57] *Report of the Preparatory Commission,* ch. XI, sec. 3.

[58] *Journal* no. 22, supp. no. 7-A/LN/2.

[59] The documents recording the negotiations of this committee are of a "restricted" character and are on file in the Department. The final report and Common Plan, A/18, Jan. 28, 1946, have, however, been published. See appendix to this article.

[60] *Report of the Preparatory Commission,* ch. V, sec. 3.

[61] *Report of the Committee on Transfer of League Assets,* A/18, par. 11.

[62] *Report of the Preparatory Commission,* ch. V, sec. 3.

[63] A/18, par. 10.

[64] *Report of the Preparatory Commission,* ch. V, sec. 3.

[65] *Journal* no. 16, Jan. 26, 1946, p. 316.

[66] Feb. 1, 1946, *Journal* no. 22: supp. no. 7-A/LN/2.

[67] *Ibid.,* p. 5.

[68] A/28, Feb. 4, 1946, sec. 4.

[69] *Journal* no. 30, p. 526: text of rapporteur's report, *Journal* no. 34, pp. 706-9. In pursuance of the resolution of the General Assembly thus adopted, the Economic and Social Council at its twelfth meeting, Feb. 16, 1946 (*Journal of the Economic and Social Council,* no. 11, p. 110), adopted a resolution, E/19, Feb. 15, 1946, requesting "the Secretary-General to undertake the survey called for by the General Assembly and to report at an early date to the Economic and Social Council" and directing him "to take the steps necessary to the provisional assumption and continuance of the work hitherto done by the League departments named" in the resolution adopted by the General Assembly. (For text of E/19, see appendix to this article.) Furthermore, the Council in setting up its commissions and committees specifically authorized certain of them to take the action within their fields necessary under the General Assembly resolution A/28 and under E/19 cited above; E/29, Feb. 22, 1946, Temporary Social Commission; E/31, Feb. 22, 1946, Temporary Transport and Communications Commission; and E/34, Feb. 27, 1946, Commission on Narcotic Drugs.

[70] *Journal* no. 30, p. 524; *ibid.,* no. 31, p. 544; *ibid.,* no. 32, p. 584.

[71] At this stage of the negotiations, Howard Elting, Jr., American Consul at Geneva, substituted for Benjamin Gerig as the representative of the United States on the Negotiating Committee.

The San Francisco UNCIO Documents

William J. Bruce

The United Nations Conference on International Organization met from April 25 to June 26, 1945. In this article, Bruce, an expert in documentation detailed to the Conference by the U. S. Bureau of the Budget, describes the process of producing and distributing the documents resulting from the conference.

An entire forty-two foot standard box car was required to transport the 3,500 cubic feet of official archives of the United Nations Conference on International Organization from San Francisco to the deck side at New York where space in the specie room of the *Queen Elizabeth* was made available to take the records to London there to be used by the Preparatory Commission. The archives consisted of all official conference documents boxed in quantities of two hundred copies of each document in English, one hundred copies in French, and fifty copies of the documents in the other languages, Spanish, Russian, and Chinese. The notes, papers, and records from the files of the executive officers and secretaries of the conference commissions and committees along with those of the secretary general, administrative secretary, executive secretary, documents officer, and their respective staffs, each file labeled to indicate its contents along with an extensive photographic record, both prints and negatives, and the complete stencil and photolith plate files, completed the seventy-ton package that will ultimately become the archives of the United Nations organization. The story of the eleven weeks of the conference at San Francisco can be found in this mass of documents. The following account gives a summary picture of the documentation with some comments on the process of its production.

The United Nations Conference on International Organization which met at San Francisco, April 25 to June 26, 1945, was called to perfect a plan of international organization developed by the four nations participating in the Dumbarton Oaks conversations in 1944. The UNCIO, in plenary session April 29, adopted the proposal of its committee of

delegation chairmen and formally organized and staffed its activities around four commissions and twelve technical committees to consider the principal items of the Dumbarton Oaks proposals. In addition, general committees essential to the basic organization and procedure of the conference were set up as follows: Steering Committee, Executive Committee, Co-ordination Committee, and Credentials Committee. The initial plans to make the small (fourteen-member) Executive Committee the principal organ of the conference ran afoul of the demands of the smaller nations to participate in all matters and as a result the Steering Committee (chairmen of all participating delegations) became the critical center of activity. [See UNCIO Doc. 67 (English) G/20, May 5, 1945, for a chart of the organization, functions, and officerships of the conference.]

During the time occupied by the first eight plenary sessions, which allowed the delegations to put their views on the Dumbarton Oaks proposals in the record, the committee and commission organization was being perfected, chairmen and rapporteurs selected from the delegation members, secretariat officers and secretaries assigned from the International Secretariat, and the general procedures agreed upon so that the spade work of the conference could be carried on by the technical committees. Each technical committee and commission had, in addition to the chairman and rapporteur, a secretary and several assistant secretaries from the International Secretariat. The four commissions each had an executive officer and small staff to coordinate the work of the various committees and subcommittees reporting to it. All commissions and committees were

SOURCE: Reprinted from William J. Bruce "The San Francisco UNCIO Documents," *American Archivist,* 9 (Jan. 1946), pp. 6–16.

serviced by the International Secretariat through the staff of the executive secretary. [UNCIO Documents No. 68 (English) G/21, May 5, 1945, and No. 578 (English) G/68 May 26, 1945, are charts of the *Organization, Functions, and Personnel of the Secretariat,* reflecting the initial and final organization of the secretariat.]

As host, the United States provided the major portion of the staff of the International Secretariat. The secretariat was under the supervision of a secretary general assisted by two principal officers, an administrative secretary and an executive secretary. Outside of the housekeeping functions of supply, space, transportation, and finance provided by the administrative secretary, the principal job of the secretariat was that of planning the work of the committees, preparing minutes and documents, providing translation and interpreters, and other technical advice necessary to the conference activities. These latter functions were performed by the staff of the executive secretary. The documentation, from debate to archives, was organized under a small supervisory staff headed by a documents officer. The subject matter of this paper concerns the functions of the documents officer whose activities the author was able to view at first hand in the capacity of deputy.

GENERAL PATTERN OF CONFERENCE DOCUMENTS

The general plan for the documentation of the conference was simply that a separate minute or report was to be prepared for each meeting of the committee or commission on its own distinguishing masthead paper, identified by document number and appropriate symbol. Complications arose out of the need for translations into the two working languages (English and French) or the five official languages (Chinese, Russian, and Spanish, in addition) and the fact that parts of the subject matter of the four commissions and their twelve committees overlapped and were interdependent, requiring reconsideration of various phases of the subject whenever significant changes were made. An illustration is found in the ramifications of the problem of the vote in the Security Council. The scope of the "veto" of a large power affected decisions in Committees 1, 2, and 3 of Commission II dealing with the General Assembly as well as the committees of Commission III, concerned with the Security Council, and of Commit-

tee 2 of Commission I when it considered the amending process. To get the exact nuances of meaning into each of the language versions of the documents required all the skill and patience of the translating staff—especially when one recalls the pressures of time imposed by the deadlines set by ten or twelve committees meeting daily—and the demand made by each succeeding meeting that the documents of the previous meeting be ready for reconsideration as part of its next agenda.

In order to handle the volume of work that it was seen would be required, an assembly-line procedure was set up under the direction of the documents officer for the preparation, processing, reproduction, and distribution of conference documents. Two or more secretaries and assistant secretaries, assisted by verbatim reporters and typists, were assigned the responsibility for the preparation of the minute or summary report of each meeting. This manuscript, properly checked and approved by the chairman of the committee was submitted to the documents officer for processing. It was decided in the pre-conference planning in Washington to routinize and control this process by adapting the standard printer's job jacket technique to the operations to be performed. Accordingly an envelope, or job jacket, was designed which showed each of the possible steps through which the manuscript might flow before it emerged as a final document. Sufficient copies of the manuscript were requested (though most often not obtained) to allow simultaneous treatment in the various languages required. The job jacket and its contents passed from the documents officer, to the editors, translators, typing pool (where stencils were cut or photo copy prepared), then to the duplicating staff (or print shop), each recording on the job jacket his receipt and completion of his part of the job. The original manuscript (for the archives) along with the required number of duplicated copies was sent to the distribution office where the delegations, secretariat, archives, and files received their copies. All these sections of the document officer's staff were operated on a three shift, twenty-four hour basis, seven days a week during their twelve weeks of operation. This use of the job jacket proved to be a farsighted decision as 5,550 jobs were processed in preparing the 1,550 conference documents in each of the five languages requested. This figure includes some three hundred papers of the working documents series, a large portion of which did not emerge as official conference documents for general distribution.

THE GENERAL, JOURNAL, PLENARY, AND PRÉCIS SERIES

The papers of general interest to all conference personnel were divided among these four series: *General* (with symbol G), *Journal* (a four to eight-page document printed daily), *Plenary* (with symbol P), and *Précis* (a summary digest of committee and commission activities issued for general distribution). In the *General* series are found such basic documents as the Dumbarton Oaks proposal (Doc. 1. G/1); the ammendments proposed by the participating nations (Doc. 2. G/7 [a through w]; G/25, G/26 [a through f]; G/28; G/29); the organization plans of the conference (Doc. 68. G/21); the Order of the Day, a listing of meeting time and place for all official sessions; the list of documents issued, showing title, document number, symbol, and date; and the final draft of the charter submitted to the conference in plenary session, January 26, 1945 (Doc. 1191, G/128). The *Journal* issued each morning contained all special conference announcements by the president or secretary general, a listing of the scheduled meetings, the documents issued the previous day, and other information on activities of interest to all delegations and the secretariat. Each issue of the printed *Journal* was identified by a consecutive volume number.

The *Plenary* series contained all documents pertaining to the plenary sessions, *i.e.,* agenda, verbatim minutes, corregenda and addenda to the minutes. In preparing these documents the verbatim reporter's transcript was checked against a sound recording of the proceedings. The corrections often reflected an after-thought of the delegation upon seeing the delegate's speech in print.

Pre-conference plans provided for a "record" to be published each day containing summaries of the proceedings of the committees during the previous day. This was to be a full official summary of each meeting prefaced by a very brief "contents-précis." By the time the technical committees were ready to meet, the document load in the two to five languages demanded was found to be so heavy that facilities were not available to print the "record." Moreover, the committees demanded their documents several hours in advance of each daily meeting and it was possible to meet this demand on time only by using the mimeograph process. Thus the "record" would have been a printed duplication of the mimeographed or multilithed documents distributed to the conference membership in as much as the documents reporting committee meetings were summaries rather than verbatim reports. As a result a series carrying the masthead, *Précis,* was issued containing a very brief (usually a single paragraph) summary of each meeting beginning with Précis No. 1, May 5, 1945, Document No. 89.

DOCUMENT AND SYMBOL NUMBERS

At this point, before continuing with a description of the committee and commission documents, it might be well to explain the numbering system and its use for control of the documents issued.

The numbering system was devised prior to the conference, although relatively little study was made either of the needs for documentation control or of alternative numbering systems. So little definitive knowledge about the documents the conference would produce was available prior to its actual operations that it was deemed advisable to spend planning time on other subjects. The system adopted and used throughout the conference with relatively minor modifications involved:

1. A document number for each separate document issued. Documents were numbered consecutively as they were received and registered by the documents officer.
2. A symbol classification and paper number indicating the organ of the conference from which the document originated and the particular paper's relation to previous documents issued by that organ.

All official papers of the conference carried document numbers. The working draft series should be considered an exception to this rule. These were considered as draft papers, some of which later became conference documents, others, like those of the Co-ordination Committee charter drafts were officially designated as restricted and unavailable for public release.

At San Francisco, 1,216 conference documents were issued. This does not comprise the whole of the documentation as several of the minutes of the concluding meetings of the Co-ordination Committee were not written up before the secretariat staff was disbanded. These documents were later prepared and issued by the U.S. Department of State in Washington. In addition what has been called Document 2, *Comments and Amendments to the Dumbarton Oaks Proposals* is in reality seventy-two separate documents. Their separate identity is maintained through the use of the symbol classification.

Neither the document number nor the date it was issued bears any necessary strict relationship to its chronological place in the conference documentation. Document numbers were assigned as the manuscripts were presented to the documents officer's staff for registry. All language versions of that document received the same document number and symbol. The date of the document was the documents officer's best estimate of when that document would actually appear in finished form ready for distribution. Usually the stenographic pool and mimeograph services had at least a twenty-four to thirty-six hour capacity load in prospect, the printers could seldom be given less than a twenty-four hour deadline, consequently many documents emerged two and at times three or four days after the secretary had finished the manuscript. Moreover, as the work load of the conference piled up few secretaries lived up to the requirement that manuscripts be ready prior to 11:00 P.M. of the day the meeting took place. All too often manuscripts received at 2 or 3 A.M. were processed for 8:30 A.M. meetings. Some types of papers had to be given absolute priority through the shop, *i.e.*, agenda, summary reports, and subcommittee reports. These, with their required French, and usually Russian, translations might take all the normal capacity of the document officer's staffs if ten or twelve committees were meeting daily. Accordingly, some documents registered early had to be shunted aside until staff time was available to complete them. This was very likely to be the case if the document was a long report.

It is by means of the symbol numbers that documents can be put together in their proper subject matter classifications. Just as

Doc. 10 (English)
P/1
April 26, 1945

was the first paper issued in English pertaining to the plenary sessions (in this case, its agenda) so also was

Doc. 70 (French)
I/1/1
May 4, 1945

the French text of the "Agenda for the First Meeting of Committee I/1." The part of the symbol I/1 indicates that the first committee of Commission I issued the report. The entire symbol indicates it was the first paper of the first committee of Commission I. Correspondingly the symbol I/2/9 indicates the ninth paper of Committee 2 of Commission I. Corregenda to reports or minutes were issued using the document number and symbol of the original report and adding a "(1)." If the document was reissued with material added to the original this fact was noted by adding to the sumbol thus: (a).

The *Journal* provided a daily listing of documents distributed the previous day showing the symbol and the language or languages in which they were prepared. A "Cumulative List of Documents Issued" was prepared approximately every other week in order that delegates and others might keep abreast of what proved to be an overwhelming stream of paper.

COMMISSION AND COMMITTEE REPORTS

The documentation of the commissions and technical committees was broken down into sixteen series in accordance with the following list of commission and committee titles showing their corresponding symbols. These separate series can be readily assembled into four volumes of commission reports which represent the major aspects of the international organization created in the charter.

	Symbol	Title
Commission I	I	*General Provisions*
Committee 1	I/1	Preamble Purposes and Principles
Committee 2	I/2	Membership, Amendment and Secretariat
Commission II	II	*General Assembly*
Committee 1	II/1	Structure and Procedures
Committee 2	II/2	Political and Security Functions
Committee 3	II/3	Economic and Social Cooperation
Committee 4	II/4	Trusteeship System
Commission III	III	*Security Council*
Committee 1	III/1	Structure and Procedures
Committee 2	III/2	Peaceful Settlement
Committee 3	III/3	Enforcement Arrangements
Committee 4	III/4	Regional Arrangements
Commission IV	IV	*Judicial Organization*
Committee 1	IV/1	International Court of Justice
Committee 2	IV/2	Legal Problems

EXECUTIVE, STEERING, AND CO-ORDINATION COMMITTEE PAPERS

The other committees of the conference each issued short series of reports. The papers of the Executive Committee (symbol EX) and the Steering Committee (symbol ST) contain some of the flavor of the political maneuvering that took place outside of the more formal proceedings of the technical committees.

The few reports of the Credentials Committee were merged with those of the Steering Committee and are distinguished by the symbol "ST/C."

One of the interesting anomalies in the documentation developed around the first meetings of secretaries general of all delegations. The organization plans for the conference provided for a Steering Committee composed of the chairmen of all delegations. The executive officer of this committee insisted, over the objections of the documents officer, that the papers and minutes of these early pre-organization meetings could not be run under the Steering Committee masthead but should be separate, restricted, and unofficial documents apart from the Steering Committee series. His thesis was based on the strict legal viewpoint that a Steering Committee could not exist until the conference had formally organized and designated such a committee. The compromise finally reached involved the creation of a separate series of reports of the "Meetings of Chairmen of Delegations" carrying document numbers and identified by the symbol "DC." Because the compromise decision was reached several weeks after the meetings had taken place the stencils were carefully rearranged, the reports properly numbered, and the series reissued to become part of the official documents. One of the sidelights of the problem was the fact that the U.S. delegation, as host, had assumed that established procedure in international conferences would be followed and had laid plans accordingly for the organization of the conference. This assumption would have made the chairman of the U.S. delegation chairman of the conference and also would have approved all the other provisional officers provided by the host nation. Banking on this assumption, the executive officer of the committee had prepared and issued a complete set of detailed recommendations for the committee's approval, hoping thus to expedite its operations. When the Russian delegation upset the apple-cart by proposing four co-equal chairmen all the nicely prepared plans had to be abandoned.

The documents officer was able to keep most of these documents as part of the conference record by establishing this separate "DC" series.

The Co-ordination Committee reports (symbol CO) enjoy the dubious distinction of being the only group of documents that were not released to the public when the matter was voted upon by the conference. The various explanations advanced for maintaining these documents in the restricted classification usually hinge around the belief that the deliberations of the Co-ordination Committee will reflect the differences of viewpoint among the "Big Five" as well as the differences between the "Big Five" and the "Little Forty-five." Much of the validity of this argument is lost, however, because a careful perusal of several of the technical committee series will reveal the various delegation viewpoints.

EXECUTIVE SECRETARY AND SECRETARIAT PAPERS

Two sets of papers comprise the record of the housekeeping procedures of the conference. One is part of the official documentation, the executive secretary series (symbol EX-SEC), the other did not carry document numbers but is a series restricted to the International Secretariat, the secretariat papers (symbol SEC). The executive secretary papers carried official announcements for the conference, organization plans, proposed procedures or procedures determined by the Executive or Steering Committees. The secretariat papers carried announcements pertinent to the staffs of the administrative secretary or the executive secretary, instructions regarding the preparation and processing of documents, entertainment and recreational programs available to the secretariat in San Francisco.

Although no index has yet been published an exhaustively complete one was maintained by the index officer at San Francisco for use by the delegations and the secretariat. This unpublished index is now on three-by-five cards in the files of the U.S. State Department. It will be a real aid to those who plan research in this field. Present plans call for the completion of the index as soon as the remaining Co-ordination Committee documents are finished and for the publication of the entire index.

DOCUMENT DISTRIBUTION AND
THE PERMANENT FILE

The process of distributing this constant stream of documents to the fifty delegations, and the approximately sixty separate officers or offices of the secretariat, press, official observers, and libraries offered almost as many problems as did the preparation of the documents. In order to fulfill the usual pattern of requests for a document, 5,000 copies in English were provided (1,500 in French, 500 each in Chinese, Spanish, or Russian) if the report was to receive unrestricted distribution. Such distribution was always given to the *Journal*, and *Plenary* series. Certain other reports, particularly those final raporteur's reports to the commissions were given similar distribution. Documents that had a restricted distribution were prepared in quantities of approximately 3,000 copies (English), 750 (French), and 200-300 in the other languages. Such "restricted" distribution meant only that official delegation members and the members of the secretary general and executive secretary's staffs dealing with commission and committee work received copies. The press and non-official observers were denied.

In every case it was the responsibility of the distribution officer to (1) transmit the original manuscript and four copies of the document to the archivist, (2) maintain two hundred copies at all times as permanent file copies for the UNO file, (3) distribute the requested number of copies to the delegation and secretariat messengers when they identified themselves and asked for their documents. This latter task meant a tremendous clerical job as each official requested a different number of copies in the various languages. The delegations' requests varied from a maximum of three hundred copies (U. S. and Chinese) to two or five copies. Each delegation requested a different number depending upon the language in which the document was written. From seventy-five to one hundred separate sorting operations had to be made for each document issued and for each of the languages in which it was prepared.

The permanent file copies were packed in specially prepared paper board document boxes measuring 9 by 11 inches and 36 inches long. As a standard 8 by $10\frac{1}{2}$ paper was used each box would hold about 3,500 sheets. The documents were stacked in the boxes and separated by a divider sheet on which was indicated the document number, symbol, language, and number of copies of each document. The purpose of this arrangement was to permit the use of these document boxes as temporary stacks while the documents are in Church House, Deans Yard, London, being used by the Preparatory Commission of the United Nations prior to their being sent to archives at the permanent seat of the United Nations Organization.

The Archives and Documents of the Preparatory Commission of the United Nations

Richardson Dougall

The United Nations Conference at San Francisco agreed on the need for a working. group to make preparations for the first session of the newly founded UN. The Preparatory Commission met in London during the period from August 16, 1945 to December 23, 1945. The document numbering system devised for the documentation produced by the Preparatory Commission is the genesis of the present UN documents numbering system.

THE PREPARATORY COMMISSION AND ITS EXECUTIVE COMMITTEE

When the Charter of the United Nations was signed at San Francisco on June 26, 1945, there was signed at the same time a much less heralded agreement known officially as the Interim Arrangements Concluded by the Governments Represented at the United Nations Conference on International Organization. This instrument "established a Preparatory Commission of the United Nations for the purpose of making provisional arrangements for the first sessions of the General Assembly, the Security Council, the Economic and Social Council, and the Trusteeship Council, for the establishment of the Secretariat, and for the convening of the International Court of Justice." It also provided for a 14-nation Executive Committee of the Preparatory Commission.[1]

The Preparatory Commission held its First Session in San Francisco on June 27, 1945, and then adjourned, leaving to its Executive Committee the task of preparing a report which could be used as a basis for Commission discussions. The Executive Committee began its labors in London on August 16, 1945, holding its meetings at Church House in Dean's Yard, near Westminster Abbey, where the British Parliament had met for a time during the "blitz." The Executive Committee and its subcommittees met from August until November, working on a report to the Preparatory Commission which included draft agenda and rules of procedure for the General Assembly, the Security Council, and other organs of the United Nations, a chapter on legal questions and the International Court of Justice, recommendations concerning the permanent Secretariat, budgetary and financial recommendations, and chapters concerning the relations of the United Nations with specialized agencies, questions involving the League of Nations, information policy, and the future permanent site of the headquarters of the United Nations.

The Second Session of the Preparatory Commission was convened in Church House, in the chamber where the House of Commons had for a time met, on November 24, 1945, and the delegates of all the United Nations then reviewed the work done by the fourteen delegations to the Executive Committee. Each chapter of the Executive Committee's report was referred to a committee of the Preparatory Commission for study. The Commission then discussed the reports of these committees and approved a report to the General Assembly of the United Nations covering all the subjects mentioned above before concluding its meetings on December 23.

ORGANIZATIONAL POSITION OF THE ARCHIVES

As at all international conferences, much of the basic work in London was done by members of

---

SOURCE: Reprinted from: Richardson Dougall, "The Archives and Documents of the Preparatory Commission of the United Nations," *American Archivist*, 10 (Jan. 1947) pp. 25–34.

the Secretariat. The International Secretariat for the Executive Committee and the Preparatory Commission was organized, under the general supervision of an Executive Secretary, and a Deputy Executive Secretary into three administrative sections—Documents, Languages, and Public Relations—and one section for each of the technical committees. The operations of the Documents Section, the largest unit of the Secretariat, were in turn divided among a group of production units (documents registration, a typing and stencil-cutting pool, a duplicating or "roneo" room, and a documents distribution office) and four units not involved in the actual production and distribution of documents, viz. the Library, the Index, the Registry, and the Archives.

The Archivist of the Preparatory Commission acted under the direct supervision of the officer in charge of the Documents Section. He carried, however, the additional assignment of Deputy Documents Officer and in that capacity had supervisory and operating functions in connection with documents production during the meeting of the Executive Committee. After the appointment of two additional Deputy Documents Officers for the meetings of the full Preparatory Commission, the Archivist's duties in his capacity as a Deputy were confined to nominal supervision of the Library, the Index, and the Registry.

CONTENTS AND ACTIVITIES OF THE ARCHIVES

When the Archivist arrived in London late in August, 1945, he found there a shipment of approximately 750 reinforced cardboard cartons containing the archives and documents of the recently adjourned United Nations Conference on International Organization (UNCIO), in the packing of which he had assisted in June at San Francisco. So far as bulk was concerned, these formed the principal portion of the Preparatory Commission Archives and, since they were needed constantly for reference, arrangements had to be made at once for opening them and storing them in such a way that their contents would be easily accessible. This involved construction of temporary shelving by the British Ministry of Works—a considerable task, inasmuch as lumber, which had been scarce enough in the United States during the war, was even harder to obtain in England.

These cartons from San Francisco included a certified copy of the Charter of the United Nations, the correspondence of the UNCIO Secretariat, the originals of the formal documents issued by the Governments or Heads of State of the various United Nations giving the UNCIO delegates full powers to sign the Charter and the Interim Arrangements,[2] the UNCIO Archivist's sets of UNCIO documents in all five of the official UNCIO languages (English, French, Chinese, Russian, and Spanish), a stock of approximately 250 copies each of most documents in one to five languages, the drafts from which the mimeographed copies and the translations of documents had been prepared, typescript verbatim minutes of the proceedings of the technical committees, and a large number of drafts and working papers submitted to the Archives by the officers of the UNCIO Secretariat.

The bulk of the Archives material which originated in London was considerably less. Inasmuch as all correspondence was kept in the Registry, the Archives received only drafts and working papers and ten copies of each document issued—so many copies were required in order to have readily available sets of the London documents for the sections of the permanent United Nations Secretariat dealing with each of the principal organs of the United Nations.

The activities carried on in London by the staff of the Preparatory Commission Archives with respect to currently issued documents consisted principally of (1) checking all documents received from the distribution office and replacing all copies found to have missing, mutilated, or illegible pages; (2) correcting the errors in assignment of document numbers which inevitably occur in the rush of an international conference; (3) filing the documents in sets; (4) filing the drafts from which the documents had been reproduced; and (5) obtaining from officers of the Secretariat and filing drafts and working papers not produced as documents. This included a considerable portion of the record of subcommittees and of such working groups as the Advisory Committee of Experts, a working group studying problems of budget and finance.

In addition to these comparatively routine duties, the Archives staff was called upon at almost any hour of the day or night to service officers of the Secretariat or of the various national Delegations with information concerning the contents of UNCIO documents and decisions reached at San Francisco. A committee secretary, for example, asked at 9 P.M. for immediate delivery of 55 copies of an UNCIO document reporting discussions at San Francisco on a question being discussed at that moment in an evening meeting of her committee of the Preparatory Commission. The Secretary to one of the large Delegations posed a series of questions concerning discussion at San Francisco of the celebrated "veto power" which required two full days of research in UNCIO committee and commission papers and minutes to answer satisfactorily. Because of the great bulk of UNCIO documentation many of the Delegations had not brought full sets of UNCIO documents to London with them. An adviser to one Delegation applied rather frequently to the Archivist for information from UNCIO documents and verbatim minutes on the stand which his country's Delegation to the San Francisco conference had taken on specific issues. A member of another Delegation inquired on his way to a committee meeting the exact date and document citation of a speech he had made in the course of the UNCIO proceedings. Delegates frequently asked for single copies of specific UNCIO documents under discussion in their committees or for French texts of UNCIO documents the English texts of which had been quoted in committee meetings, or vice versa. By and large, this servicing function was the most interesting as well as the most immediately useful part of the Archivist's work.

Another duty of considerable importance which devolved upon the Archivist in London was the preparation and binding of a complete and definitive set of UNCIO documents in the five official languages.[3] The basis for this set was the UNCIO Archivist's set of documents, but this set was not absolutely complete, besides which approximately five per cent of the copies were defective in one way or another, and the summary records of the last meetings of the UNCIO Coordination Committee had not been issued in San Francisco but had been prepared later in the Department of State at Washington. The checking of the UNCIO documents for defects was a laborious task, but an essential one in view of the fact that the San Francisco Archives staff had not had time to do it. In most cases a defective copy of a document could be replaced by a copy drawn from the extra stock of UNCIO documents shipped from San Francisco to London, but in some cases no extra stock had been provided and copies had to be obtained from the Department of State in Washington, to which the UNCIO document stencils had been sent.

More important was the checking of the UNCIO Archives set against the records of the UNCIO Documents Office to ensure that the definitive set would include (1) every paper issued originally as an UNCIO document or working document, including papers later withdrawn from the documents series, and (2) every UNCIO issuance appearing originally as a miscellaneous paper to which a document number had later been assigned. Errors in the assignment of document numbers and symbols were also corrected and cross references inserted to ensure that anyone having a citation to an uncorrected document could find the corrected document in its proper place. All important variants of a document—some documents were "rerun" as many as three times with occasional variations—were either bound in or explained in notes. All revisions and corrigenda were bound in.

A master set in English was prepared first, as almost all the 1216 UNCIO documents and the 442 UNCIO working documents had been issued in English, while a good many of them had not been issued in French, fewer still having been put out in Russian, Spanish, and Chinese. The master English set was completed and was bound as a permanent record by the British Museum Bindery during the term of the Preparatory Commission, with the exception of two volumes which could not be completed until after the Archivist had returned to the United States and, by research in the Department of State files, found the most elusive document in the entire set.

The master English set was arranged as follows: volumes 1 to 19, Documents 1 to 1216 arranged numerically by document serial number; volume 20, list of documents by document serial number; volumes 21 to 25, Working Documents 1 to 442 arranged by working document number; volumes 26 to 49, documents and working documents arranged by symbol, that is, according to committee or commission;[4] volume 50, list of documents by symbol. Bound in volumes 51 to 100 were the typescript verbatim minutes of the UNCIO technical committees and of meetings of the Coordination Committee and the Advisory Committee of Jurists for which verbatim minutes had been taken.

French having been the second working language under the UNCIO rules of procedure, work on a definitive set of French UNCIO documents was begun before the binding of the master English set was completed. The process of preparation was roughly the same, but certain French documents presented special problems where their English counterparts had presented none. The French text of the Report of the Rapporteur of UNCIO Committee IV/1 serves as a case in point: because of a misunderstanding the text circulated in San Francisco contained a number of pages in which linguistic corrections in the French text of the Statute of the International Court of Justice had not been made. This misunderstanding almost caused the accuracy of the report to be questioned in a plenary session of UNCIO Commission IV, but objections were quelled in advance by the preparation of an extremely limited number of corrected copies, none of which were filed in the UNCIO Archives. A considerable number of corrected copies with an explanatory cover-sheet were subsequently prepared by the Department of State in Washington and circulated to all of the United Nations, but once again no copy reached the Preparatory Commission Archives. In these circumstances it was only the interest and care of the Secretary of UNCIO Committee IV/1, who was also an Adviser to the United States Delegation to the Preparatory Commission, that assured the inclusion of both the uncorrected and the corrected report, with a note of explanation, in the master French set. Because of the limitations of time and staff, only about ten volumes of the master French set were sent to the British Museum for binding during the term of the Preparatory Commission, but the other volumes were turned over in a state of partial readiness to the Archivist of the First Session of the General Assembly of the United Nations for further work.

It was not possible to do more than begin the checking of the Russian, Spanish, and Chinese master sets of UNCIO documents during the term of the Preparatory Commission and these too were turned over to the General Assembly Archivist, who would probably have completed them in London had it not been for the necessity of packing the Archives early in March for shipment to New York. The two UNCIO documents issued in Portuguese were also turned over to the General Assembly Archivist for attention.

THE DOCUMENTS SYSTEM OF THE PREPARATORY COMMISSION

The documents system of the Preparatory Commission and of its Executive Committee was planned on the basis of UNCIO experience. Where each UNCIO document had carried both a document serial number and a committee symbol and number,[5] Preparatory Commission documents bore only one designation, based upon the UNCIO system of committee symbols and numbers. The document serial number was done away with entirely, for the reasons that (1) most Delegations had kept files of documents both by serial number and by symbol, thus doubling the number of copies requested and imposing an unnecessary burden on the Secretariat, and that (2) the possibility of errors in documentation was lessened by having only one number instead of two. Each document number of the Preparatory Commission began with PC/ to identify the Preparatory Commission documents easily from documents to be issued later by permanent organs of the United Nations. Each document number assigned during the session of the Commission's Executive Committee began with PC/EX/.

After this initial identification came either (1) an arabic number in series, if the document pertained to the full Commission or to the full Executive Committee, or (2) a further committee symbol followed in turn by arabic numbers in series. The reorganization of the ten committees of the Executive Committee into the eight committees of the Preparatory Commission was accompanied by a few changes in these committee symbols. These changes are reflected in the following table, which gives the designation of the first document in each series during the session of the Executive Committee and the first document in each series during the Second Session of the Preparatory Commission.

Revisions, corrigenda, and addenda to documents were indicated by adding /Rev. 1,/Corr. 1, or /Add. 1 to the number assigned the original document, and except in a few cases this made the relationship clear without becoming unduly cumbersome. One of the cumbersome examples, however, will best illustrate the system: Document PC/EX/SC/39/Rev. 1/Add.1 was the first addendum to the first revision of the thirty-ninth document pertaining to the Committee on the Security Council appointed by the Executive Committee of the Preparatory Commission. Likewise Document PC/LEG/9/Rev. 2/Add. 2 was the second addendum to the second revision of the ninth document pertaining to the Committee on Legal Questions of the Preparatory Commission. The ultimate in a document number was not reached until the final day of the Commission's session, when Document PC/AB/31/Rev. 1/Add. 1/Corr. 1 had to be issued. In addition to these regular series of documents,

Committee (Short Name)	Executive Committee	Preparatory Commission
Plenary Session	PC/EX/1[6]	PC/1
General Assembly	PC/EX/A/1	PC/GA/1
Security Council	PC/EX/SC/1	PC/SC/1
Economic and Social Council	PC/EX/ES/1	PC/ES/1
Trusteeship Council	PC/EX/TC/1	PC/TC/1
International Court of Justice (subsequently Legal Problems)	PC/EX/ICJ/1	PC/LEG/1
Secretariat	PC/EX/SEC/1 ⎫	These two committees were merged in the
Finance	PC/EX/FI/1 ⎭	Administrative and Budgetary Committee
Administrative and Budgetary		PC/AB/1
Specialized Agencies	PC/EX/SA/1	This committee was merged in the Economic and Social Council Committee
League of Nations	PC/EX/LN/1	PC/LN/1
General	PC/EX/G/1	PC/G/1
Steering		PC/ST/1
Coordination and Drafting		PC/CD/2[7]
Administrative Documents	PC/EX/AD/1	PC/AD/1
Technical Advisory Group on Information		PC/INF/1
Advisory Group of Experts		No documents issued[8]

the Preparatory Commission issued a *Journal* from November 24 to December 24. The *Journal,* which included general notices, programs of meetings, agenda for meetings, verbatim minutes of plenary sessions, summary minutes of meetings of the Steering Committee, and lists of documents issued, was numbered serially but did not bear a document number. Supplements to the *Journal,* however, in which were printed minutes of meetings of the eight principal committees, and which were usually stapled to the *Journal* but sometimes distributed separately, bore regular document numbers so that they could be filed with mimeographed documents pertaining to the same committees.[9]

The working languages of the Preparatory Commission and its Executive Committee were English and French and the great bulk of documents was issued in both these languages. Ordinarily the English and French texts were mimeographed separately and distributed as soon as available. The *Journal* and its Supplements, however, were printed in double-column form, with English in the left-hand column and French in the right-hand column. A very few documents were also produced in each of the other official languages, viz. Chinese, Russian, and Spanish. The final report of the Executive Committee, for example, was printed from type in English, French, and Spanish; a Russian text was reproduced by a photo-offset process from a typewritten text; and a Chinese text was similarly reproduced from a master copy written by hand. When it came to producing the final report of the Preparatory Commission to the General Assembly, however, objection was made to the reproduction of a Russian typewritten text and arrangements were made for two members of the Secretariat to supervise the printing from type of the Russian report in Paris, it being impossible to print it in England on the time schedule demanded.

While the documents of the Preparatory Commission and of its Executive Committee are now primarily of historical value, an understanding of the documents system is useful not only to those performing research in the United Nations Archives on the machinery by which the United Nations as an organization was brought into being but also to those wishing a full appreciation of the documents system of the present organs of the United Nations. This is true because the documents system now used by the United Nations Secretariat is to a considerable extent based upon that of the Preparatory Commission, with modifications drawn from the system used by the League of Nations. The initial PC/ has of course disappeared, but the relation of document numbers such as A/LN/1 (the first document of the League of Nations Committee of the General Assembly) or E/ORG/1 (the first document of the Committee on Organization of the Economic and Social Council) to the system discussed above is apparent. Thus the first document of Committee 4 of the General Assembly was numbered A/C.4/1.

A thorough description of present United Nations documentation, however, cannot be attempted here. It must await the establishment of all the principal organs of the United Nations and the evolution, with experience, of a stable documentary practice.

NOTES

[1] The following countries were represented on the Executive Committee: Australia, Brazil, Canada, Chile, China, Czechoslovakia, France, Iran, Mexico, the Netherlands, the Union of Soviet Socialist Republics, the United Kingdom, the United States of America, and Yugoslavia.

[2] Photostats of these full powers were subsequently made by the British Air Ministry, and these photostats were retained in the United Nations Archives, while the originals were transmitted to the United States Government, with which the original Charter of the United Nations is deposited. The original of the Interim Arrangements was delivered in London during the session of the Executive Committee but was not deposited in the Archives.

[3] The most complete set generally available is the photo-offset *Documents of the United Nations Conference on International Organization, San Francisco, 1945* (15 volumes), published by the United Nations Information Organizations, London and New York, 1945. A considerable number of deliberate omissions were made in the preparation of these volumes, however, including all the working documents of the very important UNCIO Coordination Committee, and there are a number of inadvertent errors as well. The charts attached to Doc. 25, for example, were inadvertently omitted, and the document included as Doc. 1160 (French) is in reality Doc. 1178 (French) with an incorrect document number, while the true Doc. 1160 (French) is omitted.

[4] For an explanation of UNCIO document serial numbers and symbols see William J. Bruce, "The San Francisco UNCIO Documents," *The American Archivist,* IX (Jan. 1946), 6.

[5] For a detailed discussion of the number system for UNCIO see William J. Bruce, article cited.

[6] There was also a set of preliminary documents, beginning with PC/EX/Prel.1, issued before the Executive Committee met.

[7] The first document issued by the Coordination and Drafting group bore the number PC/CO/1.

[8] All papers of the Advisory Group of Experts were working drafts and bore numbers indicating the fact, e.g. PC/AGE/W1.

[9] Research in Supplements to the *Journal* is complicated by the fact that Supplements were numbered serially in eight new series unconnected with any other series of documentation, one for each of the eight principal committees of the Preparatory Commission. They also failed to carry the number of the *Journal* to which they were attached, although they bore its date, and only the first page bore the document number. Consequently, in using Supplements which have been detached from the *Journal* and filed separately, researchers should bear in mind the fact that pages were easily lost or misfiled and that it is difficult to identify the document to which a misfiled page belongs.

League of Nations Documents and Publications Comparable with or Continued in United Nations Publications[1]

Marie J. Carroll

The UN inherited many of the functions of the League, maintained much of the administrative organizational pattern, and absorbed a number of personnel from the predecessor agency. A natural result of this continuity was a continuity in publications. As noted in this article a large number of serial publications continued often with the same title used before 1945.

Now that the United Nations has completed its 5th year as a publisher of official documents, it seems fitting and appropriate that a survey of the scope of its documentation in comparison with that of the League of Nations should be made for those interested in this field.

To a considerable number of librarians the vast collection of League publications, which were acquired by many American libraries in the period 1920–1946 covering the activities of a now defunct international organization, may appear to have only a historical value for the student of international affairs. But an examination of the various series of official documents of the United Nations reveals that some serials have been continued with only slight changes in title while in many fields there is a continuity of subject matter in the publication, even though the form may be somewhat altered. In carrying out its work in the technical field, the United Nations has taken over the powers and functions assigned to the League of Nations under the terms of more than 50 international conventions. These were transferred to the United Nations as of October 1946 and cover such broad subjects as communications and transit, economic and financial questions, the work of narcotic drug control, health questions, legal questions and those of a social and humanitarian character.

On 18 April, 1946, the 21st, and last, Assembly of the League of Nations adopted a resolution for the dissolution of this great international organiza-tion and a Board of Liquidation was appointed to give effect to the decisions in this resolution. The League Assembly of 1946 also adopted three resolutions concerning the assumption by the United Nations of functions, powers and activities hith-erto performed by the League. These resolutions deal with: (1) the transfer to the United Nations Secretariat of the original texts of treaties and international agreements, with the exception of the Conventions of the International Labour Organisation; (2) the assumption without interruption, by the United Nations or by Specialized Agencies of functions and powers performed by the League under international agreements of a technical and non-political character; and (3) the assumption by the United Nations of any non-political activities of the League which the United Nations might decide to undertake.

For the present study and for greater ease of comparison, the publications of the League of Nations and those of the United Nations may be divided into four main groups:

1. General periodical and serial publications;
2. Publications prepared by the Sections of the League of Nations Secretariat and by the substantive Departments of the United Nations Secretariat;
3. Document series issued by the principal organs of the League of Nations and the United Nations;
4. Studies and reports, or monographs.

SOURCE: Reprinted from: Marie J. Carroll, "League of Nations Documents and Publications Comparable with or Continued in United Nations Publications," *College and Research Libraries*, 13 (Jan. 1952) 45–52, 64.

It is obviously impossible to analyze these four categories in any detail in a paper of this sort, but attention should be directed to the continuance of the subject contents of some of the most important League of Nations publications in those now issued by the United Nations.

1. GENERAL PERIODICAL AND SERIAL PUBLICATIONS

The basic serial publication covering the activities of the two principal organs of the League of Nations—the Assembly and the Council—was the *Official Journal* and its Special Supplements; which first appeared in 1920 and was published as a monthly until March 1940. The Assembly or the Council could deal at its meetings "with any matter within the sphere of action of the League or affecting the peace of the world." Commencing with its 16th session in January 1922 and continuing to its 107th session in 1939 the Minutes of the Council were incorporated in the *Official Journal.* In the first two years, the edition was bilingual, English and French, but from January 1922 two separate editions were issued. The *Official Journal* also contained the texts of reports adopted by the Council, as well as the principal documents received or despatched by the Secretariat of the League.

The Assembly of the League met annually in ordinary session and could be convened in extraordinary or special sessions by request, accepted by a majority of the Member States. The *Records* of the first three sessions, 1920–1922, were published as a separate series. From the 4th to the 21st ordinary sessions (as well as the special sessions) the *Records,* which included the texts of the debates of the plenary meetings, the minutes of the committees, the resolutions adopted, and an index, appeared in the numbered series of *Official Journal, Special Supplements.*

Publications of the United Nations comparable with the Minutes of the League Council and the Records of Assemblies, though differing in form, and not classed as periodicals, are the *Official Records* of the five organs and the supplements and annexes thereto. These comprise five series: (1) the *Official Records* of the General Assembly, (2) of the Security Council, (3) of the Economic and Social Council, (4) of the Trusteeship Council and (5) of the Atomic Energy Commission.

The annual reports of the three Councils to the General Assembly of the United Nations are published as Supplements to the *Official Records of the General Assembly.*

The *Annual Report of the Secretary-General on the Work of the Organization,* published as a Supplement to the *Official Records of the General Assembly,* is a United Nations publication similar in scope to the annual report, with its supplement, made by the Secretary-General of the League of Nations to the Assembly on the work of the Council and the Secretariat, entitled *Reports on the Work of the League since the . . . Session of the Assembly,* which was issued in the numerical Assembly Documents series for each ordinary session.

Monthly Summary of the League of Nations and United Nations Bulletin

The *Monthly Summary of the League of Nations* contained a general survey of the work of the League and the Permanent Court of International Justice, including the text of the resolutions of the annual session of the Assembly. Important documents on a wide variety of subjects were printed as supplements at irregular intervals.

It was first issued by the Information Section of the Secretariat in April 1921 and appeared in six language editions: English, French, German, Italian, Spanish and Czech. The last issue is dated January–February 1940. The periodical which is comparable with the *Monthly Summary* is the *United Nations Bulletin,* published by the United Nations Department of Public Information twice each month. From August 1946 to December 1947 it was issued weekly under the title *United Nations Weekly Bulletin.* Each issue contains an authoritative account of the work of the Organization and the Specialized Agencies. Reports and analyses of the current activities of all the United Nations organs, as well as background articles, appear regularly. Special articles and statements by leading United Nations personalities surveying their particular work are featured. *The Bulletin,* which is currently issued in separate English, French and Spanish editions, is illustrated with photographs, charts and maps, and includes digests of United Nations meetings and a monthly calendar of international meetings.

Library Publications

Two periodicals have been continued in the same volume series by the United Nations Library at

Geneva under the same titles used for many years. They are the *Monthly List of Selected Articles,* which first appeared under that name in January 1930 and the *Monthly List of Books Catalogued in the Library of the League of Nations,* (now *United Nations*) Volume I of which appeared in January, 1928. At present both are issued for sale not monthly, in spite of their titles, but at intervals in the form of combined numbers.

The United Nations Headquarters Library at New York issues a monthly list of all books published in the current or the preceding year, which have been added to the library collections, entitled *New Publications in the United Nations Headquarters Library,* and also publishes irregularly a *Selected List of Periodical Articles in the United Nations Headquarters Library.*

2. PUBLICATIONS PREPARED BY SUBSTANTIVE DEPARTMENTS OF THE UNITED NATIONS OR SECTIONS OF THE LEAGUE OF NATIONS SECRETARIAT

The publications described below which emanate from departments of the Secretariat of the United Nations—the Department of Economic Affairs, the Department of Social Affairs, Department of Trusteeship and Information from Non-Self-Governing Territories and the Legal Department—may be classed as periodicals and serials. A number of these publications are, in effect, continuations of similar ones prepared by the various Sections of the Secretariat of the League of Nations, such as the Financial Section and Economic Intelligence Service, Economic Relations, Social Questions, Mandates, Legal, Communications and Transit, and Traffic in Opium and Other Dangerous Drugs.

Economics, Finance and Statistics

The Statistical Office of the United Nations, in the Department of Economic Affairs, compiles and publishes the *Monthly Bulletin of Statistics.* This compares with the same title begun in 1919 by the Supreme Economic Council and issued from 1921 through July 1946 by the League of Nations Economic Intelligence Service, and continued from August 1946 by the United Nations. The *Bulletin* keeps up to date the United Nations

Statistical Yearbook. Each issue of the *Bulletin* contains over 170 pages of tables and charts with data from more than 70 countries, with figures reduced to common units of measurement to facilitate international comparison. The text and explanatory notes appear in both English and French.

With the publication in 1949 of the first volume of the new series entitled *Statistical Yearbook,* the United Nations has taken up one of the most valuable traditions of the League of Nations. Its predecessor, the *International Statistical Year-Book 1926,* was first published by the League in 1927 and changed its name in 1931 to *Statistical Year-Book of the League of Nations.* Seventeen issues appeared, ending with the one dated 1942/44, published in 1945.

The Statistical Office of the United Nations has been able to improve upon the high standards set by the League and has enriched the contents. In the second issue published in 1950, international statistical data are presented from 250 countries and territories for the two decades 1930-1949, covering a wide variety of subjects.

A further collection of international demographic statistics, formerly published by the League of Nations in its *Monthly Bulletin of Statistics* and in the annual *Statistical Year-Book,* is now available in the *Demographic Yearbook* which is prepared by the Statistical Office of the United Nations in collaboration with the Department of Social Affairs. The volume for 1948 covers the available figures for all major countries and territories for the period 1932-47 and has a 50-page bibliography. The second issue appeared in 1951 and includes data for 1948 and 1949.

The Population Commission of the Economic and Social Council of the United Nations is continuing the series of *Population Studies* which were initiated by the Committee of Experts for the Study of Demographic Problems, appointed by the Council of the League of Nations on 16 January 1939.

The League of Nations Economic, Financial and Transit Department during the period of 1944-46, when it was on mission at Princeton, published studies on the economic demography of Europe and the Soviet Union.

In addition, the Statistical Office is continuing many other former League statistical publications in the field of international trade and balance of payments. For example, it has just issued the *Yearbook of International Trade Statistics 1950* which carries on the League publication, discon-

tinued in 1939, entitled *International Trade Statistics.*

The volume bearing the title of *Balance of Payments, 1939-1945*, while appearing under United
Nations imprint, was prepared by the Secretariat
of the League of Nations. It concludes the series
of balance-of-payments reviews begun by the
League in 1924 under the title *Memorandum on
Balance of Payments and Foreign Trade Balances,
1910-1923.* The work on the series, discontinued
during the war period, was resumed in the latter
part of 1945 by the League of Nations Economic,
Financial and Transit Department, (then at Princeton, N.J.), with a view to bringing out in one volume the information on balance of payments that
had become available since 1938, the last year
previously covered. The data which were available
by the middle of 1946 were largely completed
when the transfer to the United Nations of the
economic and statistical activities of the League of
Nations took place. Certain additional information has become available since the substantive
work on the volume was closed. Meanwhile, the
International Monetary Fund has begun collecting
information on post-war balances of payments.

In 1938 the League of Nations Committee of
Statistical Experts began studying the classification of international business transactions with a
view to the framing of a new model scheme. The
war interrupted the work, but in 1945 a draft
classification was ready and was circulated to governments for observations and comments in the
early part of 1946. This *Note on Balance of Payments Statistics* has been published by the United
Nations Statistical Office in the former League of
Nations series of *Studies and Reports on Statistical
Methods* as No. 7. Six issues have appeared with
League of Nations imprint and the series is being
continued by the United Nations under the same
title.

Annual Surveys

One of the most significant and widely used of
the annual surveys was the League of Nations
World Economic Survey, which numbered 11 volumes in the period 1927-1944. The subject matter is now covered in the United Nations *World
Economic Report* and in the special annual area
studies, such as the *Economic Survey of Europe,*
the *Economic Survey of Asia and the Far East,* the
Economic Survey of Latin America; and the *Review of Economic Conditions in the Middle East*

and the *Review of Economic Conditions in Africa,*
both of which have been issued as supplements to
the *World Economic Report 1949-50.*

These annual publications are supplemented by
the *Economic Bulletin for Europe* and the *Economic Bulletin for Asia and the Far East,* prepared
by the Economic Commission for Europe and the
Economic Commission for Asia and the Far East,
respectively. Three separate issues covering the
first, second and third quarters of the year are
published, providing a statistical summary and
periodic review; the analyses for the fourth quarter are included in the annual volume.

Additional statistical data on timber, steel and
coal may be found in the quarterly bulletin on
Timber Statistics, prepared jointly by the secretariats of the United Nations Economic Commission for Europe and the Food and Agriculture Organization of the United Nations; in the *Quarterly
Bulletin of Steel Statistics for Europe;* and in the
Monthly Bulletin of Coal Statistics, both of which
are issued by the secretariat of the Economic Commission for Europe in bilingual English-French editions.

Transport and Communications

The Communications and Transit Organisation
of the League of Nations had the task of studying
measures likely to ensure the freedom of communications and transit by land and sea, on navigable
waterways and in the air, and to co-ordinate the
work of the numerous international bodies dealing
with these questions. It carried on these functions
through (1) general and special conferences; (2) an
Advisory and Technical Committee; (3) the Communications and Transit Section of the League
Secretariat; (4) Permanent Committees; and
(5) Temporary Committees.

The comparable work under United Nations auspices may be found in the reports of the Transport
and Communications Commission (a functional
commission of the Economic and Social Council)
which are published as Supplements to the *Official
Records of the Economic and Social Council* and
in the *Transport and Communication Review,*
quarterly publication of the Division of Transport
and Communications of the United Nations Department of Economic Affairs. *The Review* serves
as a medium for the publication of special studies
and information on the co-ordination of the work
and activities of various international agencies con-

cerned with transport and communications. The first number was issued in 1948 and superseded the *Monthly Summary of Important Events in the Field of Transport and Communications* (first published by the League of Nations in separate English and French editions).

In 1950, the Transport Division of the secretariat of the Economic Commission for Europe published the first volume of the *Annual Bulletin of Transport Statistics, 1949,* which is a general review of the transport situation in Europe with special reference to the volume of traffic, networks of inland transport, mobile equipment, etc. The statistical information in this annual is an expansion of figures given in the League of Nations *Statistical Year-Book.*

The United Nations has convened in the past two years a series of conferences on maritime transport, road and motor transport, customs conventions on touring, etc., which have resulted in international conventions either amending or carrying forward the work begun in similar conferences under the League of Nations.

A revision was made by the United Nations in 1948 of the valuable compilation published in 1945 by the Communications and Transit Section of the League of Nations Secretariat, entitled *List of Multilateral Conventions, Agreements, etc. Relating to Transport and Communications Questions.*

Social Welfare Publications

The publications covering social questions, formerly issued as *Annual Reports* by the League of Nations Advisory Committee on Social Questions and by the Child Welfare Information Centre, are continued by the United Nations Social Commission and the Department of Social Affairs of the United Nations Secretariat. Under the terms of the international conventions on traffic in women and children and the suppression of the circulation of obscene publications, the League of Nations received annual reports from governments on violations of these agreements. The *Summary of Annual Reports on Traffic in Women and Children* and the *Summary of Annual Reports on Traffic in Obscene Publications* are prepared by the United Nations Department of Social Affairs.

The former publication of the League of Nations Child Welfare Information Centre entitled *Summary of the Legislative and Administrative Series*

of Documents now appears as a United Nations publication, which summarizes the texts of legislation passed during the year, and the annual reports on child and youth welfare submitted by governments. It now bears the title *Annual Report on Child and Youth Welfare.* The first issue under its new title, placed on sale, covered information received between 1 April 1947 and 31 March 1948.

The reports of the sessions of the Social Commission, whose functions may be regarded as comparable with those of the League of Nations Advisory Committee on Social Questions, are published as Supplements to the *Official Records of the Economic and Social Council.*

Narcotic Drug Control

The United Nations Commission on Narcotics Drugs has undertaken the preparatory work on the replacement of the eight international conventions on narcotic drugs by a single agreement which would strengthen and simplify the international control of the drug traffic. The first of these conventions was signed at The Hague on 23 January 1912 and the others resulted from international conferences held in the years 1925, 1931 and 1936 under League of Nations auspices. The United Nations Commission on Narcotic Drugs replaces the former League of Nations Advisory Committee on Traffic in Opium and Other Dangerous Drugs and makes its reports to the Economic and Social Council. These are printed as Supplements to the *Official Records of the Council.* The Commission continues the League publication of the *Summary of Annual Reports of Governments,* and also the *Summary of Illicit Transactions and Seizures* reported to the Secretariat of the United Nations.

The two other bodies dealing with the control of traffic in drugs—the Permanent Central Opium Board, set up by the League of Nations Council in December 1928 under the Geneva Convention of 1925, and the Drug Supervisory Body, provided for in the 1931 Convention—continue to submit their reports to the Economic and Social Council, namely: *Statistics of Narcotics and the Work of the Board* and the annual statement by the Drug Supervisory Board entitled *Estimated World Requirements of Narcotic Drugs.*

The Commission on Narcotic Drugs has been responsible for carrying on the work of the League Secretariat by the publication of the *Annual Summary of Laws and Regulations Relating to Control of Narcotic Drugs.*

In October 1949, the first issue of the *Bulletin on Narcotics,* a quarterly prepared by the Division of Narcotic Drugs of the United Nations Secretariat, was published in separate English and French editions. This periodical contains technical and scientific studies on narcotic drugs, articles on legislation and administration in various countries, and a bibliography of current literature.

Trusteeship Publications

The international trusteeship system set up under Chapters XII and XIII of the Charter of the United Nations supersedes the mandates system provided for by the terms of Article 22 of the Covenant of the League of Nations, which was designed to secure the well-being and development of the peoples in the territories who have not yet attained their independence or self-government. A Permanent Mandates Commission, consisting of experts, was constituted by the League Council to receive and examine the annual reports submitted by the governments which had received the mandates for these territories at the close of World War I. This examination was recorded in the published *Minutes of the Commission.*

Nine trusteeship agreements covering the former mandated territories in Africa and the Pacific were approved by the General Assembly of the United Nations in 1946. In 1947 the Security Council approved a trusteeship agreement for the strategic area of the Pacific Islands under United States administration—the Marshalls, Marianas and Carolines—formerly under Japanese mandate.

The approval of the trusteeship agreements made possible the formation of the Trusteeship Council which operates under the authority of the General Assembly and assists it in carrying out functions under these agreements. The Trusteeship Council also assists the Security Council with respect to strategic areas under trusteeship. An annual report, based on a questionnaire prepared by the Trusteeship Council, is required from the administrative authorities for each trust territory. These reports continue the series issued as government documents, not League of Nations publications, by the mandatory States.

The Trusteeship Council now examines these annual reports and issues *Official Records* which are comparable with the *Minutes of the Permanent Mandates Commission* of the League of Nations. Resolutions and reports of visiting missions to these territories appear in the Supplements. Reports of the Trusteeship Council to the General Assembly are issued as *supplements* to the *Official Records* of the General Assembly.

The texts of the League of Nations mandates were re-published by the United Nations in 1946 and the Trusteeship Agreements for nine territories were placed on sale in 1947.

Legal Publications

The Legal Department of the United Nations Secretariat, among its many other functions, maintains liaison with the International Court of Justice; carries on research work; prepares studies and memoranda to facilitate the work of the International Law Commission in the field of development and codification; prepares publications consisting of judicial reports, collections of agreements and collections of national legislation. Under the terms of Article 102 of the Charter of the United Nations it is responsible for the registration, recording and publication of treaties and agreements, which are printed in the United Nations *Treaty Series.*

This series is, in effect, a continuation of the League *Treaty Series,* published for more than 25 years and containing 205 volumes and 9 general indexes. The texts of the treaties and international agreements are published in their original languages, and English and French translations are provided when the official texts are not in these languages.

Each volume of the United Nations Treaty Series is divided into two parts. The first part contains treaties and international agreements registered with the Secretariat by States Members of the United Nations since 24 October 1945, and the second part contains instruments filed and recorded.

In order to avoid any gap between the last volume of the League of Nations *Treaty Series* and the first of the United Nations series, the Secretary-General invited the Members of the United Nations and the non-Member States to transmit to him for filing and publication all treaties and international agreements which had been entered into prior to the date of entry into force of the Charter on 24 October 1945, and not previously published in the League of Nations *Treaty Series.*

More than 50 volumes, containing some 1000 treaties and agreements, have been published to date. General index volumes for each 15 volumes will be published in English and French editions; two have appeared to date.

Two other publications for which the Legal Section of the League Secretariat was responsible have been brought up to date by the Legal Department of the United Nations. The first volume of a series which will report periodically on the status of international conventions and agreements, for which the Secretary-General of the United Nations acts as depository, has been published under the title of *Signatures, Ratifications, Acceptances, Accessions, etc. Concerning the Multilateral Conventions and Agreements, etc.* Formerly this information was published annually in a list in the League of Nations *Official Journal, Special Supplement.*

The study of arbitration conventions and security treaties, issued by the League in 1927, has been published under practically the same title, and reproduces in full, in chronological order, the texts of treaties concluded from 1928–1948. This *Systematic Survey of Treaties of the Pacific Settlement of International Disputes* contains an analysis of the provisions of over 200 treaties dealing with procedures and machinery.

3. DOCUMENTS SERIES OF ORGANS OF THE LEAGUE OF NATIONS AND THE UNITED NATIONS

The two most important and most comprehensive series of documents issued by the League of Nations were the so-called C.M. and A. Series. The first designation included all documents circulated to the Council of the League and to the Member States. They were numbered in sequence of circulation for each calendar year, and included both mimeographed documents circulated within the League organs and those printed and placed on public sale.

The Assembly documents, or A. series, were issued in numerical sequence for each Assembly in the order of publication date and have the number, assigned to a particular document, in Arabic numerals, after the "A," the year of the Assembly (if extraordinary session, the abbreviation Extr. followed), and the Roman numeral of the Section of the Secretariat responsible for its publication, or indicative of its subject matter.

The series of abbreviations used as document symbols on some 757 additional series was based to a large extent on the French name of the Committee, Commission, etc., from which it emanated. These were issued in sequence without regard to year of publication. An explanation of these symbols together with a list of those which appeared on sales publications from 1920–1936 will be found in Carroll's *Key to League of Nations Documents Placed on Public Sale* (5 vols., 1930–1938).

The comparable series in United Nations documentation are identifiable as Security Council or S/ documents in the general series of the Security Council, and the A/ documents in the general series of the General Assembly. Document numbers are assigned in a continuous numerical order in the same series in accordance with the order of registration with the United Nations Bureau of Documents. Three other series appear as a basic symbol of an organ on United Nations documents: E/ for the Economic and Social Council; T/ for the Trusteeship Council; and AEC/ for the Atomic Energy Commission.

The League of Nations documents issued by its Economic Committee bore the symbol E. and the Permanent Mandates Commission which was superseded by the Trusteeship Council used the symbol C.P.M. (Commission permanente des mandats).

Symbols Compared

In addition to the general series of the main organs of the United Nations there are many other series which are designated by adding the symbols for committees or commissions, subcommittees or subcommissions, regional and special bodies to the basic symbol, which forms the first part of the symbols of all subseries. Within each of the five general series a document presented to the principal organ for consideration, or issued by it, is identified by an Arabic numeral following the symbol. For instance, A/800 is the 800th document in the General Assembly series.

Numbering of Sales Publications

The numbering of the sales publications, begun by the League of Nations in 1926, has been continued by the United Nations with some additions in the Roman numeral classification used to denote note subject fields. Thirteen Roman numerals in addition to "General" appeared on League publications, whereas the United Nations publications offered for sale have categories I to XVII. The general publications of the United Nations which include rules of procedure, lists of delegations to the General Assembly, publications of the Department of Public Information, etc. are issued in category I. Every sales publication, except *Official Records,* the *Treaty Series,* and the various periodicals, carries on the inside front cover or on the reverse of the title page, a box containing "United Nations Publications. Sales No.: . . ., the year of publication, the category number of the publication (in Roman numerals) and the number of the publication within the category (in Arabic numerals)." Thus, 1951.IV.1 indicates that this publication was the first issued in category IV (Social Welfare Publications) for the year 1951. The official document symbol and date of registration should not be confused with the "Sales Number." The Department of Public Information assigns "sales numbers" comparable with the "Series of League of Nations Publications" used on publications offered for sale in 1926 and thereafter by the League.

All of the League of Nations category numbers were used for United Nations publications, but some categories have been subdivided and four new sales categories were added. The following chart may be of interest in a comparison of the two systems of sales publication numbers.

Language Editions

The majority of League of Nations documents were printed in English and French editions, the two official languages. Some were issued in bilingual form and a very limited number of studies on economic and financial subjects were translated into Spanish.

The official languages of the United Nations are five in number: Chinese, English, French, Russian and Spanish. The working languages for most of the organs and subsidiary bodies, including the International Court of Justice and the Secretariat, are English and French, but the working languages of the General Assembly are English, French and Spanish; those of the Economic Commission for Europe are English, French and Russian, and those of the Economic Commission for Latin America are English, French and Spanish.

CATEGORIES OF DOCUMENTS WITH SALES NUMBER DESIGNATIONS

League of Nations		United Nations	
General		I.	General
I A.	Administrative Commissions		
I B.	Minorities		
II A.	Economic & Financial	II A.	Economic Stability & Employment Studies
II B.	Economic Relations	II B.	Economic Development Studies
		II C.	Economic Reports
		II D.	Trade, Financial & Commercial Studies
		II E.	Report of the Economic Commission for Europe
		II F.	Report of the Economic Commission for Asia and Far East
		II G.	Report of the Economic Commission for Latin America
III.	Health	III.	Health Publications
IV.	Social Questions	IV.	Social Welfare Publications
V.	Legal	V.	Legal Publications
VI A.	Mandates	VI A.	Trusteeship Publications
VI B.	Slavery	VI B.	Studies and Reports on Non-Self-Governing Territories
VII.	Political	VII.	Publications on Political Affairs
VIII.	Communications & Transit	VIII.	Transport & Communications Publications
IX.	Disarmament	IX.	Publications on Atomic Energy and Armaments Control
X.	Financial Administration	X.	Publications on International Administration
XI.	Traffic in Opium and Other Dangerous Drugs	XI.	Publications on Narcotic Drugs
XII A.	Intellectual Cooperation	XII.	Publications on Educational, Scientific and Cultural Affairs
XII B.	International Bureaux		
XIII.	Refugees	XIII.	Demographic Publications
		XIV.	Human Rights Publications
		XV.	Relief and Rehabilitation Publications
		XVI.	Fiscal Publications
		XVII.	Statistical Publications

The *Official Records* eventually appear in each of the five official languages. Until the latter part of 1949 the *Official Records* of the General Assembly, the Economic and Social Council, and the Trusteeship Council appeared in bilingual English-French editions and in separate monolingual editions in the three other official languages; now they appear in monolingual editions in each of the official languages. The *Official Records* of the Security Council and of the Atomic Energy Commission continue to appear in a bilingual English-French edition and separate Chinese, Russian and Spanish editions.

Catalog Cards

Over 300 American public and university libraries have acquired, through global subscription, collections of League of Nations documents placed on sale, which included the Records of the Assembly, Minutes of the Council and printed reports of committees and commissions, as well as periodicals, research studies and documents of conferences.

The Library of Congress has printed catalog cards for both the sale and non-sale publications. In 1921 the Catalog and Card Division of the Library of Congress began to supply cards for periodicals and documents available to libraries, but not until October 1945, through a grant from the Rockefeller Foundation to the Woodrow Wilson Memorial Library was it possible to undertake the cataloging of the thousands of documents issued in mimeographed form. A cooperative cataloging arrangement was made by the Woodrow Wilson Memorial Library with the Library of Congress and continued until February 1950 when the project was completed at a cost of $60,000. The United Nations Library received in June 1950 as the generous gift of the Woodrow Wilson Foundation this comprehensive card Catalog and its collection of League of Nations documents.

Catalog cards are now available from the Library of Congress for some serials and printed publications of the United Nations.

League Publications on Sale

The great majority of the publications of the League of Nations are still in print and are available through the United Nations. Catalogs cover-

ing the period 1920-1946 may be obtained by writing to the Sales and Circulation Section, United Nations, New York. The mimeographed documents of the League of Nations were not placed on sale. The unrestricted mimeographed documents of the United Nations, however, may be obtained on an annual global subscription through the Sales and Circulation Section. The United Nations publications are available in 58 countries through 63 official sales agents or co-operating bookshops. The official sales agent in the United States is the International Documents Service, Columbia University Press, 2960 Broadway, New York 27, N.Y.[2]

4. STUDIES AND REPORTS, OR MONOGRAPHS

The studies and reports prepared by the Secretariat of the United Nations cover to a large extent the same subject fields, or a development of them, as those issued under the League of Nations imprint.

In addition to the serial publications discussed above, the following types of printed publications have been made available in League of Nations documentation: proceedings of international conferences including conventions, agreements, etc.; reports on a wide variety of topics submitted to these conferences, or to Member States for comment and observations, and special studies or inquiries requested by the Assembly and Council of the League of Nations. In view of the fact that space does not permit a more detailed comparison by title of these valuable contributions of the League of Nations to an understanding of international problems with those issued by the United Nations, it may be stated briefly that the counterpart of such studies or monographs can readily be found in the catalogs issued by the United Nations Department of Public Information describing publications offered for sale, 1945-48-49-50.

It must also be noted that many of the activities and publications of the League of Nations are not continued by the United Nations but have been assumed by the Specialized Agencies, which make annual reports to the Economic and Social Council on their work. These specialized agencies cover such fields as international labor relations, food and agriculture, educational, scientific and cultural problems, civil aviation, monetary, economic reconstruction and development questions, postal communications, telecommunications, refugee and displaced persons, international trade, meteorology, and world health.

Each of these agencies issues its own publica- tions and no attempt is made in this paper to describe the continuance by them of former League periodicals or documents series, or to trace their ancestors in the League of Nations publications.

NOTES

[1] Paper presented at meeting of Public Documents Committee, A.L.A., July 12, 1951, Chicago.
[2] The present official sales agency is: UNIPUB, 650 First Avenue, P.O. Box 433, New York, N.Y. 10016.

Publications of the United Nations[1]

José Meyer

This article explains the steps leading to the founding of the United Nations. The major documents emanating from the preparatory conferences and commissions are listed.

There were four stages in the establishment of the United Nations as an organization. The *first* includes a series of preliminary steps which began with the Moscow Declaration of the Foreign Ministers of China, the Soviet Union, the United Kingdom, and the United States in October 1943.[2]

This stage was completed when the Dumbarton Oaks Proposals, which were agreed to in October 1944, were supplemented by decisions made at Yalta in the Crimea by President Roosevelt, Prime Minister Churchill, and Marshal Stalin in February 1945, in regard to the voting procedure in the proposed Security Council and the place and date for a general United Nations conference to prepare a charter for a permanent world organization.

The end of the *second* stage was reached at San Francisco on June 26, 1945, when fifty nations signed the United Nations Charter and established the Preparatory Commission.

Seven weeks later the *third* stage began in London with the opening session of the Executive Committee on Aug. 16, 1945, and closed October 27 of the same year with the adoption of its report.

The *fourth* stage is represented by the work of the Preparatory Commission in London, Nov. 24-Dec. 23, 1945.

The document which served as the starting point for the United Nations is known as the Dumbarton Oaks Proposals, a tentative plan for a world organization drafted in the autumn of 1944 after informal exploratory discussions by representatives of China, the Soviet Union, the United Kingdom, and the United States, for consideration by their governments and subsequent submission to all the United Nations.

All together, there were four separate official editions of these proposals:

Dumbarton Oaks Documents on International Organization. [Washington, D.C., Government Printing Office, 1944.] 22p. (Department of State Publication 2192, Conference Series 56).

Dumbarton Oaks Documents on International Organization: together with Chart and Questions and Answers. [Washington, D.C., Government Printing Office, 1944.] 22p. (Department of State Publication 2223, Conference Series 60). A reprint combining two previously printed pamphlets, *i.e.,* the foregoing title, and *Questions and Answers on the Dumbarton Oaks Proposals,* issued as Publication 2218, Conference Series 58.

The United Nations: Dumbarton Oaks Proposals for a General International Organization, to Be the Subject of the United Nations Conference at San Francisco, April 25, 1945. [Washington, D.C., Government Printing Office, 1945.] 8p. including chart. (Department of State Publication 2297. Conference Series 66).

The United Nations: Dumbarton Oaks Proposals for a General International Organization. (For the use of the delegates). [Washington, D.C., Government Printing Office, 1945.] 22p. At head of title: The United Nations Conference on International Organization. General. Dec. 1. G.T. Interlined, lines numbered.

One of the provisions of the Dumbarton Oaks Proposals called for an International Court of Justice as principal judicial organ of the new organization. A draft statute for this court was prepared for submission to the United Nations Conference at San Francisco by the United

SOURCE: Reprinted from José Meyer, "Publications of the United Nations," *College and Research Libraries,* 7 (Oct., 1946) pp. 311–318.

Nations Committee of Jurists, a group of legal experts from forty-three countries who met in Washington, Apr. 9-20, 1945, under the chairmanship of Green H. Hackworth of the State Department. Its records consist of eighty-seven mimeographed documents numbered consecutively throughout, Jurist I to Jurist 87. These are of two kinds: summary reports of the thirteen meetings, and draft proposals submitted by delegations and various draft statutes. The final document, *Report on Draft of Statute of an International Court of Justice,* was submitted to the United Nations Conference at San Francisco, and was known as Jurist 86 (in English) and Jurist 87 (in French). These documents, with the exception of the Chinese, Russian, and Spanish texts of the draft statute, were reproduced as Volume XIV of the UNIO-LC edition of the San Francisco documents.[3]

PRECONFERENCE PUBLICATIONS

On the eve of the conference, the State Department issued two pamphlets in the now familiar "Stettinius blue" covers. One was a guide to the conference entitled *Guide: The United Nations Conference on International Organization, San Francisco, 1945.* [Washington, D.C., Government Printing Office, 1945.] 28p. The other, an oblong album, consisted of a set of charts and pictographs with some explanatory text, showing the structure and functions of the proposed organization and of its organs. There were Chinese, English, French, Russian, and Spanish editions.[4]

The original documentation of the United Nations Conference on International Organization has been fully and expertly described by Nelle Marie Signor, librarian of the History and Political Science Library, University of Illinois, in *Special Libraries* 37:3-6, January 1946. A few additional comments only, based on the experience gained in preparing these documents for publication, may be made here.

The consecutive numbers assigned to the documents run from 1 to 1216. There were two lists:

Document 1184: Cumulative List of Documents Issued During the United-Nations Conference on International Organization. 101p.
Document 1216: [List of documents arranged by symbol.] 110p.

When using these lists, however, caution should

be exercised, as they were found to be inaccurate in places. This is especially true of the listing of various language editions which often does not correspond to actual fact. Also, the titles given do not always correspond to the titles of the documents themselves. Another point worthy of mention is the discrepancy frequently found between the English and French versions of a document.

There is further a most helpful chapter:

"Conference Documentation and Records" in *Charter of the United Nations: Commentary and Documents* by Leland M. Goodrich and Edvard Hambro. (Boston, World Peace Foundation, 1946, p. 16-18.)

DOCUMENTATION OF CONFERENCE

The entire documentation of the conference, as rehearsed upon the recommendation of the Secretariat in the final plenary session, June 25, 1945, was published by the United Nations Information Organizations, New York and London, in cooperation with the Library of Congress in photo-offset in fifteen volumes. In this edition the documents are arranged in logical order, by commissions, committees, and subcommittees. Each volume is preceded by a table of contents listing all the documents included, together with a finding list by symbol which indicates the location of any document in any volume. Only English and French texts are included, except in Volume IV, where proposed amendments to the Dumbarton Oaks Proposals in the original Spanish, Portuguese, or Russian are included. An index to the fifteen volumes has been prepared but has not yet been published.

The original edition of the Charter has a bibliographically interesting story. How and by whom the text in five languages was printed, how many copies were printed on treaty paper, how the deadline for the signing ceremony had to be met in spite of continual changes almost up to the last minute, is told in detail by Samuel L. Farquhar, manager of the University of California Press, originally in the *Publisher's Weekly* of July 7 and 14, 1945, in two papers entitled "Printing the United Nations Charter" and "Binding the Atlantic [*i.e.,* United Nations] Charter," respectively, and later in book form *Printing the United Nations Charter.* (Berkeley, University of California Press, 1946, 56p.).

CHARTER

Immediately after the close of the conference, the State Department arranged for a large printing of the text of the Charter for mass distribution. This was the pocket edition:

Charter of the United Nations, Together with the Statute of the International Court . . . Signed at the United Nations Conference on International Organization, San Francisco, Calif., June 26, 1945. [Washington, D.C., Government Printing Office, 1945.] 58p. (Department of State Publication 2353, Conference Series 74).

Simultaneously, a facsimile edition of the original Charter in five languages with the signatures affixed at San Francisco was printed and placed on sale:

Facsimile of the Charter of the United Nations, Statute of the International Court of Justice and Interim Arrangements, in Five Languages. Signed at the United Nations Conference on International Organization, San Francisco, California, June 26, 1945. [Washington, D.C., Government Printing Office, 1945.] Various paging. (Department of State Publication 2368, Conference Series 76).

An excellent over-all account of the background of the San Francisco Conference and the drafting of the Charter, primarily from the American point of view, can be found in the so-called Stettinius report:

Charter of the United Nations. Report to the President on the Results of the San Francisco Conference, by the Chairman of the United States Delegation, the Secretary of State, June 26, 1945. [Washington, D.C., Government Printing Office, 1945.] 266p. (Department of State Publication 2349, Conference Series 71).

This contains, as appendices, the text of the San Francisco Charter and on opposite pages the text of the corresponding Dumbarton Oaks Proposals, with a key to chapters and paragraphs; the text of the Statute of the International Court of Justice; the text of the Interim Arrangements; a list of delegations; the complete composition of the U.S. delegation including consultants; and a chart of the organization.

INTERIM ARRANGEMENTS

A separate edition of the Interim Arrangements was issued by the State Department in the Conference Series, uniform with the pocket edition of the Charter:

Interim Arrangements, Concluded by the Governments Represented at the United Nations Conference on International Organization, San Francisco, California, June 26, 1945. Washington, D.C., Government Printing Office, 1945. 4p. (Department of State Publication 2357, Conference Series 75).

This agreement called for the establishment of a Preparatory Commission of the United Nations, consisting of all the members of the organization, and entrusted it with certain duties. The commission was to function until the Charter came into force and the United Nations was established.

The first meeting of the Preparatory Commission, purely formal in character, was held in San Francisco on June 27, 1945. The documentary record of this meeting consists of two documents, the *Agenda* and the *Summary Report*, both issued in photo-offset from typed copy.

The Executive Committee held its first meeting in London, Aug. 16, 1945, and during nine weeks of intensive labor proceeded to carry out the recommendations provided for in the terms of reference of the Preparatory Commission. For this purpose, it set up ten technical committees dealing with the various organs of the United Nations, financial arrangements, relations with specialized agencies, the winding up of the League of Nations, and general questions such as selection of the site. By Oct. 27, 1945, the reports of the ten committees had been approved by the Executive Committee and had been assembled into a single 144-page document entitled:

Report by the Executive Committee to the Preparatory Commission of the United Nations. [London] Preparatory Commission of the United Nations. [H. M. Stationery Office] 1945. 144p. (PC/EX/113/Rev. 1, Nov. 12, 1945).

The current documentation of the Executive Committee was in the form of mimeographed papers not available for public distribution.

In the meantime, the Charter of the United Nations had become a part of the law of nations when, on Oct. 24, 1945, the Soviet Government deposited its instrument of ratification with the State Department, thereby achieving the required number of ratifications to make the organization operative.

PREPARATORY COMMISSION

The full Preparatory Commission, consisting of the delegates of the fifty-one United Nations, convened in London on Nov. 24 and completed its work on Dec. 23, 1945. The Executive Committee became the Steering Committee of the Preparatory Commission. The report of the Executive Committee was taken as the basis for the work of the commission and was apportioned for detailed consideration among eight technical committees: (1) General Assembly, (2) Security Council, (3) Economic and Social, (4) Trusteeship, (5) Legal Questions, (6) Administrative and Budgetary Matters, (7) League of Nations, (8) General Questions. In addition to these, there were also a number of special committees and subcommittees and a drafting committee. Not all the recommendations of the Executive Committee were adopted, still others were supplemented, a few were the subject of discussion. The result of these debates, primarily in the form of recommendations, was incorporated in the report which was adopted Dec. 23, 1945:

Report of the Preparatory Commission of the United Nations. [London, H. M. Stationery Office] 1945. 151p.

The report also contains draft provisional staff regulations, the provisional rules of procedure for the General Assembly, the Security Council, the Economic and Social Council, and the Trusteeship Council; also the draft agenda for the first meetings of these bodies, with the exception of the Trusteeship Council.

The original documents of the Preparatory Commission consist of:

(a) A printed *Journal,* no. 1–27, Nov. 24-Dec. 28, 1945, English and French in parallel columns, including in the form of supplements, the summary records of meetings of the eight technical committees.

(b) A printed *Handbook,* Nov. 23, 1945, containing a list of the delegates and their staffs and of the Secretariat officials and staff. Revised edition, Nov. 24, 1945. The latter

was published also in French as Commission Préparatoire des Nations Unies. Manuel, édition révisée.

(c) Mimeographed reports and documents identified by symbols corresponding to the above-mentioned committees and subcommittees. These were not available to anyone except the delegations and the Secretariat. The more important ones, however, are included in their final form in the report of the Preparatory Commission.

At the close of the meetings, the *Journal* and its supplements containing the summary records of the meetings of the eight technical committees, together with the list of delegates, were reprinted in nine parts as:

United Nations. *Journal of the Preparatory Commission, 24 November–24 December 1945.* London, Church House, Westminster [Printed and published by H. M. Stationery Office, 1946] 146p. in double columns, 3s.6d.

—Committee 1: General Assembly. *Summary Record of Meetings, 24 November–24 December 1945.* 55p. 1s.3d.

—Committee 2: Security Council. *Summary Record of Meetings, 24 November–24 December 1945.* 30p. 1s.3d.

—Committee 3: Economic and Social. *Summary Record of Meetings, 24 November–24 December 1945.* 30p. 1s.3d.

—Committee 4: Trusteeship. *Summary Record of Meetings, 24 November–24 December 1945.* 41p. 1s.3d.

—Committee 5: Legal Questions. *Summary Record of Meetings, 24 November–24 December 1945.* 19p. 1s.3d.

—Committee 6: Administrative and Budgetary. *Summary Record of Meetings, 24 November–24 December 1945.* 56p. 1s.3d.

—Committee 7: League of Nations. *Summary Record of Meetings, 24 November–24 December 1945.* 16p. 1s.3d.

—Committee 8: General Questions. *Summary Records of Meetings, 24 November–24 December 1945.* 70p. 1s.3d.

The General Assembly met in London at Central Hall, Westminster, Jan. 10–Feb. 13, 1946. It was attended by delegates from all the fifty-one United Nations. On January 11 six main committees were set up to carry out the work of the General Assembly: (1) Committee on Political Security, (2) Economic and Financial Committee, (3) Social,

Humanitarian, and Cultural Committee, (4) Trusteeship Committee, (5) Administrative and Budgetary Committee, (6) Legal Committee.

The report of the Preparatory Commission was the basic document before the assembly.

GENERAL ASSEMBLY DOCUMENTS

The documentation of the General Assembly consists of a printed *Journal* which includes, as supplements, the summary records of meetings of the six main committees and two *ad hoc* committees set up to deal with specific questions regarding the League of Nations. The first part of the first session of the General Assembly was covered by *Journal*, No. 1–34, Jan. 10–Mar. 7, 1946. The *Journal* was printed and placed on sale by H. M. Stationery Office at 6d. per number. *Journal*, No. 34, which was compiled after the close of the meetings, contains the text of the resolutions adopted on the reports of the six main committees, on the report of the Committee on the League of Nations, on the report of the Permanent Headquarters Committee, and on the proposals of the General Committee. These resolutions include, in the form of annexes, such documents as the terms of appointment of the secretary-general, the organization of the Secretariat, the recommendations of the Technical Advisory Committee on Information concerning the policies, functions, and organization of the Department of Public Information, the provisional staff regulations, budgetary and financial arrangements, a convention on the privileges and immunities of the United Nations, etc. Two other printed documents have emanated from the General Assembly:

United Nations. *Provisional Rules of Procedure for the General Assembly.* London [H. M. Stationery Office] 1946. 17p.
United Nations. *First Session of the General Assembly* [*Handbook*]. London [H. M. Stationery Office] Jan. 10, 1946. 88p. fold. plans.
–Revised edition, February 1946.

A convenient account of the work achieved by the General Assembly in January and February of 1946 will be found in:

The United States and the United Nations. Report of the United States Delegation to the

First Part of the First Session of the General Assembly of the United Nations. London, England, Jan. 10–Feb. 14, 1946. Submitted to the President of the United States by the Secretary of State . . . Mar. 1, 1946. Washington, D.C., Government Printing Office, 1946. 54p.

The General Assembly proceeded on Jan. 12, 1946, to the election of the six nonpermanent members to sit on the Security Council in addition to the five permanent members—China, France, the Soviet Union, the United Kingdom, and the United States. The way was thus open for the first meeting of the Security Council which took place on Jan. 17, 1946, at Church House, Westminster.

In the course of twenty-three meetings lasting until February 16, the council transacted procedural business. Since the council functions continuously, the first meeting to be held at Hunter College in the Bronx, after the members of the council and the Secretariat had established themselves in New York, was numbered the twenty-fourth.

SECURITY COUNCIL RECORDS

The records of the Security Council consist of the *Journal,* which like the journals of the Preparatory Commission and of the General Assembly is in English and French in parallel columns. Nos. 1–16, Jan. 18–Mar. 1, 1946, were published in London and printed by H. M. Stationery Office. Single issues were available for 6d. each.

The first *Journal* issued in the United States was Number 17 and dated Mar. 25, 1946. Beginning with this number, all important documents mentioned in the text of discussions are printed in the *Journal.*

To date, there have been two editions of the following:

Security Council of the United Nations, New York. *Provisional Handbook, March 1946.* 41p. Mimeographed.
– Apr. 30, 1946. Supersedes the above-mentioned earlier edition.

The *Handbook* contains certain useful information on location of offices and available services and facilities, a list of the delegates and their staffs, and a list of the personnel of the Secretariat. It is planned to publish frequent revisions, possibly monthly editions.

In accordance with the terms of the Charter, the eighteen members of the Economic and Social Council were elected by the General Assembly on Jan. 14, 1946. The council held its first meeting on Jan. 23, 1946, at Church House in London. During this first session, thirteen meetings in all were held in London, the last one on Feb. 18, 1946. The second session opened at Hunter College in the Bronx on May 25, 1946.

COMMISSIONS

As proposed by the Preparatory Commission, the council established a Commission on Human Rights, including a Subcommission on the Status of Women; an Economic and Employment Commission; a Statistical Commission; a Temporary Social Commission; a Temporary Transport and Communications Commission; and a Commission on Narcotic Drugs. The council further set up a Negotiating Committee to contact the specialized agencies and decided to convene an International Health Conference to be held by June 20, 1946, and an International Conference on Trade and Employment in the latter part of 1946. In accordance with the General Assembly's recommendations, a Committee on Refugees and Displaced Persons was appointed, which met in London during April 1946.

The record of deliberations and work achieved by the Economic and Social Council is embodied in its *Journal.* The first session of the council is covered by Numbers 1-12, Jan. 25-Apr. 10, 1946. All but No. 12 were printed in London by H. M. Stationery Office and placed on sale at 6d. per copy. No. 12 was issued in New York and contains the text of resolutions adopted for these journals. While those of the Security Council are yellow, the journals of the first session of the Economic and Social Council are printed on pink paper, and those of the second session on blue paper. The journals of the General Assembly are white. The first journal covering the second session now being held is numbered 13 and is dated May 22, 1946.

INTERNATIONAL COURT

With the election of the fifteen judges of the International Court of Justice in February 1946 by the Security Council and the General Assembly

sitting separately in plenary sessions, the court, one of the main organs of the United Nations, was established. Its seat, like that of its predecessor, the Permanent Court of International Justice, is in The Hague. A first session, mainly organizational in character, took place in April 1946. For a well-documented account of the drafting of the court's statute covering the work of the United Nations Committee of Jurists in Washington and of Committee IV/1 of the San Francisco Conference, see the following:

Preuss, Lawrence. "The International Court of Justice and the Problem of Compulsory Jurisdiction." In *Department of State Bulletin* 13:471-78, Sept. 30, 1945.

Thus all the main divisions of the United Nations, with the exception of the Trusteeship Council, have come into existence. It was fully realized in the preparatory stages that this body could not be set up at the first assembly since the Charter provides that prior to the formation of the council a number of territories must have been placed under the trusteeship system. It is possible that the council will be established during the second part of the first session of the General Assembly to be held in September 1946.

PROSPECTIVE PUBLICATIONS

The Official Record is to be issued some time after the closing of each session. It will consist of the official verbatim text of the proceedings and their translations, together with the text of all relevant documents. It will be issued in five separate editions, in Chinese, English, French, Russian, and Spanish.

Then, there will be the annual report of the secretary-general, a basic document which, it is expected, will become available each year about the time of the General Assembly session in September.

At the present time, plans for two publications other than documents are well advanced. One is a weekly bulletin containing regular accounts of the activities of the United Nations, of its various branches and related agencies, background articles on topics under discussion, biographical notices on delegates and officials, and a bibliographical section. The other is a United Nations yearbook which will include, among other things, a chronology of United Nations activities, an account of the work achieved by each organ, with the resolutions passed, the structure of the United Nations, with the names of delegates and officials, a who's who, a list of publications issued during the year, a calendar of forthcoming United Nations events, and basic texts such as the Charter, together with amendments, if any. Both of these publications will be issued by the Department of Public Information.

It is likely that in addition there will be specialized and technical publications, for example a treaty series to take the place of the treaty series issued by the League of Nations.

All publications of the United Nations intended for public distribution will be available from Columbia University Press, International Documents Service, 2960 Broadway, New York City 27.

NOTES

[1] Abridgment of a paper presented at the meeting of the Committee on Public Documents, American Library Association, Buffalo, June 19, 1946.

[2] Complete text in *Toward the Peace: Documents.* [Washington, D.C., Government Printing Office, 1945] (Department of State Publication 2298) p. 33–36.

[3] See p. 313.

[4] Because of a misprint on the verso of the front cover, giving February 1944 instead of 1945 as date of the Crimea Conference, the English edition was withdrawn: U.S. Department of State. *Proposals for a General International Organization as Developed at Dumbarton Oaks, 1944.* [Washington, D.C., Government Printing Office, 1945.] 24p., charts.

V

THE UNITED NATIONS

With the death of the League of Nations its successor the United Nations became the most important and the largest international organization. The scope of its activities is reflected in the more than 7,000 documents produced each year. This section introduces writings that explain the structure and function of the United Nations. The problems of acquiring, processing and servicing UN documents are covered by the writings of librarians practicing in the UN Library itself or in other research libraries housing comprehensive collections of UN documents. The work of the UN Library is detailed in a summary journal article and in an annual report.

The United Nations

This excerpt from an official handbook about the United Nations provides a brief history of the organization. It explains also the functions and purposes of the UN and describes this body's internal organization.

The deep-felt needs and intentions which inspired the founding of the United Nations are proclaimed in the preamble to the Charter, signed at San Francisco on June 26, 1945:

We the peoples of the United Nations determined to save succeeding generations from the scourge of war, which twice in our lifetime has brought untold sorrow to mankind, and to reaffirm faith in fundamental human rights, in the dignity and worth of the human person, in the equal rights of men and women and of nations large and small, and to establish conditions under which justice and respect for the obligations arising from treaties and other sources of international law can be maintained, and to promote social progress and better standards of life in larger freedom,

And for these ends to practice tolerance and live together in peace with one another as good neighbours, and to unite our strength to maintain international peace and security, and to ensure, by the acceptance of principles and the institution of methods, that armed force shall not be used, save in the common interest, and to employ international machinery for the promotion of the economic and social advancement of all peoples,

Have resolved to combine our efforts to accomplish these aims. Accordingly, our respective governments, through representatives assembled in the city of San Francisco, who have exhibited their full powers found to be in good and due form, have agreed to the present Charter of the United Nations and do hereby establish an international organization to be known as the United Nations.

PURPOSES AND PRINCIPLES

The purposes of the United Nations are set forth in Article 1 of the Charter. They are:

1. to maintain international peace and security;
2. to develop friendly relations among nations based on respect for the principle of equal rights and self-determination of peoples;
3. to co-operate in solving international problems of an economic, social, cultural or humanitarian character, and in promoting respect for human rights and fundamental freedoms for all; and
4. to be a centre for harmonizing the actions of nations in attaining these common ends.

To fulfil the purposes for which it was established, the United Nations acts in accordance with the following principles, as set forth in Article 2 of the Charter:

1. the Organization is based on the principle of the sovereign equality of all its members;
2. members are to fulfil in good faith the obligations they have assumed under the Charter;
3. they are to settle their international disputes by peaceful means;
4. they are to refrain in their international relations from the threat or use of force in any manner inconsistent with the purposes of the United Nations;
5. they are to give the United Nations every assistance in any action it takes in accordance with the Charter, and to refrain from giving assistance to any state against which the Organization is taking preventive or enforcement action;
6. the United Nations is to ensure that non-members act in accordance with these principles so far as is necessary for maintaining international peace and security;
7. the Organization is not to intervene in matter essentially within the domestic jurisdiction of any state. This provision does

SOURCE: Reprinted from "The United Nations," *Everyman's United Nations; A Complete Handbook of the Activities and Evolution of the United Nations During Its First Twenty Years, 1945-1965.* N.Y., United Nations, 1968. pp. 3-28.

not, however, prejudice the application of enforcement action with respect to threats to the peace, breaches of the peace and acts of aggression.

STEPS TO THE CHARTER

Inter-Allied Declaration

The first of a series of steps which led to the establishment of the United Nations was the Inter-Allied Declaration, which was signed on June 12, 1941, at St. James's Palace, London, by the representatives of Australia, Canada, New Zealand, the Union of South Africa and the United Kingdom, of the exiled Governments of Belgium, Czechoslovakia, Greece, Luxembourg, the Netherlands, Norway, Poland and Yugoslavia, and of General de Gaulle of France. In the Declaration, the signatories, recognizing that "the only true basis of enduring peace is the willing co-operation of free peoples in a world in which, re-lieved of the menace of aggression, all may enjoy economic and social security," stated that it was their intention "to work together, and with other free peoples, both in war and peace, to this end."

Atlantic Charter

Two months later, on August 14, 1941, President Franklin D. Roosevelt of the United States and Prime Minister Winston Churchill of the United Kingdom, meeting "somewhere at sea," issued a joint declaration in which they set forth "certain common principles in the national policies of their respective countries" on which they based their hopes for a better future for the world. In the document, known as the Atlantic Charter, the two signatories stated that: "after the final destruction of the Nazi tyranny, they hope to see established a peace which will afford to all nations the means of dwelling in safety within their own boundaries, and which will afford assurance that all the men in all the lands may live out their lives in freedom from fear and want."

They also stated that: "they believe that all of the nations of the world, for realistic as well as spiritual reasons, must come to the abandonment of the use of force. Since no future peace can be maintained if land, sea, or air armaments continue to be employed by nations which threaten, or may

threaten, aggression outside of their frontiers, they believe, pending the establishment of a wider and permanent system of general security, that the dis-armament of such nations is essential. They will likewise aid and encourage all other practicable measures which will lighten for peace-loving peoples the crushing burden of armaments."

The two statesmen also expressed, in the docu-ment, their desire "to bring about the fullest col-laboration between all nations in the economic field with the object of securing, for all, improved labour standards, economic advancement and social security."

Declaration by United Nations

On New Year's Day 1942, the representatives of twenty-six nations that were fighting against the Axis aggressors signed at Washington, D.C., the Declaration by United Nations. (This document marked the first formal use of the term "United Nations," which had been suggested by President Roosevelt.)

In the Declaration, the signatory Governments:

"Having subscribed to a common program of purposes and principles embodied in the . . . At-lantic Charter,

"Being convinced that complete victory over their enemies is essential to defend life, liberty, independence and religious freedom, and to pre-serve human rights and justice in their own lands as well as in other lands, and that they are now engaged in a common struggle against savage and brutal forces seeking to subjugate the world,

"Declare:

"(1) Each Government pledges itself to employ its full resources, military or economic, against those members of the Tripartite Pact and its ad-herents with which such Government is at war.

"(2) Each Government pledges itself to co-operate with the Governments signatory hereto and not to make a separate armistice or peace with the enemies."

The Declaration was left open for signature by other nations "which are, or may be, rendering material assistance and contributions in the strug-gle for victory over Hitlerism."

The twenty-six signatories of the Declaration of United Nations were:

United States	Czechoslovakia	Netherlands
United Kingdom	Dominican Republic	New Zealand
USSR	El Salvador	Nicaragua
China	Greece	Norway

Australia	Guatemala	Panama
Belgium	Haiti	Poland
Canada	Honduras	Union of South
Costa Rica	India	Africa
Cuba	Luxembourg	Yugoslavia

Later adherents to the Declaration were (in order of the dates of adherence):

Mexico	Colombia	Venezuela
Philippines	Liberia	Uruguay
Ethiopia	France	Turkey
Iraq	Ecuador	Egypt
Brazil	Peru	Saudi Arabia
Bolivia	Chile	Syria
Iran	Paraguay	Lebanon

(*Note:* France and Denmark were generally regarded as having been identified with the United Nations from the beginning. Free French Forces had fought against the Axis powers and the Danish Minister in Washington had signified the adherence of all free Danes to the Allied cause. Since the Declaration was signed by Governments, they could not at that time, however, formally adhere to it. When the French National Committee was constituted as a Government, France adhered formally to the Declaration. Denmark, which was not liberated until after the opening of the San Francisco Conference, was admitted as one of the United Nations by the Conference.)

Moscow and Teheran Conferences

In a declaration signed in Moscow on October 30, 1943, by V. M. Molotov of the USSR, Anthony Eden of the United Kingdom, Cordell Hull of the United States, and Foo Ping-sheung, the Chinese Ambassador to the Soviet Union, the four Governments proclaimed that:

"they recognize the necessity of establishing at the earliest practicable date a general international organization, based on the principle of the sovereign equality of all peace-loving states, and open to membership by all such states, large and small, for the maintenance of international peace and security."

A month later, on December 1, 1943, President Roosevelt, Premier Stalin and Prime Minister Churchill, meeting at Teheran, declared the following:

"We recognize fully the supreme responsibility resting upon us and all the United Nations to make a peace which will command the goodwill of the overwhelming masses of the peoples of the world and banish the scourge and terror of war for many generations."

Dumbarton Oaks and Yalta Conferences

The first concrete step towards the creation of the United Nations was taken in the late summer of 1944 at a mansion known as Dumbarton Oaks in Washington, D.C. In the first phase of the Dumbarton Oaks Conference, from August 21 to September 28, 1944, conversations were held between the representatives of the USSR, the United Kingdom and the United States; in the second phase, from September 29 to October 7, conversations were held between the representatives of China, the United Kingdom and the United States. (This arrangement served to respect USSR neutrality in the war against Japan.) As a result of the conference, the four powers reached a number of agreements which were embodied in proposals for the establishment of a general international organization.

The Dumbarton Oaks proposals were primarily concerned with the purposes and principles of the organization, its membership and principal organs, and arrangements for the maintenance of international peace and security and for international economic and social co-operation. According to the proposals, the key body in the United Nations for preserving world peace was to be the Security Council, on which the "Big Five"—China, France, the USSR, the United Kingdom and the United States—were to be permanently represented. Agreement was not, however, reached on the question of voting procedure in the Security Council.

This question, among others, was discussed by President Roosevelt, Prime Minister Churchill and Premier Stalin at a conference at Yalta in February, 1945. On February 11, 1945, following the conference, a report was issued in which the three leaders declared:

"We are resolved upon the earliest possible establishment with our Allies of a general international organization to maintain peace and security. We believe that this is essential, both to prevent aggression and to remove the political, economic and social causes of war through the close and continuing collaboration of all peace-loving peoples.

"The foundations were laid at Dumbarton Oaks. On the important question of voting procedure, however, agreement was not there reached. The present Conference has been able to resolve this difficulty.

"We have agreed that a Conference of United Nations should be called to meet at San Francisco in the United States on the 25th April 1945, to prepare the charter of such an organization, along the lines proposed in the informal conversations of Dumbarton Oaks."

The report further stated that the Government of China and the Provisional Government of France would be invited to sponsor invitations to the Conference jointly with the United States, the United Kingdom and the USSR and that as soon as consultations with China and France had been completed, the text of the proposals on voting procedure would be made public.

The Chinese Government agreed to join in sponsoring the invitations. The French Government agreed to participate in the Conference but decided not to act as a sponsoring nation.

The invitations to the Conference were issued on March 5 to those nations which had declared war on Germany or Japan by March 1 and had signed the Declaration by United Nations. The text of the invitation contained the provisions for voting in the Security Council which were subsequently adopted at San Francisco.

San Francisco Conference

Before the start of the San Francisco Conference, the Dumbarton Oaks proposals were studied and discussed by the nations of the world, both collectively and individually. From February 21 to March 8, 1945, for instance, the representatives of twenty Latin American nations met in Mexico City and adopted a resolution suggesting points to be taken into consideration in the drawing up of the charter of the proposed international organization. From April 4 to 13, 1945, talks were held in London between representatives of the British Commonwealth, and a statement issued at the close of the meetings indicated agreement that the Dumbarton Oaks proposals provided the basis for a charter, while recognizing that clarification, improvement and expansion were called for in certain respects.

On April 25, delegates of fifty nations met in San Francisco for the conference known officially as the United Nations Conference on International Organization. Working on the Dumbarton Oaks proposals, the Yalta Agreement and amendments proposed by various Governments, the delegates, meeting both in plenary sessions and in committees, drew up the 111-article Charter.

The heads of the delegations of the sponsoring countries took turns as chairman of the plenary meetings: Anthony Eden, of the United Kingdom,

Edward R. Stettinius, Jr., of the United States, T. V. Soong, of China, and V. M. Molotov, of the Soviet Union. At the later meetings, Lord Halifax deputized for Mr. Eden, V. K. Wellington Koo for Mr. Soong, and A. A. Gromyko for Mr. Molotov.

The Conference formed a Steering Committee, composed of the heads of all the delegations, which decided all matters of major principle and policy. An Executive Committee of fourteen heads of delegations was chosen to prepare recommendations for the Steering Committee.

The proposed Charter was divided into four sections, each of which was considered by a commission. Commission I dealt with the general purposes of the organization, its principles, membership, the secretariat and the subject of amendments to the Charter; Commission II considered the powers and responsibilities of the General Assembly; Commission III took up the Security Council; and Commission IV worked on a draft for the Statute of the International Court of Justice, which had been prepared in Washington in April 1945 by a 44-nation Committee of Jurists.

On June 25, the delegates met in full session in the Opera House in San Francisco and unanimously adopted the Charter, and the next day, they signed it at a ceremony in the auditorium of the Veterans' Memorial Hall.

The Charter came into force on October 24, 1945, when China, France, the USSR, the United Kingdom and the United States and a majority of the other signatories had filed their instruments of ratification.

United Nations Day

On October 31, 1947, the General Assembly decided that October 24, the anniversary of the entry into force of the Charter of the United Nations, should thenceforth be officially called "United Nations Day," and be devoted to informing the peoples of the world of the aims and achievements of the Organization and to obtaining support for its work. Member governments were invited to co-operate in the observance of the anniversary.

Amendments to the Charter

Amendments to the Charter come into force for all members of the United Nations when they have been adopted by a vote of two-thirds of the members of the General Assembly and ratified by two-thirds of the members of the United Nations, including all the permanent members of the Security Council.

Amendments to Articles 23, 27, and 61, which had been approved by the General Assembly on December 17, 1963, came into force on August 31, 1965. The amendment to Article 23 increases the membership of the Security Council from eleven to fifteen. The amended Article 27 provides that decisions of the Security Council on procedural matters shall be made by an affirmative vote of nine members (formerly seven) and on all other matters by an affirmative vote of nine members (formerly seven), including the concurring votes of the five permanent members. The amendment to Article 61 enlarges the membership of the Economic and Social Council from eighteen to twenty-seven.

Consequent upon the entry into force of these amendments, the General Assembly, at its twentieth session, adopted, on December 20, 1965, an amendment to Article 109 of the Charter to reflect the change in the number of votes (seven to nine) in the Security Council on procedural matters, and called on all member states to ratify the amendment, "in accordance with their respective constitutional processes," at the earliest possible date.

MEMBERSHIP

The original members of the United Nations, numbering fifty-one, are those states which took part in the San Francisco Conference or had previously signed the Declaration by United Nations, and which signed and ratified the Charter. They are:

Argentina	China
Australia	Colombia
Belgium	Costa Rica
Bolivia	Cuba
Brazil	Czechoslovakia
Byelorussian	Denmark
Soviet Socialist	Dominican
Republic	Republic
Canada	Ecuador
Chile	Egypt

El Salvador	Peru
Ethiopia	Philippines
France	Poland[1]
Greece	Saudi Arabia
Guatemala	South Africa
Haiti	Syria
Honduras	Turkey
India	Ukrainian
Iran	Soviet Socialist
Iraq	Republic
Lebanon	Union of Soviet
Liberia	Socialist Republics
Luxembourg	United Kingdom of
Mexico	Great Britain and
Netherlands	Northern Ireland
New Zealand	United States of
Nicaragua	America
Norway	Uruguay
Panama	Venezuela
Paraguay	Yugoslavia

Membership in the United Nations is open to all peace-loving states which accept and, in the judgment of the Organization, are able and willing to carry out the obligations of the Charter. Any state desiring to become a member must submit an application containing a declaration that it accepts the obligations contained in the Charter of the United Nations.

New members are admitted by a two-thirds vote of the General Assembly upon the recommendation of the Security Council. Membership becomes effective on the date the Assembly accepts the application.

The additional members admitted to the United Nations from 1946 to 1966 are listed on the following page by date of admission. At the end of 1966, United Nations membership totalled 122 states.

A member of the United Nations against which preventive or enforcement action has been taken by the Security Council may be suspended from the exercise of the rights and privileges of membership by the General Assembly on the recommendation of the Security Council. The exercise of these rights and privileges may be restored by the Security Council.

A member of the United Nations which has persistently violated the principles of the Charter may be expelled from the Organization by the General Assembly on the recommendation of the Security Council.

There is no provision in the Charter concerning

---

[1] Poland did not attend the San Francisco Conference because the composition of its new government was not announced until June 28—too late for the Conferece. A space, however, was left for the signature of Poland, one of the original signatories of the Declaration by United Nations. Poland signed the Charter on October 15, 1945, thus becoming one of the original members.

the re-entry into the Organization of an expelled member.

After lengthy debate, it was agreed at the San Francisco Conference not to include any provision in the Charter for the withdrawal of members. It was made clear, however, that it was not the purpose of the Organization to compel a member "to continue its co-operation in the Organization," if that member "because of exceptional circumstances" felt constrained to withdraw.

Permanent Missions to the United Nations

Since the creation of the United Nations, the practice has developed of establishing permanent missions of member states at the seat of the Organization. The General Assembly sought to regulate the submission of credentials of permanent representatives on December 3, 1948, when it recommended that credentials be issued by the head of the state, by the head of the government,

Member	Date of Admission	Member	Date of Admission
Afghanistan	November 19, 1946	Congo	
Iceland	November 19, 1946	(Leopold-	
Sweden	November 19, 1946	ville)[2]	September 20, 1960
Thailand	December 16, 1946	Cyprus	September 20, 1960
Pakistan	September 30, 1947	Dahomey	September 20, 1960
Yemen	September 30, 1947	Gabon	September 20, 1960
Burma	April 19, 1948	Ivory Coast	September 20, 1960
Israel	May 11, 1949	Madagascar	September 20, 1960
Indonesia	September 28, 1950	Niger	September 20, 1960
Albania	December 14, 1955	Somalia	September 20, 1960
Austria	December 14, 1955	Togo	September 20, 1960
Bulgaria	December 14, 1955	Upper Volta	September 20, 1960
Cambodia	December 14, 1955	Mali	September 28, 1960
Ceylon	December 14, 1955	Senegal	September 28, 1960
Finland	December 14, 1955	Nigeria	October 7, 1960
Hungary	December 14, 1955	Sierra Leone	September 27, 1961
Ireland	December 14, 1955	Mauritania	October 27, 1961
Italy	December 14, 1955	Mongolia	October 27, 1961
Jordan	December 14, 1955	Tanganyika[3]	December 14, 1961
Laos	December 14, 1955	Burundi	September 18, 1962
Libya	December 14, 1955	Jamaica	September 18, 1962
Nepal	December 14, 1955	Rwanda	September 18, 1962
Portugal	December 14, 1955	Trinidad and	
Romania	December 14, 1955	Tobago	September 18, 1962
Spain	December 14, 1955	Algeria	October 8, 1962
Sudan	November 12, 1956	Uganda	October 25, 1962
Morocco	November 12, 1956	Kuwait	May 14, 1963
Tunisia	November 12, 1956	Kenya	December 16, 1963
Japan	December 18, 1956	Zanzibar[3]	December 16, 1963
Ghana	March 8, 1957	Malawi	December 1, 1964
Federation		Malta	December 1, 1964
of Malaya[1]	September 17, 1957	Zambia	December 1, 1964
Guinea	December 12, 1958	Gambia	September 21, 1965
Cameroon	September 20, 1960	Maldive Islands	September 21, 1965
Central African		Singapore[1]	September 21, 1965
Republic	September 20, 1960	Guyana	September 20, 1966
Chad	September 20, 1960	Botswana	October 17, 1966
Congo		Lesotho	October 17, 1966
(Brazzaville)	September 20, 1960	Barbados	December 9, 1966

[1] The name of the Federation of Malaya was changed to Malaysia following the admission, to the new federation, of Singapore, Sabah (North Borneo) and Sarawak. Singapore became an independent state on August 9, 1965, and a member of the United Nations of the following month.

[2] Officially renamed the Democratic Republic of the Congo in July 1964.

[3] Following the ratification in April 24, 1964, of Articles of Union between Tanganyika and Zanzibar, the United Republic of Tanganyika and Zanzibar continued as a single member of the United Nations, later changing its name to United Republic of Tanzania.

or by the Minister for Foreign Affairs, and be transmitted to the Secretary-General. It was further recommended that the permanent representative, in case of temporary absence, should notify the Secretary-General of the name of his replacement; that member states which wanted their permanent representatives to represent them on one or more organs of the United Nations should specify in their credentials the organs concerned; and finally, that changes of members of permanent missions, other than the permanent representative, should be communicated in writing to the Secretary-General by the head of the mission.

Permanent Observers

The following non-member states maintain offices of permanent observers to the United Nations: Federal Republic of Germany, Holy See, Republic of Korea, Monaco, Switzerland and Republic of Viet-Nam.

THE PRINCIPAL ORGANS

The Charter established six principal organs of the United Nations: the General Assembly, the Security Council, the Economic and Social Council, the Trusteeship Council, the International Court of Justice and the Secretariat.

In all organs of the United Nations other than the International Court of Justice, the official languages are Chinese, English, French, Russian and Spanish, and the working languages are English and French. In the General Assembly and the Economic and Social Council, Spanish is also a working language.

The official languages of the International Court of Justice are English and French.

General Assembly

The General Assembly consists of all the member states of the United Nations, each of which has one vote in the Assembly.

Functions and Powers

The General Assembly may discuss any questions or any matters within the scope of the Charter or relating to the powers and functions of any organs provided for in the Charter. It may make recommendations on these questions and matters to the member states or to the Security Council or to both, with one exception—it may not make recommendations on any dispute or situation which the Security Council has under consideration unless the Council so requests.

The Assembly may consider the general principles of co-operation in the maintenance of peace and security, including those governing disarmament and the regulation of armaments.

It may discuss any questions relating to the maintenance of international peace and security brought before it by a member state, by the Security Council or by a non-member state, if that state accepts in advance the obligations of pacific settlement contained in the Charter, and, unless the matter is already being dealt with by the Security Council, may make recommendations on any such question to the state or states concerned or to the Security Council or to both.

Subject to the same exception, the Assembly may recommend measures for the peaceful settlement of any situation, regardless of origin, which it deems likely to impair the general welfare or friendly relations among nations. It may also call to the attention of the Council situations which are likely to endanger international peace and security.

The Assembly initiates studies and makes recommendations for the purpose of: *(a)* promoting international co-operation in the political field and encouraging the progressive development of international law and its codification; and *(b)* promoting international co-operation in the economic, social, cultural, educational and health fields and assisting in the realization of human rights and fundamental freedoms for all.

Through the Trusteeship Council, the Assembly supervises the execution of Trusteeship Agreements for all territories except those designated as strategic. It approves the terms of these agreements and any alterations or amendments.

The Assembly receives and considers reports of the other organs of the United Nations. It elects the ten non-permanent members of the Security Council, all twenty-seven members of the Economic and Social Council and those members of the Trusteeship Council which are elected. Voting independently, the Assembly and the Security Council elect the members of the International Court of Justice, and, on the recommendation of the Security Council, the Assembly appoints the Secretary-General.

The finances of the United Nations are controlled by the Assembly, which considers and approves the budget and apportions the expenses among the members. It also examines the administrative budgets of the specialized agencies.

Voting

Decisions on important questions, such as recommendations on peace and security, election of members to organs, admission, suspension and expulsion of members, trusteeship questions and budgetary matters, are taken by a two-thirds majority of members present and voting. Other questions require a simple majority.

Sessions

The Assembly meets once a year in regular session, commencing on the third Tuesday in September. Special sessions may be called at the request of the Security Council, a majority of member states, or one member state with the concurrence of a majority. An emergency special session may be called within twenty-four hours of a request by the Security Council on the vote of any nine of its members, or by a majority of the United Nations members.

Structure

The Assembly elects its President and Vice-Presidents for each session and adopts its own rules of procedure. At each session, the Assembly distributes most agenda items among its seven Main Committees, on which every member state has the right to be represented. These committees, which prepare recommendations for approval in plenary meetings of the Assembly, are:

First Committee (Political and Security, including the regulation of armaments)

Special Political Committee (shares the work of the First Committee)

Second Committee (Economic and Financial)

Third Committee (Social, Humanitarian and Cultural)

Fourth Committee (Trusteeship, including Non-Self-Governing Territories)

Fifth Committee (Administrative and Budgetary)

Sixth Committee (Legal)

Voting in committees or sub-committees is by simple majority. Agenda items not referred to a Main Committee are dealt with by the Assembly itself, in plenary meetings.

The organization of the work of each session is the responsibility of the General Committee, which is composed of the President of the Assembly, the seventeen Vice-Presidents and the Chairmen of the seven Main Committees. The Credentials Committee, consisting of nine members appointed by the General Assembly on the proposal of the President, reports to the Assembly on the credentials of representatives.

The Assembly is assisted by two standing committees—the twelve-member Advisory Committee on Administrative and Budgetary Questions, and the ten-member Committee on Contributions, which makes recommendations to the General Assembly on the percentage scale for members' contributions to the United Nations. Members of these two committees are selected on the basis of broad geographical representation, personal qualifications and experience.

In addition, the Assembly has, from time to time, set up a number of subsidiary, *ad hoc* and related bodies.

Security Council

The Security Council is composed of five permanent members—China, France, the Union of Soviet Socialist Republics, the United Kingdom and the United States—and ten non-permanent members, elected by the General Assembly for two-year terms and not eligible for immediate re-election.

Functions and Powers

Under the Charter, the members of the United Nations confer on the Security Council primary responsibility for the maintenance of international peace and security in accordance with the purposes and principles of the United Nations.

The Council may investigate any dispute or situation which might lead to international friction, and may recommend methods of adjusting such disputes or the terms of settlement.

Disputes and situations likely to endanger international peace and security may be brought to the attention of the Council by any member state, by a non-member which accepts in advance the obligations of pacific settlement contained in the Charter, by the General Assembly, or by the Secretary-General.

The Council may determine the existence of any threat to the peace, breach of the peace or act of aggression. It may make recommendations or decide to take enforcement measures to maintain or restore international peace and security. Enforcement action may include a call on members to apply economic sanctions and other measures short of the use of armed force. Should it consider such measures inadequate, the Council may take military action against an aggressor. (Under the Charter, all members have undertaken to make available to the Council on its call, in accordance with special agreements to be negotiated on the Council's initiative, the armed forces, assistance and facilities necessary for maintaining international peace and security.) The Council is also responsible for formulating plans to regulate armaments. In addition, the Security Council exercises the trusteeship functions of the United Nations in those areas classed as strategic.

The Security Council makes annual and special reports to the General Assembly.

The Security Council and the General Assembly, voting independently, elect the judges of the International Court of Justice. On the Security Council's recommendation, the General Assembly appoints the Secretary-General.

Voting and Procedure

Voting in the Security Council on all matters other than questions of procedure is by an affirmative vote of nine members, including those of the permanent members. Any members, however, whether permanent or non-permanent, must abstain from voting in a dispute to which it is a party. On questions of procedure, a decision is by an affirmative vote of any nine members.

The Security Council is so organized as to be able to function continuously, and a representative of each of its members must be present at all times at United Nations Headquarters. The Council may meet elsewhere than at Headquarters.

A country which is a member of the United Nations but not of the Council may take part in its discussions when the Council considers that that country's interests are specially affected. Both members and non-members are invited to take part in the Council's discussions when they are parties to disputes being considered; in the case of a non-member, the Council lays down the conditions under which it may participate.

The presidency of the Council is held monthly in turn by members in English alphabetical order. The Council decides its own rules of procedure and may establish subsidiary organs.

There are two standing committees—the Committee of Experts, which studies and advises the Council on rules of procedure and other technical matters, and the Committee on Admission of New Members; each is composed of representatives of all Council members. Over the years, the Council has also established many *ad hoc* bodies.

The Military Staff Committee, composed of the Chiefs of Staff of the five permanent members or their representatives, was established under the Charter to advise and assist the Security Council on such questions as the Council's military requirements for the Maintenance of peace, the strategic direction of armed forces placed at its disposal, the regulation of armaments and possible disarmament.

Economic and Social Council

The Economic and Social Council is composed of twenty-seven members, nine of which are elected each year by the General Assembly for a three-year term of office. Retiring members are eligible for immediate re-election.

Functions and Powers

The Economic and Social Council is the organ responsible, under the authority of the General Assembly, for the economic and social activities of the United Nations. Its functions are: to make or initiate studies, reports and recommendations on international economic, social, cultural, educational, health and related matters; to promote respect for, and observance of, human rights and fundamental freedoms for all; to call international conferences and prepare draft conventions for submission to the General Assembly on matters within its competence; to negotiate agreements with the specialized agencies, defining their relationship with the United Nations, and to co-ordinate the activities of the specialized agencies by means of consultation with them and recommendations to them, and by means of recommendations to the General Assembly and members of the United Nations; to perform services, approved by the Assembly, for members of the United Nations and, upon request, for the specialized agencies; and to consult with non-governmental organizations concerned with matters with which the Council deals.

Voting

Voting in the Economic and Social Council is by simple majority; each member has one vote.

Subsidiary Bodies

The Council works through commissions, committees and various other subsidiary bodies. It has six functional commissions: the Statistical Commission, the Population Commission, the Commission for Social Development, the Commission on Human Rights, the Commission on the Status of Women and the Commission on Narcotic Drugs.

Representatives on the Commission on Narcotic Drugs are appointed directly by their respective Governments. For the other five Commissions, the member countries nominate representatives, after consultation with the Secretary-General, with a view to securing balanced representation in the various fields covered by each Commission; these nominations are in turn confirmed by the Council.

There are also four regional economic commissions: for Europe; for Asia and the Far East; for Latin America; and for Africa, as well as an Economic and Social Office in Beirut.

Other related bodies include the Executive Board of the United Nations Children's Fund; the Governing Council of the United Nations Development Programme; the United Nations/FAO Inter-Governmental Committee on the World Food Programme; the Trade and Development Board of the United Nations Conference on Trade and Development which reports to the General Assembly through the Economic and Social Council; the Permanent Central Opium Board; and the Drug Supervisory Body.

Inter-Governmental Agencies

The inter-governmental agencies are separate, autonomous organizations related to the United Nations by special arrangements. They have their own membership, their own legislative and executive bodies, their own secretariats and their own budgets, but they work with the United Nations and with each other through the co-ordinating machinery of the Economic and Social Council.

The inter-governmental agencies are:

International Atomic Energy Agency (IAEA)
International Labour Organisation (ILO)
Food and Agriculture Organization of the United Nations (FAO)
United Nations Educational, Scientific and Cultural Organization (UNESCO)
World Health Organization (WHO)
International Bank for Reconstruction and Development (World Bank, IBRD)
International Finance Corporation (IFC)
International Development Association (IDA)
International Monetary Fund (Fund, IMF)
International Civil Aviation Organization (ICAO)
Universal Postal Union (UPU)
International Telecommunication Union (ITU)
World Meteorological Organization (WMO)
Inter-Governmental Maritime Consultative Organization (IMCO)

The General Agreement on Tariffs and Trade (GATT) is not a specialized agency but is often listed among them because of its relationship with some of the agencies.

Non-Governmental Organizations

Non-governmental organizations may be consulted by the Economic and Social Council on matters with which they are concerned and which fall within the competence of the Council. The Council recognizes that these organizations should have the opportunity to express their views and that they often possess special experience or technical knowledge which will be of great value to the Council in its work.

Organizations in consultative status are divided into three categories: those with a basic interest in most of the activities of the Council (Category

A); those which have a special competence in, and are concerned specifically with, only a few of the Council's fields of activity (Category B); and those which have a significant contribution to make to the work of the Council which may be placed on a register for *ad hoc* consultations. As of December 1965, ten organizations were in Category A, 131 organizations were in Category B and 219 were on the Register.

The non-governmental organizations may designate authorized representatives to sit as observers at public meetings of the Council and its bodies, and they may submit written statements relevant to the work of the Council and its bodies for circulation as United Nations documents. All three categories of consultative non-governmental organizations may consult with the United Nations Secretariat on matters of mutual concern.

Trusteeship Council

The Trusteeship Council is the principal organ of the United Nations responsible for the supervision of territories placed under the International Trusteeship System. The Council consists of member states administering trust territories, permanent members of the Security Council which do not administer trust territories, and enough other non-administering countries elected by the Assembly for three-year terms to ensure that the membership is equally divided between administering and non-administering members.

At the beginning of 1966, the Trusteeship Council was composed of four administering authorities (Australia, New Zealand, the United Kingdom and the United States), and four non-administering members, of whom three (China, France and the USSR) are members by virtue of being permanent members of the Security Council; the fourth, Liberia, was elected by the Assembly in December 1965 for a period of three years.

Functions and Powers

The Trusteeship Council, under the authority of the General Assembly, carries out the functions of the United Nations with regard to trust territories except in those areas which are des-ignated as strategic. The Security Council exercises the functions of the United Nations in "strategic areas," with the assistance of the Trusteeship Council in political, economic, social and educational matters.

The Trusteeship Council considers reports submitted by the administering authority on the basis of a questionnaire prepared by the Council, and examines petitions in consultation with the administering authority. It provides for periodic visiting missions to trust territories at times agreed upon with the administering authority, and takes other actions in conformity with the terms of the trusteeship agreements.

Three of the original eleven trust territories remain: Nauru, administered by Australia on behalf of Australia, New Zealand and the United Kingdom; New Guinea, administered by Australia; and the Trust Territory of the Pacific Islands, a "strategic" Territory administered by the United States.

Voting

Voting in the Trusteeship Council is by simple majority; each member has one vote.

The Council meets once a year, usually during June.

International Court of Justice

The International Court of Justice is the principal judicial organ of the United Nations. The Court functions in accordance with its Statute, which is an integral part of the United Nations Charter. The Statute is based upon the Statute of the Permanent Court of International Justice, which functioned under the League of Nations.

The Court is open to the parties to its Statute, which automatically includes all members of the United Nations. A state not belonging to the United Nations may become a party to the Statute on conditions to be determined in each case by the General Assembly on recommendation of the Security Council. Switzerland (1948), Liechtenstein (1950) and San Marino (1954) are the three non-member states which are presently parties to the Statute. The Court is also open to states which are not parties to its

Statute on conditions laid down by a Security Council resolution of October 15, 1946. Such states must file with the Registrar of the Court a declaration by which they accept the Court's jurisdiction in accordance with the Charter of the United Nations and the Statute and Rules of the Court, undertaking to comply in good faith with the decision or decisions of the Court and accepting all the obligations of a member of the United Nations under Article 94 of the Charter. Such a declaration may be either particular or general. A particular declaration is one accepting the Court's jurisdiction in respect of a particular dispute or disputes which have already arisen. A general declaration is one accepting the jurisdiction in respect of all disputes, or of a particular class or classes of dispute, which have already arisen or which may arise in the future. General declarations have been filed by the Federal Republic of Germany and the Republic of Viet-Nam under certain treaties. The Court is not open to private individuals.

Jurisdiction

The jurisdiction of the Court comprises all cases which the parties refer to it, and all matters specifically provided for in the Charter or in treaties or conventions in force. In the event of a dispute as to whether the Court has jurisdiction, the matter is settled by the decision of the Court.

To preserve continuity with the work of the Permanent Court of International Justice, the Statute of the International Court of Justice stipulates that whenever a treaty or convention in force provided for reference to the Permanent Court, the matter is referred to the International Court as between the parties to its Statute.

States are not forced to submit cases to the Court. The Charter provides that members of the United Nations may entrust the solution of their differences to other tribunals.

States parties to the Statute may at any time declare that they recognize as compulsory, *ipso facto* and without special agreement, in relation to any state accepting the same obligation, the jurisdiction of the Court in all legal disputes concerning: (*a*) the interpretation of a treaty; (*b*) any question of international law; (*c*) the existence of any fact which, if established, would constitute a breach of an international obligation; and (*d*) the

nature or extent of the reparation to be made for the breach of an international obligation.

Advisory Opinions

The General Assembly or the Security Council may request the Court to give an advisory opinion on any legal question. Other organs of the United Nations or specialized agencies, when authorized by the Assembly, may also request advisory opinions on legal questions arising within the scope of their activities.

The Law Applied by the Court

In accordance with Article 38 of the Statute, the Court applies: (*a*) international treaties and conventions; (*b*) international custom; (*c*) the general principles of law recognized by civilized nations; and (*d*) judicial decisions and the teachings of the most highly qualified publicists as subsidiary means for the determination of the rules of law. Furthermore, the Court may decide a case *ex aequo et bono,* that is, according to the principles of equity, if the parties concerned agree.

The Security Council can be called upon by one of the parties in a case to determine measures to be taken to give effect to a judgment of the Court if the other party fails to perform its obligations under that judgment.

Composition of the Court

The members of the Court are fifteen independent judges, of different nationalities, elected by the General Assembly and the Security Council from candidates nominated, after consultation with national and international law bodies, by government-appointed national groups of highly reputed international law experts.

The General Assembly and the Security Council hold separate elections independently of one another. They must be satisfied not only that the persons to be elected individually possess the qualifications required in their respective countries for appointment to the highest judicial offices or are recognized authorities on international law, but also that, in the Court as a whole, the result will be the representation of the main forms of civilization and the principal legal systems of the world. To be elected, a candidate must obtain an absolute majority of votes, both in the Assembly and in the Council. The voting in the Council is without distinction as between its permanent and non-permanent members.

The Statute provides for a special joint conference procedure to be applied, if after three meetings, concurring majorities have not been achieved in the two organs for all the vacant seats. Parties to the Statute which are not members of the United Nations may nominate candidates and take part in the elections in the General Assembly.

Judges are elected for terms of nine years and are eligible for reelection. The terms of five of the fifteen judges expire at the end of every three years. The Court itself elects its President and Vice-President for three-year terms.

If there is no judge of their nationality on the bench, the parties to a case are entitled to choose *ad hoc,* or national, judges, to sit only in that particular case. Such judges take part in the decision on terms of complete equality with the other judges. All questions are decided by a majority of the judges present, with nine constituting a quorum. In the event of an equality of votes, the President of the Court has a casting vote.

Administration

The International Court of Justice has its seat at The Hague, Netherlands. Its administration is directed by the President and carried out by a Registrar and Deputy-Registrar elected by the Court, assisted by Registry officials responsible to the Registrar and appointed by the Court.

The Court issues its own publications, which may be obtained wherever United Nations publications are distributed. They include the full texts of the Court's decisions, in the *Reports* series; case documents and speeches, printed after a case is over in the *Pleadings* series; a *Yearbook* of current information on the work of the Court; the instruments governing the Court's operation, in *Acts and Documents;* and an annual *Bibliography.*

The channel of communication with the Court is the Registrar.

Secretariat

The Secretariat is composed of a Secretary-General, appointed by the General Assembly upon the recommendation of the Security Council, and "such staff as the Organization may require."

The Secretary-General's functions are: to be the chief administrative officer of the Organization; to act in his capacity as Secretary-General in all meetings of the General Assembly, the Security Council, the Economic and Social Council and the Trusteeship Council and to perform such other functions as are entrusted to him by these organs; to make an annual report and any supplementary reports necessary to the General Assembly on the work of the United Nations; and to appoint the staff.

Under Article 99 of the Charter, the Secretary-General may bring to the attention of the Security Council any matter which in his opinion may threaten the maintenance of international peace and security.

The first Secretary-General of the United Nations was Trygve Lie, of Norway, who was appointed on February 1, 1946, for a five-year term. On November 1, 1950, he was continued in office for a period of three years. He tendered his resignation on November 10, 1952, and, on April 10, 1953, was succeeded by Dag Hammarskjöld, of Sweden. Mr. Hammarskjöld was appointed on September 26, 1957, for a further five-year term beginning April 10, 1958. Following Mr. Hammarskjöld's death on September 17, 1961, in an airplane crash on his way from Leopoldville in the Congo to Ndola in Northern Rhodesia, the General Assembly, on November 3, 1961, appointed U Thant, of Burma, as Acting Secretary-General for a term of office extending until April 10, 1963. On November 30, 1962, the Assembly, acting on the recommendation of the Security Council, unanimously appointed U Thant Secretary-General for a term of office expiring on November 3, 1966. On November 1, 1966, the General Assembly extended the appointment of U Thant as Secretary-General until the end of the Assembly's twenty-first session and on December 2, 1966, appointed U Thant Secretary-General for another term of office ending December 31, 1971.

The staff of the United Nations is appointed by the Secretary-General under regulations established by the General Assembly. Under the Charter, the "paramount consideration" in employing staff and in determining conditions of service is the necessity of securing the highest standards of efficiency, competence and integrity, with due regard paid to the importance of recruiting on as wide a geographical basis as possible.

Article 100 of the Charter provides that the Secretary-General and the staff, in the performance of their duties, shall not seek or receive instructions from any government or any other authority external to the United Nations. They must also refrain from any action which might reflect on their position as international officials responsible only to the United Nations. For its part, each member of the United Nations is bound by the Charter to respect the exclusively international character of the responsibilities of the Secretary-General and the staff and not to seek to influence them in the discharge of their responsibilities.

The Secretariat is divided into major units, the heads of which are directly responsible to the Secretary-General.

The structure of the United Nations Secretariat is as follows: the Offices of the Secretary-General, consisting of the Executive Office of the Secretary-General, the Offices of the Under-Secretaries for Special Political Affairs, the Office of Legal Affairs, the Office of the Controller and the Office of Personnel; the Department of Political and Security Council Affairs; the Department of Economic and Social Affairs, including the regional economic commissions; the Department of Trusteeship and Non-Self-Governing Territories; the Office of Public Information; the Office of Conference Services; the Office of General Services; the Secretariat of the United Nations Conference on Trade and Development and the United Nations Office at Geneva; and the separate staffs serving the following subsidiary organs established by the General Assembly or the Economic and Social Council: the United Nations Children's Fund (UNICEF), the United Nations Development Programme (UNDP), the Office of the United Nations High Commissioner for Refugees (UNHCR), the United Nations Relief and Works Agency for Palestine Refugees (UNRWA), the United Nations Institute for Training and Research (UNITAR) and the

United Nations Industrial Development Organization (UNIDO).

HEADQUARTERS OF THE UNITED NATIONS

Site for Permanent Headquarters

On December 10, 1945, the Congress of the United States unanimously resolved to invite the United Nations to establish its permanent home in the United States. The invitation was accepted by the General Assembly in London on February 14, 1946, after offers and suggestions for permanent sites had also been received from many other parts of the world. At the time, the first part of the first session of the General Assembly was meeting in London's Central Hall, Westminster, while the Secretariat was in nearby Church House.

Early in 1946, the Secretariat was established provisionally at Hunter College in the Bronx, New York, and in the middle of August the United Nations moved to the Sperry Gyroscope plant at Lake Success in Long Island. A few meetings of the Security Council were held at the Henry Hudson Hotel and at 610 Fifth Avenue, New York, prior to the move to Lake Success. Several General Assembly sessions took place in the New York City Building at Flushing Meadow, and on two occasions—in 1948 and 1951—the Assembly met in Paris.

On December 14, 1946, the General Assembly accepted an offer by John D. Rockefeller, Jr., of $8.5 million for the purchase of the present eighteen-acre site between 42nd and 48th streets on Manhattan's East Side, bounded on the west by United Nations Plaza (formerly a part of First Avenue) and on the east by the East River. Concurrently with the Rockefeller gift, the City of New York offered certain lands within and adjacent to the site, together with waterfront rights and easements. The City also undertook a $30 million improvement programme in the immediate area, including the construction of a vehicular tunnel under First Avenue.

Once the site was decided on, the first Secretary-General, Trygve Lie, appointed the architect Wallace K, Harrison, of the United States, to guide the architectural and development plans in co-operation with an international board of design consultants from ten countries.

The plans prepared by the international board of consultants were unanimously adopted by the General Assembly on November 20, 1947. Demolition of the existing structures on the site had already begun in July. The cornerstone of the buildings was laid on October 24, 1949– United Nations Day–at an open-air plenary meeting of the General Assembly at which the President of the United States, among others, spoke. Occupancy of the Secretariat building began in August 1950 and was completed the following June. The Security Council held its first meetings in its new chamber early in 1952 and in October of the same year the General Assembly convened for the first time in the new Assembly Hall.

The four main structures, all interconnected, that comprise Headquarters, are the thirty-nine-story office building of the Secretariat; the long, low Conference Building paralleling the East River; the General Assembly Hall; and the Dag Hammarskjöld Library.

The official address is United Nations, New York. Telephone: 754-1234.

United States Loan and Total Construction Costs

In approving the plans prepared by the international board, the Assembly also authorized the Secretary-General to negotiate with the United States Government for an interest-free load of $65 million to finance the cost of construction. An agreement was signed on March 23, 1948, by the Secretary-General and the United States representative to the United Nations providing for repayment of the loan, without interest, over a period of thirty-one years from July 1, 1951, to July 1, 1982, in annual instalments ranging from $1 million to $2.5 million. The agreement was approved by the United States Congress and signed by the President of the United States on August 11, 1948. By the end of 1965, the United Nations had repaid $30 million to the United States Government.

The General Assembly, in February 1952, approved an additional sum of $1.5 million (provided from the United Nations budget) to complete construction of the Headquarters.

Headquarters Agreement

On June 26, 1947, the Secretary-General and the Secretary of State of the United States signed an agreement dealing with the privileges and immunities of the United Nations Headquarters. Under this agreement, which came into force on November 21, 1947, the United Nations has the power to make necessary regulations for the Headquarters district.

Dag Hammarskjöld Library

The Dag Hammarskjöld Library is located at the south-west corner of the Headquarters site, adjoining the Secretariat building. Its construction and furnishing were made possible by a gift from the Ford Foundation in 1959 and, at the Foundation's request, it was named for the late Secretary-General, who met his death just before the Library's dedication in 1961. It was designed to accommodate 400,000 volumes, 175 readers in the principal reading rooms and a staff of upwards of 100 persons.

The Library is highly specialized in the subjects of international law and in political, economic and social affairs and is devoted primarily to providing information, research materials and library services required by delegations and the Secretariat. It includes a collection of documents and publications of the United Nations and the specialized agencies, as well as books, periodicals and pamphlets concerning them. The Woodrow Wilson Memorial Collection, a gift of the Woodrow Wilson Foundation, contains documents of the League of Nations and publications dealing with the League, the peace movements and international relations between the two World Wars. There is also a special collection of maps and geographical reference books.

The services of the main Library are supplemented by two branch collections in the Secretariat building–for Economic and Social Affairs, and for Legal and Security Council Affairs.

Official Seal, Emblem and Flag of the United Nations

The official seal and emblem of the United Nations is a map of the world, as seen from the

North Pole, surrounded by a wreath of olive branches. When the General Assembly approved the design in 1946, it also recommended that members should adopt legislation or other appropriate measures to protect the emblem against use not authorized by the Secretary-General. In particular, the Assembly called for prohibition of the use for commercial purposes of the official seal, emblem, name or initials of the world organization.

The United Nations flag was adopted by the General Assembly in 1947. Its design consists of the official emblem in white, centered on a light blue background. In accordance with Assembly directives, the Secretary-General drew up regulations concerning the dimensions of the flag and issued, on December 19, 1947, a Flag Code to govern the use and protect the dignity of the flag. The Code was amended in November 1952 to permit display of the flag by organizations and person desiring to demonstrate their support of the United Nations.

Among the matters covered by the Flag Code are the protocol to be followed in display of the flag, its use in specified circumstances and its manufacture and sale. Under one of the provisions of the Code, any violation of the Code may be punished in accordance with the law of the country in which such violation occurs.

The text of both the Flag Code and the regulations is contained in a pamphlet, entitled *The United Nations Flag Code and Regulations,* issued by the United Nations.

ECAFE's Twenty-Fifth Anniversary; National Progress Through Regional Cooperation

U Nyun

In this article U Nyun, Executive Secretary of the United Nations Economic Commission for Asia and the Far East, reviews the programs of the Commission. Parallel regional economic commissions have been established in Africa, Europe, Latin America, and the middle East. A result of this decentralization is a substantial number of specialized publications issued by the regional offices. While some of the regional studies are issued in the UN series and are in the depository set, many are not, and direct arrangements for acquisition must be made with the individual regional offices.

On a hillside north of Vientiane, overlooking a reservoir that did not exist a year ago, the King of Laos recently pushed a button to unleash turbines with a capacity of 30,000 kilowatts of power for development in his country and neighbouring Thailand. Behind him flew the flags of more than a dozen countries and the United Nations—symbols of an international partnership in planning, financing and construction that has stretched around the world from the Mekong Basin of South-East Asia. In microcosm, this reservoir and power station on the Nam Ngum tributary of the Mekong provide a tangible illustration of "National Progress through Regional Co-operation"—the theme chosen for this year's observances of the Twenty-Fifth Anniversary of the United Nations Economic Commission for Asia and the Far East (ECAFE).

This project, in fact, typifies something of the spirit that has enabled ECAFE, in the quarter-century since its establishment, to lead a successful search for regional solutions to regional problems in a wide range of fields. In the beginning, some called Nam Ngum a job that could not be done; they said it would be too expensive, too isolated, in an area of too much conflict. But today it rises, massive and solid, across a valley that has been reshaped because nations dared to stand together.

The same determination to join hands in the face of diversity has enabled ECAFE members to combine their strength in projects stretching across Asia, in a physical sense, and to seek common ground in less tangible fields ranging from trade and commodity problems to development planning and public administration.

This year, when Commission members gather in Bangkok for their annual session from 15–27 March, they will look back over the 25 years since ECAFE was founded on 28 March 1947 by the Economic and Social Council as one of the four regional commissions of the United Nations. Taking stock, they will find, in essence, a new Asia—an Asia still beset by problems, certainly, but a region marked by dynamism and countless examples of multinational co-operation.

A QUARTER-CENTURY OF CHANGE

Indeed, to see how great the change has been, in Asia itself and in ECAFE, it is necessary to look back to the early post-war years. When ECAFE took its first exploratory steps, Asia as a community of nations was still being formed. Its first session, held in Shanghai in June 1947, was attended by 10 countries, but only four were from Asia (China, India, the Philippines and Thailand). Today, ECAFE has 35 members, including five associates; its geographical area stretches from Iran to Western Samoa, from Mongolia to New Zealand, and its composition is predominantly Asian.

SOURCE: Reprinted from: "ECAFE'S Twenty-Fifth Anniversary; National Progress Through Regional Cooperation," *UN Monthly Chronicle,* 9 (Feb., 1972) pp. 45–52.

Side by side with the expansion in ECAFE membership, the quarter-century has brought sweeping changes in international and regional relationships. At the end of the Second World War, based on the pattern of the colonial period, the lines of communication flowed outward from Asia to the West; in consequence, interaction among Asian nations was limited, and in many fields the professionals of Asia knew their European counterparts better than colleagues on their own continent. Today, our countries are linked by new highways and communications, the visible symbols of change; by a new intensity in hopes for intra-regional trade and improved monetary arrangements, for example; and—in a deeper, more spiritual sense—by a new feeling of Asian identity.

A special challenge for Asian development, and for ECAFE, lay in the vastness and diversity of the region. No one formula could be prescribed for nations with widely differing levels of economic growth, social traditions, and political institutions. Rather, one step at a time, the Commission and its secretariat sought to identify common interests and draw nations together—perhaps only a few at first—in co-operative undertakings.

FROM DATA COLLECTION TO ACTION PROJECTS

From the perspective of 1972, a historian can trace a progression of different phases in ECAFE's work, each reflecting the possibilities of a particular period and each later stage growing out of the previous achievements. Early in its lifetime, ECAFE sought as one major goal to build up a central storehouse of information on the region, like a bank on which the whole region could draw. Early studies were launched at a time when basic statistics and projections were scarce and unreliable; some, such as the *Economic Survey of Asia and the Far East,* have become standard, authoritative works still eagerly sought by scholars of the world.

The search for information drew specialists closer, and ECAFE became known as a meeting place for professionals of the region in numerous fields. In its seminars, working parties, study tours and expert-group meetings, members could exchange views on the best ways to improve practices in their own countries. Political relationships, sometimes tenuous, could be forgotten in the sharing of specialized knowledge in fields ranging from population problems and social needs to flood control and industrial technology. The pooling of skills expanded further in a period when United Nations technical assistance opportunities gave ECAFE a new dimension, and soon major problems could be attacked through knowledge shared by all.

By the early 1960s, with the first United Nations Development Decade getting under way, the fabric of Asian relationships had been woven firmly enough to permit new experiments in concerted action.

POLICY DECISIONS LAY BASIS FOR PRACTICAL CO-OPERATION

In response to an ECAFE resolution, the first Ministerial Conference on Asian Economic Co-operation met in Manila in December 1963. Its participants agreed on steps to achieve "an increasing measure of economic co-operation" in the region, based on mutual respect for national sovereignty, "with due recognition of the different stages of development of the countries of the region and of the importance of co-operation of countries outside the region."

Two years later, at Manila in 1965, the Second Ministerial Conference adopted a "Resolution on Dynamic Asian Economic Co-operation" which set the stage for intensified regional work. As one immediate action, it adopted the Agreement Establishing the Asian Development Bank.

The drive for regional co-operation continued with adoption of the "Tokyo Declaration," urging development of a "common will" among ECAFE members, at the Commission's annual session in 1967; and with agreement on a "Strategy for the integrated development of regional co-operation in Asia" at the Third Ministerial Conference in Bangkok, in December 1968.

Again, in a resolution on plans for the Second United Nations Development Decade adopted at its Singapore session in 1969 and in the "ECAFE Declaration" approved at the 1970 session in Bangkok, the Commission sought maximum regional co-operation, with support by developed countries.

In a landmark decision of 19 December 1970, the "Kabul Declaration" called for specific new efforts to expand regional trade, improve monetary mechanisms, and speed balanced development through joint action. It urged a concerted drive to solve a series of priority problems, with special concern for the least developed of the region's developing countries. This Declaration was adopted by the Council of Ministers for Asian Economic Co-operation (successor to the earlier Ministerial Conferences), which is composed of ECAFE's regional members.

FROM PRINCIPLES TO ACTION: A PROFILE OF REGIONAL PROJECTS

Meanwhile, the principles drawn up in parliamentary-type meetings were being put into effect in actual field projects. Since the mid-1960s ECAFE's day-to-day work shows two major trends—a sharpening focus on action-oriented projects designed to produce maximum tangible impact, and increasing stress on regional co-operation to speed up growth and raise living standards.

Perhaps the best way to trace the gathering momentum is simply to list succinctly the regional, subregional and multinational projects launched under ECAFE's auspices, or with its aid or as an outgrowth of its work.

The projects were undertaken at an exploratory pace at first—three major projects launched in the eight years between 1957 and 1965. Then, in the next six years, more than a dozen co-operative undertakings came into being and still others are taking shape.

A profile of regional projects related to ECAFE in various ways—including some financed with the aid of the United Nations Development Programme (UNDP) or other types of international support—would include the following:

- Committee for the Co-ordination of Investigations of the Lower Mekong Basin (Khmer Republic, Laos, Republic of Viet-Nam and Thailand). Established in 1957, based in Bangkok. Works under ECAFE auspices with support from UNDP and other international aid.
- Asian Institute for Economic Development and Planning, 1964. Operates in Bangkok under ECAFE auspices, with UNDP aid and contributions from participating Governments.
- Asian Highway Co-ordinating Committee, 1965. Its Transport Technical Bureau (secretariat) is based in Bangkok and works under ECAFE auspices, with the aid of UNDP.
- Asian Development Bank, which grew out of an ECAFE resolution and since 1966 has

operated as an independent institution in Manila.
- Asian Industrial Development Council, 1966. Serviced by the ECAFE secretariat in Bangkok.
- Committee for Co-ordination of Joint Prospecting for Mineral Resources in Asian Offshore Areas (CCOP), 1966. ECAFE's Mineral Resources staff serves as CCOP's secretariat, based in Bangkok, and UNDP support has been approved.
- Asian International Trade Fairs, organized periodically since 1966 in response to an ECAFE proposal. The first was held in Bangkok and the second in Teheran; the third is scheduled for New Delhi in November-December 1972.
- Typhoon Committee, set up under the auspices of ECAFE and the World Meterological Organization, 1968. Orginally was based in Bangkok and now has headquarters in Manila.
- Asian Coconut Community, first association of Asian producers organized on a commodity basis, under ECAFE auspices, 1969. Originally based in Bangkok; now has permanent headquarters in Djakarta.
- Feasibility study for a Regional Telecommunication Network (plan of operation signed in 1970). ECAFE is providing support facilities. Financing is shared by UNDP and participating Governments.
- Asian Statistical Institute, inaugurated in Tokyo on 3 June 1970. Operates under ECAFE auspices with UNDP aid and contributions from participating Governments.
- South-East Asia Iron and Steel Institute, formally opened in March 1971, with headquarters in Singapore.
- Trans-Asian Railway Project, a continuing undertaking in the ECAFE secretariat. It is designed to bring about greater uniformity and improvements in regional rail services and thus speed transport.
- Pepper Community (agreement signed in April 1971). ECAFE is providing secretariat service on request, in Bangkok, pending establishment of a Community secretariat.
- Asian Centre for Development Administration, now in organizational stages, with the ECAFE secretariat working on final aspects, following approval in June 1971 of a plan for joint financing by UNDP and contributing Governments.
- Trade and payments arrangements. In November 1971 ECAFE launched an Asian

Trade Expansion Programme; in March 1971 a draft agreement for an Asian clearing union was drawn up and has been placed before Governments; and proposals have been outlined for an Asian reserve bank.

INTRA-REGIONAL TRADE EXPANSION; OTHER NEW PROJECTS

The newest co-operative project, calling for an "Asian Trade Expansion Programme among Developing Countries," is a direct response to the Kabul Declaration but also represents a culmination of years of groundwork laid in ECAFE consultations, field missions and expert meetings. In November 1971 an intergovernmental committee convened by ECAFE agreed unanimously on the urgent need for such a programme and requested an early beginning to specific trade negotiations with a simple flexible approach.

Still other regional projects are taking form. They relate, for example, to:

- Commodity projects, including efforts to devise machinery to deal with rice surpluses emerging from the "green revolution" in agriculture.
- Training facilities in data processing.
- Development of intra-regional shipping, port-improvement, and maritime personnel training programmes.
- Industrial development through joint ventures.
- Mineral resources development.
- Co-operation in international river basin development.

A TANGIBLE CONTRIBUTION TO ASIAN GROWTH

Such a profile is, of course, only a skeleton. A few examples may show something of how the regional projects are actually contributing to Asian growth. One of the best known undertakings—the Mekong project—has drawn together not only the four countries of the Lower Basin but also 26 outside Governments as well as intergovernmental organizations and private institutions in imaginative development of a rich natural resource, with growing attention to human needs. However, as the recent inauguration of the Nam Ngum dam in Laos has shown, the Mekong effort

has become more than a project; it is, indeed, a symbol of constructive growth in an environment of violence and destruction.

Another of ECAFE's older regional projects, the Asian Highway Network extending through 14 countries, has had perhaps the widest geographic impact, from a physical point of view. Looking back to the goal set in the early 1960s, the Asian Highway Co-ordinating Committee recently reported: "In scarcely more than a decade, what had been to most people an impractical dream had been translated into a reality. The objective of an all-weather through-route from east to west, with suitable connexions to other countries not falling on that route, had been nearly achieved."

Although newer, the Trans-Asian Railway Network project and the Asian Telecommunication Network project are similarly gaining ground in attempts to improve the region's physical infrastructure.

Meanwhile, possibilities of undersea wealth for part of the region are being investigated by a partnership of developing and developed countries under ECAFE auspices, through the work of the Committee for Co-ordination of Joint Prospecting for Mineral Resources in Asian Offshore Areas. Specially equipped vessels and aircraft have been provided by industrialized countries for offshore reconnaissance in wide areas, and the Committee recently expressed belief that its technical publications on the findings "have undoubtedly been a major factor in attracting risk capital to explore in more detail the prospects for mineral resources on the marine shelves of Asia, particularly for petroleum."

Development efforts ranging over a broad spectrum have received financial assistance from the Asian Development Bank, one of the key regional projects growing out of ECAFE efforts.

Because of projects such as these, ECAFE has become known as a catalyst, a springboard, "a poor man's development agency." Even though ECAFE does not itself distribute capital aid, it has helped set up and attract funds for regional activities that, in turn provide specific development assistance.

Other co-operative undertakings have sought to help participating countries make the most of their human resources. One of the oldest ECAFE-linked projects, the Asian Institute for Economic Development and Planning, has trained hundreds of senior specialists, and additional hundreds of middle-level professionals, from virtually every corner of the region. Now a second-generation project, the

Asian Statistical Institute, is following a somewhat similar pattern. Other regional institutes are providing the framework for a pooling of skills and a transfer of knowledge from the relatively more developed countries of the region to those less advanced in particular specialities.

THE INTANGIBLE SIDE-EFFECTS OF CO-OPERATION

Over and above the physical benefits, ECAFE's co-operative regional projects have led to other advantages—sometimes indefinable, intangible, but nevertheless real. Some of the projects have, for example, brought participants into close contact even when their Governments had no diplomatic relations.

Certainly the day-to-day companionship of shared tasks in regional undertakings has led to a greater warmth in official sessions, and a deeper understanding of the problems of the region as a whole. Consequently, in Commission meetings, countries have supported each other's projects even while politically at odds. Not long ago, two countries for the first time issued transit visas to each other's nationals travelling along the Asian Highway.

DAY-TO-DAY WORK: ACCENT ON ACTION

ECAFE's increasing emphasis on action projects has been reflected not only in specific regional undertakings but also in day-to-day work of the secretariat in carrying out decisions by policy-making bodies. For example, studies are now viewed primarily as steps towards setting action projects in motion; advisory services have expanded with more field missions and fewer meetings; and a comprehensive approach to development is stressed, with staff activities cutting across individual sectors in line with the concept of an integrated strategy.

As the regional arm of the United Nations in Asia, ECAFE sought to mobilize the region behind the targets for the first United Nations Development Decade, and with increasing impetus it focussed on efforts to help members chart and carry out plans for balanced growth, launch new industries, make maximum use of resources, enlarge the scale of investment, harmonize produc-

tion programmes, increase international and regional trade, lay a solid base of transport and communication facilities, intensify attention given to population problems, integrate social with economic policies, and improve administrative and statistical services.

As new priorities have become evident, ECAFE expanded its services in a number of sectors or entered totally new fields to meet emerging needs. As one example, a new Population Division was set up in 1968 and has organized advisory services, training programmes and workshops, among other activities, seeking to help Governments work out far-sighted policies to cope with larger manpower supplies, expanding urban populations, and specific family planning problems on request.

Surveying the results of the first Development Decade, ECAFE found that a number of promising trends had been recorded in Asia's developing countries but that "general living conditions did not show much of an improvement for large sections of the population." At its 1971 session in Manila, the Commission therefore called for comprehensive development policies that would ensure "social justice hand-in-hand with economic growth."

Reflecting the concern for human needs, ECAFE has taken in the past year its first steps in the environmental field. Participants in a seminar on environment and development urged developing countries to meet environmental threats as early as possible, with special concern for problems such as inadequate housing and transport, water pollution, industrial wastes and deterioration of natural resources.

THE "DECADE OF IMPLEMENTATION": A FORWARD LOOK

Now, with the Second United Nations Development Decade under way, ECAFE is undertaking a series of experimental approaches designed to uncover the root causes of persisting problems, with emphasis on the needs of the least developed of the region's countries. As one illustration, ECAFE recently sent its first "interdisciplinary mission" to three land-locked members, hoping to help Governments map out a co-ordinated attack on problems in the fields of planning, fiscal policies, social development, roads, railways, trade and industry.

As one means of seeking continuous momentum

in the current decade, ECAFE has laid plans for periodic evaluations of regional progress in the 1970s.

Here in Asia, we hope that by combining our ancient heritage with a fresh, innovative spirit, we can make this Second United Nations Development Decade a true "Decade of Implementation." Sometimes we hear that current conditions will make any real progress impossible, and that major development projects must await the return of greater serenity.

ECAFE, however, holds a more confident view. Asia has lived with problems before, throughout the centuries. With continued determination of the type that has brought us through the early years of independence, and intensified co-operation of the type already proved so fruitful, Asia can move forward through the 1970s to a new partnership that will ensure progress and prosperity, a new era in our ancient lands.

United Nations Documents and Their Accessibility

Joseph Groessbeck

Most documents of the United Nations are produced as working materials for the officials of the organization. In this article, Joseph Groessbeck, for many years Deputy Director of the Dag Hammerskjold Library, United Nations, New York, explains why the purposes of the UN are at odds with the purposes of librarians who want to acquire the documentation. He explains also the 1962 decision to restrict the United Nations Document Index *to UN publications only.*

I am aware that there is among American librarians a sense of puzzlement, frustration, and irritation in their good-willed approach to the heterogenous issuances that are loosely labelled "UN documents" and in their conscientious effort to control and to make use of a tantalizing corpus that they sense may be an important auxiliary source of information on a vast variety of subjects. I know, too, that the puzzlement, the frustration, and the irritation all are justified. However, I think these natural reactions are exaggerated, and I hope that I can allay them to a degree by describing in broad terms the patterns of publishing and distribution of UN documents in such a way that the possible approaches to them are illuminated somewhat, and the impossible approaches are recognized as inevitable.

First, let me explain that, counter to the general opinion, there is no closely-knit family of United Nations agencies. The relationships among them are those of half-brothers and half-sisters, guardians and wards, cousins and cousins-twice-removed, a loosely-united clan of which the individual members are loyal to certain common principles but are independent in action and equal in authority. It is not a family with a single responsible head and properly-obedient children.

The clan numbers fifteen agencies of which the United Nations itself is the largest, followed in size and influence by UNESCO, ILO, FAO, and WHO, each pre-eminent in a broad but special area, and by GATT, IBRD (together with the IDA and the IFC), ICAO, IMCO, IMF, ITU, UPU, and WMO, all smaller and more specialized, but extremely influential, each in its own sphere. The fifteen agencies have in common the fact that they are inter-governmental organizations dedicated to improvement of the conditions of life on this earth and that they all are organized in a roughly-similar pattern. Beyond that, they have really little in common. GATT is concerned with questions of tariffs, WHO with the eradication of disease, ICAO with the regulation of air transport, ILO with labor problems, WMO with the weather, IMF with the fate of the pound sterling, and UPU with postal systems, Each has its own constitution, rules of procedure, budget, and administrative head, even its own membership, for although most sovereign states belong to most of the organizations comprising the group, there are notable exceptions (e.g. the USSR and other socialist republics do not belong to the International Bank; the Federal Republic of Germany and the Republic of Viet-Nam are members of WHO but not of the UN; Indonesia has withdrawn from the UN but not from FAO).

In many efforts, especially those aimed at providing technical assistance to underdeveloped countries, there is a community of interest among several agencies and a consequent co-ordination of operations, but such projects are joint undertakings and there is no suggestion of one agency's taking direction from another. These and other matters of common concern are reviewed periodically by an Administrative Committee on Co-ordination composed of the executive heads of the agencies and some other related organizations (e.g. IAEA, UNICEF), with the Secretary-General of the UN

SOURCE: Reprinted from Joseph Groessbeck, "United Nations Documents and Their Accessibility," *Library Resources and Technical Services,* 10, (Summer 1966) pp. 313–318.

as Chairman. The ACC is a useful instrument at the administrative level, and it has been effective in establishing a reasonable degree of uniformity among the agencies in personnel policies, salaries, and other common administrative functions. However, it does not have any positive authority over any one of the member organizations.

One of the areas in which efforts have been made through the ACC to achieve conformity among the related agencies is that of the preparation, external distribution, and indexing of their documents and publications. Those efforts have achieved little, for a variety of reasons, good and bad, but mostly a matter of extreme variation in the nature of the publications produced and the machinery of publication and distribution, the emphasis on public relations, the availability of technical staff, the degree of interest on the part of the executive heads, the proportion of documentation which is classified "Restricted," and even such apparently unlikely factors as the place and the language of publications of the several agencies.

Let me illustrate by reference only to the UN itself: The United Nations issues documents and publications which range from a one-line note transmitting a report, to the *Proceedings of the Second Conference on the Peaceful Uses of Atomic Energy,* offered for sale in 33 volumes at a price of $500.

Broadly speaking, the "publications" of the United Nations are intended for public consumption. They comprise, on the one hand such books as *Everyman's United Nations* and *The United Nations Yearbook* and periodicals such as *The UN Monthly Chronicle* which are specifically designed for wide external distribution, and on the other hand such works as the *Official Records* of the General Assembly, the aforementioned *Proceedings of the Second Conference on the Peaceful Uses of Atomic Energy,* and a host of reports, studies, bulletins, etc., which, while they are prepared for internal use, are felt to be of some public interest and so are issued, as it were incidentally, as "publications." Materials in these two categories generally are offered for sale. They bear sales numbers and prices, they are listed in UN sales catalogs and in PTLA, and they may be purchased directly from the Sales Section of the United Nations in New York or Geneva or through bookstores.

The "documents" of the United Nations, in contrast to the "publications," are not intended, either primarily or secondarily, for public use.

Most of them are ephemeral mimeographed issuances produced for the information of States Members and the Secretariat. They include draft resolutions, verbatim records of meetings, working papers, preliminary reports, administrative announcements, press releases, etc. They are produced very rapidly, in small editions, and, for the most part, they are of no interest outside the House or beyond the immediate present.

Insofar as they are thought to have any lasting value or usefulness to the public they are reprinted in final corrected form and are issued as "publications." Thus, the verbatim records of meetings, after they have been corrected, edited, and summarized, are released as part of the *Official Records* of the appropriate organ (the General Assembly, the Security Council, etc.). So, also, are the final texts of resolutions, which in their existence as "documents" may have gone through any number of redraftings, with attendant revisions, corrections, and additions. Other "documents," such as some preliminary studies and reports, are refined and released as "publications" in the form of monographs or series.

And, finally, to make the full record of the Organization's work publicly available, sets of its publications and documents, including even the ephemeral mimeographed material intended only for internal use and not scheduled for inclusion in the *Official Records* or for other republication, are deposited in selected libraries around the world, and are made available to other libraries by subscription to entire series in their original mimeographed form, on microfilm, or in a microprint edition offered by the Readex Microprint Corporation.

Such is the general nature of the printed material produced by the United Nations and the general pattern of its distribution. I think it must be clear that these demonstrate a clear recognition of obligation to inform the world about the Organization's activities and an effort to do so economically and usefully. Indeed, publication and distribution are major concerns of two departments: the Office of Conference Services, of which the Publishing Service is a part, and the Office of Public Information. The Publishing Service has a staff of about 250 persons; it produces, distributes, and stocks some 45,000,000 pages of text each month. The Office of Public Information numbers about 500 people, including the staffs of nearly fifty overseas information centers, of which probably one hundred are more or less continuously engaged in writing or in facilitating the distribution of UN publications. To all of this publishing and distributing, the Secretary-General, as represented by a high-level Publications Board, gives encouragement and support.

Nonetheless, neither the machinery of publication nor that of distribution runs smoothly. And it never will, because at best "publishing" is incidental to the work of the Organization; in some ways it is even contraventual. For example, the Economic Commission for Europe, which sits in Geneva, is an influential body which, uniquely among economic associations, enjoys the participation of West Germany and the USSR, as well as that of the West European countries and the United States. If it is to function effectively in its role of collecting and analyzing economic data, in facilitating economic agreements, in conducting long-range regional economic studies and forecasts, or in whatever similar role, it must maintain an atmosphere of mutual trust among the representatives of its constituent Member States. This can only be done if care is taken to embargo preliminary reports and draft resolutions which might be seized upon by the press or by commercial interests, to the possible embarrassment of one or another Member, or to the misleading of the business community. Understandably, therefore, to avoid an endless weighing of potential combustibility, and to eliminate the constant risk or errors of judgement, the Commission considers all such preliminary papers to be "Working Papers" and restricts their circulation to the appropriate working parties. This means that unless the Working Papers are republished as parts of final studies, reports, or Official Records, or unless they are in due course declassified—which is not done routinely—they never are generally available. Some of them, indeed, never even reach the Dag Hammarskjold Library.

To cite another situation, the Economic Commission for Latin America, isolated from the rest of the Organization in Santiago, Chile, plainly cannot turn to the Publishing Service in New York or Geneva for reproduction of every document it requires, there and then. Inevitably, it has become its own publisher, at least of some series of mimeographed documents, and because its sphere is regional, it also is its own distributor. In this situation, mimeographed documents originating in Santiago are rerun in New York and are given normal worldwide distribution if they are documents of some consequence; if they are not—or if they are not thought to be—they are not rerun, and so they never receive more than regional dis-

tribution. Moreover, depending upon their considered significance, they are, or are not, translated from the original Spanish into English and French, and because distribution is on a basis of language, it can happen that some interesting material issued in Spanish and distributed from Santiago never reaches English- and French-speaking depository libraries or subscribers.

I have dwelt at some length on the complexity of the publication and distribution machinery of the United Nations—and believe me, I have not touched on many idiosyncratic variations—because I wish to show that in the fairly-well thought-out and adequately-supported system for the reproduction and distribution of the publications and documents of even one international organization—in this case the UN—there are complications and anomalies aplenty. To add the other agencies to the publications-distribution complex multiplies the complications and the anomalies by fourteen.

I began by saying that in our efforts through the ACC to achieve a degree of conformity among the fifteen agencies which make up the UN clan in the supposedly-simple area of production, distribution, and indexing of our respective publications, we met extreme variations in the nature of the publications produced and in the machinery of publication and distribution operative in the several agencies. I trust that my description of the vagaries within the UN itself will suggest the vagaries compounded among the total fifteen members. Still, to drive the point home, let me note simply that, whereas the United Nations employs 250 people in its Publishing Service and maintains a worldwide system of sales agents and has established 250 depository libraries, at the other end of the scale the WMO relies on external printing, sells its modest list of technical reports and its *Bulletin* directly, and deposits its publications in five libraries; whereas the UN makes full use of a large and sophisticated Office of Public Information to spread its gospel, the ITU manages nicely with a Public Relations Officer; whereas ILO is developing an advanced system of computerized controls of its documentation, the IMCO finds it sufficient to assign one officer and two clerks to the task of keeping its own documents in order and to provide a basic library service; whereas the publications of the UPU are exclusively concerned with the regulation and techniques of national postal administrations and international postage agreements, UNESCO both publishes voluminously and also subvents numerous interesting books and journals on a wide gamut of subjects, authored by private individuals or institutions and published commercially; whereas the Dag Hammarskjold Library has a staff of one hundred, including twenty-five editors, indexers, and technicians who are occupied exclusively in preparing indexes to UN documents, the Geneva Library of the UN (the former League of Nations Library) has a total staff of twenty-eight, none of whom is thus engaged.

Against this background let me review the effort that has been made over fifteen years to bring documentary unity out of diversity. The effort began in 1949 when the libraries of the agencies concerned agreed that there should be a single monthly publication which would list and index all of the documents published by all of the agencies in the preceding calendar month. It was further decided that this should be a cooperative undertaking with each agency sending its documents promptly to the UN Headquarters Library and supplying a monthly check-list of them together with a subject index prepared in an agreed-upon sytle. The *United Nations Documents Index,* which commenced publication in January, 1950, was the result.

From the start, the effort was less than completely successful, not for want of good will, but by reason of the extreme variance I have suggested in the publishing and distribution patterns of the members of the clan, the varying attention paid to public relations, the availability or the lack of technically-qualified staff, the degree of interest on the part of the executive heads of the respective agencies, the proportion of classified documentation, and even the place and language of a participating agency's publications. It was apparent quite soon that the consolidated UNDI was neither comprehensive nor truly co-operative, because some agencies were without the means or the incentive to carry their share of the responsibility to make it so. Increasingly, the indexing burden was shifted to the UN Headquarters Library, and what had been conceived as a relatively simple job of editing submitted copy, became for the Library an onerous task involving the acquisition of the agencies' documents, the indexing of materials in technical subjects far removed from the day-to-day work of the UN itself, and the editorial chore of accommodating within one publication references to a widely-diverse body of documents.

The conviction grew with the years that we were trying to bag together oranges and apples, a few figs and many thistles, and that UNDI did not in fact provide what it was presumed to provide, i.e. a current and comprehensive bibliographical record of the documents and publications of all the members of the clan. Moreover, the mixed bag prevented our introducing a number of clearly-desirable changes in the method of compilation and the editorial presentation of the major portion of UNDI, that portion devoted to the listing and indexing of documents and publications of the United Nations itself. Accordingly, in 1962 it was decided, with the relieved consent of most of the specialized agencies, to give up the frustrating and unsuccessful effort to make UNDI an omnibus index to everything.

This made it possible to effect several improvements in UNDI, among them direct reference in the subject index to the symbol numbers of the documents themselves rather than to entry numbers in the checklist section, so it is now possible to go directly from the subject index to the shelves. It also allowed us to produce an annual cumulation of the check list (the subject index has been cumulated annually from the start), and to project a French language version of UNDI, unhappily not yet realized owing to the Organization's financial difficulties.

Subscribers to UNDI have been delighted with these and other improvements made in the past three years, but they have also decried the elimination of the specialized agencies' material, uneven and undependable as that coverage was. The fact is, however, that the documents of the agencies do not by any means go unrecorded. Several of the agencies, notably GATT, ICAO, ILO, IMCO, ITU, UNESCO, and WMO issue frequent comprehensive lists of their documents, and virtually all of them publish sales catalogs. Moreover, much of the most useful material issued by the agencies is picked up by such subject indexes as *The Bibliography of Agriculture, Index Medicus,* and *PAIS.* Still, the demand persists for a single index such as UNDI set out to be. Thus, most recently a proposal has been made to the newly-organized Association of International Libraries, an offspring of IFLA, that a counterpart to UNDI be established, to cover the specialized agencies and other international organizations, such as the Council of Europe, the OAS, and the OECD. I am sceptical, personally, of the feasibility of the proposal, in the light of our experience, but indeed it merits study, and if at its Helsinki meeting next month the Association decides to explore such a possibility, we shall co-operate in every way we can.

Documents and Publications of the United Nations

Harry N. M. Winton

Within a few years after the founding of the United Nations the pattern of production, numbering and distributing UN documents was set. The categories of publications issued, the numbering scheme applied, and some information about the in-house indexing and control used to provide service to UN officials is described in this piece by Winton.

Two years ago in this city, on June 26, 1945, the representatives of fifty-one governments signed the charter of the United Nations and the statute of the International Court of Justice. The six main organs of the United Nations have since been established, the eleven commissions of the Economic and Social Council have been set up, and the major relationships between the specialized agencies and the United Nations have been defined for most of the agencies by agreement so that the initial period of basic organization may be said to have been completed.

During these two years of efforts to revivify and coordinate international activities disrupted by the late war, to grapple with the first substantive problems laid before the United Nations, the Secretariat itself has been in process of organization. The work of building a new Secretariat, while at the same time serving the new organs engaged in their first tasks, has not been made easier by the two great removes of the organization, from London to the Bronx in New York City, and thence to Lake Success in Long Island, which in turn will be only a temporary headquarters until the erection of the permanent buildings on the East River side in Manhattan. It is not surprising, therefore, if the swirl of activities, sweeping across the Atlantic to the New World and back again through conferences and commissions of inquiry and new specialized agencies, has prevented Secretariat procedure from settling into recognizable patterns which may be described and cataloged with assurance. For the methodically-minded observer, the situation is still not clear, and to the Secretariat itself only the grander outlines and some details here and there emerge with clarity. But we are beginning to see our way and to order and coordinate our activities. It will be reasonable enough, therefore, simply to outline in this paper the situation concerning documents and publications of the United Nations, without pretending to finality in description.

DEFINITIONS

Certain definitions may be conveniently laid down and certain areas marked off as outside the scope of the present paper. The term "United Nations documents" covers only those papers submitted, records of meetings, resolutions and reports adopted by organs and suborgans of the United Nations, which are published in a series under an official symbol or in the official records, whether the distribution be unrestricted or restricted, whether the documents be processed or printed. Drafts, Internal Secretariat studies, and delegation papers, which are not so published or which remain in typescript are excluded from that definition. Press releases and publications of the Department of Public Information of the Statistical Office of the United Nations, and of other divisions of the Secretariat are likewise excluded. Furthermore, of the documents and publications of the United Nations, four groups will not be described in this paper. (1) The documents of the specialized agencies are outside the scheme of documentation developed at the headquarters. The specialized agencies are relatively autonomous

SOURCE: Reprinted from: Harry N. M. Winton, "Documents and Publications of the United Nations," *College and Research Libraries*, 9 (Jan. 1948) pp. 6–14.

and vary considerably in their methods of documentation, publication, and distribution. Some agencies, such as the International Labour Organization, are older than the United Nations itself; others, such as the International Refugee Organization, are not yet completely established; and most of them are not seated at the headquarters. (2) The documents of the Military Staff Committee are produced and distributed by that body alone. (3) The circulars and bulletins of the Secretariat are primarily of internal interest and circulation. (4) The documents issued away from headquarters, at the European office in Geneva, for example, have not yet been received with sufficient speed and regularity for the Documents Index unit at the headquarters to make any reasonable observations in the matter.

The documents of the International Court of Justice, which is seated at The Hague, lie outside the scheme of publications and distribution developed at the headquarters. They are printed in Leiden and are distributed by the court, which will, however, use the regular sales agents of the United Nations. Six series are planned: A. Judgments; B. Advisory opinions; C. Documents presented in cases; D. Statutes and treaties governing the organization of the court; E. Annual reports; F. Indexes to the judgments, etc. So far, only the first number in Series D has appeared.

DOCUMENTS SERIES

Returning to an outline of the present situation with respect to United Nations documentation for the General Assembly, the councils, and commissions, we may observe that there are several salient categories by which it may be described. First, documents appear on paper of a distinctive color and masthead and under a series symbol. Second, nearly all documents are issued both in English and in French, the working languages, and key documents usually appear also in Russian, Spanish, and Chinese editions. Third, most documents issued for current use in discussion are processed (mimeograph or offset reproduction) a fact which sets a limit to the quantity which may be produced and which under the present distribution policy excludes such processed documents from sale, in order to assure an adequate supply for official use. Fourth, a considerable number of documents are reissued in printed form in the official records of the various main organs, so that they are generally available to the public through sale or subscription; and, furthermore, a growing number of key reports, from the Secretary-General and from subordinate bodies to the main organs, for instance, will appear initially in printed form either as separate documents in series or as separate supplements to official records of the main organ concerned. Fifth, documents are classified as to distribution into the categories "unrestricted," "restricted," and "secret." The last category requires the written approval of the Secretary-General for issue and so far has not been used. "Restricted" documents, including "restricted working papers," are circulated primarily to the members of the body of issue, usually a drafting subcommittee or body in which certain questions of policy are being initially discussed, or which meets in "closed" or "private" session. "Secret" and "restricted" documents are not distributed to the so-called depository libraries.

We may now take up in greater detail each of the five broad groupings outlined above. First, the identification of documents. The use of colored sheets for processed documents and colored covers for printed documents permits quick recognition of the issuing body in rapid sorting of masses of documents, whatever may be thought of the variations in hue which arise from the present exigencies in the paper supplies. All documents in the General Assembly, its committees and other subordinate bodies appear on white paper under a bilingual General Assembly masthead. Documents of the Security Council and its subordinate bodies appear on yellow under a Security Council masthead. The documents of the Economic and Social Council and its commissions appear on blue paper (although the documents of the first session issued in London were pink). The Trusteeship Council documents are green. The important Atomic Energy Commission, although not one of the six main organs under the charter, issues documents on salmon paper. The Secretariat circulars and bulletins appear on white paper under a bilingual "United Nations" masthead, which is also used for documents of any joint body composed of representatives of two of the six main organs. The covers only of the official records of the General Assembly and the councils are colored in the distinctive manner just described. The former journals, however, were printed on paper of these distinctive colors, with the journal of the first session of the Economic and Social Council, like the documents of that London session, in pink. So far as one can at present see, this policy will remain unchanged.

The system of document series symbols is more complex. The present system was laid down in New York and modifies the arrangements prevalent in the London period by discarding emphasis on letter symbols for a system which is primarily numerical in character. The modifications are really less severe than they have appeared. Most of the purely alphabetical series symbols which were superseded relate either to documents of *ad hoc* committees which have been dissolved or to documents of the "nuclear" commissions of the Economic and Social Council which have been succeeded by full commissions regarded as new bodies. There remain to be sure, certain inconsistencies, but the following brief outline describes the basic features. Since the work of the main and subordinate organs during the years 1946 and 1947 has been essentially organizational in character, there is still, here and there, an area of uncertainty in symbol series of subordinate bodies, especially where certain bodies have not yet established a characteristic pattern of work and organization. Furthermore, anomalies have appeared and will appear when documents are produced away from the headquarters by members of the Secretariat not entirely familiar with the scheme.

Each of the main organs covered by the scheme and the Atomic Energy Commission has a characteristic symbol for its own plenary or general documents series: A/ for the General Assembly, S/ for the Security Council, E/ for the Economic and Social Council, T/ for the Trusteeship Council, and AEC/ for the Atomic Energy Commission. Documents presented to the main organ for consideration or issued by it are identified by a number following the characteristic basic symbol for the organ. Thus, A/182 is the 182nd document in the general series of the General Assembly, S/27 is the twenty-seventh document in the general series of the Security Council, and so on.

Subordinate to the General Assembly and the councils, is a ramifying complex of committees, commissions, subcommittees, and other bodies. Most of the permanent subordinate bodies have been now established, but there is no end to the number of *ad hoc* subordinate bodies which are created for specific tasks and are dissolved when these are accomplished. This is not the place to describe their documentation in detail, but the general scheme may be outlined rather simply, with the reminder that the present arrangements have superseded the initial pattern devised in London.

The documents of any permanent or standing committee of a main organ are identified by a symbol composed of the basic symbol for the main organ and the component for committee numbered to correspond with the particular committee. Thus documents of the first or Political and Security Committee of the General Assembly are identified by the symbol A/C.1/; the documents of the Committee on Arrangements for Consultation with Nongovernmental Organizations of the Economic and Social Council are identified by the symbol E/C.2/.

Similarly, documents of *ad hoc* committees are identified by a symbol composed of the basic symbol for the main body and a component for the *ad hoc* committee numbered to correspond with the order of its establishment. Thus, E/AC. 17/ is the series symbol for the *ad hoc* Committee on the Economic Commission for Europe, the seventeenth *ad hoc* committee established by the Economic and Social Council. Committees appointed before the institution of the present symbol scheme have been counted in determining the number of *ad hoc* committees so far established, but their old alphabetical symbols remain unchanged since most of these committees have expired. The permanent headquarters Committee of the General Assembly (symbol, A/SITE/) was the second *ad hoc* committee to be established by the General Assembly but its documents will continue to bear the old symbol until the committee is discharged.

Subcommittee series are indicated by fixing the number symbol component SC.1/, /SC.2/, etc., to the symbol for the parent committee or *ad hoc* committee.

Outside the Economic and Social Council proper are its subordinate commissions now numbering eleven. The documents of each of these are distinguished by a numbered component indicating a commission (/CN.1/, /CN.2/, etc.) affixed to the basic symbol for the council. Thus the documents of the Economic and Employment Commission bear the symbol E/CN.1; the Statistical Commission, the symbol E/CN.3/; the Population Commission, the symbol E/CN.9/. It was felt by the Documents Index unit that a numerical designation would be less confusing in the long run than purely alphabetical symbols, because the innumerable alphabetical designations for various national and intergovernmental bodies already in existence narrow the choice of meaningful letter combinations available, while the problem of creating letter symbols meaningful in both English and French further narrows the area of choice. In the case of the Economic Commission for Europe the series symbol E/CN.10/ was overruled in favor of E/ECE/, but the latter symbol, completely alphabetical, may easily be confused by the unwary with the current abbreviation EECE for the Emergency Economic Committee for Europe, an older organization which is about to be dissolved.

Subcommissions series are indicated by affixing the numbered component/SUB.1, /SUB.2, etc., to the series symbol for the parent body. Thus E/CN.4/SUB.2/ designates the Subcommission on Prevention of Discrimination and Protection of Minorities established by the Commission on Human Rights.

Conferences under the auspices of the Economic and Social Council or its commissions have been variously designated, but henceforth, will be designated with a numbered conference component E/CONF.1/, E/CONF.2/, etc.

Preparatory committees established to prepare for such conferences will issue documents bearing the affix /PC/ attached to the conference symbol.

In addition to their general series, there are for most of the main organs and subordinate bodies, certain subseries also embracing information series, records of meetings, and working papers. The symbol components for these types of subseries are affixed to the basic symbol for the organ. Thus, instructions to delegations, lists of members of delegations, and similar purely informative documents are issued in an information series with the affixed secondary symbol /INF/, so that the symbol A/INF/3 is to be interpreted as the third document in the information series of the General Assembly.

Records of meetings appear either as verbatim records with the affixed secondary symbol /PV., indicating procès-verbal *in extenso*, or as summary records with the affixed secondary symbol /SR., indicating summary record, so numbered that the document number corresponds with the meeting number in a continuous series. Thus, S/PV.53 indicates the verbatim record of the fifty-third meeting of the Security Council, while T/AC.2/ SR.6 indicates the summary record of the sixth meeting of the *ad hoc* Committee on Questionnaires established by the Trusteeship Council. It should be observed that verbatim records are provisional in character both as to original and interpreted text. They are prepared during the course of the plenary meetings for immediate issue to delegations, the Secretariat, and the press. Delegations are requested to forward any corrections within forty-eight hours to the Editorial Division, which is charged with preparing copy for the official records. The Economic and Social Council, unlike its sister organs, publishes only summary records in its *Official Records* (as formerly in its *Journal*), so that the verbatim records remain in processed form only. Beginning with the fifth session, the summary records of this council will appear in a summary record series, instead of being scattered through its plenary series. The General Assembly, the Security Council, the Atomic Energy Commission, and the Trusteeship Council, which reissue the final texts of their verbatim records in their official records, do not issue summary records of plenary meetings.

With the exception of the first special session of the General Assembly, and the public meetings of the Subcommittee on the Spanish Question of the Security Council, verbatim records are not published for committees, commissions, and other subordinate bodies of the main organs but remain in manuscript form (if verbatim reporters were available to record the proceedings) in the files of the Secretariat or in the archives of the United Nations. Committees, commissions, and other subordinate bodies which issue records of their proceedings publish summary records. So far, only the summary records of the committees of the General Assembly (with the exception of the Credentials Committee) have been reissued in the printed official records. The summary records of the committees, commissions, and other subordinate bodies of the councils, as well as the subcommittees of General Assembly committees remain in processed form.

The last of the subseries embraces the working papers, always of restricted distribution, and usually composed of drafts and other documents for preliminary consideration or for discussion in closed meetings. Such a subseries is indicated by affixing the secondary symbol /W. to the basic symbol for the issuing body. The issue of such working papers is usually confined to committees and other subordinate bodies. Thus, document A/AC.7/W.3 is the third working paper of the headquarters Advisory Committee.

In addition to symbols for these subseries and to the series of subordinate bodies, certain other secondary symbols are employed to indicate revisions of texts and corrigenda and addenda.

When the text of a document has been formally revised by action of the issuing body, or a delegation or the Secretariat has prepared a revised text of a document submitted by it, the secondary symbol /Rev.1 is added to the symbol and number assigned to the original text. Thus E/INF/1/Rev.1 denotes the first revision of document one in the information series of the Economic and Social Council.

If new material is issued which should be appended to a document already published, such as an appendix, tables, charts, maps, additional clauses or paragraphs, later information and the like, the addendum is issued with the secondary symbol /Add.1 added to the original symbol and number of the main document. Thus T/15/Add.1 would be the first addendum to document fifteen in the general series of the Trusteeship Council. E/INF/1/Rev.1/Add.1 would be the first addendum to the first revision of document one in the information series of the Economic and Social Council.

Secretarial or editorial correction of errors in the text, title, data or classification of a document, including the emendation of the translation or the addition of text erroneously omitted may be accomplished by issuing a corrigendum bearing the secondary symbol /Corr. 1 attached to the original symbol and number of the main documents. Thus, S/PV.82/Corr.3 is the third corrigendum to the verbatim record of the eighty-second plenary meeting of the Security Council. The time has not yet arrived when the Secretariat may produce documents with an Olympian calm and decisiveness which precludes the necessity of issuing occasional revisions, corrigenda, and addenda, but the line is drawn at the issuance of corrigenda to corrigenda, and instead a second or third corrigendum is issued.

PRINTED DOCUMENTS

Of the processed documents described above, many are destined to be reissued in the printed official records and in the supplements thereto. The official records of the General Assembly, of the Security Council, the Economic and Social Council, the Trusteeship Council, and the Atomic Energy Commission comprise the records of the plenary meetings. These are usually verbatim records, but in the case of the Economic and Social Council, they are summary records only. The supplements contain the principal documents discussed at these meetings. The official records will replace entirely the former journals of the General Assembly, the Security Council, and the Economic and Social Council, and the former *Journal of the United Nations*, all of which, like the processed verbatim records, are only provisional in character. It is true that a great back log of older records has not been printed because of the priority given to the heavy demands for printing of current records for the Security Council and Atomic Energy Commission, but before very long all the records for meetings in 1946 should be in print.

The official records are issued initially in bilingual editions in English and French and eventually appear also in Chinese, Russian, and Spanish editions.

The official records are sold or exchanged, so that they will be the means for making available to all libraries the bulk of the processed documents in the plenary series, the verbatim records of meetings of the main organs, and the reports of committees and commissions to those main organs. The remaining processed documents in the plenary sales which are not reissued in the official records are not sold or exchanged, so they must be consulted in the so-called "depository libraries" or at the headquarters of the United Nations. Except for the main committees of the General Assembly and its League of Nations and permanent headquarters committees, it is not intended that summary records of committees and commissions of the councils or of the other *ad hoc* committees of the General Assembly be published in the official records; likewise the papers of subcommittees will be excluded.

Certain important documents in any series, when they can be prepared sufficiently far in advance of a session, are printed rather than processed, such as the annual report of the Secretary-General on the work of the organization. Reports of commissions to the Economic and Social Council would probably appear only in draft form in the commission series and in final form as printed documents in the council series as supplements to its official records. For example, document E/436, the *Report of the Meeting of Experts to Prepare for a World Conference on Passport and Frontier Formalities*, appears as *Supplement No. 1* to the official records of the fifth session of the council. It seems clear that eventually the major portion of the general documents of the General Assembly and the councils will appear in print, and that an increasingly large part of the key reports will appear initially in printed form in advance of the meeting or session at which they will be considered.

SERIAL PUBLICATIONS

In addition to the documents of the United Nations and the official records, there are a number of official serial publications which may here be briefly mentioned. Some of these publications have not yet appeared, while others have not yet acquired that regularity of appearance which marks the transition from the organizing period of the parent body. It is, therefore, fitting that only brief mention be made of them at this time and that, rather, attention be directed at certain aspects of their appearance. The Economic and Social Council was charged by the General Assembly with the task of surveying certain functions and activities of the League of Nations, with a view to determining which of them should, with such modifications as are desirable, be assumed by organs of the United Nations or be entrusted to specialized agencies which have been brought into relationship with the United Nations.

Among such league functions and activities to be considered were certain periodical publications and special studies. The continuance of such publications and the initiation of new series by the United Nations may be undertaken at the headquarters by the appropriate divisions of the Secretariat, by the European office (Geneva), by the office for Asia and the Far East, or by various specialized agencies now or later brought into relationship with the United Nations, with the consequence that existing publications of the agencies must also be considered and that a period of time must elapse before a firm picture can be obtained of the new situation. The Statistical Office of the United Nations at the headquarters now publishes the *Monthly Bulletin of Statistics* in English and French, which in its new form replaces the former league *Monthly Bulletin of Statistics.* The Transport and Communications Division of the Department of Economic Affairs prepares the *Monthly Review of Important Events in the Field of Transport and Communications* in a provisional form for limited distribution which continues the similar publication of the League of Nations Economic, Financial, and Transit Department.

Two former publications of the League of Nations library are being continued in Geneva as the *Monthly List of Selected Articles* and the *Monthly List of Books Catalogued in the Library of the United Nations,* although not yet on a monthly basis.

The General Assembly approved regulations for the registration of treaties and for their publication in a treaty series of the United Nations. This project is well under way in the Legal Department and will be carried out in the tradition of the League of Nations Treaty Series.

Besides those publications and studies of the League of Nations which are to be continued, and the technical publications and studies inaugurated by the United Nations, is the considerable volume of informational material prepared and planned by the Department of Public Information. The department is well-known to libraries through its *United Nations Weekly Bulletin,* published in English, French, and Spanish editions. It issues also a wide variety of processed materials for the benefit of the press and schools, and reaches the public through other media less familiar to libraries, such as the radio, still and motion pictures, posters, and public speakers. The full round of its activities is beyond the scope of this paper.

PUBLICATION SALES NUMBERS

The Sales Section of the Division of Documents and Sales has established a series of standing-order categories for individual publications apart from periodicals and the official records. The categories cover fifteen fields, which are outlined in *United Nations Publications Catalogue No. 1.* Beginning in 1947 each publication carries on the reverse of the title page a box containing a publications sales number consisting of the year of publication, the category number of the publication in Roman numerals, and the number of the publication in the particular category in Arabic numerals.

DISTRIBUTION

The problem of distributing the unrestricted materials described in this paper may only be touched upon briefly. For the printed materials, the problem is not so difficult, since most of these are obtainable by exchange or sale through arrangements with the regular sales agents of the United Nations. The problem in this field is rather of coordinating the activities of the various specialized agencies and nongovernmental organizations throughout the world which are associated with the United Nations, so that at least information concerning separate and serial publications is readily available through some uniform method of listing or cataloging, even though publication and distribution may not be centralized. So far as the processed documents are concerned, it is difficult to see a better solution for a wide distribution to useful purpose of the immense bulk of unrestricted documents (in two working languages) than some arrangement for strategically located "depository libraries." The governments, the delegations, the Secretariat departments, the specialized agencies, and the nongovernmental organizations working with the United Nations must be assured of a distribution of documents sufficient to further their work, but an additional complete distribution beyond a select number of national libraries and research institutions making daily use of such documents seems uneconomic. For the general library, the printed official records will probably suffice. How the documents in the so-called "depository libraries" are to be made available to users elsewhere is a problem for the libraries themselves to solve.

The work of the Documents Index unit has so far been chiefly to locate for the delegations and the Secretariat documents currently under discussion in the sessions of the various organs of the United Nations—speeches, draft resolutions, reports, and the like, to identify documents referred to or quoted, and to bring together documents dealing with any particular subject. The card index files cover a vast range of documents from the San Francisco Conference, through the Preparatory Commission, the General Assembly, the three councils, and the various commissions and other

ad hoc bodies established by the main organs, as well as the circulars and bulletins of the Secretariat. But the efforts of a small staff to establish clues to all this material through cards, indexes, and other devices have left little time for publication of up-to-the-minute checklists or of detailed subject-indexes. Gradually, however, the backlog of checklists to documents is being whittled away by the issue of individual checklists to each committee series of the General Assembly for 1946. The Documents Index unit also issues at the close of sessions of any organ during 1947, checklists which also list under each agenda item the documents submitted concerning it, the records of meetings in which it was discussed, and the section of the final report concerning the item. These checklists are themselves processed documents, but it is hoped that before the end of the year the unit will be able to publish this material in its own periodic checklist on a sales or subscription basis.

SUMMARY NOTE

This survey has been of necessity brief, but it has possibly clarified the picture in some degree, and has suggested some of the documentary questions facing the United Nations and its associated bodies. The magnitude of the problem of international documentation demands that the best of technical skill and imagination be employed toward its solution for the benefit of all peoples. The cooperation and advice of American librarians in meeting this challenge will certainly be both warmly welcomed and expected.

The Use of United Nations Documents

William H. Patch

In this most useful document, William Patch, Documents Librarian, Wisconsin University, provides a guide to reference work with UN documents. The document numbering system is briefly described, the important reference tools and indexes analyzed, and a general search strategy suggested.

INTRODUCTION

The great value of United Nations documents lies in their wide range of subject matter as well as in the accuracy and authority with which they are prepared. Because of the belief that peace may be encouraged and maintained by many different means, the United Nations has undertaken work in many fields other than the strictly diplomatic proceedings of the General Assembly and Security Council, about which so much is heard.

One of the first things a student notices when he begins work with the U.N. material is the almost overwhelming volume of it. A few figures will suffice to impress this point, for it is this tremendous number of individual pieces that causes the difficulty in finding specific information. The following figures represent the total number of entries year by year in the *United Nations Documents Index* since its beginning in 1950:

1950	7,502
1951	6,859
1952	6,886
1953	6,015
1954	5,731
1955	6,170
1956	5,019
1957	7,022
1958	6,776
1959	6,583
1960	6,094

Although this tabulation is not strictly accurate as a count of documents, it does come reasonably close. If we take the figure given by Harry N. M. Winton of 41,000 documents[1] for the period from 1946 through 1949, we arrive at a total of well over 100,000.

This paper will describe the various types of material available in libraries and give suggestions on how to locate specific titles or bits of information. In using this great mass of paper, a student will best be aided by a thorough knowledge of the organization. It will also help to have done some previous reading on the subject. A good place to start is with the two basic reference books issued by the United Nations: *Everyman's United Nations*[2] and the *Yearbook of the United Naitons*.[3] It is also wise to consult other books and periodical articles found through such indexes as the *Readers' Guide to Periodical Literature*[4] and the *Public Affairs Information Service*.[5]

The student should also be aware of the relationship of the specialized agencies of the United Nations, such as the International Labour Organization (ILO) and the United Nations Educational, Scientific, and Cultural Organization (UNESCO). These are not a part of the United Nations organization, and their documents are issued quite separately although they are indexed in the *United Nations Documents Index* (UNDI). Such regional international organizations as NATO, SEATO, and the Organization of American States (OAS) have even less affiliation with the United Nations, and their documents do not appear in UNDI.

UNITED NATIONS DOCUMENTATION

When it began its publications program, the United Nations had the advantage of the experience of the League of Nations. In some cases it

---

SOURCE: Reprinted from William H. Patch, *The Use of United Nations Documents.* Urbana, University of Illinois Graduate School of Library Science, 1962. (Graduate School of Library Science. *Occasional Papers* 64).

copied League practice very closely. For example, Secretariat Publications bear sales numbers very similar to those of the older organization. Sometimes the United Nations continued titles originated by the League, but with new numbering. Such a title is the *Treaty Series.* Marie J. Carroll has described these documents in an excellent article on this subject.[6]

Even with the League experiences to rely upon, the United Nations' early publications and documents showed many changes in format, numbering, and titles before they became standardized. There have been few changes since 1950. In the matter of indexing, there were also experiments and false starts. With the publication of UNDI and the near completion of the *Check Lists,* most of the previous efforts at indexing have been discontinued. Since most of the articles and pamphlets describing the use of U.N. documents and publications were written in the early 1950s, they do not take these two excellent indexes into full consideration and, consequently, have become less valuable than when written.

This pamphlet was issued to help the student to locate documents and publications with the use of the catalogues and indexes published by the United Nations. Many of the procedures necessary before 1950, but no longer of use, have been omitted.

DOCUMENTS (MIMEOGRAPHED)

Almost everything issued by the United Nations, except periodicals and some public relations pamphlets, appears originally in document form. Many items, including very important ones, never appear in any other way. Each document bears a characteristic symbol by which it is always identified, even when the document is reprinted in another form. Some libraries shelve the printed versions with the mimeographed, although it is believed that most prefer to use other means of shelving the more permanent forms. The document symbol is composed of letters and Arabic numbers, the different parts of which are divided by slashes, e.g., E/CN.11/Trans/Sub. 2/6. The parts of the symbol are identifiable thus:

6 indicates that this is the sixth document issued by *Sub. 2,* which is the Highway subcommittee of *Trans,* which is the Inland transport committee of *CN. 11,* which is the Economic Commission for Asia and the Far East. *E* indicates

that the parent body is the Economic and Social Council.

A key to this numbering system is found in the booklet *United Nations Document Series Symbols.*[7] Except upon the rare occasions when the work of an agency or committee is being studied as a whole, it is seldom necessary to analyze these numbers. Most documents are sought by specific subject and found through the use of the *Check Lists* and UNDI.

Document symbols are arranged by alphabetical-numerical order and shelving usually follows the same system:

A/3761
A/3765
A/AC.34/25
A/AC.34/SC.1/15
E/CN.4/569
E/CN.11/243
S/984

OFFICIAL RECORDS

A. General Assembly.
   Printed records of each session consist of the following parts:

1. Records of the Plenary Meetings.
   These are verbatim reports of the proceedings, except for the 2nd, 3rd, and 4th special sessions, for which the printed records give only summarized versions of the speeches. Verbatim records for these are only in the preliminary mimeographed documents, which are quite rare.
2. Annexes.
   These volumes comprise a selection of the mimeographed documents printed for permanent preservation. Beginning with the 4th session, the reprinted documents are arranged by agenda item number. There is a check list of documents in each volume giving the location of each if printed, and if not, the statement "Mimeographed document only." This is the only guide to reprinted documents; and since it is neither cumulative nor complete, it is not wise to depend upon it entirely. Before the 4th session, documents were printed in numerical order.
3. Main and procedural committees.
   Summary records only for each of the nine

committees. Some sessions have committee *Annexes* of documents.

4. Supplements.

These are numbered reports of various agencies required to submit reports to the General Assembly. Since the 2nd session the *Annual Report of the Secretary-General on the Work of the Organization* has held the place of *Supplement No. 1* in regular sessions. The first report submitted by that official was issued only as a document (A/65). Most supplements also contain a documents number, although the original mimeographed copy is not often distributed. In addition to the above, there are many annual reports and some final reports of committees. Resolutions have been made the last supplement since the 5th session; previously they have been an unnumbered supplement.

As an example, the following is a list of the supplements to the 11th session:

No. 1   Annual Report of the Secretary-General on the Work of the Organization, 16 June 1955–15 June 1956 (A/3137).

No. 1A   Introduction to the Annual Report of the Secretary-General on the work of the Organization, 16 June 1955–15 June 1956 (A/3137/Add. 1).

No. 2   Security Council Report to the General Assembly, 16 July 1955–15 July 1956 (A/3157).

No. 3   Economic and Social Council Report to the General Assembly, 6 August 1955–9 August 1956 (A/3154).

No. 4   Trusteeship Council Report to the General Assembly, 23 July 1955–14 August 1956 (A/3170).

No. 5   Budget Estimates for the Financial Year 1957 and Information Annex (A/3126).

No. 6   Financial Reports and Accounts for the year ended 31 December 1955 and Reports of the Board of Auditors (A/3124).

No. 6A   United Nations Children's Fund (UNICEF). Financial report and accounts for the year ended 31 December 1955 and report of the Board of Auditors (A/3129).

No. 6B   United Nations Relief and Works Agency for Palestine Refugees in the Near East. Accounts for the financial year ended 30 June 1956 and report of the Board of Auditors (A/3211).

No. 6C   United Nations Korean Reconstruction Agency. Financial report and accounts for the year ended 30 June 1956 and report of the Board of Auditors (A/3206).

No. 6D   United Nations Refugee Fund. Accounts for the year ended 31 December 1955 and report of the Board of Auditors (A/3128).

No. 7   Advisory Committee on Administrative and Budgetary Questions. Second report to the eleventh session of the General Assembly (A/3160).

No. 8   United Nations Joint Staff Pension Fund. Annual report of the United Nations Joint Staff Pension Board for the year ended 30 September 1955 (A/3146).

No. 9   International Law Commission. Report of the eighth session, 23 April–4 July 1956 (A/3159).

No. 10   Report of the Committee on Contributions (A/3121).

No. 11   Report of the United Nations High Commissioner for Refugees (May 1955–May 1956) (A/3123/Rev. 1).

No. 11A   Addenda to the Report of the United Nations High Commissioner for Refugees (A/3123/Rev. 1/Add. 1 and Add. 2).

No. 12   Report of the Committee on South West Africa to the General Assembly (A/3151).

No. 13   Report of the United Nations Commission for the Unification and Rehabilitation of Korea. Covers the period 7 September 1955–24 August 1956 (A/3172).

No. 14   United Nations Relief and Works Agency for Palestine Refugees in the Near East. Annual report of the Director, covering the period 1 July 1955–30 June 1956 (A/3212).

No. 14A   United Nations Relief and Works Agency for Palestine Refugees in the

Near East. Special report of the Director, covering the period 1 November to mid-December 1956 (A/3212/Add.1).

No. 15   Report of the Committee on Information from Non-Self-Governing Territories (A/3127).

No. 16   United Nations Korean Reconstruction Agency. Report of the Agent General, for the period 1 July 1955–30 June 1956 (A/3195).

No. 17   Resolutions adopted by the General Assembly from 12 November 1956–8 March 1957 during the eleventh session (A/3572).

No. 17A   Resolutions adopted by the General Assembly from 10 to 14 September 1957 during the eleventh session (A/3572/-Add.1).

No. 18   Report of the Special Committee on the Problem of Hungary (A/3592).

B. The Security Council.

   1. Meetings.
   Since the Security Council does not have specific sessions at set times of the year, the meetings are numbered consecutively, and the records are verbatim.

   2. Supplements.
   These are now issued quarterly. They contain documents which in the other organs would be included in annexes. The deliberations of the few committees created by the Council are not reprinted in the *Official Records*.

C. The Atomic Energy Commission.
   This commission was in existence from 1946 to 1952. Its *Official Records* follow the pattern of those of the Security Council.

D. The Disarmament Commission.
   This commission took the place of the Atomic Energy Commission and the Commission for Conventional Armaments. Its *Official Records* follow the pattern of those of the Atomic Energy Commission.

E. The Economic and Social Council.

   1. Proceedings of the plenary meetings.
   The 1st and 2nd sessions and 1st special session were all recorded verbatim. Beginning with the 3rd session, all plenary meetings have been summarized in the printed *Official Records*.

2. Annexes.
As in the General Assembly, selected mimeographed documents are printed. The Records of the 1st session contain no annexes. In the 2nd, 4th, and 5th sessions, annexes were included in the same volume with the proceedings of the plenary meetings. In the 3rd session, annexes were included in supplements. In these first five sessions, there was no clear statement as to the principle of arrangement of the documents. Beginning with the 6th session, they are arranged by agenda item. Although each volume contains a table of contents, there is no actual check list of all documents issued and their printed location, if any, until the 10th session. In that session the annexes are printed for the first time by fascicles for each agenda item, with a check list of documents applying to that item at the end. In the 10th session there is also a single check list for all agenda items. This list is not a complete listing of documents of the regional economic commissions and other series of less import. After the 10th session, the only check lists appear at the end of each fascicle.

3. Supplements.
As with the General Assembly, these supplements consist mainly of the various annual reports required to be submitted. Resolutions were included in the same volume with verbatim records of the plenary meetings and annexes for the 1st and 2nd sessions. From the 3rd session through the 7th, they are printed separately but are not a part of the supplements. During this period they bear a sales number as well as a documents symbol. In some collections, therefore, they might be shelved with the sales number publications rather than with the Official Records where they belong.

Because there are two sessions of the Council each year, reports tend to appear every second session, and the number of supplements alternates from many to few. For example, here are the supplements to the 23rd and 24th sessions:

Supplements to the 23rd session:

No. 1   Resolutions adopted by the Economic and Social Council during the twenty-third session, 16 April–2 May 1957 (E/3009).

No. 2   United Nations Children's Fund. Report

of the Executive Board, 22 October–2 November and 11 December 1956 (E/2937).

No. 3   Transport and Communications Commission. Report of the eighth session, 7–16 January 1957 (E/2948).

No. 4   Population Commission. Report of the ninth session, 25 February–8 March 1957 (E/2957/Rev.1).

Supplements to the 24th session:

No. 1   Resolutions adopted by the Economic and Social Council during the twenty-fourth session, 2 July–2 August 1957 (E/3048).

No. 1A   Resolutions adopted by the Economic and Social Council during the resumed twenty-fourth session, 10–13 December 1957 (E/3048/Add.1).

No. 2   Economic Commission for Asia and the Far East. Annual report, 15 February 1956–28 March 1957 (E/2959).

No. 3   Commission on the Status of Women. Report of the eleventh session, 18 March –5 April 1957 (E/2968).

No. 4   Commission on Human Rights. Report of the fourth and fifth session, 28 November–7 December 1956 and 6–17 May 1957 (E/2970/Rev.1).

No. 5   Technical Assistance Committee. Annual report of the Technical Assistance Board for 1956 (E/2965).

No. 6   Economic Commission for Europe. Annual report, 22 April–15 May 1957 (E/2989).

No. 7   Commission on International Commodity Trade. Report of the fourth and fifth sessions, 28 November–7 December 1956 and 6–17 May 1957 (E/3003).

No. 8   Economic Commission for Latin America. Annual report, 15 May 1956–29 May 1957 (E/2998).

No. 9   Social Commission. Report of the eleventh session, 6–24 May 1957 (E3008).

No. 10   Commission on Narcotic Drugs. Report of the twelfth session, 29 April–31 May 1957 (E/3010/Rev.1).

F. The Trusteeship Council.

1. Proceedings of the plenary meetings.
   Like the Economic and Social Council, the first meetings were recorded verbatim. The 1st session and the 1st part of the 2nd session were done in this way, but beginning with the 2nd part of that session, they were summarized. In the 414th meeting held during the eleventh session, it was decided to print the verbatim records for discussion of substantive matters and summarize discussions of procedural questions. This was done for the 414th meeting and continued through the 12th session; but beginning with the 13th session, all discussion was again summarized. Verbatim records appear only in mimeographed documents, which are not generally distributed.

2. Annexes.
   Annexes are included in supplements until the 4th session, when the practice of an annex and numbered supplement became the rule.

3. Supplements.
   The *Special Supplement* to the 2nd session is the first report to appear in this form. Beginning with the 4th session, practice was standardized in the current system, and the Resolutions were included in the numbering. A typical list of supplements is that of the 13th session:

No. 1   Resolutions adopted by the Trusteeship Council during the thirteenth session, 28 January–25 March 1954 (T/1106).

No. 2   United Nations Visiting Mission to Trust Territories in West Africa, 1952. Report on Togoland under United Kingdom administration (T/1107).

No. 3   United Nations Visiting Mission to Trust Territories in West Africa, 1952. Report on Togoland under French administration (T/1108).

No. 4   United Nations Visiting Mission to Trust Territories in West Africa, 1952. Report on the Cameroons under United Kingdom administration (T/1109).

No. 5   United Nations Visiting Mission to Trust Territories in West Africa, 1952. Report on the Cameroons under French administration (T/1110).

SECRETARIAT OR "SALES NUMBER" PUBLICATIONS

The third form of U.N. documentation consists of Secretariat or "Sales Number" publications. These are printed and are on sale to the public at book stores through regular trade channels. They are identified by the fact that each bears a Sales Number made up of the year of publication, a Roman numeral indicating the category, and an Arabic number indicating the order in which titles in a given category were issued for that year. When this method is used, it is very helpful to know the category numbers as follows:

I.   General
IIA.   Economic Stability and Employment
IIB.   Economic Development
IIC.   World Economy
IID.   Trade, Finance, and Commerce
IIE.   European Economy
IIF.   Economy of Asia and the Far East
IIG.   Latin American Economy
IIH.   Technical Assistance
III.   Public Health
IV.   Social Questions
V.   International Law
VIA.   Trusteeship
VIB.   Non-Self-Governing Territories
VII.   Political and Security Council Affairs
VIII.   Transport and Communications
IX.   Atomic Energy and Armaments Control
X.   International Administration
XI.   Narcotic Drugs
XII.   Education, Science, and Culture
XIII.   Demography
XIV.   Human Rights
XV.   Relief and Rehabilitation
XVI.   Public Finance and Fiscal Questions
XVII.   International Statistics

The volumes range from slim pamphlets for public relations work to large scholarly multi-volume works on international law or statistics. Some examples follow:

1952.I.32	Teaching about the United Nations and the Specialized Agencies
1954.I.15	Yearbook of the United Nations, 1953
57.XIV.3	Study of Discrimination in Education

58.II.C.1	World Economic Survey, 1957. (Beginning in 1957, the first two figures from the date of the Sales Number have been omitted.)
58.V.4, Vols. 1–7	United Nations Conference on the Law of the Sea. Geneva, 24 February–27 April 1958. Official Records. 7 v.
58.IX.1	Atomic Energy Glossary of Technical Terms.

Libraries vary widely in their handling of these titles. Some treat them as other books and classify them with other materials on the same subjects in widely scattered parts of the stacks. Others, particularly those with complete sets, keep them together and arrange them by Sales Numbers. Most of the Secretariat publications were originally published as mimeographed documents and bear a documents number as well as the Sales Number. While a few libraries may shelve them under this number, which keeps them with other material issued by the same agency, most libraries consider that this practice tends to make the materials too difficult to locate.

PERIODICALS

The United Nations publishes a number of periodicals, some of which are listed below. A complete list appears in the February issue of UNDI each year. Although many of the titles are intended for purely regional use, those listed here are considered to be of a more general nature and use. Since March, 1958, more important articles have been indexed in UNDI. A few are also included in more general periodical indexes as indicated.

Asian Bibliography. Bangkok, Jan/June 1952–. Twice a year. An accession list of the Library of the Economic Commission for Asia and the Far East. For some reason, titles in oriental languages are translated.

Bulletin on Narcotics. Geneva, v. 1, no. 1, Oct., 1949–. Quarterly. This periodical contains articles concerned with the scientific, legal and economic aspects of narcotics. It is indexed in *Chemical Abstracts* and *Public Affairs Information Service.*

Commodity Trade Statistics. New York, v. 1, no. 1, Oct/Dec. 1949–. Quarterly. A list of reporting countries is given at the end of the table of contents. This title is Series D of the United Nations Statistical Office's *Statistical Papers.* It also bears the Documents Series Symbol: ST/STAT/Ser.D/. Since it consists entirely of statistical tables, it is not indexed elsewhere.

Direction of International Trade. New York, v. 1, no. 1, Jan/Mar. 1950–. Eleven monthly issues plus 1 annual issue. This is a joint publication of the U.N. Statistical Office, the International Monetary Fund, and the International Bank for Reconstruction and Development. It is issued as Series T of the *Statistical Papers* of the U.N. Statistical Office, and bears the U.N. Documents Series Symbol: ST/STAT/Ser.T/. It consists entirely of statistical tables.

Economic Bulletin for Africa. Addis Ababa, v. 1, n. 1, Dec., 1960–. Twice a year. The first two issues are accompanied by statistical supplements. The first issue and its supplement were issued as mimeographed documents, E/CN.14/67 and E/CN.14/67 Stat. App.

Economic Bulletin for Asia and the Far East. Bangkok, v. 1, no. 1, 1st quarter 1950–. Three times a year. *The Economic Survey of Asia and the Far East* constitutes the 4th issue and appears in March. The June issue contains articles and notes on subjects related to the Asian economy. The September issue is devoted to a summary of the economic situation in the preceding year, both for the region as a whole and for the countries individually, along with an assessment of the economic situation in the early months of the current year. The December issue features special studies and reports relating to economic development and planning. All four issues include a compendium of Asian economic statistics. It is indexed in *Public Affairs Information Service.*

Economic Bulletin for Europe. Geneva, v. 1, no. 1, 1st quarter 1949–. Three times per year plus the annual *Economic Survey of Europe.* Each issue emphasizes some aspect of the European economy. It is indexed in *Public Affairs Information Service.*

Economic Bulletin for Latin America. Santiago de Chile, v. 1, no. 1, Jan. 1956–. Twice a year. This is similar to the above three bulletins. Indexed in *Public Affairs Information Service.*

International Review of Criminal Policy. No. 1, Jan. 1952–. Twice a year. Formerly sold on a subscription basis, this is now a Sales Number publication in Category IV. It also bears the Document Series Symbol: ST/SOA/Ser.M/. The contents are published in English, French, and Spanish. Résumés appear in the language not used in the articles.

International Social Service Review. New York, no. 1, Jan. 1956–. Twice a year. This periodical includes articles and news of social work and services. There are also bibliographies.

Monthly Bulletin of Statistics. New York, v. 1, no. 1, Jan. 1947–. This keeps up to date the annual *Statistical Yearbook* of the United Nations.

Population and Vital Statistics Reports. New York, v. 1, no. 1, Jan/Mar. 1949–. Quarterly. This is Series A of the *Statistical Papers* issued by the Statistical Office of the United Nations. It bears the Documents Series Symbol: ST/STAT/Ser.A/, as well as a Sales Number in Category XIII. It is made up entirely of statistical tables.

Quarterly Bulletin for Coal Statistics for Europe. Geneva, no. 1, 1st quarter 1952–. This is issued by the Economic Commission for Europe.

Quarterly Bulletin of Electric Energy Statistics for Europe. Geneva, v. 1, no. 1/2–. First and second quarters 1956–. Issued by the Economic Commission for Europe.

Quarterly Bulletin of Housing and Building Statistics for Europe. Geneva, no. 1, 1st quarter 1953–. Issued by the Economic Commission for Europe.

Quarterly Bulletin of Steel Statistics for Europe. Geneva, no. 1, Dec. 1950–. Issued by the Economic Commission for Europe.

Timber Bulletin for Europe. Geneva, v. 1, no. 1, June 1948–. Quarterly. Before v. 8, no. 1, Jan/Mar. 1955 issued as *Timber Statistics for Europe.* Published jointly by FAO, U.N. Department of Economic and Social Affairs, and the Economic Commission for Europe.

Transport and Communications Review. "Publication of the *Review* has been discontinued with volume VIII, no. 1, issued in 1955. The first issue in this series was v. 1, no. 1, July–Sept., 1948. The *Review* was issued quarterly during these years in separate English and French editions."–*United Nations Publications,* 1955, p. 38. The *Review* contained articles and news notices on legal and technical matters concerned with transportation and communication.

United Nations Bulletin. New York, v. 1-16, 1948-1954. Volumes 1-3 had title *United Nations Weekly Bulletin.* Now replaced by the *United Nations Review,* it is very similar to the new magazine. It was indexed in the *Readers' Guide to Periodical Literature* and the *Public Affairs Information Service.* It is useful in supplementing and bringing up to date the account of work of the United Nations found in the *Yearbook of the United Nations.*

TREATY SERIES

Section 1 of Article 102 of the United Nations Charter states "Every treaty and every international agreement entered into by any member of the United Nations after the present Charter comes into force shall as soon as possible be registered with the Secretariat and published by it."

When registered, the treaty is listed in the monthly *Statement of Treaties and International Agreements Registered or Filed and Recorded with the Secretariat.* The complete text of the treaty appears eventually in the *Treaty Series.*

Treaties listed by title in the *Statement of Treaties and International Agreements* are arranged chronologically according to the date of registration and numbered consecutively. This number and arrangement carry over into the final *Treaty Series.* There is, however, no index published to the former title. The *Treaty Series* includes official texts in all official languages plus translation into English and French if those languages are not used in the original versions. Part I of the series contains treaties registered by members of the organization. Part II contains treaties filed and recorded. These include treaties between nonmembers of the U.N. not bound by Article 102 and treaties ratified before the date of entry into force of the Charter.[8] Part II also includes ratifications, accessions, revisions, and other changes in status of treaties already published. Both parts appear in the same volumes.

While several volumes of indexes have been prepared, there are now only two which need be consulted, *Cumulative Index No. 1* (volumes 1 to 100) and *Cumulative Index No. 2* (volumes 101 to 200). These are arranged by a chronological list of all treaties, a chronological list of General International Agreements, and an alphabetical list of all treaties by country and subject. Volume and page references are given. It is assumed that this *Cumulative Index* will continue to be published.

INDEXES

An awareness of how documents and publications are arranged is only part of the knowledge needed to locate a specific document, or documents on a specific subject. It is also necessary to know what indexes there are, what they include, and how to use them.

United Nations Publications, 1945/1948–. Since the first issue, covering three years, this catalog has been annual. The issue for 1954 cumulated the first ten years, through the end of 1954, and bears the somewhat misleading title *Ten Years of United Nations Publications, 1945 to 1955, a Complete Catalogue.* This cumulation and the annual issues following it are described below.

As the title implies, this is a catalog of publications. No mimeographed documents are included. The first portion is a list of Secretariat publications arranged by the category number. Annual issues list the individual titles within the category, first by date and then by the third number indicating the order of issue for that year. Thus, when one uses a collection of Secretariat publications arranged by Sales Number, this catalog is a convenient index to them.

The ten-year cumulation follows this system but groups the publications under each category by title of series or specific subject rather than by a strictly chronological and numerical arrangement. It also omits superseded editions. Thus, all volumes of the *Yearbook of the United Nations* are listed together in Category I, rather than separated as they would appear on the shelves in order of publication. On the other hand, only the 1953 edition of *Everyman's United Nations,* for instance, is listed in this issue of the catalog.

Following the Secretariat publications, there is a complete listing of *Official Records* published during the period covered by the particular issue. They are arranged in the following order:

1. General Assembly
2. Security Council
3. Atomic Energy Commission
4. Disarmament Commission
5. Economic and Social Council
6. Trusteeship Council

This arrangement is the same as that usually used in shelving the volumes and makes a very convenient key to the material. The *Catalog* does not, however, analyze the contents of either the proceedings of the meetings or the many documents included in the annexes.

The classified listing of records is followed by miscellaneous descriptions of sources of information other than those included in the catalog. This includes information on League of Nations publications, addresses of the specialized agencies, lists of depository libraries, etc. Finally there is an excellent index listing all entries in the book by subject and title.

For most purposes *United Nations Publications* forms an adequate index to materials published by the United Nations. It is necessary to turn elsewhere only when an exhaustive search is made on some subject, or when a speech is to be located in the *Official Records.*

United Nations Books in Print; Nations Unies: Ouvrages en Vente; Naciones Unidas: Obras en Vente, 1960. This is the most recent catalog of publications. It lists all publications in print at the time of publication. As the title indicates, it is divided into three sections according to language.

It is unfortunate that the United Nations has not issued its excellent *United Nations Publications* since 1958 because this volume by no means takes its place as a reference work. First of all, it includes no *Official Records.* The three sections are completely separate. Thus, if a book appears in the list of Spanish or French titles, but not in the English list, it is impossible to ascertain whether the book has never been published in English or is simply out of print.

In addition the entries are very brief and include no series notes and no document numbers. The latter can be useful in identifying the series when it is not otherwise identified. The index, divided into three alphabets and containing subjects and titles, seems adequate.

Check Lists of United Nations Documents. When completed, these volumes will form a complete listing of all publications and mimeographed documents from 1946 through 1949, with the exception of periodicals. Since the *Check Lists* are being published retrospectively, it has been possible to divide the contents into parts, making each part a complete listing of a single organ. Unlike the *United Nations Document Index,* the lists do not include the documents of specialized agencies. Each volume has its own alphabetical index.

The numbers refer to entry numbers of specific documents in the particular *Check List.* There is no overall index to the set; so it is necessary to know what organ issued the item or handled the subject being sought.

Part 1:   General Assembly (and subsidiary organs) [Not yet published.]

Part 2: No. 1: Security Council 1946–1949 (1953.I.3)

Part 3:   Atomic Energy Commission, 1946–1949 (1953.I.3)

Part 4: No. 1: Trusteeship Council, 1947/48; 1st and 2nd sessions (1949.I.2)

No. 2: Trusteeship Council, 1948; 3rd session (1949.I.5)

No. 3: Trusteeship Council, 1949; 4th and 5th sessions, 1st and 2nd special sessions (1951.I.17)

Part 5: No. 1: Economic and Social Council, 1946–1947; 1st to 5th sessions (1949.I.4)

No. 2: Economic and Social Council, 1948; 6th and 7th sessions (1951.I.27)

No. 3: Economic and Social Council, 1949; 8th and 9th sessions (1952.I.4)

Functional Commissions of the Economic and Social Council

Part 6A: No. 1: Economic and Employment Commission, 1947–1949; 1st to 4th sessions, including Economic and Employment Commission (Nuclear), 1946; Temporary Sub-Commission on the Economic Reconstruction of Devastated Areas; Sub-Commission on Employment and Economic Stability, 1st to 3rd sessions (1952.I.10)

Part 6B: No. 1: Transport and Communications Commission, 1946–1949; 1st to 3rd sessions, including Temporary Transport and Communications Commission, 1946 (1951.I.18)

Part 6C: No. 1: Statistical Commission, 1947–1949; 1st to 4th sessions, including Statistical Commission (Nuclear), 1946; Sub-Commission on Statistical Sampling, 1st to 3rd sessions, United Nations World Statistical Congress, Washington, D.C., 1947, Regional Meeting of European Statisticians, Geneva, 1949 (1951.I.19)

Part 6D: No. 1: Commission on Human Rights, 1947–1949, 1st to 5th sessions, including Commission on Human Rights (Nuclear), 1946; Sub-Commission on Freedom of Information and of the Press, 1st to 3rd sessions; Sub-Commission on Prevention of Discrimination and Protection of Minorities, 1st and 2nd sessions (1952.I.6)

Part 6E: No. 1: Social Commission, 1946–1949, 1st to 5th sessions, including Temporary Social Commission, 1946 (1951.I.20)

Part 6F: No. 1: Commission on the Status of Women, 1947–1949, 1st to 3rd sessions, including Sub-Commission on the Status of Women, 1946 (1951.I.21)

Part 6G: Commission on Narcotic Drugs (not yet published)

Part 6H: No. 1: Fiscal Commission, 1947–1948, 1st session (1949.I.6)

No. 2: Fiscal Commission, 1949, 2nd session and interim (1951.I.22)

Part 6I: Not assigned

Part 6J: No. 1: Population Commission, 1947–1949, 1st to 4th sessions (1951.I.23)

Regional Economic Commissions of the Economic and Social Council

Part 7A: Economic Commission for Europe (not yet published)

Part 7B: No. 1: Economic Commission for Asia and the Far East, 1947–1949, 1st to 5th sessions (1951.I.26)

Part 7C: No. 1: Economic Commission for Latin America, 1946–1949, 1st and 2nd sessions (1951.I.28)

Part 8: No. 1: United Nations International Children's Emergency Fund and United Nations Appeal for Children, 1946–1949 (1953.I.5)

Part 9: Secretariat: Publications (not yet published)

United Nations Documents Index

Since 1950, this monthly compilation has been the most comprehensive list of U.N. documents and publications. The only materials which it has not covered thoroughly are speeches made in the various meetings and magazine articles. However, "beginning in March of 1958 articles of general interest appearing in the United Nations periodicals" have been included.[9] Speeches from meetings are to some extent indexed, at least by subject, but are much more thoroughly listed in the *Index to Proceedings,* which will be described in the next section. Periodicals have been listed with bibliographical descriptions in the February issue of each year, except those of 1951, when they were listed more briefly in the December issue.

The section of each issue devoted to U.N. material includes the publications and documents of the International Court of Justice. Following the entire section are separate listings of the specialized agencies of the United Nations, such as UNESCO, WHO, etc. UNDI does not include the various regional organizations like the International Federation for Documentation.

UNDI appears monthly, as indicated above, and the simplest way to understand its arrangement is to examine the Table of Contents for a monthly issue. That of November 1961 is reproduced on the following page. It will be seen immediately that each organization has a symbol and an entry number. These numbers continue numerically through the twelve months of each year, beginning with '1' again the next year. The numbers are used only to locate titles in UNDI. They have no relation to the Documents Series Symbols or Sales Publications Numbers.

When issued, each monthly number has a fascicle printed on yellow paper and bound in the center.

This constitutes the General Index for that month. It is alphabetical by subject, distinctive title, and some personal authors. Care must be taken when one is looking up subjects under the names of countries to distinguish documents bearing on a matter related to the country and documents submitted by the country's government, often having little direct connection with that country. An example from January 1959 will help to explain this and will also show how the index lists the entry numbers of the various specialized agencies:

France:
  documents submitted concerning:
    Hungarian situation   UN 27
    International Computation Centre: Convention, 1951: acceptance   UNESCO 15
    Korea, Republic of: UN, admission to UN 73
    UN: Members: admission to   UN 75
    Viet-Nam, Republic of: UN, admission to Un 75
  museums   UNESCO 15
  refugees: assistance: eligibility   UN 40
  uranium   UN 61

At the end of the year the yellow index pages are removed and the twelve monthly issues are bound with a cumulative index. This combines, in a single alphabet, all of the material from the yellow pages and is arranged in the same way.

The procedure for using UNDI is simple enough. Once the subject is found, it is necessary to look up only the entry number, and the title of the document is given along with the document series symbol, sales publication number, or location in the *Official Records*. The following item contains material on refugees in France, taken from the above example of the General Index:

40 A/AC.96/12   Programme for non-settled refugees living outside camps. Submitted by the High Commissioner, 20 Dec. 1958 ii, [24 p., including annex]

The difficulty in using UNDI lies in the great number of documents included. It is often impossible to tell from the General Index which entry is for a substantive document and which refers only to an administrative paper, such as a letter of transmittal, a note accepting credentials of a delegate, or some other routine matter. In the use of UNDI, especially for locating material from the specialized agencies, it is well for one to remember that the compilers depend upon submission of documents from widely separated sources, and this sometimes means a delay of several months before a document is listed.

Disposition of Agenda Items and Index to Proceedings

These two titles are essentially the same. The *Disposition of Agenda* Items was a mimeographed sub-series of the *Information Papers* of the General Assembly, the Economic and Social Council, and the Trusteeship Council. Beginning in 1953 these series became Sales Publications and their titles were changed to *Index to Proceedings*. At the same time they were placed in the *Bibliographical Series* of the U.N. Headquarters Library and given the appropriate Documents Series Symbols in addition to the Sales Numbers.

The issues of the *Disposition of Agenda Items* which are still used in the original follow:

GENERAL ASSEMBLY

1st session, part 2:	A/283
1st special session:	A/INF/7 & Adds. 1 and 2
2nd session:	A/INF/15 & Corr. 2, 3 and Add. 1 and Corr. 1
2nd special session:	A/INF/24
3rd session, part 1:	A/INF/28
4th session:	A/INF/35 & Corr. 1

ECONOMIC AND SOCIAL COUNCIL

4th session:	E/INF/13
5th session:	E/INF/16
6th session:	E/INF/22 and Add. 1
7th session:	E/INF/29
8th session:	E/INF/28 and Add. 1, 2
9th session:	E/INF/32 and Add. 1
10th session:	E/INF/38
11th session:	E/INF/40
12th session:	E/INF/44
13th session:	E/INF/48 and Add. 1

TRUSTEESHIP COUNCIL

1st session:	T/INF/3/Rev. 1
2nd session:	T/INF/6 and Add. 1

3rd session: T/INF/8
4th session: T/INF/10
5th session: T/INF/12
6th session: T/INF/23
7th session: T/INF/20
8th session: T/INF/21

9th session: T/INF/22
10th session: T/INF/24

At the time of writing, the following *Indexes to Proceedings* have been published:

GENERAL ASSEMBLY

5th regular session:	(ST/LIB/SER.B/A.1)	(Sales No. 1953.I.8)
6th regular session:	(ST/LIB/SER.B/A.2)	(Sales No. 1954.I.23)
7th regular session:	(ST/LIB/SER.B/A.3)	(Sales No. 1953.I.26)
Resumed 7th session:	(ST/LIB/SER.B/A.3/Add. 1)	(Sales No. 1953.I.38)
8th session:	(ST/LIB/SER.B/A.4)	(Sales No. 1954.I.13)
9th session:	(ST/LIB/SER.B/A.5)	(Sales No. 1955.I.15)
10th session:	(ST/LIB/SER.B/A.6)	(Sales No. 1956.I.21)
1st emergency special session; 2nd emergency special session; 11th session:	(ST/LIB/SER.B/A.7)	(Sales No. 1957.I.25)
12th session:	(ST/LIB/SER.B/A.8)	(Sales No. 58.I.15)
3rd emergency special session: 13th session:	(ST/LIB/SER.B/A.9)	(Sales No. 59.I.14)
13th session: Addendum:	(ST/LIB/SER.B/A.9/Add. 1)	(Sales No. 59.I.14, Add. 1)
14th session:	(ST/LIB/SER.B/A.10)	(Sales No. 60.I.11)
4th emergency session: 15th session:	(ST/LIB/SER.B/A.11)	(Sales No. 61.I.18)

ECONOMIC AND SOCIAL COUNCIL

1st special session: 14th session (resumed)	(ST/LIB/SER.B/E.5)	(Sales No. 1953.I.9)
15th session:	(ST/LIB/SER.B/E.6)	(Sales No. 1953.I.23)
16th session:	(ST/LIB/SER.B/E.7)	(Sales No. 1954.I.11)
17th session:	(ST/LIB/SER.B/E.8)	(Sales No. 1954.I.16)
18th session:	(ST/LIB/SER.B/E.9)	(Sales No. 1955.I.9)
19th session: 19th session (resumed)	(ST/LIB/SER.B/E.10)	(Sales No. 1955.I.20)
20th session: 20th session (resumed)	(ST/LIB/SER.B/E.11)	(Sales No. 1956.I.11)
21st session:	(ST/LIB/SER.B/E.12)	(Sales No. 1956.I.26)
22nd session: 22nd session (resumed)	(ST/LIB/SER.B/E.13)	(Sales No. 1957.I.8)
23rd session: 23rd session (resumed)	(ST/LIB/SER.B/E.14)	(Sales No. 1957.I.16)
24th session: 24th session (resumed)	(ST/LIB/SER.B/E.15)	(Sales No. 1958.I.5)
25th session:	(ST/LIB/SER.B/E.16)	(Sales No. 58.I.12)
26th session: 26th session (resumed)	(ST/LIB/SER.B/E.17)	(Sales No. 59.I.8)
27th session:	(ST/LIB/SER.B/E.18)	(Sales No. 59.I.13)
28th session:	(ST/LIB/SER.B/E.19)	(Sales No. 60.I.5)
29th session:	(ST/LIB/SER.B/E.20)	(Sales No. 60.I.9)
30th session:	(ST/LIB/SER.B/E.21)	(Sales No. 61.I.5)
31st session:	(ST/LIB/SER.B/E.22)	(Sales No. 61.I.14)

TRUSTEESHIP COUNCIL

11th session (1st and second parts):	(ST/LIB/SER.B/T.6)	(Sales No. 1953.I.17)
12th session:	(ST/LIB/SER.B/T.7)	(Sales No. 1954.I.12)
13th session:	(ST/LIB/SER.B/T.8)	(Sales No. 1954.I.24)
14th session:	(ST/LIB/SER.B/T.9)	(Sales No. 1955.I.18)
15th session:	(ST/LIB/SER.B/T.10)	(Sales No. 1955.I.21)
16th session:	(ST/LIB/SER.B/T.11)	(Sales No. 1955.I.31)
5th special session: 17th session:	(ST/LIB/SER.B./T.12)	(Sales No. 1956.I.27)
18th session:	(ST/LIB/SER.B/T.13)	(Sales No. 1957.I.2)
6th special session: 19th session:	(ST/LIB/SER.B/T.14)	(Sales No. 1957.I.19)
20th session:	(ST/LIB/SER.B/T.15)	(Sales No. 1957.I.26)
7th special session: 21st session:	(ST/LIB/SER.B/T.16)	(Sales No. 58.I.8)
22nd session: 8th special session: 9th special session:	(ST/LIB/SER.B/T.17)	(Sales No. 59.I.4)
23rd session:	(ST/LIB/SER.B/T.18)	(Sales No. 59.I.11)
24th session:	(ST/LIB/SER.B/T.19)	(Sales No. 59.I.18)
10th special session: 25th session:	(ST/LIB/SER.B/T.20)	(Sales No. 60.I.4)
26th session:	(ST/LIB/SER.B/T.21)	(Sales No. 61.I.2)
11th special session: 27th session:	(ST/LIB/SER.B/T.22)	(Sales No. 62.I.5)

Both old and new titles have basically the same table of contents for each issue. That for the *Index to Proceedings of the General Assembly,* twelfth session, is given as an example:

Explanatory note v
Abbreviations vii
A. Checklist of meetings 1
B. Agenda 4
C. Subject index 8
D. Index to speeches. 65
E. Numerical list of documents. 104

Documents as well as speeches are included in the subject index, but only those of committees which meet during the sessions. Thus, while there is some overlapping with UNDI, the *Index to Proceedings and Disposition of Agenda Items* cannot be depended upon for a complete listing of documents on some subjects.

The index to speeches is arranged alphabetically under the name of the member country. The subjects of the speeches are given under these names. However, since delegates are not listed by name, it is necessary to know on what organs and committees a delegate served in order to locate all of his speeches.

One finds these two series of great value when tracing a single issue through the United Nations, and also when finding out the attitude of a country on any issue.

Directory of Economic and Statistical Projects. Catalogue of Economic and Social Projects

In 1948 the Department of Economic Affairs issued No. 1 of the *Directory* as a Sales Publication. The following year an enlarged volume was issued, again as No. 1, but with a new title: *Catalogue of Economic and Social Projects.* Five annual volumes and a supplement to No. 3 of the *Catalogue* appeared, the last being for 1954. The subtitle to No. 1 of the *Catalogue* well describes the contents: "An annotated list of work planned, in progress or completed by United Nations and Specialized Agencies." These catalogs are still very useful for the period covered because they not only describe the various projects, but also list the documents and publications emanating from them. It is to be regretted that the series was not continued.

Other sources:

United Nations Yearbook

This set is not only invaluable for obtaining a background knowledge of the work of the United Nations, but through its abundant footnotes and bibliographies it also provides a valuable source of information of the documentation of each subject.

Public Affairs Information Service

This index has been mentioned in the Introduction to this paper in connection with background reading. It also lists under appropriate subjects the Secretariat publications. It does not include mimeographed documents.

Periodicals

Many periodicals list documents and publications, either in footnotes or in separate bibliographical articles and lists. Among the most important of these are *International Organization, The Department of State Bulletin,* and the *United Nations Review.*

CONCLUSION

The various indexes and catalogs described above form an adequate, if cumbersome, apparatus for using the documents and publications of the United Nations. One problem remains to bother librarians and students. There is still no generally available, satisfactory key to the more than 13,000[10] documents that have been printed in annexes, supplements, and Sales Number publications. Many of these documents are cited by document series symbol only. With no other information, it is extremely difficult to locate the document if the original is not available. The University of Wisconsin has solved the problem by making a list on cards of all of these reprints, arranged by documents series symbol. There are several reasons for the importance of this list. It permits the easy location of documents which were never possessed in the original and thus effectively increases the resources of the library. It also permits the discarding of thousands of documents mimeographed on short-lived paper and at the same time limits the space needed to shelve all of this material.

Since this paper was prepared with the user rather than the librarian in mind, nothing has been said about the technical aspects of arranging, binding, and records keeping. It will have served its purpose if the student can locate his material more efficiently than before.

NOTES

[1]Winton, Harry N. M. "Documentation," *Annual Review of United Nations Affairs, 1949.* New York, New York University Press, [c1950], p. 52.

[2]*Everyman's United Nations: the structure, functions and work of the organization and its related agencies during the years 1945-1958.* 6th ed. New York, United Nations Office of Public Information, 1959.

[3]*Yearbook of the United Nations.* New York, Columbia University Press, 1946/47—.

[4]*Readers' Guide to Periodical Literature.* New York, H. W. Wilson, 1900 .

[5]*Bulletin of the Public Affairs Information Service, A Cooperative Clearing House of Public Affairs Information.* 1st—. 1915—.

[6]Carroll, Marie J. "League of Nations Documents and Publications Comparable with or Continued in United Nations Publications," *College and Research Libraries,* 12:44-52, 64.

[7]United Nations Library. *United Nations Documents Series Symbols* (U.N. Headquarters Library, Bibliographical Series No. 5). New York, United Nations, [1956]. (Sales No. 1956.I.4).

[8]An explanation of the procedures and history of Article 102 is found in *Repertory of Practice of United Nations Organs.* New York, United Nations, 1955, vol. 5, pp. 279-313 (Sales No. 1955.V.2, Vol. V).

[9]Footnote from UNDI, February 1958, p. 86.

[10]From the finding list on cards at the Memorial Library, University of Wisconsin.

Acquiring Publications of the United Nations and Its Agencies

E. M. Ronquillo

Those libraries not fortunate enough to be designated as UN depositories must acquire the documentation by other means, primarily by purchase. E. M. Ronquillo, Librarian-Documentalist, UNESCO Research Center on Social and Economic Developments in Southern Asia, Delhi, sets forth some acquisitions considerations and lists sources of purchase.

0. INTRODUCTION

The United Nations Organization has grown tremendously in size and complexity from the time it was conceived in 1945 to the present. Its membership has increased and so with the problems it has to handle. Time and again the member states have called on it to assist them in their manifold problems covering practically every field of human activity and interest—problems which are of varying urgency and importance. Some need immediate action while others are long-range plans. This variety demands, therefore, that the Organization be flexible enough, be so designed and so organized structurally as to be able to meet them all without any rupture or complication in the structure. Committees of individuals and of nations are convened to look after every sort of problem; conferences at various levels are planned to discuss matters; specialists are despatched for on-the-spot studies; centres are established to study long-range implications, and so on. This complexity in structure, methods and functions of the Organization has no doubt created a lot of confusion in the minds of the public. It has become imperative, therefore, that such doubts and confusions be cleared if it were to inspire support to its benevolent ideals: peace among nations and the welfare of humanity as a whole.

One fact is sure: that the United Nations believes in the importance of libraries in pushing through its mission and so libraries are in a very strategic position to assist the Organization in erasing mis-conceptions and further an understanding of the Organization itself, of its various organs, their separate missions and the processes by which the nations and the Organization work to promote common interest. It becomes a must for everyone to know the administrative offices that handle the different jobs, because every branch of the Organization is a productive group: every office, a veritable mine of literature, as every activity performed is properly documented for use. Being an Organization of governments, the results of deliberations and the studies of its bodies bear the stamp of authority: they are documents and as such, are so much sought for in all quarters. Invariably, it becomes the task of the librarians to produce them on request. May I say in this connection that around a third of correspondence received at the Unesco Research Centre, for instance, are questions regarding United Nations documents: what there are, where and how to get them. Such questions come not only from the public, but also from librarians themselves since ours is a Unesco Centre and, therefore, believed to be knowledgeable in the ways of the Organization and its agencies, and of its publications. Frankly speaking, however, we ourselves get puzzled sometimes over such literature. We have likewise to wade through catalogues, advance publications notices, despatch lists, and so on, to be able to know what there are. Even librarians of depository libraries cannot calmly sit by and wait for the documents to automatically come to their libraries *en toto*, as one library may be a depository for United Nations publications or of a series but may

SOURCE: Reprinted from: E. M. Ronquillo "Acquiring Publications of the United Nations and its Specialized Agencies," *Library Herald* 8 (July 1965), pp. 65–81.

not be for other agencies or for all serials. It is doubtful if in this region any library can claim to have a complete collection of the Organization and agencies' publications. It is the objective of this paper therefore to guide the librarians on methods of finding out what is being issued, where and how to acquire it.

1. ORGANIZATION

It is accepted that a good librarian knows the various organizations existing around, especially those working along the line of his own organization's interest—besides knowing the people working in them. The knowledge would be useful to him in creating contacts and eventually understanding that organization's activities and the results of such activities. The knowledge may come in handy when acquiring publications too. So will the knowledge of the structure of more complex organizations like the United Nations—the Organization that plays a vital part in our time, and is affecting us vitally, the Organization acknowledged to be the most prolific publisher of our age—be essential. To know its whole structure, therefore, is a must to a librarian. This we give hereafter. The main Organization consists of 6 main organs, namely:

1. The General Assembly
2. The Security Council
3. The Economic and Social Council
4. The Trusteeship Council
5. The International Court of Justice
6. The Secretariat

The General Assembly takes up the problems on hand and decides what steps to take. The rest executes that decision. Most of these offices are housed in the Headquarters in New York, but each of them has committees, agencies or commissions of some sort distributed all over the world. Of the six organs, the Economic and Social Council is one of the biggest and potentially the more important one in the Organization. It has regional economic commissions, of which ECAFE is one. The others are in Africa, Europe and Latin America. To implement decisions taken up by the General Assembly, specialized agencies are entrusted to deal with governments directly. These are the ILO, FAO, GATT, UNESCO, ICAO, IBRD, IMF, WHO, UPU, ITU, WMO, IFC, IAEA, IMCO.[1]

Each of these agencies is by itself an autonomous body, each with its own policy and programme-making executives, secretariat and administration. They also have commissions, branches, and centres by which they implement decisions taken up at the Assembly for every country. All specialize in one or two special fields and are potential sources of literature, so that, altogether the UN's publications programme cover a wide range of subjects. This being so, the United Nations Organization as a whole has attained the title of being the most prolific single publisher in the world today.

2. WHERE TO ORDER

Everyone of the agencies mentioned maintain separate publications programmes and facilities for distribution and sale of its publications. However, the United Nations includes descriptions of such work in its own catalogues. These catalogues are issued regularly in the form of cumulative lists, loose leaf notices, advance releases, etc. Some of these UN catalogues are listed below:

21 For Older Publication

United Nations publications (ST/DPI/SER,FO1–). UN, Department of Public Information. Issued annually in English and French (discontinued).

Ten years of United Nations publications, 1945-1955 (ST/DPI/SER,F/–). UN, Department of Public Information. Issued in English and French.

Current United Nations publications.
Produced in the interval between the annual catalogues and contains descriptive notes or a selection of current United Nations publications.

United Nations documents index. Compiled by the UN Library Documents Index Unit, in co-operation with specialized agencies, V. 1, no. 1–, 1950–.
Issued monthly. Lists, describes and indexes by subject all documents and publications of the United Nations and specialized agencies received in the United Nations Library. In English. This title succeeded the *Checklist of United Nations Documents*, 1946 through 1948.

United Nations book in print (ST/CS/SER.J/1—).
UN, 19—. Issued annually in English, French
and Spanish; kept up to date with supplements.
United Nations publications. Yellow sheets issued
each time a publication is released. This is cumulated monthly in a white sheet.

211 For Catalogues

UN catalogues may be had from the:
  Sales and Circulation Section, United Nations,
  New York, U SA .;
  The Office of Public Information, United Na-
  tions, New York, U S A.; and
  The Sales Section, European Office of the
  United Nations, Palais de Nations, Geneva;

or from the UN Information Centres distributed
all over the world (details sec 62), of which one is
in Delhi on 21, Curzon Road, and from the UN National Distributors (details sec 61). The distributors for India are:

  Messrs Orient Longmans Ltd, 17, Chittaranjan
  Avenue, Calcutta 13, with branch on 24/1,
  Asaf Ali Road, New Delhi 1,
  Messrs Oxford Book and Stationery Co; 17, Park
  Street, Calcutta 16, with branch in Scindia
  House, New Delhi-1.

Both booksellers handle the publications of the
International Court of Justice, the FAO and the
UNESCO in India. The latter store, Oxford, also
handles those of ICAO and WHO besides.

Should it be difficult to obtain them from these
national booksellers, let us say for free materials,
one may always write directly to the main office
of each specialized agency.

  1. International Court of Justice publications
     may be had from the UN Sales Sections and
     Sales Agents of the UN.
  2. Besides the Sales Agents mentioned above,
     FAO publications may be ordered also di-
     rectly from:

     The Distribution and Sales Section.
     Food and Agriculture Organization of the
     UN,
     Viale Delle Terme di Caracalla,
     Rome, Italy.
  3. IAEA publications may be had directly
     from its offices in Geneva.
  4. Orders for IBRD publications should be ad-
     dressed to their publishers:

     The John Hopkins Press, Baltimore 18,
     Maryland, USA, or to its only agent in the
     United Kingdom:

     The Oxford University Press, Amen House,
     Warwick Square, London, EC 4,
     England.
  5. ICAO—As mentioned ahead, the Oxford
     Book and Stationery Co, in Calcutta and
     Delhi handles ICAO publications.
  6. IFC has no sales publications.
  7. ILO—One can subscribe to all ILO publica-
     tions for $50.00 or £15. Publications may
     also be purchased individually in the cur-
     rency of each country. Publication informa-
     tion and catalogues may be obtained from
     the head offices in Geneva, from the ILO
     Liaison Office with UN on 345 East, 46th
     Street, New York 17, the ILO Field Offices
     which in case of India is the ILO Asian Field
     Office, P O Box No 4, Bangalore, Mysore
     State, or from the ILO Branch Offices, as
     the one in New Delhi:

     The Director, Mandi House, New Delhi,
     and from national correspondents of the
     ILO.
  8. IMF has no sales agent, except in the United
     Kingdom. Its only priced publications are
     International financial statistics, (monthly)
     Balance of payments year book, and *IMF
     staff papers* for which payment is accepted
     in national currencies by central banks of
     many member countries. Orders may be
     sent to:

     The Secretary, International Monetary
     Fund, 1818, H Street, NW,
     Washington 25, DC, USA
  9. IRO—International Refugee Organization
     has no sales publications.
  10. ITU has no sales agent. Orders should be
      addressed to:

      The General Secretariat, International
      Telecommunication Union, Palais Wil-
      son, Geneva, Switzerland.

The complete list of ITU publications with
prices may be obtained from the General
Secretary. A selective list is published each
month in the organ of the ITU, the *Telecommunication journal.*
  11. UNESCO—Unesco publishes general cata-
      logues, periodic and yearly checklists, a se-

ries of specialized (subject) lists, advance information sheets on its publications. Its most recent one which covers 1946–1959 is the *General catalogue of Unesco publications and Unesco sponsored publications.* (Unesco, 1962, 217 p.) (DP. 60/11.19/AF). Such catalogues may be had from its Headquarters in:

The United Nations Educational, Scientific and Cultural Organization, Palace de Fontenoy, Paris 7e. France.

Publications and catalogues as well may also be had from Unesco's national distributors. Where there are no distributors, orders may be placed with the Headquarters in Paris. There are certain publications sponsored by Unesco or in which Unesco is associated with but which are not issued by Unesco. Orders and enquiries for them should be sent to their respective publishers. A list of such publications is to be found also in the *General catalogue of Unesco publications and Unesco sponsored publications* and in the *List of publications and documents* (ARC/Lists) issued quarterly. And so, with requests for free publications: they should also be addressed to the publisher, not to the national distributor or sales agent, as they do not handle distribution of free publications. Publications prepared locally and distributed free of charge by Unesco Regional Offices and Science Co-operation Offices should be requested direct from these offices, in spite of the Unesco imprint. Thus our Centre's publications may be had from us, except for the priced ones which would be with M/s Orient Longmans Ltd, the national distributor of Unesco.

12. UPU—Publications of the Universal Postal Union are listed in the *Union postale*, monthly journal of UPU. UPU has no sales agents. Orders may be addressed to:

The International Bureau, Universal Postal Union, Schossholdenstrasse 46, Berne 15, Switzerland.

13. WHO—Requests for catalogues of WHO publications may be had from Sales Agent, Oxford Book and Stationary Co., for India as

previously mentioned or from the Sales Section, World Health Organization, Palais des Nations, Geneva, Switzerland.

14. WMO—WMO has no sales agents. Orders should be addressed to:

World Meteorological Association, Campagne Rigot, 1 Avenue de la Park, Geneva.

3. HOW TO ORDER

Mimeographed documents and meeting records of the plenary meetings of the General Assembly, the Economic and Social Council, the Security Council, and the Trusteeship Council are largely reproduced in the printed *Official records* of these bodies primarily for the use of the Member States and of the Secretariat. It should be noted that, while documents and meeting records of sessional committees of the General Assembly also reappear in its printed *Official records*, no documents and meeting records are republished in the *Official records* of the three Councils, nor are inter-sessional committee documents published in the *Official records* of the General Assembly. Furthermore, the majority of other documents and meeting records of the commissions under the Economic and Social Council, the documents of the United Nations Children's Fund, the United Nations Special Fund, and the petitions series of the Trusteeship Council remain permanently in mimeographed form. Mimeographed meeting records and documents of the International Law Commission reappear in the two volumes of the printed *Yearbook* of the Commission. Arrangements, have been made to enable interested parties or individuals to purchase certain classes of these mimeographed documents by annual subscription. For convenience in location they are subdivided by classes. These classes are as follows:

I Plenary documents of the General Assembly

II Documents of the Committees of the General Assembly

III Plenary documents of the General Assembly and documents of the Committees of the General Assembly

IV   Documents of the Economic and Social
Council
V   Documents of the Commissions and Com-
mittees of the Economic and Social
Council
VI   Documents of the Economic and Social
Council and of the Commissions and Com-
mittees of the Council
VII   Documents of the Security Council and the
Disarmament Commission
VIII   Documents of the Trusteeship Council
IX   All mimeographed documents, class I—
VIII.

When ordering the printed *Official records* of the
General Assembly, Economic and Social Council
and the Trusteeship Council, the purchaser should
give the session number, the title (indicating
whether meetings or annexes) or supplement meeting and language required. For those of the Security Council and of the Disarmament Commission,
give the year, the number of the meeting or title
of the supplement. Orders for subscriptions
should be sent directly to the Sales and Circulation Section, United Nations, New York.

Secretariat publications, likewise have been divided into 17 sales categories, each indicated by a
Roman numeral for easy identification. The sales
categories are:

I   General
II-A   Economic stability and employment
II-B   Economic development
II-C   World economy, Middle East economy
II-D   Trade, finance and commerce
II-E   European economy
II-F   Asian economy
II-G   Latin American economy
II-H   Technical assistance
II-K   African economy
III   Public health (not used since 1948;
WHO commands this field)
IV   Social questions
V   International law
VI-A   Trusteeship
VI-B   Non-self-government territories
VII   Political and Security Council affairs
VIII   Transport and Communications
IX   Atomic energy and armaments control.

These categories together with the year of publication and final identity number of the particular
publication, make up the sales number. This number and the language desired must be stated when
ordering. Obviously, one purpose of the sales pub-

lication categories—apart from its brief identification of a specific item without having to copy the
title, date of publication, and number of pages—is
to allow standing order arrangements with sales
agents or the Sales Section, so that all items in the
category of Asian economy (II. F), for instance,
may be sent and billed upon publication.

4. PAYMENTS

Orders for United Nations Organization materials invariably make the purchaser think of
foreign exchange. This worry is generally unwarranted, as publications when ordered through sales
agents may be paid in the national currency. Even
when ordering must be done straight to the main
offices, certain agencies still accept payment in the
national currency by arrangement with the central
banks. Where there is no such agreement, Unesco
Book Coupons may be purchased from the Ministries of Education or the National Commissions.

5. UNITED NATIONS DEPOSITORY LIBRARIES IN INDIA

The United Nations has established a network of
depository libraries so that its documents and publications will be available for reference. Most of
these libraries are open to the public; a few are
restricted to members.

The Central Library.
Government of Maharashtra,
Bombay.

University of Bombay Li-
brary, Bombay.

The Servants of India Society
Library,
Poona, Maharashtra.

The Delhi School of Eco-
nomics Library.
University of Delhi,
Delhi 6.

The Central Secretariat
Library,
New Delhi 1.

The Indian Council of
World Affairs Library,
Sapru House, New Delhi 1

The Parliament Library.
New Delhi 1.

The Connemara Public
Madras.

Banaras Hindu Univer-
sity Library,
Varanasi, Uttar Pradesh.

Uttar Pradesh Civil Secretariat Library,
Lucknow, Uttar Pradesh.

The National Library,
Belvedere,
Calcutta, West Bengal.

6. NATIONAL DISTRIBUTORS AND INFORMATION CENTRES

To facilitate the acquisitions of publications
by libraries and others, UN and other agencies

have set up a network of distributors in most countries of the world. All orders can be placed through these distributors in respective countries. UN has further facilitated the availability of its publications for use through a number of UN Information Centres in various countries. These Centres acquire and preserve a copy each of all UN documents and the same are made available for reference on demand. A list of distributors and centres is provided herewith for reference.

61 List of National Distributors for UN and UNESCO Publications

AFGHANISTAN
Panuzai, Press Department,
Royal Afghan Ministry of Education,
Kabul.

ALBANIA
N. Sh. Botimeve Naim Frasheri,
Tirana.

ARGENTINA
Editorial Sudamericana, S.A.
Alsina 500,
Buenos Aires.

AUSTRALIA
Melbourne University Press,
369 Lonsdale Street,
Melbourne C 1 (Victoria).

AUSTRIA
Verlag Georg Fromme & Co.
Spengergasse 39,
Wien V.

BELGIUM
Office de publicite, S.A.
16, rue Marcq,
Bruxelles 1.

N V Standaard Boekhandel,
Belgielei 151,
Antwerpen.

For "The Courier":
Louis de Lannoy,
22, palace de Brouckere,
Bruxelles.

BOLIVIA
Libreria Selecciones,
avenida Camacho 369,
La Paz.

Libreria Universitaria,
Universidad de San Francis
Xavier, Sucre

Libreria "Los Amigos del Libro,"
calle Peru 11,
Cochabamba.

BRAZIL
Fundacao Getulio Vargas,
186 praia de Botafogo,
caixa postal 4081,
Rio de Janeiro

BULGARIA
Raznoisnos,
1 Tzar Assen.
Sofia.

BURMA
Burma Translation Society,
361 Prome Road,
Rangoon.

CAMBODIA
Librairie Albert Portail,
14, avenue Boulloche,
Phnom-penh,

CANADA
The Queen's Printer,
Ottawa (Ont.)

CEYLON
Lake House Bookshop,
P. O. Box 244,
Lady Lochore Building,
100 Parsons Road,
Colombo 2

CHILE
Editorial Universitaria, S.A.,
avenida B. O'Higgins 1058,
casilla 10220,
Santiago.

For "The Courier":
Comision Nacional de la Unesco en Chile,
calle San Antonio 255,
7.0 piso,
Santiago.

CHINA
The World Book Co, Ltd,
99 Chungking South Road,
Section 1,
Taipeh (Taiwan/Formosa).

COLOMBIA
Libreria Central,
carrera 6-A no 14-32,
Bogota.

Libreria Buchholz Galeria,
avenida Jimenez de Quesad:
8-40,
Bogota.

J. Germàn Rodriguez N.,
oficina 201,
Edificio Banco de Bogota,
apartado nacional 83,
Girardot.

COSTA RICA
Imprenta y Libreria Trejos, S.A.,
apartado 1313,
San Jose.

CUBA
Libreria Economica,
Pte Zayas 505-7,
apartado 113,
La Habana.

CZECHOSLOVAKIA
Artia Ltd.,
30 Ve Smeckach,
Praha 2.

DENMARK
Ejnar Munkagaard, Ltd.,
6 Norregads,
Kobenhavn K.

DOMINICAN REPUBLIC
Libreria Dominicana,
Mercedes 49,
apartado de correos 656,
Ciudad Trujillo.

ECUADOR
Casa de la Cultura Ecuatoriana
Nucleo del Guayas,
Pedro Moncaya y 9 de Octubre,
casilla de correo 3542,
Guyaquil.

EL SALVADOR
Manuel Navas & Cia.,
1.a avenida Sur 37,
San Salvador.

ETHIOPIA
International Press Agency,
P.O. Box 120,
Addis Ababa.

FINLAND
Akateeminen Kirjakauppa,
2 Keskuskatu,
Helsinki.

FRANCE
Librairie de l'Unesco
place de Fontenoy,
Paris–7e.

FRENCH WEST INDIES
Librairie J. Bocage,
rue Lavoir, B.P. 208,
Fort-de-France (Martinique).

GERMANY (FEDERAL REPUBLIC)
R Oldenbourg Verlag,
Unesco-Vertrieb fur,
Deutschland,
Rosenheimerstrasse 145,
Munchen 8.

GHANA
Methodist Book Depot Limited,
Atlantis House,
Commercial Street.
P.O. Box 100,
Cape Coast.

GREECE
Librairie H. Kauffmann,
28, rue du Stade,
Athens.

GUATEMALA
Comision Nacional de l'Unesco.
5.0 Calle 6-79,
zona 1 (Altos),
Guatemala.

HAITI
Librairie "A la Caravelle,"
36, rue Roux,
B.P. 111,
Port-au-Prince.

HONG KONG
Swindon Book Co.,
25, Nathan Road,
Kowloon.

HUNGARY
Kultura,
P.O. Box 149,
Budapest 62.

INDIA
Orient Longmans Ltd.:
17, Chittaranjan Avenue,
Calcutta 13;

Nicol Road, Ballard Estate,
Bombay 1;

36a Mount Road, Madras 2;

Kanson House,
1/24 Asaf Ali Road,
New Delhi-1.

→   Sub-depots:
Oxford Book and Stationery Co.
17, Park Street, Calcutta 16.
and
Scindia House, New Delhi.

INDONESIA
Bappit Pusat PERMATA,
Djalan Nusantara 22,
Djakarta

IRAN
Commission nationale iranienne pour l'Unesco,
avenue du Musee,
Teheran.

IRAQ
McKenzie's Bookshop,
Baghdad.

IRELAND
The National Press,
2 Wellington Road,
Ballsbridge,
Dublin.

ISRAEL
Blumstein's Bookstores Ltd.,
35 Allenby Road and
48 Nahlat Benjamin Street,
Tel Aviv.

ITALY
Libreria Zanichelli,
Portici del Pavaglione,
Bologna.

Libreria Commissionaria
Sansoni (Agente Generale),
via Gino Capponi 26,
casella postale 552,
Firenze.

Hoepli,
via Ulrico Hoepli, 5,
Milano.

Libreria Internazionale
Ulrico,
Hoepli,
Largo Chighi,
Roma.

Libreria Paravia,
via Garibaldi, 23,
Torino.

JAMAICA
Sangster's Book Room,
91, Harbour Street,
Kingston.
Knox Educational
Services,
Spaldings.

JAPAN
Maruzen Co., Ltd.,
6 Tori; Nichome,
Nihonbashi,
P.O. Box 605,
Tokyo Central,
Tokyo.

JORDAN
Joseph I. Bahous & Co,
Darul-Kutub, Salt Road,
P.O. Box 66,
Amman.

KOREA
Korean National Com-
mission for Unesco,
P.O. Box Central 64,
Seoul.

LEBANON
Librairie Antoine.
A. Naufal et Freres,
B.P. 656,
Beyrouth,

LIBERIA
J. Momolu Kamara
69 Front and Gurley
Streets,
Monrovia.

LUXEMBOURG
Librairie Paul Bruck,
22 Grand-rue,
Luxembourg.

MALAYSIA/SINGAPORE
Federal Publications Ltd,
Times House,
River Valley Road,
Singapore.

MALTA
Sapienza's Library,
26, Kingsway,
Valletta.

MAURITIUS
Nalanda Co. Ltd,
30 Bourbon Street,
Port-Louis.

MEXICO
Editorial Hermes,
Ignacio Hariscal 41,
Mexico, D.F.

MONACO
British Library,
30, Boulevard des
Moulins,
Monte–Carlo.

MOROCCO
Centre de diffusion docu-
mentaire, du BEPI,
B.P. 211,
Rabat.

NETHERLANDS
N.V. Martinus Nijhoff,
Lange Voorhout 9,
's–Gravenhage.

NETHERLANDS ANTILLES
G.C.T. Van Dorp & Co.
(Ned. Ant.) N.V.,
Willemstad (Curacao,
N.A.).

NEW ZEALAND
Unesco Publications
Centre,
100 Hackthorne Road,
Christchurch.

NICARAGUA
Libreria Cultural Nicara-
guense,
calle 15 de Septiembre
115,
Managua

NIGERIA
CMS (Nigeria) Bookshops,
P.O. Box 174,
Lagos.

NORWAY
A.S. Bokhrnet,
Lille Greoen 7,
Oslo.

PAKISTAN
The West-Pak Publishing
Co. Ltd,
Unesco Publications House,
P.O. Box 374,
56 N. Gulberg Industrial
Colony,
Lahore.

PANAMA
Cultural Panamena,
avenida 7a no. T1-49,
apartado de correos 2018.
Panama.

PARAGUAY
Agencia de Librerias,
de Salvador Nizza, Yegros,
entre
25 de Mayo y Mcal. Esti-
garribia,
Asuncion.

PERU
"ESEDAL–Oficina de Ser-
vicios,"
Dpto. de Venta de Publica-
ciones,
Jiron Huancavelica (calle
Ortiz), 368,
apartado 577,
Lima.

PHILIPPINES
Philippine Education Co.
Inc.
1104 Castillejos,
Quiapo,
P.O. Box 620, Manila.

POLAND
Osrodek Rozpowszechni-
ania
Wydawnictw Naukowych
PAN,
Patac Kultury i Nauki,
Warszawa.

PORTUGAL
Dias & Andrade Lda,
Livraria Portugal.
rua do Carmo 70,
Lisboa.

REPUBLIC OF SOUTH
AFRICA
Van Schaik's Bookstore
(Pty.),
Libri Building,
Church Street,
P.O. Box 724,
Pretoria.

RHODESIA AND NYASA-
LAND (FEDERATION)
The Book Centre
First Street,
Salisbury (Southern
Rhodesia).

RUMANIA
Cartimex,
Str. Aristide Briand 14-18,
P.O. Box 134-135,
Bucuresti.

SENEGAL
La Maison du livre,
13, avenue Roume, Dakar.

SPAIN
Libreria Cientifica
Medinaceli,
Duque de Medinaceli 4.
Madrid 14.

For "The Courier":
Editiones Iberoamericanas
S.A.,
calle de Onate 15,
Madrid.

SWEDEN
A/B C.E. Fritzes Kungl.
Hovbokhandel,
Fredsgatan 2.
Stockholm, 16.

For "The Courier"
Svenska Unescoradet,
Vasagatan 15-17,
Stockholm C.

SWITZERLAND
Europa Verlag,
Ramistrasse 5,
Zurich.

Payot,
40, rue du Marche,
Geneve.

TANGANYIKA
Dar es Salaam Bookshop.
P.O. Box 9030,
Dar es Salaam.

THAILAND
Suksapan Panit,
Mansion 9,
Rajdammern Avenue.
Bangkok.

TURKEY
Librairie Hachette,
469 Istiklal Caddesi,
Beyogiu,
Istanbul.

UGANDA
Uganda Bookshop,
P.O. Box 145,
Kampala,

UNITED ARAB REPUBLIC
La Renaissance d'Egypte,
9, Sh. Adly Pasha,
Cairo (Egypt.)

UNITED KINGDOM
H.M. Stationery Office,
P.O. Box 569,
London, S.E. 1.

UNITED STATES OF
AMERICA
Unesco Publications
Center,
801, Third Avenue,
New York 22, N.Y.

and except for periodicals:
Columbia University
Press,
2960 Broadway,
New York 27, N.Y.

USSR
Mezhdunarodnaja Kniga,
Moskva G-200.

URUGUAY
Unesco Centre de Coop-
eracion Cientifica para
America Latina,
bulevar Artigas 1320-23,
casilla de correo 859,
Montevideo.

Oficina de Representacion,
de Editorales,
plaza Cagancha 1342, ler
piso,
Montevideo.

VENEZUELA
Libreria Politecnica,
calle Villaflor,
local A, lado General
Electric,
Sabana Grande,
Caracas.

Libreria Selecta,
Avenida 3, no 23-23,
Merida.

VIET-NAM
Librairie-papeterie Xuan-
Thu,
185-193 rue Tu-Do,
B.P. 283,
Saigon.

YUGOSLAVIA
Jugoslovenska Knjiga,
Tetaziji 27,
Beograd.

62 U N Information Centres

Accra, Ghana. Covering Gambia, Ghana, Nigeria, Sierra Leone.

Addis Ababa, Ethiopia. ECA Information Officer, Ethiopia.

Athens, Greece. Covering Greece, Israel and Turkey.

Bangkok, Thailand. ECAFE Information Officer, covering Cambodia, Laos, Thailand, Federation of Malaya and Singapore, Viet-Nam.

Belgrade, Yugoslavia. Covering Albania and Yugoslavia.

Buenos Aires, Argentina. Covering Argentina, Paraguay and Uruguay.

Cairo, United Arab Republic (Egypt). Covering Iraq, Jordan, Lebanon, Libya, Saudi Arabia, United Arab Republic, Yemen.

Copenhagen, Denmark. Covering Denmark, Finland, Iceland, Norway, Sweden.

Djakarta, Indonesia. Information Officer for Indonesia.

Geneva, Switzerland. Information Service of the European Office, covering Australia, Bulgaria, Germany, Hungary, Poland, Rumania, Switzerland.

Kabul, Afghanistan. Covering Afghanistan.

Karachi, Pakistan. Covering Pakistan

Lima, Peru. Covering Bolivia, Peru.

London, United Kingdom. Covering Ireland, Netherlands, United Kingdom.

Manila, Philippines. Covering the Philippines.

Mexico City, Mexico. Covering Costa Rica, Cuba, Dominican Republic, El Salvador, Guatemala, Honduras, Mexico, Nicaragua, Panama.

Moscow, USSR. Covering Byelorussian SSR, Ukrainian SSR, USSR.

New Delhi, India. Covering Ceylon, India, Nepal.

Paris, France. Covering Belgium, France, Luxembourg.

Prague, Czechoslovakia. Covering Czechoslovakia.

Rangoon, Burma. Covering Burma.

Rio de Janeiro, Brazil. Covering Brazil.

Rome, Italy. Covering Italy.

Santiago, Chile. ECLA Information Officer.

Sydney, Australia. Covering Australia, New Zealand.

Teheran, Iran. Covering Iran.

Tokyo, Japan. Covering Japan.

Washington, United States of America.[1]

7. CONCLUSION

Lest one be more confused about the profusion of the information just given, let me summarize this paper briefly.

Orders for catalogues and publications of United Nations and all its agencies may be had from the national distributors. Most publications of the Organization repeat this list in the back covers. Should this be difficult, as in cases of mimeographed documents, official records, periodicals and free publications, one may write directly to main offices, preferably to their sales and distribution sections, or the information centres, field offices and branches, addresses of which are given in this paper.

Orders for UN publications, particularly, should bear the sales number and the language desired. Except for United Nations publications, those of other agencies may be ordered directly or through their agents through the usual orders, giving author, title and date of publication and language, if published in two or more languages. Payments may be made in national currencies when ordered through sales agent in one's country or in Unesco coupons when ordering outside the country. In the case of India, these coupons may be had from the Ministry of Education upon presentation of an official bill. These coupons are simply made to the seller who in turn endorses them to the Unesco Coupon Office. The Unesco Coupon Office instructs its bank to transfer the amount of the coupon to the seller's bank. Thus the payment is finalized.

[1] For addresses of Information Centers *see* Everyman's United Nations, 8th ed. N.Y., United Nations, 1968, pp. 591–594 [*Eds.*]

NOTE

[1] International Labour Organization, Food and Agriculture Organization of the United Nations, General Agreements on Tariffs and Trade, United Nations Educational, Scientific and Cultural Organization, International Civil Aviation Organization, International Bank for Reconstruction and Development, World Health Organization, Universal Postal Union, International Tele-communications Union, World Meteorological Organization, International Finance Corporation, International Atomic Energy Agency, Intergovernmental Maritime Consultative Organization.

United Nations Documents Collection at New York University·

Waldo Chamberlin and Carol Carter Moore

With the decision to establish a Graduate Program of Studies in United Nations and World Affairs in 1947 New York University found it mandatory to establish a comprehensive collection of United Nations documents. The authors, Dr. Chamberlin, Professor of Government, and Miss Moore, Librarian of the N.Y.U. United Nations Collection, outline here the entire range of library processes involved from the planning of an acquisitions program through staffing, processing and providing reference service on a meager collection.

The United Nations Documents Collection at New York University represents an attempt to solve, by a combination of conventional and unconventional means, a number of problems that exist in all large libraries without decreasing the usefulness of the material and, where possible, making it more usable. The result has been to develop one of the most complete and usable collections of English language United Nations documents in the world. The interest of scholars in the New York University collection, and the number of questions concerning it from librarians engaged in coping with the same vast material, were the reasons for preparing this account of the procedures used.

NEED FOR COLLECTION

The need for such a collection sprang from two sources: first, the decision of the university in 1947 to establish a Graduate Program of Studies in United Nations and World Affairs, and second, the realization that the United Nations and specialized agencies were entering into the discussion and study of such a wide range of human activities that the documentation which would be produced would be useful to virtually every department and discipline in the university. The Graduate Program of Studies in United Nations and World Affairs was designed to provide M.A.

and Ph.D. degrees that would permit candidates to cut across the usual departmental lines—a clear recognition that the United Nations system would do the same. The physical proximity of the university to the headquarters of the United Nations presented unusual opportunities and unusual responsibilities to collect U.N. documents and to provide adequate facilities for the study of the international organization and its operations.

It was immediately recognized that one of the first steps required would be the creation of an exceptionally complete and usable documents collection. While the university had had global subscriptions for all published United Nations material, it had not undertaken to acquire the mimeographed papers. The decision to create such a collection was followed by investigation of collections of United Nations documents in other libraries. The number of instances found where libraries had extensive holdings, but where the material was virtually unusable, were numerous enough that the problem of making the future collection available and usable for library patrons was fully as important as acquiring the material in the first place.

THREE YEAR PLAN

Because, as is often the case in libraries, both funds and floor space were limited, it was de-

SOURCE: Reprinted from: Waldo Chamberlin and Carol Carter Moore, "United Nations Documents Collection at New York University," *College and Research Libraries*, 12 (Jan. 1951) pp. 52–61.

cided to build the desired type of collection according to a "three-year plan," as outlined below:

1948-1949 Academic Year:
1. Acquire all the processed and printed English language documents of the United Nations.
2. Accession all documents and begin preparations for binding (this required that approximately 250,000 documents be sorted, arranged in symbol series, checked, missing numbers obtained or noted, and duplicates discarded).
3. Complete the binding of the printed United Nations publications already owned by the university.

1949-1950 Academic Year:
1. Bring the United Nations documents up to date, including accessioning, shelflisting and binding.
2. Start to acquire the documents of the specialized agencies on an extensive basis and process them in temporary form. (The university was already receiving the published documents of some agencies.)
3. Expand the collection of United States government documents relating to the United Nations system.
4. Merge the university's League of Nations documents with the United Nations documents after rechecking and reconditioning the former.

1950-1951 Academic Year:
1. Continue the United Nations collection.
2. Continue the specialized agency collection and complete the accessioning and binding.
3. Continue the United States government collection.
4. Expand the collection of the documents, of other governments which relate to the United Nations.
5. Start to acquire the papers of nongovernmental organizations whose work is relevant to the United Nations.

DISTINCTION BETWEEN DOCUMENTS AND OTHER MATERIALS

It will be noted that no mention has been made of books about the United Nations which are not published by the organization. A clear distinction was made between such books and periodicals, on the one hand, and documents on the other. Desirable as amalgamation of the two types of material relating to the same subject might be, the practical reality of space available made separation necessary. Certain advantages have accrued from the separation; notably, the development of a reference staff expert in its knowledge of primary source material. Thus the books and periodicals about the United Nations are not part of the collection and are cataloged and shelved in the usual manner.

SPACE PROVIDED

When the decision to create the collection was made in the summer of 1948, the printed publications of the United Nations were housed in the Serials Division and arrangements were concluded to acquire and process the mimeographed documents in another building. The separation of the two types of material was a matter of expediency, rather than choice. In the summer of 1949, extensive remodeling of the library's plant permitted the assignment of an alcove in the Serials Reading Room which made it possible to bring all the material together. This alcove has approximately 300 linear feet of shelving and space for a desk and two reading tables, with additional table space adjacent. A work room with 125 linear feet of shelving and large enough for a six-foot table has been provided nearby, thus making it possible to have room for sorting and other mechanical processes outside the stack-reading room area. It is estimated that the present available space will be adequate for the expanding collection through the summer of 1951, at which time the whole problem of the collection and its future will be surveyed.

STAFFING ARRANGEMENTS

To put this plan into operation in 1948, two part-time students were employed, one a graduate student with some knowledge of United Nations documents and the other an undergraduate without such knowledge. The personnel was selected so that there would be continuity of trained staff to serve the collection. The undergraduate chosen was one who intended to continue on in graduate study leading to the Ph.D. degree and would presumably be available for two or more years. These two part-time students spent the first year in sorting, checking and listing the mimeographed material as fast as it was obtained. At the end of the year they had done the preliminary sorting and had begun the preparation of some volumes for binding. In the summer of 1949 it became evident that increased staff would be necessary to complete the sorting and arranging of the immense mass of mimeographed documentation obtained from friends and other institutions. The director of libraries and the librarian of the Washington Square Library approved the appointment of one full-time and three part-time students for the academic year 1949–50 with a view to completing the sorting and processing of the approximately 250,000 items.

The full-time student, the former part-time undergraduate in 1948–49 and the three half-time students completed the work on the backlog in June 1950, and have also provided reference service to the users of the collection on a five and one-half day per week basis, including evenings until 8:30 P.M.

ACQUISITIONS

The university maintains three global subscriptions for the published United Nations material from the international documents service of the Columbia University Press and, in addition, receives one copy of all unrestricted mimeographed and printed documents by virtue of the gracious decision of the librarian of the United Nations that the university is one of the recognized centers for the study of international affairs. One of the subscription sets is deposited in the Law Library, one in the School of Commerce Library and the third in the United Nations Collection in the Serials Division of the Washington Square Library. It is this latter set, plus the free set of printed and mimeographed documents, which constitutes the collection described herein.

The three subscription sets are mailed to the Acquisition Division of the university's libraries, where they are checked against bills and accessioned before being distributed. The fourth set, that received directly from the United Nations, is picked up each morning at the United Nations building in New York City by the university's messenger and brought directly to the United Nations Collection.

This fourth set is processed in a somewhat different manner from the other three because of the desire to have the current documents available for faculty and student use within 24 hours of the date of issue by the United Nations. Such a service is maintained because of the need for most recent information available by classes, seminars and faculty members engaged in research and because of the belief that processing that is to be done eventually can just as well be done currently and promptly. In other words, the policy is to avoid the creation of an anathema to all librarians, the back-log or the arrearage.

The result of this policy has been that in many instances, printed publications are available for users of the collection at the same time they are provided to official delegations and to members of the Secretariat of the United Nations. Numerous instances have occurred when the university has received publications in its free set as much as several weeks ahead of the general distribution to subscribers to United Nations documents. The benefit to those engaged in research on current problems is evident.

Materials received on this daily basis are listed on visible card files under the symbol or series in which they are issued. The printed items are then shelved according to the plan explained below, and the mimeographed documents are placed in four-drawer vertical steel files, of which there are only two. The volume of papers maintained in vertical files is kept at a minimum by the binding policy observed, also explained below, and it is thought that two vertical files will continue to be adequate for all foreseeable needs.

BINDING

The policy governing binding requires that the collection be maintained in usable condition at all times and that items should not be missing for any considerable period of time because they are "at the bindery."[1] To meet such a standard, both from the point of view of budget and time, three processes are used.

The first is the normal commercial contract binding in full board and buckram, at the usual range of prices, ranging from $2.00 upward per volume depending upon size and requirements determined by the librarian.

The second is a form of pamphlet binding which is done in the library by staff employed for this purpose.

The third binding process appears to be unusual, judging by the number of visitors to the collection whose only interest is in seeing the volumes so bound. Actually there is nothing new in the method, as it is simply an adaptation of the pad-binding used in manufacturing scratch pads or other stationery in pad form. The university adopted the method as the result of observance of its application by the Secretariat of the United Nations, where the deputy director of the Publications Division, D. D. DeWalt, had experimented for three years and had developed a very satisfactory inexpensive binding. The process is used primarily for the mimeographed documents but is not limited thereto, as it is adequate for any non-permanent items. It is this method and the pamphlet binding which have made it possible to limit the current material maintained in vertical files to two four-drawer cases.

The pad-binding is done in the university's duplicating shop at a cost of approximately 25¢ per volume. Twenty to 50 volumes are prepared for binding at one time and normally are not out of the collection more than 48 hours. Preparation for binding includes typing of a title page containing a list of the documents in the volume, and the removal of all staples. A 3″ x 5″ card is then prepared as a binding record and serves as a shelflist card when the volume has been bound. The use of the one card for two purposes is possible because the instructions to the bindery are standard and do not vary from volume to volume.

The technique of pad-binding is simple. When the documents are received in the bindery, each volume is placed in a paper cutter and the binding edge is trimmed enough to insure that each sheet will touch the binding material. Pieces of pressboard cut to size, or trimmed to fit each volume as the case may be, are then placed on the front and back of the volume. The volumes, 20 or more, are then stacked one on top of another, with the binding edges true and square to one another. A layer of thick binders glue is then applied to the area of the binding edges of the stacked volumes in one application. If the documents to be bound are 10″ long and the 20 volumes average $1\frac{1}{2}$″ in thickness, the area to which the glue is applied by paint brush in one operation is 300 square inches, thus reducing the labor costs per volume. After the glue has been applied, a layer of cloth (crash) is applied to the glue, following which a second layer of glue is applied over the cloth. Heavy weights are then placed on top of the pile of volumes and they are allowed to dry overnight. If a press of sufficient capacity is available, it is used instead of the weights, but such a press is not required as the weight of the volumes supplies all the pressure necessary except to the few top items.

On the following day, the volumes with their pressboard covers are sliced apart with a sharp knife and vellum tape is placed over the spine of each volume, overlapping on each cover not less than one inch. The volumes are then returned to the collection and are ready for lettering and shelving. The experience at the United Nations and at the university leads to the belief that this form of binding will last as long as will the woodpulp paper used for mimeographed documents.

The pad-binding is an inexpensive process and requires no equipment or capital investment other than a paper cutter powerful enough to trim a volume that may be as much as 2″ thick. All that is needed in addition is a homemade rack to hold the volumes while they are being glued and dried plus the supplies of glue, crash, pressboard and vellum tape. The process is adaptable because of the small amount of floor space required. It should be understood that it is as easy to bind 100 volumes at a time as it is to bind 20; in fact, it is cheaper by volume. The only limit is the height of the ceiling of the room in which the work is done.

SHELVING

The documents are all shelved according to the documents symbol system of the United Nations. The decision to follow this course was dictated by the structure of the United Nations itself, which is in many ways a subject structure, and by the realization that most users of the documents would request them by name of organ or documentary series. The manner of shelving was closely related to the decision regarding cataloging described in detail below. Thus all documents of the General Assembly are shelved together. All Secretariat documents are shelved together and all items bearing sales numbers are shelved together. Such a system is recognition of the fact that there are four principal categories of United Nations documents, though they sometimes cross and duplicate one another:

  I. The printed official records of the main organs.
  II. The mimeographed series (some individual items of which are occasionally printed in one or more of the other categories).
  III. The Secretariat series.
  IV. The sales series.

The documents not included in the sales series are shelved in the following order:

  I. The United Nations Conference on International Organization
    A. Printed 16 volumes
    B. Mimeographed documents
  II. Executive Committee of the Preparatory Commission of the United Nations (follows same general plan as under General Assembly below)
  III. Preparatory Commission of the United Nations
  IV. General Assembly by session in chronological order
    A. Each session in this order
      1. Index to session (if any)
      2. Resolutions of each session (will be shifted to supplements to the official records for past session if the U.N. decides to print future resolutions in that subseries)
      3. Plenary meeting documents
        a. Printed official records
        b. Printed official records annexes
        c. Mimeographed verbatim records
        d. Mimeographed summary records
        e. Mimeographed A/- documents
      4. General Committee documents
        a. Printed official records
        b. Printed official records annexes
        c. Mimeographed summary records
        d. Mimeographed A/-BUR documents
      5. Documents of committees, 1, 2, 2 & 3, 4, 5, 6 and sessional *ad hoc* committees in which all members are represented are shelved in the same manner as those of the general committee
        a. Subcommittees and drafting subcommittees documentation are shelved at the end of the papers for the relevant committee for the session.

      6. Supplements to the official records of each session
      7. Documents of all other *ad hoc* bodies are shelved after the most recent sessional papers, because these documents are not sessional, for the most part, and originate from bodies meeting between sessions, and in some instances, meeting over a period of several regular sessions.

Essentially the same pattern is followed for the documents of the Economic and Social Council and the Trusteeship Council, both of which meet by sessions each year.

The Security Council and Atomic Energy Commission documentation also follows the same basic pattern, except that the documents are shelved by month of issue because the two bodies are theoretically in permanent session. The order on the shelves is as follows:

  1. January printed official records
  2. January printed official record annexes and supplements
  3. January mimeographed verbatim records
  4. January S/- documents
  5. At the end of the Security Council Collection are shelved the documents of all *ad hoc* committees, subcommittees, field missions, etc.

The publications issued within the sales number series are shelved under such series because of the subject arrangement of the series themselves. Because adequate research tools prepared by the United Nations Secretariat are available as guides to this material, it is more usable when shelved in this manner than if broken up under some other system which would make the reference tools available relatively useless.

The Secretariat documentation, which is voluminous and cuts across virtually all subject fields used by the organization, is shelved according to the unified system of symbols recently adopted. Items issued before this unified system was in use are arbitrarily assigned to positions on the shelves in keeping with the new symbols.

CATALOGING (OR NONCATALOGING)

Very few of the documents in the United Nations Collection are cataloged, a sharp break with traditional practice which was not determined until all concerned had been consulted. There are four basic reasons upon which this decision was based:

1. The United Nations Secretariat has produced many excellent reference tools and checklists which go far beyond anything that any catalog can ever be expected to accomplish with the funds likely to be provided.
2. The arrearage in cataloging of United Nations documents by the Library of Congress, or anyone else, was so great as to make it unlikely that it could ever become current. (Perhaps an arrearage of as much as 40,000 documents in one language by the end of 1948.
3. The inadequacy of any catalog as a guide to the best items on any subject within a large block of material of this nature.
4. Cost of cataloging and maintaining such a catalog, particularly in the light of the reference tools described in "1" above.

The essential feature of the plan is that in place of the usual author, title or subjects cards the catalog contains "see also" cards directing the user to the United Nations Collection. One such card appears under the catalog entry, UNITED NATIONS, in front of the cards for books about the United Nations which are not published by that organization. Subject cards are inserted throughout the catalog thus:

HUMAN RIGHTS
see also
United Nations Collection in Serials
Reading Room

The users of the library are best served by being guided by the catalog to the reference staff of the collection where the wealth of reference tools are put at their disposal and where trained staff can assist them.

The operation of the plan may be described by explaining in some detail one example, although the method is equally applicable to any subject discussed or studied by the United Nations.

The average lower division student represents the level of user of documents whose needs are normally the simplest. Such a student, looking under the heading HUMAN RIGHTS, finds in the catalog only cards for items about the subject which are not issued by the United Nations. He also finds the "see also" card described above. If the non-United Nations publications are not adequate for his need, he proceeds to the United

Nations Collection and explains that need to the librarian on duty. In all probability, he would be given a mineographed document prepared by the Department of Public Information of the Secretariat of the United Nations bearing the title, *Commission on Human Rights, Background Paper no. 25,* and simultaneously handed the volumes of the *United Nations Bulletin.* In many instances, these two items, or one of them, are adequate for his need. Yet neither would normally have been cataloged because of the ephemeral nature of the first as a processed document, and because analytics do not exist for the *Bulletin.* The student would not have been aware of the existence of either item and could not, therefore, have called for either. The result is that this student with his limited interest or need, has left the library satisfied. Most important of all, perhaps, is the fact that he was supplied with the type of material best suited to his need and he was not required to leaf through a large number of cards while simultaneously attempting to form a judgment as to which item would best suit his need, a judgment that he had neither the experience nor training to make. This is not the place to discuss why he was not equipped to make such a judgment, and the procedure described herein was devised to meet the situation that exists.

Consider now the better lower-division student or the upper-division student engaged in the preparation of a term paper on "Human Rights." In this case, the initial approach to the catalog is the same as that of the first student, but the need is entirely different. One or two papers of a background character will not be sufficient. Yet neither should the student be forced to consider the whole range of material on the subject. This is particularly true when normal methods of cataloging would not direct him to a large segment of the most important material. Finally, reliance on the catalog may deprive the student of knowledge of the existence of excellent available tools of reference, obviously the first place to start his research.

The important United Nations documentation and publications on human rights are listed below in a tabular form in order to give a graphic representation of the problem the potential user must face when he begins his search. The items listed are by no means the only ones which cover the subject, but they are the most important and the student should be guided to them in the fastest and most efficient manner possible.

UNITED NATIONS DOCUMENTS AND PUBLICATIONS ON "HUMAN RIGHTS"

	Items which would usually: not be cataloged under Human Rights	be cataloged under Human Rights
Reference tools		
1. *United Nations Documents Index*	X	
Check List of United Nations Documents:		
2. Part 1: *General Assembly*	X	
3. Part 4: *Trusteeship Council*	X	
4. Part 5: *Economic and Social Council*	X	
5. Part 6D: *Human Rights Commission*		X
6. Part 6E: *Social Commission*	X	
7. Part 6F: *Commission on the Status of Women*	X	
8. A/INF papers	X	
9. E/INF papers	X	
Index Notes:		
10. *Cumulative Index to the Resolutions of the Economic and Social Council*	X	
11. *Cumulative Index to the Resolutions of the General Assembly*	X	
Documentation and publications		
12. *Human Rights Yearbook*		X
13. Mimeographed papers of the Commission on Human Rights		X
General Assembly Official Records:		
14. *Plenary Meetings*	X	
15. *Resolutions*	X	
16. *General Committee*	X	
17. *First Committee*	X	
18. *Third Committee*	X	
19. Mimeographed verbatim records (PVs) of the Plenary meetings of the General Assembly	X	
20. *For Fundamental Human Rights*		X
21. *Economic and Social Council Official Records*	X	
22. *Resolutions*	X	
23. *Report of the Commission on Human Rights* (Annual Supplement to *Official Records*)		X
24. Mimeographed papers of the Conference on Freedom of Information	X	
25. Mimeographed papers of Committee on Non-Governmental Organizations	X	
26. Documents of the Preparatory Commission of the United Nations and of its Executive Committee	X	
27. Documents of the United Nations Conference on International Organizations (San Francisco 1945)	X	
28. *United Nations Bulletin*	X	
29. *United Nations Yearbook*	X	
30. Miscellaneous papers and publications of the Department of Public Information of the United Nations Secretariat	X	
Total	25	5

Thus there will normally be five important items or series cataloged under the heading HUMAN RIGHTS and 25 items or series not so cataloged. This score of five to one against cataloging of this type of material is quantitative but a case can be made for the contention that most of the best material would not be subject cataloged. Evaluation of the 30 items, listed above would result in some such standard of relative usefulness to the advanced undergraduate student as is outlined on page 225.

According to this scale of values, the qualitative measurement of seven to three against cataloging is almost as strong as the quantitative one. This conclusion determined, more than any other factor, the decision not to catalog.

	Subject Cataloging	
	Yes	No
A. *For Fundamental Human Rights*	X	
B. *United Nations Yearbook*		X
C. *General Assembly Resolutions*		X
D. *United Nations Bulletin*		X
E. *General Assembly Official Records– Plenary Meetings*		X
F. Mimeographed documents and summary records of the Commission on Human Rights	X	
G. *Check list of UN Documents:* Part 6D *Commission on Human Rights*	X	
H. *General Assembly Official Records– Third Committee*		X
I. *Economic & Social Council Resolutions*		X
J. *Economic & Social Council Official Records*		X

REFERENCE CARD FILE

The "see also" subject cards are made up at the same time as cards are prepared for the reference card file which is maintained in the collection. This is done by taking the subjects which are used by the *United Nations Documents Index* in the subject indexes in each of the reference tools. Each such card bears a notation in the lower left hand corner indicating in which reference tool or tools the subject heading appears A card appearing thus:

```
HUMAN  RIGHTS
CL, Pt. 5–1    DI–50 Ja.
CL, Pt. 6D     PUB
IN–15          A/INF.28
```

would mean that material on human rights is indexed in the following reference tools:

CL, Pt. 5–1 *Checklist of U.N. Documents,* Part 5, no. 1
    Economic & Social Council, 1946-1947
CL, Pt. 6D *Commission on Human Rights,* Part 6D
IN–15 Index Note No. 15. *Cumulative Index to the Resolutions of the General Assembly*
DI–50 Ja. *United Nations Documents Index,* January, 1950
PUB *Publications 1945-1948*
A/INF *Disposition of Agenda Items of the*

3rd Regular Session (of the General Assembly)

Anyone engaged in serious research on the subject of "human rights" presents himself to the librarian on duty in the collection, having first been referred there by the "see also" card in the catalog. He is then given the various reference tools listed above and the librarian assists him in making his selection of which documents he wishes to consult first.

This type of card is kept in the collection in the reference card file and is the key to the use of the documents therein. As each new reference tool arrives from the United Nations, the staff of the collection add an indication of new material on old subjects by listing a new symbol on the subject cards. These symbols are determined from a master guide and the librarian in charge is the only one authorized to create new symbols, such as the six listed on the sample card above. When a new subject appears, a card is typed bearing that subject and it is taken to Catalog Division of the library where it is either accepted for insertion as a new "see also" card in the catalog or adapted to meet the system of subject headings used by the library. Should the subject chosen by the librarian in the collection not meet the subject cataloging policy of the library, the library policy prevails. However, the collection files its own subject card, under the heading used by the United Nations, with a "see also" card in its reference card file stating that the catalog has material on the particular subject listed under a different heading. This makes it possible to use the subject headings appearing in United Nations documents and cited and quoted in the press and periodicals, without checking and cross checking to find out what the catalog subject heading may be. This practice of having the catalog adhere to the standards of the library profession, and the collection adhere to the United Nations standards, works out well in practice. The staff of the Cataloging Division is thus freed from cluttering up the catalog with innumerable confusing subject headings which apply almost exclusively to the United Nations material and to no other.

The *United Nations Documents Index,* issued monthly, is checked against the reference card file within 48 hours after receipt, thus assuring that this key guide to the reference tools is as current as physically possible. Any other reference tools received are similarly processed. When the number of symbols at the bottom of any card in the reference card file becomes too numerous for the one card, a second card is made and the first card is retyped to include only the references to the more significant reference tools.

IMPORTANCE OF TRAINED STAFF

Trained staff is important in the satisfactory maintenance of such a collection and will always be so. However, the procedures described above were designed to make it possible to operate an adequate collection with a nonpermanent staff, that is, with one person who would probably not remain more than three years, supplemented by others who might remain as little as one year.

NOTE

[1] The quicker the documents kept in file folders can be bound, the less opportunity there is for pilferage and other forms of loss.

United Nations Documents in the Medium-Sized University—Nuisance or Necessity

Thomas R. Cassidy

Not all institutions need the complete range of UN documents to meet the needs of their teaching programs. A program of selective acquisition based on the needs of the faculty of the University of Oregon is described here.

The world, as it grows older, is becoming ever more garrulous. By the middle of 1947, only two years after it had come into existence, the United Nations had spoken—and printed—more words than its predecessor, the League of Nations, produced in a quarter of a century. Today, the General Assembly by itself is responsible for some 1800 documents, ranging from one page to several thousands of pages. The Security Council has issued about 2000, the Economic and Social Council 1900 more. Minor divisions of the larger agencies—committees, subcommittees, drafting subcommittees, commissions and conferences, permanent and temporary—have yet other thousands to their credit, in some instances nearly as many as the parent body.

Much of this mass of wordage is given over to matters in which few people are interested, to questions of parliamentary procedure to the endless, confused maneuvers of international politics, to the clumsy legislative machinery of fifty-nine nations with fifty-nine separate sets of interests and nearly as many languages in which to voice them. Indeed, most United Nations documents have the single purpose of straightening out some aspect of this confusion. Of this genre are such titles as, "Procedure in handling items proposed for insertion in the provisional agenda of the Council by Specialized Agencies and non-governmental organizations," "Memorandum, draft resolutions, draft protocols and annex on transfer to the United Nations of functions and powers exercised by the League of Nations under the Conventions on the traffic in women and children, and in obscene publications," "Summary report of financial implications of resolutions involving expenditures from United Nations funds." These documents make up a detailed record of the United Nations at work and in this respect they are valuable, but their application is limited and their use confined to the specialized worker following a single line of research.

There are, however, scattered among these publications of limited value, a great many reports and studies of economic and social matters which are international in scope, timely and of which fairly constant use can be made. Among these, to give only a few random samples, are studies of housing, of communications, of comparative marriage laws, of drug consumption, of the development of backward countries, of foreign exchange, of international law. Within this material—and in many libraries only within this material—may be found such varied information as the extent of postwar railroad construction in South Africa, the current production of iron ore in Mexico, the death rate in India, or the main causes of discrimination.

All universities have some courses in economics, geography, history, political science, sociology and law; and in all these fields United Nations publications provide excellent source material. But not all universities will be able to make the same amount of use of this material. A large university with a great many students and a correspondingly well-rounded faculty naturally lends itself to a greater degree of specialization than a small or medium-sized university. Where in a large university there may be, as there is at New York University, a whole group of courses

SOURCE: Thomas R. Cassidy, "United Nations Documents in the Medium-Sized University—Nuisance or Necessity?" *College and Research Libraries*, 13 (April 1952) pp. 107–110.

built around the study of the United Nations, a smaller institution will usually have to confine itself to a single class on international organization.

This, of course, affects the library. The library of a large university can much more easily provide the money, space and personnel for processing, storing and making available all the thousands of United Nations documents. Probably such a library will even be one of the thirty-two United Nations depositories, receiving at no charge all but restricted documents. On the other hand, the smaller university library, even if it were able to bind, shelve and index the complete body of United Nations publications, would find that demand was not great enough to justify the required expense of money and space.

The problem is, therefore, that while the medium-sized university urgently needs much of the material published by the United Nations, this material is too bulky and requires too much handling to warrant its complete acquisition. The solution, of course, is a policy of limited acquisition, a policy which is at once favored and made tantalizingly difficult by United Nations publication practices.

This is true because United Nations publications (excluding periodicals) are issued in three different formats—mimeographed documents, the *Official Records,* and the publications of the Secretariat. Each of these divisions duplicates a large amount of the material in the two others, and each contains much that appears in no other place.

The mimeographed documents are the most inclusive, containing all published material except the most lengthy and important studies and reports. Since they are issued when needed by the various organs, they are also the most up to date. However, because of their number, because each document appears separately and because they make use of a poor quality of paper, they are also the most fragile and the most generally difficult and expensive to handle. They must be sorted and arranged according to a fairly complex and not always consistent system of symbols, they must be bound and some method of indexing them must be found. Finally, they require the greatest amount of space and contain the largest number of non-utilizable documents. If they are not to be tied up and put away in some basement stack to rot or allowed to become mixed-up piles of dog-eared papers, they will require the full time services of at least one trained librarian and several assistants—more than the medium-sized library can allot to such a job.

The *Official Records* are the printed accounts, either verbatim or summary, of the meetings of the chief deliberative bodies which make up the United Nations and of certain of their permanent *ad hoc* committees. These are issued in five sets—for the General Assembly, the Security Council, the Economic and Social Council, the Trusteeship Council and the Atomic Energy Commission. (Publications of the International Court of Justice are not a part of the *Official Records* and, being few in number and of a specialized, legal nature, need not be taken up here.) In addition, many of the more important mimeographed documents are reprinted in the *Official Records,* usually as supplements or annexes, occasionally as a part of the records of the meetings. In format the *Official Records* are much more permanent than the mimeographed documents, less space is required for their shelving, and their arrangement is simple. A little later we can consider a few of the difficulties they present.

The surveys, reports and bibliographies prepared by the Secretariat are the most useful of all United Nations publications for general reference work in questions involving either United Nations activities or world social and economic conditions. Since these are issued in book or pamphlet form and with a ready-made subject classification which divides them into fifteen broad categories, and since they are comparatively few in number, they offer no special problems.

Acquisition of the two latter types of United Nations publications will probably be as much as the library of the medium-sized university can manage. As far as space and expense are concerned, this is a good compromise, but as a complete solution it has several major weaknesses. For one thing, the *Official Records* contain many of the important documents, but they do not contain all of them. Again, the Economic and Social Council's resolution to send a group of experts to South America for a study of the effects of chewing coca leaves may, for instance, be reprinted in three different parts of the *Official Records,* while a much more frequently cited analysis of comparative methods of compiling vital statistics, since it was considered by a commission rather than the whole Council, never goes beyond the mimeographed stage. There are also parts of the *Official Records*—a great many of them—which have not been printed because of lack of funds and time. Someday, of course, these will be available, but that is no help when a document they are going to contain is needed now.

But perhaps the greatest disadvantage of using the *Official Records* as a substitute for a set of mimeographed documents is the difficulty of locating a document which has been reprinted there. Nearly all citations to United Nations publications are made to mimeographed documents: except for the Secretariat publications and those of the committee reports which appear in individual *Official Records* supplements, references are usually made only to document symbols. Thus, for instance, "Establishment of relationship between the United Nations and the Universal Postal Union" may be cited in *Publications of International Organizations* simply as E/278, with no indication that it has been reprinted in an annex to the records of the Economic and Social Council. And, since the *Official Records* do not reproduce documents in accordance with the numerical order of the symbols, if E/278 is wanted, all one can do is to hunt for it, more or less blindly and with no certainty that it has ever been reprinted. There have been published, it is true, a few check lists which aid in this search, but they are far from complete and are particularly weak on documents issued by committees, commissions and other minor bodies.

For the past several sessions, however, the task of the digging material out of the *Official Records* has been growing less difficult. The General Assembly, for example, now begins its annexes with location lists of its documents and those of its committees. Somewhat similar lists are also being put out by the Economic and Social Council and the Trusteeship Council. The *United Nations Documents Index,* published since January of 1950, also has a section devoted to republications. These and other improvements are still no substitute for the knowledge gained by experience in using the *Official Records,* nor will they be of much value without such experience. Nevertheless, they are indicative of the United Nations' willingness to disseminate knowledge of its work as broadly as possible. They help to make it possible for United Nations documentation, in spite of its bulk and complexity, to be fitted into a medium-sized library without demanding a disproportionate slice of budget and stacks. And even a limited collection of these documents, aided when necessary by interlibrary loan from one of the depository libraries, can be an extremely valuable possession at a time when world wide understanding and knowledge are needed more than they have ever been before.

United Nations Documents in the United Nations Library: Organization and Servicing

Fernando Caballero-Marsal, Jorgen K. Nielsen, and Harry N. M. Winton

Caballero-Marsal, Chief of the Documents Index Unit, Nielsen, Chief of the Catalog Unit, and Winton, Librarian-in-Charge of the United Nations Documents Collection of the UN Library, detail the procedures for preparing the United Nations Documents Index, *the provision of reference service to UN staff, and the procedures for selecting and cataloging certain categories of documents.*

In an effort to give a clear idea of what the United Nations Library does with the documents of the United Nations and the specialized agencies, the authors of this article felt that it would be helpful to organize it by following the route that the documents travel within the library.

DISTRIBUTION OF DOCUMENTS

The United Nations Library has no control over the distribution of documents. As a matter of fact, it is at the receiving end of the distribution line and, consequently, has to contend with its imperfections. All the documents are delivered to the Library by the Distribution Section of the Bureau of Documents.

CHECK-LISTING AND INDEXING

All documents are first brought to the Documents Index Unit on the fifth floor of the Library Building. This Unit, with a permanent staff of nine professionals and eight clerks and clerk-typists, keeps bibliographical control of all the documents and publications of the United Nations and the specialized agencies received by the United Nations Library at headquarters. The control is maintained by daily registration, check-listing, and indexing on cards.

The documents are registered in a visible card index by series symbols and by numbers within the series. Non-symbolized material is registered by sales number, if any, or by title. The languages of issues and the number of copies received are also recorded. This register constitutes an accurate record of the holdings of the United Nations Documents Collection, and provides the basis for claiming missing items.

After the documents have been registered, they are check-listed and indexed on 3 X 5 cards, with the bibliographical information entered on the upper half of the card, and the author and subject headings listed on the lower half. The typewritten master cards—the text of which must be letter-perfect for photographing later on—reproduce beneath a hectograph, or Ditto, master for the reproduction of cards on the Ditto machine operated in the Unit itself. A sufficient number of hectographed cards is made for distribution to the United Nations Documents Collection and to the sub-stations of the Bureau of Documents. These cards are not sent outside the United Nations Secretariat at headquarters.

These typewritten master cards are used by the

SOURCE: Reprinted from: Fernando Caballero-Marsal, Jorgen K. Nielsen, and Harry N. M. Winton "United Nations Documents in the United Nations Library: Organizing and Servicing," *Journal of Cataloging and Classification,* 7, (Summer 1951) pp. 65-72.

*Editor's Note: Presented in an abbreviated form at a meeting of the A. L. A. Public Documents Committee in Chicago, July 12, 1951. We are indebted, not only to the authors, but also to Mrs. Violet A. Cabeen, Chief of the Acquisition Unit, United Nations Library, for planning and making arrangements for the paper.

Unit in the copy preparation of the monthly *United Nations Documents Index* by a method of mounting the cards on sheets which are photographed and reproduced by offset.

The monthly *United Nations Documents Index* (document series ST/LIB/SER.E/) is the most important publication issued by the Unit. The first issue appeared in February, 1950, covering the documents received by the Unit during January, and in the first year and a half of its existence, the *Index* has established itself as an indispensable reference tool and guide to the documents of the United Nations and the specialized agencies.

The *Index* lists all the documents and publications received by the Documents Index Unit from the United Nations and the specialized agencies, excepting restricted or confidential material and internal papers. In general, each monthly issue covers the documents and publications received by the Unit during that month. Periodicals and press release series, first listed in the February issue for 1950, are listed annually thereafter in the December issue of every year.

Each issue comprises:

(a) General Introduction
(b) List of Abbreviations
(c) Lists of Documents and Publications—a section for the United Nations, followed by a section for each of the specialized agencies in the alphabetical order of their abbreviated names: Bank, FAO, Fund, ICAO, etc. Each section is arranged in three parts: 1) a list of documents and publications; 2) revisions, addenda, corrigenda, and non-English language editions; 3) republications. In each part, materials are arranged as far as possible in alphabetical order by symbol numbers. Only in part 1 are complete bibliographical details given. Parts 2 and 3 are arranged in tabular forms, giving only the information needed to identify the documents and publications in these categories.
(d) General Index.

The General Index covers all documents and publications listed in every section. All references in this index are to the entry numbers in the respective sections. The United Nations list and each of the specialized agencies lists has its own series of entry numbers, each series being consecutive for one calendar year. Entry numbers have been used because of the divergency of practice among the organizations with respect to the use and non-use of symbols and sales numbers, and the complexity of direct reference to these symbols or to titles. The indexes in the monthly issues are cumulated into an annual index at the end of the year. The first cumulative index, covering the year 1950, appeared in May, 1951.

An asterisk [*] distinguishes those documents and publications which summarize the work of an organ, represent the final results of international conferences or research projects, or are works of reference such as bibliographies, handbooks and yearbooks. This minimum selection from thousands of documents and publications is intended to assist the general user in understanding the current work of the organizations and in finding the basic documents.

It is intended to publish occasional self-contained, special supplements to the *Index* during the year. So far, the Unit has published one supplement containing consolidated lists of depository libraries and sales agents and offices. The first revision of these lists appeared as Part 2 of the April, 1951, issue. All changes affecting these lists are noted in the section for errata of the following monthly issues and are incorporated in the next annual revision. The Unit is now considering the publication of some other documents regularly produced by it, as supplements to the *Index*.

Since January, 1951, the International Labour Office has been responsible for the listing and indexing of the documents of the International Labour Organisation, and the Documents Index Unit retains only the editorial and co-ordinating control of the material submitted by the International Labour Office from Geneva for incorporation in the *Index*. Similar arrangements with the Food and Agriculture Organization of the United Nations, the International Bank for Reconstruction and Development, the International Civil Aviation Organization, the International Monetary Fund, the International Telecommunication Union, and the Universal Postal Union are now under active consideration. All the other specialized agencies have also been invited to participate more directly in the production of the *Index*.

In addition to its major publication, the Documents Index Unit produces the following documents at irregular intervals:

(a) *Dispositions of Agenda Items* (e.g., document A/INF/36), covering the various sessions of the General Assembly, the Economic and Social Council, the Security Council, and the Trusteeship Council. These documents constitute a chronological-historical index of all the topics discussed during the sessions of the various organs, with separate indexes to the speeches made during each session. While the organs concerned are in session, the draft dispositions of agenda items are distributed on sheets to the United Nations Documents Collection and to the sub-stations of the Bureau of Documents in order to relieve them of the pressure for immediate information. After the end of each session of each organ, the respective dispositions of agenda items are edited and published in the information series of the organ concerned (A/INF/, for the General Assembly; E/INF/, for the Economic and Social Council, etc.) Most of the dispositions of agenda items have been published in mimeographed or photo-offset form only. Some have been incorporated in the Official Records which are printed and more generally available.

(b) *Indexes to the United Nations Treaty Series:* The Documents Index Unit of the Library has been entrusted by the Legal Department with the current indexing of the *United Nations Treaty Series,* and it publishes (in separate English and French editions) one index volume for every fifteen volumes of treaties.

(c) *Cumulative indexes to resolutions* (e.g., documents ST/LIB/SER.D/35, and ST/LIB/SER.D/35/Add.1): The Documents Index Unit also prepares cumulative indexes to the resolutions of the General Assembly, the Economic and Social Council, and the Trusteeship Council. (The Department of Security Council Affairs produces similar documents covering the resolutions and decisions of the Security Council.) These indexes are issued in photo-offset form only.

(d) *Index Notes:* The Documents Index Unit publishes in this series, guides to the symbol series of the various organs of the United Nations, lists and indexes of the reports submitted by subsidiary bodies to the Economic and Social Council, lists of official records, etc.

In order to bring under control all the documents produced by the United Nations prior to the inauguration of the *United Nations Documents Index* in 1950, the Unit has been engaged during the past two years in the preparation of a definitive check-list and index covering the documents that appeared during the period 1946–1949. While working on this vast project, the Unit was given sufficient temporary assistance to enable it to complete the listing and indexing of the documents by July 1951. This goal was reached recently, and the results of the project will be embodied in the 31 volumes of the *Check List of United Nations Documents.* Four of the volumes are already available in printed form, and the Unit has now a program calling for the publication of at least 17 additional volumes between July and November, 1951. The remaining 10 volumes will be issued in 1952.

Here it should be explained that the Documents Index Unit has built up a master list of subject-headings which is very much its own. When adopting new headings, due attention is always paid to the well-established and consecrated lists prepared and used by other institutions and organizations; but, whenever there is a choice of terms, the terminology used in the international documentation is preferred. Thus, the Unit uses the heading "Human rights" rather than the Library of Congress heading "Civil rights" because the former is the familiar one in the vocabulary of the United Nations.

SERVICING THE UNITED NATIONS COLLECTION

When the Documents Index Unit finishes processing the United Nations and specialized agencies documents, they are sent to the United Nations Documents Collection, which occupies one floor of the Library Building. It comprises in a single collection the official documents and other publications of the United Nations and of the specialized agencies, as well as the non-official books, pamphlets, periodicals, and Government documents concerning these organizations.

When the removal of the Library from Lake Success to Manhattan was completed in February, 1951, it was possible for the first time to bring together this material in one place. During 1950 certain steps were taken in anticipation of this consolidation of material, and, in line with the administrative policy, that responsibility for comprehensive reference service covering books, periodicals, documents, and similar material rests with the United Nations Library. The document files of the Archives were transferred to the Library. The only permanent reference collection of documents received from specialized agencies is to be maintained in the Library.

In view of the remarkable completeness of the League of Nations collection, largely because of the gift to the United Nations Library of the Woodrow Wilson Memorial Library by the Woodrow Wilson Foundation, it has been decided that older material of the specialized agencies or certain of their predecessor organizations associated with the League should be serviced by the staff of the Woodrow Wilson Memorial Collection. Thus, reference queries concerning the International Labour Organisation prior to January, 1946, or the International Institute of Intellectual Co-operation are handled by the Woodrow Wilson Memorial Collection staff, while reference queries concerning the International Labour Organisation since January 1, 1946, and the United Nations Educational, Scientific, and Cultural Organization are the responsibility of the United Nations Documents Collection staff. Some documents and publications have been re-located in the two collections in accordance with this division of responsibility.

In the United Nations Documents Collection, a staff of two professionals and two professional assistants does reference work, which includes answering inquiries (during January through June, 1951, a total of 5,470 inquiries were answered: 4,450 by telephone, 977 in person, and 43 in writing), circulating books and documents (during January through June, 1951, a total of 1,044 books and documents were circulated), and occasional bibliographic work.

The staff makes extensive use of card indexes covering United Nations documents prepared by the Documents Index Unit during 1945 to 1948; of card indexes covering documents of the United Nations and the specialized agencies prepared by the Unit since January 1, 1950 in connection with the *United Nations Documents Index;* of check-lists, dispositions of agenda items and other indexes prepared by the Unit; of other official and non-official aids, including, as far as they exist, guides to the materials of the specialized agencies prior to January 1, 1950; and of the personal experience of the staff, three of whose members have worked for four years or more in this field. In addition to these indexes, cards for a floor catalog are being prepared by the Catalogue Unit which catalogs a selection of printed official material and nearly all of the non-official material.

During 1951 and 1952 an extensive program of binding the documents and publications of the Collection will be carried out. The set of United Nations documents recently transferred from Archives is being bound and shelved as rapidly as possible, and the unbound United Nations and specialized agencies material already possessed by the Collection is being transferred to shelves and will also be prepared for binding. Much material hitherto in storage, both official and non-official, must be unpacked, sorted, and absorbed or discarded. Current 1951 United Nations material will be collated for binding by the Bureau of Documents. A considerable amount of the older material issued by the specialized agencies must be checked and missing copies claimed prior to binding. Non-official material will be cataloged according to the classification scheme (which is described below), some material being transferred and reclassified from the general reference, periodical, or government document collections in the Library. When these operations have been completed upon the basis of the classification schemes, the collection will be grouped into three parts:

1. official United Nations material,
2. official material of the specialized agencies, and
3. non-official material concerning these organizations.

It is expected that the staff of the Collection shall become generally familiar with its whole contents now that the collection has been physically brought together.

The United Nations Documents Index, since 1950, reveals to the readers outside the Collection most of its official contents whether printed or mimeographed. A wide selection of the printed, official material and nearly all of the non-official material will be known eventually to the users of the general catalog.

The Librarian in charge of the United Nations Documents Collection takes part in the selection of books to be bought for the Collection, and he is also responsible for the establishment of series symbols for United Nations documents.

The United Nations Documents Collection is maintained to serve the staff of the Secretariat and the delegations, as is the Library as a whole. Both staff and budgetary limitations prevent the extension of Library services too generously to outsiders. It is the intention of the Library to assist, whenever possible, qualified outside users such as teachers, graduate students preparing doctoral theses and dissertations, newspaper and radio correspondents accredited to the United Nations, and other research workers with a genuine need for access to documentation of the United Nations and the specialized agencies not available elsewhere. The question is now under official consideration as to how the Library can best fulfill these intentions with due regard to its primary duties towards the official clientele.

CATALOGING

In view of the fact that the index cards produced by the Documents Index Unit are filed in the floor catalog of the United Nations Documents Collection, elaborate cataloging of the documents of the United Nations and specialized agencies is deemed unnecessary.

Instead, it was decided that only very few titles would be cataloged in the ordinary way for inclusion in the main catalog. The principal problem for the Catalogue Unit, therefore, was establishing a classification scheme for the bound volumes, and shelflisting these volumes for a record of physical holdings. In addition, the Library staff had to devise a special classification scheme for the non-official material about the United Nations which is also housed in the United Nations Documents Collection, and which will be cataloged in the normal way.

A special staff committee selects the material to be processed by the Catalogue Unit. This committee has decided that all publications in the following categories will be so processed:

(a) Periodicals, whether printed or reproduced in another form
(b) Yearbooks
(c) Bibliographies published as separate monographs

(Documents containing extensive bibliographies may be proposed for cataloging by the Reference Librarian in charge of the United Nations Documents Collection.)

The committee has further decided that only a selection of titles in the following categories will be cataloged:

(a) Serials (other than periodicals and yearbooks)
(b) Publications of the Department of Public Information
(c) Comprehensive monographic studies issued by the various departments

Although all of the United Nations Documents Collection are housed in the United Nations Collection, the committee may select titles to be cataloged and shelved elsewhere in the Library as well, usually in the general reference collection and the departmental libraries. Such selections are documents of permanent topical interest. They are processed like any other material in the Library.

CLASSIFICATION

Nearly all documents appear under symbols identifying them with the organ of issue. Citations of United Nations documents in both official and non-official papers customarily refer to the document symbols. The Library, therefore, has not attempted to fit this great mass of material into the Universal Decimal Classification but uses instead the document series symbols as the basis for classifying these documents.

A classification scheme based on document series symbols is not really a subject classification, but is rather an arrangement scheme by issuing body. In many cases, however, the series symbol is equivalent to a subject classification because many organs deal with special subject fields: thus, the documents of the Statistical Commission relate to statistics, and they will be shelved together according to the series symbol of the Commission (E/CN.3/).

Because the classification is based on symbols, documents are bound strictly according to symbol order. However, some documents appeared without symbols prior to January 1950, and some periodicals such as *United Nations Bulletin* will never bear a symbol. For this material Universal Decimal Classification notations and Cutter numbers are used after the basic symbol for the organ or department of the Secretariat. (The Universal Decimal Classification is used elsewhere in the Library, so these notations are already a familiar feature.)

The best way to illustrate what the United Nations Library is doing is to give examples of the treatment given to various types of material:

In order to distinguish material of the United Nations from that of the specialized agencies, the letters "UN" precede the basic series symbol for each organ:

UNA   General Assembly documents (A/ documents)

UNS   Security Council documents (S/
           documents)
UNST   Publications of the United Nations
           Library
LIB   (ST/LIB/ documents)

The call numbers for bound volumes are arranged alphabetically by symbols:

UNA 1-76	General Assembly. Documents A/1 to A/76
UNA 77-102	General Assembly. Documents A/77 to A/102
UNA AC.18 SR.1-20	General Assembly: Interim Committee. Documents A/AC.18/ SR.1 to A/AC.18/SR.20
UNA C.1 1-46	General Assembly: First Committee. Documents A/C.1/1 to A./C.1/46.

Certain discontinued Secretariat series which were issued between 1946 and 1949 bore no symbol. For those series UDC notation (05) for serials is used after the basic departmental symbol:

UNST DPI(05) C3	Department of Public information. "Checklist of Publications of Specialized Agencies, 1947-1948"

Certain current series which bore no symbol prior to January 1, 1950, are now issued under a series symbol. Issues in these series published prior to January 1, 1950, are classed with issues published after January 1, 1950:

UNST DPI SER.A 1-55	Department of Public Information. Background Papers, No. 1 to 55. These issues were numbered but bore no symbols. They are classed with subsequent issues which bear a symbol. See the next example.
UNST DPI SER.A 56-75	Department of Public Information. Background Papers, No. 56-75. These issues bore symbols ST/DPI/SER.A/56 to ST/DPI/ SER.A/75.

Certain series in this category starts the numbering with no. 1 after January 1950. Volumes of issues prior to January 1950 are numbered 01, 02, etc., in order to bring these volumes in front of those published after January 1950:

UNST   Department of Administrative and

AFS SER.B 01	Financial Services. "Statements on the Collection of Contributions." 1947-1949. Dated but unnumbered and bearing no series symbol.
UNST AFS SER.B 1-	Department of Administrative and Financial Services. "Statements of the Collection of Contributions." No. 1-, 1950-.

Certain Secretariat publications were issued prior to the establishment of departmental series symbols. For such material the UDC notation (02) for monographs is used after the basic departmental classification symbol:

UNST
ECA(02)
Cutter by title

NON-SYMBOL SERIALS

For serials which do not bear a symbol either before or after January 1, 1950, UDC notations are used:

a. *Official Records:* For these the notation (01) is used in order that they be shelved immediately after the symbol documents:

UNA UNA(01) R3	General Assembly. Documents. General Assembly. Official Records. (Note that Cuttering after "Official" is avoided because the letter "O" can easily be confused with the figure "0."

b. For other non-symbol serials, such as the *United Nations Bulletin,* the notation (05) is used:

UNST DPI(05) U5	Department of Public Information. *United Nations Bulletin.*

PRESS RELEASES

For press releases of Department of Public Information, which bear their own series symbols not in line with other symbols used elsewhere, the word PRESS is used after the basic departmental symbol:

UNST DPI PRESS 1949	Department of Public Information. Press Releases, 1949.

For press releases of the United Nations Information Centres, the following arrangement is used:

UNST   United Nations Information Centre
DPI.PAR   (Paris). Press Releases, 1949.
PRESS
1949
UNST   United Nations Information Centre
DPI.RIO   (Rio de Janeiro). Press Releases,
PRESS   1949.
1949

LANGUAGE NOTATION

To distinguish material in the different official languages the name of the language in full in English is added under the call number:

UNE   UNE
INF   INF
1-17   1-17
English Spanish

ARRANGEMENT OF LANGUAGE VERSIONS ON SHELVES

Material in different official languages is arranged series by series in the following sequence of languages within each series:

a. English or bilingual English/French
b. French
c. Spanish
d. Russian
e. Chinese

CATALOGING OF NON-OFFICIAL MATERIAL ABOUT THE UNITED NATIONS

"Non-official" material in the United Nations Documents Collection is defined as all material which is not published by the United Nations. This material includes both publications of any kind about the Organization published by national governments, other organizations, and commercial publishers, as well as republications of United Nations documents by any of these sources.

The acquisition and preservation of such material is a duty of the United Nations Library.

The treatment of this material may also be of interest:

All non-official material is processed by the Catalogue Unit. To keep all non-official material together and to distinguish it from official material the letter "X" is added after the prefix "UN" to form the prefix "UNX."

Non-official republications of United Nations documents are classed under UNX followed by the symbol of the original document:

UNX
E/76
Spanish

For non-official material other than republications, the following classification scheme is used. It is based on Universal Decimal Classification numbers and notations. Only the basic scheme is given below. Breakdowns and additions are made as needed, and the full scheme is appended to the general Universal Decimal Classification scheme used in the Library.

UNX.016	Bibliography
UNX.04	Miscellaneous pamphlets. Periodical articles, etc.
UNX.049	Collections of documents on the United Nations
UNX.05	Periodicals (e.g. United Nations World)
UNX.058	Yearbooks
UNX.06	Publications of United Nations associations (subdivided by country). Here are classed only reports on their activities. Monographic studies on special subjects are classed with subject.
UNX.09	History (General)
UNX.091	1941–45 (Formation of a world organization)
UNX.0912	Atlantic Declaration
UNX.0913	Moscow
UNX.0914	Dumbarton Oaks
UNX.0915	Yalta Conference
UNX.0916	San Francisco Conference
UNX.1	United Nations in general
UNX.12	Charter (text), arranged by language editions
UNX.122	Commentaries on the Charter, and works on special articles of the Charter
UNX.13	General Assembly
UNX.15	Security Council
UNX.161	Military Staff Committee

UNX.162	Atomic Energy Commission
UNX.165	Commission on Conventional Armaments
UNX.17	Economic and Social Council
UNX.19	Trusteeship Council
UNX.21	International Court of Justice
UNX.23	Secretariat in general
UNX.232	Headquarters site
UNX.233	Department of Administrative and Financial Services (AFS)
UNX.235	Department of Conference and General Services (CGS)
UNX.238	Department of Public Information (DPI)
UNX.24	Department of Economic Affairs (ECA)
UNX.243	Legal Department (LEG)
UNX.245	Library (LIB)
UNX.248	Department of Security Council Affairs (SCA)
UNX.25	Executive Office of the Secretary-General (SG)
UNX.255	Department of Social Affairs (SOA)
UNX.258	Department of Trusteeship and Information from Non-Self-Governing Territories (TRI)
UNX.26	European Office
UNX.27	Staff
UNX.275	Staff Association
UNX.28	Specialized agencies (general)
UNX.29	United Nations and religion
UNX.330.4	United Nations and technical assistance
UNX.341	United Nations and international law
UNX.370	United Nations and education
UNX.371	Education and study books. Teaching about the United Nations
UNX.372	Children's books
UNX.81	Poems, songs about United Nations
UNX.82	Dramatic works about United Nations
UNX.83	Novels
UNX.84	Pictorial works, caricatures
UNX.87	Satires, humorous works, parodies about United Nations
UNX.88	Curiosa
UNX.971	United Nations and Canada (Geographical numbers are used for relations with countries)

CONCLUSION

By performing the various functions described above and encouraging cooperation among the United Nations organizations in the field of documentation, the United Nations Library is endeavoring to establish and to maintain full and accurate control of their documents and to assist librarians and research workers who use these materials.

Report of the Headquarters Library, 1970

United Nations Library

This annual report of the United Nations Headquarters Library shows graphically the programs and functions of a large specialized library attached to a major international organization. Additional descriptive and historical material about this library may be found in The Libraries of the United Nations; a Descriptive Guide. *N.Y. United Nations, 1966 or in the monographs listed at the end of this reading.*

I. ADMINISTRATION

1. During the year, several changes occurred in the Library's top administrative and supervisory level. In June the Director, Mr. Lev I. Vladimirov, left the Organization and was succeeded, by the middle of July, by Mrs. Natalia I. Tyulina. His departure was preceded by the retirement, in April, of the Deputy Director, Mr. Joseph Groesbeck. The Deputy Director's post was filled by the promotion of Mrs. M. Toerien, formerly Chief of the Readers' Services Division, whose post, in turn, was filled by the promotion of the Chief of the General Reference Section, Mr. P. K. Gardé. The Acting Chief of the Documents Processing Section, Mrs. G. Faridi, was confirmed in the post and promoted to the proper level. Several promotions in the Professional, General Service and Manual Worker categories were also effected.

2. The staffing required for the projected expansion of the Computer-assisted Indexing Programme was completed by the addition to the Library manning table of seven Professional and two General Service posts. The incumbent of one of these posts was assigned to the preparation of the index to resolutions of the General Assembly—a long-standing commitment which could not be met until now for lack of staff.

3. One Professional and one General Service post were also added in order to enable the Library to expand the indexing of legal texts prepared by the Office of Legal Affairs which has been repeatedly requested by that Office for many years.

4. The four extra-budgetary posts provided by the United Nations Development Programme for non-Library acquisitions were approved again this year. Thus the Library manning table totals 141 posts, 62 of which are professional.

5. As in the preceding year, the planned expansion of the computer-assisted operations was severely affected by delays in recruitment. Half of the newly established posts were filled only in the second part of the year, the last one as late as in December 1970. The operations of other sections of the Library too suffered serious setbacks due to turnover in personnel and delays in filling posts vacated through resignations, transfers and retirement both in Professional and General Service categories. With the annual and sick leave absences added, the 35,673 man-days available were reduced by $8,388\frac{1}{2}$ with the result that the overall effectiveness was 0.6 per cent lower than last year in spite of the increase in manpower.

6. The budget appropriation of $220,000 for books, serials, supplies and services was sufficient to enable the Library to satisfy most of the needs of its clientèle and provide materials and services requested. The contracts with the State University of New York, Stony Brook, for computer services, the National Cash Register for microfiching, the IBM for rental of keypunch machines and the New York Public Library for interlibrary loans were approved and the services were rendered as required. The cost of the New York Public Library and the IBM contracts was adjusted downward toward the end of the year. The request for equipment was not approved fully. Nevertheless, it was possible to obtain some of the most urgently needed items such as a microfiche duplicator, a few portable readers and other minor items.

7. The Library's holdings having reached some 335,000 volumes and the upper floors of the Library being increasingly used to accommodate new staff and expanding operations, the problem of space was rapidly becoming acute. It was

solved at last toward the very end of the year when the Archives Section vacated the third basement of the building after nearly 10 years of occupancy.

8. Twenty meetings of division and section chiefs with the Director were held at which administrative and professional matters were discussed. The division and section chiefs also held regular or *ad hoc* meetings with their staff to consider and resolve problems and difficulties encountered in the performance of their duties. Such meetings are of great practical value to all participants inasmuch as they provide on the job training for new recruits and broaden the experience of older staff as well.

9. In order to improve their linguistic proficiency, 54 staff members followed the language courses organized by the Training Service of the Office of Personnel: 13 in English, 26 in French, 9 in Spanish, 5 in Russian and 1 in Chinese. Twelve participants passed the proficiency examination.

II. ACQUISITION

10. The efforts of the Organization towards the limitation of documentation are clearly reflected in the number of documents received. The receipts of the United Nations documents dropped sharply by 23,250 (104,411 in 1970 as against 127,661 in 1969). Documents received from the specialized agencies, on the other hand, increased by some 1,600. This is due to the active claiming with a view to completing broken sets ensuring that materials needed by the Library are received and made available promptly. Nevertheless, the total of documents received (119,556) decreased by 21,564 as compared to 1969 (141,120).

11. On the non-UN side, the Library has not received more books than in the previous year. It has, however, checked in more serial publications, as shown below:

	1968	1969	1970
Books received	9,979	11,146	11,148
by purchase	3,651	3,999	4,228
by gift and exchange	6,328	7,147	6,920
Serial pieces received	227,438	241,545	258,534

Following the trend of the past years, about 65 per cent of the Library's allotment for publications were spent on the acquisition of serials.

12. The Library continued its extensive exchange programme in order to obtain publications either not available at all, or not promptly enough, from commercial sources. During the year, 49 new exchange agreements were concluded. Under this programme a review of non-governmental and inter-governmental organizations receiving United Nations publications free of charge was initiated. The review which will continue next year has so far resulted in 24 new exchanges. The other 25 were arranged with various organizations and learned institutions throughout the world. Several among these were concluded under the provisions of the *Principles governing United Nations depository libraries* (ST/PB/Rev. 2). By the end of 1970, the Library's partial or total exchange agreements reached a total of 643.

13. Records were also set up for 10 major gift agreements, whereby the Library receives regularly publications without having to reciprocate.

14. A great deal of effort was devoted to the acquisition of the official publications of Member States which are the core of the collections and the basis for much of the work of the Organization. At present the Library receives some 7,200 government serials. Because of the quantity and complexity of production and distribution, this material often presents problems in checking, claiming and maintenance of orderly records. For instance, much time was devoted to reviewing all official Canadian publications prior to claiming and setting up records for the French language versions. Similarly, all holdings were completed and records closed for the 1960/61 population censuses in anticipation of the forthcoming publications resulting from the 1970/71 censuses, etc.

15. In April, H. E. Mr. Yakov A. Malik, Ambassador Extraordinary and Plenipotentiary Permanent Representative of the USSR, presented the Library on behalf of his Government with a collection of works of V. I. Lenin on the occasion of the latter's one hundredth anniversary. The books were put on exhibit in the Periodical Reading Room and the titles not yet in the Library will be incorporated in the collection at a later date.

III. PROCESSING OF MATERIALS

16. The preparation of machine readable annotations relating to United Nations documents and publications, which had started late in 1969, continued at an increased rate. By the end of the

year, 9,700 indexing annotations and 4,750 quadrilingual indexing expressions had been prepared. The information stored related to documents issued currently in the series of the Economic and Social Council and its functional commissions and to a selected portion of documents issued in connexion with the twenty-fifth session of the General Assembly in the Plenary series. The addition of two IBM 029 Keypunch machines to the two already on rental made possible the preparation of a much larger number of cards, 65,600 as against 13,500 in 1969. By the end of 1970, the information stored in the Indexing Data File had increased by 5,315 records, for a total of 6,502 records. The information stored in the Quadrilingual Terminology File increased in 1970 by 3,570 records, for a total of 4,612 records.

17. Concurrently with the computer-assisted indexing of selected United Nations documents the conventional indexing continued at the same rate and coverage as last year. The indexing of specialized agencies material was much slowed down and a backlog developed because of the prolonged absence on sick leave of the staff member assigned to this work. On the other hand, the filing of some 86,000 cards in the UNSA index/catalogue has cancelled a backlog which persisted for several years. The assigning of symbols and call numbers to new documents series continued as the need arose. A total of 134 call numbers and 19 new series symbols were assigned.

18. The cataloguing of incoming books and serials was brought on a current basis and the minor backlog of materials in less known languages, outstanding from 1969, was eliminated altogether. With the staff gaining progressively more experience, the speed of cataloguing increased and it was possible to reduce the priority system from three levels to two. The number of titles catalogued in 1970 was five per cent higher than in the two previous years (1968: 6,078; 1969: 6,068; 1970: 6,367). It was also possible to make changes and adjustments in records for certain older materials pertaining to some 50 present and former non-self-governing territories.

19. The consolidated list of subject headings used in the catalogue of the general collection was kept up to date. The Bibliographical Terminology Committee continued to work on the co-ordination of subject headings used in the card catalogues and indexes produced by the Library. Some of the decisions taken were implemented and the relevant catalogue cards were changed. The progress is

necessarily slow on account of lack of manpower both on the professional as well as the clerical side.

20. Housekeeping chores, such as combining the holdings of government gazettes in hard copy and on film in one shelflist, weeding, consolidation or reorganization of various files and other unglamorous but necessary and time-consuming tasks were undertaken and completed according to urgency and time available.

IV. ORGANIZATION OF THE COLLECTIONS

21. Toward the very end of 1970, the Archives Section vacated the third basement of the building and the Library moved immediately to relieve some of the most crowded areas of the stacks and to provide space for additional offices and work areas needed for expanding operations. Although a large part of that basement is occupied by air-conditioning and other machinery, enough space was gained to accommodate materials which are less frequently called for, such as non-English versions of specialized agencies documents, back runs of bound periodicals, gift and sale material, etc. As a corollary, the relocation of the collection of government documents to wider range areas in the second basement was also initiated. The move, executed mostly by the Library staff, will be completed early next year.

22. The Serials Committee, in addition to its normal functions, continued and completed by the end of June the review of the periodical collection which was begun in 1968. As a result, out of a total of 2,500 titles examined, 205 titles were withdrawn, 286 were moved from the permanent to the limited retention group, 33 were moved in the converse direction and 54 were transferred to other sectors of the collections. Former retention schedules were changes on 445 titles and binding decisions were taken and recorded for 665 classified periodicals. The subsequent changes in relevant records were carried out by the sections concerned.

23. In connexion with the transfer of registration of United Nations and specialized agencies periodicals from the Acquisition Section to the Documents Processing Section, the Committee examined the constitutional status of those bodies whose relationship with the United Nations or the agencies was not clear and established a loose-leaf "List of specialized agencies and bodies affiliated

with the United Nations and the specialized agencies." The list will be used as authority for placement of periodicals in the proper parts of the collections and will be amended as necessary.

24. The programme of selective conversion to microform of portions of the documentary collections, which got underway in 1969, continued in 1970 at a slightly reduced pace due to changes in the procedures for the preparation of material for filming brought about by the adoption of a revised inter-agency standard. The revised standard, prepared in December 1969 by an ACC *ad hoc* Meeting on Microfiche Matters and later endorsed by the Preparatory Committee of the Administrative Committee on Co-ordination, was issued in March 1970 with the document symbol ST/PB/30. During the year, 306,500 pages of documents and publications were prepared for filming. Some 6,000 microfiche masters and the required number of duplicates were produced under contract. The microfiches produced contain the texts of the English, French and Spanish versions of documents issued currently in the series of the Economic and Social Council and its functional commissions, as well as selected portions of the *Official records* of the General Assembly, the Security Council, the Economic and Social Council and the Trusteeship Council from 1946 on. Also converted to microfiche were the resolutions of the four afore-mentioned organs from 1946 to 1969. Due to shortage of qualified staff only a very limited number of microfiches containing Russian versions of documents could be prepared. Several requests for the supply of microfiches were received during the year from missions of Member States, libraries and research institutions. Since no decision has been taken yet as to the extension of the microfiching service to such users or as to the offering of microfiches on sale, these requests could not be satisfied.

25. The programme of conversion of the gazette collection to microfilms also continued, the deteriorating hard copies being thus gradually substituted by film and holdings completed where necessary. The progress of the programme is largely dependent on the availability of films produced commercially.

26. In line with the policy of encouraging commercial publishers in undertaking initiatives which are in the interest of the Organization, the Publications Board has approved in 1969 the microfilming of the League of Nations documents and publications preserved in the collections of the Headquarters Library. The filming was completed during the summer of 1970.

V. SERVICES TO READERS

(a) Loans and Related Services

27. Compared to last year, there were some slight variations in the number of books borrowed at various service points. The total count, however, remained almost the same (60,326 in 1970; 60,129 in 1969). The inter-library loan service was more in demand than in 1969, showing an increase of nearly 25 per cent and, analyzed by the type of material, reflecting the Organization's growing involvement in science and technology. The loans from the general collections, on the other hand, show a slight decrease, while those from the Statistical Collection increased.

28. As to the circulation of serials, an effort was made to consolidate the routing by directing the material to substantive units rather than to individuals wherever such arrangement was possible. The merit of the system is that the unit members are assured of prompt receipt in spite of absences, changes in assignments or room numbers of individual recipients. Out of the total of 112,240 issues circulated, some 80,000 are routed directly from the Acquisition Section and the rest from the Periodical Reading Room and the departmental branches.

29. There was a steep increase in demand for copying services. The number of requests rose from 435 in 1969 to 753 in 1970, and the number of pages copied increased from 10,713 in 1969 to 22,385 in 1970. One of the reasons for this increase is the fact that, as the Organization grows older, more and more documents are out of stock and the users from all over the world turn increasingly to the Library for copies. It was therefore most timely that an additional manual post was added to the Library's manning table in 1970 to meet this increase in clerical work load, and that the Xerox 914 copier was replaced by the new and faster 720 model. Additional equipment bought in 1970 also enabled the Library to offer complete, albeit limited, microfiche viewing, enlarging and copying facilities.

30. The Library was again heavily used by outside readers and the number of passes issued was higher than last year (674 in 1970, 612 in 1969). The majority of readers were scholars, researchers,

doctoral students, representatives of business firms and publishing houses mostly from other states of the USA and from abroad, who came to consult United Nations and specialized agencies documents not available elsewhere. Many law firms in the City were also given assistance in locating texts of laws, treaties and agreements of various countries. That the wealth of the statistical data contained in the Library continued to attract researchers of various business firms and organizations is evident from the fact that nearly 25 per cent of admission passes were directed to the Statistical Collection. All study carrels, reserved for long-term researchers, were occupied throughout the year.

(b) Information Tools

31. The computer-assisted indexing having become operative, the Library began to issue a new series of indexes to the documents of United Nations under the name *UNDEX*. Two issues of a *Subject index* and two issues of a *Country index*, in four languages, were compiled by computer from the records stored during the year. Two more issues were in preparation by the year's end. It is expected that the frequency of publication of these indexes will increase gradually in the future.

32. In response to requests of permanent Missions and substantive departments of the Secretariat several reading lists and selective bibliographies were prepared. Examples of these are a bibliography on the definition of aggression prepared for the Bulgarian Mission and a bibliography on planning-programming-budgeting system for the Office of the Controller. The Library also introduced, tentatively, a current awareness service whereby the latest articles and publications relevant to the various work programmes are immediately brought to the attention of the staff concerned with the subject. So far, this service is extended to the Department of Political and Security Council Affairs, to the Division of Public Administration and to the Social Affairs Division. It will be continued and expanded in the coming year and then evaluated as to its effectiveness. All other established publications (*United Nations documents index* and its cumulations, indexes to proceedings, *Current issues, New publications in the Dag Hammarskjold Library,* etc.) continued to be issued as scheduled. (Cf. section VIII.)

(c) Reference Services

33. The number of queries directed orally or in writing to the various service points reached nearly 102,000. They conformed to the usual pattern, ranging from simple call number or fact-finding type to those requiring extensive research, the latter category having risen considerably over the last year. The thinking of the international community on the contamination of outer space, the significance of the North Pole in the emblem of the United Nations, apportionment of expenses of the League of Nations, United States legislation dealing with environmental pollution are a few examples of the variety of topics dealt with by the Documents and General Reference Sections. The Map Collection had its usual fare of questions relating to measurement of road mileages, spelling of place names, in addition to queries requiring locating targets of air raids near Cairo, highjacking of airplanes in the Middle East, tidal waves in the Gulf of Bengal, etc. The Legal Branch continued to give customary service within its field of specialization and, in addition, prepared several selective lists of references on such subjects as ombudsman, collective security, South West Africa cases before the International Court of Justice and others.

VI. SERVICES AND ASSISTANCE RENDERED TO OTHER PARTS OF THE SECRETARIAT AND OTHER LIBRARIES

34. The Acquisition Section continued to provide acquisition services to various units having their own funds (UNCTAD, UNITAR, etc.) and took over all subscriptions for UNICEF. It also continued to maintain exchange records and to acquire and forward United States government publications for the Geneva Library. The service to UNDP continued to increase as follows:

	1968	1969	1970
UNDP items processed	6,978	7,668	8,073
Invoices processed	3,448	3,809	4,848

To improve the service to UNDP projects in the field, arrangements have been made for consultations with project managers to discuss, when necessary, the problems connected with requests for publications. Several such meetings were held and proved mutually most useful.

35. The repeated requests by the Office of Legal Affairs, that the Library undertake page indexing of the most important legal texts published by that Office were finally met this year when additional manpower was provided for that purpose. The preparation of the Spanish version of the *Index to the repertory of practice of United Nations organs* was begun immediately after the professional post was filled in May. The other two standing commitments to the Office of Legal Affairs, namely the indexing of the *United Nations Treaty series* and the preparation of the legal bibliography for inclusion in the *United Nations juridical yearbook* were met on target.

36. The participation of the Library in the inter-office activities directed to the application of modern techniques to the storage, retrieval and dissemination of information, with particular reference to the needs of the development assistance cycle, continued. The Chief of the Documentation Division chaired an Inter-Office Technical Group which submitted in May 1970 a report on the feasibility of the establishment of an information sub-system covering technical co-operation reports. He also supervised the technical aspects of the preparation of materials for a demonstration project on modern methods of information retrieval applied to the technical documentation output of United Nations field projects.

37. The meetings of the Publications Board, in which the Library participates in an advisory capacity, were attended regularly throughout the year by the Chief of the Documentation Division.

38. In line with its responsibility, the Library continued to submit to the Publications Board the requests for depository status with appropriate recommendations. Ten new depository libraries were designated in 1970: one each in Australia, India, Japan, Jordan, Kuwait, Nigeria, Pakistan, Rwanda, and two in France. At the end of the year, there were 310 depositories in 108 countries. Nevertheless, there were still the following Member States without a depository library at the end of December 1970: Albania, Botswana, Burundi, Cameroon, Central African Republic, Chad, Congo (People's Republic), Congo (Democratic Republic), Dahomey, Equatorial Guinea, Gabon, Gambia, Guinea, Ivory Coast, Malawi, Maldive Islands, Mali, Mauritania, Mauritius, Niger, Sierra Leone, Southern Yemen, Swaziland, Tunisia, Upper Volta and Yemen.

VII. EXTERNAL RELATIONS

(a) Staff Activities

39. The Library staff participated in various meetings and conferences of professional interest. The Deputy Director attended the 35th Conference of the FID and the International Congress on Documentation, held in Buenos Aires, 14–24 September 1970. From there she proceeded to the Meeting of Experts on Documentation in Santiago, Chile, convened by the Economic Commission for Latin America in connexion with the proposed establishment in ECLA of a regional documentation centre.

40. The Chief of the Documentation Division attended two OECD meetings held in Geneva, 7 to 11 December 1970: the Expert Group Meeting on the Aligned List of Descriptors and the Annual Meeting of the Correspondents of the Development Enquiry Service, where matters of exchange of information, and of co-ordination and standardization of methods and services between international, intergovernmental and governmental agencies were discussed.

41. The Chief of the Acquisition Section served as President of the New York Technical Services Librarians end in this capacity organized the first seminar in systems analysis for librarians held in New York. She also attended the annual Conference of the American Library Association and chaired the meeting of the International Relations Committee of the Resources and Technical Services Division. During the Conference she met with representatives of the Library's suppliers in Europe, Middle East and Latin America—all important sources of acquisition, some of which had caused problems in the past. She further attended several special conferences on problems of government publications, reprints, library/ bookdealer relations, and the annual General Assembly and the Symposium on Bibliographical Problems of International Organizations, convened in Vienna by the Association of International Libraries.

(b) Visitors

42. As every year, the Library received many distinguished visitors and scholars who came to inquire about the Library's activities in general or

in specific fields. Thus, several directors of United Nations information centres were briefed on the Library's relations and co-operation with the centres. Assistance was provided to the permanent missions of Barbados, Cuba, Japan and Sierra Leone in the organization and maintenance of their documentary collections. The scope, functions, procedures and techniques of the computer-assisted indexing programme and of the microfiching programme were described to numerous visitors, who, individually or in groups, came to the Library seeking such information. Among others, particular mention should be made of a study team from the British Foreign Office, a group of experts from the Swedish Ministry of Justice, two teams of experts from the International Bank for Reconstruction and Development and the Inter-American Development Bank, and the two experts provided by the Government of the Netherlands to make a feasibility study for the establishment of an ECLA documentation centre at Santiago, Chile.

43. Among the many visitors who came to discuss their problems and interests with the Director or the respective chiefs of divisions and sections were Mr. E. W. Dawy, bibliographer for economic development, Princeton University; Mr. A. E. Grundy, British Embassy, Washington; Mr. M. H. Khan, Central Board for Development of Bengal, Dacca, Pakistan; Mr. H. Liebaers, President of IFLA, Director of the Bibliothèque Royale, Brussels, Belgium; Mr. B. C. Malla, Chairman, Department of Political Science, Tribhuvan University, Kathmandu, Nepal; Mr. McDowel, Department of Lands and Surveys, New Zealand; Mrs. O. Orimalde, Librarian, National Library of Nigeria, Lagos; Mrs. A. Popescu-Bradicini, Director of the National Library of Romania, Bucharest; Mrs. G. Soriano-Llave, Chief, Library Service of the House of Representatives, Congress of the Philippines, Manila.

44. Talks to various groups of visiting colleagues, students of the profession and new staff members undergoing the orientation courses and subsequent tours of the premises have become an accepted part of the Library's normal activities. Several such talks were given and tours conducted during the year.

VIII. BIBLIOGRAPHY FOR THE YEAR 1970

45. Publications relating to documents of the United Nations and the specialized agencies:

Development bibliographies a listing of United Nations and specialized agencies material. March 1970. 7 p.
Unpublished; typewritten
Index to proceedings of the Economic and Social Council, 46th session, 1969. 1970. vi, 45 p. (ST/LIB/SER.B/E.37)
Sales No.: E.70.I.8
Index to proceedings of the Economic and Social Council, 47th session, 1969. 1970. vi, 46 p. (ST/LIB/SER.B/E.38)
Sales No.: E.70.I.16
Index to proceedings of the General Assembly, 24th session, 1969. 1970. vi, 248 p. (ST/LIB/SER.B/A.20)
Sales No.: E.70.I.25
Index to proceedings of the Security Council, 24th year, 1969. 1970. vi, 56 p. (ST/LIB/SER.B/E.6)
Sales No.: E.70.I.18
Index to proceedings of the Trusteeship Council, 37th session, 1970. 1970. vi, 10 p. (ST/LIB/SER.B/T.31)
Sales No.: E.71.I.2
List of depository libraries receiving United Nations material, 1970. 28 p. (ST/LIB/12/Rev. 4)
List of United Nations document series symbols, 1970. iv, 171 p. (ST/LIB/SER.B/5/Rev.2)
Sales No.: E.70.I.21
UNDEX; index des documents de l'Organisation des Nations Unies, série A: Index par matière, V. 1 : 1–2, janvier-août 1970 (ST/LIB/SER.I) A.1–2)
UNDEX; index des documents de l'Organisation des Nations Unies, série B: Index par pays, V. 1:1–2, janvier-août 1970 (ST/LIB/SER.I/B. 1–2)
UNDEX; indice de documentos de las Naciones Unidas, serie A: Indice de materias, T. 1:1–2, enero-agosto 1970 (ST/LIB/SER.I/A.1–2)
UNDEX; indice de documentos de las Naciones Unidas, serie B; Indice de paises, T. 1:1–2, enero-agosto 1970 (ST/LIB/SER.I/B.1–2)
UNDEX; Указатель Документов Организации Объединенных Наци . Серия А: Предиетныи указатель. Т. 1:1, январь 1970. (ST/LIB/SER.I/A.1)
UNDEX: Указатель Документоз Организации Объединенных Наци . Серия В: Указатель но странам. Т.1:1, январь 1970. (ST/LIB/SER.I/B.1)
UNDEX; United Nations documents index. Series A: Subject index, V. 1:1–2, January-August 1970 (ST/LIB/SER.I/A.1–2)

UNDEX; United Nations documents index.
Series B: Country index, V. 1:1-2, January-August 1970 (ST/LIB/SER.I/B.1-2)

United Nations documents index, V. 21, No. 1-9, January-September 1970 (ST/LIB/SER.E/259-267)

— Cumulative index, V. 19, pt. 1, 1968. 1970. vi, 407 p. in 2 v. (ST/LIB/SER.E/CUM. 12, pt. 1, v. 1-2)

— Cumulative index, V. 19, pt. 2, 1968. 1970. v, 141 p. (ST/LIB/SER.E/CUM.12, pt. 2)

46. Other publications (titles marked x are for internal distribution only):

Annual report of the Headquarters Library, the Geneva Library, and the libraries of the economic commissions, 1969. 1970. 48 p. (ST/LIB/25)

Apartheid; a selective bibliography on the racial policies of the Government of the Republic of South Africa, February 1970, 57 p. (ST/LIB/22/Rev. 1)

x Bibliography on planning-programming-budgeting system (PPBS), December 1970, 5 p. Unpublished; typewritten

x Bibliography on the definition of aggression, May 1970, 8 p. Unpublished; typewritten

Current issues; a selected bibliography on subjects of concern to the United Nations, No. 10, spring 1970, xxi, 94 p. (ST/LIB/SER.G/10) Sales No.: E.70.I.13

Current issues; a selected bibliography on subjects of concern to the United Nations, No. 11, autumn 1970, xviii, 68 p. (ST/LIB/SER.G/11) Sales No.: E/71.I.3

x Dated list of publications received; ESA Statistical Collection, No. 1-92, 1970 Unpublished, hectographed

x The diplomatic recognition of the People's Republic of China, November 1970, 5 p. Unpublished; hectographed

Legal bibliography of the United Nations and related inter-governmental organizations. *In* United Nations juridical yearbook, 1968. 1970. p. 264-299 (ST/LEG/SER.C/6) Sales No.: E.70.V.2

x List of newspapers currently received in the Dag Hammarskjold Library, September 1970, 12 p. Unpublished; hectographed

New publications in the Dag Hammarskjold Library, V. 21, No. 1-12, January-December 1970 (ST/LIB/SER.A/244-255)

x Publications related to the Persian Gulf States, May 1970, 24 p. Unpublished; typewritten

Short bibliography (on treaties concluded between states and international organizations or between two or more international organizations) *In* A/CN.4/L.161. 28 December 1970, p. 3-8

47. Publications on the Headquarters Library, or by staff members:

Dale, Doris Cruger. *The United Nations Library; its origin and development.* Chicago, American Library Association, 1970. xvi, 236 p. illus.

Gardé, P. K. *The United Nations family of libraries.* New York, Asia Publishing House (1970), 252 p. (Ranganathan series in library science, 22)

Groesbeck, Joseph. *Introducing UNDEX. Special libraries* 61:265-270, 1970, No. 6

VI

THE SPECIALIZED AGENCIES OF THE UNITED NATIONS

Some of the specialized agencies of the United Nations date their founding to the period prior to the League of Nations. Others were established as League affiliates. Still others were established after 1945. Each specialized agency places its major emphasis on a specific substantive field or fields of interest. Most concentrate on a relatively narrow field such as meteorology, banking, or aviation. An agency such as UNESCO on the other hand has programs on education, sciences, culture and communication.

The specialized agencies have a common pattern of organization. Each agency maintains its own headquarters with a central secretariat, is formed by agreement among a number of governments and is funded in large measure by these governments, and each maintains a close affiliation with the United Nations. Most of the agencies receive some funding from or carry out programs in cooperation with or on behalf of the United Nations. In recent years many of these special programs have been coordinated and funded through the United Nations Development Program.

A few of the publications of the specialized agencies, particularly the annual reports, are issued in an UN edition as well as an agency edition. Most of the publications appear only in the agency edition and are available only from the agencies themselves or through designated special sales agents.

The readings in this chapter explain the organization and functions of the specialized agencies and their documentation and publishing programs. Also included are some articles describing the activities and programs of the special libraries developed to meet the information needs of the central secretariat and staff of a specialized international organization.

United Nations and the Specialized Agencies: Documents and Publications

A. D. Roberts

In this article A. D. Roberts explains the use of the United Nations Documents Index *as a primary means of access to the documents of the specialized agencies. This approach formerly used by most documents librarians in the U. S. is unfortunately no longer possible since the UNDI ceased indexing the documents of specialized agencies at the end of 1962. Roberts suggestions about checking records and arrangements of documents still apply.*

This article deals with the problems facing libraries which are receiving the great majority of the documents and publications of either the United Nations and/or one or more of its Specialized Agencies. Libraries whose intake is restricted to sales publications should be able to treat these books, periodicals and pamphlets as they do works issued by commercial publishers. We are, then, concerned with libraries receiving extensive sets of documents and publications, "documents" to mean papers which are not normally obtainable separately and most of which are mimeographed and in numbered series. By "publications" is meant those items which have either been placed on public sale individually or which are distributed free as informational material.

The means of most, if not all, libraries do not permit them to catalog individually all the items issued by the United Nations or one of its prolific agencies. A number of libraries catalog only the publications placed on general sale, or perhaps only a selection of these. Some libraries have made "open entries" for the periodicals and the various series of mimeographed documents bearing symbol numbers. Many libraries are unhappy about what they have done and their catalogs are not indicative of what they have.

The purpose of this article is to examine the possibility of using the *United Nations Documents Index* and other bibliographies of United Nations and Specialized Agency materials as substitutes for entries in the catalog itself. *United Nations Documents Index* records United Nations and Special-ized Agency documents and publications received in the library at Lake Success; publication of it began in January 1950. It is a monthly checklist with a subject index; the latter is to be cumulated annually. Most of this present article deals with its adequacy as a record of the key to a library's holdings of United Nations materials.

Before examining the uses of *United Nations Documents Index,* however, the value of the library's checking record of United Nations and/or Specialized Agency materials should be mentioned. Such a record is necessary to control the intake of documents and publications. The great majority of mimeographed documents bear symbols, and it is according to these that the record should be arranged. Since these symbols in many cases represent a brief "author entry" for the items in question, the checking record will often answer "author" questions about a library's holdings.

Speaking now only of the United Nations, if its documents and publications are arranged in the library in the order of their symbols (which for the most part agrees with the order in *United Nations Documents Index*), no further investigation is necessary in order to find an item marked as received in the checking record. If it is wished to shelve certain items outside the general sequence, the checking record must be marked accordingly. A dummy for a volume or a reference sheet filed with the mimeographed documents would be an added help. There are certain other decisions to be made; one would be whether to file all sales publications together or whether to treat them in

SOURCE: Reprinted from A. D. Roberts, "United Nations and Its Specialized Agencies: Documents and Publications," *College and Research Libraries,* 12 (April 1951), pp. 166-170.

the way they are listed in *United Nations Documents Index*.

If a library does attempt descriptive cataloging of a selection of its mimeographed documents and then interfiles these cards with those for the United Nations sales publications, the result is a sequence of author cards which both librarians and readers find most difficult to follow. Only librarians specializing in United Nations material and readers who have spent some time working with it and who know something of the structure of the United Nations will be able to find their way easily among these cards. It is suggested that under the heading "United Nations" cards be placed explaining the holdings of the library in general (e.g. mentioning the date from which it holds mimeographed material) and explaining the uses of the checking record, *United Nations Documents Index* and other bibliographies.

It would be possible, then, for a library wishing to effect cataloging economies to dispense with corporate author entries under "United Nations" for United Nations material if its United Nations collection was well organized, had checking records and was adequately serviced. Sales publications, except those recently published, can, for example, be rapidly identified by consulting *Publications 1945–1948* and *United Nations Publications 1949* issued by the United Nations Department of Public Information. *United Nations Documents Index,* the two bibliographies of sales publications just cited and other appropriate bibliographies would need to be shelved near the public catalog. If necessary they could be annotated to show exact holdings and call numbers. If it was decided that some corporate author cards should be filed (perhaps because subject entries for these items had been decided upon) the detailed statement of the library's holdings and cataloging policies should still be retained on the first cards under "United Nations."

The next part of this article is an attempt to answer questions which arise about the use of *United Nations Documents Index* as a substitute for full cataloging.

WHAT DOES THE LIBRARY OF CONGRESS DO?

The Library of Congress has cataloged a number of United Nations and Specialized Agency documents and publications and has cards available for them. They represent, however, only a portion of the documents of importance. The Library of Congress makes author entries under "United Nations" for publications prepared by national delegations and published by their governments. These items are not recorded in *United Nations Documents Index* and would, presumably, be dealt with by a library in the same way as other government publications.

Would *United Nations Documents Index* record everything in the Library? In nearly every case it will record far more than the holdings of any library outside Lake Success, partly because it includes documents with a limited distribution. Because its listing of Specialized Agency material is limited to items received at Lake Success, a depository of a Specialized Agency could receive material not in *United Nations Documents Index*. The United Nations has not yet perfected its arrangements for obtaining all Specialized Agency material at Lake Success.

HOW UP TO DATE IS UNITED NATIONS DOCUMENTS INDEX?

An issue of *United Nations Documents Index* recording documents and publications received at Lake Success during one month appears on the fifteenth of the following month. Generally speaking it is quicker in recording items issued by the United Nations than it is in entering those of the Specialized Agencies, because the latter items have to travel first; the majority of the former are produced at Lake Success.

What treatment would be given to such items as monographs by individual authors and serials with distinctive titles? A small minority of documents and publications bear the names of individual authors. Examples are to be found among papers prepared for the International Law Commission of the United Nations; one of these is, for example, a "Report on the High Seas," by J. P. A. Francois (U.N. document A/CN.4/17, 1950). Unesco has published a number of works bearing their authors' names, among them *Education for Librarianship,* by J. P. Danton and *Food and the Family* by Margaret Mead. These works are particularly likely to be looked for in the catalog under their individual authors' names. Reference librarians may not recognize them as having been issued by the United Nations or one of the Specialized

Agencies if imprints are omitted from references. It might well be decided that these items should have individual author entries, especially if the library concerned specialized in the topics dealt with. If individual author entries are to be made for a limited number of items, the selection could be made either at the time of receipt or by a perusal of *United Nations Documents Index.*

Similarly, serials with individual titles like the *Transport and Communications Review* and the *Demographic Yearbook* of the United Nations or *Industry and Labour* of the International Labour Office might be cataloged under their titles. In any case, if special lists of periodicals, perhaps of those currently received, are made for reference use apart from the general catalog, titles of United Nations and Specialized Agency periodicals should be included.

Would not the absence of subject cards mean that readers would miss important materials? This is probably the gravest accusation against the proposed scheme. In assisting readers, reference librarians would have to be constantly on the watch to see that they did not neglect items receiving this special treatment. The present writer feels that some subject treatment is necessary. The following suggestions are put forward with the view of giving some subject coverage in an economical way. We have seen that Library of Congress cards are available for most sales publications and for a number of mimeographed documents. These cards could be filed by subject.

Form references to the library's holdings of United Nations material, and to *United Nations Documents Index* in particular, might be inserted under other appropriate headings. An examination of the subject entries in the catalog of one library housing United Nations documents and publications showed a number of subject entries for sales publications but not much else. There was nothing for the United Nations under "International law—Codification," though a relevant League of Nations publication was there. This was because the work of the United Nations in this field is reported in supplements to the General Assembly's *Official Records;* many mimeographed documents are also concerned with this subject. Nor were there entries under a number of other subjects for which United Nations documents and publications in that library probably give the most detailed, the most authoritative, or the most up-to-date information available. This library is, in general, taking good care of its United Nations collection. Though a thorough investigation has not

been made, it is probable that conditions in this one library are paralleled elsewhere.

If Library of Congress cards for United Nations materials are filed by subject and form cards are also used, sometimes they would come together under the same heading. In the great majority of cases all that would be necessary would be to add a word to the form card, so that instead of reading "Information . . . " they would read "Additional Information . . . " Most printed United Nations publications and the more substantial mimeographed documents will be found to be supported by other related mimeographed items.

It has already been suggested that United Nations documents and publications arriving in a library be screened for works by individual authors, titles of serials, etc. They might also be screened from the subject point of view and new form cards made when appropriate. For this purpose a separate United Nations form card file would be needed as a working tool. It is also suggested that the cards be dated. The interests of the United Nations do change; after the passage of a number of years it might be necessary to add to the form cards a fuller indication of the years concerned. The procedures outlined would not take much time and they would provide a minimum coverage by subject in the public catalog. They are suggested because it is realized that fuller subject cataloging is often not possible.

It should be noted that in each issue of *United Nations Documents Index* "an asterisk distinguishes those documents and publications which summarize the work of an organ, represent the final results of international conferences or research projects, or are works of reference such as bibliographies, handbooks and yearbooks."

The monthly subject index at the end of *United Nations Documents Index* does, however, provide an analytic index far superior to anything libraries can afford to produce themselves for their own catalogs. It includes index entries for parts of documents and publications as well as for these items as a whole. In this respect it is more detailed than the subject indexes in the general catalogs of the publications of national governments. As has already been noted, the plan is to cumulate annually its subject index.

What treatment would be given to items which the library wished to shelve outside the main United Nations and/or Specialized Agencies Collection? Notes in the checking records and possibly a marked copy of *United Nations Documents Index* would show this. It might be decided that extra copies of the publications concerned were needed for such purposes. If special catalogs were provided for these other locations, e.g. in departmental or seminar libraries, the extra copies could be cataloged for this purpose. If the main catalog of the library is a union catalog of all holdings, the checking record and/or the copy of *United Nations Documents Index* serving as a catalog would be marked accordingly.

What of the material that appeared before "United Nations Documents Index" began? Some 41,000 documents and publications in English had been issued by the United Nations alone before *United Nations Documents Index* began. Some of these are carefully recorded in *Checklists:* these have subject indexes. The preparation and publication of checklists for the documents not so far covered is continuing. For coverage of the Specialized Agencies in pre-*United Nations Documents Index* times, only the catalogs and indexes produced by these agencies themselves are available.

A case can, then, be made for using *United Na-*

tions Documents Index as part of the catalog of a library's contents and for not cataloging at all or adopting a scheme of highly selective cataloging in the card catalog itself. It should be added that, in addition to *United Nations Documents Index,* some agencies have detailed catalogs of their own documents and publications. If a library is a depository of one of these agencies, it most certainly should shelve the relevant agency bibliography with *United Nations Documents Index*. In at least one case the agency bibliography is fuller than *United Nations Documents Index*.

The International Civil Aviation Organization publishes a monthly *Index of ICAO Documents.* This is in alphabetical order of subjects and it is cumulated annually. Alternatively, or in addition, one can receive monthly, by subscription, cards containing abstracts. Subject headings are printed at the top of the cards. These headings are, however, specialized ones, so that the cards could hardly be interfiled in the catalog of a general library.

Significant Early Documents of the Specialized Agencies Related to United Nations

José Meyer

In this article Meyer covers the history of the founding or re-establishment of the specialized agencies associated with the United Nations and notes the major sources of documentation.

The Economic and Social Council of the United Nations, at its final meeting in London on Feb. 18, 1946, set up, together with other commissions and committees, a negotiating committee of twelve members to study methods of bringing the International Labour Organization, the Food and Agriculture Organization, the World Bank and Fund, and UNESCO into relationship with the United Nations and to work out preliminary draft agreements with these agencies. The draft agreements were submitted to the second session of the Economic and Social Council which opened at Hunter College on May 25, 1946.

The International Labour Conference, at its twenty-seventh session, adopted on Nov. 5, 1945, an instrument for the amendment of the Constitution of the International Labour Organization, enabling it to establish a cooperative relationship with the United Nations. The text may be found in the *Official Bulletin of the International Labour Office,* v. 28, Dec. 15, 1945, p. 1-4.

The other three agencies have in their constitutions special clauses providing for a relationship with the United Nations.

FOOD AND AGRICULTURE ORGANIZATION OF THE UNITED NATIONS (F.A.O.)

F.A.O. was the first of the new permanent United Nations organizations. It was originally planned at the United Nations Conference on Food and Agriculture at Hot Springs, Va., from May 18 to June 3, 1943. The first step was the setting up of an Interim Commission on Food and Agriculture, July 15, 1943, for the purpose of formulating and recommending for consideration by all member governments a specific plan for a permanent organization in the field of food and agriculture.

The original documents of the Hot Springs Conference were in the form of loose mimeographed papers, not for general circulation. The final act and relevant documents were published in the United States as:

United Nations Conference on Food and Agriculture, Hot Springs, Virginia, May 18-June 3, 1943. Final Act and Section Reports. Washington, Government Printing Office, 1943. 59p. (Department of State Publication, 1948, Conference Series 52.)

In Great Britain, the final act and accompanying documents were issued in two separate publications as:

Final Act of the United Nations Conference on Food and Agriculture. London, H.M. Stationery Office, 1943. (Cmd. 6451.)

United Nations Conference on Food and Agriculture. Section Reports on the Conference. London, H.M. Stationery Office, 1943. (Cmd. 6461.)

After a year's work, the interim commission completed the draft of a constitution for the Food and Agriculture Organization of the United Nations. This, together with a detailed report on its activities, was submitted in the following form to each of the forty-four governments represented at the Hot Springs Conference:

SOURCE: Reprinted from José Meyer, "Significant Early Documents of the Specialized Agencies Related to the United Nations," *College and Research Libraries,* 8, (Apr. 1947), pp. 142–146.

First Report to the Government of the United Nations by the Interim Commission on Food and Agriculture. Washington, Aug. 1, 1944. 55p.

On Dec. 14, 1944, the British Government accepted this constitution. The text of its instrument of acceptance, together with the text of the constitution itself and, as an appendix, the first report of the interim commission, were published as:

Documents Relating to the Food and Agriculture Organization of the United Nations, 1st August-14th December 1944. London, H.M. Stationery Office, 1945. 42p. (Cmd. 6590.) Miscellaneous No. 4 (1945)

By May 30, 1945, twenty-two nations had accepted the constitution, making it possible for the organization to come into existence. The interim commission carried out its final function before being automatically dissolved upon the coming into being of F.A.O.; it convened the first plenary session of F.A.O. at Quebec City in Canada, Oct. 16, 1945.

Five technical committees of the interim commission had, in the meantime, conducted research on agricultural production, nutrition and food management, forestry, fisheries, and statistics respectively and submitted the results of their findings in the form of reports to the Quebec Conference:

Five Technical Reports on Food and Agriculture, Submitted to the United Nations Interim Commission on Food and Agriculture by Its Technical Committees on Nutrition and Food Management, Agricultural Production, Fisheries, Forestry and Primary Forest Products, Statistics. Washington, D.C., Aug. 20, 1945. 313p. Issued also in five separate parts.

Other documents distributed to member governments at the time of the Quebec Conference were:

Second Report to the Governments of the United Nations by the Interim Commission on Food and Agriculture. Washington, D.C., July 15, 1945. 3p.

This contained recommendations concerning the future of the International Institute of Agriculture in Rome.

Third Report to the Governments of the United Nations by the Interim Commission on Food

and Agriculture, Transmitting the Report of the Technical Committee on Forestry and Primary Forest Products. Washington, D.C., Apr. 25, 1945. 47p.

The Work of FAO: A General Report to the First Session of the Conference of the Food and Agriculture Organization of the United Nations, Prepared by the Reviewing Panel and Circulated to Members of the Interim Commission by the Executive Committee. Washington, D.C., Aug. 20, 1945. 57p.

The conference lasted from Oct. 16 to Nov. 1, 1945. Two commission, A and B, were set up, one technical, comprising the above five committees, the other administrative. The principal documents of the conference were the journal and the final reports of these two commissions, which were unanimously adopted. There were, in addition, a large number of other papers, including reports of meetings of subcommissions, all of them mimeographed. These were not available for general distribution. The commission reports, together with a number of other documents, were published later by F.A.O. as:

First Session. Conference of the Food and Agriculture Organization of the United Nations. Journal. v. 1, no. 1-15, Oct. 16-Nov. 1, 1945. Quebec City, Canada, 1945.

Food and Agriculture Organization of the United Nations. *Report of the First Session of the Conference, Held at the City of Quebec, Canada, October 16 to November 1, 1945. Containing the Reports of Commission A (Policy and Program) and Commission B (Organization and Administration) with Supplementary Data Relating to Resolutions and Recommendations, the Budget, Rules of Procedure, Financial Regulations, and the Constitution.* Washington, January 1946. xxi, 89p. in double columns.

In Great Britain, these documents were published as:

Documents Relating to the First Session of the Food and Agriculture Conference of the United Nations, Quebec, Canada, 16th October-1st November, 1945. London, H.M. Stationery Office, January 1946. 62p. (Cmd. 6731.) Miscellaneous No. 3 (1946)

There is also available from F.A.O. a limited number of copies of a made-up volume entitled

Basic Documents of F.A.O., at $2.50 per copy, containing the following documents:

Report of the First Session of the Conference, Held at the City of Quebec, Canada, October 16 to November 1, 1945.

FAO Conference. First session. *Draft: Provisional Program of Work for the First Session.* Washington, Aug. 4, 1945.

United Nations Interim Commission on Food and Agriculture. *The Work of FAO.* [Washington, Aug. 20, 1945.]

Third Report to the Governments of the United Nations by the Interim Commission on Food and Agriculture. Washington, Apr. 25, 1945.

Second Report to the Governments of the United Nations by the Interim Commission on Food and Agriculture. Washington, July 16, 1945.

First Report to the Governments of the United Nations by the Interim Commission on Food and Agriculture. Washington, Aug. 1, 1944.

United Nations Conference on Food and Agriculture, Hot Springs, Va., May 18-June 3, 1943. *Final Act and Section Reports.* Washington, 1943.

At Quebec a resolution was adopted calling for the taking over by F.A.O. of the library, archives, and properties of the International Institute of Agriculture in Rome, the Centre International de Sylviculture, and the Comité International du Bois. It was further decided that English, French, Spanish, and Russian were to be the official languages, with English and French to be used in debates and documents.

During the first part of April 1946 F.A.O. held a meeting in London of a panel of experts from various international and regional organizations for consultation in connection with the setting up of permanent services in the field of statistics, scientific abstracting, library service, and bibliographic information.

Additional early publications of F.A.O. which have been widely circulated are:

FAO Information Service Bulletin, no. 1, Dec. 3, 1945; no. 2, Apr. 2, 1946. Irregularly issued.

FAO, Cornerstone For a House of Life by Gove Hambidge. [Washington, 1946.] 24p.

Facts about FAO. Washington, D.C., Apr. 12, 1946, 7p.

BRETTON WOODS AGREEMENTS

The United Nations Monetary and Financial Conference at Bretton Woods, N.H., July 1-22, 1944, attended by experts of forty-four nations, dealt with machinery for currency stabilization and to provide long-term credit for permanent reconstruction and the development of untapped productive resources. For this purpose, draft constitutions for an international monetary fund and for a bank for reconstruction and development were drawn up. Each of these bodies is to be headed by a board of governors composed of representatives of all the member countries and a board of executive directors of whom there are to be always at least twelve, with five of their number to represent the five members having the largest national quotas.

The original documentation of the Bretton Woods Conference consisted of over five hundred separate mimeographed papers, comprising in addition to reports of meetings and technical papers submitted, the following:

Journal of the United Nations Monetary and Financial Conference. Bretton Woods, N.H., no. 1-22, July 1-22, 1944. Mimeographed.

The only printed document of the conference was:

United Nations Monetary and Financial Conference. *Officers of the Conference, Members of the Delegations, Officers of the Secretariat.* Revised to July 9. Bretton Woods, N.H., July 1944. 32p.

These were available only to delegations and their staffs. The text of the final agreements was issued in the United States as:

Articles of Agreement: International Monetary Fund and International Bank for Reconstruction and Development, United Nations Monetary and Financial Conference, Bretton Woods, N.H., July 1 to 22, 1944. Washington, D.C., U.S. Treasury [1945]. 89p.

United Nations Monetary and Financial Conference, Bretton Woods, N.H., July 1 to July 22, 1944. *Final Act and Related Documents.* Washington, Government Printing Office, 1944. 122p. (Department of State Publication 2187, Conference Series 55.)

In an effort to win support for United States

participation in the fund and the bank, the U.S. State Department and Treasury, besides reprinting various statements made by officials in support of the measure, issued the followng pamphlets, which are available free:

Conference at Bretton Woods Prepares Plans for International Finance by John Parke Young. Washington, Government Printing Office, 1944. 28p. (Department of State Publication 2216, Conference Series 57.)
U.S. Treasury. The Bretton Woods Proposals. Washington, D.C., Feb. 15, 1945. 13p.
——The Bretton Woods Proposals. Questions and Answers on the Fund and Bank. Washington, D.C., Mar. 15, 1945. 16p.
——Charts Relating to the Bretton Woods Proposals [Washington, D.C.] Apr. 30, 1945. 18p. and charts. Oblong.

The British Government, in the meantime, published the documents relating to the Bretton Woods Conference as:

United Nations Monetary and Financial Conference, Bretton Woods, N.H., U.S.A., July 1 to July 22, 1944. Final Act. London, H.M. Stationery Office, 1944. 70p. (Cmd. 6546.)
United Nations Monetary and Financial Conference, Bretton Woods, N.H., U.S.A., July 1 to July 22, 1944. Documents Supplementary to the Final Act. London, H.M. Stationery Office [1945] 24p. (Cmd. 6597.)

The agreements became operative Dec. 27, 1945, only a few days before the deadline set at Bretton Woods, when twenty-nine countries representing 65 per cent of the total quotas allotted by the agreements for the bank and the fund had ratified the Bretton Woods instrument. The United States, as the largest contributor, then called a preparatory conference for setting up the organization for the world fund and bank at Wilmington Island, Savannah, Ga., which lasted from March 8 to 18, 1946. Two full sessions of the boards of governors were held.

A journal was issued during the conference, but of the conference documents, only the following have come to hand so far:

World Fund and Bank. Inaugural Meeting. [Savannah, Ga.] Fund Documents 1-30. [n.p., 1946] Mimeographed.

UNESCO

At the invitation of the British Government, representatives of forty-four United Nations met in London from Nov. 1 to 16, 1945, to discuss the adoption of a draft constitution for educational and cultural collaboration between the United Nations. This document had been prepared by the Conference of Allied Ministers of Education in cooperation with United States educational authorities. The text of the draft consituation may be found in:

Proposed Educational and Cultural Organization of the United Nations. Washington, Government Printing Office, 1945. 27p. (Department of State Publication 2382.)

The London Conference ended on November 16 with the adoption of the draft constitution of UNESCO, whereby the signatories pledged themselves to collaborate in the advancement of mutual knowledge and understanding of peoples; to give fresh impulse to popular education and to the spread of culture; and to maintain, increase, and diffuse knowledge. The organization was formally established in November 1946, when the first general conference was held in Paris.

The early documents of the United Nations Conference for the Establishment of an Educational and Cultural Organization were in the form of mimeographed papers, solely for the use of the delegations. The final documents comprise the final act, the constitution of the United Nations Educational, Scientific, and Cultural Organization, and an instrument establishing a preparatory educational, scientific, and cultural commission, also several resolutions. They were issued in the United States as:

"the defenses of peace": Documents Relating to UNESCO, the United Nations Educational, Scientific, and Cultural Organization.
Pt. 1. Washington, Government Printing Office, 1946. 31p. (Department of State Publication 2457, Conference Series 80.)

And in Great Britain as:

Final Act of the United Nations Conference for the Establishment of an Educational; Scientific, and Cultural Organization. (With related documents.) London, Nov. 16, 1945. London, H.M. Stationery Office, 1945. 25p. (Cmd. 6711.) Miscellaneous No. 16 (1945)

UNRRA

UNRRA is a wartime agency established by virtue of an agreement signed in Washington Nov. 9, 1943, by representatives of forty-four countries. Its purpose is limited strictly to relief and immediately needed rehabilitation, not long-term reconstruction.

Due to UNRRA's temporary character, an organic connection with the United Nations is not possible at this stage, but there is nevertheless close cooperation. The publications of UNRRA have been fully described by Olive L. Sawyer in an article entitled "Information Please, on UNRRA," which appeared in *The Booklist*, July 15, 1945, p. 328-31.

All the more important early publications by and about UNRRA will be found in:

Selected Reading List on United Nations Relief and Rehabilitation Administration, Prepared by the United Nations Information Office in Consultation with the United Nations Relief and Rehabilitation Administration. New York [1945], a 10-page folder, with its supplement [1946], an 8-page folder.

Libraries and the Publications of the UN Specialized Agencies[1]

Janet F. Saunders

This piece reviews the questions of acquiring, arranging and providing reference service on collections of documents of the specialized agencies. An updated and more extensive list of lists, indexes, and catalogs than the one at the end of this article may be found in UNESCO Bulletin for Libraries, *21, (Sept.–Oct., 1967) pp. 263–270.*

At first sight, the handling of documents of Specialized Agencies of the United Nations seems even more complicated than that of United Nations documents. There are 11 agencies, each with its own peculiar system of publication, of document notation, and of distribution. Some of them are highly technical. All in all, it is perplexing to find a common method of treatment for the whole family. Some of them are so little known even to librarians that it seems worth while to enumerate them before beginning to discuss their publications. They are the following: Food and Agriculture Organization of the United Nations (FAO), International Bank for Reconstruction and Development (Bank), International Monetary Fund (Fund), International Civil Aviation Organization (ICAO), International Labour Organisation (ILO), Interim Commission for the International Trade Organization (ICITO), International Telecommunication Union (ITU), United Nations Educational, Scientific and Cultural Organization (Unesco), Universal Postal Union (UPU), World Health Organization (WHO), World Meteorological Organization (WMO).

Let us assume that the medium-sized library, for which this article is intended, is interested in keeping a representative collection of the publications of all the agencies. Even so, it will be outside its scope to keep anything like a complete collection of all of them, even if it were possible to obtain them. Only the largest libraries, or those having a special interest in international affairs, would attempt to do so. A threefold problem arises: first, size and importance of the international collection and selection of documents; second, classification; and third, means of utilization.

SIZE OF COLLECTION AND SELECTION OF DOCUMENTS

In the *United Nations documents index (UNDI)*, that indispensable tool of all librarians using international documents,[2] there is an introductory statement to the lists of publications of each agency which explains the system of publication, the notation, sources of information, etc. The lists themselves give an idea of the quantity of material issued and its nature. The quantity varies from 715 items listed in 1952 for Unesco and 319 for the ILO, to 5 for WMO.[3] In 1953, the number of documents indexed increased materially for FAO and WMO (from 5 in 1952 to 182 in the first 10 months of 1953), and decreased for ICAO and Unesco, in the latter case by almost 50 per cent. In addition, there are of course, periodicals which except in the case of WHO are not indexed in *UNDI.* They range in number from 1 each for ICITO, ITU and WMO to 11 for ILO, 12 for FAO, 12 for WHO and 11 for Unesco. A large proportion of the documents, particularly of agencies such as ICAO, ITU, UPU and WMO are purely technical, if one may be allowed to use that term for such documents as sections of the *Formulaire de l'UPU,* for example, *Liste des formules de l'arrangement concernant les virements postaux.* Others are working papers, notifications, circulars

SOURCE: Reprinted from Janet F. Saunders "Libraries and Publications of the UN Specialized Agencies," *UNESCO Bulletin for Libraries,* 8, (Aug.–Sept., 1954) pp. E103–E108.

and other papers of interest only to the specialist and are outside the scope of the moderate-sized library.

Of course, if a library is a depository, it has certain obligations in the matter of conserving the material it receives, and of making that material available to the public. If the library is not a depository and is permitted to use its discretion in selecting the ingredients of its international collection, it will find that general documents in their final text; periodicals, particularly the chief organ of the issuing body; special studies, such as monographs on a specific question; and reports of missions, which frequently are equivalent to important monographs, will form in a very few years a good-sized collection, representative of all the agencies, and of permanent value.

TYPES OF PUBLICATIONS

The type of publication varies from agency to agency. All, of course, publish the proceedings of their general conferences and executive boards. FAO issues a great many monographs, and indexes in *UNDI,* in addition to its printed documents, the working papers of its general and technical conferences. The Bank and Fund issue *Statistical papers,* loan agreements, schedules of par values, and one or two yearbooks. The Bank, for the last two or three years, has been issuing most valuable reports of economic and financial missions to Ceylon, Nicaragua, Chile, Jamaica, Mexico and other countries. The Interim Commission for ITO is responsible for the documents of the Interim Commission and also for the documents of the Contracting Parties to the General Agreement on Tariffs and Trade (GATT). ICAO's documents are largely technical. ITU documents are for the most part working documents essential for the day to day operations of international telecommunication service: *List of international monitoring stations, List of point-to-point radio channels, Radio frequency record,* etc. They are of little interest to the general public. UPU and WMO documents are for the most part of the same general type, except for UPU's *Dictionnaire des bureaux de poste* (2 vols.) and WMO's *Technical notes* (of general interest) and such special publications as the recent *World distribution of thunderstorm days* and the forthcoming *International cloud areas 1953,* which promises to be a definitive work.

ILO publishes quite a number of special studies

each year in its *Studies and reports* series. In addition, the working papers of its conferences and of its principal committees, notably the industrial committees, are often valuable background studies of industrial, economic and social questions. Others are analyses of reports of government on national conditions concerning certain topics under discussion by the ILO.

Unesco issues single studies and monograph series in the category termed "Publications". Official documents indexed in *UNDI* and available to the public include, in addition to final records of conferences and committees, some of their working papers, departmental publications, and circular letters.

More than any other agency, Unesco issues publications sponsored jointly with some other institution, such as those prepared by the International Bureau of Education: *The Teaching of reading, Introduction to mathematics in primary schools, The Teaching of handicrafts in secondary schools,* etc.

Most of the special studies of WHO are issued in the *Bulletin of the World Health Organization,* which is its chief scientific organ. It publishes two special series, its *Technical report series,* which contains reports of expert committees, and its *Monograph series* for important contributions of international significance. The latter also occasionally includes reprints and complete translations of material originally published in the *Bulletin.* The *Supplements* to the *Bulletin of the World Health Organization* constitute a third special series, containing technical contributions such as the *Manual of the international statistical classification of diseases, injuries and causes of death,* and the *Pharmacopoeia internationalis,* of too special a character for inclusion in a periodical.

CLASSIFICATION

The basic problem of classification of international documents is whether to group all the documents of the international organizations together, or whether to disperse them according to subject interest. The library which is making a speciality of international documentation will probably consider it essential to group together at least the general documents, such as the proceedings of the general assemblies, or the minutes of the executive body. These probably include as annexes or otherwise the reports of the principal committees of the organization, and some at least of the preparatory documents or working papers of the meetings to which they refer. It might be well to include in this group all official reports on the activities of the organization, reports of missions or committees, minutes of technical or regional conferences, annual reports such as those submitted to the United Nations on the work of the organization as a whole, periodicals which are the official organ of the agency and contain the important texts, such as the *Official bulletin of the ILO, Unesco official bulletin, Union postale, Chronicle of the world health organization, WHO bulletin,* and so on. If the library does not have a strictly subject classification, then by all means keep all the documentation of each agency together, even the periodicals dealing with special subjects, such as the *Fisheries bulletin* of FAO, or the *Copyright bulletin* of Unesco. If it does have a subject classification, then it would be more practical to class according to their subject interest the monographs, special studies, and even reports of missions such as those conducted by the International Bank, which constitute studies of the economic and financial conditions of certain countries. Periodicals, except the main organ, under this system would be classed like other periodicals in the library, either by principal subject interest or in the periodicals division of the library.

For the classification of agency documents, in so far as these are kept in a group by themselves, some system such as that used by the UN Library in New York is practical. Each document bears as the first part of its classification number the combination of letters commonly used as the abbreviation of its agency's name. This is followed by the official notation of the document if such exists. If there is no official symbol, a very simplified form of decimal classification is used.

The general principle of documents symbols as used by the Agencies is the same as that used by UN. However, it has its variations, and certain documents, notably proceedings of the various general assemblies, bear no symbol at all. The symbol is applied pretty regularly to committee documents, and processed material. The general rule is that the symbol for each series of documents begins with a letter or letters representing the initials of the issuing body—committee, conference, department, etc.—and is followed sometimes by a session or year number, subdivided by the serial number of the group of documents; sometimes merely by the serial number. Here are a few examples:

FAO. Committee documents bear the initials of the name of the committee in English, followed by the year without indication of century, subdivided by the individual document number; e.g., Committee on Commodity Problems, Series of 1952 documents, No. 70, is numbered CCP 52/70.

ICAO. Documents are identified by their title and by a reference symbol. The reference symbol consists of two groups of figures separated by a hyphen, a letter symbol and an oblique stroke.

Example: Doc 5000-AT/200. The first figure (5000 in the example given) is the serial number in the general listing of ICAO documents. The letter symbol (AT in this example), separated from the figure by a hyphen, indicates the category of activity concerned (in this case, Air Transport). An oblique stroke is placed before the second figure (in this case 200) which is the serial number allotted to the document within that particular category.

ILO. Governing Body documents bear the initials of the issuing body in English, followed by the number of the session, subdivided (something peculiar to the ILO) by the agenda item number, and subdivided again by the serial number of the documents of that session; e.g., G.B. 122/15/7, would be the fifteenth item on the agenda of the 122nd session of the Governing Body, and the seventh document issued. Committee documents, or the documents of special conferences do not include the agenda item number. Committees of the Governing Body have, first, the initials G.B. and the session number, then the initials of the committee, then the document number preceded by "D" (document).

Unesco. The session number appears before the symbols of the General Conference and the Executive Board, which are followed by symbols of committees, commissions, etc., and serial numbers of working documents or summary records; e.g., 5C/PRG/23 (twenty-third document of the Programme Commission of the fifth session of the General Conference); 25 EX/CF/SR. 3 (third summary record of the Finance Commission of the twenty-fifth session of the Executive Board). The reference number of the documents of the secretariat departments consists of the symbol of the originating department, followed by a serial number; e.g., CUA/3 (third document of the Department of Cultural Activities). A *Guide to reference numbers and to the classification of documents and correspondence* was published in July 1953. (Document ODG/6.)

With a little thought the symbol is quite easily understood, and is really the only practical way of classing such documents as bear it, even if the library set happens to be incomplete.

UTILIZATION

The most serious problem of all to the library is the utilization of the documents. Having acquired them, and classed them, there remains the question of how best to get the meat out of them. Here surely is the outstanding claim for co-operative indexing. Here, too, in a special collection, is the case where the printed index can and should replace formal cataloging of individual documents. This is particularly true of general documents such as the records of general conferences, which treat each year different questions of world interest. It was to meet this need that the *United Nations documents index* was started in 1950.

The printed index of international documents, however, is not entirely adequate for the needs of the library. It is excellent for the readers who are already interested in a question from an international standpoint, but for those who do not know, so to speak, that they want to study their subject from a world standpoint and so do not think to look at international publications, an international index is not much use. It must constantly be brought to the readers' attention by the librarian. This is particularly true of monographs and special studies, the material most easily lost sight of, if they are classed in a special group with other documentation of the agencies. They are the publications of most value to the reader who is making a study of a special subject, not of an international organization. For this reason, it was suggested

earlier that they should be classed independently, and apart from the other publications of the agencies. Even though they are indexed in *UNDI,* it is important that they should receive full subject cataloguing, or subject classification, if the Library does one or the other or both, just as much as other works.

UNDI began only in January 1950, and several of the agencies had been hard at work for some time already. ILO, for instance, has been going since 1919. FAO took over from its predecessor, the International Institute of Agriculture (IIA) which had been in existence since 1910. WHO, too, is the direct heir of the Health Section of the League of Nations and the committees it served. Almost all began life in their present incarnation several years before *UNDI* made its first appearance. A list of indexes, sales catalogues, and announcements of recent publications issued by the different organizations is given below as a general guide to librarians who wish to complete their collection of these important bibliographical tools.

The work of the Specialized Agencies is of such vital importance in the world today that it should be made known as widely as possible, and every facility given to those who wish to study it.

REFERENCES

Indexes prior to 1950

ICAO:
Index of ICAO documents. Special issue, PICAO and ICAO assembly documentation 1946 to 1950. $0.75.
Index of ICAO publications (book-form index). Cumulative edition 1947 and 1948 (out of print). Annual cumulation, 1949 and 1950. $0.75 a year. Card index, annual sets, averaging 5,000 cards for 1949 and 1950. $18 a year.
ILO:
Catalogue of the publications in English of the International Labour Office, 1919-1950 (ILO Library, *Bibliographical contributions,* 5). Subject and title index and classified catalogue of all printed documents of the ILO from the beginning up to the end of 1950. Free on request. Limited stock.
WHO:
Bulletin of the Health Organization, 1945, vol. II. Lists all documents and publications issued by the Health Organization of the League of Nations, as well as articles published in technical periodicals, during the years 1920-45.

Current (1950 to date)

United Nations documents index (UNDI), January 1950 to date. Complete subject coverage of non-confidential unrestricted documents, and in the case of some agencies of limited documents and working papers.
ICAO:
Index of ICAO publications (book-form index), monthly edition with cumulation in June and December of each year. Covers the more important publications, such as Council and Assembly documents, the final reports of divisional

meetings and the reports to the Council made by the Air Navigation Commission and the Air Transport Committee, 1949 to date. Card index, annual sets, $18 (discontinued 1952).

UNESCO:
Subject list of publications and documents of Unesco. Monthly. A classification of the content of Unesco documents in the main series, and titles of publications issued.

Sales Catalogues

BANK:
Publications of the International Bank, 31 May 1950.
List of publications, 12 May 1947.
Checklist, 10 June 1948.

FAO:
Catalogue of publications 1945-1954, including available publications of the former International Institute of Agriculture 1910-1946, March 1954.
FAO documentation. Monthly publications list, no. 1, January/February 1954, issued in March 1954. Title and introductory page in English only. Items are listed in the language of publication with indication of other language editions. Supplements and brings up-to-date the *Catalogue.*
FAO documentation. Publications sales bulletin. Irregular. Issued for sales purposes to point out outstanding items.

FUND:
Publications (folder) March 1950, July 1950.

ICAO:
Salable publications, 1946-1953, 3rd ed., Jan. 1954.
Price list of PICAO publications to May 1, 1947.

ILO:
Catalogue of publications of the International Labour Office, 1953.
ILO new publications, May 1952-Aug. 1953. nos. 1-5, irregular.

ICITO:
ICITO Checklist, 1st-6th ed., Nov. 1948-Sept. 1950.
Short list of official material relating to the GATT. 1st-3rd ed., March 1951-Jan. 1953.

ITU:
Complete catalogue, brought up to date, monthly in *Telecommunication journal.*

UNESCO:
Unesco publications general catalogue, 1954.

WHO:
Publications of WHO, June 1947, June 1948, 1949, 1950.
Catalogue of publications, 1951, and July 1952, 1954.[4]
Recent and forthcoming publications. Autumn 1952.

WMO:
A complete list of publications of the International Meteorological Organization (predecessor of WMO) is available as an annex to IMO publications nos. 75 and 79, on sale by WMO. (WMO *Bulletin,* vol. 1, no. 1, p. 24.)

Announcements of Recent Publications

ICAO:
ICAO weekly list of publications. Roneoed. Also listed in *ICAO monthly bulletin,* sometimes with reviews.

ILO:
The most important printed publications are reviewed each month in the *International labour review,* at the beginning of the book review section.

UNESCO:
Listed each month in the Unesco *Official bulletin.*

UPU:
Listed each month in *Union postale.*

WHO:
Listed each month in the *Chronicle of the World Health Organization.*

WMO:
Listed in the monthly WMO *Bulletin.* Since July 1953, summaries of the publications are included.

Announcements of Recent Publications: Unofficial Lists

International organization. Boston, World Peace Foundation. Monthly. Contains an important bibliography on international questions, including a list of UN and Specialized Agencies publications.
Bulletin of the Public Affairs Information Service. New York. Weekly, with five cumulated issues yearly. Includes many of the publications of the Specialized Agencies.
Government publications monthly list. London, H.M. Stationery Office. Monthly. Contains a section listing UN and Specialized Agencies publications on sale by the Stationery Office.
Biblio. Catalogue des ouvrages parus en langue française dans le monde entier. Paris, Service bibliographique de la Librairie Hachette. Monthly with annual cumulative issue. Includes some publications of the Specialized Agencies.

NOTES

[1] This article is in continuation of a previous article *Libraries and United Nations publications,* which appeared in the *Bulletin,* vol. VIII, no. 2–3, item 137.

[2] This is fully described in *Libraries and United Nations publications* (*Bulletin* vol. VIII, no. 2–3, item 137).

[3] WMO started its activity in 1951, and the low number of documents in 1952 is due to the fact that not all were sent in for indexing at that time.

[4] New edition recently issued, containing a detailed author and subject index to all publications so far issued by WHO.

Specialized Agencies and the IAEA

U. S. Department of State

This annual report presents in summary the activities of all of the specialized agencies during a recent calendar year. More detailed information about a sampling of these agencies and their library and documentation activities will be found in the pieces following this one.

INTERNATIONAL BANK FOR RECONSTRUCTION AND DEVELOPMENT AND INTERNATIONAL DEVELOPMENT ASSOCIATION

With its membership increased to 115 by the addition of Yemen, Cambodia, and Equatorial Guinea, the IBRD by December 1970 had increased its authorized capital from $24 billion to $27 billion, of which $23.207 billion has been subscribed. Of this, the United States has subscribed $6.35 billion, or 27.36% of the total, of which $635 million has been paid in. With weighted voting, the United States has 63,750 votes, or 24.44% of total voting power.

The Bank relies for its sources of funds on borrowings in international capital markets, which by December 31 had grossed over $9 billion, as well as on its capital and reserves. Its reserves as of July 1970 were in excess of $1.3 billion. By contrast, its affiliate, the IDA, with 107 members,[1] depends in part on the annual allocation of a share in the IBRD profits, and in part on replenishments from members. In July 1970, a "third replenishment" was agreed upon, by which a total of approximately $813 million per year would be provided for 3 years; the first payment was scheduled for November 1971.

Whereas IBRD loans carry an interest rate of 7¼%, IDA credits bear no interest charge, and their service charge is only ¾%. IDA thus provides its members that are in the most difficult circumstances with a supplement or alternative to the IBRD loans. These differences aside, IDA has the same management and staff as the Bank, and finances the same general range of projects. Some projects, in fact, are financed in part by IBRD loans and in part by IDA credits.

Lending totals for the IBRD and IDA, for calendar years 1969 and 1970, are as follows:

	1969	1970
	(In millions of dollars)	
IBRD Loans		
Number	73	68
Amount	1,225.2	1,615.1
IDA Credits		
Number	39	59
Amount	463.2	604.8

Development lending by the IBRD and IDA combined in calendar year 1970 focused on the following principal areas:

	(In millions of dollars)
A. *Agriculture*	
Number	33
Amount	357.78
No. of countries including	22
1. *Irrigation*	
Amount	48.5
2. *Investment Credit*	
Amount	58.7
3. *General Agriculture*	
Amount	209
4. *Agriculture/Industries*	
Amount	41.8
B. *Education*	
Number	12

SOURCE: Reprinted from "Specialized Agencies and the AIEA," U.S. Department of State *U.S. Participation in the UN; Report by the President to the Congress for the Year 1970.* Washington, Government Printing Office, 1971. pp. 130-161.

Amount	101.5
No. of countries	11

C. *Public Services Infrastructure*

Number	55
Amount	1,281.55
No. of countries	44

including
1. *Transportation*

Amount	552.10

2. *Electric Power*

Amount	615.25

3. *Telecommunications*

Amount	114.2

D. *Industry*

Number	3
Amount	51.5
No. of countries	3

E. *Family Planning*

Number	1
Amount	2.00
No. of countries	1

A noteworthy agricultural project was a $26 million IDA credit to the U.A.R. for drainage of the Nile Delta.

The IBRD regards educational loans and credits, which enhance students' subsequent employment opportunities and national reservoirs of badly needed skills, as among the soundest forms of investment to be made in the developing world. Among these in calendar 1970 were an $11 million IBRD loan to the Ivory Coast for a project which included educational TV (see also p. 142) and an IDA credit of $6.1 million to Kenya to establish its first University Faculty in Agriculture.

Infrastructural lending included a $125 million loan to Mexico for electric power and a $40 million loan to Yugoslavia for a telecommunications project.

A $2 million loan went to Jamaica, the first to be used to support family planning.

INTERNATIONAL FINANCE CORPORATION

An affiliate of the IBRD, the IFC encourages investment in private enterprises in developing countries through both lending and equity participation. In contrast to the IBRD, which requires host government guarantees for its loans and IDA credits, the IFC operates without such guarantees. With the accession of the Congo (Kinshasa), Gabon, and Yemen, the IFC's membership in calendar 1970 reached 95, and total subscriptions to capital, $107 million. In addition to capital subscriptions, the IFC also obtains funds from repayments of investments, sales of equity and loan investments, and net income.

During calendar year 1970, the IFC invested $118.6 million in developing countries, an increase of $30.6 million over the year before. Since its establishment in 1956, the IFC's total investments by June 30, 1970, had reached $476.5 million in 153 businesses in 43 countries. Others had invested $2,132.7 million in these ventures, making a total of $2,609.2 million.

Some of the IFC's recent commitments have been for a polyethylene plant in Brazil, textile and synthetic fiber plants in Ceylon, Colombia, Ethiopia, Malaysia, and Nigeria; tourism in Colombia; and an automobile plant in Yugoslavia. The financing of development banks in four countries, as well as the regional ADELA Investment Company in Latin America, are other important projects.

The IFC expects that investments in which it was associated during 1970 will provide over 19,000 new jobs, add $53 million in new export capacity, and reduce needs for imports by approximately $167 million. The internal rate of return to the IFC over the years has averaged 9.08% per annium.

INTERNATIONAL MONETARY FUND

The basic objectives of the IMF are to promote exchange and monetary stability and to provide, under adequate safeguards, medium-term financial assistance to member countries in temporary balance-of-payments difficulties. Yemen and Barbados joined during 1970 and by year's end the IMF had 117 members with quotas totaling $28,433 million, of which the U.S. quota was $6,700 million. This reflects the implementation through the end of 1970 of the general quota increase agreed to earlier in the year. Total quotas will eventually reach $28.9 billion if all members accept their full quota increases.

IMF resources are supplemented by the General Arrangements to Borrow, which became effective in 1962 and were renewed in 1966 and again in 1969 for a 5-year period to begin in October 1970. Under these Arrangements, the main industrial countries undertook to lend the IMF specified amounts of their currencies up to the equivalent of $6 billion in the event that the stability of the international monetary system were endangered.

As a result of subsequent exchange rate changes, the total commitment is now $5.9 billion. The U.S. commitment under the Arrangements is $2 billion.

On July 28, 1969, the Amendment to the IMF Articles of Agreement for the establishment of a facility based on special drawing rights (SDR) entered into force, following its acceptance by the required 60% of the Fund's members having 80% of the total voting power. In accordance with a resolution adopted by the Board of Governors at its 1969 annual meeting, the IMF made an initial SDR allocation equivalent to $3,414 million, effective January 1, 1970, to 104 participants in the Fund's special drawing account. The second allocation, approximately $3 billion, was made on January 1, 1971; and a similar allocation will be made on January 1, 1972. The SDR allocation received by the United States for the first year was $866,880,000. Its second year allocation was $716,900,000.

FOOD AND AGRICULTURE ORGANIZATION

The celebration of FAO's 25th anniversary on October 16 provided opportunity for it and its member nations to rededicate themselves to raising levels of human nutrition and standards of living, improving the production and distribution of food, bettering the living conditions of rural populations, and ensuring man's freedom from hunger.

A World Agricultural Census was completed in 1970. This was the third in a series of 10-year censuses sponsored by FAO to provide basic data for use by the organization and its member governments in program planning, agricultural development, and other activities.

Some 1,800 persons attended the Second World Food Congress, held at The Hague, June 16-30. The main themes were conservation of man's environment, population growth in relation to economic development, and the role of youth in development. The final declaration of the Congress called upon governments to increase drastically the supply of resources for development and to channel an increasing proportion of agricultural development assistance and economic aid through an improved system of international cooperation.

FAO's field program continued to grow, and some 1,000 professional staff members at FAO headquarters in Rome devoted close to one-half of their time to providing support services to projects financed from UNDP and other sources. The field program in 1970 employed approximately 2,270 experts in 105 countries and dependent territories. The U.S. contribution to FAO's regular program budget in 1970 amounted to $10,083,458.

World Situation

Total agricultural production in the developed regions of the world remained relatively stable, with little or no increase in Western Europe and Oceania, some increase in Eastern Europe, and a decline in total production in North America. Among the less-developed areas, food production increased somewhat. East Asia showed the largest increase, with lesser gains in Latin America, while food production in Africa remained about the same as in 1960.

Although gross agricultural output in the developing countries rose continuously during the 1960's, per capita production declined in all of the developing regions except East Asia. Thus the problem of adequate food production and distribution on a worldwide basis remains paramount. The further development and introduction of high-yielding crop varieties; the expansion of livestock, dairy, and poultry production; the continuing increase in fertilizer usage; and the improvement of marketing and distribution processes are more important than ever in meeting the world's need for food and clothing.

The Indicative World Plan for Agricultural Development, completed in 1969, defined the magnitude of the world food problem and pointed out that by 1985, given the present population growth rates, the developing countries would require 80% more food than in 1962 merely to maintain existing nutrition levels. Thus continuing rapid agricultural growth is the alternative to starvation.

Agriculture

The FAO Agriculture Department conducts its activities through four divisions: Land and Water Development, Animal Production and Health,

Plant Production and Protection, and the Joint FAO/IAEA Division of Atomic Energy and Agriculture. The work of these divisions in 1970 was again geared to the five areas of program emphasis: (1) development of high-yielding varieties, (2) closing the protein gap, (3) war on waste, (4) development of human resources, and (5) increasing foreign exchange earnings and savings.

Specific projects covered a wide range of activity. For example, more than 700 FAO specialists worked in developing countries on improving food, industrial crops, and pastures. New high-yielding varieties of wheat were identified through a 23-country project including the Near East, Africa, and southern Europe. Soybeans suitable to tropical conditions were introduced and tested in Burma, Malawi, and Latin America, and soybean cultivation was started in West Pakistan. Continuing their joint efforts to find safer and more effective uses of pesticides, the FAO and WHO recommended more than 250 pesticide residue levels as internationally acceptable for crops. By promoting and encouraging new techniques in farm management, agricultural mechanization, food processing and storage, and agricultural engineering, FAO helped many developing countries in making the transition from subsistence to commercial agriculture.

FAO continued to support animal health and protection research projects, including one to develop and improve vaccines for tick-borne diseases in Kenya, and one to establish facilities for diagnosis of animal diseases and vaccine production in the Near East. The FAO also established regional livestock training programs in Latin America, Africa, and the Near East.

The United States took part in the FAO study groups, working parties, and committees on the establishment and operation of these programs and furnished technical experts and research data to assist FAO in carrying on its worldwide program on agriculture.

Forestry

During the year FAO's Forestry Department published a report on inputs and costs of logging and transportation in tropical countries; promoted and coordinated various bilateral tree seed exchange programs; established forest tree seed centers to improve species; began to revise the document, "Forest Policy, Law, and Administration,"

taking into account the broad need for attention to the environment; and began preparation of a "Handbook on Forest Concessions" to assist governments in exercising control over forest exploitation in order to assure sustained forest production and achievement of long-term forestry development goals.

The United States participated in the meeting of the Committee of Alternates of FAO's North American Forestry Commission held in Washington, D.C., the 11th session of the Latin American Forestry Commission held in Ecuador, FAO's Regional Consultation on Forest Industrial Development in Latin America held in Mexico, the FAO/U.S.S.R. Seminar on Forest Influences held in the U.S.S.R., the FAO Study Tour of Forest Genetics and Tree Breeding in Hungary, and the third session of FAO's Committee on Wood-Based Panel Products held in Italy. Participation in these meetings enabled the United States to gain new information, to encourage the application of modern technology, and to promote national development of forests and forest industries in the developing countries. It also fostered within the United States an increased appreciation of the relationship of forestry development to total economic and social development.

Fisheries

FAO is the only global forum concerned with fisheries and its Fisheries Department, which is headed by a U.S. citizen, provides leadership in the effort to safeguard the living resources of the oceans. FAO was one of the first international organizations to respond to world concern about ecology and marine pollution when it organized and convened the FAO Technical Conference on Marine Pollution and its Effects on Living Resources and Fishing, December 9-18, in Rome. This Conference, attended by 415 environmentalists, focused world attention on the marine pollution problem, and developed conclusions that should be helpful in attacking the problem.

In 1970 FAO established a Fishery Industry Division to assist the building of such industries in interested developing countries. In addition it continued to encourage the developing countries to collect adequate data and statistics in order to assess the stocks of fish for management or development.

As more countries become interested in utilizing the fishery resources off their coasts, there are more UNDP fisheries projects carried out by FAO. In addition there are more expressions of concern about foreign exploitation of offcoast fisheries. The FAO African Regional Conference recognized this problem and requested that an African fisheries conference be convened to consider possible solutions. In view of the General Assembly proposal in December 1970 for a Law of the Sea Conference in 1973 that would include fishery matters (see p. 25) all of FAO's activities in this area have gained added importance.

The United States attended meetings of two major FAO regional fisheries bodies. The second session of the Indian Ocean Fishery Commission in Rome, and the 14th session of the Indo-Pacific Fisheries Council in Bangkok discussed needs for management of such stocks as tuna and considered means of developing and coordinating fishery development activities. An outstanding example of the latter is the International Indian Ocean Fishery Survey and Development Program which will be coordinated and executed by the Indian Ocean Fishery Commission under the leadership of a U.S. citizen. The United States is supporting this new project which should be in draft form by early 1971.

Economic and Social Affairs

FAO's work on economic and social problems is organized into five divisions: Economic Analysis, Commodities and Trade, Statistics, Nutrition, and Rural Institutions.

In the field of economic analysis, FAO stressed country program planning assistance, project evaluation, program appraisal, and economic intelligence. The country approach to all FAO-administered programs was followed for the first time in 1970, projects under Special Fund type UNDP-financing in 20 countries were reviewed, and all FAO programs were evaluated in five countries. Also, a feasibility study was completed for the Comahue region of Argentina, resulting in 38 specific project proposals, and FAO sponsored a regional training course in agricultural development, planning, and project analysis in New Delhi with 50 participants from 22 countries.

FAO's work on commodities and trade centered on problems of promoting commodity export earnings and import savings in developing countries. It established a Central Information Service on Food Aid Operations to assemble data relating to trade transactions subject to the new consultative and reporting procedures accepted by the principal trading countries. It also established a study group on meat to deal with livestock and meat trade problems. Study groups for grains, rice, tea, hard fibers, jute, and kenaf continued to deal with commodity trade problems. The United States is represented on all of the study groups.

The United States continued its participation in the statistical development and analysis work of FAO, with agencies of the U.S. Government cooperating with FAO in a comprehensive program to train English-speaking technicians in the methods and procedures required for planning and conducting agricultural censuses. (The French Government conducts a similar program for French-speaking nations.) Food balance sheets were prepared showing the flow of agricultural production, utilization, and trade for the period 1961–67 for use in program evaluation and analysis, and FAO index numbers of food and agricultural production for the years 1961–65 were revised as the basis of a new country classification by economic region and subregion.

The FAO's nutrition program focused on the mobilization of human resources for rural development, planning at the family level, and women's participation in rural cooperatives and agrarian reforms. The program supported over 250 field projects, typical examples of which were the project in Senegal which established nutrition education and school feeding programs throughout the country, and the FAO-WIIO-UNICEF 10-week course in Lebanon for nutrition policy planners which was attended by 31 participants from 13 countries. The United States contributed to the nutrition program through its participation in the World Food Program (see below) as well as in other ways.

A World Conference on Agricultural Education and Training was held in Copenhagen July 28–August 8 with the cooperation of UNESCO and ILO. Ninety-five countries (including the United States) sent 350 participants, who urged a comprehensive approach to the problems of rural development through more efficient planning, better preparation of teachers, and establishment of coordinating bodies in the agricultural sector of member countries.

A Special Committee on Agrarian Reform established in 1970 and composed of leaders from both developed and developing countries, recommended action to modify land tenure systems and development of related institutions.

Development

FAO continued its efforts to stimulate investment in agricultural development. The FAO/IBRD cooperative program financed 21 projects amounting to $275 million, and FAO recommendations to regional banks raised the volume of agricultural investment still higher. FAO's Industry Cooperative Program, which helps stimulate private investment in developing countries, continued to grow and by the end of the year 90 private firms were participating in the program. Some 30 investment proposals ranging from the production of small farm equipment in Pakistan to pulp milling in Central America were under consideration. Also, the nucleus for a similar program with private banks was established in 1970.

The FAO participated in the design or implementation of a large number of UNDP-financed development projects, and administered many projects financed under trust funds provided by the Freedom-from-Hunger Campaign and other private and governmental donors. FAO participation in the design, administration, and implementation of projects supported by the World Food Program also contributed to international economic development in 1970.

Fifty-five FAO country representatives, who also serve as senior agricultural advisers to the UNDP resident representatives, provide a link between Rome Headquarters and the member nations participating in the UNDP. They work in cooperation with both the UNDP resident representatives and country officials to develop and carry out national development programs and projects.

The United States participates in FAO's development efforts in a variety of ways. The U.S. Agency for International Development (AID) and FAO engage in frequent consultation and exchange of information concerning specific development projects. In addition, the two agencies are jointly devising a methodology and model for agricultural sector analysis. Through its membership in FAO committees on agriculture, forestry, and fisheries, the United States contributes to the formulation of FAO developmental policy, and through its participation in regional commissions and attendance at conferences, the United States provides policy review and technical guidance to FAO development experts.

UN/FAO World Food Program

The WFP, a joint undertaking by the United Nations and the FAO, was established on an experimental basis in 1962 and placed on a continuing basis in 1965. This multilateral food assistance program was supported by contributions of commodities, services, and cash from 80 member nations in 1970.

WFP provides food at the request of governments of less developed countries to help carry out economic and social development projects and to meet emergency/disaster situations. Special emphasis is given projects related to preschool and school feeding activities, and labor intensive and rural welfare projects. The United States has played a major role in encouraging WFP to assume greater responsibility and larger program operations in the multilateral food assistance effort.

Resources available to the WFP since its inception, including pledges for 1971-72, totaled $719 million through the third quarter of 1970: $513 million were in commodities and $206 million in cash and services. An additional $42 million worth of food grains were made available by the signatories of the Food Aid Convention of the International Grains Arrangement.

From the beginning of the program through 1970 a total of 478 economic development projects were approved in 83 countries involving commitments of more than $1 billion. Of these projects, ranging from 3 to 5 years in length, 74 have been completed and 404 are in various stages of implementation. In addition, 122 emergency operations costing nearly $100 million have been undertaken in 67 countries. More than $18.3 million of this total was extended during 1970 to victims of floods, droughts, earthquakes, and other disasters.

In January 1970 the United States pledged to contribute up to $125 million toward the WFP goal of $300 million for the 1971–72 biennium. The pledge includes up to $85 million in commodities, an estimated $37 million in ocean freight required to ship the commodities, and up to $3 million in cash for administrative support of the program. The U.S. commodity contribution is subject to the condition that it does not exceed 50% of the total contributions from all governments in commodities and cash used for the purchase of commodities. By the end of 1970, 59 other states had pledged a total of $91,131,014 toward the WFP target of $300,000,000.

INTERNATIONAL LABOR ORGANIZATION

International Labor Conference

The International Labor Conference, which normally meets once each year, is the standard-setting body of the ILO. Member states are represented by tripartite delegations: One worker, one employer, and two government delegates, each with a separate vote. In 1970 the Conference held two sessions, one in the spring and one in the fall that was devoted entirely to maritime questions.

The 54th session, June 3-25, was attended by delegations from 111 of the 121 ILO member states. The Conference adopted four new international instruments: a convention and a recommendation on minimum wage-fixing, with special reference to developing countries; a new convention concerning annual holidays with pay, revising former standards; and a recommendation concerning special youth employment training schemes.

The Conference also considered the reports of the Governing Body's Working Party on the Program and Structure of the ILO, which for the past 7 years had been considering proposals to revise the ILO structure. The Conference decided to refer to the Governing Body for further consideration certain important outstanding questions concerning structure (particularly the transfer of authority from the Governing Body to the Conference, and the composition of the employer group of the Governing Body). It requested the Governing Body to provide for a special intersessional committee of the Conference to consider further matters of structure should the Conference consider it necessary in 1971. This, in effect, would transfer the consideration of structure from the Governing Body to the Conference where the states wishing to make radical changes in the character of the organization exercise greater influence.

The Conference also decided, over the opposition of the U.S. Government, to adopt a supplement to the 1970-71 biennium budget for the purpose of providing a $700,000 subsidy in 1971

to the ILO's International Center for Advanced Technical and Vocational Training at Turin, Italy. The United States took the position that training provided at the Center, which is a form of UN technical assistance for economic development, should be financed through the UNDP.

The 55th (Maritime) session of the International Labor Conference met October 14-30. This was the eighth maritime session held since the ILO was founded in 1919 and the first since 1958. Sixty-five member states were represented at the session which adopted eight new international instruments: a convention and a recommendation on accident prevention; a convention and two recommendations on crew accommodation, air conditioning, and the control of harmful noise; a recommendation on employment problems; a recommendation on vocational training; and a recommendation on seafarers' welfare at sea and in port.

Governing Body

The Governing Body consists of 24 government members—14 elected and 10 who hold seats as the states of chief industrial importance;[2] 12 employer members, and 12 worker members. Twelve deputy seats for each of the three groups are also elected. The government, worker, and employer groups of the Conference form separate electoral colleges for the purpose of choosing the members of their respective groups on the Governing Body; the 10 states of chief industrial importance are excluded from participation in the government electoral college. The Governing Body serves for 3 years, and was last elected at the Conference in 1969. The next Governing Body election will take place at the 1972 Conference.

The most significant action by the Governing Body in 1970 was the election of a new Director General to succeed David A. Morse (a U.S. national) who in February announced his intention to resign effective May 31. There were two principal candidates: C. Wilfred Jenks of the United Kingdom, the Principal Deputy Director General of the ILO, and Francis Blanchard of France, a Deputy Director General of the ILO. In a close election on May 20, Mr. Jenks by a vote of 25 to 23 was elected to succeed Mr. Morse for a 5-year term beginning June 1. The U.S. government, employer, and worker members of the Governing Body supported the election of Mr. Jenks.

Crisis in U.S.-ILO Relations

A serious crisis in relations between the United States and the ILO occurred when the Congress on October 7 took final action on the State Department Appropriation Bill from which it had cut $3.7 million of the funds requested to pay the assessed contribution to the ILO for calendar year 1970 ($7,458,875). In a letter of August 24 to the Chairman of the Senate Appropriations Subcommittee, the Department pointed out that "the United States has undertaken an international legal duty to pay the share of the budget that has been voted by the ILO General Conference" and would be in violation of that obligation if it did not pay the full assessment. The Department pointed out that "aside from broader foreign policy implications, failure to pay our obligatory assessment would seriously weaken the ability of the United States to exert influence within the organization."

The congressional action was a reflection of a deep U.S. concern over the steady erosion of the tripartite concepts and practice of the ILO following the U.S.S.R.'s resumption of membership in 1954. Some results of this erosion were (1) the weakening of the autonomy of the employer and worker groups; (2) the introduction of special procedures to offset Eastern European inability to participate on a tripartite basis; (3) the development of a double standard by which the Eastern European states were granted a degree of immunity from discussion of their obligations with respect to ILO conventions; (4) the increased use of the ILO Conference for political attacks on free institutions in general and the United States in particular, and (5) the use of official ILO publications for articles by Soviet writers espousing views contrary to the very principles of this tripartite organization.

Between 1954 and 1959 the employer group of the Conference did not elect any Communist state delegates as voting employer members of tripartite committees because they did not represent employer interests, but were in fact government-instructed delegates. In 1959, however, the Conference (over U.S. objections) adopted new procedures that resulted in giving two Communist state representatives voting "employer" membership on the tripartite committees of the Conference, thus overruling the determination of the group of delegates accredited to the Conference to represent employer interests. This, of course, imposed a limitation on the autonomy of the nongovernment groups and, by imposing government-instructed representatives as employer members of the committees, tended to weaken the influence of the employer group in the work of those committees.

In 1965 special arrangements were made to modify the results of the tripartite elections for membership on the 10 ILO industrial committees. The applications of Eastern European states for membership on these committees did not fare well in the elections, failing to win much support from the employer and worker groups which knew that the employer and worker delegates sent by Communist states to those committees could not represent independent employer and worker interests. In response to Soviet charges of "discrimination," and threats of retaliatory action unless the election results were "rectified," arrangements were made to increase the membership of each committee and to add a Communist state to 8 of the 10 committees.

Under standing procedures, the ILO Conference considers placing on a "special list" those member states which have persistently violated their treaty obligations to give effect to the provisions of ILO conventions that they have ratified. The U.S.S.R. and a number of other Eastern European states have ratified the ILO Convention on Freedom of Association. A committee of experts, which reviews the reports of member states on the manner in which they apply ILO conventions, had since 1959 determined that the U.S.S.R. and the other Eastern European states were in violation of the provisions of that convention. After acrimonious debate over those findings in 1961 and 1962, the Conference in 1963 decided that, rather than engage further in such debate, it would adjourn any discussion of the application of the Freedom of Association Convention by the Eastern European states and Cuba (which had also ratified the convention). At each subsequent Conference a similar decision has been taken. Thus, those states enjoyed an immunity from the application of procedures which are regularly applied as necessary to other member states. This double standard not only protects one group of ILO members from criticism, but undermines respect for this important human right which is central to the tripartite character of the ILO.

Before Mr. Jenks' election the U.S. Government had informed him, as well as his predecessor, of its grave concern that the appointment of a Soviet national to a top policy-level position in the International Labor Office would tend to damage further the ILO's constitutional adherence to tripartism which is alien to Communist concepts. He was informed that the appointment of a Soviet national as Assistant Director General would raise very serious problems in the United States.

The decision by the new Director General, within a month of his assumption of the Director Generalship, to appoint a Soviet national to that post was seen as a cause for concern that under his leadership the trend of accommodation to Soviet pressures at the expense of the ILO's constitutional commitment to its tripartite character was likely to continue.

In response to continued expressions of concern by the United States some steps were taken in the ILO in the latter half of 1970 which demonstrated its awareness of and greater willingness to apply the fundamental standards of the organization more rigorously. For example, the normally scheduled 5-year election of industrial committee memberships was held by the Governing Body in November. When the Eastern European states fared no better than in the previous election, the Governing Body did not arrange to add Eastern European states to the committees as it had in 1965. The Director General issued instructions to the staff regarding the objectivity of ILO publications. There were also some indications of resistance to Soviet proposals for further erosions of the autonomy of the nongovernment groups to determine their own representation on tripartite bodies. It is hoped that these changes reflect the intention of the ILO to adhere to those standards which have in the past enabled it to bring to bear the independent views of governments, employers, and workers on a wide range of social problems affecting the welfare of workers.

UN EDUCATIONAL, SCIENTIFIC, AND CULTURAL ORGANIZATION

16th General Conference

The UNESCO General Conference, which meets every 2 years to discuss and approve the program and budget, held its 16th session in Paris, October 12-November 14. It approved a program for 1971-72 that will continue to emphasize education and the natural sciences, and adopted a budget for

the biennium of $89,898,560. The U.S. assessed contribution will be $12.2 million per year, compared with $10.6 million in 1970. The United States voted against the budget because it considered certain of the increases unjustified, including one for construction of a new building not expected to be fully utilized until 1985.

The Conference also adopted, by a vote of 63 to 1, with 8 abstentions (U.S.), a resolution calling upon UNESCO to place the Arabic language on the same level as the four working languages of the organization (English, French, Spanish, and Russian) by the 18th General Conference in 1974. This culminated a drive by the Arab countries, begun several years ago, to give Arabic full equality with the four working languages. The United States abstained because it believed that UNESCO's Rules of Procedure already adequately provided for the use of other languages, as appropriate, and that this resolution would result in unnecessary expense.

The United States also abstained on a lengthy resolution, adopted by a vote of 68 to 1, with 28 abstentions, that dealt with a number of topics, including "UNESCO's tasks with respect to the elimination of colonialism." The resolution reaffirmed UNESCO's earlier decision not to accord any help to the governments of Portugal, South Africa, or the illegal regime in Southern Rhodesia, and not to invite them to participate in UNESCO activities "until such time as the authorities of those countries desist from their policy of colonial oppression and racial discrimination." The resolution also requested the Director General "to undertake investigations of all international nongovernmental organizations enjoying relations with UNESCO which have branches, sections, affiliates or constituent parts" in those countries "with respect to the practice of racial discrimination or racial segregation in their policies, activities, or membership or their cooperation in any way with the apartheid policy of the Government of the Republic of South Africa." The resolution further called on the Executive Board, in light of the Director General's report to it on his investigations, to break off, as of December 31, 1971, all relations with those international nongovernmental organizations that had not established to the Board's satisfaction that they neither practiced racial discrimination or segregation in their policies, nor cooperated with South Africa in its apartheid policy.

The United States believed that this proposed

action would undermine the effectiveness of many UNESCO-affiliated professional and technical organizations which maintain a presence in southern Africa and in their own ways work against apartheid and discrimination in any form. Such action would also have an adverse effect on UNESCO, depriving it of useful contacts in the countries and territories concerned as well as of the assistance which the organizations render to the UNESCO program and operation. Although U.S. opposition to apartheid is clear and long-standing, it believed the issue was properly the concern of the political organs of the United Nations. The introduction of such political matters into the deliberations of technical bodies such as UNESCO could only serve to diminish the effectiveness of those bodies in their area of prime responsibility.

Education

International Education Year

The 24th UN General Assembly in December 1969 unanimously approved the designation of 1970 as International Education Year. Two of the themes emphasized for the Year were lifelong education and democratization of education. UNESCO coordinated activities within the UN system and provided guidance to member states and many nongovernmental organizations, concentrating its efforts on assisting each country and organization to reevaluate its own educational goals and its plans for the Second Development Decade.

Some 86 member states indicated an interest in the worldwide program to further education, and 42 of these states planned substantive programs including such activities as special television broadcasts and films, seminars and symposia, competitions in the field of education, original exhibitions, organization of training courses, production of posters and postage stamps, publication of articles and journals, and a special review of their national educational systems. Some countries organized campaigns to collect funds to improve their own educational systems, and 13 countries, including the United States, increased their aid to developing countries in this area.

Other Activities

One of the ways that UNESCO furthers its education program is by organizing and sponsoring international conferences. In 1970 the United States participated in a number of these conferences, including: (1) a conference of Ministers of Education and Economic Planning in the Arab States, which inventoried educational progress and analyzed the problems involved in expanding and improving education at all levels; (2) the 32nd session of the International Conference on Education, which considered current trends in world education, and, specifically, ways to reduce the dropout rate among primary school children; and (3) a world conference on agricultural education and training which was also sponsored by FAO and ILO.

The UNESCO/IBRD cooperative program in educational planning, financing, and development, begun in 1964, continued to expand during the year. One of its major undertakings was the launching of a nationwide "teaching by television" project in the Ivory Coast. The IBRD provided about $1 million for the television facilities and $10 million for the overall education project which includes creation of a TV production center and the building and equipping of 11 experimental schools. The project's goal is the complete reorganization of the Ivory Coast's primary school system by 1976 through the systematic employment of new educational methods and techniques in the training and retraining of teachers.

UNESCO continued its 10-year experimental project, begun in 1969, to improve education in the rural areas of Upper Volta for women and girls who are illiterate or have had only minimal schooling. The project, which received 2 million CFA francs from the Upper Voltan government in 1969 and 2.5 million in 1970, will encompass a wide range of literacy and educational activities, including health, social welfare, agriculture, and rural development, to permit women and girls to participate more effectively in the economic and social development of their country.

UNESCO continued to emphasize educational publications. During 1970 it published, *inter alia,* a booklet on world progress in literacy during 1967-69 based on data from 93 governments and 9 organizations. The booklet provides for the first time a statistical analysis of world literacy, including data on teaching methods and techniques, and the relations of the literacy programs carried out by member states to UNESCO's World Experimental Literacy Program.

Natural Sciences

UNESCO's scientific program covers a wide range of activities including hydrology, environmental sciences, oceanography, natural resources, and science education.

As the sponsor of the International Hydrological Decade (IHD), begun in 1964 on U.S. initiative, UNESCO's work in the field of water resources continued to be both extensive and important. A project of special interest to the United States was the inauguration of an international field year for the Great Lakes to coordinate data collection by the United States and Canada. Other activities included the publication of handbooks and manuals, the sponsoring of graduate training courses in universities, and the sponsoring—often in cooperation with other interested agencies, such as the WMO, IAEA, and WHO—of conferences and seminars in all parts of the world. Symposia of particular interest to the United States were held in Germany in September on problems of surface water measurement, and in New Zealand in December on the results of research on representative and experimental basins.

A mid-Decade conference, held in December 1969, had recommended, *inter alia,* that the program in the second half of the Decade be reoriented away from the purely scientific toward the solution of more practical problems in hydrology. During 1970 the Coordinating Council of the IHD began to implement this recommendation by reviewing its working groups and panels and redefining their terms of reference. In addition, a working group composed of the United States and eight other countries continued its effort to develop a long-term system of international hydrological cooperation for the years after the close of the IHD.

UNESCO has for several years demonstrated a growing concern for international environmental problems. The United States both shares and encourages this concern. In 1970 the 16th General Conference decided to launch a long-term intergovernmental and interdisciplinary program on "Man and the Biosphere," which will involve a study of the structure and functioning of the biosphere; systematic observation of changes brought about by man in the biosphere and its resources; a study of overall effects of these changes on the human species; and education and information concerning these subjects. The Conference also established an International Coordinating Council to plan the program, define its priorities, supervise its execution, and make any necessary proposals for coordinating UNESCO's program with those conducted by other international organizations concerned. The United States was one of 25 member states elected to the Coordinating Council for 1971–72.

During the year UNESCO and the International Council of Scientific Unions completed a feasibility study for the establishment of a proposed jointly sponsored world scientific and technical information system. The study confirmed the feasibility of the concept and suggested a number of ways to expedite the establishment of the program. The United States supports selective implementation of this system which will further worldwide scientific activities by providing a flexible network for voluntary exchanges of information among various information systems.

(For the work of UNESCO's Intergovernmental Oceanographic Commission see p. 113.)

Social Sciences and Humanities

UNESCO's program in the social sciences and humanities during 1970 was designed to (1) improve international cooperation among social scientists and humanists, (2) provide clearinghouse services, (3) increase social science teaching and research, and (4) apply the social sciences to specific problems of economic and social development.

Largely as a result of U.S. recommendations this program has become less fragmented and more concentrated on specific problems requiring international cooperation. In 1970 the General Conference assigned high priority for the next biennium to four themes: (1) the contribution of the social sciences to development, particularly during the Second Development Decade; (2) human environment and population studies; (3) the introduction of social science perspectives into studies in the natural sciences, mathematics, and engineering; and (4) the contribution of the social sciences and humanities to human rights and peace.

In addition the Conference unanimously approved a U. S.-initiated resolution that called for the development of an international interdisciplinary program against drug abuse. This program will be financed initially by the UN Fund for Drug Abuse Control (see p. 100).

In 1965 UNESCO began an international study on "Main Trends of Research in the Social and Human Sciences." The first volume, subtitled "Social Sciences," was published in 1970 and covers such disciplines as sociology, political science, social and cultural anthropology, economics, demography, and linguistics. The work was carried out by UNESCO in collaboration with national and international organizations, social science research centers, and some 300 specialists (including 33 Americans) who were consulted individually. The study is intended for the use of both professional social scientists and the national and international institutions responsible for organizing and financing scientific research programs.

American experts participated in all four of the international symposia in social science fields that UNESCO sponsored during 1970: (1) the implications of recent scientific research on the understanding of aggressiveness, (2) man and his environment, (3) the role of the social sciences in development, and (4) the present state of teaching of the management sciences.

Culture

Eighty-eight states took part in the UNESCO-sponsored Intergovernmental Conference on the Institutional, Administrative, and Financial Aspects of Cultural Policies, which was held in Venice from August 24 to September 2. The U.S. delegation was headed by Nancy Hanks, Chairman of the National Endowment for the Arts. This Conference was the first government-level meeting held on a world scale to discuss matters related to culture. It provided an opportunity for the comparison of experiences regarding programs, management, administration, and budgeting; the discussion of common problems and solutions; and the consideration of ways to achieve greater international cooperation. The Conference stressed the importance of cultural considerations in environmental planning; the need for creative education in the arts in order to encourage artists and to raise audience standards; the need to train administrators or managers of cultural programs; and the importance of UNESCO as a clearinghouse for worldwide experience in the arts.

UNESCO maintains an extensive cultural publication program including *inter alia* art books, translations of classics of world literature, bibliographies, and historical and anthropological studies. In 1969 it had launched, with a volume on the United States, a new series called "Studies and Documents on Cultural Policies." Six additional booklets, on Japan, France, Tunisia, the United Kingdom, the U.S.S.R., and Czechoslovakia, were published in 1970. Other publications of considerable use in the United States were two film catalogs—one on ethnographic films in the Pacific region, and the other a comprehensive one on archaeological, ethnographic, and historical films.

UNESCO continued to encourage and further the preservation of monuments and sites of historical interest and value. In response to a request from Cambodia under the terms of the Convention for the Protection of Cultural Property in the Event of Armed Conflict, UNESCO sent an expert to Cambodia to examine steps which might be taken to preserve Angkor Wat and other monuments and works of art. In light of the expert's suggestions, two missions were organized to pack and store 3,000 art items from Cambodian museums, to train local technicians for protective work, and to draw up a long-term program to protect cultural property.

In most instances, the preservations activities were related to tourism as a factor of economic development. In 1970 this work concentrated on three sites, preparatory to mobilizing international assistance for their preservation: Borobudur in Indonesia, Mohenjo Daro in Pakistan, and Philae in the U.A.R. As another aspect of preservation UNESCO continued to conduct extensive regional training programs for museographers and restorationists in Jos (Nigeria), Mexico City, and New Delhi.

On May 9 the President signed P.L. 91-243, as amended, which provided for U.S. accession to the Statutes of the International Center for the Study of the Preservation and Restoration of Cultural Property.[3] The Center's training programs and its willingness to study the particular preservation problems of member states will be helpful to the United States in connection with the implementing of the Historic Preservation Act which, among other things, authorizes a program of matching grants to the States and the National Trust for Historic Preservation for the acquisition of historic sites and buildings.

Another notable cultural development during

1970 was the adoption by UNESCO's General Conference on November 14 of the Convention on the Means of Prohibiting and Preventing the Illicit Import, Export, and Transfer of Ownership of Cultural Property. American experts, both governmental and nongovernmental, played important roles in preparing the final text of the Convention, which reflects the serious concern of states at the illegal movement of national art treasures and the destruction through pillage and other means of the remains of ancient civilizations.

Communication and Copyright

The General Conference took a number of actions related to communication and copyright. The most important was its declaration of 1972 as International Book Year, which will highlight the importance of books in modern life. This decision is in line with the U. S. position of encouraging a much freer flow of information and materials throughout the world and it has been endorsed by U. S. publishers and librarians.

As the culmination of several years of work, to which Americans had contributed substantially, the General Conference adopted a formal Recommendation on the Standardization of Library Statistics, and decided to support a program for improving international statistics available on education, manpower, and libraries.

At meetings held in Paris and Geneva in September, revisions were proposed to both the Universal Copyright Convention and the Berne Convention for the Protection of Literary and Artistic Works. These draft proposals, which will be the subject of an international conference, incorporate U. S. suggestions for protecting an author's basic intellectual property rights while still providing certain privileges for developing countries. In a related move, the General Conference authorized the establishment of an International Copyright Information Center to assist developing countries to make greater use of copyrighted books.

UNESCO also cooperated closely with the Customs Cooperation Council in preparing the text of a Customs Convention on the Temporary Importation of Pedagogic Material. The Convention, which covers a variety of materials manufactured in the United States, such as programed instruction material, language laboratories, closed-circuit television, and mobile libraries, was done at Brussels on June 8. The Convention will enter into force after five states have ratified or acceded to it.

WORLD HEALTH ORGANIZATION

World Health Assembly

The 23d World Health Assembly, WHO's governing body, met May 5–22 in Geneva. Of WHO's 128 members and 3 associate members, 124 sent delegations totaling 415 public health professionals. In addition, some 120 persons attended as official observers from the United Nations, the specialized agencies and nongovernmental organizations having official relations with WHO. Dr. Jesse L. Steinfeld, Surgeon General of the Public Health Service, served as the U.S. Chief Delegate.

Financial Matters

A major Assembly function is to review and approve the program and budget. The Director General presented a 1971 budget totaling $73,230,000, an increase of $5,580,000 (8.25%) over that for 1970. The U.S. position was that a slower organizational growth rate was preferable; nevertheless, the Assembly approved the budget by a vote of 86 to 5, with 2 abstentions (U.S.). By a simple majority, the Assembly also approved a 1972 "order of magnitude" providing for a 10% increase, plus additional costs that might result from any salary increases recommended by the UN General Assembly. The level for the order of magnitude, i.e., the suggested increase for the second ensuing year, serves as a guide and is not binding on the Director General. The approved level was higher than the Director General's own planning figure of $79 million (7.9%) and was opposed by the United States and most other large contributors.

The Assembly decided that its working capital fund would be a fixed dollar amount rather than a percentage of the budget and that the disposition of "casual income" was a matter to be decided annually. These interrelated actions established the principle, which the United States has long supported, that all of WHO's expenditures should be under direct membership control.

The Assembly also established a real estate fund

for the purchase or construction of new office space and the purchase or repair of staff housing in the field. The United States voted against the resolution providing an initial $3 million for the fund because it questioned the need for such an amount since cost estimates were not definitive enough to make sound judgments. However, the resolution was adopted by a vote of 56 to 6 (U.S.), with 4 abstentions.

Program Review

The Assembly gave considerable attention to the revised global strategy for malaria eradication, making a thorough review of the administrative, financial, and technical problems relating to complete eradication. It was noted that of the 1,300 types of insecticides tested in WHO's evaluation program, none had been found as inexpensive nor as effective as DDT, and few as safe. The Assembly concluded that malaria continued to be a major public health problem in many tropical countries where eradication at present is impractical. In a resolution on this subject the Assembly called for intensified research, stressed the need for personnel training, and urged governments manufacturing insecticides to continue to make them available to the developing countries.

In considering the question of human environment the Assembly reaffirmed WHO's leading role in the prevention and control of environmental factors adversely affecting health. It requested the Director General to formulate a long-term program, to be submitted to the 24th Assembly, for environmental health including "insofar as practicable, a program for a worldwide system of surveillance and monitoring" of adverse environmental health factors.

The Assembly also approved expanding a pilot research project on the international monitoring of adverse reactions of pharmaceutical drugs into a primary operational stage. The project, launched in 1967 at U.S. initiative with 10 participating nations, was transferred from the United States to WHO headquarters and will be treated as a regular program activity.

The Assembly also reviewed problems concerning yellow fever in Africa, research on alternate methods of vector control, quality control of drugs, and the community water supply program.

The Assembly gave special attention to the question of dependence on and abuse of narcotic and dangerous drugs. It requested the Director General to develop a plan for the international collection and exchange of data on the prevalence and incidence of drug dependence, and to seek the most effective ways of examining the medical, scientific, and social factors involved.

Program Activities

WHO has two major areas of activity: technical assistance to governments and the establishment of international standards in health protection. As always emphasis continued to be on the former. In 1970 WHO had planned approximately 900 projects. The majority were single country projects, but some were intercountry or interregional. In addition to its regular budget, WHO administered funds made available by organizations such as UNICEF and UNDP, and special contributions earmarked for specific activities. The total funds administered by WHO in 1970 exceeded $112,000,000.

Cholera

The importance and predominance of WHO in international health was underscored by its work in connection with the 1970 pandemic of cholera. Although the outbreak of El Tor cholera first appeared in 1961, in mid–1970 it spread rapidly through much of the Near East and North Africa, and then jumped, for the first time in a century, to Africa south of the Sahara. By the end of the year 34 countries had reported 40,000 cases and it was generally conceded that there was a far larger number of unreported cases. It was immediately recognized that only WHO had the staff, communications system, and expertise to coordinate the counter-attack, which began immediately and continues.

Malaria

Reducing the worldwide incidence of malaria remained WHO's largest single program. By year's end 74.1% of the world's population was protected: 39.4% through the maintenance phase (the disease reported as eradicated), 16.4% in the consolidation phase (free from endemic malaria), and

18.3% in the attack phase (protected through spraying operations). A total of 55 countries received assistance in combating malaria and there were 21 regional or interregional projects.

Smallpox

The complete eradication of smallpox within a decade became a WHO priority in 1967. The organization is rapidly moving toward that goal. In 1970, there were reports of 27,369 cases of smallpox, a decrease of 77% from 1967, the first year of the campaign. During the year 43 countries received assistance.

Other Communicable Diseases

WHO continued to assist governments in attacking other communicable disease problems, through various programs designed to meet specific needs. In Cambodia, for example, WHO assisted in assessing the extent of the tuberculosis program and in planning and carrying out a control program which will eventually cover the whole country. In Uganda, WHO is assisting in establishing an epidemiological and health statistical service to be responsible for control of all communicable diseases.

Environmental Health

WHO continued in 1970 to place major emphasis on environmental health, and a long-term program for environmental health began at WHO headquarters in Geneva. In its direct assistance to governments, WHO places particular emphasis on development of adequate water supplies and sanitary facilities. In 1970 over 200 separate projects were underway in 86 countries, supported by over 50 interregional activities. As always WHO tailored the project to a country's need: in Barbados it assisted the Sanitation Board in reorganizing its refuse collection and disposal services; in Nepal it assisted in the preparation of a plan for the development of water supply and sewerage in greater Kathmandu and Bhaktapur.

Health Promotion

Improvement of public health administration is a prerequisite for the infrastructure needed for all other health activities. WHO assisted 124 countries (virtually its entire membership) with over 350 projects, supported by 48 intercountry activities. Examples show the variations. In Thailand assistance was supplied for integrating specialized programs into the general health services. Morocco continued to receive aid in developing national public health services and implementing the public health program within the framework of its economic and social development plan.

There were also some 79 countries and intercountry programs in population dynamics or in maternal and child health care, which often contain a large component for family planning. Further, many of WHO's other projects had activities related to family planning or population dynamics. In Ceylon, for example, a health education project in behavioral studies was designed to assist with baseline studies of knowledge, attitudes, and practices related to maternal and child health, family health, human reproduction, and related fields.

Education and Training

Strong emphasis has always been given to the need for more, and better trained, public health personnel. In addition to specific or general fellowships, many programs designed for other purposes necessarily contained an element for education and training: e.g., in Mali under the nursing program two nurse educators worked at developing training programs for nurses, midwives, and medico-social workers at the state-diploma and auxiliary levels. In Venezuela fellowships were provided to buttress an environmental health project on the health aspects of the planning and implementation of housing programs, particularly in rural areas.

Other Activities

WHO partially underwrites more than 150 international reference centers, of which more than 40 are in the United States. These centers collect and correlate data on various health problem areas through research carried out under different conditions throughout the world.

WHO also continued in 1970 its publications program to disseminate information on public health matters through distribution of material designed both for the public health administrator and the layman.

Finally, WHO sponsors more than 30 expert committees, each designed to bring together, in an individual capacity, outstanding men who will examine a specific topic. Fourteen expert committees met in 1970 on such topics as drug dependence, family planning, and pesticide residues.

INTERNATIONAL CIVIL AVIATION ORGANIZATION

The U.S.S.R., Southern Yemen, and Mauritius adhered to the Convention on International Civil Aviation in 1970, increasing ICAO membership to 120 governments. On August 1 Dr. Assad Kotaite of Lebanon began a 3-year term as Secretary General, succeeding B. T. Twigt of the Netherlands.

Revision of Warsaw Convention

The 17th session of the ICAO Legal Committee, meeting at Montreal February 9–March 11, recommended important revisions to the passenger liability limits of the Warsaw Convention of 1929. Under that Convention, as amended by The Hague Protocol of 1955, the air carrier, unless it proves that an accident resulting in death or injury to a passenger could not have been prevented by it, shall be liable up to $16,600. The ICAO Legal Committee recommended raising the air carrier's liability to $100,000 under a new rule which would make the carrier liable, regardless of whether it was at fault, except where the negligence of the claimant contributed to the damage. These and certain other improvements in the Warsaw Convention will be considered at a diplomatic conference convened by the ICAO Council in 1971.

Extraordinary Assembly on Aviation Security

Following mid-air explosions on board both Swiss and Austrian aircraft in February, 11 Euro-

pean nations requested an extraordinary session of the ICAO Assembly, which was held at ICAO's headquarters in Montreal June 16–30. The Assembly was attended by 91 member governments, the U.S.S.R. as a nonmember government, and 12 international organizations including the International Air Transport Association, the International Federation of Airline Pilots Associations, three associations of international airport operators, and the International Criminal Police Organization.

The agenda called for the development of both technical and legal measures to prevent further acts of unlawful interference with international civil aviation and its facilities, including hijacking of aircraft, sabotage, and armed attacks. The United States played an active role in proposing action by the Assembly.

The Assembly was highly successful in reaching agreement on a long list of special security measures to be followed by governments, air carriers, and airport operators, and it recommended that these authorities coordinate their efforts through the development of international airport security committees. Appropriate international organizations were requested to continue their cooperation with ICAO to solve problems of unlawful interference. Governments were asked to exchange information—both directly and through ICAO—on physical security controls in airport plans and on research and development regarding weapons and explosives detection.

The Assembly requested (1) the urgent development by its Legal Committee of a treaty dealing with sabotage and other violent unlawful acts against international civil aviation, (2) completion and ratification of an ICAO-sponsored convention providing for punishment of aircraft hijackers, and (3) enactment by governments of national legislation providing severe penalties for hijacking and other forms of unlawful interference with international civil aviation. In a spirit of international cooperation the governments represented at the Assembly unanimously adopted a solemn declaration and resolution condemning all acts of violence against international civil air transport and its facilities and calling upon governments to take concerted action to suppress such acts.

Council Action on Unlawful Interference

The ICAO Council on October 1 adopted a U.S.-sponsored resolution proposing concerted international action to suspend air services to and from states which after a hijacking (1) detain passengers, crew, and aircraft contrary to the principles of article 11 of the 1963 Tokyo Convention on Offences and Certain Other Acts Committed on Board Aircraft, or (2) fail to extradite or prosecute persons responsible for such acts. The ICAO Legal Committee was directed to consider an international convention or other instruments to provide the legal framework for states to take joint action in the form of sanctions and other measures after a hijacking.

A second resolution, presented by Canada and also adopted on October 1, directed the Legal Committee to consider a special clause which might be incorporated in bilateral air transport agreements to provide for the enforcement of international legal obligations relating to unlawful interference with international civil aviation.

Legal Committee Consideration of Unlawful Interference

In accordance with the directive given it by the Assembly, the ICAO Legal Committee, meeting in London, September 29–October 22, completed a draft convention on unlawful interference (other than hijacking) with international civil aviation. This draft convention, which the ICAO Council decided should be submitted to a diplomatic conference for adoption in 1971, declares as severely punishable offences various acts such as an armed attack against the life of a person on board an aircraft in flight and intentional acts that seriously damage aircraft or endanger safety of flight.

The ICAO Legal Committee, in accordance with the U.S.-sponsored and Canadian-sponsored resolutions adopted by the ICAO Council, also began consideration of what sanctions might lawfully be undertaken against a government that failed to perform its international obligations in those cases of unlawful interference with international civil aviation that involve international blackmail. A subcommittee of the Legal Committee, consisting of representatives of 11 governments including the United States, was established to consider the subject further in 1971.

Adoption of Hijacking Convention

A diplomatic conference was convened by the ICAO Council at The Hague December 1–16 to complete the draft hijacking convention. The conference was successful, and 74 of the 77 governments attending voted in favor of adopting the Convention for the Suppression of Unlawful Seizure of Aircraft. Fifty of these nations, including the United States, signed the Convention at The Hague. As of January 1, 1971, the Convention was opened for additional signatures at Washington, London, and Moscow until such time as it comes into force after ratification by 10 governments that had attended the conference.

The Convention is designed to ensure the prosecution of hijackers no matter where a hijacking takes place or a hijacker is found. States that become parties to the Convention will be required to initiate criminal proceedings against hijackers if they do not extradite them. (See also p. 215 for consideration of aircraft hijacking by the Security Council and General Assembly.)

Personnel Standards

Forty-seven member states and six international organizations attended the meeting at Montreal of ICAO's Personnel Licensing, Training Practices, and Medical Division, October 20–November 14. This division has the task of ensuring that ICAO standards for flight and ground personnel are in line with the higher safety requirements of advancing technological development in civil aviation. At this meeting extensive revisions were proposed to the international standards and recommended practices for training, licensing, and medical requirements. Strengthened requirements were recommended for pilots and flight instructors, air traffic controllers, and aircraft maintenance technicians. In some instances, medical requirements were made more demanding, and various new subjects of a medical nature were identified for special study in consideration of current and future effects on civil aviation activities.

INTERGOVERNMENTAL MARITIME CONSULTATIVE ORGANIZATION

Much time and effort was spent by IMCO in 1970 in forwarding its work on preventing pollution of the sea, with particular emphasis on the prevention of oil spills and the mitigation of the effects of spills. To this end IMCO's Maritime Safety Committee, of which the United States is a member, adopted a resolution urging member states to implement unilaterally the provisions of the 1969 amendments to the 1954 Oil Pollution Convention, even before these provisions come into effect multilaterally as the result of their ratification by the requisite number of states. IMCO, through the Maritime Safety Committee, also considered the preparation and adoption of standards to limit the size of individual tanks in tankships. This work began in 1970 on the understanding that it would be a significant part of IMCO's program for the mitigation of oil spills. IMCO also developed specifications for oily water separators and devices to measure content of oil in ballast water.

In the general field of safety of navigation, IMCO formulated traffic separation schemes to lessen the possibility of accident in such areas as the Hook of Holland and the English Channel. Additionally, it drew up final specifications regarding standards for shipboard navigational equipment, including radar, gyrocompasses, echo sounders, and radio direction finders. In this connection work has accelerated in preparation for the conference to be called by IMCO in 1972 on the Revision of the International Collision Regulations.

During the year plans were made for IMCO's participation in the 1972 Conference on International Container Traffic which will emphasize the safety aspects of container operation. IMCO also brought to virtual completion a code for the safe carriage by ship of noxious chemicals and made considerable progress on a basic code governing the safety of fishing vessels. IMCO also adopted in 1970 a document providing guidance on the training of seafarers. It is believed that this document will be particularly helpful to the authorities of developing countries.

The United States took an active part in IMCO's Legal Committee which in 1970 continued its review of the texts of the proposed conventions on Ocean Data Acquisition Systems, the Combined Transport of Goods, and the Carriage of Nuclear Substances. The Legal Committee also gave intensive consideration to the formulation of basic principles and the development of language for an International Compensation Fund for Oil Pollution Damage. IMCO will convene an international conference in 1971 to finalize a convention with respect to this Fund if the necessary preliminary work has been completed. Such a convention would supplement the Convention on Civil Lia-

bility for Oil Pollution Damage which was adopted at a conference held in Brussels in 1969.

During 1970 IMCO significantly expanded its technical assistance activities. It undertook a 31-country survey to determine the needs of developing countries with respect to programs within its competence. The survey indicated a widespread need by developing countries for help in applying the international safety regime for shipping and in training their nationals in the manning of ships and the administration of their merchant marines. IMCO now has on its staff a full-time consultant for technical assistance activities.

INTERNATIONAL TELECOMMUNICATION UNION

Membership in the ITU increased from 137 to 139 in 1970 with the accession of Equatorial Guinea and Swaziland to the International Telecommunication Convention. During the year the ITU continued to function as the specialized organization for maintaining and extending international cooperation for the improvement and rational use of telecommunications of all kinds. The ITU also continued to work closely with the United Nations during the year, especially in its role as a UNDP executing agency in the telecommunications field.

Administrative Council

The United States is a member of the Administrative Council which held its 25th session in Geneva, May 23–June 12 and completed its arrangements for convening a World Administrative Radio Conference for Space Telecommunications in Geneva in June 1971. The Council also set the dates for several major ITU conferences during the next 4 years, including the convening of an ITU Plenipotentiary Conference in the fall of 1973. The Council reviewed and approved a 1971 budget of 27,571,500 Swiss francs of which the U.S. share of the assessment on member countries is approximately $700,000. In addition, the Council took action on a number of other staff, organization, operational, and financial matters, including a decision to rent a new computer. The results of the Council's session were consistent with U.S. interests, and should result in greater efficiency and effectiveness for the organization.

Other Permanent Organs

The permanent technical organs of the ITU—the International Radio Consultative Committee (CCIR), the International Telegraph and Telephone Consultative Committee (CCITT), and the International Frequency Registration Board (IFRB)—all met during the year. The United States is a member of the first two bodies.

The 12th plenary assembly of the CCIR met in New Delhi January 21–February 11 to consider and approve nearly 600 texts on technical radio matters. The texts resulted from the work of the 15 CCIR Study Groups which met during 1969. Among these documents were important recommendations on (1) use of satellites for the transmission of telephony and television, (2) use of computers to improve reliability of forecasts of usable radio frequencies, and (3) reliability of radio services. In addition, the Assembly modified the structure of the CCIR Study Groups to bring them into line with current progress in radio communications.

The CCITT's Plan Committee for Asia and Oceania met in Tehran April 20-30 and the Plan Committee for Europe and the Mediterranean Basin met in Warsaw September 14-23. Both meetings produced useful work toward the objective of an orderly development of telecommunications on a worldwide basis. In addition, various CCITT Study Groups met during the year to amend international standards for telephone and telegraph operations, switching, and signalling systems, and to consider other technical and tariff matters.

The essential function of the IFRB is the technical examination and registration of radio frequency notifications to insure interference-free radio operations throughout the world. The IFRB and its staff continued to carry out this function completely and effectively. During the year the IFRB conducted a radio frequency management seminar, primarily for the benefit of developing countries. Such seminars are part of a continuing program that provides the developing countries with the information necessary for a proper administration of national and international telecommunications.

Technical Assistance

Through technical advisory services, fellowships, and seminars the ITU, as a UNDP executing agency, provides much needed technical assistance to the developing nations in increasing their capabilities in the management and operation of telecommunications systems. A major project of the technical assistance program is the establishment and staffing of telecommunications training institutes to provide expertise to the developing countries. In addition, and as the result of requests from the developing countries, the ITU is expanding its program of technical telecommunications seminars. Finally, increasing numbers of technical experts from the developed countries, including the United States, have been recruited for advisory positions on specific telecommunications projects and for studies in developing countries.

UNIVERSAL POSTAL UNION

A new headquarters building for the UPU was formally inaugurated on May 20, 1970, in the presence of the President of Switzerland, a personal representative of UN Secretary-General Thant, and ranking postal officials from many parts of the world. The ceremonies in celebration of the opening of the new headquarters building in Bern began with an address to the assembled delegates which recalled the growth of the Union (whose membership increased to 143 during 1970 with the addition of Equatorial Guinea) and the evolution of the Union's importance for coordinating the development of postal services among all nations.

International Postal Communications Matters

The new rate structure for international mail approved by the UPU Congress in Tokyo in 1969 was agreed upon at the expense of compromising a basic principle of the Union, the uniform application of rates to mail categories. At the first meeting of the Executive Council after the Congress, it was decided that before further steps could be taken to simplify the rate structure, UPU members would have to decide whether their interests would be better served by more freedom in setting rates or by a return to uniformity.

The 1969 Congress had also approved a temporary scheme whereby countries that receive substantially more mail than they send out will have the right to demand reimbursement from those countries in which the excess mail originates. The Executive Council established a working party, of which the United States is a member, to study the elements involved in such compensation. The fact that some countries might have to increase rates in order to pass on to the public the cost of reimbursing other countries for imbalances in the exchange of mail will be a significant factor in the Council's study of the rate structure.

Current UPU regulations require that all articles mailed at a reduced rate must be prepared so that the contents can be easily inspected. The growing volume of printed matter exchanged between countries and the increasing use of mechanical equipment—by publishers for packaging and by postal facilities for sorting and routing purposes—has given rise to studies in both the Executive Council and the Consultative Council for Postal Studies of ways to facilitate modernization of mail processing without jeopardizing customs procedures and postal revenues.

The Executive Council initiated on the instructions of the Tokyo Congress, a study to identify and provide special treatment for the official correspondence of diplomatic missions, consulates, and international organizations.

Organizational Matters

The developing countries had expressed their dissatisfaction at the Tokyo Congress with the present scheme for apportioning the expenses of the Union. They emphasized that under the present UPU system, the large industrial countries bear a relatively light financial burden, since no member now pays more than 4.8% of the expenses of the Union. A report will be submitted to the 1971 Executive Council which may provide the basis for new recommendations to the next Congress, scheduled for 1974.

In 1970 the United States chaired the Finance Committee of the Executive Council, which reviews the budget of the Union. The expenses of the Union were $1,582,000, and the U.S. contribution was $66,546, or approximately 4.2% of the total. The United States also became a member of a new working party formed to study the organization and structure of the International Bureau. In carrying out its task the working party will review practices in other UN specialized agencies related to the appointment and promotion of staff, and to the creation and classification of posts.

Technical Assistance

During discussions at the Executive Council of the UPU's financial needs in the area of technical assistance, developing countries renewed their call for increased contributions to the UPU's Special Fund. A proposal was made to ask all members to donate to the Special Fund each year a fixed percentage of their regular contribution to the Union. This proposal was dismissed at the initiative of the U.S. delegation, which pointed out that the UPU Congress had called on member countries to increase their contributions to the Special Fund only to the extent that such contributions were compatible with the technical cooperation policies of their individual governments. In many donor countries, it was pointed out, the established policy is to funnel all multilateral technical assistance funds through the UNDP, and not to support voluntary special funds in specialized agencies.

In 1970 the UPU had over half a million dollars in UNDP funds to carry out postal projects under the technical assistance component of that program. In addition, it was the executing agency for five regional projects—centered in Syria, Afghanistan, Turkey, Ivory Coast, and Thailand—under the UNDP preinvestment component.

Political Matters

The Executive Council had before it a number of resolutions of the 24th UN General Assembly dealing with colonialism and apartheid. Of particular relevance was one adopted December 23, 1969, recommending that all specialized agencies, and in particular ICAO, ITU, and the UPU, work out measures aimed at discontinuing collaboration with the governments of Portugal and South Africa and the regime in Southern Rhodesia. It was suggested that in compliance with this resolution the International Bureau should publish, at regular intervals, a list of those countries that have suspended postal services with Rhodesia. The United States pointed out, however, that the resolution was not addressed to individual countries and did not speak of the interruption of postal services, but rather of "measures aimed at discontinuing any collaboration" between the UPU and the Southern Rhodesian regime. This view was accepted and it was decided that further efforts should be made to determine more precisely what purpose this resolution has in reference to the UPU, and to communicate to the United Nations the difficulty that the UPU would have in complying with it.

WORLD METEOROLOGICAL ORGANIZATION

World Weather Watch

For planning purposes the WMO has divided the World Weather Watch (WWW) program into two phases: (1) the period 1968-1971 during which major effort would be placed on the implementation by members of the WWW plan by conventional observing techniques, and (2) the period 1972-1975 where emphasis would be placed on development of modern technology to achieve WWW goals.

The principal goals to be achieved by the end of 1971 are (1) substantial improvement in the global observing system, (2) implementation of the global data processing system, (3) improvement of the global telecommunication system, (4) acceleration of the program to educate and train meteorologists, and (5) development of a global atmospheric research program.

Adequate weather data is generally unavailable for over 80% of the earth's surface, primarily the oceans and developing countries. A successful implementation of the WWW plan should overcome part of this deficiency and improve weather forecasts for such end-users as farmers and the construction, transportation, and fisheries industries.

Under the WWW each of the 133 WMO members[4] is called upon to implement needed improvements in observations, data processing, and communications in their territories. To the extent that members lack the resources required for implementation in their own territories, the WMO Voluntary Assistance Program (VAP), established by the fifth WMO Congress in 1967, can assist them in procuring radiosonde ground equipment, observational balloons, radiosondes, communications equipment, and long-term training. The VAP assistance is provided only to the extent that such assistance is not feasible under UNDP or other bilateral or multilateral arrangements. The assisted countries provide counterpart resources, usually local facilities and personnel.

At its annual meeting, October 8-16, the WMO Executive Committee, of which Dr. Robert M. White, Administrator of the U.S. National Oceanic and Atmospheric Administration (NOAA) is a member, reviewed requests from developing countries for assistance from VAP and reviewed the status of 295 projects that have already been approved for circulation to WMO members. Of these projects over 100 had received offers of whole or partial support from members and 9 projects had been completed by October. The United States contributed to projects in Bolivia, Brazil, Republic of China, Colombia, Costa Rica, Ethiopia, Guatemala, Honduras, India, Indonesia, Paraguay, Somalia, Turkey, and Venezuela. The U.S. contribution to these projects during 1970 totaled $1,500,000: (1) $200,000 to the Voluntary Assistance Fund on a matching basis at a rate of 40% of the total unrestricted cash contributions of all WMO members; and (2) $1,300,000 for contributions-in-kind to the Equipment and Services Program. The contributions-in-kind included U.S. equipment, experts, services, and U.S. training in meteorology for personnel from developing countries. This program is administered by NOAA.

A key part of the WWW is research to improve the understanding of the basic structure of the atmosphere. For this purpose a Global Atmospheric Research Program (GARP) is underway. To bring nongovernmental scientists fully into this program, the WMO planned GARP in cooperation with the International Council of Scientific Unions. WMO and ICSU established a Joint Planning Staff to develop research plans, and tentatively agreed that the project on a hemispheric or global basis would be undertaken in 1976 with several interim experiments over a more limited geographical area. WMO's Executive Committee agreed to establish with ICSU a GARP Tropical Experiment in the South Atlantic and arranged for meetings to work out the details of the program and to receive commitments from the governments concerned.

Related Activities

The WMO Executive Committee also considered environmental questions, particularly pollution problems and the possible economic benefits of meteorology. It approved (1) the establishment of a network of stations to measure background air pollution on both worldwide and regional bases, (2) a statement on the present state of knowledge and possible practical benefits in some fields of weather modification, and (3) closer working arrangements with ICSU in the field of solar-terrestrial monitoring.

The United States attended three regional WMO meetings during the year—the fifth session of the Asian Regional Association held in Tokyo July 20-31, the fifth session of the Southwest Pacific Regional Association held in Kuala Lumpur August 3-15, and the fifth session of the South American Regional Association held in Bogota July 6-20. At these meetings the associations reviewed their plans for the WWW with particular attention to detailed arrangements for the regional networks of stations, communications, and data processing.

The United States also took part in the fifth session of the Commission for Synoptic Meteorology, held in Geneva June 15-July 3. The Commission developed procedures and regulations in the fields of weather forecasting, communications, global networks, and training and recommended improvements with particular emphasis on the problems relating to the WWW.

Technical Assistance

In addition to directing its own Voluntary Assistance Program, the WMO serves as executing agency for UNDP projects pertaining to meteorology and hydrometeorology. Many countries and territories received assistance during 1970 from the approximately $1.3 million that WMO administered under the UNDP's technical assistance component. In addition, 12 large-scale preinvestment projects were being carried out. Two new projects started in 1970: one in Guinea and Mali on a flood forecasting and warning system in the Niger River Basin, and another in Bolivia on development and improvement of the meteorological and hydrological services.

U.S. Satellites

During 1970 the United States launched three new meteorological satellites: TIROS M, NOAA 1, and NIMBUS 4. All carried Automatic Picture Transmission System (APT) cameras, enabling users throughout the world to receive pictures on local inexpensive ground equipment. These satellites and four earlier weather satellites (NIMBUS 3, and ESSA, 2, 8, and 9) that continued to perform satisfactorily enabled the United States to make available data on weather conditions to all nations of the world.

INTERNATIONAL ATOMIC ENERGY AGENCY

The IAEA was established in 1957 as a result of President Eisenhower's atoms-for-peace proposal before the United Nations in December 1953. During 1970, the Agency continued to pursue its broad statutory objectives of promoting the peaceful uses of atomic energy throughout the world and ensuring, so far as it is able, that assistance provided by it, or at its request, or under its supervision or control, is not used in such a way as to further any military purpose.

Work was given a new impetus with the entry into force of the nonproliferation treaty in March 1970. By the end of the year 64 countries were parties to the treaty and an additional 34 had signed but not yet ratified. The treaty gives the IAEA the responsibility for safeguarding nuclear materials intended for peaceful application in nonnuclear weapon states that accept its terms.

As in past years, the United States participated in all areas of the IAEA's activities and took the initiative in many of its major programs.

Safeguards

The IAEA Board of Governors established a committee open to all member states to advise it on the IAEA responsibilities under the nonproliferation treaty, and in particular on the content of the agreements that will be required between the Agency and the parties to the treaty. The committee, in which the United States played a major role, met June 12-July 3, October 13-November 4, and December 1-11. The substance of the draft agreement drawn up so far provides for independent IAEA verification of the data and findings of national systems of control of the use of nuclear materials. By the end of December, 24 governments had entered into formal negotiation of such agreements with the IAEA.

Work with respect to the IAEA's previously established safeguards system continued to expand during the year. IAEA safeguards are now applied to 10 nuclear power stations comprising about 12% of the total world nuclear electrical generating capacity; to 68 other reactors; and 4 conversion, fabrication, and reprocessing plants; and to 74 other separate accountability areas. Of a total of 44 safeguards agreements that the IAEA Board has approved, 22 concern the transfer to the IAEA of the safeguards responsibilities provided for in U.S. bilateral Agreements for Cooperation.

In addition to safeguards applications, the development and improvement of safeguards methods and techniques was given a great deal of attention. A symposium on progress in safeguards techniques, organized by the Agency in Karlsruhe, Germany, showed that there have been substantial improvements in methods of systems analysis, techniques of verification based on correlation of fuel cycle data, and new instruments. Panels of experts drew up recommendations on technical objectives of safeguards work, principles of inspection, requirements for information on the design of nuclear installations, and verification of nuclear materials.

Nuclear Power and Reactors

The number of new nuclear power plants on order or being built continued to grow and, consequently, the IAEA continued to emphasize the provision of practical services to member states during the early stages of a nuclear power project, including economic studies, siting surveys, and safety evaluations.

National programs for the use of nuclear power were reviewed at a symposium, organized jointly by the IAEA and ECE, on the economic integration of nuclear power stations in electric power systems. The Agency held a symposium in Oslo, Norway, on technical and economic aspects of small- and medium-sized power reactors, in

which various developing countries have a special interest.

IAEA began to prepare estimates of the financial requirements of developing countries for their nuclear projects in the next decade and to survey possible sources of finance. Information received by year's end indicated that developing countries expect to install 20,000 to 25,000 megawatts of electricity of nuclear capacity between 1970 and 1980, which would require foreign exchange resources of 3 to 4 billion dollars.

More countries, including a few of the developing ones, are taking an interest in the development of fastbreeder reactors, and the IAEA therefore sponsored a symposium on progress in sodium-cooled fast reactor engineering. Following this symposium, the annual meeting of the Agency's International Working Group on Fast Reactors was held. This group exchanges information and coordinates international meetings on fast reactor development programs.

The IAEA serves as a focal point for international cooperation in the field of nuclear power desalting, and continued to participate in a study by the U.S. Atomic Energy Commission's Oak Ridge National Laboratory on the potential application of nuclear powered energy centers to provide large amounts of fresh water and electricity for arid regions in the Middle East.

The IAEA and the European Nuclear Energy Agency of the OECD published a review of uranium resources including production and demand; and the IAEA convened a symposium to discuss the recovery of uranium from its ores and other sources. A panel of experts met to discuss uranium exploration geology.

The first international meeting on the peaceful uses of nuclear explosions, convened in Vienna, provided an important exchange of information which had not been available previously. A panel of experts also met at IAEA Headquarters in Vienna and considered the question of international observation of peaceful uses of nuclear explosions in the context of the NPT. The United States made important contributions at both of these meetings.

Isotopes and Radiation Sources

The Joint FAO/IAEA Division of Atomic Energy in Food and Agriculture continued many programs aimed at improving food crops. At meetings throughout the year, experts reviewed the uses of nuclear techniques in increasing the protein content of various plants, in pest control, and in plant metabolism. Organizations in 19 countries including the United States, agreed to take part in a new international project under the joint auspices of the IAEA, FAO, and OECD, devoted to the testing of irradiated food products for wholesomeness, research on the methodology of such testing, and dissemination of information resulting from this work. The United States pledged to contribute $25,000 a year to the project for 3 years, subject to the availability of funds.

The program on medical applications and radiation biology continued to emphasize the physical aspects of nuclear medicine. In coordination with WHO, research was supported on diseases such as parasitic infections, deficiency diseases, and tropical anemias. A joint IAEA/WHO meeting helped to prepare international recommendations on absolute dose measurement.

The Agency continued its work on the use of nuclear techniques in hydrology, within the program of the International Hydrological Decade and in cooperation with UNESCO. It organized a symposium on the use of isotopes in hydrology and a special panel meeting on the use of carbon isotopes.

Industrial nuclear techniques were pursued, including work on the processing of fiber plastic composites for use as building materials. Research was performed on techniques for oil field evaluation and prospecting for nonnuclear minerals. The increasing interest of developing countries in industrial uses was shown in several proposals for UNDP projects which were being reviewed by the IAEA from the standpoint of their technical feasibility.

Atomic Energy and the Environment

The IAEA is well aware of the growing public interest in maintaining the quality of the environment and can point to a strong, continuing program on matters of health and safety and the management of radioactive wastes. This was evident at a symposium on environmental aspects of nuclear power stations organized at UN Headquarters by the Agency and the U.S. Atomic Energy Commission, August 10-14. At this symposium, AEC Chairman Seaborg suggested that the Agency establish a central repository of data on the amounts and concentrations of radioactivity released in the environment in connection with civilian uses of atomic energy, and at year's end the IAEA was formulating plans to do so. The Agency has had under consideration for several years the desirability and practicality of instituting an international register of disposals of radioactive waste in the sea.

Since 1961, as part of its hydrology program and in cooperation with the WMO, the Agency has collected and published data from a worldwide network, involving about 65 countries, on the occurrence of tritium, deuterium, and oxygen-18 in precipitation. U.S. organizations and laboratories have cooperated in providing data and in performing analyses for this program.

Since its inception the Agency has been involved, with U.S. assistance, in such activities as establishing basic safety standards, disseminating information, and supporting research in the radiological safety field. During 1970, IAEA symposia reviewed work in radioactive waste management and in the use of nuclear techniques in the measurement and control of environmental pollution. One program in the latter field which may have wide-ranging results concerns the use of radioisotope tracer techniques to study the course of pesticide residues.

Information and Laboratories

IAEA launched the International Nuclear Information System (INIS) on a limited basis in 1970, following initial proposals and continuous support from the United States. Under INIS, the Agency receives reports of new nuclear literature from members, prepares bibliographic indexes, assigns keywords, and makes them available to members in published as well as computer format. By the end of the year 36 countries and 8 international organizations were taking part in this work, thus assuring INIS of over 90% coverage of the world's publications on nuclear subjects. One component of INIS supplies microfiche copies of all reports received by the Agency.

Technical Assistance

During 1970 IAEA made expert services, equipment, and fellowships available to 52 countries—

19 in Africa and the Middle East, 11 in Asia and the Far East, 11 in Latin America, and 11 others, mainly in Europe. The Agency organized 13 interregional training courses, 1 seminar, and 2 study tours for participants from developing countries—one in the U.S.S.R. on the uses of isotopes and radiation in agricultural research and the other in the United States and Canada on the industrial application of radioisotopes and radiation. Two training courses were held in the United States, one at Cornell University on the use of radioisotopes and radiation in animal science and veterinary medicine and the other at the Puerto Rico Nuclear Center on dosimetry in radiotherapy.

The United States has been a strong supporter of the IAEA technical assistance program, and for many years has furnished fellowships, experts' services, training courses, and items of equipment as well as cash contributions. In 1970 the cash contribution was about $650,000 and the value of the contributions-in-kind was about $750,000. In addition the United States urged upon all members the obligation to devote an increasing amount of resources and constructive attention to this aspect of the IAEA program.

Organizational Matters

The IAEA is financed by means of a regular or administrative budget, supported largely by assessments levied on the member states according to a scale developed by the United Nations, and an operational budget, supported mainly by voluntary contributions from member states. The operational budget covers some laboratory work and all technical assistance activities other than those carried out by the IAEA on behalf of the UNDP.

At its 14th General Conference, September 22–28, the IAEA adopted a regular budget for 1971 of $13,778,000, an increase of 10.1% over 1970, and a scale of assessments under which the United States would pay 31.45%, compared to its 1970 rate of 31.5%. The General Conference further adopted an operational budget for 1971 of $3,251,000, of which $2,500,000—an increase of $500,000 over 1970—was the target for voluntary contributions, with the remainder to be funded from special contributions and other sources. The United States announced that, subject to congressional approval, it would contribute in 1971 at least an amount equivalent to its 1970 contribution.

By a vote of 54 to 9, with 13 abstentions, the 14th General Conference also approved an amendment to the IAEA Statute that will increase the membership of the Board of Governors from 25 to 34, if it is ratified by two-thirds of the 102 member states.[5] The amendment, sponsored by Italy and 33 other states including the United States, will increase the representation of the developing countries on the Board and will also increase from 5 to 9 the number of "designated" or permanent seats for the member states most advanced in nuclear technology.

NOTES

[1] Yemen, Cambodia, and Southern Yemen joined during 1970.
[2] Canada, China, France, Federal Republic of Germany, India, Italy, Japan, U.S.S.R., United Kingdom, and United States.
[3] The U.S. declaration of accession was deposited with UNESCO Jan. 20, 1971.
[4] The Bahamas joined during 1970.
[5] Ireland joined and Nicaragua withdrew during 1970.

Food for the Family of Nations; The Purpose and Structure of the Proposed Food and Agriculture Organization of the United Nations

Howard R. Tolley and LeRoy D. Stinebower [1]

In this reading the authors describe the steps leading to the founding of FAO, its initial organizational structure and functions. Additional information about FAO will be found in the section on the transition from League to UN and in the description of the FAO library later in this section.

The United Nations Conference on Food and Agriculture, which met at Hot Springs, Virginia, in May 1943, has been called the first of the peace conferences for World War II. It probably fully deserves that title.

It was called, at the invitation of President Roosevelt, while the war was still far from over, to consider ways of removing one of the basic causes of war—perennial want of food. It had no authority to consider *terms* of peace—and thus in an exact sense it was no peace conference at all—but it did have full authority to explore one of the underlying *conditions,* freedom from hunger, which predispose nations to peace. Its purpose thus was not to seek to end war but to explore what could be done by united action in the field of food and agriculture to help lay the foundations for economic improvement and stability, without which the prospects for peace cannot remain secure.

The working committees at the Conference were composed of experts in agriculture and nutrition. Almost unanimously they had two outstanding convictions, if one is to judge by the recommendations and resolutions adopted by the Conference: (1) with recent progress in the science of agricultural production and of nutrition, there is no longer any real excuse for mankind's indifferent success in the age-long struggle for adequate food; and (2) the time is at hand for the peace-loving nations of the earth to better the conditions of rural populations everywhere by cooperative action

to secure increased efficiency in the production and distribution of agricultural products.

Shortly after the Hot Springs conference the Interim Commission on Food and Agriculture was established in Washington to formulate "A specific plan for a permanent organization in the field of food and agriculture," including forestry and fisheries. Delegates to the Interim Commission were designated by the governments of all the United and Associated Nations, and the Commission was convened in Washington on July 15, 1943.[2] A little over a year later—in August 1944—the Interim Commission made its first official report to the governments it represented.[3]

It had completed its major task—the formulation of a "specific plan for a permanent organization." It was ready to dissolve as soon as the constitution which it had prepared for the Food and Agriculture Organization of the United Nations (FAO) had been accepted by 20 of the nations, as required by the constitution, and the first FAO conference had been convened. Meanwhile, the Commission would continue its "preliminary statistical investigations and research into the problems with which the permanent organization will deal," as required by the resolution of the United Nations Conference on Food and Agriculture which had called it into being.

The Interim Commission recommended that FAO be established as soon as possible and that "Governments in a position to do so should make

SOURCE: Reprinted from Howard R. Tolley and LeRoy D. Stinebower, "Food for the Family of Nations; the Purpose and Structure of the Proposed Food and Agriculture Organization of the United Nations," U. S. Department of State. *Bulletin,* 12 (Feb. 18, 1945) pp. 225–230.

every contribution in their power, by releasing suitable personnel and otherwise, towards making it"—even in its beginning stages—"an effective and authoritative nucleus for dealing with both immediate and long-term problems of adjustment in food and agriculture." The Commission had carefully weighed the considerations which favored deferring establishment of FAO until after the war—such as the difficulties of recruiting qualified personnel and the preoccupation of many of the governments and other bodies with other matters—but believed that the considerations which favored immediate action were more important. Immediately after the war many serious problems in nutrition, food, and agriculture would be calling urgently for solution, and the fluid political, economic, and social conditions then obtaining "would be particularly favorable to the adoption of sound and thorough-going measures to meet these problems." Unless FAO were actually in existence at that time to give the international advice and influence which it is designed to provide, effective dealing with these problems might be delayed for many years.

"The sooner it is established," the Commission concludes, "the sooner will it be able to bring to bear upon post-war problems of reconstruction the disinterested, international, and instructed advice and influence the provision of which is the essential purpose of the Organization." To insure the broadest possible continuing influence for the Organization, provision was made in its constitution to enable it to take its proper place in any general organization for world security which might be established at a later date.

As of early February 1945, 17 governments had indicated their intention to accept the constitution. In his message to the Congress of February 12, 1945, President Roosevelt indicated his expectation that the proposed constitution would shortly be submitted to the Congress. It would appear probable that the first conference of FAO could be convened within a few months after favorable action by the Congress and that the Organization could then begin its work of building a secure and lasting peace on the solid foundation of the "things that make for peace."

THE PURPOSE OF THE ORGANIZATION

Although twice as many people are engaged in agriculture as in all other occupations combined, two thirds of the people of the world have never had enough of the right kinds of food. The purpose of FAO is to work toward correcting that situation, for which there is no longer any excuse.

There was a time, before the modern industrial era, when it seemed impossible to relieve the pressure of a constantly increasing world population on the world's supply of food. The gloomy predictions of Malthus seemed inescapable. Malthus would have been incredulous had he been told that in the United States in the third and fourth decades of the twentieth century the major concern of farm leaders would center on the so-called problem of surplus agricultural production. Knowing as he did the unrelieved poverty and perennial hunger of millions of people in his day, and knowing also that the malnutrition and disease associated with such hunger and poverty were the primary checks against vast increases in population, Malthus would have found it impossible to believe that any great nation could actually be concerned about producing too much food and would actually take steps to restrict its production.

Malthus, however, could not foresee the tremendous increases in agricultural production which modern science was to make possible. In fact, most of us even today do not fully realize what potentialities still lie ahead. In Malthus' time—and even now in many areas of the world—from 7 to 9 out of every 10 persons capable of work were engaged in agriculture. A century or more ago it required that many people merely to maintain the extremely low level of subsistence which to Malthus seemed to be the inescapable fate of the great mass of the world's people throughout time.

Today in the United States less than one person out of five is working in agriculture. Because of the manpower requirements of war, many of those now working in agriculture are too old or too young to be viewed as fully able-bodied. Yet on the average our civilian population, after more than two years of war, actually ate last year more food and nutritionally better food than at any other time in our history. Civilian per-capita consumption of food was 9 percent greater than in the years just before the war (1935–39), even though we were devoting almost a quarter of our total food production to military and lend-lease uses. Such an achievement—and it is truly amazing—was possible only because of the remarkable increases in agricultural production per acre and per hour of labor which technological improvements have brought about.

This is not to argue, of course, that Malthus' fears were unwarranted. They are warranted even today. The world's population still presses against the world's food supply and will probably continue to press against it for decades to come. We do know, however, that the techniques of agricultural production, transportation, and food preservation now employed by the more developed countries of the world are capable of relieving this pressure not only for their own peoples but also— if extended to other areas through education and trade—for other peoples throughout the world. In actuality, the pressure has been fully relieved nowhere. Even in the United States, better nourished on the whole last year than in any year in the past, millions of people subsisted on diets which were inadequate for proper health and well-being. For many areas of the world the pressure of population on the available supply of food has not been eased at all since Malthus' time. This vast difference between what we have achieved in the production and distribution of food and what we now know we can achieve if we want to is the impelling—and appalling—circumstance which has called FAO into being.

In the language of the preamble to the proposed constitution, the nations "accepting this Constitution" and thereby establishing the Food and Agriculture Organization of the United Nations are "determined to promote the common welfare by furthering separate and collective action on their part for the purposes of

"(1) raising levels of nutrition and standards of living of the peoples under their respective jurisdictions,

"(2) securing improvements in the efficiency of the production and distribution of all food and agricultural products.

"(3) bettering the condition of rural populations.

"(4) and thus contributing toward an expanding world economy."

SPECIFIC FUNCTIONS OF FAO

These broad objectives set forth in the preamble to the constitution are immediately followed by a list of specific functions of the Organization. This list (art. I) together with article XI and the "purposes" quoted above from the preamble constitute the essential working program of FAO. The other 24 articles deal principally with the

structure of the Organization, which will be discussed later in this paper, and sundry operating procedures and relations which are a necessary legal concomitant of all constitutions but are important chiefly from the standpoint of administration.

Two very brief articles, however, are of special interest to the people of the United States. The first of these (art. XVI) specifies that the term *agriculture* as used in the constitution includes fisheries, marine products, forestry, and forestry products; and the second (art. XXIV) states that the "temporary seat of the Organization shall be at Washington unless the Conference should otherwise determine."

The Conference referred to here, and in later pages, is the policy-making body of FAO. It is composed of one representative from each of the member nations. Except for such powers as it may delegate to an executive committee, it is the sole governing body of the Organization.

Articles I and XI are given in full below:

Article I (Functions of the Organization)

1. The Organization shall collect, analyze, interpret, and disseminate information relating to nutrition, food and agriculture.

2. The Organization shall promote and, where appropriate, shall recommend national and international action with respect to

(a) scientific, technological, social, and economic research relating to nutrition, food and agriculture;

(b) the improvement of education and administration relating to nutrition, food and agriculture, and the spread of public knowledge of nutritional and agricultural science and practice;

(c) the conservation of natural resources and the adoption of improved methods of agricultural production;

(d) the improvement of the processing, marketing, and distribution of food and agricultural products;

(e) the adoption of policies for the provision of adequate agricultural credit, national and international;

(f) the adoption of international policies with respect to agricultural commodity arrangements.

3. It shall also be the function of the Organization

(a) to furnish such technical assistance as governments may request;

(b) to organize, in cooperation with the governments concerned, such missions as may be needed to assist them to fulfill the obligations arising from their acceptance of the recommendations of the United Nations Conference on Food and Agriculture; and

(c) generally to take all necessary and appropriate action to implement the purposes of the Organization as set forth in the Preamble.

Article XI (Reports by Members)

1. Each Member nation shall communicate periodically to the Organization reports on the progress made toward achieving the purpose of the Organization set forth in the Preamble and on the action taken on the basis of recommendations made and conventions submitted by the Conference.

2. These reports shall be made at such times and in such form and shall contain such particulars as the Conference may request.

3. The Director-General shall submit these reports, together with analyses thereof, to the Conference and shall publish such reports and analyses as may be approved for publication by the Conference together with any reports relating thereto adopted by the Conference.

4. The Director-General may request any Member nation to submit information relating to the purpose of the Organization.

5. Each Member nation shall, on request, communicate to the Organization, on publication, all laws and regulations and official reports and statistics concerning nutrition, food and agriculture.

Two things become clear from a study of this list of functions: (1) The Organization is intended to serve primarily as an expert advisory center which member nations can use to help them achieve better levels of living for themselves; (2) it has no coercive power, except that which it can bring to bear on the *conscience* of each nation by requiring it to report periodically on the progress it has made toward achieving what it agreed to try to achieve when it joined the Organization.

Both these points are extremely important, for between them they insure that the Organization shall not, on the one hand, assume any authority which a sovereign nation rightfully reserves to itself, nor shall it, on the other hand, forego any influence for greater national welfare which it can properly bring to bear on a nation as a result of its findings and recommendations in the field of food and agriculture. FAO is quite properly viewed as a research and statistical clearinghouse in the field of food and agriculture, with expert advisory functions, but it is not solely that; it is, in addition, a perpetual international reminder that facts and statistics and advice must find ultimate expression in human betterment. Or, to look at FAO in another way, the Organization agrees to gather facts, to advise, and to help member nations in the field of food and agriculture; the member nations, in turn, agree to keep the Organization informed as to the extent to which they have used the facts, the advice, and the help the Organization has provided.

Because of the emphasis the Hot Springs conference rightly placed on better nutrition, there has been some tendency to view the proposed Organization as being primarily concerned with the consumer of agricultural products. An analysis of the provisions of article I of the constitution does not substantiate this view. The misinterpretation probably arises from a confusion of the means used with the end sought.

The farmer himself is the world's greatest consumer of food—two thirds of the world's people are farmers—and hence he himself gains directly from any efforts to raise levels of nutrition. Moreover, he also profits indirectly through the expansion in markets resulting from better nutrition among non-farm consumers. Better food for the entire family of nations, from any angle one looks at it, means better living conditions for the farm families or fisher-folk who must produce that food.

FAO, with its dual emphasis on food *and* agriculture, promises to approach the basic problem of freedom from want of food from the standpoint of both consumer and producer. This is apparent throughout article I, where the agricultural emphasis dominates but nutrition is stressed equally with agriculture in each of the first three provisions. The reason for this is to be found in the varied specific problems the Organization will have to face. The facilities of FAO will be available to all member nations, but the nature of the service it can render most appropriately will vary with the most pressing needs of each country. For many undeveloped nations, where expanding populations continue to press unrelentingly on the food supply, its primary service will be to aid them in adopting the technical improvements—including both scientific research and educational and extension activities—which have been of such outstanding help in developing the agriculture of the more advanced nations. Such aid will enable them not only to provide more adequate food for themselves but also to contribute their share to the universal benefits arising from an expanding world economy, in which a more efficient agriculture must be matched by greater industrial production and greater buying power among farm and industrial producers alike.

For the already highly developed nations, FAO's primary service will be in the statistical and technical aid it can give in adapting agricultural production as equitably and as efficiently as possible to changing world needs. By seeing the world situation as a whole, FAO will be in a position to grapple with international problems in food and agriculture as they arise and to suggest solutions which can forestall serious national and international difficulties.

Although today less than one person in five in the United States is engaged in agriculture, the perennial peacetime farm problem in this country has been one of how to keep a constantly expanding production from pressing against the available market outlets without disastrous declines in farm income and prices. FAO offers invaluable aid in solving this problem. Its world-wide statistical and economic services will provide a greatly improved basis for planning production and marketing programs. The conferences it is empowered to convene will provide means for working out early and equitable answers to international commodity problems that tend to grow more vexatious the longer they are postponed.

The unhappy experience of United States farmers in the period between the two world wars demonstrated conclusively that the farm problem cannot be solved by divorcing our markets from those of the rest of the world. The world has become too small for that. In the even smaller world which will be our home after the war because of recent advances in transport and communication, the family of nations will find it necessary more than ever before to plan its living, including its food supply, together.

This is not to propose, in any sense at all, that the FAO should seek to provide through international charity the basic food needs of ill-nourished peoples; it is simply to point out that in a world so small as ours has become any help that can be given to enable these peoples to produce better food for themselves means better food and better living for us. A full-employment economy for the United States, through which every American child can have the food he needs for vigorous growth and through which every American farmer can be assured of the living conditions he deserves, is not attainable unless we can trade with other than hungry and impoverished peoples in other parts of the world. The broad purpose of FAO, as revealed by the specific functions set forth in article I of its constitution, is to provide the framework by which a start can be made toward seeing clearly the world's needs in food and agriculture and toward making available to any nation which desires it the technical help or advice it may require to adapt its agricultural economy to those needs.

FAO'S RELATION TO OTHER INTERNATIONAL ORGANIZATIONS

At the time the first report was prepared by the Interim Commission, the Dumbarton Oaks conference on international security had not been held, but provision was made in the proposed constitution to permit FAO to fit into any general world organization which may be established.

As envisaged, FAO will be coordinate in function with the International Labor Office, the International Monetary Fund and the International Bank for Reconstruction and Development (both proposed at Bretton Woods), and such other international bodies in allied social and economic fields as may eventually be established. All these agencies would be under the high coordination of the Economic and Social Council, which would be responsible to the General Assembly. Under such arrangements FAO would be autonomous in its fields of endeavor but would yet function in such a way as to collaborate with its coordinate organizations in attaining the over-all objectives of world security.

Close working relations with the United Nations Relief and Rehabilitation Administration (UNRRA) have already been established by the Interim Commission. Although UNRRA is a temporary organization designed only to meet the immediate relief and rehabilitation needs occasioned by the war, its rehabilitation work must be guided so far as possible by the longer term objectives of FAO if the difficulties of post-war transition are to be minimized. This cooperative working relation will necessarily be continued by the permanent Organization.

The constitution provides for similar cooperation by FAO with other public international organizations with related responsibilities. Part of the work proposed for FAO has been pioneered by existing international organizations, such as the International Institute of Agriculture and related agencies in the fields of forestry and fisheries. FAO will work out arrangements for utilizing fully the experience of these predecessor agencies.

STRUCTURE OF THE ORGANIZATION

The specific functions of FAO have made possible a relatively simple operating structure. Lacking authority to carry out its recommendations—which, indeed, can be carried out only by the nations concerned—it will not need the elaborate structure or the huge sums of money required by even a national "action" agency. Moreover, the Organization proposes to utilize to the fullest extent possible the facilities and resources of other organizations, both national and international, which are already established or may be established. Thus its own staff of technical experts need not be large.

The budget for the first year has been fixed at $2,500,000, toward which the United States would contribute $625,000. The annual budget for the next five years has been estimated at about double the amount set for the first year. On this basis the cost of membership to the people of the United States would be about $1,250,000 a year.

Original membership in the Organization is limited to the 44 nations represented at the Hot Springs conference, but other nations may be admitted to membership later by a two-thirds majority vote of all the member nations. Initial membership is for a period of not less than five years. At the end of an initial four-year period any member nation may withdraw upon a year's notice.

In addition to making the periodic reports required under article XI, member nations in accepting the constitution assume only three specific obligations to the Organization: (1) to contribute to its expenses, (2) to accord appro-

priate diplomatic privileges to the Organization and its staff, and (3) to respect the international character of the staff's responsibilities. The last provision is designed to safeguard the Organization against any strictly national influence or pressure which might otherwise be exerted against nationals of any country on its staff.

The Conference will meet at least once a year, and each member nation will have one representative and one vote. The Conference will appoint the Director General, who will direct the work of the Organization subject to the general supervision of the Conference and the Executive Committee. The latter will be composed of from 9 to 15 members—appointed by the Conference from among its members or alternates or associates and their advisers—with each nation again limited to one member.

Broad policy-making control of the Organization thus rests with the member nations on a democratic and representative, one nation, one vote basis. The carrying out of the Conference's policies rests with the Director General, appointed by the Conference and subject to its supervision through the Executive Committee. In addition, the Director General will be informed and advised by technical and regional standing committees which the Conference is authorized by the constitution to establish as well as by special conferences of representatives of interested groups or organizations which the Conference is authorized to convene. These standing committees and special conferences will enable the organization to keep in close touch at all times with expert thought and public opinion. They will also help to enlist the public support through which alone the recommendations of the Organization can be carried out in any given country.

The very nature of the Organization, which is primarily advisory in character, requires that it achieve its ends almost exclusively through the excellence of its work and the resulting influence and prestige it is able to build up among the member nations. As a consequence its success or failure as an international body will be determined almost entirely by the competence of its working staff. The Interim Commission was well aware of this, and in article VIII of the constitution it bound the Director General—who will appoint the staff "in accordance with such procedure as may be determined by rules made by the Conference" and to whom the staff is responsible—to select his staff on as wide a geographic basis as possible but "subject to the paramount importance of securing the highest standards of efficiency and of technical competence."

This excellent provision is strengthened by an injunction to further caution which is contained in the explanatory first report. There the Interim Commission advises that in making initial appointments "due regard should be had to the importance of retaining freedom of action to enable the Organization to include in its staff, at a later date, personnel from areas not yet liberated from enemy occupation" and urges that the Organization "make a number of temporary appointments at the outset while taking ample time to choose the permanent staff carefully and awaiting the release from war service of persons of the ability and training needed for its work."

A staff of this caliber, dedicated to the work outlined in the proposed constitution, should assure producers of food everywhere of the firm voice in international councils to which they are entitled. Backed by the authority of knowledge, FAO should be able to point the way to unyielding progress toward freedom from want.

NOTES

[1] Mr. Tolley, Chief of the Bureau of Agricultural Economics, U.S. Department of Agriculture, is the U.S. representative on the United Nations Interim Commission on Food and Agriculture; Mr. Stinebower, Deputy Director, Office of Commercial Policy, Department of State, is the alternate U.S. representative on the Interim Commission.

[2] BULLETIN of July 17, 1943, p. 33.

[3] BULLETIN of Aug. 27, 1944, p. 207.

The General Agreement on Tariffs and Trade; An Article-by-Article Analysis in Layman's Language

Honoré M. Catudal

Only the first portion of Catudal's article summarizing the provisions of the Agreement is presented here. At the time this article was written the author was adviser in the Trade Agreements Division of the Department of State.

INTRODUCTION AND SUMMARY STATEMENT

What Is GATT?

The General Agreement on Tariffs and Trade, or GATT, as it has come to be called, is an international trade agreement entered into by the United States under the Trade Agreements Act. Virtually all of the important trading nations of the free world participate in the GATT.

A technical and complex document, because the problems of international trade are technical and complex, the GATT can be reduced to three simple essentials. It consists, first, of *"schedules"* or lists of tariff "concessions" (i.e. named products for which maximum tariff treatment has been agreed upon), with separate schedules for each "contracting party" (i.e. signatory or participating country). Second, there is a *code* of agreed principles and rules governing the import and export trade of the contracting parties. Third, through periodic meetings of representatives of the participating countries, GATT provides a broad international *forum* for the friendly discussion and settlement of mutual problems of international trade.

The General Agreement is the most comprehensive agreement ever concluded for the reduction of barriers to, and hence for the expansion of, international trade, having regard to the number of participating countries, to the scope of its provisions, and to the volume of trade affected.

Thirty-nine countries are now full contracting parties to the GATT, and in addition several other countries also participate in their work under special, temporary arrangements. Besides the United States, the contracting parties include the countries of the British Commonwealth, most of the countries of Western Europe, and a number of Latin American, African, and Asiatic countries, including Japan. These countries together account for over 80 percent of the international trade of the whole world.

The schedules of tariff concessions in the General Agreement include about 60,000 items in the tariff classifications of the contracting parties and cover more than half of the world's total foreign trade. These tariff concessions include reductions in import duties or commitments to "bind" (i.e. to "freeze" or agree not to increase) specified duties or duty-free treatment and, in some cases, the complete elimination of duties or the reduction or elimination of tariff preferences.

The general provisions of the GATT provide a framework or code of principles and rules to safeguard the tariff concessions against nullification or impairment by other restrictive devices and to supplement the tariff concessions by relaxing other barriers to international trade. These provisions include such basic rules as most-favored-nation treatment (i.e. equal treatment or nondiscrimination) for all contracting parties in tariff, customs, and tax matters, and a general prohibition of quantitative import and export restrictions (e.g. quotas) against the trade of other contracting parties. There are agreed qualifications and exceptions to the general rules under certain carefully defined circumstances. The general provisions also deal with procedural matters, such as the geographic areas covered by GATT, the accession of new countries, amendments, the termination or waiver of obligations, consultation, administration, and various other matters relevant to the agreement as a whole.

Genesis and Development of GATT

From 1934 to World War II the United States used the authority under the Trade Agreements Act to negotiate bilateral trade agreements. In some 10 years such agreements were concluded with 29 countries. It is generally agreed that these bilateral trade agreements helped to slow down the worldwide trend toward ever higher barriers to trade.

By the end of the war, however, it was evident that much remained to be done in the reduction of world trade barriers and that the bilateral agreement had serious limitations as a method of effecting further important reductions.

This was especially true as regards barriers other than tariffs. For example, import quotas, which had become widespread in the period between the two world wars, were being used or held in readiness by many countries as a bargaining weapon or threat against the use of quotas by other countries. Significant limitations could not be agreed to in such fields until most or all important trading countries were ready to undertake similar obligations on a reciprocal basis.

Even in the field of tariffs it was clear that bilateral agreements could not achieve the needed reductions. Countries tended to hold back tariff concessions for fear that other countries not party to such agreements would obtain benefits without giving concessions or assuming corresponding obligations.

Furthermore, the process of negotiating bilateral agreements one by one with each country was extremely time-consuming. At the end of the war there was a pressing need to get agreement among as many nations as possible in order further to reduce trade barriers and avoid the economic conflicts which would inevitably arise if each country

were left to deal with its own difficulties without regard to the effect of its action on other countries. Some other technique which would achieve broader and faster results than bilateral trade agreements was clearly needed.

To meet these difficulties the United States took the initiative in developing a "multilateral" (i.e. many-country, as opposed to the "bilateral" or two-country) approach to the solution of international trade problems. After several years of intensive preparation both here and abroad, including 6 months of continuous negotiations among 23 countries at Geneva in 1947, the General Agreement on Tariffs and Trade was completed on October 30, 1947, and came into force on January 1, 1948, as a "provisional" or interim undertaking by eight important trading nations, including the United States. Since that time many more countries have agreed to apply the GATT and several new rounds of intergovernmental tariff negotiations have taken place—at Annecy, France, in 1949, at Torquay, England, in 1950-51, and again at Geneva in 1955 and 1956. At the present time (early 1961) another general tariff conference is taking place at Geneva.[1]

Today 39 countries are full contracting parties to the General Agreement, others are in the process of accession, and several other countries participate on an interim basis or have become associated with it. The steady growth of this unique international cooperative association reflects the increasing worldwide acceptance of the principles and aims of the GATT and the widely held realization that GATT's practical, commonsense approach and working methods are achieving good results.

The Trade Agreements Authority

The United States is taking part in the 1960-61 GATT tariff conference at Geneva, as it has in previous trade agreement negotiations, under the authority granted by Congress in the trade agreements legislation and in accordance with several Executive orders issued by the President.

The Trade Agreements Act of 1934, as extended and amended, gives the President limited authority to enter into trade agreements with foreign countries whereby the United States agrees to modify, or to bind against increase, tariff duties applying to specified imported products in return for similar concessions by foreign countries on products exported by the United States.

THE CONTRACTING PARTIES TO THE GENERAL AGREEMENT ON TARIFFS AND TRADE

At the present time (June 1961) there are 39 contracting parties to the General Agreement on Tariffs and Trade:

Australia	Italy
Austria	Japan
Belgium	Luxembourg
Brazil	Malaya
Burma	Netherlands
Canada	New Zealand
Ceylon	Nicaragua
Chile	Nigeria
Cuba	Norway
Czechoslovakia	Pakistan
Denmark	Peru
Dominican Republic	Rhodesia and Nyasaland,
Finland	Federation of
France	Sierra Leone
Germany, Federal	South Africa, Republic of
Republic of	Sweden
Ghana	Turkey
Greece	United Kingdom
Haiti	United States of America
India	Uruguay
Indonesia	

Under the Trade Agreements Extension Act of 1958 (Public Law 85-686), extending the authority until June 30, 1962, the President is authorized generally to reduce U.S. duties, in annual stages, by not more than 20 percent of the rates existing on July 1, 1958. Alternatively, he may reduce any rate of duty by 2 percentage points ad valorem, and he may reduce to 50 percent ad valorem any rate which is in excess of 50 percent. The law also authorizes him to agree to bind duty-free treatment for articles on the free list and to bind existing customs or excise treatment of imported goods. The 1958 act likewise authorizes the President to increase tariff rates up to 50 percent above the rates existing on July 1, 1934; generally speaking, these latter are the rates of the Smoot-Hawley Tariff Act of 1930.[2]

In carrying out his responsibilities under the Trade Agreements Act, the President is assisted by a network of interdepartmental committees, so organized as to make available to him information and advice from all Departments and agencies of the Government concerned with foreign trade— from the technical level up to the Cabinet and from interested persons and organizations, as well

as the general public. Three principal interdepartmental committees have been established by Executive order, the Committee on Trade Agreements, the Committee for Reciprocity Information, and the Cabinet-level Trade Policy Committee.[3]

Summary of General Provisions and Protocol of Provisional Application

Before beginning an article-by-article analysis of GATT, it will be helpful to keep in mind a summary of the principal parts of the General Agreement and the Protocol of Provisional Application.

The general provisions of GATT are divided into a preamble and three parts, as follows:

1. The preamble states the broad objectives of the agreement.
2. Part I gives legal effect to the schedules of tariff concessions and lays down the basic rule of most-favored-nation treatment, or nondiscrimination, in tariff and customs matters generally (articles I and II).
3. Part II covers trade barriers other than tariffs, including internal taxes, quotas, and customs formalities, as well as the "escape clause," general exceptions, etc. (articles III-XXIII).
4. Part III deals mainly with procedural matters, such as the territorial application and administration of GATT, its definitive entry into force, amendments, the accession of new contracting parties, the modification of schedules, withdrawal from the agreement, etc. (articles XXIV-XXXV).

The Protocol of Provisional Application of October 30, 1947, is the formal instrument or document whereby the United States and other countries which took part in the original GATT negotiations undertake to apply the General Agreement. In substance, in this protocol the signatory countries agree to apply *provisionally* (a) parts I and III of the General Agreement and (b) part II of the GATT to the fullest extent not inconsistent with legislation existing on October 30, 1947. Such provisional application may be withdrawn upon 60 days' notice by a country desiring to terminate its GATT obligations. This is equivalent to saying that contracting parties, under the Protocol of Provisional Application, undertake to put into effect the schedules of tariff concessions and to grant general most-favored-nation treatment on and after agreed dates but are not required immediately to make changes in their existing laws which are inconsistent with the GATT provisions relating to nontariff trade barriers (e.g. quotas), and, finally, that they may withdraw from GATT on 60 days' notice.

Since the original GATT negotiations in 1947, new contracting parties acceding to the General Agreement have, in subsequent protocols or other instruments, undertaken to apply GATT in substantially the same way as set forth in the 1947 Protocol of Provisional Application.

In 1954-55 a thoroughgoing review of all the general provisions of GATT was undertaken at Geneva by representatives of the contracting parties for the purpose of strengthening the agreement and making it a more effective instrument for the development of a sound system of world trade. After months of intensive intergovernmental negotiations, this review resulted in the drawing up of several protocols to amend various provisions. In accordance with the terms for amending GATT contained in article XXX, some of these amendments could not become effective until accepted or ratified by all the contracting parties, while other amendments were to go into effect for those parties accepting them upon acceptance by two-thirds of the contracting parties. A considerable number of the amendments drawn up at the 1954-55 review session were of the latter kind and became effective for two-thirds of the contracting parties, including the United States, on October 7, 1957.

The article-by-article analysis of the provisions of the General Agreement which follows is based on the text of the GATT as amended to include the amendments which became effective for the United States on October 7, 1957, and February 15, 1961.[4]

NOTES

[1] For an article by Mr. Catudal on "The 1960–61 GATT Tariff Conference," see BULLETIN of Feb. 22, 1960, p. 291.

[2] For a two-part article by Mr. Catudal with a section-by-section analysis of the trade agreements legislation, see *ibid.*, Dec. 22, 1958, p. 1013, and Dec. 29, 1958, p. 1050.

[3] For an article by Mr. Catudal on "How a Trade Agreement Is Made," see *ibid.*, Feb. 24, 1958, p. 286. This article gives detailed information concerning the interdepartmental trade agreements organization and procedures.

[4] This amended text is printed in *The General Agreement on Tariffs and Trade,* Department of State publication 7182, which will be available from the Superintendent of Documents, U.S. Government Printing Office, Washington 25, D. C.

The International Atomic Energy Agency, The First Year

U. S. Department of State

This report of the first year's activities includes some historical background. Included also is information about the purposes and structure of the Agency as well as its relationships with other international organizations.

INTRODUCTION

On July 29, 1957, a new international organization came into being—the International Atomic Energy Agency. Formed with the unanimous approval of 80 members of the United Nations, this organization is designed "to accelerate and enlarge the contribution of atomic energy to peace, health and prosperity throughout the world."

The IAEA is not a political assembly but a technical organization which, it is hoped, may eventually pay its own way.

. . . The Agency will supply nuclear fuels and act as a wholesaler, distributor, and purveyor for international transactions involving atomic energy supplies and equipment.

. . . It will function as a supplier of scientific, technical, and engineering services.

. . . It will sponsor and assist research activities throughout the world and may establish its own facilities for research.

. . . It will assist member states in constructing reactors and will procure and supply reactor fuels.

. . . It will undertake to establish international regulation of the disposal of radioactive wastes and standards of health and safety for the guidance of users of atomic energy throughout the world.

. . . It will conduct an extensive program to train scientists and technicians to meet the needs of developing atomic energy programs all over the world.

. . . It will be a center for the collection and distribution of information on peaceful uses of atomic energy.

The IAEA has wide powers of inspection and control to make sure that none of the assistance it gives, nor any of the materials it supplies, are diverted to military purposes. The Agency's experience in devising and implementing effective safeguards may well serve as a useful precedent and guide for future disarmament proposals.

The agency provides a means by which fissionable material may be progressively removed from military stockpiles and placed at the service of science and industry. With the assurance that Agency assistance cannot be used to enhance the military potential of other countries, the atomically advanced nations of the world can share their knowledge and their materials with confidence.

THE FIRST YEAR

The IAEA has now completed its first year of operation. This has been a year necessarily devoted in considerable measure to organizational problems. However, the Agency has also begun its program of operations and has undertaken a number of important projects.

This year has been marked by a significant increase in the Agency's membership. On July 29, 1957, when the IAEA treaty entered into force, 26 members had ratified the statute. By the opening session of the first General Conference on October 1, the membership was 54 nations, and by the end of the conference, 59. On August 1, 1958, 67 nations were IAEA members.

During this year the Agency's operations continued to be characterized by the same spirit of cooperation, of practical realism, and of determina-

SOURCE: Reprinted from *The International Atomic Energy Agency, the First Year.* Washington, Government Printing Office, 1958 (U.S. Department of State. *International Organization and Conference Series*, I, 37.)

tion to devise new approaches to the problems of atomic energy that marked the early negotiations which established the Agency. The IAEA today gives promise of having made an effective start on the road to achieving the goal set by President Eisenhower in 1953 when he first proposed the Agency's creation—". . . To find the way by which the miraculous inventiveness of man shall not be dedicated to his death, but consecrated to his life."

HOW THE AGENCY BEGAN

From the first days when scientists released the power of the atom, the U.S. has sought to find a way by which the destructive power of atomic energy could be controlled and its potential for bettering human life made available throughout the world. In 1946 when we still had a monopoly of the techniques of producing nuclear explosions, we offered to give to an international agency the exclusive right to manufacture, own, and utilize atomic energy materials. A vital part of our plan was an effective and thorough system of inspection and control to insure that no nation could secretly manufacture nuclear weapons. Despite years of negotiation within and outside the United Nations, this plan as well as others to control the destructive force of the atom have been denied to the world because of the refusal of the Soviet Union to agree to any kind of an effective inspection system.

Seeking a way to end this stalemate and to bring to a halt the costly and dangerous trend toward amassing ever-larger stocks of nuclear weapons, President Eisenhower on December 8, 1953, proposed to the U.N. General Assembly that there be created under the aegis of the United Nations an International Atomic Energy Agency, which would "initiate at least a new approach to the many difficult problems that must be solved . . . if the world is to shake off the inertia imposed by fear, and is to make positive progress toward peace."

The President's plan was designed to accomplish the following purposes:

It would provide a way to bring the benefits of peaceful uses of atomic energy to all the peoples of the world despite the deadlock with the Soviet Union over the question of disarmament.

It would encourage worldwide investigation into the peaceful uses of atomic energy by making radioactive research tools available to scientists all over the world.

It would begin to diminish the potential destructive power of the world's atomic stockpiles by encouraging the channeling of atomic energy materials into an international pool for peaceful purposes.

It would demonstrate to the peoples of all nations that the great powers of the world are interested in human aspirations rather than armaments of war.

The President's proposal was widely acclaimed throughout the world and there was evidence of new hope that the material benefits of atomic energy might contribute to the solution of some of the world's most pressing economic problems and that the establishment of the agency might have great significance in the attainment of the peaceful world which all mankind so earnestly desires. The Soviet Union, which first evidenced a negative attitude toward the President's proposal, was eventually led to cooperate in the face of a world public opinion which universally favored the Agency's creation.

While the initial obstruction of the Soviet Union delayed the formation of the IAEA, the United States proceeded with its own atoms-for-peace program. The U.S. program has made available to other free countries both technical and material assistance in the training of nuclear scientists and technicians and in the building in other countries of nuclear reactors.

Throughout 1954 and 1955 negotiations looking toward the establishment of the IAEA continued. By the fall of 1955 the Soviet Union had reversed its negative position and entered into the ever-widening group of nations actively preparing the Agency's statute.

In October 1956, at the largest international conference ever convened in world history, unanimous agreement was reached on the Agency's statute. Representatives of 70 nations signed the statute before this conference adjourned. The statute provided that the Agency would come into being with the deposit of the ratifications of 18 nations, including at least 3 of the principal atomic powers. This condition was fulfilled on July 29, 1957, with the deposit of the U.S. ratification, and the International Atomic Energy Agency was born.

ORGANIZATION

The IAEA is an autonomous international organization which makes regular reports to the appropriate organs of the United Nations. An 18-member Preparatory Commission[1] drafted a treaty defining the organization's relationship with the United Nations, which was approved by the member nations at the first General Conference in the fall of 1957. The Agency will also establish treaty relationships and cooperative working arrangements with the specialized agencies of the United Nations.

Any nation which is a member of the United Nations or of the specialized agencies was eligible to become a charter member of the IAEA. In addition, other countries may be admitted by the General Conference on the recommendation of the Board of Governors if these countries are deemed willing and able to carry out the obligations of membership and observe the principles of the U.N. Charter.

The IAEA has a *General Conference* composed of representatives of all member nations, each nation having one vote. Its responsibilities include giving approval to Agency budgets, applications for membership, and amendments to the statute. The General Conference also has advisory functions and may discuss any matter relating to the work of the Agency and make recommendations to the Board of Governors.

The *Board of Governors* is composed of 23 members, 10 of which are elected by the General Conference, the remaining 13 being chosen by the outgoing Board of Governors (or, in the case of the first Board, by the members of the Preparatory Commission). The atomically advanced countries (Canada, France, the United Kingdom, the United States, and the U.S.S.R.) are, in effect, granted permanent representation on the Board. Provision is also made for membership for the most atomically advanced nations in each of the geographic areas of the world not represented by the above group, and for adequate representation from all areas regardless of the state of atomic technology in the member states.

The nations designated as Board members by the Preparatory Commission were as follows:

*Canada *France *United Kingdom *United States *U.S.S.R.	World leaders in atomic energy technology
*Australia *Brazil *India *Japan *Union of South Africa	Most advanced nations in the geographical areas not represented by the first five

Czechoslovakia Portugal	Suppliers of source materials
Sweden	Supplier of technical assistance

Elected by the General Conference were:

*Argentina	*Republic of Korea
Egypt	*Pakistan
(United Arab Republic)	Peru
Guatemala	*Rumania
Indonesia	*Turkey
Italy	

*Indicates nations which will serve 2-year terms. The others will be replaced at the close of the 2d General Conference, which will convene at Vienna on September 22, 1958. Czechoslovakia and Portugal will be replaced by Belgium and Poland and Denmark will replace Sweden; and replacements will be elected by the General Conference for Guatemala, Indonesia, Italy, Peru, and the United Arab Republic. (The latter five countries may succeed themselves.)

Dr. Pavel Winkler of Czechoslovakia served as the Board's chairman during the Agency's first year, and representatives of Canada and Japan were chosen as vice-chairmen.

The statute provides for a permanent *staff* which is selected on the basis of scientific and technical qualifications from all member countries. The staff is headed by a *Director General,* who is appointed by the Board for a 4-year term. The first Director General, unanimously chosen by the Board, is W. Sterling Cole of the United States, Member of Congress from 1935 to 1957, and a member of the Congressional Joint Committee on Atomic Energy from the time of its creation in 1946 until 1957. The 1958 budget authorized the hiring of 167 officers and 202 general service personnel.

The staff and its Director General are responsible to the Board of Governors and are independent of control by any national government.

The staff has been divided into various specialized units which will handle the Agency's functions. There are, for example, Divisions of Isotopes, Reactors, Exchange and Training, and Technical Information.

THE FIRST GENERAL CONFERENCE

The concept of an international organization dedicated to the peaceful uses of atomic energy holds great promise for the welfare of the world's peoples and for the attainment of world peace. The statute of the organization is broad and flexible and provides an adequate framework for the Agency's potential growth. But that statute had to be translated into a practical working organization which could effectively deal with the problems which must be solved if the Agency is to fulfill its promise. The organizational problems facing the first meetings of the Board of Governors and the General Conference and the newly recruited staff, while less dramatic and perhaps less inspiring than the substantive problems of atomic energy utilization, were none the less of vital importance to the ultimate success of the Agency's mission.

Careful preparations were made for the Agency's first session. The 18-nation Preparatory Commission had worked for many months to make recommendations and formulate specific problems on which the Board of Governors and the General Conference were to take action.

The first General Conference convened on October 1, 1957, at Vienna with delegates from 54 member nations, observer delegates from 11 nations, and representatives of the United Nations and seven specialized agencies attending.

President Eisenhower, in his message sent to the members at the opening session of the General Conference, set the keynote for the meeting. He said:

"No other Conference in history has ever begun more auspiciously. The Statute . . . which you are about to implement, represents the will and the aspirations of more nations than ever before subscribed to an international treaty.

". . . The peoples of the world . . . look hopefully to you to further the practical program whereby the fissioned atom will cease to be a symbol of fear and will be transformed into the means of providing them with richer, healthier and happier lives. . . .

"The opportunities which now lie before you are many; the challenges which you will have to meet and solve will be great. But with faith and continued friendly cooperation, such as has marked the creation of the Agency, our generation can make of atomic energy a gift for which mankind will be forever grateful."

While most of the members revealed their high ambitions and fervent hopes for the eventual broad role of the Agency, there was also evidence throughout the meetings of an acute awareness of the enormity of the problems faced. As a consequence the initial program for the Agency, which was adopted by the General Conference on the recommendation of the Board of Governors, was realistic and cautious.

The first steps taken by the Board and the General Conference were to adopt rules of procedure, to attend to housekeeping details such as arrangements for the Agency's permanent headquarters in Vienna, to approve the treaty defining the Agency's relationship with the United Nations, to provide for the recruitment of a competent staff, and to prepare regulations governing its conduct.

It was decided that member states which were not represented on the Board of Governors should be allowed to have permanent nonparticipating observers at sessions of that body so that all members could be fully informed of the Agency's plans and activities.

THE BUDGET

Under the terms of the IAEA statute, the administrative expenses of the organization, such as salaries for the staff, costs of maintaining IAEA information facilities, and the cost of common operational programs, are assessed to member states on roughly the same basis as contributions to the United Nations. However, the expenses incurred in connection with particular technical assistance projects and the supply of atomic energy materials are not assessed to members. The supplying of materials will be done on a business basis. Countries making materials available to the Agency will be reimbursed and countries receiving the materials will pay for them. It is anticipated that eventually such transactions will generate revenues which can be used for technical assistance purposes.

However, until the supply function of the Agency is in full-scale operation, technical assistance and other operating activities must depend upon voluntary contributions by member states. (The Board of Governors has recommended that the Agency participate in the U.N. Expanded Program of Technical Assistance, under which it would be entitled to receive funds from the United Nations, as do the specialized agencies such as the World Health Organization and the Food and Agriculture Organization.)

The regular administrative budget totaled $4,089,000, including $624,000 to be used to repay a loan from the United Nations for the costs of the operation of the Preparatory Commission. The Agency also programed a Working Capital Fund of $2 million. The United States was assessed $33\frac{1}{3}$ percent of the administrative budget and contributed a similar percentage to the Working Capital Fund, making a total contribution of $2,029,465. In addition, the Agency provided for a General Fund of $250,000 to be raised by voluntary contributions. This fund is being used exclusively to provide fellowships for training in aspects of nuclear science. The United States has agreed to match contributions made by other nations to the fund up to a maximum U.S. contribution of $125,000.

INITIAL PROGRAM

The initial program established by the Agency was not intended to be limited to the 1958 calendar year. Many of the projects already undertaken or in the planning stage are to be continued and expanded during 1959 and succeeding years.

Technical assistance to underdeveloped areas is cited in the IAEA statute as a major element of the Agency's program and forms an important part of many of its initial undertakings. Because Agency membership extends to all regions of the world and includes countries advanced in the technology of atomic energy as well as underdeveloped countries, the Agency is uniquely suited to foster the use of atomic energy to narrow the tremendous gaps in economic development and well-being which exist in the world.

One of the immediate forms of technical assistance to be provided by the Agency will be surveys made, on request, by fact-finding teams and expert missions in the underdeveloped countries with the purpose of determining how the services of the Agency can best be utilized in applying atomic energy to the solution of that country's problems.

RADIOISOTOPES

Initially the Agency will probably concentrate upon the application of radioisotopes, since this is a field in which immediate and important benefits can be gained without the expenditure of large amounts of capital.

Radioisotopes are substances made radioactive artificially by being placed in a reactor. They have the unique property of being detectable by means of a Geiger counter in quantities as small as a billionth of a billionth of a gram. By introducing a small quantity of these substances into plants or into the bodies of animals or man, it is possible to study the complex processes of life and growth. When radioisotopes are introduced into industrial processes, they act like a powerful X-ray machine, detecting flaws or weaknesses in the densest metals.

Since 1946, when radioisotopes first became available in the United States, science and industry have developed thousands of new uses for them. They are being used in the diagnosis and treatment of cancer, leukemia, and disorders of the thyroid gland. In the laboratory they provide vital information about the cause, control, and cure of countless other diseases. They can be used to sterilize antibiotics and hospital equipment and to preserve foods.

In agriculture, radioisotopes have shown farmers how to use fertilizers more efficiently to increase crop yields. Mixed with fertilizers, they have shown when and how the vital nutrients are absorbed into growing plants, thus demonstrating the most efficient method of applying fertilizers. Radioisotopes have been used to trace cattle and poultry feed through the bodies of the animals. Scientists have been able to tell farmers how to correct deficiencies in poultry and cattle diets. Radiation is being used to develop better varieties of some staple crops.

In industry today radioisotopes are commonplace, and their use is doubling each year. The applications range from testing the efficiency of washing machines to new techniques of production control in steel plants.

In order to spread the knowledge of these and other applications of radioisotopes throughout the world, the IAEA will send special isotope teams to member states at their request to demonstrate the uses of these materials in the solution of particular problems and to assist in the training of technicians in the proper methods of using them.

The United States has already made available to the Agency two complete mobile isotope laboratories to be used for training and demonstration purposes.

THE FELLOWSHIP PROGRAM

One of the most lasting effects of the Agency's activities will be achieved through its training and fellowship activities. The scientists and technicians so trained will be able to apply their new knowledge to the problems of their countries, and they will, in turn, give further training to their own nationals.

The $250,000 appropriated this year for fellowships in the Agency's General Fund will provide training for about 50 individuals for periods up to 2 years. In addition, a number of member states have made available about 140 fellowships for 1958 in the institutions of their countries.

The Board of Governors has already established the criteria for awarding these fellowships and is accepting and reviewing applications. The fields covered by this fellowship training are many and include techniques of discovering and processing radioactive ores, operation techniques for nuclear reactors, and the application of nuclear tools in biological, medical, and agricultural research.

By 1959 the fellowship program will be in full operation. Besides its contribution of $125,000 to the Agency fellowship fund, the U.S. has offered 120 scholarships to foreign nationals to be selected by the Agency. Other member states, too, have offered similar training opportunities in their institutions. Once this program becomes more widely known throughout the world, the number of applicants requesting training is bound to increase, and it is hoped that the services of the Agency and of the member states in offering opportunities for study will be able to keep pace with the increased demand. The 1959 program will, in addition, provide not only training fellowships but also research fellowships to enable scientists to conduct research using nuclear tools which are not available in their own countries.

REGIONAL TRAINING CENTERS

One of the important projects in the Agency's initial program is the initiation of procedures for studying the needs for cooperatively financed regional training centers in various areas. At the request of member states, teams of experts will survey the needs and resources for training in atomic energy techniques in a given area and, on the basis of these studies, may decide to assist the requesting countries in planning, building, and operating such centers. Early in 1958 a working group of six experts, including two members of the Agency's staff, was sent to Latin America to make the first such survey.

It is anticipated that during 1959 there will be other requests for similar surveys.

EXCHANGE OF SCIENTISTS

A number of member states have already requested the Agency to provide them with the services of experts and consultants to assist them in solving particular problems involving atomic energy. The Agency is compiling information on the availability of scientists for such assignments, and it is likely that exchange activity will begin during the latter part of 1958.

The program will provide for the exchange of professors between universities to give special courses in fields such as nuclear physics and radiochemistry. Visiting scientists will be asked to hold courses and seminars in special techniques applied to research problems. Experts and consultants will also be sent to requesting countries to advise on problems related to the training of technical and scientific personnel in the universities and institutes of the requesting countries.

THE LIBRARY

Member states have already contributed more than 40,000 volumes and documents to the IAEA to form the nucleus of its basic technical library. In addition the Agency has made an arrangement with the central library of the Physical Institute of the University of Vienna so that the Agency staff and scientists of member nations receiving Agency assistance will also have access to that extensive collection.

The Agency's library will not only be of direct use to the IAEA staff but will also make it possible for the Agency to supply information to member states.

In 1959 the library will initiate a comprehensive documentation service covering the laws and regulations of member states which apply to peaceful uses of atomic energy, since there is no world center for information of this nature. The library will also act as a clearinghouse for current papers and information on developments in the field of atomic energy. It will receive and classify documents from member states and on request will supply bibliographies, translations, or abstracts of special interest to requesting states.

TERMINOLOGY

Nuclear science is today is its infancy compared to other fields of science. Each day in laboratories all over the world new terms are developed to describe materials and phenomena. One of the Agency's functions will be to coordinate and standardize this terminology so that scientists the world over will, in a sense, speak the same specialized language of nuclear science.

CONFERENCES

An important way in which the Agency will promote the exchange of information on peaceful uses of atomic energy will be through international meetings. Here the world's scientists can exchange ideas and describe the results of their studies. The Agency is planning during 1959 to sponsor meetings to discuss such topics as radioactive waste disposal and the economics of nuclear energy. The Agency is also engaged in compiling a catalog of all international scientific meetings sponsored by private organizations whose discussions may have a bearing on the peaceful uses of atomic energy.

One of the Agency's first tasks in the conference field was to render assistance in the preparations for the 2d International Conference on Peaceful Uses of Atomic Energy, which will convene at Geneva, Switzerland, on September 1, 1958.

NUCLEAR POWER

During the next 10 years the world's requirements for electric power are expected to double. But in many countries large-scale expansion of electric power output is virtually impossible. Adequate supplies of the conventional fuels used for power generation—coal and oil—are not available in all countries. And many countries do not have the economic means to increase their imports of these fuels. Even in countries which are well supplied with coal and oil the future demands of industry and individual consumers may deplete existing resources and result in high production costs and shortages.

In countries such as the United States, which today have plentiful supplies of conventional fuels, nuclear power generation is not yet economically competitive with conventional methods of power generation. But in the countries where conventional fuels are expensive or in short supply, even at the present state of reactor technology, nuclear power is economically feasible. In these countries nuclear power plants can bring the most immediate large-scale benefits.

Before the use of nuclear power can become widespread throughout the world, there are many problems which must be solved. Developments in less costly methods of constructing reactors will be important if underdeveloped countries are to be able to afford nuclear power. Countries building reactors must have access to reliable supplies of the special reactor fuels such as uranium-235 and plutonium, which are expensive and difficult to produce. Other problems include the development of health and safety standards which will insure that the workers in nuclear power installations and the people residing in the vicinity will not be exposed to dangerous amounts of radiation. Nuclear reactors generate radioactive waste materials which remain dangerous for many years. Studies must be made to discover methods of disposing of these wastes so that they do not contaminate the earth's surface.

It is anticipated that eventually the largest part of the Agency's operations will be devoted to dealing with fuels for nuclear reactors. The atomically advanced nations will make these available for purchase by the Agency, which in turn will be able to guarantee to member states dependable supplies of these fuels at stable prices.

The initial program of the Agency in the reactor field is concentrated on the collection and dissemination of information on reactor technology and related problems. During 1959 it will devote itself particularly to the study of small and medium power reactors which are needed in certain of the less developed areas.

A number of countries have already offered to make available to the Agency supplies of nuclear fuels and source materials. The United States has offered 5,000 kilograms of uranium-235 and has offered to match all contributions made by other nations until mid-1960. The Soviet Union has offered 50 kilograms and the United Kingdom, 20. Brazil, Canada, Portugal, the United States, and the U.S.S.R. have also offered source materials, and Australia and Yugoslavia have indicated that they may be able to make source materials available at a future date.

The staff is now collecting information on the exact nature of the materials offered for purchase and the terms under which they can be acquired by the Agency. Its task will then be to determine the methods by which these materials will be transported and stored and made available to requesting countries.

HEALTH AND SAFETY AND WASTE DISPOSAL

The widespread use of atomic energy for peaceful purposes could well be delayed for many years because of fears on the part of potential user-nations that atomic energy installations might constitute a threat to the life and health of their people. One of the Agency's most important tasks will be to establish standards of health and safety for all operations conducted by the organization or under its auspices and to evaluate the specific hazards of each project submitted to the Agency. The Agency is to undertake studies leading to the establishment of regulations for the international transport of radioactive materials. It will also promote research and develop standards with respect to waste disposal.

Since the initial program of the Agency will concentrate upon the utilization of radioisotopes, its first health and safety activities will be related to this field. A large number of users of radioisotopes will be provided with information and advice on the proper methods of handling these radioactive materials. Eventually, of course, the Agency will also fill a regulatory role with regard to health and safety in connection with reactors and other major installations assisted by the Agency, and the standards it establishes will serve as a guide for atomic energy installations all over the world.

During 1959 the IAEA will give assistance to less developed countries having special health and safety problems, particularly those incidental to accidents in isotope work. Small countries cannot afford to set up and train an extensive staff in the wide variety of procedures which may well never be required but which must be on hand for a possible emergency. The Agency is preparing itself to provide emergency services to such countries and will be able to undertake such functions as the performance of tests to determine the gravity of any accident and advise and assist on corrective steps to be taken.

During 1959 the Agency will also undertake a special study with regard to the disposal of radioactive wastes in the sea. This study was requested by a resolution adopted on April 27, 1958, by the U.N. Conference on the Law of the Sea meeting at Geneva. In consultation with other bodies having an interest in marine biology or oceanography, the Agency is acquiring information and basic knowledge which will make it possible to formulate proposals for regulations regarding this aspect of radioactive waste disposal.

The Agency is also cooperating with the International Labor Organization, which is particularly interested in the protection of industrial workers, in drawing up regulations and codes of safety for workers in atomic energy installations. In addition the Agency will also assist member states to secure the technical services needed to implement such regulations.

SAFEGUARDS AND INSPECTION

In the Agency statute, East and West for the first time agreed that an international body should have wide powers to insure the observance of an international agreement. The statute provides that the Agency's inspectors "shall have access at all times to all places and data and to any person" involved in Agency-assisted projects, to make sure that Agency assistance is not diverted to any military purpose.

Eventually this safeguard and inspection purpose will be of great importance. Its development will go hand-in-hand with the development of the supply function of the Agency, and the first phase of the Agency's work in this field is necessarily of a preparatory character.

The IAEA is collecting information on the problems involved in accounting and controlling the materials produced in atomic energy installations which could be used for military purposes. It may in the near future place contracts for certain types of studies and research. A director of the Division of Safeguards, Roger Marshall Smith of Canada, has been appointed, and the Agency is engaged in recruiting additional personnel to assist in the development of an effective inspection system.

As the Agency's safeguard procedures are developed, it is hoped that they will be applied to atomic energy activities other than those assisted by the Agency itself. In June 1958 the United States and the European Atomic Energy Community (EURATOM) agreed that, when the Agency procedures have been developed, they will consider the feasibility of asking the Agency to apply

safeguards to EURATOM projects assisted by the
United States.

THE SECOND GENERAL CONFERENCE

The 2d General Conference of the IAEA will
convene at the Agency's headquarters at Vienna
on September 22, 1958. Among the items on the
provisional agenda are the question of the Agency's participation in the U.N. Expanded Technical
Assistance Program, measures to obtain voluntary
contributions to the General Fund, relations with
specialized agencies as well as relations with regional intergovernmental organizations such as
EURATOM, and rules for granting consultative
status to nongovernmental organizations.

The most important measure will be adoption of
the 1959 program and budget, which will probably
include items such as: technical assistance to member states, particularly in the field of isotope utilization; the development of information, training,
and exchange activities; a series of conferences and
studies looking toward the formulation of health
and safety and waste disposal regulations; and
further work on the development of a system of
inspection and safeguards in connection with the
Agency's supply functions. The proposed administrative budget to be assessed to member states in
1959 is $5,225,000. A General Fund of
$1,500,000, to be raised by voluntary contribu-
tions, has also been proposed by the Board of Governors for projects such as the building of an
Agency laboratory, an expanded fellowship program, and economic, technical, and research assistance programs.

PROMISE OF THE FUTURE

In future generations mankind may well look
back to the founding of the International Atomic
Energy Agency as one of the first great steps toward ending the "balance of terror" wherein the
great powers have confronted one another in fear
and in the hostility born of fear. For, while much
remains to be done, the IAEA is at least making a
start toward solving some of the world's great
problems which contribute to international
tension.

The Agency's work, coordinated with the programs of the specialized agencies of the United

Nations, can help in the attack against man's common enemies—hunger, disease, and poverty. It can
help the world's farmers to raise their production
of food. It can help man to understand and eventually to cure some of the world's dreaded diseases. It can help to provide the electric power
by which underdeveloped nations can increase
their industrial productivity, and it can provide
assistance in utilizing radioisotopes to promote industrial efficiency throughout the world.

Through the cooperation of all nations in the
struggle against man's common enemies, the
Agency can help build the habits of cooperation
and the mutual confidence and trust on which
world peace must be based.

Through the standardization of health and safety
practices, the Agency can help to assure that the
widespread use of atomic energy will not constitute a threat to the health and safety of the
world's people.

By promoting the exchange of information and
encouraging international cooperation in research,
it can accelerate the development of new and better methods of using atomic energy for peace.

The inspection functions of the IAEA, unique
among international organizations, can be a first
step toward the real goal of universal atomic inspection. Through the Agency's work, some of
the great scientists of our time can devote their efforts to devising and testing the practical measures
which will make it possible to assure that the
power of the atom is used only for mankind's
benefit.

The IAEA provides a way by which the great
powers of the world may be encouraged to diminish their stockpiles of nuclear weapons by channeling atomic energy materials into peaceful uses.
The world can in this way create a device which
will siphon off nuclear materials from weapons
stockpiles into productive uses which will result in
financial gain and economic benefits.

The United States, which took the lead in establishing the International Atomic Energy Agency,
will continue to devote itself wholeheartedly to
the accomplishment of the Agency's great objectives. It will encourage the widest possible participation by nations great and small in the work of
the Agency.

While the IAEA is not a panacea which can solve
all of mankind's problems, the United States
firmly believes that it provides a means by which
men today may take practical and important steps
toward a better world and a peaceful world.

NOTES

[1] The members of the Preparatory Commission were Argentina, Australia, Belgium, Brazil, Canada, Czechoslovakia, Egypt (the United Arab Republic), France, India, Indonesia, Japan, Pakistan, Peru, Portugal, the Union of South Africa, the U.S.S.R., the United Kingdom, and the United States.

Report of the United Nations Educational, Scientific, and Cultural Organization (1970)

UNESCO

This annual report by UNESCO to the United Nations Economic and Social Council is an example of the reports made to the UN by the specialized agencies. The report covers the programs carried out during the year and the administration of the agency during the period under review.

1. The Director-General has the honour to present to the Economic and Social Council, at its fifty first session, the report of the Organization's activities in 1970.

2. This short analytical summary of the major developments which are likely to be of interest to the Council is presented in compliance with the requests contained in the Council's resolutions 1458 (XLVII) and 1548 (XLIX) regarding the form and contents of these analytical summaries.

3. Pursuant to the recommendation contained in paragraph 7 (f) of resolution 1450 (XLVII), this summary also refers to the Implementation of the Declaration on the Granting of Independence to Colonial Countries and Peoples by the Specialized Agencies and the international institutions associated with the United Nations, notably in connexion with general resolution 8 adopted on 7 November 1970 by the General Conference of Unesco at its sixteenth session.

4. Council members wishing to have more details concerning Unesco activities listed in this analytical summary or on items not included are invited to refer to the *Report of the Director-General on the Activities of the Organization in 1970* which has been submitted to all Member States in March 1971 in accordance with Article VI.3 b of the Constitution. Copies of the report are available to members of the Council.

5. By definition the following analytical summary is selective; it describes the most important activities of the Organization during 1970, but does not review the developments of all of its traditional on-going projects. This summary does reflect, however, the general orientation of Unesco's programme, as determined by its governing organs in the light not only of the Organization's constitutional responsibilities in its fields of competence, but also of overall efforts and trends of the United Nations system, as expressed in various resolutions of the Economic and Social Council and the General Assembly.

6. This general orientation permeated the activities of the Organization, starting with International Education Year which was called for by the General Assembly, the Economic and Social Council and the General Conference of Unesco and conceived as a special contribution to the preparations for the Second United Nations Development Decade. Whether in the fields of education, science, culture or communication, not only has Unesco been furthering the rôle of man as a resource of development, but it has been concerned with the effects of development on man and his relations to the environment. It has pursued its objectives of peace and the promotion of human rights through appropriate activities which include actions in favour of racial equality in a world free of colonial or other domination.

CONSTITUTIONAL DEVELOPMENTS AND ACTIVITIES OF THE MAJOR ORGANS OF THE ORGANIZATION

7. There have been no constitutional developments in 1970. As requested in Council resolution 1548 (XLIX), two organizational charts are included in this report; one describes the structure

SOURCE: Reprinted from *Report of the United Nations Education, Scientific and Cultural Organization*. N.Y., United Nations, 1971. (UN Doc. E/4975) pp. 1-34.

of the Secretariat of Unesco in 1969-1970, the other the structure approved in 1970 for 1971-1972. At its sixteenth session (October-November 1970) the General Conference approved the following three changes: (a) the establishment of an Office of Pre-Programming, under the supervision of a new Assistant Director-General and directly responsible to the Director-General; (b) the creation of a Department of Preservation and Development of Cultural Heritage in the Sector of Social Sciences, Human Sciences and Culture; (c) the creation of a Bureau of Relations with Member States and International Organizations and Programmes as a result of the merger of the Bureau of Relations with Member States and the Bureau of Relations with International Organizations and Programmes. Furthermore, the Management Division previously under the Bureau of the Budget, was given full responsibility for the organization of electronic data processing and made a part of the Office of the Director-General as Office of Management and Data Processing.

8. *The Executive Board* of Unesco held three sessions in 1970:

    84th session—4 May to 19 June
    85th session—21 September to 8 October and
        10 November
    86th session—16 to 18 November

9. *The General Conference* of Unesco held its sixteenth session from 12 October to 14 November 1970. The resolutions which it adopted as well as the decisions of the above-mentioned sessions of the Executive Board are referred to under relevant programme activities or administrative and budgetary questions, respectively in Chapter II and Chapter V of the present report. Three significant resolutions of a more general character which determine the orientation of the Unesco programme and the Organization's overall policy were adopted by the General Conference:

    —Resolution 7 on Directives concerning future programme;
    —Resolution 8 which deals inter alia with Unesco's contribution to peace and the Organization's tasks with respect to elimination of colonialism;
    —Resolution 9 on the Evaluation of the results of the First Department Decade in Unesco's field of competence, and draft programmes of the Organization for the Second Decade. In view of the importance of resolutions 8 and 9 in relation to the Economic and Social Council and the General Assembly resolutions, their full texts are reproduced in annexes I and II of this report.

10. As regards resolution 7 it invites the Director-General to continue to present every two years a *six-year medium-term outline plan* as "it constitutes a suitable framework for the formulation of directives concerning future programmes and makes possible the rationalization of the methods employed for preparing draft programmes and budgets for ensuing biennia," making it even more possible to translate into action the Organization's desire for renovation on a continuing basis.

11. The resolution also instructs that in addition to activities pursuing its objective of peace, development and the promotion of human rights, Unesco's priorities established for education in 1960, and for science and its application to development in 1964, remain valid and should be maintained for the period 1971-1976. At the same time, greater importance should be gradually given to the cultural sector while "social sciences should play a more active part in the conception and implementation of the whole of the Organization's programme, in particular as regards development and promotion of peace."

12. Other general directives on the future programme given in resolution 7 of the General Conference include a 7% real growth rate of the Budget for 1973-1974 and 1975-1976, the rationalization of meetings and conferences, the slowing down of the growth of the Secretariat and the securing of increasingly effective execution of the programme at regional and national level by means of decentralization. An appeal is also made to Member States to co-operate with the Organization in ensuring that "the modern media of communication play their vital part in the promotion of the ideals of peace, justice and progress sought by the international community."

13. Special directives endorse the Director-General's main guidelines for future programmes in education, science, culture and communication, as contained in the *long-term outline plan for 1971-1976* (document 16 C/4 stating inter alia that Unesco's work must contribute to a regeneration of education which "must cover simultaneously quantitative expansion and qualitative improvement and tend towards the *life-long education* which the new techniques and methods of education and communication render possible." The Director-General is also authorized to include in the future draft programmes activities relating to *population* and family planning to be carried out within the competence of Unesco and in co-operation with other competent international organizations . . . "

DEVELOPMENTS IN MAJOR PROGRAMMES

A. Education

14. The crisis in education which has been affecting to varying degrees most parts of the world calls for profound changes in approach to all aspects of education. In continuing to develop the multitude of methods and techniques required for this purpose, Unesco has been reaching for two broad objectives: the *democratization* and the *regeneration of education;* the former leading to quantitative, the latter to qualitative improvement, each strengthening the other. While both are being pursued actively, 1970 witnessed a marked emphasis on the regenerative process.

15. At the same time, multidisciplinary approaches have been adopted to make educational planning more responsive to specific needs of Member States and more readily integrated into overall *country planning and programming.* Unesco has thus participated with ILO, FAO, IBRD and/or UNDP in country missions financed by either of these institutions or by Unesco. Such missions, organized upon a country's request, are doubly interdisciplinary in that in addition to members from different agencies, they include staff from various parts of the Unesco Secretariat, in order to obtain a composite view of the country's entire educational sector and to be in the best position to redefine the country's educational goals, having had the opportunity of measuring them against such other vital national objectives as employment (for which Unesco in close cooperation with ILO is testing new manpower survey models), population and other social and economic requirements.

16. Seventeen such interdisciplinary missions have been carried out in 1970. In addition to the results of these missions Unesco will soon be able to draw upon the report of the *International Commission on the Development of Education.* The establishment of this Commission has been approved by the General Conference at its sixteenth session on recommendation of the Executive Board, its purpose being to formulate educational strategies at the international level, in the framework of the Second Development Decade. The Commission, whose members are appointed by the Director-General, is headed by Mr. Edgar Faure, former Prime Minister and Minister of Education of France. The other six members are: Mr. Felipe Herrera (Chile); Mr. Abdul-Razzak Kaddoura

(Syria); Mr. Henri Lopes (People's Republic of the Congo); Mr. Arthur Vladimirovitch Petrovsky (USSR); Mr. Majid Rahnema (Iran); Mr. Frederick Champion Ward (U.S.A.). Its report is expected by the end of 1971.

17. Three examples of projects launched in 1970 as a follow-up of the Inter-disciplinary missions may be cited. They have led to the development of entirely new techniques to meet the needs of the countries concerned; in time they may bring fundamental changes to the educational systems of the countries concerned. (a) *Ivory Coast:* an experimental teacher-training project, sponsored jointly by several international and bilateral aid-donors, based on current closed-circuit television and other educational techniques; (b) *Indonesia:* an application of systems analysis in developing an integrated system of education which would best meet the social and economic needs of the country; (c) *Spain:* use of computers in a long-term programme for the intensive training of secondary school teachers.

18. *The International Education Year* (1970) resulted in considerably greater activity in promoting ideas, activities and standards than could have been expected, thanks to the active participation in special activities of large numbers of local and national authorities as well as international organizations, both governmental and non-governmental. A detailed critical analysis is currently being prepared and will be issued as a supplement to the Report of the Director-General on the Activities of the Organization in 1970. Pending its publication, it is worth noting that the two overriding themes of the Year—democratization of education and life-long education—appear to have found acceptance as major objectives of participating governments.

19. The publication by Unesco in early 1970 of a booklet entitled *Introduction to life-long Education* may well have contributed to the acceptance of this concept, which was further supported during the debates of the sixteenth session of the General Conference. At its second session in December 1970, the International Consultative Committee on Out-of-School Education recommended an agenda for the Third International Conference on Adult Education, to be held in 1972, whose theme will be "Adult Education as an Integral Part of life-long Education." Coincident with the renovation of school education from primary to university levels, new meaning and substance must be given to adult education and youth activities. This is intended to achieve a total restructuring of

education—both in and out of school—to meet the requirements of modern society.

20. As requested in General Assembly resolution 2573 (XXIV), Unesco co-operated in the preparation of the feasibility study on the establishment of an *International University* which the Secretary-General was invited to prepare. By its resolution 1542 (XLIX), the Council had requested the General Conference of Unesco to make its views available to the General Assembly, at its twenty-fifth session, "on the goals and objectives and also optional models of an international university and at an appropriate time to put forward proposals as to how Unesco might participate in such a university." In its resolution 1.242, the General Conference responded by stating that "it would be premature to take a decision on the establishment of an international university until further careful and objective studies of the educational, financial and organizational factors involved are completed and considered." It expressed the hope that "the General Assembly will invite Unesco to take steps with a view to presenting a full feasibility study to a subsequent meeting of the Economic and Social Council or of the General Assembly" and invited the Director-General "in the event of the General Assembly's acting accordingly, to undertake the feasibility study jointly with the Organizations of the United Nations system concerned, and the university community throughout the world."

21. By its resolution 2691 (XXV), the General Assembly, taking note of the Director-General's report on this matter submitted to the General Conference (document 16 C/72), and of the latter's resolution 1.242, invited Unesco to undertake the studies recommended by its General Conference and requested the Secretary-General to "continue consultations and studies, in close cooperation with Unesco and UNITAR, relating to the problems which are primarily of concern to the United Nations, in the context of the establishment of an international university." The General Assembly also noted that the Secretary-General and the Director-General "are arranging to conduct the relevant studies in such a manner as to be complementary to each other." Consultations have started in 1970, and will be intensified during 1971 following the first meeting in March of experts called upon to advise the Director-General on various aspects of the feasibility study.

22. Two high level governmental conferences in the field of education, one regional, the other international, were held under the aegis of Unesco in 1970: (a) the third *Conference of Ministers of Education and of Ministers in charge of Economic Planning of Arab States,* which took place in Marrakesh in January 1970 and discussed the considerable quantitative expansion of education in that region during the past decade; the Conference paid special attention to the continuing needs of functional literacy and for technical and vocational education, with particular concern for the access of girls to the latter; (b) the thirty-second *International Conference on Education* which was held in Geneva in July 1970. Its principal theme was the vital question of improving the effectiveness of educational systems, particularly through reduction of wastage at all levels of instruction. This was a theme which had already pre-occupied several regional ministerial meetings. In its recommendations to Member States, the Conference suggested practical measures and technical studies in the light of its general debate on important world trends in education today.

23. 1970 has witnessed the consolidation of the *International Bureau of Education,* located in Geneva, in its new functions. Structurally and administratively becoming an integral part of Unesco, its intellectual and functional autonomy within the framework of Unesco's programme is assured by its own Council, comprising representatives of 21 States designated by the General Conference. While continuing to prepare, organize and follow-up the International Conference on Education (see para. 22 above) now to be held biennially alternating with the General Conference, the Bureau is a world-wide information and documentation centre in the field of education. It undertakes comparative studies and, in addition to such publications in 1970 as the *International Yearbook of Education* (Vol. XXX–1969), the *Annual Educational Bibliography–1969* and periodical information on significant educational developments in its quarterly *IBE Bulletin,* it maintains the Co-operative Educational Abstracting Service, for use of educational policy-makers, senior administrators and other educational documentation and research specialists.

24. *Educational assistance to refugees* has continued to afford Unesco the opportunity of applying both ethical and operational action to one of the most important problems facing this special group of people. While pursuing cooperation—all too modest for lack of resources—with the United Nations High Commissioner for Refugees, 1970 witnessed an intensification of Unesco educational

assistance to refugees placed under the authority of UNRWA. As heretofore, financial, political and administrative responsibility of what is in fact the largest internationally-operated educational activity, has been assumed by UNRWA, while Unesco held technical responsibility for educational programmes, mainly by supplying relevant senior staff. To ensure that the education of refugees is fully consonant with the principles of the Universal Declaration of Human Rights, even under conditions of belligerency, Unesco not only succeeded, by agreement with the Governments concerned, in repeating the holding of school-leaving examinations in occupied territory but, notably also to secure government acceptance of international authority as to the content and use of textbooks.

25. In view of the rapidly increasing deficit of UNRWA's budget, the Commissioner-General announced, at the twenty-fifth session of the General Assembly that unless assistance was forthcoming, he would be compelled to reduce substantially the educational programme, representing 45% of the budget, as no reduction was possible in the existing minimal provisions for food, medical service and sanitation. In the face of this emergency and following the wish for such assistance, expressed by the Marrakesh Conference of Ministers of Education and of Ministers in charge of Economic Planning of Arab States, the Executive Board requested the Director-General to launch a special appeal for support of the UNRWA educational programme thus endangered, which he did on 1 January 1971. In its resolution 2728 (XXV), the General Assembly urged all Member States to respond generously to such appeals for the support of UNRWA.

26. *Regional Offices for Education* – The increasing experience of operational activity of the Organization as well as the changes in programming procedures for international aid currently introduced by the United Nations Development Programme, point to the desirability of pursuing and amplifying the efforts of de-centralizing a certain number of Unesco activities. Thus a new Regional Office for Education for Africa was established in Dakar in 1970, while that for Asia, in Bangkok, and that for Latin America, in Santiago, have been developed and reinforced.

B. Natural Sciences and Their Application to Development

27. In 1970 Unesco's action has been focused particularly on three domains: (i) science policy,

(ii) development of science and technology, and (iii) international programmes of scientific co-operation. The Organization has not only upheld the priority for natural sciences and their application to development which the General Conference decided in 1964, but has endeavoured to have this priority fully recognized in the International Development Strategy for the Second Development Decade adopted by the General Assembly at its twenty-fifth session.

(i) Science Policy

28. Following research and promotional work over a number of years concerning *Science policy,* the governments of 23 developing countries requested missions in this field which were carried out by Unesco in 1970. These missions advised governments on the establishment of appropriate national structures for science policy and in some cases also assisted in the development of such policy. The financial assistance of UNDP made possible the establishment of the first national science policy institution in a developing country, the National Centre for Planning Scientific and Technological Research in Senegal.

29. A major regional event in the realm of science policy was the first *Conference of Ministers of the European Member States responsible for Science Policy* (MINESPOL), held at Unesco Headquarters in Paris in June 1970, with the active participation and co-operation of the United Nations Economic Commission for Europe. This conference provided a rare opportunity for high officials from countries of divergent socio-economic and political interests to explore their respective views on a number of common concerns. Their deliberations resulted in the unanimous adoption of a series of Conclusions and Recommendations relating to the themes of the Conference: (a) the selection, training and utilization of scientists and engineers; (b) the choice of national scientific research priorities arising from economic, social and cultural development goals; (c) national aspects of fundamental research; (d) European co-operation in fundamental research.

30. The Conference also adopted other recommendations dealing inter alia with co-operation in science and technology between European and developing countries and with the rôle of fundamental sciences in the evolution of societies and the living condition of mankind. A number of recommendations adopted by MINESPOL were

translated into programme action proposals for Unesco in 1971-1972 and subsequently adopted by the General Conference. It included not only various studies, meetings and symposia concerning science policy and research, but also regarding scientific and technical information, ecology, statistics, human resources, etc. Mention should also be made of the decision to establish within Unesco, as from 1971, a Science Co-operation Bureau for Europe, and to hold a MINESPOL follow-up meeting of governmental experts on science policy in 1972.

(ii) Development of Science and Technology

31. The four pilot projects in the *Teaching of Basic Sciences* which combined national study groups, regional seminars, international working groups, writing sessions and workshops for the modernization of science education, completed their work in 1970. These pilot projects centered on physics in Latin America, chemistry in Asia, biology in Africa and mathematics in the Arab States. Results of these efforts are already being applied in a number of projects at the secondary school and university levels in countries of all four areas. At the same time, there has been increasing demand for Unesco's series *New Trends in the Teaching of the Basic Sciences* and the *Unesco Source-Book for Science Teaching* which have been instrumental in reforming the teaching of sciences in developing countries. It is hoped that even wider application of the experience gained over these years of experimentation will be possible in coming biennia by increasing the number of joint projects financed by UNDP, Unicef or the World Bank.

32. At its forty-ninth session ECOSOC adopted resolution 1545 (XLIX) by which it requested Unesco to take the necessary steps for further implementation of the recommendations of the Advisory Committee on the Application of Science and Technology to Development (ACAST) in its report on science education. This resolution was brought to the attention of the Executive Board of Unesco at its 85th session (September/October 1970) which adopted decision 7.1, paragraph 5 of which reads as follows: "Invites the Director-General to include in his next annual report to the Economic and Social Council a detailed account of Unesco's science-teaching programme and its relation to the recommendations of the Advisory Committee on the Application of Science and

Technology to Development." In compliance with that decision, a detailed account of Unesco's science-teaching programme and its relation to the recommendations of the Advisory Committee on the Application of Science and Technology to Development is appended to this report as annex III.

33. In the field of training of engineers and technicians, and technological research, Unesco's rôle is predominant. A meeting of experts, held in May, reviewed the changing problems, and the needs and conditions to be taken into account when planning these activities, and gave valuable advice for future action. But 1970 was not only a year of reflection. It was also the occasion of operational activities in the *transfer of science and technology* and their application to development to which considerable resources were devoted. Some 35 projects were implemented in 1969-1970, in all areas of the world. The new or expanded teaching and research institutions, as well as the governments concerned, benefit also from the guidance and recommendations of a number of meetings of experts, symposia and conferences which Unesco organized or sponsored in 1970. In arranging such regional or international exchanges of ideas, Unesco aimed at stimulating the reform and regeneration of technological education, and providing developing countries with the latest scientific and technological achievements. Emphasis was put on the questions of structures for training activities, notably on a regional basis, the planning and development of curricula, and the rôle of the engineer in adapting modern technology to the requirements of economic development.

34. Some of these meetings in 1970, were the Regional Seminar on Engineering Education in Algiers; the Regional Conference of Representatives of African Engineering Societies, in Nairobi; the Regional Seminar on the Problems of Transition from Laboratory Research to Industrial Application, in Poona, India; the Regional Symposium on the Utilization of Science and Technology for Development in Africa, held in Addis Ababa jointly with the United Nations Economic Commission for Africa. Work in this field is also carried out by the Latin American Centre for the Application of Science and Technology to Development in Sao Paulo, Brazil.

35. Two other important meetings in this field were held at Unesco Headquarters in 1970: (a) an international working group of high-level experts considered the *training of technicians,* their special rôle and the relation of their training to that of engineers; (b) a meeting of consultants on *engineering education and research.* This latter in-

cluded representatives of the International Council of Scientific Unions (ICSU), The World Federation of Engineering Organizations (WFEO) and the Union of International Technical Associations (UATI) and provided the Director-General with valuable recommendations as regards the Organization's future programme.

36. The FAO/Unesco/ILO Inter-Secretariat Working Group on *Agricultural Education, Science and Training* met four times in 1970 to implement the recommendations of the Joint FAO/Unesco/ILO Advisory Committee in that field. A notable manifestation of the three Agencies' co-operation in this field was the World Conferences on Agricultural Education and Training, held in Copenhagen in July-August 1970, which they prepared, sponsored, and organized jointly. The Conference yielded valuable recommendations, the implementation of which should contribute to raise the level of agricultural education, heretofore often considered a second-class branch of education, and provide the much needed boost to rural development which affects two-thirds of the world population. The effects of this inter-agency co-operation condition not only the nature and direction of the three organizations' programmes, but also those of their field activities which deserve more substantial additional budgetary and extra-budgetary resources.

(iii) International Programmes of Scientific Co-operation

37. Considerable progress was accomplished in 1970 in the preparation or implementation of major programmes of scientific co-operation with the United Nations, Specialized Agencies and other bodies of the United Nations system, as well as with governmental and non-governmental international organizations. Two characteristics of such programmes should be noted: (a) their preparatory stages are mostly devoted to studies and activities designed to promote, co-ordinate and launch a programme. So the apparent modesty of the initial Unesco budget is not indicative of the magnitude of the programme to be developed; once in operation, its implementation normally requires additional funding on the part of all co-operating organizations; (b) to enable developing countries to benefit fully from such programmes, Unesco supplements its own budgetary contribution with extra-budgetary resources for the train-

ing of staff and specialized research designed to reduce the inherent scientific and technological underdevelopment of these countries.

38. In launching The Man and the Biosphere programme in 1971, the General Conference described it as "focusing on the general study of the structure and functioning of the biosphere and its ecological regions, on the systematic observations of the changes brought about by man in the biosphere and its resources, on the study of the overall effects of these changes upon the human species itself, and on the education and information to be provided on these subjects" (cf. 16 C/Resolution 2.313). As recalled in the Director-General's report on the activities of the Organization in 1970, "two features of this programme merit special emphasis. In the first place, it is truly a scientific and educational programme, the purpose of which is to provide guidance for governments and to support them, by creating a suitably informed public opinion, in the measures they take, within their own countries and internationally, for the preservation of the resources of the biosphere and for the maintenance of a harmonious relationship between man and his environment. The programme does not bear on those measures themselves. On the other hand, it is a multidisciplinary[1] programme; it cannot be carried out without the active participation of many international organizations which are variously concerned with the great complex of studies involved." As such the programme Man and the Biosphere is a positive contribution in the solution of problems which have justified the convening of the forthcoming United Nations Conference on the Human Environment, to be held in Stockholm in 1972, in the preparation of which Unesco has been playing an active rôle from its earliest stages, as requested in Council resolution 1536 (XLIX) and acknowledged in General Assembly resolution 2687 (XXV). With the help of the governmental Council it has set up to guide the destinies of this programme, the General Conference will review its development at its next session in the light of the results of the Stockholm Conference.

39. Whereas the programme of Unesco's Office of Oceanography has been devoted mostly to the advancement of marine sciences through various forms of training, its *Intergovernmental Oceanographic Commission (IOC)* responded to General Assembly resolution 2467 D(XXIII) by intensifying its activities, in co-operation with other interested agencies, in particular with regard to coordinating the scientific aspects of a long-term and

expanded programme of world-wide exploration of the oceans and their resources. To enable the IOC to play this wider rôle and to broaden its base to facilitate such co-operation with the interested organizations of the United Nations system, particularly through their contributing to its secretariat, the Commission proposed appropriate changes in its statutes, which were approved by the General Conference with some revisions. While the Inter-Secretariat Committee on Scientific Programme Related to Oceanography (ICSPRO), which includes representatives of the United Nations, FAO, WMO, IMCO and Unesco, met regularly in 1970 in support of IOC's enhanced co-operative effort, the first meeting of the ICC Group of Experts on the Long-Term Science Policy and Planning took place in Monaco in November 1970 and developed a first list of "co-operative exercises" to be completed at forthcoming meetings. Three new member-countries joined IOC in 1970, bringing its total membership to 70.

40. Under the guidance of the Co-ordinating Council for the *International Hydrological Decade* (IHD), Unesco continued to serve as the secretariat for the Decade in co-operation with the United Nations, FAO, WHO, WMO, and IAEA and to co-ordinate six permanent and one ad hoc IHD Working Groups, while co-operating with the other four IHD Working Groups whose technical secretariat is provided by other agencies. The sixth session of the Co-ordinating Council met in July 1970 at WMO Headquarters in Geneva and took action as to the future orientation of IHD in the light of the recommendations of the Mid-Decade Conference held in Paris in December 1969.

41. Finally, among 1970 developments concerning international programmes of scientific co-operation is the completion of the Unesco-ICSU (International Council of Scientific Unions) feasibility study for the establishment of a *World science information system (UNISIST)*. The first session of the Central Committee of the Unesco-ICSU joint project on this subject concluded that a world science information system was not only necessary but feasible. It recommended that Unesco sponsor an international serials data system and agreed to advise the Director-General in planning an intergovernmental conference on UNISIST to be held in October 1971. At its sixteenth session, the General Conference in its resolution 2.141 expressed support for this conference to be prepared jointly with ICSU "with the aim of establishing and putting into operation a World

Scientific and Technical Information System." Related undertakings of the Organization included completion of the first draft of "Guidelines for the Establishment and Development of Multilingual Scientific and Technical Thesauri for Information Retrieval" and the compilation and study of an inventory of sources of scientific and technical terminology.

C. Social Sciences, Human Sciences and Culture

(i) Social and human sciences

42. Most of the activities of the Organization in this field during the course of 1970 were devoted to studies and meetings of experts designed to re-think and restructure Unesco's programme of promotion and assistance (a) to the development of the social sciences documentation and information services, (b) to social science teaching and research (with emphasis on international law, the management sciences and development problems); (c) to the application of the social sciences to the problems of human rights, peace and development, as well as to human environmental and population problems. As regards the application of social sciences to development, the General Conference in its resolution 3.24 adopted at its sixteenth session, authorized the Director-General inter alia to pursue general studies relating to (a) the identification and use of social and economic indicators, (b) the promotion and utilization of human resources, (c) the rôle of the social sciences in development planning and policy formulation, and (d) the human rôle in development.

43. However, the *training of specialists* and research in various fields and techniques of the social sciences, with increasing emphasis on their application to development, were continued in such regional centres as the Latin American Faculty of Social Sciences (FLACSO) in Santiago, Chile; the African Centre for Administrative Training and Research for Development (CAFRAD) in Tangiers, the Institute of Economic Growth in Delhi, the Latin American Social Sciences Research Centre (CENTRO) in Rio de Janeiro and the European Co-ordination Centre for Research and Documentation in the Social Sciences in Vienna.

44. In response to several resolutions of the General Conference and of the General Assembly, studies dealing with the eradication of racial discrimination, human rights, peace research and the

relationship between development and peace, were initiated in 1970. Among them, were studies on the "Assessment of the rôle of education in eliminating racial prejudice and racial discrimination" and the "Economic Aspects of the Race Question," as well as a comparative study on "The Right to Privacy"—the latter following a meeting of experts on that subject, held in Paris in February 1970. As an activity related to peace research, a meeting of eighteen experts in both social and biological sciences took place in Paris (19 to 23 May) at which was discussed the implications of recent scientific research on the understanding of human aggressiveness. The meeting received considerable attention from the press and was fully reported in the August-September 1970 issue of the Unesco *Courier*.

45. The programme *Man and his Environment* gives primary emphasis to the human and social aspects of the environment problem and complements that on Man and Biosphere which is largely oriented towards bio-physical and ecological investigations; both programmes respond to General Assembly resolution 2657 (XXV). A symposium on *Man and his Environment–Design for Living* was held in Helsinki in June 1970 and dealt with man's rôle in changing his environment, with special reference to architecture and urbanism for growth and change. The results of the symposium were subsequently evaluated by a group of consultants, with a view to defining priorities for the relevant parts of the Unesco programme and to enhance Unesco's contribution to the 1972 Stockholm Conference on the Human Environment.

(ii) Culture

46. The single most striking activity of Unesco in this field was the *Inter-governmental Conference on Institutional, Administrative and Financial Aspects of Cultural Policies* held in Venice in August-September 1970, with the participation of representatives from over 80 Member States, half of whom were ministers. The Conference marked a new departure in the general conception of culture, its nature and its rôle in society, and of Member States' obligations to it. At its sixteenth session, the General Conference fully endorsed the conclusions of the Venice Conference in its resolution 3.3. It was emphasized that "culture should not be restricted to a few artistic activities reserved for an elité: it is culture which gives daily life its

particular quality, adapting and subordinating to that quality the transformation of the urban or natural environment; it assimilates the techniques which form the context of modern life and it enables each man to make scientific progress an integral part of his way of living and thinking."

47. Two notable concepts emerged from the Venice Conference: (a) *Cultural development* is part and parcel of development as a whole, of which it is both a precondition and an ultimate objective. The implications of this conclusion were incorporated in General Conference resolution 9 concerning the assessment of the first Development Decade and Unesco's programme for the Second Decade, particularly in parts 9.11 and 9.133 of that resolution (see annex II); (b) Cultural development requires action on the part of public authorities whose purpose it is "to ensure the full and entire participation of each person without distinction of race, nationality, social category, creed or opinion in the cultural life of his own community and of mankind as a whole" (16 C/Resolution 3.3). Thus *cultural policy* has now joined educational planning and science policy as one of the Organization's main concerns for action.

48. Work on Unesco's programme of *Cultural Studies* has continued satisfactorily. Studies on the different cultures of Asia have been considerably developed, dealing increasingly with contemporary problems while continuing to promote research into and reflection about the past. The African cultures and languages programme has also been forging ahead. Thus, a meeting of experts held in Yaoundé, Cameroon, in August 1970, recommended the establishment of a ten-year plan of action for the promotion of African languages; while another group of experts, meeting in Addis Ababa two months earlier, gave shape to what should become an eight-volume General History of Africa to be drafted under the supervision and responsibility of an International Scientific Committee consisting of eminent Africanists, for the most part Africans themselves. With regard to the studies of Latin American and of Balkan and South-East European cultures, work is progressing under very favourable conditions.

49. With reference to preservation and presentation of the cultural heritage, the General Conference adopted, at its sixteenth session, the *International Convention on the Means of Prohibiting and Preventing the Illicit Export and Transfer of Ownership of Cultural Property* which had been many years in preparation under the guidance of a

Special Committee of Government Experts which had revised the last draft of the Convention at its April 1970 meeting.

50. Operational activities, combining Unesco's tasks in the preservation and restoration of cultural heritage with the promotion of economic and social development through what may be termed *cultural tourism,* have progressed considerably in 1970. During 1969-1970, aid of up to $691,000 in this field was provided to 80 countries, under the Organization's Participation (Regular) programme by way of Technical Assistance. Another fact of importance to be noted is that for the first time, the United Nations Development Programme agreed to finance a project for the preservation and development of an archaeological and artistic zone with a view to promoting tourism. The project concerns the *Tunis-Carthage* region where a team of experts has begun operations in 1970.

51. Missions with a view to assisting governments with similar endeavours in other parts of the world have been undertaken in numerous countries, notably with regard to the "*Andean Route*" (Bolivia, Chile, Colombia, Ecuador, Peru), *Mohenjo-Daro* (Pakistan) and *Borobudur* (Indonesia). In many cases, efforts have been made to mobilize various forms of international assistance with a view to financing activities such as those contained in the Plan for the development of the monuments of the Altiplano (Peru), and in the six-year plan prepared by Unesco for the Borobudur project.

52. Pursuing the International Campaign to Save the Monuments of Nubia, arrangements have been concluded in 1970 for the remaining work to save *Philae* for which the Executive Committee for the Campaign has expressed the view that Unesco should try to raise at least $6,000,000 of the estimated cost of $13,300,000. While still below the $6,000,000 target, the contributions received or pledged—including a substantial amount from the World Food Program—were held to be adequate for the work to be started, hopefully in early 1971, as soon as the relevant contract is signed by the Government of the United Arab Republic.

53. Unesco has continued to assist the Government of Italy in the scientific and technical research and other preparations which led the International Advisory Committee for *Venice* in September 1970 to draw up a minimum plan for emergency action. The Italian Government has declared its intention of implementing a comprehensive plan for the preservation and development of Venice, subject to budgetary appropriations.

The Unesco publication "Rapporto su Venezia" was so successful in bringing to the public the problems connected with the physical protection and socio-cultural development of Venice, that a third edition in Italian is to appear in early 1971. While the French edition appeared in December 1970, the English version is planned for Autumn 1971.

C. Communication

54. The Organization's work in this domain has gradually been extended to new fields, and has involved use of new techniques, notably the use of space communication to promote Unesco's aims, the development of information media, book production and distribution, the computerization of documentation, and statistics. Considering the media of communication as essential tools not only for the mobilization of public opinion but for development itself, the General Conference, at its sixteenth session, emphasized this aspect in its resolution 9.134 (see annex II).

55. As regards the promotion of the use of *space communications* to further Unesco's aims, and in conjunction with the forthcoming World Administrative Radio Conference for Space Telecommunications, to be convened by the International Telecommunication Union in 1971, the Unesco Advisory Panel on Space Communication meeting in Paris in April 1970 reviewed the progress in Unesco's programme and, at a session with representatives of several regional broadcasting organizations, recommended that the Unesco Secretariat undertake a survey on the professional aspects of the use of space communication for broadcasting. In response to requests from the United Nations Working Group on Direct Broadcast Satellites, reports have been initiated on the effects of the content of satellite broadcasts on cultural and social standards and the use of space communication for national development, education and cultural exchanges. The General Assembly acknowledged Unesco's activities in this field and urged their intensification in resolution 2733 (XXV), which has been reflected in the Organization's programme approved by the General Conference at its sixteenth session.

56. The increased interest of developing countries in the possibilities of using satellite broadcasting for educational purposes have led to several missions in various parts of the world and

notably in Latin America where the Ministers of Education of the Andean region asked Unesco for a thorough study of the possibility and advisability of a project for using space communications to develop educational television. Following the ensuing requests from several Latin American countries the United Nations Development Programme agreed to provide the necessary assistance which would enable Unesco, in co-operation with the International Telecommunication Union, to carry out this study which is thus the first UNDP project in this field.

57. As regards the *training of information personnel,* the network of institutions set up with the Organization's assistance to provide education and training for mass communication personnel was extended with the establishment in April 1970 of a School of journalism at Nairobi University. Training activities in other components of this network were pursued in all parts of the world. It should be noted that as another first project of its kind, the United Nations Development Programme granted support of $1,147,000 for the establishment of a training centre for television personnel in India so as to enable the government to carry out its programme for the development of educational television.

58. The *book development programme* was taken a step further with the establishment of a regional book development centre for Latin America in Bogota. Along with the centres of other regions, it will play an important part in the implementation of the International Book Year in 1972 which the General Conference proclaimed at its sixteenth session in resolution 4.121. At the same time, the General Conference, by its resolution 4.122, authorized the establishment of an international Copyright Information Centre on books which will afford developing countries greater access to protected works and help in promoting the free flow as well as the development, distribution and production of books.

59. Two activities relating to the use of mass media should be mentioned as examples of different aspects of the work carried out by Unesco under this heading but in different fields: (a) the *Symposium on the Impact of Violence in the Mass Media* held in Paris in July 1970 as a result of which an international non-governmental organization contemplates awarding an annual prize for television programmes for children and adolescents, that are free of violence; (b) the training course in the *Use of Mass Media in Family Planning Programmes* in Asia, which took place in

Seoul in September-October 1970, and led to the preparation of a draft handbook on mass media and family planning programmes in individual countries, to be completed in 1971. The interest of Asian countries in the services which Unesco could perform in this field has made it possible to appoint a regional consultant and an assistant at the Unesco Regional Office for Education in Bangkok.

60. In addition to continuing its programme of assistance, particularly to developing countries, for the strengthening and improving of their *documentation, library and archives services,* Unesco has been active in promoting research and international co-operation in these fields. Examples of studies completed or initiated in 1970 are Public library legislation, the Rôle of Libraries and documentation services in economic and social development, Trilingual terminology of documentation, and the Function of archives and records management in public administration.

61. Continuing its early studies concerning information storage and retrieval, Unesco has been responding to the concerns for close co-ordination by the organizations of the United Nations system in the establishment of computers and other relevant services, expressed in various resolutions of the Council and by the Committee on Programme and Co-ordination. Based on the results of the feasibility study on the application of mechanized methods for the dissemination of Unesco documents, preliminary systems analysis and design were carried out with a view to establishing a *Computerized Documentation Service* for the processing, storage and dissemination of information on Unesco documents and publications and, at a later stage of development, on external documents relevant to the execution of the programme of the Organization.

62. In the field of *statistics* there has been a marked increase and broadening of Unesco activities during 1970. A number of studies, meetings and seminars have been carried out in various parts of the world in relation to the advancement of education and research, and assistance was provided to Member States for the development of their statistical services and activities in matters within Unesco's purview. While continuing its basic work of collecting, analysing and publishing international statistics on education, science, culture and communication—including the publication of its seventh edition of the "Unesco Statistical Yearbook" for 1969—the Office of Statistics has been called upon increasingly to service the

various sectors of the Secretariat and contribute to the preparation of a growing number of international and regional governmental and other conferences as well as reports, requiring considerable statistical data. Thus, the co-operation of the Office has enabled the Human Resources Analysis Division to elaborate simulation models for education, and for scientific and technical manpower, which are being used increasingly in planning for economic and social development (see para. 17 above).

CO-ORDINATION WITH OTHER ORGANIZATIONS OF THE UNITED NATIONS SYSTEM

63. In an endeavour to co-ordinate as far as possible its programmes with those of the other Specialized Agencies concerned, Unesco has adopted the practice of forwarding its draft Programme and Budget for the forthcoming two-year period to the United Nations Organization (since 1947) and to the other Specialized Agencies (since 1955), requesting their comments thereon. The comments received from these organizations are then reproduced, *in extenso,* in a special document which is presented to the biennial session of the Unesco General Conference. Delegations to that Conference are thus enabled to make their decisions on the Unesco Programme and Budget in the light of the comments from other organizations of the United Nations system.

64. The present chapter refers to activities undertaken by Unesco in co-operation with other United Nations bodies. It deals with inter-agency missions aimed at assisting Member States in country planning and programming, agricultural education, oceanography, man and the biosphere, and hydrology. The latter portion of the chapter refers to some difficulties which have been encountered in co-ordination with the Regional Economic Commissions.

Inter-Agency missions

65. During 1970 Unesco participated with ILO, FAO, IBRD and/or UNDP in 17 inter-agency missions with a view to assisting Member States in overall country planning and programming (cf. paragraph 15 above).

Agricultural Education

66. The *World Conference on Agricultural Education and Training,* jointly organized and sponsored by FAO, Unesco and ILO, is one of the most notable examples of inter-agency co-operation in 1970. Held in Copenhagen, Denmark, in July/August, it was attended by representatives from 95 countries, the Directors-General of the three co-sponsoring organizations, and by representatives from other organizations of the United Nations system. The results of this Conference, details of which are given in paragraph 36 above, will largely influence the nature and direction of the future programmes and field activities of the three organizations concerned.

Oceanography and marine science

67. Further progress has been made in broadening the base of the participation in the work of the Intergovernmental Oceanographic Commission (IOC), in response to General Assembly resolution 2467 (XXIII). The Inter-Secretariat Committee on Scientific Programmes Related to Oceanography (ICSPRO), which now includes representatives of the United Nations, FAO, WMO, IMCO and Unesco, meets regularly in support of IOC's intensified co-operative effort (cf. paragraph 39 above).

Man and the Biosphere

68. Extensive consultations were carried on with other agencies, particularly FAO, WHO and WMO, prior to the discussion of this programme at the sixteenth session of the Unesco General Conference last October/November. This multidisciplinary programme is a positive contribution to the solution of some of the problems which are to be discussed at the United Nations Conference on the Human Environment, in the preparation of which Unesco is playing an active rôle (cf. paragraph 38 above). Unesco also collaborated in the meeting of senior governmental officials and scientific advisers of ECE countries, held last November/December, for the purpose of exchanging views on governmental objectives and policies in the field of the environment.

Hydrology

69. In co-operation with the United Nations, FAO, WHO, WMO and IAEA, Unesco continued to serve as the secretariat for the International Hydrological Decade (IHD) (cf. paragraph 40 above). Additional activities for the promotion of the general advancement of hydrology, many of which were carried out particularly in co-operation with WMO, are outlined in part II, chapter 2.D of the Report of the Director-General on the Activities of the Organization in 1970.

Co-operation with Regional Economic Commissions

70. There have been many instances of close and fruitful co-operation between Unesco and the various Regional Economic Commissions as evidenced in the report of the Director-General on the Activities of the Organization in 1970, notably part I, chapter 2.

71. Despite this, a co-ordination problem exists which has still to be solved, since, as inferred by ECPC at its resumed second session, there has been a tendency on the part of some of these Commissions to embark on activities which may duplicate those normally falling within the purview of the Specialized Agencies (document E/4C.51/GR/20, Annex I.F., para. 9).

72. It is worth recalling that at the July 1969 meeting of the Executive Secretaries of the Regional Economic Commissions, the Unesco representatives had the opportunity of referring to this situation. A consensus was then reached on how best to organize co-operation between the Regional Economic Commissions and Unesco, particularly in the field of science and technology. Chapter VI of document E/4709 (Report of the meetings of the Executive Secretaries of the Regional Economic Commissions held in 1969) concerns these discussions. The document was subsequently noted by ECOSOC.

73. Some positive achievements have been recorded—as, for example, the recent establishment of the ECAFE/Unesco Science and Technology Unit in Bangkok, fruitful co-operation with ECE within the framework of the Conference of European Statisticians and its various working groups, and work with ECA on the revision of the educational targets previously established by the Conference of African States on the Development of Education in Africa (Addis Ababa, 1961). Difficulties however have been experienced with the Economic Commission for Africa in relation to its Programme of work and priorities for 1971/1973 with projections to 1967, as well as with the Economic Commission for Europe which was seized with a proposal for the creation of a permanent principal subsidiary body called "Senior Advisers to ECE governments on science and technology," the terms of reference of which show clearly a possible duplication with responsibilities being carried out by Unesco. In this case, the Unesco Secretariat requested that the provision of paragraph 5 of the Terms of Reference of the Commission, which call for prior consultation between the Commission and the Specialized Agency concerned, be fully respected.

TECHNICAL ASSISTANCE ACTIVITIES

74. The substantive elements relating to Unesco's technical assistance activities have been touched upon in Chapter II. The information given below is solely of a statistical nature to indicate general trends in this aspect of the programme.

75. Under the UNDP/Special Fund component, Unesco's expenditure in 1970 amounted to $23,198,396, representing an increase of $1,941,810 or 9% over the 1969 expenditure which was $21,256,586. During 1970 four additional projects in the field of education and five in the field of natural sciences and their application to development became operational (while five projects were completed), making a total of 126 operational projects for which Unesco was the Executing Agency. Whereas 23 new or extended projects were entrusted to Unesco during 1969, 19 such projects were approved during 1970.

76. Unesco implemented 413 projects at a value of $7,902,346 under the UNDP/Technical Assistance component in 1970. Compared with the previous year during which 349 projects involving $6,487,580 were implemented, the 1970 record shows an increase of 22% in the amount and of 18% in the number of projects.

77. The regular Technical Assistance budget of Unesco is called the Programme of Participation in the Activities of Member States, which differentiates itself from the UNDP in that all Member States of Unesco are eligible and that it covers all Unesco's fields of competence. Under this pro-

gramme 121 countries received allocations totalling $2,738,661 for 825 projects to be implemented in 1969-1970 compared with the 1967-1968 allocation of $2,105,804 for 629 projects in 109 countries. The 1969-1970 allocation represents an increase of 30% in the amount, 31% in the number of projects and 11% in the number of beneficiary countries.

ADMINISTRATIVE AND BUDGETARY QUESTIONS

(a) Budgetary Trend

78. The expenditure for 1970 under Unesco's Regular budget and under the UNDP (Special Fund and Technical Assistance) projects entrusted to Unesco for execution is as shown in the following table:

heavier than that for the first year. Under Part I, General Policy, the 1970 expenditure ($868,102) is 80.2% more than that for 1969 ($481,844), which is explained by the fact that Unesco's biennial General Conference (budgeted under this Part) took place in 1970. Under Part II, Programme Operations and Services, the 1970 expenditure of $23,440,963 is 0.9% more than that for 1969 ($23,228,172).

80. Taking the Regular budget and the UNDP (Special Fund and Technical Assistance) projects together, the total 1970 expenditure of $70,426,552 is 9.8% greater than the total 1969 expenditure ($64,134,165), whilst the 1970 expenditure of $54,543,704 for Part II, Programme Operations and Services, is 9.5% more than the 1969 expenditures ($49,825,945).

81. The total 1970 expenditure of $39,323,812 under the Regular budget includes the 1970 portion of the amount of $1,288,000 transferred, with the prior approval of the Executive Board,

| | Regular budget | UNDP | | Total |
		S.F.	T.A.	
	$	$	$	$
Part I				
General Policy	868,102	–	–	868,102
Part II				
Programme Operations and Services				
Education	8,710,305	11,726,352	4,842,190	25,278,847
Natural Sciences	5,320,067	11,430,310	1,705,771	18,456,148
Social Sciences, Human Sciences and Culture	4,036,638	–	557,861	4,594,499
Communication	4,961,513	41,734	798,523	5,801,770
International Standards Relations and Programmes	412,440	–	–	412,440
Total Part II	23,440,963	23,198,396	7,904,345	54,543,704
Part III				
General Administration and Programme Supporting Services	6,637,862	–	–	6,637,862
Part IV				
Documents and Publications Services	3,161,125	–	–	3,161,125
Part V				
Common Services	3,446,678	–	–	3,446,678
Part VI				
Capital Expenditure	1,769,082	–	–	1,769,082
Total Parts I to VI	39,323,812	23,198,396	7,904,345	70,426,553

79. Under the Regular budget, the total expenditure of $39,323,812 is 4.8% more than the total 1969 expenditure ($37,536,392), thus reflecting the normal tendency of the Organization's expenditure for the second year of the biennium to be

from the Appropriation Reserve in order to meet part of the costs of the increases that had occurred during 1969-1970 in staff salaries and allowances, as well as in the costs of goods and services. (The unused balance, $649,662, of the Reserve, together with other budetary surpluses, will be surrendered to Member States at the end of the liquidation period, 31 December 1971). The remaining costs of the staff salary and allowance increases were covered from the savings, in terms of U.S. dollars, that had occurred as a result of the change in the parity of the French franc visa-à-vis the U.S. dollar on 8 August 1969, as well as from "natural" savings that had occurred in the course of programme implementation.

(b) Implementation of the recommendations of the Ad Hoc Committee of Experts to Examine the Finances of the United Nations and the Specialized Agencies

82. In conformity with a resolution adopted by the Unesco General Conference at its fifteenth session, in which the Director-General was requested to implement fully Recommendation 29, the Director-General submitted to the General Conference at its sixteenth session in October-November 1970 a long-term outline plan for the period 1971-1976 (document 16 C/4). This plan will be duly up-dated and extended so that at each biennial session the General Conference will have before it a six-year plan of the Organization's activities.

83. Unesco has continued to participate in the Working Parties of CCAQ and their studies at the inter-agency level concerning a number of other recommendations of the Ad Hoc Committee, in particular Recommendation 4 (uniform budget layout), Recommendation 24 (standardization of financial regulations), and Recommendation 26 (standardization of nomenclature).

(c) Developments regarding the Joint Inspection Unit

84. During the year 1970, the Chairman of the Joint Inspection Unit continued to transmit to the Director-General reports, observations and notes on matters of concern to the Organization. On a number of occasions the Director-General has expressed his appreciation for the valuable contribution made by the Inspection Unit, especially those reports which made a detailed examination of project operations in the field, and those dealing with the procedures and administration of the Organization. The executive Board itself has often commended the work of the Unit. This appreciation has also been expressed by the representatives of Unesco during discussions on the Joint Inspection Unit in the Fifth Committee of the General Assembly of the United Nations, and in the Committee for Programme and Co-ordination.

85. In addition, the Director-General has taken the initiative in requesting the assistance of the Unit in evaluating certain activities undertaken by the Organization: an inspection of regional centres and institutes established or assisted by Unesco, and a study of the horizontal structures which could be established within the Secretariat for the implementation of interdisciplinary programmes.

86. The reports of the Joint Inspection Unit are distributed to the senior officials of the Secretariat concerned including officers responsible for field projects. The reports, with the Director-General's comments thereon, are then made available to the Executive Board, which has entrusted to its Special Committee a preliminary examination of reports of concern to Unesco.

87. The following reports, observations and notes of the Joint Inspection Unit of concern to Unesco were submitted by the Director-General to the Executive Board in 1970:

Rationalization of Proceedings and Documentation of the Unesco General Conference (JIU/REP/69/4)

Report on the Overhead Costs of Extra-Budgetary Programmes and on Methods of Measuring Performance and Costs (JIU/REP/69/2)

Report on Economic Commission for Asia and the Far East (JIU/REP/69/6)

Report on Programming and Budgets of the United Nations Family of Organizations (JIU/REP/69/7)

Report on Malaysia and Singapore (JIU/REP/69/8)

Report on Selected Ideas for Improving Field Operations (JIU/REP/69/9)

Notes on Field Inspection in Morocco (JIU/REP/69/1)

Observations arising from a Visit of Inspection to Malawi (JIU/REP/69/11)

Note on the Educational Broadcasting Project in Malawi (JIU/REP/69/2/2-2)

Observations on the Activities of Unesco in Colombia (JIU/REP/70/2-3)

A report on the United Nations Activities and Operations in Nepal (JIU/REP/70/4)

Observations on the Work of Unesco in Madagascar (JIU/REP/70/6-4)

Second Report on the Activities of the Joint Inspection Unit, 1969-1970.

88. Recognizing the importance for Member States of reports made by the Unit on activities carried out in their countries the Executive Board at its 85th session (21 September to 10 November 1970) decided to invite the Member State concerned to be represented by its permanent delegate when such reports are discussed. This procedure would enable Member States to be fully informed of the views of the Executive Board and would also provide an opportunity for the Board members to benefit from any observations which the delegate of the Member State may wish to present. Increased participation by Member States concerned can enhance the Board's appraisal of the recommendations of the Inspectors and contribute to the formulation of directives to the Secretariat for the improvement of the efficiency and the use of the resources of the Organization.

89. A mechanism has been established within the Secretariat to ensure appropriate follow-up on the recommendations of the Joint Inspection Unit. The proposals of the Inspectors have resulted in improvements in project planning and execution and in the administration of projects. A few recent examples follow:

(a) School of Engineering, National University of Bogota, Columbia (SF project COL.8):

The Inspector commented on the production of textbooks in this project and recommended that they be given wide distribution. These textbooks cover fields which were not adequately treated in available Spanish language textbooks. Unesco is making efforts to have the nineteen technical textbooks produced by this project widely distributed in Latin America;

(b) Educational Training and Research Institute in Madagascar (SF project MAG 1): The Inspector proposed that local purchase of equipment be authorized when appropriate. Unesco has revised its purchase rules to permit direct purchase of equipment by the Chief Technical Adviser at the project site, up to specified limits without referral to Headquarters;

(c) Secondary Teacher Training School, Guatemala (SF project GUA 11): In view of the difficulties reported by the Inspector he proposed a mission to review the project. As a result project operations were temporarily suspended and expert contracts not renewed; but now that the Government has approved the statutes, plan of studies and budget for the School it seems likely that the project can get off to a new start.

NOTE

1 The social science component of this programme is described in para. 46.

Twenty-Fourth World Health Assembly

World Health Organization

The following is an account of the principle topics discussed and the decisions taken at the Twenty-Fourth World Health Assembly which met in Geneva from 4 to 20 May 1971. The Assembly is the governing body of the World Health Organization.

BUDGET

The Twenty-fourth World Health Assembly adopted an effective working budget of $82,023,000 to finance the Organization's programme for 1972. This figure represents an increase of 9.05% over the 1971 budget as revised by the Assembly.

THE CHOLERA PANDEMIC

The Health Assembly considered the cholera situation[1] at some length. The course of the pandemic was predictable from the time the disease left its traditional foci until its arrival in north-east Africa. It then jumped a stage and appeared unexpectedly on the west coast of the continent during a period of floods and seasonal epidemics of waterborne infections. The countries of Africa responded admirably to the threat, and WHO, by organizing courses in the control of cholera, was able to prepare African health administrations to deal with the disease. There is at present no further risk of a country being taken by surprise, and emergency supplies for diagnosis, treatment, and prevention are ready in the most exposed areas. Such supplies are expensive because of the high cost of air freight, and African countries need assistance to ensure their continued flow. The readiness of African countries to notify WHO of the evolution of the epidemic has enabled the Organization to keep countries informed of the situation. Vaccination is of limited effect, and while it may be useful in reducing transmission in epidemic foci it should not be relied on to prevent the introduc-

tion of the disease. The USA no longer requires cholera vaccination for those travelling from infected countries.

The Health Assembly requested the Director-General to give high priority to programmes aimed at improving water supplies, environmental sanitation, and personal hygiene. Further research should be undertaken on the vaccine prophylaxis and treatment of cholera, and the national production of rehydration fluids, antibiotics, and effective vaccines should be encouraged. The Assembly asked the Director-General to study the implications of removing cholera from the International Health Regulations. It also called on Member States not to impose an unjustified embargo on foodstuffs imported from countries reporting cholera cases.

HUMAN ENVIRONMENT

Hundreds of millions of people are affected by preventable diseases originating in the environment in which they live. One major difficulty encountered by many Member States in their efforts to control pollution of the environment is the lack of internationally agreed criteria and guides on environmental quality, and the Assembly considered that WHO should establish such criteria, paying particular attention to occupational exposure, water, food, air, and wastes. Agreement could be reached on codes of practice based on provisional criteria and guides. In endorsing the Director-General's long-term programme on the human environment, the Assembly emphasized the need to improve basic environmental health and sanitation,

SOURCE: Reprinted from "Twenty-Fourth World Health Assembly -2," *WHO Chronicle,* 25 (Aug., 1971) pp. 337–342.

notably in the developing countries, by the provision of adequate quantities of potable water and the sanitary disposal of wastes. WHO should stimulate the development and co-ordination of epidemiological health surveillance and environmental monitoring systems and promote knowledge of the effects of environmental factors on human health by collecting and disseminating information, supporting and co-ordinating research, and assisting in the training of personnel.

In preparing their contributions to the United Nations Conference on the Human Environment to be held in Stockholm in 1972, Member States should, it was recommended, regard health considerations as a major concern. The Director-General was requested to implement his proposals as fully as possible within WHO's regular programme and to submit to the Conference on the Human Environment a statement on the capabilities of WHO in the field of the environment, so that the Organization would be in a position to carry out the work required if funds were made available as a result of the Conference. He was also asked to invite voluntary contributions from governments and other sources to accelerate the existing programme and extend its scope.

SMALLPOX ERADICATION

The smallpox eradication campaign is now in its fifth year. Between 1967 and 1970, the incidence of the disease declined by over 75%, from 131,000 to 31,000 reported cases per annum. From January to May 1971, the number of cases reported (nearly 14,000) showed no reduction on the figure for the comparable period of 1970, but over half of the cases were reported by Ethiopia, where surveillance activities have greatly increased following the recent start of an eradication campaign. During the first months of 1971, the smallpox incidence in the rest of the world declined by about 50%—the sharpest decline yet observed. Smallpox is now endemic in fewer than 10 countries, and it is expected that by the end of 1971 the number will be reduced to five—Ethiopia, India, Nepal, Pakistan, and Sudan.

The Assembly believed that intensified effort is needed to reach the objective of global eradication in the shortest possible time. It asked all countries to give priority attention to the further improvement of case reporting and the immediate investigation and containment of all outbreaks of smallpox and urged Member governments to provide additional assistance to countries where the disease is still endemic.

COMMUNITY WATER SUPPLY

The community water supply programme proposed for the United Nations Second Development Decade (1971–80) aims at providing all town dwellers and 20% of the people in rural areas with a safe and abundant water supply. At present, only 51% of town dwellers and less than 10% of country dwellers in the developing countries have such a supply. The estimated total expenditure required to achieve this aim is $9100 million.[2] The resources available to WHO through the United Nations Development Programme (UNDP) and other assisting agencies will meet the cost of pre-investment studies, but WHO itself would have to provide for an additional 110 staff members to be assigned to Member governments for varying periods, and for a corresponding increase in supervisory and supporting staff. Some fourteen man-years of consultantships would be needed every year, and allowance would have to be made for an increase in training activities and an expansion of the fellowship programme. The financial commitment of WHO for an accelerated programme of assistance would thus be $26 million over the next nine years, and a further $20 million would be required from UNDP.

The Assembly recommended that each Member State concerned should carry out a nation-wide assessment of urban and rural water supplies, promulgate a national policy and create the infrastructure to implement it, prepare a 10-year national programme and individual projects capable of attracting investment, and foster interest among the people to be served. The needs for public water supply and sewerage should also be fully considered when formulating national economic development plans. The Director-General was asked to promote research and development activities leading to more efficient and economical water supply systems, to assist in the training of personnel in the developing countries, and to help Member States to mobilize all possible sources of technical and financial co-operation in the provision of community water supplies.

OCCUPATIONAL HEALTH FOR MINERS

The extraction of ores and other substances from the earth was described in a report of the Director-General to the Health Assembly as one of the most hazardous occupations known to man. The report shows that, in spite of prolonged efforts to improve them, the living and working conditions of miners in many areas remain dangerous and unhealthy. Among the subjects discussed are the optimum length of the working day in hot climates or at high altitudes, the employment of children in heavy mining work, and the housing of miners and their families, who often live in overcrowded, damp, and insanitary dwellings lacking a water supply. Small mines and quarries, which may at times employ the majority of a country's mining workers, present extensive health problems owing to their limited economic and technical resources.

The Health Assembly stressed the need for further efforts to improve the occupational health of miners and in particular for Member States, with WHO assistance, to develop occupational health services for miners and train the necessary personnel to man them. It requested the Director-General to study ways of establishing a standard medical reporting system to improve the health statistics relating to diseases and injuries in the industry, and to expand the current research programme on the health of miners, particularly in different geographical and sociocultural environments.

QUALITY CONTROL OF DRUGS

The Health Assembly considered that the production and distribution of drugs, the control of drug quality, safety, and efficacy, and the monitoring of adverse reactions, including dependence-producing properties, should be viewed as a whole. Owing to the continuous development of medical science and of the pharmaceutical industry, new and more effective drugs are constantly being produced, and there is an increasing need for prescribing physicians to know the effects, side reactions, and possible interactions of drugs. The Health Assembly believed that WHO must assume responsibility for helping to keep national health authorities and the medical profession abreast of the latest developments through expanded information facilities on pharmacotherapy and through continuing education in clinical pharmacology. It asked the Director-General to consider the creation of a system for collecting and disseminating information on the results of safety and effectiveness trials of new drugs and their registration. It also requested the publication of a list of countries where the authorities implement the requirements for good practices in the manufacture and quality control of drugs and the certification scheme on the quality of pharmaceutical products moving in international commerce.

DRUG DEPENDENCE

A proposal for the extension of WHO activities in the field of drug dependence was approved by the Health Assembly. The programme is concerned with the collection and exchange of data, the analysis of medical, social, cultural, and economic factors contributing to drug dependence, the conduct of research and training activities, and evaluation. The Assembly urged Member States that have not already done so to accede to the Convention on Psychotropic Substances.

TRAINING OF NATIONAL HEALTH PERSONNEL

Because the extreme shortage of health personnel is one of the major obstacles to the development of effective health services in the developing countries, the Health Assembly resolved to extend still further the co-operation of WHO with governments and with other international organizations in the training of national health personnel. Despite the difficulties involved, the shortage can and should be overcome much more rapidly than it was in the developed countries. A necessary condition is the co-operation and co-ordination of efforts of Member States and the relevant international organizations in order to make use of all available resources and experience. The Assembly stressed the importance of current and long-term health manpower planning and called on Member States to pay attention in their social and economic development plans to the problems of training and utilizing health personnel. High priority should be accorded to developing and strengthening educational institutions offering optimum conditions for the training of personnel drawn from all strata and social groups of the population. The training given in them should be flexible, not only applying internationally acceptable standards for the teaching of medical and allied health personnel, based on advances in educational science, but also taking into account the circumstances that influence health in a particular country or region.

The Director-General was asked to intensify the study of criteria for assessing the equivalence of medical degrees in different countries and to formulate a definition of the word "physician." WHO will study the curricula and syllabuses of existing medical teaching institutions with a view to drawing up models that will help in establishing medical schools in developing countries. Studies are also to continue on the outflow of trained personnel from developing to developed countries (the so-called "brain drain"), the continuing education of health personnel, and the training of medical teachers.

HEALTH CONSEQUENCES OF SMOKING

In view of the relationship between smoking and the development of pulmonary and cardiac disease, including lung cancer, ischaemic heart disease, chronic bronchitis, and emphysema, the Health Assembly considered that a sustained effort by health and education authorities and others is needed to reduce tobacco smoking and to prevent the extension of the habit, especially among young people and pregnant women. The Organization will produce a code of practice to guide governments in formulating legislation on smoking.

The Assembly endorsed the recommendations contained in a report of consultants submitted by the Director-General, which call for:

- the establishment by governments of national committees to supervise anti-smoking programmes,
- studies of the nature and magnitude of the smoking problem and of behaviour and attitudes towards smoking, particularly among opinion leaders,
- the curtailment and eventual elimination of cigarette advertising, increased taxation on cigarettes, and differential taxation according to the content of tar or nicotine,
- the education of medical students in the hazards of smoking,
- the discouragement of smoking in hospitals and

other health institutions and in public places, and
- the discouragement of smoking among health workers, especially in the presence of patients and young people.

The Director-General was asked to draw the attention of the Food and Agriculture Organization to the necessity of undertaking a study on crop diversification in tobacco-growing areas in view of the expected decrease in tobacco consumption.

MEDICAL USE OF IONIZING RADIATION

The exposure of populations to ionizing radiation is growing, owing partly to the increasing use of radiation for diagnostic and therapeutic purposes and partly to the development of nuclear energy and the use of radioisotopes. The Health Assembly recognized that this trend heightens the probability of deleterious biological effects in both the present and future generations, but it was also well aware of the important role of radiation in preventive medicine and therapy. It decided that WHO should study the use of ionizing radiation in medicine and the risks to health arising from its excessive or improper use. The Director-General was asked to draw up a programme of activities based on the rational use of ionizing radiation and on improved diagnostic and therapeutic techniques and equipment, including clinical dosimetry and radiological protection.

At the same time, Member States were invited to co-operate in epidemiological studies on the effects of ionizing radiation, to promote studies on improved radiodiagnostic and radiotherapeutic techniques that would be more effective but would minimize human exposure, and to set up radiation protection services to provide advice and for the purposes of supervision and inspection.

HEALTH ASSISTANCE TO REFUGEES IN THE MIDDLE EAST

Since the inception of the United Nations Relief and Works Agency for Palestine Refugees in the Near East, WHO has borne responsibility for the technical direction of UNRWA's health services, to which it provides certain WHO staff members including the Director of Health. As customary, the Health Assembly considered the annual report of the Director of Health for the year 1970. It adopted two resolutions relating to health assistance to refugees and displaced persons in the Middle East, requesting the Director-General to expand WHO's programme of assistance and to take all measures in his power to safeguard the health conditions in the area concerned.

ADMISSION OF A NEW MEMBER

The Sultanate of Oman was admitted to membership of the World Health Organization, becoming WHO's 130th Member State.

MEMBERSHIP OF THE EXECUTIVE BOARD

The Health Assembly elected the following eight Member States to designate persons to serve for three years on the WHO Executive Board: Denmark, Ecuador, Italy, Lesotho, Syria, Thailand, Trinidad and Tobago, and Uruguay. The remaining 16 members of the Executive Board are designated by: Algeria, Austria, Bulgaria, the Central African Republic, Cyprus, Ethiopia, France, Japan, Kenya, Laos, Nepal, Nicaragua, Saudi Arabia, Upper Volta, the USA, and the USSR.

OTHER DECISIONS OF THE ASSEMBLY

Consideration of the participation of the German Democratic Republic in WHO was deferred until the Twenty-fifth World Health Assembly. It was decided that the Twenty-fifth World Health Assembly would be held in Switzerland.

• • • •

TECHNICAL DISCUSSIONS

The subject of the technical discussions held during the Assembly was "Mass health examinations as a public health tool."

Dr. H. E. Hilleboe, Clinical Professor of Comprehensive Medicine, Medical School, University of South Florida, USA, was appointed General Chairman of the discussions.

The 221 participants, from 57 countries and nine international organizations, attended informally and not as delegates of their governments or as officials of their organizations.

The field of mass health examinations is expanding rapidly and already covers a very wide range of health activities, from checking smallpox vaccination scars to applying a battery of automated biochemical, haematological, and other screening tests. Mass examinations fall into several basic categories. Some aim at acquiring information on the health status of a population. Others try to detect changes in health status. Another form seeks to discover conditions such as heart disease or cancer of the cervix before symptoms have become overt.

Mass health examinations are primarily concerned with preventing disease, or reversing or arresting its course in the individual or the community, by the application of various investigative techniques to large numbers of people. They should be considered within the general framework of national health programmes and not as an isolated activity. In the developing countries they are likely to be used principally to detect and combat communicable diseases, in the developed countries to control chronic non-communicable diseases.

Where sufficient medical manpower is available, screening can be carried out mainly by doctors, but most countries lack sufficient professional staff and less skilled personnel have been trained to carry out a variety of important tasks. Auxiliary workers can be trained to do some kinds of laboratory work, to perform initial tests of sight and hearing, and even to interpret radiographs. In one country, participants were told, quarantine inspectors were trained to carry out mass radiography work. After a 10-week course they were able to screen films as rapidly and accurately as professionals.

Mass examinations raise ethical and legal problems regarding the extent to which people should be compelled to undergo them and the degree of confidentiality of the data gathered. In some countries, it is held that there should be compulsory examinations for people in certain occupations, such as food-handlers or school-teachers, because they may be a risk to the community. As with all medical examinations, there may be considerable consequences for the individual, and medical confidentiality must be maintained. The importance of obtaining public participation through health education was emphasized.

The possible dangers of mass examinations were well brought out in the discussions. These include physical dangers from irradiation, hepatitis caused by blood tests, iatrogenic disease (for example, neuroses that may develop because a person is informed of slight abnormalities in the electrocardiogram that are really of no significance), and the danger of false security due to error in the examination technique.

Mass examinations also raise practical problems. For instance, in screening for disease, borderline groups may be discovered consisting of people who are not demonstrably diseased, yet not clearly free from the risk of developing the disease. It is often difficult to decide whether such people should be treated and, if so, what form the treatment should take.

The introduction of automated analysis in the laboratory has possibly been the most significant innovation in mass health examinations for many years. Today there are rapid and accurate automatic methods of carrying out biochemical tests on a large number of specimens. Automatic methods in microbiology and immunology are being developed. Automation is also making progress in the recording of body measurements, the reading of electrocardiograms, and the analysis of heart sounds. These procedures are likely to revolutionize mass health examinations in the future, making the surveillance of large populations a more manageable task.

However, a note of caution was sounded by the participants. As the Chairman observed, automated and computerized techniques are complex and their application not universally desirable. Techniques and tests must be evaluated before embarking on sophisticated programmes, which may turn out to be unexpectedly expensive and to yield a lower return in improved health than was anticipated.

NOTES

[1] See *WHO Chronicle,* 1971, 25, 155.
[2] See *WHO Chronicle,* 1971, 25, 70.

Annual Report of the World Meteorological Organization 1967

World Meteorological Association

The following general review of the activities of WMO in 1967 is the first section of the Secretary General's voluminous annual report to the member states of WMO and to the Economic and Social Council of the United Nations. Information about the documentation activities of WMO will be found in the article following this one.

GENERAL REVIEW

1.1 Major Developments

1.1.1 General

The year 1967 was a very important and eventful year for the World Meteorological Organization.

The World Meteorological Congress, which meets at intervals of four years to adopt the policy, programme and budget of the Organization for the subsequent four-year period, held its fifth session in Geneva in April 1967. Each Congress is an event of the highest importance in the life of the Organization, but Fifth Congress was, however, of unprecedented importance and significance because it saw the unanimous adoption by the Organization of a new world weather system—World Weather Watch. It may be recalled that the World Weather Watch Plan had been developed by WMO in response to a request of the United Nations General Assembly to ensure that modern scientific and technological developments (particularly in the field of outer space) are fully used to improve the basic knowledge of the atmosphere and that this knowledge is applied in practical and peaceful ways for the benefit of all peoples in the world. The plan was the outcome of intensive activity within WMO during the four-year period following the previous Congress held in 1963, and its adoption by Fifth Congress in 1967 marked a culmination of this activity.

U Thant, Secretary-General of the United Nations, honoured Congress by addressing a plenary session. He commended WMO for the manner in which it had responded to the request of the General Assembly of the United Nations by preparing the plan for the World Weather Watch.

It is of interest to record that, at its meeting in September 1967, the United Nations Committee on the Peaceful Uses of Outer Space expressed great appreciation of the World Weather Watch Plan, which it considered to be an excellent demonstration of the practical benefits which could be derived from the peaceful uses of outer space. Keen interest in the plan has also been shown by the specialized agencies, other international organizations in the field of science and the scientific community in general.

Congress also took important decisions regarding the steps to be taken to implement the World Weather Watch Plan. Among the several ways in which it is envisaged that implementation shall be effected is the establishment of a new WMO Voluntary Assistance Programme, which has been designed to meet the specific needs of Member States, especially developing countries, which cannot be met through other sources such as the United Nations Development Programme (UNDP) or bilateral assistance. The WMO Voluntary Assistance Programme envisages contributions by Members in cash, equipment and services on a purely voluntary basis. The Executive Committee, which was requested by Congress to approve the rules of this new programme, fulfilled this task at its nineteenth session held immediately after Congress (May 1967).

SOURCE: Reprinted from Annual Report of the World Meterological Association, 1967. Geneva, World Meteorological Association, 1968. pp. 1-1–1-8.

Immediately afterwards, the Secretariat began extensive studies, based on correspondence with individual Members of WMO, on the arrangements for the implementation of national projects within the over-all plan for the World Weather Watch.

Congress also endorsed the concept of a Global Atmospheric Research Programme (GARP) as a framework within which all research activities relating to World Weather Watch should be undertaken and decided that it should be planned and implemented on a joint basis with the International Council of Scientific Unions (ICSU). For this purpose Congress gave appropriate directives to the Executive Committee to negotiate an agreement with ICSU for the implementation of this programme. The formal agreement for the joint sponsorship of this scientific project by the two organizations was concluded later in the year. In accordance with this agreement, a Joint Organizing Committee for GARP was also established at the same time, composed of twelve scientists selected by mutual agreement between ICSU and WMO, whose main tasks would be to recommend to these two organizations the scientific goals and plans for GARP and to lay down the requirements for the implementation of the whole programme.

The collaboration between ICSU and WMO in this joint enterprise is in fulfillment of a request of the General Assembly of the United Nations. Its ultimate goal is to increase the understanding of the general circulation of the atmosphere and thereby develop the physical and mathematical basis for methods of extended prediction.

An item of great interest during the Fifth Congress of WMO was the first IMO Lecture, delivered by Dr. Edward N. Lorenz of the Massachusetts Institute of Technology on "The nature and theory of the general circulation of the atmosphere." It may be recalled that the IMO Lecture was instituted by a decision of Fourth Congress (1963) to commemorate the International Meteorological Organization, the non-governmental body created in 1873 and replaced by WMO in 1951.

Some of the other major decisions of Congress are reviewed in the following paragraphs.

Congress recognized that there was a need for a thorough review of the present structure of WMO for carrying out its scientific and technical work, especially in view of the activities related to the World Weather Watch. It requested the Executive Committee to make a detailed study of this question with a view to preparing comprehensive proposals for desirable modifications in the structure and method of functioning of the Organiza-

tion and gave detailed guidance as to the principles to be followed in carrying out this task.

A major item in the programme of technical activities approved by Congress was in the field of agrometeorology. Provision was made for the establishment and implementation of an expanded world programme for achieving the maximum contribution from meterology, at both the international and national levels, to increasing world food production and conserving world food resources and supplies. Dr. B. R. Sen, the then Director-General of the Food and Agriculture Organization, made a statement before Congress offering the full collaboration of FAO in a programme of this nature, and since then, in addition to FAO, UNESCO and UNDP have formally agreed to participate in this programme.

Congress reviewed the activities of WMO related to meteorological training and took a number of decisions with a view to further expansion in this field. Among these, special mention may be made of the provision of funds in the regular budget for long-term fellowships. The purpose of these fellowships is to enable candidates from developing countries to obtain the basic university education in science required for specialized studies in meteorology and thereafter to pursue a career in the Meteorological Service.

Other important decisions of Congress with regard to the technical activities of the Organization will be found in section 1.1.2.

Congress reviewed the participation of WMO, as a United Nations specialized agency, in the technical co-operation programmes under the United Nations Development Programme (UNDP). Congress noted with satisfaction that the activities of WMO in this field have increased steadily over the past years and received with great interest the statement made personally by Mr. Paul Hoffman, Administrator of UNDP, confirming the continued collaboration of UNDP in the technical assistance work of WMO. In view of the important part which Meteorological Services can play in economic development and of the possibility of providing aid to them through technical co-operation programmes, Congress considered it necessary for these Services to be represented on the national planning bodies of their respective countries and recommended appropriate action to that end.

Other decisions of Congress of particular interest in the field of technical cooperation activities of WMO are summarized in section 1.1.3.

Congress adopted some amendments to the Convention of the Organization which are mentioned in Part 3 of the present report. One important change in the Convention was to increase the membership of the Executive Committee from twenty-one to twenty-four.

Congress decided that the close collaboration of WMO with the United Nations and its specialized agencies as well as with other international organizations whose activities have meteorological aspects should be maintained and further strengthened whenever possible in order to assist in achieving the most effective application of meteorology to human activities and the complete success of the World Weather Watch Plan.

The Executive Committee at its nineteenth session (1967) approved the award of the IMO Prize to Professor K. Y. Kondratyev, Rector of the University of Leningrad and Chairman of the Atmospheric Physics Division of the University. Professor Kondratyev, who is a member and former chairman of the WMO Advisory Committee, is also well known for his activities within the International Association of Meteorology and Atmospheric Physics (IAMAP) of the International Union of Geodesy and Geophysics.

The seventh World Meteorological Day was celebrated throughout the world on 23 March 1967, the anniversary of the day on which the Convention of WMO came into force in 1950. The selected theme for this occasion was "Weather and water" in support of the International Hydrological Decade in which WMO is participating together with some other international organizations, notably UNESCO. An illustrated booklet describing the role played by WMO in the field of water resources development was published and distributed as part of the literature made available to Members of the Organization in celebration of the World Meteorological Day.

The close collaboration between WMO and the United Nations in various fields was continued during the year, particularly in matters relating to the application of science and technology to development, outer space, marine sciences and evaluation of technical co-operation programmes. Collaboration was also maintained with the Economic Commissions of the United Nations, the specialized agencies and other international organizations through joint projects and in other ways. Activities in this respect are reported in detail in Part 4 of the present report.

The steady increase in the Membership of WMO has continued, three new Members having joined the Organization during the year, making a total of 132.

Relations with the authorities of the Swiss Federal Government and of the Canton and City of Geneva continued to be cordial. In this connexion it may be mentioned that the Swiss authorities indicated their willingness to make a loan for the construction of an extension to the Headquarters building of the Organization, an offer which the WMO Congress was happy to accept. Further information on this subject is given in Part 8 of the report.

The year 1967, which was the last year of the fourth financial period (1964-1967), was a reasonably satisfactory one from the financial point of view, an over-all budgetary surplus for the period as a whole being recorded. As regards contributions, about 86 per cent of the contributions for 1967 had been received by the end of the year, as compared with the corresponding figure of about 88 per cent for 1966.

1.1.2 Technical development

The year under review saw much progress and development in the technical activities of the Organization.

Reference has already been made in the previous section to the adoption of the World Weather Watch Plan by Fifth Congress. The main features of this Plan are described in Part 7 of the present report. The full texts of the plan and its implementation programme together with the relevant decisions of Congress and of the subsequent session of the Executive Committee were included in a publication which was widely distributed. It may be mentioned that the plan calls for continuing studies both with regard to the agreed operational system and new techniques to be introduced into the operational system as soon as they have been proved to be sufficiently reliable and economical. Both types of study were continued during the period following Fifth Congress and the results of some of these studies were published in the World Weather Watch Planning Reports series. Six such publications were issued during the year.

In connexion with the joint WMO/ICSU Global Atmospheric Research Programme, which will constitute the main activity on the research aspects of the World Weather Watch, WMO co-sponsored a study conference which was organized jointly by the ICSU/IUGG Committee on Atmospheric Sciences and the Committee on Space Research (COSPAR) of the ICSU. The main purpose of this conference, which was attended by a large number of specialists, was to identify some of the basic problems requiring study, determine the requirements of observational systems and data, and formulate plans for theoretical studies and observational experiments in order to be able to realize the objectives of this scientific programme. Fuller information about this conference will be found in section 7.6 of the present report.

Some of the other important decisions of Fifth Congress in the technical field are reviewed briefly in the following paragraphs.

While no changes were made by Congress in the present system of technical commissions through which the technical activities of the Organization are largely carried out, some essential modifications were made in the terms of reference of most of the commissions. In particular, the terms of reference of the Commission for Synoptic Meteorology were expanded to include the co-ordination of the various aspects of the Global Observing System and of the Global Data Processing System which are two of the components of the World Weather Watch Plan. Congress also decided that the Commission for Aerology should be renamed Commission for Atmospheric Sciences and agreed that Members of the Organization should be invited to take due account of any important research activities outside their respective Meteorological Services when nominating experts to participate in the work of this commission.

Several important decisions were taken by Congress for the promotion of meteorological research. To ensure that meterological data are readily available to research workers, it was decided to expand the publication "Catalogue of meterological data for research" with priority to a section containing information on the data archived on media suitable for machine processing. Congress considered that a WMO-sponsored programme of visiting scientists to research institutes would further the promotion of international research in meteorology, and established principles to be followed by Members in making specific requests under this programme. It may be noted in this connexion that a programme of this nature had earlier been recommended by the WMO Advisory Committee and approved by the Executive Committee but, for financial reasons however, the plan was of a short-term nature and was restricted to the field of tropical meterology. The first project under this interim arrangement was carried out during the year by sponsoring the visit of a well-known expert in tropical meteorology to Australia.

Congress recognized that the publications programme of the Organization constituted one of its most important activities and in order to provide greater assistance to Members decided that as many as possible of the publications should be issued in the four official languages.

Congress examined the position regarding the preparation and publication of regional climatic atlases and in view of the financial difficulties which had proved a great handicap in the successful implementation of this project in the past, it made budgetary provision to ensure that at least some of the planned regional atlases shall be published in the fifth financial period (1968-1971). Under the authority given by Congress, negotiations with UNESCO have since been successfully concluded under which UNESCO will contribute to the cost of printing the charts of the European Atlas.

WMO continued its active role in the programme of the International Hydrological Decade (IHD) in which UNESCO is acting as the central co-ordinating agency. In particular WMO provided the technical secretariat for a number of projects included in the programme of IHD. A new series of technical publications entitled "Reports on WMO/IHD projects" giving the results of studies undertaken on such projects was introduced and the first four reports in this series were published by WMO during the year. Two international symposia dealing with floods and their computation and hydrological forecasting were organized by WMO in Australia and U.S.S.R. jointly with other international organizations and the authorities of the host countries.

The Typhoon Survey Mission, jointly sponsored by ECAFE and WMO, which commenced its survey visits to countries in east Asia and the northwest Pacific towards the end of 1966, completed its work early in 1967. The report of the mission was thereafter examined by a meeting of experts held in Bangkok in order to suggest ways of translating the recommendations into a programme of action. It was agreed to set up an intergovernmental typhoon committee with a regional typhoon centre to serve as its executive arm. Action was in hand at the end of 1967 to convene, in collaboration with ECAFE, a meeting of governments in the ECAFE region with the object of formally setting up the typhoon committee.

The General Assembly of the United Nations at

its twenty-first session (1966) adopted Resolution 2172 (XXI) on Resources of the Sea in which it requested the Secretary-General of the United Nations, in co-operation with other international organizations and interested governments, to undertake a comprehensive survey in marine science and technology and formulate proposals for ensuring the most effective arrangements for an expanded programme of international co-operation in this field. WMO participated actively in the work of the group of experts set up by the United Nations pursuant to this resolution. WMO also collaborated closely with SCOR, IOC and the FAO Advisory Committee on Marine Resources Research in a study of some aspects of the resolution.

WMO continued its collaboration with FAO in the United Nations Special Fund project on Desert Locust Control. The series of joint FAO/UNESCO/WMO projects in agroclimatology, the purpose of which is to demonstrate how climatological data can be used in helping to solve problems in agricultural planning in semi-arid and arid zones, was continued. The third project of this kind was started in 1967, the area selected for the study being the highlands of eastern Africa. The report of the second project, completed in 1966, was published in 1967 in the WMO Technical Note series.

The WMO Advisory Committee which meets annually held its fourth session during the year when it gave special attention to the research aspects of the World Weather Watch and the role of WMO in the Global Atmospheric Research Programme.

The normal technical activities of the regional associations and of the technical commissions were carried out as usual. Two of the technical commissions held their fourth sessions while a few of the working groups of all the eight commissions held a session each during the year.

The Commission for Agricultural Meteorology held its fourth session in Manila (Philippines). Among the new subjects to be studies by the commission are the meteorological factors affecting the disease "rice blast" and methods of forecasting the quantity and quality of crop yields.

The fourth session of the Commission for Aeronautical Meteorology was held at the ICAO headquarters in Montreal. The major part of the session was held conjointly with the fifth Air Navigation Conference of ICAO. Discussions during this part of the session related exclusively to the meteorological services required in the ap-

proach, landing and take-off phases of aircraft operations. Among other matters of concern to the commission which were considered in a separate session may be mentioned; questions relating to the qualifications and training of aeronautical meteorological personnel and the preparation of a handbook on aviation forecasting techniques and practices.

A large number of publications were issued during the year including seven additions to the WMO Technical Note series. The publication of the WMO Bulletin was continued on a quarterly basis and there seems little doubt that it continued to be well received by meteorologists both within and outside national Meteorological Services as well as by all those interested generally in the applications of meteorology to economic development.

1.1.3 Technical co-operation

The participation of WMO in the various technical co-operation programmes of the United Nations continued to be one of the major activities of the Organization.

As already indicated in section 1.1.1, Fifth Congress reviewed the activities in this field and took some important decisions.

Congress noted with satisfaction that during the period 1963-1966 the participation of WMO in the various technical co-operation programmes had substantially increased and that during that period projects in the field of meterology costing more than nine million US dollars had been carried out from which nearly one hundred countries had benefited. Congress also recognized that technical co-operation programmes will assume an even greater importance in the implementation of World Weather Watch and noted with satisfaction that the UNDP authorities had expressed their interest in the WWW Plan.

Congress gave much attention to the systematic evaluation being carried out by WMO on all assistance rendered under UNDP. It expressed the view that such evaluation should in future not only be based on reports received from the permanent representatives of the Members of WMO, but that, in an increasing manner, personal visits should be made to recipient countries by members of the Secretariat and, where necessary and appropriate, by special consultants.

In view of the great importance and usefulness

of regional projects, particularly with regard to meteorological training, Congress decided that the appropriate United Nations authorities should be approached with a view to increasing the allocation for regional projects. It is gratifying to report that the Governing Council of the UNDP, at its session in June 1967, decided to increase the share of regional projects from 16 to 17 per cent of the total field programme.

Some of the salient features of the technical cooperation activities of the Organization during 1967 are briefly reviewed in the following paragraphs.

1967 was the first year of the biennial programme cycle 1967-1968 of the Technical Assistance component of the UNDP. The rate of implementation of the approved programme was very satisfactory and it is gratifying to report that in 1967 the largest technical assistance programme so far (about 1.3 million US dollars) was carried out in the first year of a programme cycle.

A special feature of the 1967 programme was an increased number of expert missions in the field of agricultural meteorology.

Training activities continued to form an important part of the technical assistance programme through the provision of fellowships or of experts serving as instructors in WMO-supported regional training centres or in country projects. Lectures at university level were also given by WMO experts in some countries. Two posts of professor for university Chairs of Meteorology were filled during the year. One of these was at the University of Lovanium in Kinshasa (Democratic Republic of Congo) and the other at the University of Costa Rica. The university Chair of Meteorology in Nairobi, previously established, continued throughout 1967 and was strengthened by the appointment of a senior lecturer to assist the professor in carrying out the training programme of the University College. A seminar for national instructors in meteorology in the countries of Latin America was organized in Santiago (Chile) as a regional project. Under its regional programme WMO also collaborated actively with the Economic Commission for Africa in the seminar organized by the latter on hydrological instruments and methods of observation and the establishment of hydrometeorological networks in Africa.

The activities of WMO under the Special Fund component of UNDP continued on an increased scale in 1967.

Implementation of four new projects was commenced: Metorological Services Development in North-Eastern Brazil, Improvement of Caribbean Meteorological Services, Expansion and Improvement of Hydrometeorological and Hydrological Services in the Central American Isthmus and the Hydrometeorological Survey of the Catchments of Lakes Victoria, Kioga and Albert.

Two new projects—Colombian Meteorological and Hydrological Services and Meteorological Training and Research in the Philippines—were approved by the Governing Council of the UNDP in 1967. Action was initiated for the implementation of these projects which are expected to become operational in 1968.

Execution of three projects was continued in 1967: Pilot Project for the Improvement and Expansion of Typhoon and Flood Warning Services in the Republic of China, Meteorological Training Centre in Kinshasa (Democratic Republic of Congo) and Meteorological Institute for Research and Training in Cairo (United Arab Republic).

Three projects were successfully completed early in 1967: Expansion of Meteorological and Hydrological Services in Burma, Institute of Tropical Meteorology and International Meteorological Centre in India and Expansion of Meteorological Services in Thailand.

Action was pursued for the implementation of projects which are of a technical assistance nature and financed from the regular budget of WMO under the New Development Fund. In several cases equipment for the improvement of telecommunications facilities approved under the relevant projects was ordered and is expected to be brought into operation in 1968. Four additional training fellowships were also approved under the WMO New Development Fund in 1967.

The New Development Fund was originally established by Fourth Congress (1963) for the fourth financial period (1964-1967). Fifth Congress (1967) authorized the carry-over of funds from this source to the fifth financial period (1968-1971) to ensure that the approved projects are successfully completed.

Appropriate steps were taken to ensure coordination between the UNDP and VAP activities, bearing in mind that the VAP should be devoted to projects which cannot be implemented by other means.

1.1.4 Future programme

The fifth World Meteorological Congress established the programme of the Organization for the four-year period 1968-1971 and it adopted the plan for the World Weather Watch as a major item in this programme. Congress also gave the directive that high priority should be given to all activities related to the implementation and further planning of the World Weather Watch.

The World Weather Watch enters into the implementation phase in 1968 and every effort will be made to ensure that the implementation is carried out efficiently and rapidly. The operation of the WMO Voluntary Assistance Programme will undoubtedly be a major activity in this connexion.

In accordance with the decision of Congress further planning studies will be continued to enable appropriate adjustments to be made by Congress or the Executive Committee in the World Weather Watch Plan in the light of the results of such studies.

Activities associated with the Global Atmospheric Research Programme, a joint ICSU/WMO enter-prise, will receive high priority to ensure that the World Weather Watch Plan not only serves operational purposes, but that research in atmospheric sciences associated with the plan also makes progress. The promotion of meteorological research in other ways will also be continued.

The technical co-operation programme through which assistance is provided not only on the national level but also on a regional basis, particularly in training programmes, will continue to be a major activity.

The normal activities of the Organization in scientific, technical and administrative fields will be continued in the usual way.

As in the past due attention will be given to ensure that WMO fully meets its responsibilities towards the United Nations and other international organizations in all matters of mutual interests.

Collection and Publication of IGY Meteorological Data

O. M. Ashford

In this piece O. M. Ashford, Chief of the Investigation Section of WMO, reports on the problem of organizing and publishing an estimated 10,000,000 individual meteorological observations made during the International Geophysical Year. The considerations leading to the decision to publish the data on microcards is stated in some detail.

INTRODUCTION

The primary object of the meteorological programme of the International Geophysical Year (1957–1958) is to assemble meteorological observations from all over the world which help the research workers to throw new light on the problem of the large-scale physical, dynamic and thermodynamic processes in the atmosphere. The present paper describes the arrangements which have been made by the World Meteorological Organization (WMO), in close collaboration with the Special Committee for the IGY (CSAGI), for collecting and publishing the IGY meteorological observations.

NATURE OF THE PROBLEM

The observations with which we are mainly concerned in this article consist of a selection of the "synoptic" surface and upper-air meteorological observations, that is the observations which are being made for routine weather forecasting purposes at standard hours all over the world in accordance with the practices laid down by the WMO. In addition to these observations, the IGY meteorological programme includes many observations in "physical" meteorology, that is radiation, ozone, atmospheric chemistry and atmospheric electricity. The synoptic observations will form by far the largest part of the material to be handled; in all they will amount to some 10,000,000 individual observations. The problem to be solved by WMO was how to ensure that this vast volume of material could be made readily available to the research worker.

EXISTING PUBLICATIONS

This problem would have been automatically solved if all the national meteorological services of the world, who are responsible for making the IGY observations, regularly published their observations, after being checked, in a reasonably uniform manner. The research worker would then simply have had to obtain a complete set of these national publications.

That this situation is far from being realized in the case of the surface meteorological observations was amply demonstrated by the results of an inquiry by WMO in 1954, when it was found that of the 60 countries from which replies were received only 38 were publishing the daily surface observations in one form or another. The publications differed greatly both as regards layout and contents; for example some contained only one observation per day for each station while others contained eight observations per day. Only 6 publications contained ships' observations and only in 5 cases was it reported that the observations were checked prior to being published, although in many cases the observations were checked subsequently and errata sheets issued.

Since 1955 the WMO has been carrying out an annual inquiry to determine the number of

SOURCE: Reprinted from "Collection and Publication of IGY Meteorological Data," *Revue de la Documentation*, 25 (Aug., 1958) pp. 74–78.

meteorological services which publish their upper-air meteorological observations, that is radiosonde, radiowind and pilot-balloon observations. In 1957 the situation was that, of the 93 services for which information was available, 56 regularly publish the data, 9 planned to do so in the near future, 9 supplied them on request in microfilm or other form and 18 did not make the data available in any form. No information was received from 16 meteorological services. As in the case of the publications containing surface observations, there is some lack of uniformity in the upper-air publications, but there has been a marked improvement in this respect since the introduction in 1953 by WMO of a recommended layout for the tables.

The only major publication which contains observations from many different countries is the *Daily Series, Synoptic Weather Maps, Part II, Northern Hemisphere, Data Tabulations,* published by the United States Weather Bureau. This contains one observation daily from approximately 240 land stations in the USA, from some 1500 land stations in other parts of the Northern Hemisphere, and from about 450 ships. Observational and transmission errors are corrected prior to publication insofar as personnel and time limitations permit. This important publication also includes a fairly complete coverage of the upper-air observations made in the Northern Hemisphere, but many of these data are unchecked. To meet the purposes of the IGY, this publication would have had to be extended to cover the Southern Hemisphere and to include four surface observations daily instead of only one. Apart from this, the publication has been criticised by research workers because the printed figures are so small that they can only be read with some difficulty.

In view of the inadequacies of the present arrangements for publishing the meteorological observations required by research workers, it was realized that it would be essential to take steps to have the IGY meteorological observations collected and published by an international centre, and this task was given to the WMO Secretariat, where the IGY Meteorological Data Centre was in fact established towards the end of 1956.

There are many thousands of meteorological stations over the world, some of which make observations every hour or even every half-hour. It was therefore essential to define precisely which observations should be collected and published, taking as a general principle that these observations should be limited to those required for the investigations included in the IGY meteorological programme. The following selection was made of the synoptic observations:

> Observations made at a selection of about 2000 land stations and on board ships at 0000, 0600, 1200 and 1800 GMT.
> All radiosonde and radiowind observations, all pilot-balloon observations made at stations south of latitude 35° N and at a selection of stations north of this latitude.

Standard forms for entering all the IGY meteorological observations were prepared by WMO, in collaboration where appropriate with other international bodies, especially the International Radiation Commission and the International Ozone Commission. Specimen forms and instructions were sent to the meteorological services of the world and to other interested institutes, and in many cases bulk supplies of the forms were also distributed at cost price.

PUBLISHING THE IGY METEOROLOGICAL DATA

General Consideration

Having decided what data to collect and how to collect them, the next major problem was to decide in what form they should be published. The primary factors to be borne in mind in this connexion were accuracy, the convenience of the user, the number of copies of the publication which would be required, the cost involved, and the need to avoid undue delay. After very careful consideration, it was decided to publish the surface and upper-air observations on Microcards. The reasons for this are given below. A final decision has not yet been taken about the method of publication of the observations in physical meteorology as there are still some unknown factors, including the total volume of the material to be published and the number of copies required.

Possible Forms of Publication

Three distinct types of publication were considered, namely (a) printed volumes, (b) punched cards and (c) microrecording. Groups (a) and (c) can be further subdivided as follows:

(a) Printed volumes
    (i) By type setting
    (ii) By offset from retyped copies of the original forms
    (iii) By direct offset from the original forms
(c) Microrecording
    (i) Microfilm
    (ii) Microcards
    (iii) Microfiches
    (iv) Microprints

The advantages and disadvantages of these various possibilities have already been described in the literature (see for example "Manual on Document Reproduction and Selection" of the International Federation for Documentation). The following paragraphs are therefore limited to the salient points with regard to the IGY material.

Accuracy

From the point of view of accuracy, a direct photographic copying of the original forms has the very great merit that not a single new error is introduced. This is an important factor in favour of processes (a iii) and (c). It should be pointed out, however, that as many of the original forms are prepared at the stations where the observations are made, there is inevitably a considerable variability in the neatness and legibility of the forms. Process (a iii) would therefore have resulted in a rather unsightly publication.

Convenience of the User

As regards the convenience of the user, it is not easy to generalize. For many, punched cards would at first sight appear to be the best way of presenting the data, as they readily lend themselves to various types of statistical analysis of the data. There are however many disadvantages in punched cards for the IGY data. Apart from the enormous number of cards required (of the order of 4 million for the surface observations from land stations alone) with the consequent high cost of production and shipping and the difficulties of storage, there is as yet no internationally agreed punched-card layout, except in the case of the surface observations from ships. Also, any given punched card cannot unfortunately be used on all the different types of machines employed by meteorological services and institutes. Many of the IGY observations will of course be put onto punched cards by national meteorological services, but this would not be a satisfactory method for the international publication of the data. An important part of the processing of the observations will be plotting them on synoptic weather maps and this cannot be done directly from punched cards—the data on the cards would first have to be tabulated.

Some form of printed volume would appear to be the next choice from the point of view of convenience, the main disadvantage apart from cost being the bulk of the material; the surface observations from land stations would alone require 220 volumes each of 500 pages, assuming that two of the original forms (21 X 15 cm) were reproduced in reduced size on a page of 16 X 24 cm.

As regards the choice between microfilm and micro-opaque cards, the advantages of the latter from the point of view of convenience have already been described by Malcolm Rigby (WMO Bulletin, Vol. V, No. 2, p. 53-60). In brief, micro-opaque cards are more compact and durable than microfilm, they are more easily transportable, more convenient for filing and for locating any given page of the original material. Microfiches also have most of the advantages of micro-opaque cards but they tend to become scratched if used frequently and they are not so easy to handle. The merits of microfiches as compared with micro-opaque cards are that more satisfactory results can be obtained from poor original material and that the design of the readers is simpler. On the whole, apart from cost considerations, the advantages for the IGY, where durability is an important factor, appear to favour the micro-opaque card.

Number of Copies Required

A world-wide survey carried out by WMO in 1956 indicated a potential demand for about 40 complete sets of the IGY meteorological data and for a smaller number of partial sets. At the time of writing it seems that this survey gave a very fair indication of the true demand and it now seems that about 50 copies of each microcard

will be required. The demand is of course somewhat influenced by the price and in its turn the
price depends very largely on the number of
copies to be sold. There is some indication that
had the price of a complete set of microcards
been considerably lower, one or two customers
would have bought complete sets instead of only
buying partial sets, but there has been no suggestion that the demand would ever have been
substantially greater.

Cost

As stated above, the cost of punched cards
would have been very high. No detailed estimates
were prepared but it is clear that they would cost
far more than either printed volumes or microrecording.

It is generally recognized that microrecording
is much cheaper than printing when only a small
number of copies are required. This can be
rapidly demonstrated by comparing the costs of
making 100 copies of the forms containing the
surface observations from land stations. If reproduced by direct offset, which can be assumed
to be the cheapest printing process, each of the
220 volumes required would cost about $20
per copy, which comes to $4,400 for a single
set of 220 volumes. The cost for a set of the
same material on Microcards would be about
$265.

To these figures must be added the distribution
costs, which would be much greater for the
printed volumes than for the Microcards, and
the overheads which can be assumed to be
roughly the same for the two methods. It is
therefore clear that the cheapest method of
printing, which in the present case would not
give a very pleasing result, would cost about 12
times as much as reproduction on Micro-cards.
This factor is so large as to render negligible any
errors in the assumptions which formed the basis
of the estimated costs.

The difference in cost between the various
microrecording processes is much smaller than the
difference in cost between any of these processes
and the cheapest printing process. Microfilm is
generally admitted to be the cheapest process
where less than 15 copies are required, while
microprints only become competitive for upwards of 100 copies. For the IGY material,
where it is estimated that 50 copies will be required, the costs of microfilm, Microcards and
microfiches are of the same order, and the final
choice between these processes must be determined from other considerations.

Speed

The microrecording systems allow much
speedier reproduction than any form of printed
volumes. In the case of the Microcards, for
example, the material can be sent for processing
as soon as all the forms (between 40 and 90) required for a given Microcard have been received.
The Microcards themselves will then be ready for
distribution within a few weeks. For a printed
volume it would be necessary to wait until all the
forms (about 1000) required for a complete
volume had been received. Depending on the
printing process adopted, the subsequent delays
might be anything from one month to six
months or more.

Conclusion

Summing up, it can be seen that the advantages
of the microrecording systems as compared with
printed volumes or punched cards are very considerable. Of the various microrecording systems,
Microcards and microprints appear to be much
more convenient and the former is cheaper for
the number of copies required. Taking account
of the favourable views expressed by CSAGI, the
WMO therefore decided to publish the IGY
synoptic meteorological data on Microcards.

WORK PLAN OF THE IGY
METEROLOGICAL DATA CENTRE

The IGY Meteorological Data Centre (MDC) is
internationally recognized as the sole centre
responsible for collecting and publishing the
IGY data relating to meteorology, including
physical meteorology. The world data centres
in USA and USSR will also collect these same
data by means of copies of the forms supplied
direct by meteorological services and by Microcards obtained from the MDC. These two world
centres will not however publish the data.

The MDC is being operated on a self-financing

basis, the necessary working capital having been provided by the Member-Governments of WMO. This means that all the direct costs in operating the MDC must be ultimately covered by revenue from the sale of Microcards and other publications. On this basis, the price of a complete set of Microcards has been fixed at U.S. $5,990 and subscribers have been requested to pay this amount in advance. This arrangement was necessary to ensure that the working capital fund would not be exhausted before payment for the Microcards had been received.

The observations to be reproduced on Microcards, that is the surface and upper-air observations, arrive at the MDC on four different standard forms:

Form No. 1–Surface observations: Land stations
Form No. 2–Surface observations: Sea stations
Form No. 3–Radiosonde and radiowind observations
Form No. 4–Upper wind observations

It was therefore decided to issue the Microcards in four parts, each part corresponding to one of the standard forms.

The main consideration to be borne in mind when deciding how to group the original forms on Microcards is that it must be easy for the user to locate any given observation. From this it follows that the same grouping should be used throughout the IGY. A relatively simple catalogue of the Microcards can then be published, from which it will be easy to determine on which particular Microcard and in what position on the Microcard a given observation will be found.

The next consideration is that the observations should be grouped regionally, so that it will be possible for somebody interested in one particular region to purchase only the Microcards for that region. Another factor is that the Microcards will be extensively used for plotting synoptic weather maps, so that so far as possible the observations should be grouped according to time and date.

Some of these considerations are to a certain extent contradictory, and the final arrangement of the forms is therefore a compromise. Each Microcard bears a 6- figure index number. The first figure is the form number, the second and third figures indicate the geographical region and the last three figures give the date. This index number will provide a convenient system for classifying, filing and ordering the microcards.

At the suggestion of Mr. Malcolm Rigby, it was also decided to have a heading on each microcard, also visible to the eye, indicating briefly the contents of the card. This should be of value to the user when searching for any particular form, especially when he does not have a key to the index-number code readily available.

On receipt at the MDC, each form is carefully examined to make sure that it has been completed correctly and that all the figures will be clearly legible when reproduced on Microcards. Some amendments of a minor nature, such as completing the headings, are done in the MDC, but if there are any doubts the forms are returned to the originator for completion or re-copying.

The forms are then registered on special cards in a Kardex visible index and placed in folders, suspended in lateral filing cabinets. When the complete material for a Microcard has been received, the relevant forms are extracted from the folders, arranged according to the planned layout, and passed to the Microcard Corporation, which has set up a special photographic unit in Geneva for the IGY.

The forms are now arriving at the MDC at the rate of about 7,000 per week from nearly 100 countries and it is anticipated that the output of Microcards will build up rapidly to nearly 100 per week. The IGY itself ends on 31 December 1958 and the complete set of Microcards should be ready before the end of 1959.

Acknowledgments

Dr. Gertrude London, Chief on the MDC, has been responsible for developing many of the procedures mentioned in this paper. The paper is published with the permission of Mr. D. A. Davies, Secretary-General of WMO, whose encouragement and advice is gratefully acknowledged.

The Development of the Scientific and Technical Documentation Services in the International Atomic Energy Agency

P. I. Nikitin

In this article, Nikitin, Officer in Charge of IAEA's Documentation Section explains the preparation and scope of the state-of-the-art reviews and bibliographies issued by the Agency.

In the Statutes of the International Atomic Energy Agency the tasks of the Agency in the field of scientific and technical information are defined in a most general way. Section III, paragraph A, n. 3 reads: "The Agency is authorized to foster the exchange of scientific and technical information in peaceful uses of atomic energy." No indication has been given of any concrete tasks or methods of developing the information services. It was therefore necessary, during the initial stage of the Section of Documentation activities, on the one hand to give the tasks a concrete form and on the other hand to devise methods of carrying them out.

After the state of affairs in the Agency had been studied and some insight into the scientific documentation methods in various countries was gained, a number of proposals concerning the development of the scientific and technical documentation services during the next years were made.

With regard to scientific documentation methods, these proposals provided for the publication of several scientific information series, which would ensure the gathering and dissemination of information material on all major topics concerning the peaceful utilization of nuclear energy.

Soon after the establishment of the Agency, Member States started sending great quantities of scientific and technical information material: books, proceedings of conferences, symposia, reports of scientific research institutes and other documents. Those contributions formed the nucleus of the library and it is continually being added to by gifts and acquisitions. In addition, a considerable number of documents are received from official organs (atomic energy commissions) of the Agency's Member States, as well as from some international organizations (UN, FAO, ISO, UNESCO and others).

The above mentioned material deals mainly with nuclear physics, techniques, energetics and related sciences.

Naturally, one of the most important tasks in the field of documentation is the organization and systematization of material. Still, this systematization is not an end in itself. It was necessary to find means by which the Agency could inform its Member States of the existence of this material. Therefore, the publication of the *List of References on Nuclear Energy* was begun.

The publication of the List of References at two-week intervals started on 1 October 1959. The List contains bibliographical descriptions in English of all scientific and technical material received by the Agency. The material is classified according to the following main categories: physics and mathematics; controlled thermonuclear processes; chemistry; biology and medicine; geology, mining and ore benefication; materials, production, technology and properties; engineering; reactors, nuclear power plants; instruments, laboratory techniques, accelerators; isotopes; health and safety; waste disposal.

During the first nine months of the List's publication 7000 bibliographical descriptions of scientific documents received by the Agency were given.

Thanks to the publication of the List, the

SOURCE: P. I. Nikitin, "The Development of the Scientific and Technical Documentation Services of the International Atomic Energy Agency," *Revue de la Documentation,* 28 (Feb., 1961). pp. 3–4.

Member States are constantly informed on the scientific and technical material available in the Agency; moreover, they may order photostatic copies of documents or borrow the originals for short periods of time.

Another means of promoting the gathering and dissemination of scientific information among the Member States has been the publication of a special series of scientific and technical reviews (*Review Series*).

The review series contains articles on individual vital problems concerning the peaceful applications of nuclear energy by prominent scientists and specialists in the various Member States. The review series is especially valuable for those countries where work in the field of atomic energy is not yet very far developed as with the help of the reviews such countries will obtain additional information on the achievements and perspectives for the development in the individual branches of atomic energy. Each review is published in one of the official languages of the Agency (English, French, Russian and Spanish), and contains resumés in the other three official languages. In some cases the reviews are published in full in two languages, namely Russian and English. To date, the following four reviews have been published:

"Surveying and Evaluating Radioactive Deposits" (Lang, Canada)
"Tritium: dosage, préparation de molécules marquées et applications biologiques" (Verly, Belgium)
"Equipement électronique pour l'industrie nucléaire française" (M. Koch, P. Desneiges, M. Doireau, J. Weill, France)
"Recent Developments in Controlled Thermonuclear Fusion Research" (Van Atta, Mills and Snell, USA).

The following four reviews are being published:

"Mass Spectrometry for Uranium Isotopic Mensurements" (C. D. Tabor, USA)
"The Behaviour of Reactor Components under Irradiation" (L. Grainger, UK)
"Application of Radioisotopes in Biology" (A. M. Kuzin, USSR)
"Research Reactors" (O. D. Kazačkovskij, USSR).

Reviews in preparation are:

"Experience in the Operation of Nuclear Power Stations" (A. K. Krasin, USSR)
"Technical Aspects of the Economics of Nuclear Plants" (L. S. Mims, L. E. Crean, R. A. Laubenstein, USA)

"Heavy Water Production" (E. W. Becker, Fed. Rep. of Germany)
"Uranium Isotopes Separation by Diffusion" (D. Massignon, France)
"The Separation of the Isotopes of Uranium with Ultracentrifuges and a comparison with Diffusion Methods" (J. Kistemaker, J. Los, D. Heymann, F.E.T. Kelling, Netherlands)
"The Application of Radioactive Isotopes in Agriculture" (V. M. Klečkovskij, USSR)
"Methods of Radioactive Waste Processing at Nuclear Plants" (C. A. Mawson, Canada)
"Powder Metallurgy in Nuclear Reactor Construction" (H. Hausner, USA)
"The Biological Effects of Small Doses of Ionizing Radiations" (F. Herčik, Czechoslovakia)
"Radioactive Isotope Therapy" (J. H. Muller, Switzerland).

Reviews on 35 topics are planned for 1960–61, including: research on thermonuclear processes (four topics); research and power reactors (7 topics); prospecting, enrichment and technology of the production of radioactive materials, including fuel elements (8 topics); production and application of isotopes in chemical processes, in industry, biology, medicine and agriculture (9 topics); utilization of radioactive wastes (1 topic, etc.) Scientists from the following countries have consented to prepare reviews: Australia, Austria, Belgium, Great Britain, Netherlands, Spain, Italy, Canada, USSR, USA, France, Fed. Rep. of Germany, Switzerland, Sweden, Czechoslovakia and the Union of South Africa.

The publication of a review series on an international basis and on such a large scale as that initiated by the Agency is a complicated and difficult enterprise, especially when it concerns such an involved field as nuclear science.

The difficulties are caused on the one hand by lack of experience and on the other hand by the complexities and peculiarities of the individual branches of nuclear science. Thus, reviews have to be prepared within a range beginning with the investigation of high-energy particles, and ending with the application of isotopes in agriculture. Difficulties also arise from the conflicting traditions in method and language which exist in individual countries.

However, it is to be hoped that these difficulties will be overcome with time, and that the scientific and technical reviews published by the Agency will be met by specialists with the appreciation they deserve.

An important function of the Scientific and Technical Information Service is the preparation of bibliographies. The Agency started this work in

1959 and in the course of one year has produced 16 bibliographies on the individual problems in the peaceful utilization of nuclear energy. (Disposal of radioactive wastes into the sea, application of radioactive isotopes in hydrology, and others.)

On the basis of experience in the preparation of bibliographies gained in 1959, proposals have been made for the publication of a special series, *Bibliographical Series,* covering bibliographies on vital problems in the development and application of nuclear energy.

The first bibliography in this series, *Application of High Energy Sources in Therapy,* appeared in May 1960. It contains 730 bibliographical descriptions. The subsequent bibliographies in the series, which have been or are being finalized for printing, as a rule give abstracts or resumés in addition to the bibliographical description. Each bibliographical description is published in the original language, with English translation. Abstracts are given in English, French and Russian.

Among the bibliographies which have been compiled the fundamental bibliographical manual on Nuclear Reactors deserves special attention. It contains 4118 references to scientific publications issued between 1947 and 1959, covering various aspects of research, technology and operation of reactors (reactor theory; research, experimental and power reactors; reactor materials; reactor control and operation; shielding and safety; economic aspects, and others). The bibliography will appear in August 1960. Bibliographies on nuclear propulsion (aircraft, ship and rocket) and on thermonuclear research are also being printed. These bibliographies will appear in 1960.

Bibliographies in the field of nuclear energy are being compiled in many countries. As this leads to some duplication, the Documentation Section is issuing a special *List of Bibliographies on Nuclear Energy* as of July 1960, in order to inform the Member States of the bibliographies which are being compiled both in the Agency and in individual countries. The first issue gave 157 references on bibliographies published in 1959/60 or in preparation in various countries. The List of Bibliographies on Nuclear Energy will appear at intervals depending on the amount of material collected.

Another reference publication being prepared by the Agency is the *List of Periodicals on Nuclear Energy.*

This list will include detailed information on all journals, reports of individual institutes and laboratories as well as annual, semi-annual and periodical publications issued in different countries. In addition to the List of Bibliographies, this publication will be an extremely important tool for scientific information services in all countries.

A part of the Agency's work in the field of Scientific and Technical documentation performed during the last three years has been described heretofore. However, the work done in organizing scientific conferences, symposia and panels and publishing the proceedings has not been mentioned. This is an extremely important and valuable activity, and we feel that it deserves a special report.

Serving Readers in a Special International Library

Robert R. Kepple

The IAEA Library and some characteristics of its users are discussed. Service to readers including the initial interview, an introduction to library tools, and the preparation of a Field-of-Interest Register and a personalized UDC schedule are explained. The author is officer-in-charge of the International Atomic Energy Library in Vienna.

The types of problems faced by an international library in serving its readers are, in general, not much different from those encountered by a library in a national organization. They vary, however, considerably in degree because of the greater differences among the backgrounds of its users. The International Atomic Energy Agency has, at the present time, ninety-seven member states from whom personnel are recruited for the secretariat. Thus, there are scientists from all the regions of the world including large countries and small ones, as well as those that are old and those that are new. Some expect very little in the way of library services, while others take it for granted that they will continue to receive the same type of service they obtained at home from their library in a large research center of a highly developed country.

The IAEA library contains, at present, over thirty-two thousand bound volumes and ninety-one thousand technical reports and receives about eleven hundred periodicals. It is a depository library for the U.S. Atomic Energy Commission, and it maintains a large collection of documents issued by the United Nations and other international organizations. It is housed in the agency's headquarters building along the Kaerntner Ring in Vienna. Its present staff numbers eighteen from six member states. Although its collection emphasizes nuclear energy and its applications, its holdings reflect the widening range of the agency's interests by including material on law, economics, medicine, agriculture and biology.

Not only does the library provide service for the technical personnel, but it also has a large collection of mimeographed documents from the United Nations, other international organizations, and the agency itself. A very active reference service is conducted for the agency's administrative personnel based on this material. A special law library also has been created for the use of the agency's legal division.

Included among the readers served by the library are those not connected with the agency but who nevertheless have a legitimate need for its facilities. These include students, teachers, writers and scientists living in Vienna. Although the collection cannot compete with those of some of its neighbors which date back for centuries, it is reasonably complete and current in its areas of specialization. Its quarters are modern and comfortable, and to the students especially open stack access is a convenience they do not ordinarily enjoy. Usage by this group is rapidly increasing as the word gets around.

This latter is perhaps the aspect of the library which surprises the most people. All collections—books, reports, periodicals, and microfiche—are available for direct consultation by the library user. Furthermore, the library never closes, and at night and on weekends, when no one is in attendance, instructions are displayed explaining how one may

SOURCE: Reprinted from Robert R. Kepple "Serving Readers in a Special International Library," *College and Research Libraries,* 28 (May, 1967) pp. 203–207, 216.

charge an item out to himself. This is incomprehensible to some users, and the inevitable question is: "But does not this cause you to have terrible losses?" When it is explained that the losses are negligible and the missing items usually turn up later anyway, they shake their heads in amazement, and one individual replied with candor: "That would never work in my country!"

As would be expected, the periodical literature and the major indexing and abstracting journals are equally well known to all of the scientists. In the field of nuclear energy, however, one abstracting journal is regarded with particular favor by users: *Nuclear Science Abstracts,* which because of its coverage of the report literature and because it provides a single source for all material in this field, is highly regarded, well known, and much used by almost everyone regardless of nationality. Two sets are maintained, one in the reports library and one in the reference section. The reports themselves are filed by their alphanumeric numbers, and NSA is relied upon for subject and author retrieval.

Although the majority of the clerical staff of the agency are Austrians and are more or less permanent, there is a rapid turnover among the professional members of the agency's secretariat. Many stay for only two or three years and very few for more than five. This presents certain difficulties for the library, particularly with the journal literature. Professor A, from country X, may request a group of journals in his subject field. Five years later, just when respectable runs are starting to develop, he leaves and is replaced by Professor B from country Y who requires an entirely different group. Since space in Vienna's busy First District is at a premium, the situation would soon lead to serious difficulties. Therefore, efforts are made to stabilize the collection with the major journals, in all languages and in each of the agency's subject fields, and grow only with the new journals (which is enough of a problem in itself). All major backruns are obtained only as microfiche. To supplement relatively small holdings, there is a large collection of abstracting and indexing journals. Since there are many good libraries in Vienna from whom the library can borrow, almost any article can usually be obtained within twenty-four hours.

Language differences do not present any particular problem. English is the working language of the agency, and those few who do not speak it when they come soon learn. Although the agency has four official languages, English, French, Russian, and Spanish, and is located in a German-speaking country, most of the material in the library is written in English, with Russian second. This is especially true of the book collection, where an effort was made initially to represent all languages as equitably as possible. Experience has shown, however, that except for major reference works, the use of non-English books is limited. This is partly due to the position of English as a universal scientific language and partly because the periodicals and reports are used by some of the non-English speaking countries in preference to books, for the scientific literature. It is interesting for librarians to note that during a training course held for library personnel, some of the professional staff presenting parts of the course preferred to do so in English, although their mother tongue was German. They felt that the terminology of library science is so English-oriented that many terms could not readily be translated.

INTRODUCING THE NEW EMPLOYEE TO THE LIBRARY

As soon as possible after his arrival in Vienna, the new agency employee will be contacted by a library staff member and a time will be arranged for them to meet in the library for an interview. During this interview, he is given a tour of the library and the various collections are explained. He is shown how to use the card catalog, the abstracting and indexing tools, and how to find material in the report and microfiche collections. He is presented with a map of the library, a directory of its services, and a publication explaining how to use its various components. He is introduced to other library staff members with whom he may have dealings.

So that the library can obtain the information it needs, part of the interview is devoted to learning as much as possible about the scientific background of the employee; his training, education, degrees, interests, languages, specialization and the particular subject interests of his present work. He is then given a list of subject headings prepared by the library which lists all subjects relating to the work of the agency. He is asked to check those headings dealing with his work and scientific interests. The information obtained during the interview and from the headings checked, is then used in two ways:

1. *Field of Interest Register.* This includes all

members of the agency's scientific secretariat and is arranged in two parts. Part I consists of cards, arranged alphabetically by the name of the individual. Under each person's name, one can learn of his fields of study, his degrees, languages, and subjects of major interest. Part II contains subject cards arranged alphabetically. On each subject card is listed the names of those persons working or interested in that field.

This register was set up initially by interviewing every member of the agency's professional staff. It is now kept up-to-date through the individual interviews held with each new staff member.

Although one could refer to this register as a simplified SDI system, it is used for this purpose only incidentally. In an organization where the personnel are continually changing and the interests are ever expanding, it is necessary to have such a register for an efficient acquisitions program. Proper advice can be obtained for purchasing new periodicals, reference works, and any material not directly related to current activities. It is also useful to consult experts when screening the items offered on exchange. Although exchange is a useful method for obtaining many items, one must be careful to refuse those items for which there is no need and which only consume valuable shelf space. The register is also useful as a reference tool. When ordinary sources fail, it is often possible to consult an expert in the field and obtain leads which the library can use or pass on to the requester for him to follow up himself. Finally, the register enables the library to route those mysterious items that are unaccountably received from time to time, to their proper recipients.

When the individual has been added to this register, which is maintained by the reference unit, the list of subject headings is sent to the cataloging unit where a personalized UDC schedule is prepared.

2. *Personalized UDC Schedule.* Probably the most difficult library tool for the new staff member to learn to use is the card catalog. The author and title sections present no particular problems, but few persons seem interested in solving the complexities of the Universal Decimal Classification, which in the best of circumstances is a difficult classification system for the average library user. However, this classification has a particular advantage to an international library since the subject headings are numbers and the word index can be in as many languages as one wishes.

To promote the UDC number catalog, the cata-

loging unit has conceived and developed a procedure for providing a personalized UDC schedule for each new staff member. This is compiled from the list of subjects headings prepared during the interview described above. The correct UDC numbers are listed for each heading and cross references are provided. When completed, it is sent to him, and the staff member then has a list of UDC numbers corresponding to those subject fields in which he is particularly interested.

To explain the UDC itself, a folder has been prepared emphasizing that it is not enough to browse in the stacks, pleasant though this may be, but in order not to miss important material (the important items are usually out, anyway) it is necessary to consult the UDC number catalog. The personal schedule is then inserted in the folder and sent to the individual.

LIBRARY PUBLICATIONS

In addition to the interview, the preparation of the Field of Interest Register, and the UDC schedules described above, the library issues a number of publications which attempt to explain the library to its users. One is a booklet describing the library, its arrangement, and how to obtain material from the book, periodical and report collections. A $5" \times 8"$ card listing all library services, their locations, and telephone numbers was prepared and sent to everyone in the agency. The library publishes a monthly *Recent Acquisitions List* which includes a "column." This is written by a library staff member and describes some particular service, new reference work, a current problem, some future plan, etc. It is hoped that this will give the reader an understanding of some of the inner workings of the library as well as give him information about items that may prove useful in his work.

The new employee is also informed at this time about the regular services that are available to him. These include: automatic journal routing, automatic routing of technical reports in special subject areas, general reference service, literature searches, and photocopying.

Of course, on the basis of a single interview and the distribution of a number of publications, it cannot be expected that every individual will have learned all there is to know in order to use the library efficiently. It is at best an introduction and one can only hope that it will encourage him to return and learn more. It is as yet too early to evaluate the success of this program. It is believed, however, that it is resulting in an increased use of the services available, thereby justifying the effort involved. It is after all not enough merely to offer good library services. They must be presented to the user in such a way that he can understand their value to him and, furthermore, be able to use them himself. Teaching the reader to use the collection and to take full advantage of the services offered is one of the most important tasks currently facing the special library for, as emphasis is placed increasingly upon the new information systems, the reader must not be forgotten. Regardless of nationality, the needs of individuals are best satisfied when they can help themselves, for they alone know what they really want. The successful library is still the one in which the reader can do this as much as possible.

I.L.O. Library

Joseph Wilson Haden

The bibliographic and documentation activities of the ILO Library are described and some account given of the internal library operations required to process and control the approximately 7,000 serial titles received. The author is librarian of the International Labor Office, Geneva.

The documentation activities of the International Labour Office Library take the form of routing of publications, indexing current periodicals, compiling reference lists and bibliographies, and maintaining various information files.

Each periodical among the approximately 7000 titles received is treated in one of two ways: either it is a regularly registered title, in which case its arrival is noted on a visible index card, or it is simply routed to the interested Division or Service of the Office, each of which has a special responsibility for following developments and trends in its field. At present, some 1200 periodicals are not registered on arrival, but marked with their regular circulation and destroyed if and when they return from circulation. These are the less used and most ephemeral materials, such as press releases, house organs, organs of local bodies and most newspapers; and the time saved in not keeping track of them is large enough to allow correspondingly more time to be spent on the more important journals. These include the publications of bodies with which the Office has relations (Government departments, employers' and workers' organisations, and other non-governmental organisations and research institutions), and commercially published journals in the social, economic, and legal fields, primarily. Official gazettes, which are the source of much information of daily use in the Office and of the *Legislative Series*, the oldest and one of the best-known of the Office's publications, are registered in the Periodicals Branch of the Library, but indexed in the Legislative Series Section, which, in addition to publishing many texts of labour interests, puts out a weekly index of labour legislation for use within the Office.

The publications which are most in demand are received in multiple copies, and some 300 of them are subject to a strictly controlled circulation, requiring each issue to return to the Library for recharging before going on to the next reader on the circulation list.

All of this periodical material, except official gazettes, is scrutinised on arrival for items concerning the I.L.O., reprints of I.L.O. material (press releases and other items), and reviews of I.L.O. publications, and for other articles of interest to the research programme of the Office. Any issue of a periodical containing an item of interest to one of the Divisions is marked to it, if it is not already on the circulation list for that title, and the more important articles, considered to be of more than passing interest and sufficient length, are indexed in the weekly *International Labour Documentation,* which the Library issues primarily for use within the Office, but also supplies to about 50 addresses outside. During the years 1949 through 1956, *I.L.D.* was issued daily except Saturdays, and contained references to articles in approximately 4000 periodical issues per year. This was a larger burden than the Library is now able to carry, and the decision to limit issuance of the list to weekly frequency was made in the interests of economy of personnel and time and of better selection of worthwhile material. An annual subject index was issued for the years 1950 to 1956, and it is contemplated to continue this practice. The resulting corpus allows reference to periodical material published during

SOURCE: Reprinted from Joseph Wilson Haden, "I.L.O. Library," *Revue de la Documentation,* 24 (May 1957), pp. 70-71

those years which is not completely covered in any of the commercial periodical indexes. An annual list was also issued of periodicals which had been referred to once or more during the year, and this also will be continued.

Books and other non-periodical material received, including pamphlets, monographs in series, and annual reports, are handled in the Catalogue Department of the Library, and given more or less full cataloguing according to their permanent value. Here again, purely ephemeral material is routed to interested Divisions of the Office without recording and destroyed if and when returned. The rest is either fully classified and catalogued (Universal Decimal Classification and Library of Congress rules are followed, with slight modifications) or grouped into pamphlet series. A particular attempt, which has been largely unsuccessful to date for lack of staff, is constantly being made to keep complete whatever series are once received. Each publication is then routed to the interested Division or Service, after preliminary examination by the Editorial Division with a view to inclusion in the "Bibliography" section of the *International Labour Review,* with or without annotation. A rough estimate shows that from 25,000 to 30,000 books are constantly on loan. This type of material is listed monthly in the *Additions to the Library,* which, again, is distributed within the Office and to a certain number of outside addresses. This is a classified list, following roughly the division of interest by Divisions and Services of the Office. An annual author index is issued to this list, making it a continuing labour bibliography which does not duplicate any other existing publication.

One official of the Library compiles bibliographical reference lists on subjects of current interest to the research programme of the Office, and *Bibliographical Contributions,* which are considered to be of more lasting value. The series of *Bibliographical Reference Lists* was at first mainly composed of lists of periodicals received in the Library, grouped by country. The need for these was diminished by the issuance of the list of periodicals indexed in *International Labour Documentation,* and by the geographical card file referred to later, and their issuance was stopped in favour of lists on subjects of immediate interest or research, such as "Living and working conditions

of indigenous populations," "Administration of labour and social legislation," "Human relations in industry" "Productivity," and "Census publications," the last-named a union list of holdings in the I.L.O., United Nations European Office and World Health Organisation Libraries. *Bibliographical Contributions,* on the other hand, began with a dictionary catalogue of I.L.O. publications since the Office's founding in 1919 through 1948, followed by further editions and expansions of the same, and various bibliographies on labour law, industrial relations, workers education, and the Catalogue of the Library of the International Management Institute which, although the Institute closed in 1933, has historical interest. Unfortunately, the production of these *Contributions* has had to be maintained in processed form, so that they go out of print very quickly, and requests for them can never be completely satisfied.

The internal files maintained in the Library include the following: the visible index alphabetical checking file for periodicals, completed by a similar file for official gazettes; and a geographical file for periodicals, classified by country, and containing a main card for each periodical by its title, and a source card indicating the issuing body. Details of the correspondence file number, the means of acquisition (purchase, exchange, or free), disposal (temporary, conservation or binding), and subject indexing by means of coloured tabs are contained in this file, which is of the hanging card type, with the coloured tabs appearing over the tops of the cards. This makes it a simple matter to locate immediately the periodicals on cooperation, labour law, industries, economics, statistics, etc., as wanted. The positions of these coloured tabs along the top of the card indicate the Divisions or Services of the Office to which the periodical is regularly circulated. The Catalogue Department maintains the usual shelflist and an alphabetical serial record, formerly held on standard sized catalogue cards, but now on larger visible index cards.

The constant need for maximum utilisation of manpower, largely trained on the spot, and for coping with an ever-increasing number of periodical titles and of subjects is the primary pre-occupation of the Library. Its ideal of giving service is never completely fulfilled, but at least no effort is spared to achieve this aim.

BIBLIOGRAPHICAL WORK OF THE I.L.O. LIBRARY TRAUVAUX
BIBLIOGRAPHIQUES DE LA BIBLIOTHEQUE DU B.I.T.

Pre-War — Avant-Guerre*

Catalogue systématique des publications sur la Russie (1917-1925) se trouvant à la Bibliothèque du Bureau international du Travail. Genève, 1926-27. 2 volumes.
  Cont.: v. 1, Publications en russe; v. 2, Publications en d'autres languas que le russe.
Exposition d'ouvrages concernant l'histoire du travail et les origines de la législation internationale du travail, organisée à l'occasion de la 20e session de la Conférence (internationale du Travail). Catalogue. Genève, 1936. 20 pages.
  ——Supplément. Genève, 1937. 4 pages.
Exposition d'ouvrages concernant l'histoire du travail maritime, organisée à l'occasion des 21e et 22e sessions de la Conférence (internationale du Travail). Catalogue. Genève, 1936. 3 pages.
List of subject headings. Répertoire des matières. Geneva, 1929. 106 pages. (With/Avec: Decimal classification. Classification décimale. Geneva, 1929. xliii pages.)
Liste alphabétique, par pays, des périodiques reçus au Bureau international du Travail, Genève, 1927. 2 volumes. (Section des renseignements généraux. Service de documentation).
  ——Genève, 1934-35. v. p.
Selection of additions to the Library. Jan. 1922-April 1940. Geneva, 1922-1940. Monthly/Mensuelle.
Bibliography of the International Labour Organisation. Bibliographie de l'Organisation internationale du Travail. Bibliographie der Internationalen Arbeitsorganisation. 1910-1938. Geneva, 1938. (D. 50. 1938)

Post-War — Après-Guerre

Additions to the Library. n.s.v.l., no 1, Jan. 1947- . Geneva, 1947- . Monthly/Mensuelle.
Bibliographical contributions. Contributions bibliographiques. no. 1- . Geneva, 1948- . Irreg.:
* 1. Catalogue-dictionnaire des publications en langue française du Bureau international du Travail, 1919-1948.
* 2. Catalogue of Russian periodicals in the International Labour Office Library. Catalogue des périodiques russes de la Bibliothèque du Bureau international du Travail. 1951.
* 3. List of periodicals indexed in the Library of the International Labour Office during 1950. 1951.
* 4. Catalogue of the Library of the International Management Institute. Catalogue de la Bibliothèque de l'Institut International d'Organisation Scientifique de Travail. 1953.
* 5. Catalogue of publications in English of the International Labour Office. 1919-1950. 1951.
  6. Catalogue des publications en langue française du Bureau international du Travail. 1919-1950. 1951.
  7. Bibliography of the International Labour Organisation. Bibliographie de l'Organisation internationale du Travail. 1954.
* 8. Bibliography on labour law. Bibliographie du droit du travail. 1953.
* 9. Bibliography of international periodicals. Bibliographie de périodiques internationaux. 1952.
 10. Bibliography of industrial relations. Bibliographie des relations professionnelles. 1955.
 11. Bibliography on workers' education. Bibliographie de l'éducation ouvrière. 1956.
 12. Bibliography on vocational training. Bibliographie sur la formation professionnelle. 1957.
Bibliographical reference lists. Listes de références bibliographiques. no. 1- . Geneva, Sept. 1949- . Irreg.:
* 1. Liste des publications périodiques sur les questions sociales. Sept. 1949.
* 2. ditto. December 1949.
* 3. Living and working conditions of indigenous population of metropolitan countries. Jan. 1950.
* 4. References on the trade union movement in Asiatic countries. Feb. 1950.
* 5. Periodicals received in the Library: Germany. March 1950. (cf. no. 32)
* 6. not issued — pas paru.
* 7. Periodicals received in the Library: Spain. March 1950.
* 8. Recent works on trade unions 1941-1949. March 1950. (cf. no. 30)
* 9. Periodicals received in the Library: France. April 1950. (cf. no. 50)
*10. Truck system. April 1950.
*11. Periodicals received in the Library: Great Britain. May 1950. (cf. no. 34)
*12. Periodicals received in the Library: Canada. June 1950. (cf. no. 29)
*13. Periodicals received in the Library: United States. July 1950. (cf. no. 69)
*14. Periodicals received in the Library: Italy. Aug. 1950. (cf. no. 36)

---

*Totalement épuisés. Out of print.

*15. Periodicals received in the Library: Belgium. Oct. 1950. (cf. no. 61)
*16. Socially depressed populations. Oct. 1950.
*17. Periodicals received in the Library: Argentina. Dec. 1950.
*18. Principal technical and industrial periodicals received in the Library. Dec. 1950.
*19. Periodicals received in the Library: Australia. Dec. 1950.
*20. Periodicals received in the Library: India. Jan. 1951. (cf. no. 53)
*21. Periodicals received in the Library: Switzerland. Jan. 1951.
*22. Periodicals received in the Library: France. Feb. 1951. (cf. no. 50)
*23. Recent references on industrial organisations and industrial relations. Feb. 1951.
*24. Periodicals received in the Library: Latin America. Feb. 1951. (cf. no. 35)
*25. Periodicals received in the Library: Scandinavian countries. Apr. 1951.
*26. Periodicals received in the Library: Netherlands. April 1951.
*27. Periodicals received in the Library: International. May 1951. (cf. no. 62)
*28. Workers' education. May 1951. Replaced by Bibliographical Contribution no. 11. (cf. no. 66)
*29. Periodicals received in the Library: Canada. June. 1951.
 30. Recent works on trade unions. June 1951. Supplement. May 1953.
 31. Trade union periodicals. June 1951.
*32. Periodicals received in the Library: Germany. July 1951.
*33. Periodicals on maritime questions. Aug. 1951.
*34. Periodicals received in the Library: Great Britain. July 1951.
 35. Periodicals received in the Library: Latin America. Oct. 1951.
*36. Periodicals received in the Library: Italy. Oct. 1951.
*37. Periodicals on cooperation. Oct. 1951.
*38. Periodicals received in the Library: New Zealand and South Africa. Nov. 1951.
*39. Periodicals on management, with addresses of national management organisations. Nov. 1951.
*40. Periodicals received in the Library: Bulgaria, Hungary, Poland, Rumania, Czechoslovakia, Yugoslavia. Dec. 1951.
*41. Periodicals received in the Library: Afghanistan, Burma, Ceylon, China, India, Malaya, Pakistan, Philippines, Thailand, Viet-Nam. Dec. 1951.
*42. Periodicals received in the Library: Costa Rica, Cuba, Guatemala, Haiti, Honduras, Jamaica, Mexico, Nicaragua, Panama, Puerto Rico, Dominican Republic, El Salvador. Dec. 1951.
*43. Periodicals received in the Library: Aden, Egypt, Greece, Iran, Israel, Lebanon, Syria, Turkey. Dec. 1951.
*44. not issued—pas paru.
*45. Periodicals received in the Library: Austria. Dec. 1951.
*46. Periodicals received in the Library: Portugal and Angola. Dec. 1951.
*47. Periodical publications of labour and social security ministeries and administrations. Dec. 1951. (cf. no. 64)
*48. Periodicals received in the Library: Scandinavian countries. Dec. 1951.
*49. Periodicals received in the Library: Canada. Dec. 1951.
*50. Periodicals received in the Library: France and French Union. Jan. 1952.
*51. Periodicals on manpower questions. Feb. 1952.
*52. Recent references on labour productivity. Feb. 1952. (cf. no. 67)
 53. Periodicals received in the Library: India. March 1952.
*54. Human relations in industry. Apr. 1952.
 ———Supplement. Dec. 1954.
 55. Reading lists on certain under-developed countries. May 1952.
*56. Books, reports and periodicals in the Library on Middle Eastern countries. June 1952.
 57. Labour productivity in agriculture. Oct. 1952.
*58. Books and pamphlets of productivity. Nov. 1952. (cf. no. 67)
 59. Technical assistance. Revised. May 1955.
 60. Periodicals received in the Library: Germany and Saar. Feb. 1953.
 61. Periodicals received in the Library: Belgium and Belgian Congo. Feb. 1953.
 62. Periodicals received in the Library: International. May 1953.
 63. Periodicals received in the Library: Statistics. May 1953.
 64. Current periodical publications of ministeries of labour and social security administrations. June 1953.
 65. Administration of labour and social legislation. June 1953.
 66. Supervisory staff development training. July 1953.
 67. Productivity. Nov. 1953.
 68. Living and working conditions of indigenous populations of States Members of the I.L.O. Nov. 1953.
 69. Periodicals received in the Library: United States. Nov. 1953.
*70. Bibliographical work of the I.L.O. Library. Feb. 1954. (Reprinted Sept. 1954). (cf. no. 80)
 71. Housing: social aspects. June 1954.
 72. List of periodicals indexed in the Library of the International Labour Office during 1953.
 73. Labour-management co-operation (with special reference to metal industries). Sept. 1954.
*74. Bibliographical work of the I.L.O. Library. Sept. 1954. (cf. no. 80)

*Totalement épuisés. Out of print.

75. Census publications (1945-1954). April 1955.
76. List of periodicals indexed in the International Labour Office Library during 1954. May 1955.
*77. Shift-work. June 1955.
78. List of periodicals indexed in the International Labour Office Library during 1955. Feb. 1956.
79. Hours of labour. June 1956.
80. Bibliographical work of the I.L.O. Library. July 1956.
81. Social aspects of automation (Preliminary list). June 1956.
Daily reference list. Liste quotidienne de références bibliographiques v. 1, no. 1, 3 Jan. 1948-v. 5, no. 241. Geneva, 1948-1953. Continued as:
International Labour documentation—Documentation internationale du travail. v. 6, no. 1, 4 Jan. 1954-   . Daily, Monday through Friday. 1954-56; weekly, 1957-   .

---

*Totalement épuisés. Out of print.

[The Library of the] Food and Agriculture Organization of the United Nations

United Nations

This article describes the administrative setting in which the FAO library operates and details the library's operations and functions. A list of FAO library publications and of other FAO bibliographic publications is included.

The Food and Agriculture Organization, first of the permanent specialized agencies of the United Nations, came into being on 16 October 1945 with the signing of its constitution at a conference held in Quebec, Canada. The draft of this constitution was prepared by a commission established for this purpose in 1943 by the first United Nations Conference of Food and Agriculture at Hot Springs, Virginia, U.S.A. The forerunner of the Organization was the International Institute of Agriculture founded in Rome in 1905.

The FAO's main objectives as expressed by the founder nations are "to raise the levels of nutrition and standards of living of the peoples under the respective jurisdiction of the member governments; secure improvements in the efficiency of production and distribution of all food and agricultural products; better conditions of rural populations; thus contribute towards an expanding world economy." To help members reach these goals, FAO provides information and advice to its States members on all aspects of the production of agricultural products, fisheries and forestry, including appraisals and forecasts of production and consumption; promotes national and international action to improve the production, marketing, processing and distribution of food products, and the conservation of natural resources; creates commodity arrangement policies; furnishes to members on request and largely through the United Nations Expanded Programme of Technical Assistance, technical advice and assistance in any of the above fields.

At present, FAO is undertaking a world-wide Freedom from Hunger Campaign which extends from 1960 through 1965. One of the highlights of this campaign was the World Food Congress held in Washington, D.C., in June 1963 which brought together 1,300 experts in sociology, economics, nutrition, science and education from developed and under-developed countries to review the progress of the Freedom from Hunger Campaign and to discuss the problems of hunger and malnutrition and their solutions. The Congress called for land reform, minimum price guarantees, the establishment of a pool of production requisites, greater efforts to obtain more complete and accurate data on world food consumption and needs, and the continuation of the Freedom from Hunger Campaign until hunger and malnutrition are defeated.

To use food in aiding programmes of economic and social development the World Food Programme was launched jointly by FAO and the United Nations; it began its operation in January 1963.

FAO works through a Conference where each member State has one vote (110 members and four associate members by the end of 1965). Between sessions of the Conference, the Council supervises the work of FAO. It consists of delegates of twenty-five member States elected for three-year terms by the Conference; the staff, or secretariat, of the permanent headquarters in Rome, is headed by a Director-General chosen by the Conference. Regional offices are maintained at Washington for North America; Cairo for the Near East; Bangkok for Asia and the Far East, with a sub-office in New Delhi; Mexico for Northern Latin America; Santiago (Chile) for Western Latin America; Rio de Janeiro for Eastern Latin America; and Accra for Africa.

SOURCE: Reprinted from "The Library of the Food and Agriculture Organization of the United Nations," *The Libraries of the United Nations, a Descriptive Guide.* N.Y., United Nations, 1966. pp. 51–57.

FAO issues regularly its Conference and Council reports and other periodicals: *The state of food and agriculture, Animal health yearbook, Plant protection bulletin, Monthly bulletin of agricultural economics and statistics, Production yearbook, Trade yearbook, Yearbook of fishery statistics, Yearbook of forest products statistics, Food and agricultural legislation,* etc.

The foundations of the FAO Library, which is now one of the largest international libraries in the world, were the world famous collection of the International Institute of Agriculture, absorbed by FAO in 1946, and the comparatively modest reference library in the FAO temporary headquarters in Washington. The real development of the FAO Library began in spring 1951 after the headquarters of the Organization was transferred to Rome.

In accordance with the 1959 reorganization of the headquarters, the Library is a branch of the Department of Public Relations and Legal Affairs where a considerable bulk of the information and documentation activities of FAO is concentrated. Library premises are in the FAO Conference Building. Reading rooms, card catalogues, reference and loan services are on the ground floor; adjoining the Readers' Services area is the stack room, three tiers centred on the ground floor.

Small reference libraries are maintained and certain special bibliographic and information services are provided by various technical subject divisions of FAO, but all acquisition operations of FAO are performed by the Central Library, which provides the necessary literature not only for its own stacks and reading rooms but also for the reference libraries in the subject divisions and field operations. On the other hand, the subject divisions assist the Central Library in solving more intricate special questions arising in the bibliographic and reference work of the Library.

The main function of the FAO central library, named after the founder of the International Institute of Agriculture, the famous American agriculturist and sponsor of the Institute's Library, the David Lubin Memorial Library, is to provide all such library services as are needed by FAO's staff at Headquarters and in the field in carrying out its programme of work and to be of assistance to member States and their institutions with library services in the subject fields of the Organization.

The Library consists of the Office of the Chief Librarian, the Processing Section (Acquisitions, Classification, and Catalogue Units) and the Reference and Loans Section (Reference, Bibliography, and Loans Units). There were forty-one established posts in 1964/65, of which eleven are professional. The budget of the Library for the biennium 1964/65 was $52,000 for books and equipment, $13,400 for book binding and $900 for travel. These figures do not cover procurement of publications needed in field development projects.

The acquisitions programme is directed toward a selective world-wide coverage of publications in the subject fields of the Organization, i.e., food and agriculture (including fisheries and forestry) in their scientific, technical and economic aspects.

The building up of a comprehensive reference collection of bibliographic source material receives special attention. Emphasis is also given to obtaining all relevant official publications of member States.

The collection of pertinent official statistical material is aimed at complete world-wide coverage. The collection of United Nations documents and those of the specialized agencies which have bearing on FAO's work is virtually complete.

The holdings of the Library amount (June 1965) to about 600,000 volumes of books and bound periodicals, approximately 500,000 documents, 3,000 microfilms and 6,500 maps. It receives currently 7,500 periodicals and 5,000 annuals.

All these collections are organized systematically according to the Universal Decimal Classification. Catalogues are in card and in printed book form. The main card catalogue covering all library holdings is located in the Reference and Loans Service area. It comprises an author and title catalogue arranged systematically with subject indexes in English and French (a Spanish index is in preparation), and a geographic catalogue arranged according to the U.D.C. with geographic indexes in English and French.

Book catalogues are: the *International Institute of Agriculture Library classified catalogue* (1948) with four supplements, the FAO *Library select catalogue of books 1957–1958* (1961), the *International Institute of Agriculture catalogue of periodicals owned by the Library* (1946), the *List of current periodicals received in the* FAO *Library* (1959).

Quite naturally, the Library's particular consideration must be given to FAO documents. Certain important items of this documentary material, mostly printed publications, have been catalogued and thus are easily retrievable through the main catalogue, which for the time being remains the first and most complete record to be consulted for all printed publications of FAO. Most of the mimeographed (provisional) documents have been arranged by symbols in chronological or numerical order and are retrievable only by means of a card-file record of FAO documentation which was initiated in January 1963 when FAO documents ceased to be listed in the *United Nations documents index.*

As substitutes for a comprehensive documents index, though by no means equivalent substitutes, are the FAO *weekly documents list* (1962, No. 1-), issued by FAO's Distribution and Sales Section, and the printed catalogues of FAO publications, issued usually at intervals of two years. Only printed FAO publications issued for subscription or sale are included in these catalogues.

Although the primary function of the FAO Library is to provide service for the Organization, it also accommodates outside institutions and research workers. In 1964 a total of 6,279 FAO staff members and 2,693 outside readers used the Library. Reference and loan services showed an increase in 1964 of 100 per cent from 39,000 queries handled in 1962/63 to an estimated 78,-000 in 1964/65. These increases reflect the growth in the potential library user population and the heavy increase in reference services required by field operations. The photo duplication service is heavily charged with internal, field and external requests. All readers have free access to the books shelved in the reading rooms but only members of the secretariat have stack privileges. The Library issues monthly the FAO *Library list of recent accessions,* which not only is distributed for internal use, but is sent to about 250 agricultural libraries and documentation centers throughout the world. A well-selected and up-to-date reference collection of bibliographic source material is located in the Reference Service area; it contains a selection of some 5,000 volumes of the most frequently used national and special subject bibliographies, periodical indexes and abstracting services.

The bibliographical activities of the FAO Library consist of assistance to readers in bibliographical retrieval and the use of bibliographical apparatus, advice and assistance in the compilation of special subject bibliographies prepared in technical units of the Organization, including bibliographical notes and references for technical publications, compilations of *ad hoc* bibliographies on topical subjects needed within the Organization, and compilation of the monthly FAO *Library list of selected articles,* covering topical problems of world agriculture and food supply, especially in relation to developing countries.

The Library has in custody the David Lubin Archives containing correspondence and documents related to the creation of the International Institute of Agriculture. A permanent exhibition, called "Archives of Agriculture", was set up in 1955 on the occasion of the fiftieth anniversary of this Institution and the tenth anniversary of FAO.

Some technical divisions of FAO (Fisheries, Commodities, etc.) have accumulated a certain volume of specialized literature and documentary material and have organized documentation systems on their own. The most complete of these is that which has been operating since 1960 in the Fisheries Biology Branch of the Fisheries Division, using its own special card-file index and a computer at Rhode Island University (U.S.A.) for bibliographic reference storage and retrieval to collect the documentary material in its fields and to make it available not only to its own experts, but to all specialists throughout the world. Some of the technical divisions have issued bibliographies covering one or other of the most important fields of FAO's activities; for example the Plant Production and Protection Division's *Publications and documents, 1947–1963;* FAO *catalogue of fisheries publications and documents* (last issue May 1962, supplements 1 and 2, 1962/63); *List of Technical Assistance reports, Forestry and Forest Products Division* (1963); *List of publications and documents issued by the Land and Water Development Division of* FAO (1963).

FAO maintains a depository library system. Responsibility for the selection of depository libraries and granting of depository status is with the Publications Service, in the Department of Public Relations and Legal Affairs. At present there are ninety-two libraries and information centres in forty-two countries on the FAO depository library list.

BIBLIOGRAPHY

Publications of the FAO Library

FAO Library list of recent accessions, 1952– . Monthly

FAO Library list of selected articles. V. 1, no. 1– ; January 1963– .
  Suspended after v. 1, no. 8, August 1963; resumed publication with v. 2, no. 1, January 1965.

FAO Library selected catalogue of books, 1951–1958. 1961, 699 p.
  Title, preliminary matter and tables of contents in English, French and Spanish.

List of current periodicals received in the FAO Library, August 1959. 1959. 224 p.

Selected bibliography on co-operation, 1957, 84 p.
  Compiled in co-operation with the Horace Plunkett Foundation. Title, preliminary matter and text of annotations in English, French and Spanish.

Catalogues of the International Institute of Agriculture Library

Catalogue of periodicals owned by the Library. Compiled by M. Camerani-Teodorova, Rome, 1946. 566 p.
  Title and text in French and English.

Classified catalogue, Rome, FAO European Regional Office, 1948, 2747 p.
  Title, preliminary matter and subject indexes in French and English
      ———— 1st supplement. 1949, 36 p.
      ———— 2nd supplement. 1949, 23 p.
      ———— 3rd supplement. 1950, 25 p.
      ———— 4th supplement. 1950, 31 p.

Other FAO Bibliographical Publications

Agrarian Research and Intelligence Service, FAO publications and documents on agrarian structure. 1963. 61 p.
  Title, preliminary matter and headings in English, French and Spanish

Bibliography on land tenure. 1955. 386 p.
  Title, preliminary matter and table of contents in English, French and Spanish
  Out of print
      ———— Supplement, 1949. 1959. 282 p.

Bibliography on the analysis and projection of demand and production, 1963. 1963. 279 p. (Commodity reference series, 2)
      Also issued in French and Spanish

Catalogue of FAO publications, 1945–1964. 1965. 94 p.
  Issued every two years in English, French and Spanish
      ———— Quarterly supplement

Edelman, C. H. and B.E.P. Eeuwens. Bibliography on land and water utilization and conservation in Europe. 1955. 347 p.
      Out of print

FAO weekly documents list. No. 1– ; 9 November 1962– .

Fisheries Division. FAO catalogue of fisheries publications and documents, 1948–May 1962. Compiled by Patricia M. Andrews. Provisional edition. 1962. 42 p.
  Title, preliminary matter and headings in English, French and Spanish
      ———— Supplement 1. February 1963. 6 p.
      ———— Supplement 2. November 1963. 6 p.

Fisheries Division. World fisheries abstracts; a quarterly review of technical literature on fisheries and related industries. V. 1, no. 1– ; January/February 1950– . Washington, D.C.; Rome, 1950– .
      Quarterly (formerly, 1950–1961, bi-monthly); published in Rome from v. 2, no. 1, January/February 1951. Also issued in French and Spanish

Forestry and Forest Products Division. List of technical assistance reports. 1964. 8 p. (PCS/3/Rev.9)
——Supplement. 1965. 2 p. (PCS/3/Rev. 10)

Jacks, G. V. *and* M. K. Milne. An annotated bibliography of rice soils and fertilizers.
Harpenden, England, Commonwealth Bureau of Soil Science; Rome, FAO, 1954. 180 p.

Plant Production and Protection Division. Publications and documents, 1947–1963. 1964. 10 p.

[The Library of the] World Health Organization (Who)

United Nations

Like the preceding piece this article details the functions and operations of a specialized international library. Similar information about the libraries of the other specialized agencies and of the UN may be found in the volume from which this article is reprinted.

The World Health Organization, a specialized agency of the United Nations designed to further international co-operation for the improvement of health conditions throughout the world, was established in 1946. The anniversary of the establishment of WHO on 7 April is celebrated in many countries as World Health Day. The precursors of WHO were the International Office of Public Health in Paris, dating from 1907, and the Health Organisation of the former League of Nations, set up in 1923. From these organizations, WHO has inherited various international duties such as epidemic control, quarantine measures and the standardization of drugs. But compared with these organizations, WHO is undertaking much broader aims and objectives, the principal of which, as determined in the First Article of its Constitution, "shall be the attainment by all peoples of the highest possible level of health." WHO has as its major activities the direction and co-ordination of international health work; advice and assistance to individual States in the improvement of their health services and a wide range of technical services. In recent years, the activities of WHO covered a wide range of measures and arrangements: a global malaria eradication campaign, and similar campaigns, particularly in the developing countries, against tuberculosis, venereal and virus diseases and leprosy; assistance to various countries in the field of community water supplies; measures against air pollution; work in vector control and insecticide resistance; assistance in the planning, running and developing of laboratory services and blood banks; improvement of nursing services; assistance in various type of maternal and

child services; work in health protection and promotion (research in cancer and cardiovascular diseases); assistance for the organization or improvement of rehabilitation services for physically handicapped children and adults; professional education and training, especially in the newly independent countries, etc.

Much of WHO's work is done in collaboration with other organizations: the Food and Agriculture Organization, UNESCO, the International Labour Organisation and others. In the study of both beneficent (radioisotopes) and maleficent (effects of fallout) aspects of atomic energy, WHO is collaborating with the International Atomic Energy Agency.

Membership of WHO numbers 122 States and three associate members. Its legislative organ, the World Health Assembly, which meets at least once a year, elects the twenty-four members of the Executive Board. The secretariat, headed by the Director-General, is in Geneva. Besides the secretariat there are six regional committees and offices composed of representatives of the members in each region (for Africa in Brazzaville, Eastern Mediterranean in Alexandria, Europe in Copenhagen, Western Pacific in Manila, South-East Asia in New Delhi and the Pan American Sanitary Bureau in Washington, D.C.).

The main periodicals of WHO are: *Bulletin of the World Health Organization,* WHO *chronicle, International digest of health legislation, Weekly epidemiological record, World health, Technical report series,* etc.

The need for an adequate library and reference service, as an essential adjunct to the technical

SOURCE: Reprinted from "[The Library of the] World Health Organization (WHO)," *The Libraries of the United Nations, a Descriptive Guide,* N.Y. United Nations, 1966. pp. 117–122.

work of the Organization, was recognized from the earliest days of the World Health Organization, and it was in December 1946 that the first books and periodicals were acquired and initial arrangements made to deal with urgent library requirements. The first issue of *Library news,* a monthly list of new accessions, appeared in May 1947 and reported that the WHO Library comprised 111 volumes and received fifty-seven current periodicals.

From these beginnings, the WHO Library has grown rapidly, its collection keeping pace with the expanding technical work of the Organization. Today, thanks in part to the inheritance of the Library of the Office International d'Hygiène Publique, Paris, one of the forerunners of WHO, it contains over 75,000 volumes, in addition to large collections of mimeographed documents and official government reports. Although a representative collection is maintained of modern works in several languages on most branches of medicine, special emphasis is placed on public health, communicable diseases, environmental sanitation and the other medical specialities of particular interest to WHO. A special feature is the large international collection of current medical and scientific periodicals, of which over 2,600 are received regularly, approximately 1,200 being in exchange for WHO publications.

The growth in size of the Library has been accompanied by a corresponding increase in the services offered and in the use made of them. For example, in 1950 the number of items lent, including the circulation of periodicals, amounted to 29,366; by 1964 it had risen to 76,933. In 1950, 163 volumes were lent to other libraries; in 1964, 2,605. In 1950, 3,077 readers were recorded in the Library reading room; in 1964, 10,138; while over the same period the number of inquiries rose from 1,509 to 3,240. The original conception of the WHO Library as a small working collection designed primarily for the use of the WHO secretariat has had to be adjusted to the fact that it is now one of the larger collections of current medical and and public health literature in Europe and is called upon more and more for loans to other libraries and for the supply of microfilms and photocopies of literature not easily obtainable elsewhere.

A distinguishing feature of the work of WHO is its use as a training centre for future medical and scientific librarians. Since 1950, WHO fellows from various countries have spent periods of from one to twelve months studying its routines and techniques and participating in its daily work.

Similar facilities have from time to time been made available to fellows from UNESCO and IAEA.

Much of the special difficulty of providing a reference service in WHO arises from its regional structure. In addition to its headquarters in Geneva, there are WHO regional offices in Alexandria, Brazzaville, Copenhagen, Manila, New Delhi and Washington, as well as teams operating in remote areas all over the world. More than two-thirds of the technical staff are thus working away from Geneva, many far removed from the most rudimentary form of medical library.

In 1949 the WHO Library began regularly indexing by subject the articles in medical and scientific periodicals that were of potential interest to WHO technical staff. The contents of approximately 1,200 periodicals are regularly scrutinized and about 1,000 articles are selected each month. From a typed transparent masterslip, which contains a full bibliographical reference and a subject heading based on those in use in *Index medicus,* cards are prepared by a cheap photographic process for weekly distribution to WHO technical staff at headquarters and in all regional offices. The indexing, it should be noted, is extremely selective, not only with regard to subject but also to aspect, the public health rather than the clinical viewpoint being emphasized. To the provision of these slips is added a photocopying service, so that staff at the periphery of the Organization may be supplied as rapidly as possible with the technical literature they require.

An alphabetical subject file of these index slips is maintained in the WHO Library for consultation by all library users. This is now restricted to the literature of the last five years, older cards being discarded annually, for it may legitimately be assumed that after that lapse of time adequate reference to the article will be found in the usual printed sources available for retrospective search in medical bibliography.

The indexes to the current periodical literature described above, together with a comprehensive international collection of medico-bibliographical tools, form an essential element in the provision of a reference service on medical and public health topics, which is available on request not only to WHO staff but also to the medical and health departments and institutions of WHO member States and to the United Nations and specialized agencies. A large number of inquiries are dealt with, ranging in scope from the identification of references to the compilation of bibliographical surveys of available literature. Much of this work is of an ephemeral character, but over a hundred more or less major bibliographies and reference lists are compiled annually to meet specific requests. In those cases where the bibliographies might have a wider application, consideration, in collaboration with the technical sections of WHO, is given to publication, and in the past few years a number of comprehensive bibliographies have been published in bilingual editions.

In addition to providing a documentation service on the technical subjects dealt with by the Organization, the WHO Library is responsible for the collection, maintenance and bibliographical control of the mimeographed documents and printed publications issued by WHO, not only in Geneva but in the WHO regional offices throughout the world. The WHO mimeographed documents of a technical nature are considered as working papers and are therefore distributed only within the WHO circle of technical collaborators. This does not, however, dispense with the necessity for a very detailed analytical index to their authors and contents. This is maintained on cards and combined with an index to the printed publications to cover all the mimeographed and printed output of the Organization both at Geneva and in the regional offices.

Comprehensive analytical bibliographies of WHO publications have been prepared and published in English and French editions. These include all articles published in WHO periodicals as well as all other WHO publications, including chapters contributed by individual authors in symposia and other collected works, grouped under subject headings, alphabetically arranged and supplemented with author and geographical indexes and a check list of publications by series. It is planned to issue such bibliographies every five years.

The regional structure of WHO has inevitably presented the library and reference services with a considerable number of problems. Small libraries have had to be established in the regional offices, and today the WHO Library in Geneva functions as the central library of the Organization providing a central acquisition service, supplying catalogue cards to all WHO documents and publications and all material acquired by the Library, and supplementing the local resources by loans, photocopies and assistance in dealing with reference inquiries.

The current acquisitions of the WHO Library are listed monthly in *Library news* which, in addition to its distribution throughout the WHO secretariat, is available on request to medical and scientific libraries throughout the world. From time to time supplements of a medico-bibliographical character are prepared and issued. One such supplement is a list of the periodical holdings of the Library revised and issued every two years; another is a list of the holdings of the three large international libraries in Geneva (WHO, International Labour Office, and the United Nations Library, Geneva) of annual governmental reports on public health and medical subjects; another is devoted to a guide to the reference sources on medicine and public health in the Soviet Union. A third edition of a supplement first issued in 1953 is now in preparation. This is a list of current indexing and abstracting periodicals in the medical and biological sciences, arranged alphabetically by title, with a subject and sponsor index, giving detailed information as to publisher, price, periodicity, number of abstracts published annually, etc.

Since its inception, the World Health Organization has been housed in the Palais des Nations, Geneva, and the WHO Library has used a make-shift reading room with accommodation for twenty readers and 6,000 volumes and stack space in the stacks of the United Nations Library, Geneva, some ten minutes' walk away. The Twelfth World Health Assembly, however, in May 1959, in view of the serious overcrowding in the Palais des Nations decided that WHO should construct a new building, and this will be ready for occupancy in the spring of 1966. There the WHO Library will be provided with accommodation for fifty readers and approximately 125,000 volumes. The main reading room with space for forty readers and the bulk of the collection of the books and monographs will be reached through a catalogue hall, while behind it a stack room containing bound volumes of periodicals and the remainder of the collection will be open to access by all readers. The loan service will be provided with an automatic book lift to all floors of the main building. The accommodation is completed by a documents room for four readers and a periodicals room accommodating six readers and the current numbers of some 2,000 periodicals.

PUBLICATIONS

Publications of the WHO Library

Bibliography on bilharziasis, 1949–1958. 1960. 158 p.
  Title, preliminary matter and subject indexes in English and French
Bibliography on hookworm disease, 1920–1962. 1956. 251 p.
  Title, preliminary matter and subject indexes in English and French
Bibliography on the epidemiology of cancer, 1946–1960. 1963. 168 p.
  Title, preliminary matter and index by anatomical site in English and French
  Also published (1964) in Russian and English edition
Bibliography on yaws, 1905–1962. 1963. 106 p.
  Title, preliminary matter and indexes in English and French. Also issued (1964) in Russian and English edition
Library news. V. 1, no. 1- ; May 1947-   . Monthly
  Title and headings in English and French
Medical education; annotated bibliography, 1946–1955. 1958. 391 p.
  Also issued in French, 1960
Publications of the World Health Organization, 1947–1957; a bibliography, 1958. 128 p.
  Also issued in French
Publications of the World Health Organization, 1958–1962; a bibliography, 1964. 125 p.
  Also issued in French

Other Publication

Catalogue of World Health Organization publications, 1947–1964. 1965. 114 p.
  Editions in French and Spanish in preparation

VII

NON-GOVERNMENTAL AND REGIONAL ORGANIZATIONS

The international organizations presented in this section are not direct affiliates of the United Nations, though many have established close ties of communication and cooperation with the United Nations or its specialized agencies. The non-governmental organizations range from international associations of florists to international learned and professional societies. The regional organizations deal with a variety of topics and problems of common concern to the countries and governments of a geographic region. Each of the international organizations covered in this section has a central office, issues publications, and maintains its own system for distribution of publications. The information in this section presents some background data about a sampling of regional organizations and conveys a notion of the numbers and characteristics of non-governmental organizations.

LC's International Organizations Section

Katherine O. Murra

In this article Katherine O. Murra who spent much of her professional career in work with the question of international bibliographic control describes the special unit set up in the Library of Congress to handle the publications of non-official international organizations. This article indicates the magnitude of the problem of comprehensive acquisition of non-official publications and describes the methods used to acquire, process, and provide reference service for this category of material.

The International Organizations Section of the Library of Congress offers a unique documentation service on the history, structure, administration, activities, and publications of international organizations and meetings, and makes its facilities available to all inquirers. Its work constitutes the first large effort of a research library to consolidate information on future international meetings found in the major published calendars, and to supplement and extend this information by further research.

The fact that it is part of a very large research library rather than being a separate library or part of an international organization secretariat has, like parents, endowed it both positively and negatively. In the beginning, 1951, Burton W. Adkinson, then an officer of the Library of Congress, assigned this writer the problem of finding out why it was so difficult to keep currently informed from the Library's collections on the activities of the International Council of Scientific Unions and its Member Unions. The Council then had 17 international organizations within 10 Member Unions as compared with the 21 organizations in 14 unions, today, and constituted, as it does today, a significant part of the whole body of international, multilateral, nongovernmental bodies.

The Library's holdings of the publications of all International Nongovernmental Organizations (INGOS, as this type of organization is commonly called) was surveyed. Astonishing gaps were revealed. An acquisitions program was begun, even before a separate administrative unit was established, to work on the problem. Each INGO listed in the 1950 *Yearbook of International Organizations* was solicited for a list of its publications. The intention was to select desired titles from the lists; in many cases, however, the request brought generous gifts of the works themselves, which immediately contributed to the strengthening of the collections. As new editions of the *Yearbook* appear, each new organization is similarly solicited.

Because of the Library's special exchange arrangements with many international intergovernmental organizations, such organizations are outside of this acquisitions program—although they are a reference responsibility of the International Organizations Section. Intergovernmental organizations in which the United States does not participate were naturally included in the Library's expanded acquisitions program.

The heartening response to the first solicitation was, nevertheless, a long way from securing specific titles—old and new—that were desired. Gradually a more rounded acquisitions apparatus and procedure was developed along conventional lines. Individual recommendations were made; national bibliographies and trade lists were checked; a variety of material was scanned for titles. Not only publications of the organizations were sought but works about the organizations—bibliographies of international publications and new serials by or about organizations. Exchange agreements with international organizations increased from 47, at the beginning, to the present 2200. Materials received are processed for the general collections of the Library of Congress and are not housed in the International Organizations

SOURCE: Reprinted from Katherine O. Murra, "LC's International Organizations Section," *Revue Internationale de la Documentation,* 31 (Nov., 1964) 138–142.

Section. A copy each of publications of international organizations reporting on other organizations, such as Unesco's *Review of the List of Nongovernmental Organizations Admitted to Consultative Status,* is retained by the Section for the reference collection it maintains.

Simultaneously with acquiring material for the Library an effort was made to identify publications which would be useful for reference, such as descriptions, histories, statutes, bibliographies, indexes, official information journals, etc. concerning international organizations. These were brought together from every class in the Library's collections to form the nucleus of this reference collection. The material acquired and that brought from other parts of the Section helped with the identification of organizations and supported further acquisition endeavors, as well as providing a basis for the Library to offer reference service in a new field.

Out of the earliest reference experience came the impetus for expanding the Section's program to cover future international meetings. The situation immediately prior to involvement in providing controls for future international meetings was described in a previous article[1]. Briefly, the multiplicity of calendars which, to a considerable extent, duplicated each other and were incomplete, singly and as a group, proved to be a dismal swamp for the lonely reference worker seeking information on an illusive forthcoming or recently adjourned meeting. In 1953, a modest program to coordinate the listings of the major calendars was begun and supplemented as manpower was made available. Three years later, current information on meetings and organizations was being regularly supplied to a number of government agencies, and a staff of five was bringing a surprising volume of facts within reach of the inquirer.

Even in the beginning, the resources of the Library of Congress for information on future international meetings contrasted markedly with those for international organizations. For meetings, they were unbelievably rich and unexploited. Through painstaking examination of unbound current serials (of which the Library now receives 100,000 titles a year), a list of those periodicals containing unique and substantial information on future international meetings was developed. The problem for the International Organizations Section of gathering information on meetings is today largely the same as it was in 1956. The amount of information that can be mined is directly proportional to the number of competent people provided to do the work[2].

Maximum exploitation of the Library's serial collection has probably not yet been achieved. The 11 professional members of the Section's staff of 17 include persons with appropriate graduate degrees who are assigned to examine and record information found in periodicals in English and Western European languages. The periodicals selected are covered but not always within the rather rigid time schedule allowed for their retention in the Section. The government and international documents containing information on future international meetings are still largely untouched for lack of staff.

Growth and development are problem-solving experiences. Accepting responsibility for developing a reference potential for future international meetings brought with it many problems. While some were solved, others continue and new ones arise. The richness of the collections did not obviate the necessity for an acquisitions effort different from, and larger than, the one for organizations. The serial collection of the Library made that effort possible. Among other items, from the serials came most of the addresses for organizers of the various meetings.

It was important to communicate with the organizers of each meeting for the latest and official facts. Thus, a form letter was dispatched asking for "current information" and "any preliminary material such as notices, the program, agenda, lists of participants, etc.". The first solicitation, a form letter sent to the organizers by one of the Library's acquisitions divisions does not always bring in the information and material wanted. Further solicitation consists of personalized follow-up letters written by staff of the International Organizations Section. Other approaches are also used in an effort to get all pertinent information and material. Those in the vicinity who may be of assistance are also contacted. This work is for future meeting information. Changes of policy and procedure have permitted and assisted systematic acquisition of pre-conference information.

This type of material is largely classed as ephemera by most libraries. It does not lend itself readily to shelving and is too inconsequential, in the long run, to bind and catalog. It is often unprepossessing in appearance and not durable. As late as the beginning of the previous decade, many, including the Library of Congress, made no effort to acquire, and usually discarded, this type of material, when it was received unsolicited. As the ephemeral type of material began coming in quantity, it became important to isolate it from the flood of more substantial materials received by the Library. Replies to form solicitations are addressed to the International Organizations Section and do not become involved in the bulk of Library receipts, even though the solicitations were sent from one of the acquisitions services of the Library. The staff examines and selects other material coming into the acquisitions divisions of the Library each week.

Storing ephemeral material for future use by the Section posed another problem. The Library of Congress has no central pamphlet collection or vertical file service for storage of such material. Specialized files are found in connection with particular services, for example the Legislative Reference Service. The International Organizations Section set up a vertical filing system with folders for each organization and each meeting for which it received publications and correspondence. An index by filing title is included in the catalog of the Section's reference collection. The vertical file now consists of 50 legal-size drawers of material including not only programs, lists of participants in meetings and publications of organizations, circulars, brochures, and pamphlets, but the correspondence, including carbons of initial form solicitations, with organizers and secretariats. Many times, letters outline plans of future meetings months and even years before any are convened or information about them is published. Thus the correspondence is reference material to be used with the publications.

The vertical file is weeded (otherwise it would have many more than 50 drawers of material) when the information it supplies is found to be outdated or otherwise inconsequential, when the information can be found in other items in the file, or in LC's permanent collections.

For the last four years a systematic endeavor has been made, and is continuing, to obtain for the Library's collections the proceedings and other permanent documents of those meetings whose subjects are within the scope of LC's collecting. A selection made from cards no longer needed for the published calendar is sent to the Exchange and Gift Division for soliciting the documents.

The record to be kept of the meetings continues to be the knottiest of technical problems. Library of Congress printed cards for proceedings

and documents of some of these future meetings will be interfiled in the Section's dictionary catalog. Therefore, any entry devised by the Section must necessarily provide hospitality in the file for the printed cards. The *ALA Cataloging Rules for Author and Title Entries,* which is used by the Library of Congress in cataloging its collections, offers limited guidance for so specialized a catalog as the one in the International Organizations Section. With insufficient technical staff, rules for the Section's catalog grew slowly, and painfully.

The format of the Library's catalog card was modified to give variety to a typed card. Originally a perforated fanfold of four bond-paper, 3 × 5 inch slips was used, enabling the typist to produce four copies at once. Not until 1959 was a multilithed card adopted. Cards are run, by another office, in twelve copies from a multilith strip mat which accommodates copy for four 3 × 5 cards.

The records made on the old fanfolds and, later, the cards constitute the largest part of a dictionary catalog of some 190,000 cards which is increasing at the rate of 57,000 cards per year. The catalog, itself, generates problems of entry, cross references, precision of subject headings, etc., etc., as well as maintenance. From 1959 on, all entries have been made in English with references from names in other languages. The inexperienced hands of the early years of struggle lay heavily on the catalog in a heritage of contradictions in entry. The newly acquired small staff of professional catalogers is large enough only to edit current input. Robert W. Schaaf, the Assistant Head of the Section, almost single-handed and, under tremendous handicaps, has maintained a reasonable coherence in the dictionary catalog. The Section's existing rules are being expanded and revised to decrease the problems in the current input, and it is hoped that the future will afford full editing of the entire dictionary catalog.

For still another problem, the solution appears illusive. As soon as one sticky spot is smoothed out another is at hand. This is the problem of timing. Libraries usually require occasional rush processing of incoming pieces for special needs. A documentation service on future international meetings requires a degree of promptness of receipt and processing of all materials which places relentless pressure on traditional services. The date on which the meeting convenes is a built-in deadline over which the service has no control. In the case of the International Organizations Section, basic facts of date, place, sponsor, and address of a source of further information, plus the program is required by the sponsor and chief users at least four months in advance of the convening date. Thus, if, for a given meeting, these are generally found in a certain journal before they appear elsewhere, it is necessary to have that journal as soon as the mails can bring it without processing delays.

Eternal vigilance is required to accomplish this for even a part of the total receipts of the Section. A serial record file has been set up in the Section which lists on 4 X 6 inch cards each of the 2000 periodicals received, the date each is received in LC, the date received in the Section, and an estimated average date for receipt of the next issue. Computation of this estimate begins after the sixth issue is received. A claiming procedure has been set up for issues of purchased serials that are not received within a few days of the anticipated date of receipt. The volume of serials received via exchange and gift is much greater than for those purchased. Like most large libraries, processing, including the all important checking in the central Serial Record of the Library, cannot keep up with the flow, so that claims can seldom be made for fear of the publication being in a Library backlog. Certain changes and adjustments of procedure have been made in response to this time pressure. There seems little more that can be done specifically for one small project. The only real solution would involve reducing the time for processing of all materials received by the Library and eliminating the backlogs. This would involve large increases of staff and revision of basic operations. A timing which would fully support the type of service given by the International Organizations Section is not anticipated for the whole Library this side of automation.

So much for the acquisition and recording of information and publications for the International Organizations Section. A reference service is offered for those who come in person or telephone or write. Those whom it serves range from graduate students to specialists in international relations, with a sprinkling of the "general public." A combination of circumstances accounts for the steady increase in the demand for reference service in this field. Professional interest of prospective participants and world events stimulate the need for such information and often infuse it with urgency. Then, too, as observed in other opera-

tions in the Library of Congress, the availability of a service tends to generate inquiries.

Up to this point, the Section has steadfastly adhered to its original scope—the description, history, structure, activities, and bibliography of international organizations and meetings. As more and more persons and groups are concerned with the many facets of international life, it becomes more difficult to confine the reference service to this first aim. Presently, the determining factors in answering or referring a question are the competence and time of the staff.

Types of questions received can be described more easily in terms of how readily an answer can be found. This changes as bibliographical control of the field improves. Many types of questions are more quickly answered by the Section now than 10 years ago because more information is organized and indexed. The usual requests for spot information—where will the International Planned Parenthood Federation meet in 1964—are quickly dispatched. Others take hours to answer and are often from specialists in the international field who have exhausted all other sources at their command. Those in the Department of State, particularly the Office of International Conferences, are regular and frequent users. The Office provides the Government and the press with information about the organizations and meetings in which the United States participates, but relies on the Section for much of its information on international nongovernmental organizations and meetings. The other specialists, such as those on the International Organizations Staff of the Department of Commerce, ask about a variety of subjects related to their responsibilities. Some of the questions are channeled through one of more than 250 research libraries and facilities in the Washington area. Many others come directly from the person who wants the answer—the administrator, researcher, scientist, etc. Inquiries from the Congress usually come through the Library's Legislative Reference Service.

Outside of the Government, international organizations, themselves, and embassies of foreign governments located in Washington, the inquirers are as varied as the inquiries—learned societies, travel agencies, airlines, industrial firms, laboratories, doctors, all types of libraries, booksellers, and so on, in this continent and abroad. Increasingly those in the United States who are organizing international meetings will telephone or write to ascertain if the date in which they are interested has been chosen by any other meeting with a subject which might compete for the audience they hope to attract. To satisfy such questions, it is frequently necessary to check national calendars, as well as our international resources, to be sure no large national or regional meeting will conflict. A selection of national calendars forms part of the reference collection of the Section.

The section's reference service supplements in depth and breadth the other bibliographical controls of the Library in this field. Its catalogs cross reference and include added entries for meetings and organizations not as fully treated in the Library's catalogs; provide additional sources to those in the official, or cataloger's catalog, of the Library; identify innumerable organizations and meetings for which no reference is found in the other catalogs of the Library; and provide authoritative forms of entry. The catalogs are consulted, among others, by the descriptive catalogers of the Library engaged in preparing new entries for material emanating from international meetings and organizations. The ephemeral material in the vertical file collection often helps to bring up to date material in the Library's collections.

Preparation of reference material for publication was an activity originally planned for the Section's reference service. However, the program was slow in beginning. The first work issued was Robert W. Schaaf's *Documents of International Meetings, 1953* published in 1959. In June of 1959, with financial assistance from the National Science Foundation, the first issue of the *World List of Future International Meetings,* a calendar in two parts[3], was published. This is sold by the Superintendent of Documents, US Government Printing Office. Beginning as a monthly, covering three years from the date of issue, it grew to such proportions that it became necessary in June 1962 to change to quarterly comprehensive issues with interim monthly supplements containing new meetings and changes. From the first, subject and sponsor indexes were included in each issue. In July 1961, a geographical index was added to the other two and that pattern is continuing. The *World List* now has subscribers in 44 countries other than the United States. This list has become a ready reference source answering many of the spot type of questions formerly sought directly by inquirers. Nevertheless, reference work has increased as users of the calendar want more information than it supplies on sources, programs, and other specifics, in addition to more meaty information about organizations.

A supplement to the December 1961 issue was printed separately under the title, *Future National and International Events, a Selected List of Calendars* compiled by Marko Zlatich, then editor the *World List.* The 396 calendars cited were offered as token assistance to those asking for a comprehensive list of national meetings 'similar to the *World List.*' The Section is not geared either to preparing such a calendar or regularly to giving information on specific national meetings.

The proliferation of scientific research has made more important knowledge of what scientists in all countries are doing. Many international organizations have become informal clearing houses for information on the work of their member scientists, and distribute reprints of their scientific papers, as well as the organization's publications. It is therefore important for the non-member scientist to know to what extent and how he can tap this cache of information. The Congress of the United States was made aware of this need by government scientists. It in turn appealed to the National Science Foundation to provide better information about sources and how they could be used. From this chain of events came the request from the National Science Foundation for the International Organizations Section to prepare, with Foundation funds, a guide to existing means of access to information in international multilateral scientific organizations. In February 1963, a guide to their library, documentation and information services was published under the title, *International Scientific Organizations.* The 794-page book reports on 449 organizations selected from a total of 781 that were questioned.

In spite of progress made in the Library of Congress toward achieving control over this burgeoning mass of information, much remains to be done in organization, service, and publishing before access to it is on a par with many of the older fields. More, in fact, than any one institution may be expected to accomplish. Fortunately, more and more groups are working on one or another facet creating a complex of tools which might, some day, be adequate for the field. Unfortunately, these efforts are largely uncoordinated. Perhaps, this decade, not yet too old, may see the beginning of serious cooperation among those already issuing reference aids in this field, and another decade or two will offer more comprehensive and reliable tools.

NOTES

[1] Murra, K. O. Organization and servicing of information about international meetings. "Bulletin NGO/ONG" (Brussels, Union of International Associations) May 1953, pp. 211–216.

[2] Futures in international meetings. "College and Research Libraries." Vol. 19, Nov. 1958, pp. 445–450.

[3] World list of future international meetings. Part I, Science, technology, agriculture and medicine; Part II, Social, cultural, commercial, and humanistic. Washington: US Government Printing Office, 1959- .

The South Pacific Commission, What It Is—What It Does

P. L. Ryan

The South Pacific Commission differs from other regional international organizations in that it is composed of colonial powers who share the common interest of controlling territory in the region. The SPC shares with other regional organizations the common characteristic of concern with problems of economic and social development.

ORIGIN

The South Pacific Commission is a regional body established under an Agreement, signed at Canberra, Australia, on 6th February 1947, by representatives of the Governments then administering territories in the area, namely Australia, France, the Netherlands, New Zealand, the United Kingdom and the United States of America, "to encourage and strengthen international co-operation in promoting the economic and social welfare and advancement of the non-self-governing territories in the South Pacific region administered by them." The Netherlands' membership terminated on 31st December 1962.

The first two Sessions of the Commission were held in Sydney, Australia, in May and November 1948. At the latter, it was decided that the permanent headquarters should be at Nouméa, New Caledonia, and since then regular Sessions of the Commission have been held there each year.

COMPOSITION

The Commission consists of not more than ten Commissioners, each of the five participating Governments being entitled to appoint two, one of whom is designated Senior Commissioner. Each Government may also appoint such alternates and advisers to its Commissioners as it considers desirable. Senior Commissioners preside over Sessions of the Commission in rotation according to the English alphabetical order of the participating Governments.

The Commission is advised by two auxiliary bodies, the Research Council and the South Pacific Conference. The Commission appoints the members of the Research Council who are selected for their special knowledge of the questions with which the Commission is concerned and the problems of the territories in those fields. The principal functions of the Research Council, which normally meets once a year, are to maintain a continuous survey of research needs in the territories within the scope of the Commission, to make recommendations to the Commission on research to be undertaken, to arrange, with the assistance of the Secretary-General, for the carrying out of research studies approved by the Commission and to co-ordinate the research activities of other bodies working within the field of the Commission's activities.

The South Pacific Conference is convened by the Commission, in terms of the 1947 Agreement, at intervals of not more than three years. The Conference is attended by representative inhabitants of all territories within the Commission's area and, by invitation, of the independent Kingdom of Tonga. Since Western Samoa attained independence on 1st January 1962, it also has been invited to continue to send delegates to the Conference. The purpose of the South Pacific Conference is to bring island representatives into close touch with the work of the Commission and to provide a regular opportunity for meeting together and for discussion of matters of common interest falling

SOURCE: Reprinted from P. L. Ryan "The South Pacific Commission, What It Is—What It Does," *South Pacific Bulletin*, (Oct. 1963) 3035.

within the Commission's competence. The Conference is entitled to make recommendations to the Commission on any such matters. The South Pacific Conference has met five times—1950 (Suva), 1953 (Nouméa), 1956 (Suva), 1959 (Rabaul), 1962 (Pago Pago).

THE SECRETARIAT

The chief officer of the Commission is the Secretary-General who is appointed by the Commission and is responsible for the administration of its programme. The other principal officers appointed by the Commission are the Executive Officers in the fields of Health, Social Development and Economic Development. The present Secretary-General is Mr. W. D. Forsyth, O. B. E., M.A., B. Litt., Dip. Ed.; Executive Officer for Health, Dr. Guy Loison, M.D., D.P.H.; Executive Officer for Economic Development, Dr. Jacques Barrau, M. Agr. Sc., D. Sc.; and Executive Officer for Social Development, Dr. Richard Seddon, Ph.D., M.A., B. Com., Dip. Ed. The Secretary-General and these three officers are members of the Research Council. The total full-time staff of the Commission, embracing professional, administrative and general service personnel, is approximately sixty, of whom all but a few are based at Nouméa. A small staff is located in Sydney and is concerned mainly with the printing and distribution of Commission publications.

ANNUAL BUDGET

The Commission's annual budget is financed by grants made by each of the member Governments in agreed proportions. Grants for specific purposes are also received on occasion from foundations, from United Nations Specialized Agencies and from territorial administrations.

COMMISSION AREA

The participating Governments are, between them, responsible for the administration of nearly all the Pacific Islands from Papua and New Guinea eastward to French Polynesia and from the Trust Territory of the Pacific Islands southward to Norfolk Island. The area thus within the Commis-

sion's competence extends over about twelve million square miles, only three per cent of which is land. Some three million people live in the area and the individual territories included in it are American Samoa, British Solomon Islands Protectorate, Cook Islands, Fiji, French Polynesia, Gilbert and Ellice Islands, Guam, Nauru, New Caledonia, New Hebrides, Niue, Norfolk Island, Papua and New Guinea, Trust Territory of the Pacific Islands and Wallis and Futuna Islands, Independent Western Samoa and the Kingdom of Tonga are within the area with which the Commission is concerned but are not, of course, counted among the "non-self-governing territories" dependent on its member Governments.

WORK PROGRAMME

The Commission's programme is in the fields of health, economic development and social development and the 1947 Agreement included recommendations for research into specific subjects within them. In the years since then the Commission has performed, promoted or assisted a very wide range of activities in each of its special fields. The programme is organized in a way that recognizes that the proper function of the Commission is to help territorial administrations to carry out their responsibilities. It does that by organizing research into unsolved problems, through training schemes, by providing experts to investigate, advise or assist, by financing study tours, and by collecting, preparing and distributing information of a general or particular kind. The nature of the Commission's programme of assistance is determined by what is believed to be the most effective use of its resources, at any time, as an aid to territorial plans. Some examples, by no means exhaustive, of the Commission's recent and current work are given in the following summaries.

HEALTH

The programme under this heading is concerned with general public health but includes such special fields as maternal and child health, nutrition, epidemiology of cardio-vascular diseases and of area diseases which create health problems, e.g. eosinophilic meningitis, fish poisoning, etc., training of personnel and health education.

The Commission has for several years assisted territories with their health education programmes. In 1957 a training course was held in this subject in Nouméa. In 1959 a Health Education Officer was appointed to the staff of the Commission and a second one in 1961. These officers make frequent visits to the territories to help local health authorities in the planning and conduct of health education programmes and training schemes. Assistance is also given in the form of written advice, printed matter (including a regular health education letter for field workers) and health education materials. The Commission convened a Conference of Directors of Territorial Health Services in May 1961 which considered health education needs of the region and recommended future lines of action. The Commission has also undertaken to assist in organizing the health education aspects of a WHO/BSIP malaria eradication programme in the British Solomon Islands Protectorate.

Mosquito-borne diseases, especially filariasis, occupied a prominent position in the Commission's health programme for many years and a full-time specialist was employed at one stage. The results of his studies and the collation of published material on this subject will be of continuing value. The work was discontinued in 1960 when it was considered that most of what could be accomplished in this field was completed. A comprehensive bibliography on the subject continues to be available.

The Commission over the years has conducted a long series of field and laboratory studies of the food and dietary conditions over much of the area. Following a review of this work, the Commission's collected material on nutrition will be published in a form suited to community needs and as a help in teaching nutrition. A socio-economic survey to determine to what extent urban living is resulting in nutritional deterioration is being organized. The Commission also appointed a Home Economics Officer within its social development section to devote special attention to nutritional problems and work in association with its women's Interests and Health Education Officers.

As fish forms an important item in the diet of many Pacific peoples, the Commission has given special attention to recurrent outbreaks of fish poisoning. This is done through its own resources and in collaboration with the University of Hawaii and the *Institut Français d'Océanie,* which are engaged in research into this problem.

The Commission also secured WHO assistance for a survey during 1962/1963 of maternal and child health services in various parts of the region. In April 1963, a conference on rural health problems with special emphasis on maternal and child health met at Tahiti. Subsequently, the Research Council considered the conference findings and reviewed the whole health programme.

Other health activities are carried on in relation to such matters as epidemiological surveys and information, the publication of a wide range of information on health subjects and the provision of financial assistance to enable Territorial health staffs to study health work in other countries.

ECONOMIC DEVELOPMENT

A three-year programme laid down at the end of 1959 developed broadly on three main themes—fisheries, plant collection and introduction, and pests and diseases of plants and animals. At the same time there was a study of capital formation as one essential element in economic development. Information related to the promotion of trade and industry in the area was also gathered. At the end of this three-year programme, the need was felt to consolidate and expand the activities of the section and it was then decided that plant production improvement, animal production improvement, plant and animal protection, and economic affairs should be the section's main fields of activity.

The Commission's special fisheries project has had as its objectives improvement in the supplies of food fishes available to the peoples of the area and the best economic use of other marine resources. The work thus has included introduction of new food fishes, the training of islanders in modern and improved fishing methods (including fish preservation, care of nets, the use and maintenance of small, powered vessels, etc.) and advice to territorial administrations for the development of fisheries based on surveys of local resources and technical knowledge. A special Fisheries Training Centre established by the Commission in association with FAO, ran for several months at Tulagi in the British Solomon Islands during 1961. Three regional boatbuilding training courses, each of two years' duration, have been initiated by the Commission at Auki in the British Solomon Islands and at Nouméa. They operate with finance and other resources made available jointly by the Commission, the United Nations and the governments of the two territories where the courses are located.

The Commission also sponsored special research

into the biology of the blacklip mother-of-pearl oyster in the Cook Islands and has since made a special grant to the Commonwealth Scientific and Industrial Research Organization (Australia) to further, through statistical analysis, this valuable research. Other fisheries work includes examination of trochus-gathering prospects in various territories and the publication or supply of literature on a variety of aspects.

Plant collection and introduction was one of the Commission's earliest projects and it has also been concerned with the improvement of existing crops in the area. Since 1961, 757 species of varieties of useful plants were introduced through its Plant Collection and Introduction Service. In the course of the search for improved cropping capacity in the breadfruit tree, cuttings of 150 "varieties" were collected in Polynesia and Micronesia and used in inter-island exchanges for comparative trials. Cuttings of 80 "varieties" were sent to Western Samoa where a central collection has been established. This work is to be intensified. Special attention was also given in the same period to the coconut palm, of which eight varieties that seemed to have interesting potentialities were sent to seven different territories for trials. Throughout its whole programme in regard to the collection, introduction and exchange of economic plants in the Pacific Islands area, special attention has been given—in addition to coconuts and breadfruit—to coffee, cacao, pepper, vegetables, bamboo, forage and pasture plants and other possible cash crops.

A primary objective of the Commission is to assist territories in their attempts to control the rhinoceros beetle which is an extremely serious threat to the coconut industry of the Pacific Islands. The Commission employs an entomologist who devotes special attention to this particular pest and who carried out investigation in East Africa during 1961-62 into insects likely to be useful in its control. The Commission has also offered grants to other institutions working on this problem and in turn has received assistance from governments in its area. A five-year programme involving approximately 1,000,000 dollars to find means of eradicating this beetle and related pests is to start early in 1964 with assistance from the UN Special Fund. A survey of plant quarantine measures and facilities has been made in the area under Commission auspices with a view to enabling territories to learn from each other and improve their services. Information is also disseminated concerning plant and animal pests and diseases occurring in the area.

The Commission convened a regional technical meeting at Rabaul (Territory of Papua and New Guinea) in November 1961. This meeting examined particularly, and recommended upon, the training of agricultural extension personnel, the promotion of rural lay-leaders and extension methods adapted to the socioeconomic conditions of the South Pacific area.

In the field of agriculture, as in others, the Commission publishes and otherwise provides much useful technical information. It financially assists study tours by agriculturists and others within its area and makes grants to experimental stations and other institutions carrying out research work of regional interest, particularly those giving attention to the coconut palm.

During the past two years, the Commission followed up a study made several years earlier, of credit arrangements and other forms of technical assistance available for islanders, by a wider survey of capital formation achievements. This led in 1962 to a special technical meeting on economic development and particularly capital formation, to compare territorial experience and to formulate basic requirements of development programmes in the region.

SOCIAL DEVELOPMENT

The Commission has always covered a very wide range of activities in this field. For example, it began work on literature promotion, literacy, library development and audio-visual aids as far back as 1952 when it established its Literature Bureau. Continuing attention and, where appropriate, financial assistance is given to all these subjects and, as well, a film appraisal service is available to territories. Through the Commission's initiative, a Literature Production Training Centre to operate for three years was established at Honjara in the British Solomon Islands in 1960. It has been supported jointly by the Commission, UNESCO and the Government of the British Solomon Islands Protectorate and, by helping to provide trained staff and by investigating practical problems, will assist territories towards self-sufficiency in the provision of printed matter designed specially for their own conditions.

Services related to education have been and continue to be undertaken. Requests for material, information and advice are met through the Social Development Clearing House. Provision is made for financial help towards inter-territorial study visits by education officers and for specialist and other assistance to territorial seminars, workshops and training courses. In 1959, the Commisssion convened a Regional Education Seminar, the outcome of which provided a basis for increased and more direct Commission activity in this field and for its planning for the future. Another such Seminar is proposed to be convened within the next two years.

The Commission has had a continuing programme to assist the development of co-operatives throughout the region and since 1955 has employed a specialist co-operatives officer. Field surveys and general advisory services have given way in recent years to direct educational and training activities. An information and clearing-house service is maintained and a comprehensive library on co-operatives has been built up. A number of specialist meetings and training courses have been held since 1958, among them a Regional Co-operatives Training Centre conducted at Suva, Fiji, for several months in 1962 in association with FAO.

The Commission, supported by funds from United Church Women of the U.S.A., appointed a Women's Interests Officer to develop its work in this field in co-operation with territorial administrations. Since then, the officer has visited and worked in most of the territories. The Commission has also contributed towards the cost of travel of representatives of women's organizations in the area for various purposes. In late 1961 a Women's Interests Seminar was convened at Apia, Western Samoa, with the collaboration of FAO, UNESCO and the United Church Women of the U.S.A.

An integrated community education project is being developed in collaboration with FAO. As a first step, and with the co-operation of the Government of Fiji, it is planned to open a Home Economics Training Centre in Fiji and conduct the first residential course there in 1963. In addition, to expand the work already commenced in the women's interests field a Home Economics Officer has been appointed to the social development staff.

An Urbanization Advisory Committee appointed by the Commission met for the first time at Honolulu in September 1961. The Committee reported comprehensively on aspects of urbanization in the Pacific, and the Commission, acting on its recommendation, has established an Urbanization Information Research Centre.

Sub-regional study groups composed of representatives of island communities are sponsored by the Commission. The first was held in 1961 on "Problems of Youth in Urban Communities" and a second has now been held in March 1963 on the topic "The Development of Small-Scale Private Enterprise." A sub-regional conference met at Papeete, Tahiti, in 1962 to discuss social and labour problems. A regional conference on low-cost housing and related problems met in Fiji during June.

The Commission convened a meeting in 1961 which led to the establishment of an Organizing Committee to promote the first South Pacific Games held at Suva in August/September 1963.

During 1963 a comprehensive survey relating to handicrafts in South Pacific territories is being undertaken.

CO-OPERATION WITH OTHER BODIES

There is liaison and co-operation between the Commission and other bodies and institutions in matters of mutual interest. Thus the United Nations, through the Technical Assistance Board and the Specialized Agencies (FAO, WHO, UNESCO), has collaborated in particular projects either by financial assistance or the provision of experts. Metropolitan governments of the member nations assist in a similar way, while there is a continuing association with institutions such as The Australian National University, the Institut Français d'Océanie, the University of Hawaii, etc. The Commission's work is also aided by Technical Advisory Committees (e.g. Fisheries, Plant Collection and Introduction) and consultants (e.g. Fiji Government Entomologist) made possible by the co-operation of governments within the area.

PUBLICATIONS

The Commission publishes an illustrated quarterly magazine, *South Pacific Bulletin,* which features articles on selected activities in the three main fields of operations, as well as articles contributed by specialists working in these and related fields in the territories within the Commission area. It is issued in two languages, English and French. A monthly news-sheet is issued for press and radio, under the title *South Pacific News.* Technical papers covering various aspects of its programme as well as reports of meetings of special groups sponsored by the Commission are also published.

The Commission maintains at its headquarters a valuable library which provides the reference material necessary for its work.

Further particulars of the Commission's activities may be obtained from the Secretary-General, South Pacific Commission, P. O. Box 9, Nouméa, New Caledonia.

A Review of the Progress and Problems of the Organization of American States[1]

Joseph John Jova

In this statement Mr. Jova, the U.S. Permanent Representative to the OAS, reviews the activities of the organization during 1970–1971.

I thank you for this further opportunity to appear before this committee to discuss the Organization of American States. When I met with you on March 17, 1970,[2] the Organization was in a period of transition, as the Protocol of Buenos Aires amending the Charter of the OAS had entered into force only 18 days before, on February 27, 1970. I also reported that the Organization had recently and successfully weathered a crisis, having brought about a cease-fire in the war between El Salvador and Honduras and having made other progressive contributions toward peace between the two countries.

Fortunately, nothing as dramatic as warfare has confronted the Organization in the intervening period. Nevertheless, there have been significant developments, and there continue to be real problems, particularly in the political, economic, and organizational fields, with which the OAS has been grappling. The process of transition continues, as does the process of confronting basic issues that face this hemisphere.

As I reported last year, the charter amendments had the purpose of making the OAS a more effective instrument for promoting the development of the hemisphere. They were designed to strengthen the structure of the Organization, to give greater emphasis to the principles and goals of the Alliance for Progress, and to enhance the Organization's peaceful settlement role. Among the principal structural changes was the establishment of a General Assembly, meeting annually as supreme organ, with three hierarchically coequal Councils operating under it; that is, the Permanent Council and two technical Councils—the Inter-American Economic and Social Council and the Inter-American Council for Education, Science, and Culture. Thus, while attempting to orient the Organization more toward its developmental functions, the changes also served to make it a more complicated and less of a unitary structure. Hence the division of responsibility between the three Councils raises problems of coordination among them. It also puts greater management responsibility upon the General Secretariat in helping to insure unity of effort.

This new structure is still going through what is essentially a "shakedown" period. The General Assembly met for the first time in June–July of last year, with most Foreign Ministers present, devoting much of its effort to setting in motion certain regulatory provisions relating to the new structure of the Organization, in addition to taking up its more routine annual responsibilities and the specific substantive issue of kidnapping and terrorism. After holding two more special sessions limited to specific subjects, the General Assembly held its first regular session in April of this year in San José, Costa Rica. With a 37-item agenda, the San José session touched on political, economic, and organizational issues of considerable importance as well as other matters reaching into the various fields of OAS activities. It thus helped establish a pattern that the General Assembly, as supreme body, must cover the spectrum of problems facing the inter-American system. The fact that the great majority of delegations were at a high level, headed by their Foreign Ministers or equivalent, also helped give the Assembly this stamp.

Returning to the question of the new structure of the OAS under the charter, the General Assembly addressed itself to certain defects or omissions which needed to be filled. It was clear, for

SOURCE: Reprinted from Joseph John Jova, "A Review of the Progress and Problems of the Organization of American States," *Department of State Bulletin,* 65, no. 1681 (Sept. 13, 1971), 284–293.

example, that a system of three autonomous Councils needed a mechanism for continuing coordination beyond the annual meetings of the General Assembly. Thus a Coordinating Committee of the three Councils was established not only to deal with problems mutual to them but also problems relating to the other organs of the OAS. Among these, for example, was and is the need to reduce the proliferating number of OAS meetings and conferences. (A phenomenon, incidentally, shared by most other international organizations today.) The Assembly also provided for improved coordination and oversight in the administrative, planning, budgeting, and evaluation functions of the Organization. Additionally, it provided for the establishment of an administrative tribunal in the General Secretariat.

This is not to say that all problems arising under the new charter structure have now been solved. There is increasing recognition, which we share, that the charter amendments failed to confer sufficient explicit central powers on the Permanent Council. The General Assembly in San José did take various actions which by implication served to increase the central responsibility of the Permanent Council. But the debate continues in the Council itself as to the extent to which it should assume certain implicit functions on behalf of the whole Organization when the General Assembly is not in session, and the question will probably come up again in next April's General Assembly session.

Mr. Chairman, before turning to other subjects I should like to mention that since our last meeting the U.S. Mission to the OAS has undergone a further slight adjustment in order to bring it in line with the practice of other missions. Our title is now Permanent Mission of the United States of America to the Organization of American States. The basic purpose when we established the mission in the first place was to provide combined and coordinated representation to the OAS as a whole, where previously we were simply a delegation to the old OAS Council.

PEACEFUL SETTLEMENT AND COLLECTIVE SECURITY

As I mentioned before, one of the advances in the amended charter—albeit a modest one—is the strengthening of the peaceful settlement machinery available to the OAS by making this func-

tion the responsibility of the Permanent Council, assisted by a subordinate body, the Inter-American Committee on Peaceful Settlement (IACPS), and by broadening somewhat the good-offices role of the predecessor organization. This new machinery still remains largely untested.

However, when Ecuador in January 1970 called for a meeting of Foreign Ministers to take up the charges of alleged "coercive" action by the United States in response to Ecuador's seizure of U.S. tuna boats (to which I refer again later), the United States formally proposed that the matter be referred instead to the Inter-American Committee on Peaceful Settlement so that the latter could propose procedures for solution. When it became apparent that the other members were prepared to accede to Ecuador's request for a Foreign Ministers meeting and that there were reasonable prospects for a balanced resolution emerging from that meeting, the United States suspended its request for the good offices of the IACPS. Nevertheless, we believe that this initiative—the first under the pertinent charter revisions —served as a reminder that this body is available as a means of helping resolve disputes in a quiet, dignified manner, away from the glare of publicity.

In my last testimony I reported at some length on the major accomplishments of the OAS in the El Salvador–Honduras conflict. Further progress has been achieved since then. The agreement that the OAS "Committee of Seven" was then in process of negotiating to establish a security zone and to govern troop dispositions in border areas was agreed to by the two countries and signed by all five Central American Foreign Ministers meeting in San José, Costa Rica, on June 4, 1970. This agreement has been in effect since then under the supervision of OAS military observers. As a result there has been a much improved atmosphere of tranquillity between the two countries, with border incidents reduced to very minor and sporadic occurrences. The situation has improved to the point where it is presently intended to terminate the OAS military observer operation on July 31, leaving liaison officers in each capital, and to transfer responsibility for maintaining the security zone to the two parties.

Meanwhile, at the close of the OAS General Assembly in San José last April, the Foreign Ministers of the two countries signed in the presence of the whole Assembly identical declarations of intention to end the anomalous situation between the two countries and to negotiate basic differences through a bilateral working group, taking up specific subjects which had already been suggested by the OAS. The bilateral working group is due to hold its next meeting in San José in a few days under the chairmanship of former OAS Secretary General José Mora, now Foreign Minister of Uruguay.

Thus, while final solutions have yet to be achieved, we can again look with satisfaction on the accomplishments of the OAS operating under the authority of the Rio Treaty (the Inter-American Treaty of Reciprocal Assistance).

Unfortunately, in another aspect of collective security under the Rio Treaty, hemispheric solidarity was somewhat weakened. As you know, the new Government of Chile in November 1970 reestablished diplomatic and commercial relations with Cuba. This step was taken despite the fact that the OAS in 1964 had taken the "binding" decision under the Rio Treaty that because of Cuban interventionist and aggressive acts, member states should have no diplomatic or consular relations, shipping, or trade with Cuba until the OAS itself by two-thirds vote decided that Cuba had ceased to be a threat to the peace and security of the hemisphere. There is still no indication that the present Cuban Government has abandoned its policy of intervention and subversion, much as the hemisphere would welcome this.

CONVENTION ON TERRORISM

A special session of the OAS General Assembly was held here in January–February of this year to consider a draft international convention on terrorism and kidnapping drawn up at the Assembly's request by the Inter-American Juridical Committee. With most Foreign Ministers participating, debate centered upon whether the convention should attempt to deal with all forms of terrorism, broadly defined, or whether it should be limited to attacks against foreign government officials and their dependents.

Six countries, led by Brazil and Argentina, argued that no convention would be meaningful in coping with the problem unless it addressed itself to all aspects of terrorism. A larger group felt that such a sweeping approach would endanger the principle of political asylum. The United States, which favored a narrower convention, nevertheless sought to bridge the gap between these two points of view, but our efforts were unsuccessful.

The result was approval by a slim majority of a convention drawn along narrower lines and aimed mainly at dealing with assaults against foreign officials and their families.[3] The six delegations who favored a hard line walked out of the Assembly session to underscore their displeasure, and a few others thought the convention went too far. Despite their criticism and despite our recognition that the convention can be no panacea, in our opinion it makes a significant contribution to building a *corpus* of international law in a comparatively new field. By declaring acts of terrorism against foreign officials and their dependents to be common crimes rather than political offenses, it deprives persons responsible for such acts of the shelter of political asylum and subjects them to extradition and prosecution.

The convention has yet to be ratified by any of the 13 signatory nations, but at least nine have indicated their intention to initiate the ratification procedure. The Department of State has presented the pertinent papers to the President, who has submitted it to the Senate for its advice and consent.

ARTICLE 19: ECONOMIC COERCION

An uncomfortable departure in our OAS affairs occurred in January of this year when Ecuador accused the United States of violating article 19 of the OAS Charter, which prohibits "use of coercive measures of an economic or political character in order to force the sovereign will of another State." Our dispute with Ecuador arose over the right of American vessels to fish off the coast of that country, in waters which Ecuador claims lie within its maritime sovereignty but which we maintain are high seas. After Ecuador had seized 14 American tuna boats in less than 2 weeks, the United States applied section 3(b) of the Foreign Military Sales Act suspending such sales to that country.

On the assertion that the United States move violated charter article 19, Ecuador called for a Meeting of Consultation of OAS Foreign Ministers, who happened to be in Washington anyway for the special General Assembly session. In their concurrent meeting on this new issue, there were severe criticisms of United States laws which allegedly apply economic sanctions and impinge upon other nations' sovereignty. For its part, the United States defended its duty to protect the legitimate rights of its citizens in international waters. The outcome, however, was a solution supported by both Ecuador and the United States, which merely stated the positions of the two disputing parties and called upon them to resolve their differences in accordance with charter principles and "abstain from the use of any kind of measure that may affect the sovereignty" of another state.[4] This in itself involved a constructive effort on both sides to calm the situation, although the basic issue continues.

While the OAS action hardly constituted an indictment of the United States in its dispute with Ecuador, the implications of the issue for the future are of concern to us should there be future applications of U.S. legislation that might be deemed by OAS members to be "coercive" and in violation of charter article 19.

ARMS LIMITATION

In April of this year, the OAS General Assembly considered a proposal by the President of Colombia that it study the feasibility of an arms limitation agreement among Latin American countries. The Colombian initiative was based on chapter VI of the 1967 Declaration of American Presidents, in which the Latin American chiefs of state expressed their intention to limit military expenditures in proportion to the real demands of national security and international commitments so as to devote maximum resources to economic and social development.[5]

The proposal was debated at length by the Assembly, but it failed to prosper in its original form. The most serious objections came from those who argued that the Presidents' intention was to promote unilateral limitation measures rather than a multilateral arms control agreement. The outcome was a resolution that merely instructed the OAS Permanent Council to study "the meaning and scope of Chapter VI" and to report on its work to the member governments in advance of next year's Assembly session. To date, Council action has made little headway, and it is clear that deep disagreement persists over both the meaning of the Presidents' declaration and the scope of the Assembly mandate.

The United States has not actively participated in the deliberations on this subject, since any

eventual agreement on arms limitation would be unlikely to include this country. Secretary Rogers, however, clearly stated to the General Assembly our willingness to cooperate in discussions of this Latin American initiative in any way other members think appropriate.[6]

HUMAN RIGHTS

The Inter-American Human Rights Commission has held three sessions of meetings since its incorporation into the new charter structure as a full-fledged organ of the OAS. Significant developments included publication of a report on the plight of political prisoners and their relatives in Cuba, which brought up to date the Commission's earlier reports on human rights there. It also issued a report on the human rights situation in El Salvador and Honduras as a result of the work of the Commission in the two countries before and after their brief war in 1969. The Commission has, in addition, undertaken a study of complaints it has received concerning alleged violations of human rights in Brazil.

Thus far only Costa Rica has ratified the Inter-American Convention on Human Rights, and no countries in addition to the 12 original signatories have signed. The convention is still under study in our Government, which has not yet signed or ratified, and the same is no doubt true in the case of other governments.

ECONOMIC, SOCIAL, AND EDUCATIONAL ACTIVITIES

As I discussed in my previous testimony before this subcommittee last year, we agreed early in 1970 to forming a continuing Special Committee on Consultation and Negotiation, a permanent committee of the IA—ECOSOC [Inter-American Economic and Social Council] , to deal with problems of trade assistance, investment technology, et cetera, on a multilateral basis. This was part of our response to the Consensus of Viña del Mar. During the 16 months since that testimony the activities in this Special Committee and its subordinate Ad Hoc Group on Trade have been extensive. In these the United States has been willing to discuss problems of protectionism and pending U.S. legislation in addition to negotiating with the Latin American countries specific items for the purpose of tariff and nontariff concessions. As a result of these intensive discussions, our generalized preference proposal was broadened and now includes some 500 of the approximately 800 items specifically requested by the Latin American OAS members. Additionally, in the same framework, there have been a number of consultations concerning other specific trade matters as well as shipping problems. Mr. Szabo in his testimony outlined in some detail the scope and results of these meetings with the Latin Americans.[7]

We are now approaching the 10th anniversary of the Alliance for Progress. In the seventh annual IA-ECOSOC meeting, now scheduled for Panama in mid-September, we and the other OAS members will be reviewing achievements of the Alliance during the past decade and seeking new and expanded roles to be undertaken during the Second Development Decade. While the hemispheric consensus is yet to be developed it is clear that greater emphasis will be given to social rather than to economic development goals. Some of the areas of concentration that have been contemplated are the growing problem of unemployment and underemployment, the social cost of the pellmell growth of urban centers, the often hidden but nevertheless real cost of pollution of the environment, and the need to bring all the population into the social and political process.

The IA-ECOSOC's permanent executive committee, the Inter-American Committee on the Alliance for Progress (CIAP), has completed its sixth cycle of country reviews. A new dimension was added to this country review cycle last year; namely, the first review of the United States, in which the impact of U.S. economic policies and trends on the hemisphere was considered. This will now be an annual affair along with reviews of other countries. We believe Latin American reaction to the first review was very favorable.

OAS technical assistance programs in the economic and social field are supervised by IA-ECOSOC, financed by voluntary contributions by member states to the Special Development Assistance Fund, and executed by the General Secretariat. They are currently funded at an annual level of about $7 million. I shall discuss this further under technical assistance.

Ambassador Henderson [Douglas Henderson,

Deputy U.S. Representative (Economic and Social Affairs) to the OAS] will give a more complete presentation on OAS economic and social activities.

The Inter-American Council for Education, Science, and Culture, created by the recent amendments to the charter, has already achieved substantial results through its regional programs of science and education. A total of 205 scientific institutions have participated in its activities while 592 visiting professors, experts, and researchers have been sent to these institutions and 1,751 scholarships for advanced studies have been granted. These programs are funded by the voluntary contributions by member states to a special multilateral fund, which is administered by the OAS Secretariat under its technical assistance activities and is budgeted at about $12 million for the current fiscal year, a more realistic figure than the earlier goal of $25 million.

OAS TECHNICAL ASSISTANCE

As I mentioned in my presentation last year, a basic premise of U.S. policy toward Latin America expressed by President Nixon on October 31, 1969, is the belief that the principal future patterns of U.S. assistance for hemispheric development must be U.S. support for Latin American initiatives and "that this can best be achieved on a multilateral basis within the Inter-American system."[8]

The Inter-American Development Bank (IDB), which is an important element of the Inter-American system but not part of the OAS, is of course primarily involved in developmental lending. The OAS itself is not involved in lending, but it does carry out significant technical assistance programs.

Three OAS organs administer the bulk of this technical assistance: the Pan American Health Organization (PAHO), the Inter-American Institute of Agricultural Sciences (IAIAS), and the OAS General Secretariat. The IDB also provides technical assistance, but this is primarily for project development in connection with potential loan applications or as a supplement to loans made, and thus it is not structured for the provision of general technical assistance.

The following table shows the current annual

level of technical assistance provided by the three OAS entities.

LEVEL OF TECHNICAL ASSISTANCE PROVIDED BY THE OAS AND ITS SPECIALIZED ORGANIZATIONS

(in millions of dollars)

	Total	From Others	U.S.	U.S. by Source Assessed (State)	U.S. by Source Voluntary (AID)
PAHO	30	12	18	18	----
IAIAS	5	2	3	3	----
OAS Secretariat	31	10	21	4	17
TOTAL:	66	24	42	25	17

For comparative purposes, the $66 million provided by the OAS entities is almost equal to the $70 to $75 million which AID provides bilaterally for technical assistance.

PAHO, in addition to being a specialized organization of the OAS, is also the regional office of WHO [World Health Organization]. It carries out a program of various technical assistance projects in the health area at a current level of roughly $30 million per year. Among its various programs, for example, it is now actively engaged in the urgent problem of equine encephalitis. Except for the population field, in which there is close liaison between PAHO and AID, the United States no longer has bilateral program activities in health in Latin America. It is reasonable to expect, therefore, that any Latin American initiatives for assistance in this area would be channeled to PAHO.

IAIAS is a specialized organization of the OAS but unlike PAHO does not also serve as a regional office of the U.N. system. It is currently in a transitional phase from being largely a research and training organization to one of assuming a broader role of providing technical assistance in areas such as agricultural production and rural development. There has been a deliberate movement to shift some activity in these fields formerly undertaken by the OAS Secretariat to IAIAS, and we encourage this shift as a logical one. AID provides bilateral assistance to the Latin American countries in agriculture. With the IAIAS currently in a transitional phase, we cannot now say what its capability will be to take on additional activities beyond its current level of $5 million a year should AID's bilateral technical assistance in

this field be reduced. As the new course for IAIAS becomes better established, the representative organs of the Institute will be the forum for expression of any new Latin American initiatives. We would expect the United States to participate fully in the development and support of its programs.

The OAS General Secretariat, through various voluntary special funds, provides technical assistance in a large number of fields at a current level of about $31 million. These include: fiscal policy and taxation, public administration, private enterprise development and marketing, labor administration, social security, urban development, housing, community development, cooperatives, statistics, natural resource and water and land development, project formulation, transportation and telecommunication, tourism development, export promotion, education, scientific and technological training and research, and library development.

The OAS has also received recently some unilateral grants from the United States for carrying out programs of technical assistance in capital markets development and marine sciences.

The annual CIAP country review provides a consultative forum in which the various donors—the OAS, IDB, international banks, U.N., and bilateral donors, including AID—can discuss and thus coordinate their programs. These reviews have been particularly useful in the lending area, but we have encouraged equal service in the technical assistance area. They provide each recipient country with an opportunity to present its plans and identify its priority needs. Thus the reviews serve as a vehicle for the expression of Latin American initiatives.

AID is providing bilateral technical assistance in many of the same areas as the OAS Secretariat. There is increasingly better coordination in such areas.

The question one might be asked, then, is: What is the OAS Secretariat's capability to expand its technical assistance programs should the United States wish to make a further shift in the emphasis from the bilateral to the multilateral channel? This involves a number of considerations and raises a number of questions.

First, there is the question of the management and technical capability of the OAS to undertake new and additional technical assistance activities. The aspect of management improvements I shall discuss a little later.

With respect to its capability to undertake effective technical assistance programs, we have, in keeping with General Accounting Office recommendations, asked our Embassies in the field to provide us with evaluations of these programs in their respective countries. As a participant and a major contributor, we felt the need to be better informed. I was gratified but almost skeptical of the preponderance of favorable conclusions regarding the usefulness and efficiency of these OAS activities. The results of our second annual canvassing have been equally favorable, so I must conclude that the OAS is, on the whole, carrying out meaningful and effective programs. This does not mean that there was no activity without problems. Any program the size of that carried out by the OAS is bound to have some, but they were few. It is obviously inherently more complex and difficult to approach maximum efficiency in a multilateral framework than bilaterally—which in foreign eyes has often meant unilaterally.

It is my conclusion, therefore, that the OAS Secretariat has the management and technical capability to carry out its current level of activity and that, given a reasonably short time to gear up, could do an effective job at a considerably larger program level provided that increases occur in a gradual manner consistent with the Organization's ability to take on increased responsibility.

Second, there is the question of the source of financing for any expanded program. This question is one faced not only by the OAS Secretariat but by PAHO and IAIAS as well. The OAS and its specialized organizations have funds only to the extent member countries make contributions, and here there is a problem.

For several years now, financing of the OAS Secretariat's regular budget and its voluntary funds (through which the technical assistance activities are financed) have been contributed at a single ratio—the United States paying 66 percent and all others paying 34 percent. The same ratio essentially is also applied in the specialized organizations, with minor variations. As I have mentioned, however, the United States has in addition made certain unilateral grants to the OAS for earmarked purposes.

For the United States to increase funds available to the General Secretariat for technical assistance programs, the following are the alternatives: (1) by making grants to the OAS outside of and above its budget, (2) by increasing the budget for the voluntary funds but keeping the current 66 : 34 ratio, and (3) by increasing the budget for the voluntary funds and at the same time permitting a change in the 66 : 34 ratio for those funds (but not for the regular budget).

Involved in these alternatives are the questions of whether or not increased U.S. contributions to OAS programs would represent an overall increase in the U.S. outlay for technical assistance in Latin America or simply a shift from bilateral to multilateral channels and whether or not an increased contribution from the Latin American countries would also be involved. These alternatives, Mr. Chairman, will have to be given careful study if we are indeed to increase our emphasis on technical assistance through multilateral channels.

OAS ROLE IN EMERGENCIES AND DISASTERS

The OAS role in disaster situations, through the Emergency Aid Fund (another voluntary fund), has become more firmly established since I appeared before you last year. I am thinking particularly of the very useful assistance provided by the OAS at the time of the earthquakes in Peru and Ecuador, especially in determining actual needs, in assisting in the movement of relief supplies tied up in distant ports, and in providing corrugated roofing for much-needed shelter for the victims of these disasters.

The bulk of the financing for this OAS assistance, largely from the United States, was forthcoming following each disaster and earmarked for it. Thus the problem remains of providing sufficient standby funds for immediate use by the Secretary General in his discretion as soon as a disaster arises.

Secretary Rogers, in his speech to the OAS General Assembly in June 1970, suggested an OAS role in ascertaining requirements and coordinating assistance in disaster situations and in providing leadership in emergency evacuations of foreign nationals.[9] We are convinced that building on its modest beginning the OAS can have a significant role to play in both natural and manmade disasters.

IMPROVEMENT OF MANAGEMENT PRACTICES

Last year I reviewed for this committee the improvements accomplished and those underway in overall OAS management practices. I am pleased to report that there has been further progress in this regard and, while there are still problems in some areas, the total reflects general improvements which I have reasonable confidence will continue.

With respect to overview and control by the representative bodies of the Secretariat's operations, there are two principal items worthy of note:

1. The latest reports of the External Auditor (Price Waterhouse) indicate that the financial controls of the OAS remain adequate.

2. In view of the concern regarding inspection and/or evaluation proposals, the General Assembly last April adopted a resolution charging its Preparatory Committee with reviewing the procedures and administrative operations of the Organization (particularly the process of budget preparation, implementation, progress reporting, and evaluation), with a view to recommending improvements in procedures and administrative operations as well as recommending means by which the representative bodies might permanently continue to review such matters. A special working group has been constituted and has commenced study.

Mr. Chairman, it should be of interest to your committee that the resolution which gave this responsibility to the Preparatory Committee requires that committee to report its findings to the General Assembly regarding the possibility and advisability of establishing a system of continuous and permanent analysis and evaluation of the activities of the three Councils and of the General Secretariat that would take into account the following matters:

1. The mandate from which each program originated, including the timeliness of the mandate;
2. The exact relationship between each mandate and its supporting programs, determining any overlapping or duplication between mandates and programs;
3. The possibility and advisability of eliminating programs considered inadequate or of combining similar programs;
4. The relationship between the objectives of each program and the effects and specific results obtained; and
5. The results of the planning and evaluation activities of the General Secretariat.

We view this new move on the part of the General Assembly as most significant. Passage of the resolution—and I must add that while it was supported by the United States, it was drafted by Latin American members and adopted at their initiative—reflects a healthy and encouraging attitude on the part of member countries. It reflects a recognition on the part of all member states that at the representative level they have an overview responsibility which they must fulfill to assure that good planning and management takes place.

From the point of internal management, major improvements have included the following:

1. The budget formation process has been through a second year of preparing consolidated budgets for all operations of the Organization, and the Secretariat now has this type of operation well in hand, an operation designed to force selection of and concentration on priority areas of activity.
2. The progress-reporting operations have continued to be improved. The quarterly progress report has reached a level of acceptance where recently it was given to the various specialized organizations of the U.N. as an example of the type of progress reporting their governing bodies desired them to produce. Thus, it is being used as a model for other international organizations.
3. The Planning and Evaluation Unit created last year has designed and is installing an Organization-wide self-evaluation system calling for a semiannual evaluation by all levels of management, with built-in ties to the progress reporting and budget preparation operations. In addition, four major activities or programs are scheduled for in-depth evaluation on an external contract basis.

While the foregoing represent an overall improvement, not all areas of operation and management have yet achieved a maximum level of efficiency. Considerable difficulties have been experienced in converting several operations to a computerized base. The Secretariat has requested and has now received the advice of the External Auditor on its computerization problems. We have been assured that this area will be given increased attention in the coming year.

RELATIONS WITH NONMEMBER STATES

There have been some interesting developments since I last met with you with respect to expanding relationships between the OAS, including its specialized organizations and agencies, and nonmember states. For example, Canada, which is already a member of the Pan American Institute of Geography and History and the Inter-American Statistical Institute, is now in process of becoming a full member of the Pan American Health Organization. (Canada has also expressed definite interest in joining the Inter-American Institute of Agricultural Sciences. Guyana is already a member of PAHO; and the United Kingdom, France, and the Netherlands, on behalf of their Caribbean dependencies, are also participants.

In addition, the General Assembly last April authorized the status of permanent observers to the OAS, leaving it to the Permanent Council to work out the criteria with respect to eligibility and prerogatives. The original proposal was that this status should be available to nonmember American states and to non-American states that participate in OAS assistance programs, and this still seems to be the most likely formula. The second category recognizes the very valuable contribution made by a number of nonmember states to OAS technical assistance and training programs. Several have shown active interest in accrediting permanent observers once the criteria are established.

As you can see, Mr. Chairman, the intervening 16 months since I last appeared before this committee have been busy ones for the OAS and, I believe, productive ones.

Improvements have been made in the structure of the Organization, but deficiencies still exist that must be dealt with. In the political arena, the mechanisms for peaceful settlement and collective security have again shown themselves to be generally adequate. On the other hand, differences have not yet been resolved on some of the important political issues the OAS has taken up. Progress has been made in collective discussion of economic and developmental questions, but we have not been able to meet all the aspirations of the other member states.

In the field of assistance, the OAS, including its specialized organizations, has continued to provide an element of multilateral coordination, has undertaken a larger portion of total external technical assistance provided in the hemisphere, and has significantly improved its management procedures for doing so. In our view, there is a capacity for the further channeling of assistance through these multilateral bodies, in keeping with President Nixon's new emphasis, provided a satisfactory contributions formula can be found.

Again, I believe, experience has demonstrated the capacity and flexibility of the OAS to grow with the times, to grapple with new issues, and to assume new responsibilities. In looking to the future, however, we must not expect too much. We must always remember that, as a multilateral organization representing diverse points of view, the extent of its achievement will continue to be dependent on the extent to which its member states can agree to delegate authority and resources for these purposes.

With its increased membership and with the change in outlook of some of its older members, the OAS has become a more diverse body and somewhat less cohesive than before. Looking back over the problems and differences that have arisen during the past 16 months, however, it seems to me that the very fact that they were aired in the OAS has made it a more vital and useful body. It would otherwise run the risk of unreality and sterility.

To quote Secretary Rogers in his address to the San José session of the General Assembly: "Such dissent, however vigorous, is not a sign of weakness but is a sign of vitality—and, in a sense, of confidence. The hemisphere is not homogeneous. The member states of this Organization are changing and becoming stronger, each in a way compatible with its social and cultural background. An Organization of American States open to different points of view can help assure that change comes peacefully and with due regard to each other's views."

Secretary Rogers went on to say: "The Organization of American States now embraces governments with several political systems, governments with differing philosophical orientations, and governments with policies often differing from ours. With all these governments the United States will continue to work as cooperatively as possible."

NOTES

[1] Made before the Subcommittee on Inter-American Affairs of the House Committee on Foreign Affairs on July 26.

[2] For Ambassador Jova's statement before the committee on Mar. 17, 1970, see BULLETIN of Apr. 20, 1970, p. 529.

[3] For text of the convention, see BULLETIN of Feb. 22, 1971, p. 231.

[4] For U.S. statements and text of the resolution, see BULLETIN of Feb. 22, 1971, p. 245.

[5] For text, see BULLETIN of May 8, 1967, p. 712.

[6] For Secretary Rogers' statement at San José on Apr. 15, see BULLETIN of May 10, 1971, p. 602.

[7] For a statement made before the committee on July 12 by Daniel Szabo, Deputy Assistant Secretary for Inter-American Affairs, see BULLETIN of Aug. 30, 1971, p. 230.

[8] For President Nixon's address at Washington, D.C., on Oct. 31, 1969, see BULLETIN of Nov. 17, 1969, p. 409.

[9] BULLETIN of July 27, 1970, p. 115.

The Organization of African Unity

U.S. Department of State

The geographic span of OAU like that of the European Communities covers a continent. OAU, however, models itself on the UN in its administrative structure and scope of interests.

". . . a single African organization through which Africa's single voice may be heard, within which Africa's problems may be studied and resolved . . . which will facilitate acceptable solutions to disputes among Africans and promote the study and adoption of measures for common defense and programs for cooperation in the economic and social fields. . . . to which we will all belong, based on principles to which we all subscribe . . . [and whose decisions] will take full account of all vital African considerations."

> Emperor Haile Selassie I
> at OAU Founding Conference
> Addis Ababa, May 1963

BACKGROUND

The formal search for African unity began in 1900, when the first pan-African conference was convened in London. From that date until World War II, however, the pan-African movement existed for the most part outside Africa and was primarily concerned with creating a sense of community among Africans living throughout the world.

The Second World War brought Africa more fully into the mainstream of world events and at the same time weakened the ability of the major colonial powers to resist the growing pressure of nascent nationalism. The new mood was reflected in the resolutions adopted in 1945 by the Fifth Pan-African Congress, which named self-government or independence as the initial goals of pan-African aspirations.

For the next decade, the energies generated by the pan-African ideal were therefore channeled into the drive for self-government and independence at the territorial level, and the search for broader African unity fell dormant.

By the late 1950's and early 1960's, however, as more and more African states became independent, pan-Africanism was reemphasized. There were two general lines of approach. One, which brought together representatives of African *peoples* rather than governments, was utilized both in African and in Afro-Asian forums. The other, which searched for unity through *intergovernmental* action, resulted in the first Conference of Independent African States at Accra, Ghana, in 1958 and several attempts at multistate regional groupings [the Mali Federation of 1959, the Council of the Entente (Ivory Coast, Upper Volta, Niger, Dahomey) of the same year, and the Ghana-Guinea-Mali Union of 1960].

By 1962 states advocating different approaches to African unity were known by the cities in which they had met. The "Brazzaville group," comprising ex-French states from West and Equatorial Africa, favored a loose grouping of states and maintenance of their own ties with France. The "Casablanca group" included states which tended to favor unity with stronger, centralized executive powers and an all-African military force. The philosophy of the "Monrovia group" fell between the other two groups and emphasized consultation among sovereign nations rather than the formation of Africa-wide executive institutions.

In late 1962 representatives of all these groups agreed to participate in a meeting of African states at Addis Ababa, Ethiopia, in May 1963. At

SOURCE: U.S. Department of State. *The Organization of African Unity.* Washington, Government Printing Office, 1970. (International Organizations Series. No. 2)

this, the founding meeting of the Organization of African Unity, representatives of 30 African states agreed to the OAU Charter on May 25, 1963. (Morocco and Togo, which had not sent representatives to the meeting, signed shortly thereafter.) Since 1963 nine more African states became independent and immediately sought and obtained admission; thus at the end of 1968 there were 41 members—all the independent African nations except the Republic of South Africa.

PRINCIPLES

OAU principles, as enunciated in the Organization's charter, reflect the historical pan-African concerns for the political independence, economic advancement, and cultural cooperation of all African peoples. The OAU Charter's preamble reaffirms the principles of the United Nations Charter and the U.N. Universal Declaration of Human Rights. It calls for the achievement of the legitimate aspirations of the African peoples and their "total advancement" through political and economic development. The OAU Charter pledges members to "coordinate and harmonize general policies," promote African progress and unity, defend their sovereignty and territorial integrity, eradicate colonialism in all its forms from Africa, and promote international cooperation. It stipulates noninterference in members' internal affairs, respect for mutual sovereignty and territorial integrity, peaceful settlement of disputes, condemnation of political assassination or subversive activity against neighboring states, liberation of the remaining dependent areas in Africa, and nonalignment with respect to great-power blocs.

The OAU Charter represents a compromise between the "Casablanca" philosophy of a continental organization with strongly entrenched executive powers and the "Brazzaville" reluctance to make extensive changes in the *status quo*. Major decisions can be made only by the heads of the member states, or their representatives, meeting at the annual (Summit) Assembly of the Heads of State and Government. The OAU, unlike the United Nations, has no provision for sanctions to enforce its decisions. It depends upon persuasion rather than punishment to bring recalcitrant members to accept the resolutions passed by the Assembly or the Council of Ministers.

In essence, therefore, the OAU seeks unity and cooperation through consensus. It reflects Emperor Haile Selassie's comment in his address to the founding meeting: "The union which we seek can only come gradually, as the day-to-day progress which we achieve carries us slowly but inexorably along this course."

Nonintervention and territorial integrity are OAU Charter principles which have become more entrenched with the passage of time. Africa's illogical and arbitrary boundaries, which have split tribal groups between or among neighboring countries, have caused many disputes. National stability is weakened by local loyalties which often outweigh a sense of national identity. The OAU has consistently opposed interference in a member's internal affairs. Its advocacy of the territorial integrity of independent states was evident in its consideration of the Congo, of several disputes involving Ghana, and, most recently, in the case of the Nigerian civil war when the Heads of State voted at both the 1967 and 1968 summit conferences that a solution should be found within the framework of a unitary Nigeria.

ORGANIZATIONAL STRUCTURE

The OAU operates through four "principal institutions," three specialized commissions, and several *ad hoc* commissions established subsequent to the charter to deal with specific functional problems or territorial disputes (see organization chart, page 3).

The *Assembly of Heads of State and Government,* which holds an annual summit meeting, is the "supreme organ" of the OAU. Although the charter provides for extraordinary Assembly sessions with the advance approval of two-thirds of the members, the Assembly has met only in its five ordinary sessions. Assembly decisions require a two-thirds majority of the membership except for procedural questions, which need only a simple majority.

In its discussions of matters of common concern to the African nations, the Assembly considers proposed resolutions prepared by the Council of Ministers, which meets immediately prior to the summit meeting, and considers reports submitted by the Secretary General and OAU specialized commissions and *ad hoc* organs. Members may also raise nonagenda questions.

The *Council of Ministers* is composed of

foreign ministers or other designated ministers. It meets at least semiannually, first in a session usually held in February and devoted primarily to budgetary and administrative questions, and again immediately before the Assembly convenes, normally in the late summer or fall. In addition, in 1963–65 the Council held six extraordinary sessions to consider pressing African problems such as the Congo and Southern Rhodesia.

Operation of the Organization between Assembly and Council meetings is the responsibility of the *General Secretariat* headed by an Administrative Secretary General. The Secretariat is responsible for executing decisions taken at the meetings; preparing the OAU budget; caring for the OAU archives; maintaining liaison with other international organizations active in Africa; facilitating participation by member states in international meetings; and preparing annual and special reports for consideration by the Assembly, the Council, and the specialized commissions.

The Secretariat is staffed by approximately 200 employees drawn from 26 member countries. At the political or executive level is the administrative Secretary General and four Assistant Administrative Secretaries General; all five are elected for 4-year terms by two-thirds vote of the Assembly of Heads of State and Governments. The present Secretary General, Diallo Telli, and his assistants were elected to office at the July 1964 summit meeting and reelected to second 4-year terms by the Assembly at the summit meeting in September 1968. Approximately 50 professional officers staff the administrative, political, economic, and cultural divisions of the Secretariat. There are about 150 support staff employees.

Another principal institution of the OAU Charter is the *Commission of Mediation, Conciliation, and Arbitration.* The Commission, which has 21 judicial representatives from different member states, is headquartered at Addis Ababa. Although established in 1963, it was not activited until April 1968. The Commission can act in disputes between or among states when all parties concerned agree to its jurisdiction. If a party to a dispute refuses such jurisdiction, the dispute is referred to the Council of Ministers for consideration. Mediation is effected by one or more mediators; conciliation by three members of the Commission plus one conciliator named by each party to the dispute; and arbitration by a tribunal of three Commission members, one chosen by each disputant and the third by the first two arbitrators named.

The charter authorized the establishment of five specialized commissions (Economic and Social Commission; Educational and Cultural Commission; Health, Sanitation, and Nutrition Commission; Defense Commission; and Scientific, Technical, and Research Commission). Two additional specialized commissions were established in 1964 (the Transport and Communications Commission and the Commission of Jurists). In 1967, when the OAU decided to streamline its organization, it abolished the Commission of Jurists and grouped the remaining six specialized functions in three larger commissions: Economic and Social; Educational, Scientific, Cultural, and Health; and Defense.

Although the original commissions met during the first 2 years of OAU operations, it became increasingly difficult to arrange separate meetings, both because of budgetary problems and because other technical organizations operating in Africa were handling a number of matters within the commissions' fields of interest. Recent practice has been for the commissions to meet in conjunction with Council and Assembly meetings. Thus the 1967 and 1968 Council and Assembly meetings gave major attention to subjects which fall within the scope of the specialized commissions.

Several *ad hoc* organs have been established by Assembly or Council resolutions. The oldest, the most controversial, and probably the most important of these is the 11-member African Liberation Committee (ALC). Established by a resolution at the OAU's 1963 founding meeting, the ALC is responsible for "harmonizing assistance from African states to national liberation movements in the dependent territories of Africa." The Committee maintains a separate fund for assistance to liberation movements, although its administrative expenses are paid from the regular OAU budget. It has its headquarters at Dar es Salaam, Tanzania, and meets semiannually in capitals of the member countries. Originally the ALC had nine members; Algeria, Congo (Kinshasa), Ethiopia, Guinea, Nigeria, Senegal, Tanzania, Uganda, and the United Arab Republic. Zambia and Somalia were added subsequently. At the 1968 Assembly meeting at Algiers several states unsuccessfully supported a move to broaden and rotate the membership on the Committee.

A seven-member *ad hoc* commission to deal with the border dispute between Morocco and Algeria was formed in November 1963. The Commission is still operative although its responsibilities may be assumed by the Commission of Mediation, Conciliation, and Arbitration.

In February 1964 a 10-member commission was established to consider the refugee problem in Africa and specifically to draw up a convention on all aspects of the problem. After several meetings the Commission approved a draft convention in June 1968. The Council of Ministers approved the draft convention at its 12th meeting in February 1969.

Other *ad hoc* bodies have been set up for OAU consideration of special problems relating to Congo (Kinshasa), Southern Rhodesia, Angola, Nigeria, and the mercenary problem in Africa. The commissions on Congo (Kinshasa) and the mercenaries are not longer active.

BUDGET

The OAU now has a budget of approximately $2 million; in the 1964–66 period the budget was more than twice as large. The level today reflects the establishment of administrative and budget review mechanisms, reduction of Secretariat staff levels, and the elimination of several functions.

The OAU budget is paid by members' assessments based on their contributions to the United Nations. However, the Secretariat has devised a new scale of assessment based on member countries' per capita national products. Approval of the new scale is pending.

In addition to the regular budget, members are assessed for contributions to the African Liberation Committee and the Commission of Mediation, Conciliation, and Arbitration. Although no outside government contributes to the Organization's administrative budget, the United States and other non-African governments participate in research projects under the OAU's Scientific, Technical, and Research Commission.

OPERATION AND ACCOMPLISHMENTS

Peacekeeping

The OAU's major accomplishments have concerned the prevention or settlement of disputes. It has assisted the amelioration or settlement of border or other disputes involving the following members: Algeria-Morocco; Somalia-Ethiopia-Kenya; Rwanda-Burundi; Sudan-Chad; Congo (Kinshasa)-Congo (Brazzaville)-Burundi-Rwanda.

In addition to interstate problems, the OAU has also assisted member governments with internal crises. A 1964 extraordinary Council of Ministers meeting considered the request of the Tanzanian Government for help in maintaining internal order and approved the dispatch of Nigerian forces to assist. Much of 1964–65 was devoted to the crisis in the Congo which had both internal and external aspects. More recently, the OAU has been active in trying to implement a political settlement in Nigeria and to expedite humanitarian assistance to victims of the conflict. The OAU Consultative Committee on Nigeria, established by a resolution passed at the 1967 summit meeting at Kinshasa, met at Lagos in late 1967; at Niamey in July 1968; and at Addis Ababa in August and September of 1968.

The OAU has also been concerned with member-nonmember disputes, e.g., the June 1967 Arab-Israeli conflict and the southern African problem. In the case of the Arab-Israeli dispute, the OAU Assembly resolved in September 1968 that members support the U.N. resolution of November 22, 1967, calling for the withdrawal of foreign troops from Arab territory. The same assembly also resolved that an attack by any southern African state on an OAU member would be considered to be an attack on all members.

The OAU hopes that future disputes can be referred to the recently activated Commission of Mediation, Conciliation, and Arbitration rather than being handled by *ad hoc* commissions as in the past.

Political Decolonization

Although the 25-percent increase in OAU membership during the past 5 years reflects continued progress in the decolonization of Africa, major obstacles still block attainment of the charter's goal of Africa-wide independence. OAU resolutions on southern African questions have advocated independence for the Portuguese territories, urged members' economic and political action against South Africa to end *apartheid* (statutory racial segregation), and sought to bring pressure on the United Kingdom to end the Ian Smith regime in Southern Rhodesia. Action recommendations have included an OAU boycott of trade with South Africa and the December 1966 resolution by the Council of Ministers that members break diplomatic relations with the United Kingdom unless the Smith regime were terminated.

Since southern African problems involve non-OAU states, the United Nations has become the major forum for international consideration and action on these issues. At U.N. debates on African questions the OAU input has been important and often decisive. Votes on southern African issues by OAU members are influenced by the resolutions of the Assembly and Council of Ministers and by consensus reached in meetings of the "African Group"—the OAU members—in New York.

While seeking to maximize international pressure for independence and majority rule in southern Africa, the OAU also operates an African mechanism, the African Liberation Committee (ALC). The ALC assesses and collects members' financial contributions and determines their distribution to nationalist organizations or "liberation groups" which are based in OAU states but active in southern Africa and Portuguese Guinea.

Economic, Social, and Cultural Activities

OAU actions in the economic field have emphasized coordinated research and expanded cooperation among members to establish the base for the economic integration of Africa envisaged in the charter. At the same time, the OAU has worked in the political field to establish the climate of confidence and solidarity necessary for expanded economic and technical cooperation.

The OAU has only limited financial resources to operate its programs. Its major role is to make policy decisions and have these policies reflected in the development programs of African national governments, African subregional organizations, and the international and external donors who have assistance programs in Africa.

The OAU attempts to coordinate the African position at international meetings which concern economic aspects in Africa. Such coordination is effected by the Secretariat circulating studies of the issues to the members; by resolutions passed by the Council of Ministers or the Assembly; and, in certain cases, by representatives of the Secretariat traveling to the conference to assist the African delegates. The OAU was actively involved in preparations for the second U.N. Conference on Trade and Development at New Delhi, February 1–March 25, 1968. It organized a conference at Algiers to coordinate the African position prior to the New Delhi meeting.

OAU efforts in the economic field rely extensively on the work of the U.N. Economic Commission for Africa (ECA), which was established in 1958 and is also headquartered at Addis Ababa. The goals of lowering inter-African trade barriers, the establishment of subregional economic communities, an eventual African common market, and inter-African monetary cooperation depend, in practice, on frequent consultation. On a day-to-day basis this consultative work is largely the function of the ECA in cooperation with the OAU Secretariat, under the general policy guidance of the OAU's Council and Assembly resolutions.

The OAU has put great emphasis on the development of transportation and telecommunications as a means to accelerate inter-African social and economic cooperation. In the field of air transportation, the ECA and the OAU have cooperated with the International Civil Aviation Organization (ICAO) in drawing up a draft constitution of an African Civil Aviation Commission (AFCAC) to maximize integration of African civil aviation. This constitution has been referred to the member states for consideration.

In the fields of health, education, culture, science, and research, the OAU has the dual function of attempting to foster African members' cooperation with each other and to coordinate their input into the international organizations active in Africa. It also operates its own subsidiary, the Scientific, Technical, and Research Commission (STRC), which has performed, pooled, and circulated research in its fields of interest to member governments and has also adminstered certain subregional economic projects, such as rinderpest (an infectious cattle disease) eradication campaigns. The STRC, which is headquartered at Lagos and has branch offices at Niamey, Niger; Bangui, Central African Republic; Yaounde, Cameroon; and Muguga, Kenya, receives approximately one-quarter of the OAU budget.

An example of a cooperative endeavor with an international organization was the Conference of Education Ministers held jointly by the OAU and the U.N. Education, Scientific and Cultural Organization (UNESCO) at Nairobi, Kenya, in 1968. On the basis of that conference's studies, the OAU has proposed the establishment of postgraduate regional education institutes which would specialize in eight scientific disciplines. The OAU plans to hold an all-African cultural festival at Algiers in 1969 and, in the sports area, is a sponsor of the All-Africa Games to be held at Bamako, Mali, in October 1969.

The OAU has attempted to bring a unified African approach to labor questions and has endorsed the creation of an African labor organization.

RELATIONS WITH OTHER INTERNATIONAL ORGANIZATIONS

The OAU has closed and fruitful relations with the United Nations and many of its specialized agencies. It is the only regional organization which has concluded a comprehensive agreement with the United Nations, spelling out mutual cooperation in several fields. In addition to the overall U.N. agreement, the OAU has concluded agreements with the U.N. Educational, Scientific and Cultural Organization (UNESCO), the Food and Agriculture Organization (FAO), and the International Atomic Energy Agency (IAEA). Similar cooperative instruments are being drawn up with the World Health Organization (WHO) and the United Nations Children's Fund (UNICEF). The attendance of U.N. Secretary-General U Thant at the 1967 and 1968 OAU summit meetings underlines the closeness of the relationship between the two organizations. The OAU maintains a small office in New York to service and to facilitate coordination of the OAU members who form the "African Group" at the United Nations.

RELATION TO AFRICAN SUBREGIONAL GROUPINGS

The recent formation of such organizations as the East African Community and the Organization of Senegal River Basin States, plus the proposed West African Regional Group, reflects the growing number of African groups organized on a regional basis. In concert with the ECA, the OAU has encouraged this subregional institutional trend as a positive step toward the economic and political cooperation envisaged in the charter. Other major bodies among the approximately 50 regional associations in Africa are the Organization Commune Africaine et Malgache (OCAM), the Central African Economic and Customs Union (UDEAC), the Council of the

Entente, the Chad Basin Commission, and the Niger River Commission.

FUTURE PROSPECTS

Many problems still face the OAU. Probably foremost is the fact that the OAU is set up as a continental organization but still lacks membership from the white-controlled areas of the southern sixth of Africa. Until there is meaningful progress in effecting independence and majority rule in the southern African territories and countries, or the OAU changes its policy toward southern Africa, the organization will have to continue to divide its efforts and resources between liberation goals on the one hand, and peacekeeping, economic, and political cooperative activities on the other.

Another problem relates to the executive function of the OAU. Under the charter, all important decisions are the responsibility of the Assembly or the Council of Ministers, with the Secretary General and the Secretariat having only limited authority to implement these decisions. In this connection, Secretary General Diallo Telli has recommended that the charter be amended to increase the executive powers of the Secretary General, a move he believes would also make it easier to obtain more qualified Secretariat personnel from the member states.

These problems notwithstanding, the OAU has made significant accomplishments to buttress its future. Despite periodic predictions that it would fall apart in disarray, that Africa's many crises and border problems would make consensus impossible, the OAU not only has continued to function but has increased the scope and influence of its activities. OAU members now constitute about one-third of the membership of the United Nations; their influence in that body continues to grow, and they hold an increasing number of executive posts on the councils of international organizations.

A change in the OAU's policy of nonalignment is unlikely: It has a consistent history of viewing international issues in the context of African interests.

U.S. POLICY

The United States has consistently supported the Organization of African Unity, although it is not a member and has no voice in its operation. On May 26, 1966, at a White House reception celebrating the OAU's third anniversary, President Johnson referred to the charter's declarations of the "inalienable right of all people to control their own destiny," that "freedom, equality, justice and dignity are essential objectives . . . of the African peoples." The President said that these concepts summed up the basic aspirations common to both American and African peoples: "to secure the right of self-government, to build strong democratic institutions, and to improve the level of every citizen's well-being." Again, in a message to the OAU on its fifth anniversary in May 1968, he said: ". . . America and Africa share a common vitality and purpose. The world looks to both of us for the answers to age-old problems. I am certain that time will not diminish the abiding faith of my countrymen in the realization of Africa's aspirations. Nor will it change our determination to help the O.A.U. to reach its goals."

The OAU's goals of a united, peaceful, and developing Africa are very much in the interests of the United States and the world community. It is clearly in the U.S. interest that Africans should develop the institutions to solve their own problems—particularly in the area of peace-keeping. It is also in our interest that Africa develop regional economic institutions of co-operation so that the external assistance so urgently needed from both private and governmental sources can be utilized most efficiently.

PRINCIPAL MEETINGS OF OAU ORGANS

Assembly of Heads of State and Government

Founding meeting—Addis Ababa, May 1963
Ordinary meetings:
  first—Cairo, July 1964
  second—Accra, October 1965
  third—Addis Ababa, November 1966
  fourth—Kinshasa, September 1967
  fifth—Algiers, September 1968

Council of Ministers

Founding meeting—Addis Ababa, May 1963

Ordinary meetings:
  first—Dakar, August 1963
  second—Lagos, February 1964
  third—Cairo, July 1964
  fourth—Nairobi, February–March, 1965
  fifth—Accra, October 1965
  sixth—Addis Ababa, February–March 1966
  seventh—Addis Ababa, October–November 1966
  eighth—Addis Ababa, February–March 1967
  ninth—Kinshasa, September 1967
  tenth—Addis Ababa, February 1968
  eleventh—Algiers, September 1968
  twelfth—Addis Ababa, February 1969
Extraordinary meetings:
  first—Addis Ababa, November 1963
  second—Dar es Salaam, February 1964
  third—Addis Ababa, September 1964
  fourth—New York, December 1964
  fifth—Lagos, June 1965
  sixth—Addis Ababa, December 1965

Specialized Commissions

Economic and Social Commission
  first—Niamey, December 1963
  second—Cairo, January 1965
Educational, Scientific, Cultural, and Health Commission
  first—Leopoldville, January 1964
  second—Lagos, January 1965
Defense Commission
  first—Accra, October–November 1963
  second—Freetown, February 1965
Commission of Mediation, Conciliation, and Arbitration
  first—Addis Ababa, December 1967

Noncharter Organs

African Liberation Committee—Fourteen meetings held; most recent, Dar es Salaam, February 1969
Ad Hoc Commission on the Moroccan-Algerian Dispute—Ten meetings held; most recent, Tangier, January 1967
Commission on the Problem of Refugees in Africa—Five meetings held; most recent, Addis Ababa, June 1968
Ad Hoc Commission on the Congo (Kinshasa)—Five meetings held; most recent, Nairobi, March 1965
Ad Hoc Consultative Committee on Nigeria—Three meetings held; most recent, Addis Ababa, August–September 1968
Committee of Five on Rhodesia—Eight meetings held; most recent, Algiers, July 1968
Ad Hoc Commission on Mercenaries—Two meetings held; most recent, Kampala, December 1967
Reconciliation Committee on Angola—Only one meeting held; Addis Ababa, June 1968

The European Communities

U.S. Department of State

This Department of State background paper presents the history and current status of three international organizations whose membership is restricted to European countries and whose interests are primarily economic. These three organizations: the European Coal and Steel Community (ECSC), the European Economic Community (the Common Market) and the European Atomic Energy Commission were created by Treaties as independent regional organizations but have since merged their separate executive bodies and are within a common institutional framework.

ORIGIN AND ESTABLISHMENT

Introduction

A unified Europe—a dream of forward-looking Europeans for centuries—has been taking shape within the last two decades. Beginning in 1951 with the signing of the Paris treaty establishing the European Coal and Steel Community (ECSC), an important series of developments has contributed steadily to that objective. Milestone steps in this process were taken in 1957 with the signing of the Rome treaties establishing the European Economic Community (the Common Market) and the European Atomic Energy Community (Euratom). The preamble to the treaty establishing the ECSC, the first of the three European Communities,[1] sets forth the basic objective of all three: "to substitute for historic rivalries a fusion of their essential interests; to establish, by creating an economic community, the foundations of a broader and deeper community among peoples long divided by bloody conflicts; and to lay the bases of institutions capable of guiding their future common destiny."

The field of action of these Communities, whose membership is identical (France, West Germany, Italy, Belgium, the Netherlands, and Luxembourg), has been largely economic; but through common tariff, agricultural, economic, social, and other policies, they are contributing to an ever closer political, as well as economic, union among the European peoples.

As used throughout this paper the term "European Communities" refers to the combined institutions of the European Coal and Steel Community, the European Economic Community, and the European Atomic Energy Community. It is proper legally to speak of the European Communities. However, they are frequently referred to colloquially as the European Community and even more often as simply the Common Market.

Historical Development

While the dream of a unified Europe is centuries old, the modern search for European unity dates from the days of World War II. The Dutch, French, and Italian resistance movements expressed strong pan-European sentiments, and in 1943 Churchill proposed the forming of a "Council of Europe" at war's end. Again, in his famous Zurich speech of 1946, Churchill made a ringing proposal to "create the European family" and "to build a kind of United States of Europe." The postwar constitutions of France, Italy, and the Federal Republic of Germany purposefully left the way open to eventual European unity through clauses permitting limitations on national sovereignty. But Europe's immediate postwar task was survival, not unification. In responding to this need in 1947 with the

SOURCE: U.S. Department of State. *The European Communities.* Washington, Government Printing Office. 1969. (International Organizations Series. No. 5.)

Marshall Plan the United States provided a catalyst for unity.

Support in the United States for European unification was particularly strong in the Congress which saw unity as the best hope that Europe would not remain dependent upon the United States. The Congress consequently made U.S. assistance contingent upon the European nations charting their recovery programs in close cooperation. In response, the Europeans created the Organization for European Economic Cooperation (OEEC) in March 1948. The intergovernmental OEEC drew the European member nations together in an unprecedented, large-scale cooperative effort to rebuild national economies as well as to prepare the way for the removal of barriers to trade and payments. Various possible regional customs unions were seriously discussed, but Benelux—a customs union between Belgium, Luxembourg, and the Netherlands—was the only one to come into being at that time (1948).

On the political side, a number of organizations dedicated to European unity held a Congress at The Hague in May 1948; more than 750 delegates attended. A European federal structure was proposed, but during the year that followed it became clear that the political will to support a supranational effort did not yet exist in all the major European countries. A compromise solution was the formation of the 15-nation Council of Europe in May 1948. The declared purpose of the Council was the promotion of closer union of its members, but the institutional structure created was too weak to achieve that end.

Other institutions were needed if European unity were to move ahead. On May 9, 1950, France's Foreign Minister, Robert Schuman, put forth a plan, incorporating some of the ideas of Jean Monnet, which focused on the placing of Franco-German production of coal and steel under an organization open to other European countries. The pooling of these vital resources would make war between France and the Federal Republic of Germany "not merely unthinkable but materially impossible;" moreover, it would set up "common bases for economic development as a first step in the federation of Europe." Britain's Labor Government, because of Commonwealth ties and other factors, turned down the French offer. Italy, Belgium, the Netherlands, and Luxembourg, however, agreed to join France and West Germany in negotiations. In April 1951 the treaty establishing the European Coal and Steel Community was signed by "the Six" at Paris, and in 1952 the

ECSC began operations under its first President, Jean Monnet.

The ECSC was a radical departure from the past. In the limited sectors of coal and steel, this new institution had some features of a supranational body. The ECSC became the basic model for future European integration.

Another step forward was to be the EDC—the European Defense Community—a joint military establishment proposed by French Premier René Pleven in December 1950, which was designed to make unilateral German rearmament unnecessary. This effort was strongly supported by the United States. The EDC proposal, however, collapsed in 1954 when the French Government refused to defend it in the French National Assembly. Its opponents brought about the treaty's defeat on a procedural motion.

Many thought the failure of the EDC had dealt a fatal blow to hopes for carrying European integration beyond the ECSC. But that same year the European Parliament, which had been established under the ECSC treaty, recommended that the Foreign Ministers of the Six meet to study the possibility of broadening the ECSC's competence. Britain was invited to participate, and plans moved forward rapidly for this meeting. The United Kingdom declined the invitation and embarked on a parallel plan to form a larger free trade area, one that would include the United Kingdom, the Six, and other Western European countries interested in free trade. Negotiations on the British proposal —the "Maudling negotiations"—were opened in 1957 within the framework of the Organization for European Economic Cooperation.

In the meantime, the Foregin Ministers of the Six had met and had adopted a plan to create two new organizations, the European Economic Community (the Common Market) and the European Atomic Energy Community (Euratom). The Common Market and Euratom treaties (the Rome treaties) were signed in March 1957 and went into force on January 1, 1958. Later that year the parallel free trade area negotiations broke up when the French announced that they could not accept the kind of free trade area sought by the British.[2]

ORGANIZATION

The three European Communities share the same institutional framework: the Commission; the

Council of Ministers; the European Parliament; and the Court of Justice.

The Commission has the sole right to initiate proposals for common policies and regulations. The Council has the sole right of decision. It may modify Commission proposals by unanimous vote. The Commission or the member states, as appropriate, implement Council decisions. Council decisions are in effect Community legislation binding on the member states. The beginnings of democratic control are exercised by the largely consultative European Parliament, while the Court of Justice is the final arbiter in all conflicts arising from the Communities treaties.

From the beginning, the Parliament and Court of Justice have been common to all three Communities. Until July 1967 each Community had its own executive body (the Common Market and Euratom Commissions and the ECSC High Authority) and its own Council of Ministers.

In April 1965 the Six signed the Brussels treaty providing for the merger of the three executive bodies in a single Commission and of the three Councils in a single Council. The merger treaty came into force on July 1, 1967. The single Council and single Commission took over from their predecessors the powers conferred by all three Communities treaties. Preliminary work is underway to merge the three treaties into a single treaty.

The Commission

The Commission consists of 14 members—three each from West Germany, France, and Italy; two from the Netherlands and Belgium; and one from Luxembourg. On July 1, 1970, membership from the first five countries is to be reduced by one each, for a total of nine. Commissioners are appointed by agreement among the six governments for a 4-year renewable term (except that the present Commission, because of the scheduled reduction in membership from 14 to nine, has only a 3-year term). Members are pledged to independence of national or other particular interests and may be removed only by censure of the European Parliament. The president and vice president are appointed by member-government agreements from among the commissioners for a 2-year term, also renewable.

The Commission implements, administers, and enforces the Paris and Rome treaties. Although the treaties state that Commission decisions in most instances require only a majority vote, most of its major decisions are made unanimously.

Two important consultative bodies, the Economic and Social Committee (created by the Common Market and Euratom treaties) and the Consultative Committee (created by the ECSC treaty) advise the Commission and the Council on major questions in economic and social fields. These Committees consist of representatives of groups of employers, workers, consumers, and others.

The Council of Ministers

The Council is the only institution of the Communities whose members directly represent member states. A representative from each state sits on the Council. He is usually the minister concerned with the question at hand—i.e., transportation, agriculture, economic affairs, etc.—but the foreign affairs minister participates in the most important sessions. Under the terms of the Rome treaties, Council decisions on most matters were to be unanimous until January 1966 and by weighted majority vote thereafter. (Weighted majority is 12 out of 17 votes, with France, West Germany, and Italy casting four votes each, Belgium and the Netherlands two each, and Luxembourg one.) In practice the Council has taken decisions on issues of major importance by unanimous vote.

The work of the Council is prepared by a Committee of Permanent Representatives of the member states. The influence of this Committee has been gradually increasing.

The European Parliament

The Parliament consists of 142 members who are elected from and by the legislatures of the member countries. The treaties envisage ultimately their direct election by universal suffrage. Plans for this were drawn up by the Parliament in 1960 and submitted to the Council of Ministers, but no action had been taken on the proposals as of July 1, 1969.

The Parliament holds plenary sessions, lasting roughly a week, about eight times a year and maintains 12 standing committees which closely follow the Commission's work. The members are divided into four political groups—Christian Democrats, Socialists, Liberals, and the European Democratic

Union (Gaullists)—and sit together in these groups irrespective of nationality. There are Communist delegates from Italy, but they do not form a parliamentary group.

The Commission must report annually to the Parliament, and consult the Parliament before decisions are taken on certain Common Market and Euratom matters. The Parliament has the right to propose changes in the Communities budget and the power to unseat the Commission, although this power has never been used. Its members frequently put questions to the Commission and sometimes to the Council of Ministers. While the Commission need not defer to the vote of the Parliament, the Commission does try to shape its proposals so as to attain majority approval.

The Court of Justice

A supreme court of seven judges has power to decide whether acts of European Communities institutions, member governments, and private organizations and firms are compatible with the Paris and Rome treaties. The Court of Justice can annul acts of the Commission itself and of the Council of Ministers. Appeals to the Court against a member state for alleged failure to meet its treaty obligations may be made by the Commission or by member states. Member states, Communities institutions, firms, and individuals may also bring actions against the Commission and Council for failure to act in accord with the treaties. The Court has power to rule in cases submitted by national courts for interpretation of the treaties and their implementing legislation. National courts *must* refer certain cases to the Court of Justice. The Court's decisions are directly binding on all parties and are not subject to appeal.

The seven judges are appointed for 6-year terms by the member governments. By the end of 1968 some 560 cases had been brought before the Court.

Location of the Major Institutions

The institutions of the European Communities are provisionally located at Brussels, Luxembourg, and Strasbourg. The Commission has its headquarters at Brussels as does the Committee of Permanent Representatives of the member states.

The Council of Ministers meets at Brussels except during the months of April, June, and October when it meets at Luxembourg. The European Parliament meets at Strasbourg, but its General Secretariat is located at Luxembourg. The Court of Justice and the European Investment Bank are at Luxembourg.

BUDGET

The general budget of the Communities is at present financed by the member governments in the following proportions: France, West Germany, and Italy 28 percent each; Belgium and the Netherlands 7.9 percent each; and Luxembourg 0.2 percent. For the Governments' contributions to farm policy financing and the Social Fund the proportions are somewhat different. The activities of the ECSC are financed by a direct tax on the value of coal and steel production in the Communities. The present rate is 0.3 percent of the value of producers' annual coal and steel sales, with an $18 million annual ceiling. The Commission has proposed financing the Communities by channeling to it the proceeds of the agricultural import levies and of all customs revenue. Such a move would greatly strengthen the Commission, but no action has been taken on these proposals.

The combined budget for all the Communities institutions in 1969 is about $2.7 billion. The staff of the Communities totals some 8,350 persons including Euratom's research personnel.

STRENGTH AND MAJOR ACCOMPLISHMENTS OF THE COMMUNITIES

Economic Strength

The European Communities are a major political and economic force by virtue of their location, population, and advanced and quickly growing economy. As the six member states are situated in the core of Western Europe, overland transportation between other nations of Western Europe must usually pass through them. They have major ports on the Atlantic Ocean and on the Mediterranean and North Seas. Their total area is 449,000 square miles.

The Communities population of 185.9 million is only slightly smaller than that of the United States. Seventy-five million of the population work. This labor force is well-endowed with skills, and unemployment is very low.

The total gross national product (GNP) of the Six is less than half that of the United States and slightly smaller than that of the Soviet Union. During the decade 1958–68, their total GNP grew at an average rate of 5.2 percent, compared to 3.9 percent in the European Free Trade Area (EFTA) countries and 4.7 percent in the United States.

The Communities account for about one-quarter of all the coal and about one-third of all the steel produced in the North Atlantic Treaty Organization (NATO) countries. They have the world's second largest output of motor vehicles and are one of the leading producers of farm produce—the second biggest milk producer and third largest meat producer.

The Communities are the foremost world trader. In 1968 they imported more than $34 billion in goods from the rest of the world and exported more than $36 billion. These trade figures are roughly double those of 1958, the year the Common Market came into being.

The Communities are a particularly important trading partner for the United States. In 1968 about $6.1 billion, or nearly 18 percent of total United States exports, went to the Six, and roughly $5.9 billion of our imports came from them.

Major Accomplishments

A. *The European Coal and Steel Community.* Substantial progress has been made under the ECSC in eliminating barriers to trade in coal and steel among the Six, including discriminatory price and transportation rates, customs duties, and quantitative restrictions. The ECSC has played a valuable role in forecasting demand and supply; providing investment guidance and cooperation through allocation of loans to firms; promoting joint research through grants; and helping regional development through loans to areas affected by declines in coal, steel, or iron-ore industries. The ECSC has been concerned with the problems of coal and steel workers, providing grants and loans for housing, ensuring free movement of skilled workers, and financing the readaptation of surplus workers.

B. *The Common Market.* The major accomplishment of the Common Market—indeed an achievement of historic proportions—was the completion of the customs union on July 1, 1968. Since that date all customs duties and quantitative restrictions on trade within the Communities have been abolished. From that same date, the six member countries have applied a common external tariff to all imports from the rest of the world. For most products the level of the common tariff was fixed at the arithmetical average of the tariffs applied on January 1, 1957, by Benelux, France, West Germany, and Italy. This made Community industrial tariff levels, even before the Kennedy Round of trade negotiations, fairly moderate. For some key products, however, common tariff levels were fixed by negotiation among the Six.

By July 1, 1968, the Communities also had put into effect a common farm policy for most agricultural products. This policy, centrally financed from a single fund, involves: 1) common marketing policies with free trade throughout the Communities and common price levels for all major products; 2) a common policy for external trade, replacing the previous complex and widely varying national structures of tariffs, quotas, and minimum prices by a Communities arrangement based on target prices, variable import levies, and export subsidies; and 3) a common policy to raise the efficiency of Communities farming. The common agricultural policy now covers virtually all of the Communities farm output, including grains, rice, pork, beef, veal, eggs, poultry, milk and other diary products, fruit, vegetables, sugar, and vegetable fats and oils. The common policy has been adapted to the particular requirements of the various product groups: In some cases (such as grains) it involves considerable market intervention; in others (such as wine) it is applied mainly through the enforcement of quality standards.

The financing of the common farm policy—which covers market support, refunds on exports, and modernization of production and distribution—comes under the Communities European Agricultural Guidance and Guarantee Fund. The Communities agriculture budget, which totaled $537 million in 1967, rose to $2.55 billion in 1969.

While the Common Market's major accomplishments are the completion of the customs union and the common agricultural policy, it has other noteworthy achievements to its credit, particularly in the development of common policies toward a full economic union and in the field of trade liberalization (notably in the Kennedy Round).

These will be dealt with below under "Present and Future Tasks" and "Relations with Third Countries."

C. *Euratom.* Euratom's role is to ensure that the Communities undertake the research necessary for the development of nuclear energy not only for power production, but also—through use of radioisotopes and radioactive sources—for agricultural, industrial, and medical purposes. Its research takes place in four research centers of its own; through association contracts under which Euratom and a partner organization in a member country jointly finance certain large-scale research projects; by contracting specific assignments to national centers or firms; and by joining international projects such as the European Nuclear Energy Agency "Dragon" project.

During the past decade Euratom has brought into being a common market for all nuclear materials and equipment, and a low or suspended common external tariff on imports of nuclear materials from nonmember countries.

Euratom has the responsibility to see that ores, raw materials, and fissile matter are not diverted from their declared peaceful uses. The Commission has Communities-wide power to inspect peaceful nuclear installations and has the legal title to all fissionable materials intended for peaceful uses. Enterprises submit to the Commission details on the equipment of their installations and regular returns on their stocks, transfers, and transactions of materials. The Commission operates an international on-the-spot inspection system to check the returns. Any enterprise breaking these regulations may be subjected to sanctions, but no significant contraventions have been detected.

PRESENT AND FUTURE TASKS

With the completion of the customs union, the next step for the European Communities is to achieve a full economic union. (NOTE: A customs union involves the elimination of internal trade restrictions and the imposition of a common external tariff. Economic union moves beyond these characteristics to ensure free mobility of the factors of production, fair competition, and the coordination and harmonization of national economic policies.) Some of the policies necessary to economic union are already far-developed. Others are just beginning to emerge.

Mobility of the Factors of Production

Free movement of unskilled labor has been largely realized. Workers have legal freedom to work anywhere in the six member countries, although a safeguards clause permits limitations if free movement results in a labor surplus in any given member state. Workers retain their social security rights when they move from one Communities country to another. Insured Communities citizens, whether in another Communities country for work, holiday, or other reason, are able to use medical services on the same terms as citizens of that country.

The *removal of restrictions on capital movements* from one member country to another is provided for in the treaties; but, while some progress has been made, much remains to be done. *Freedom of establishment* (of firms, branches, agencies, and professional men) and *freedom to supply services* are also provided for in the treaties; here again major work remains to be done. The member states are not pledged to adopt identical legislation and regulations, but must ensure that nationals of the other Communities countries enjoy equal rights with their own citizens.

Fair Competition

Considerable progress has also been achieved in assuring fair competition. Agreements and practices preventing, restraining, or distorting competition are banned by the Common Market treaty if they are likely to affect trade among member states. The Commission has important powers of inspection and control and can impose heavy penalties for infringements of fair-competition rules. Since 1961 decisions by the Commission and the Court of Justice have begun to lay the basis of a case law whereby specific types of intercompany agreement are judged.

Common Policies

A *common transport policy* for road, rail, and inland-water transport is to be adopted by 1970. Agreement was reached in July 1968 on rules of competition; trucking quotas; fuel reserve allowances; and harmonization of truck driver safety regulations, trucking rates, and double taxation.

While this was a significant breakthrough, the Communities must still deal with the major aspects of a common transport policy, including rationalization of this exceedingly complex sector of the Communities economy.

The Communities have made a modest start in the field of *economic and financial policy*. A Short-Term Economic Policy Committee examines the current economic situation and urgent policy requirements. The Medium-Term Economic Policy Committee recommended a 5-year plan which was adopted by the Commission in 1966 and approved by the Council in February 1967. The plan lays down commonly agreed goals of economic growth and the general lines of policy needed to reach them and to bring about a fairer distribution of increasing prosperity between the regions and between the social classes.

Agreement by the Six in February 1967 to adopt the *added-value (TVA) system* of indirect taxation will put producers throughout the Communities on a more equal competitive footing. The TVA is similar to a sales tax but is collected each time a product changes hands and is imposed on the difference between the price which the seller paid for the item (or material used in its fabrication) and the sale price. The TVA system by mid-1969 was in effect in France, the Netherlands, and West Germany (although not at identical rates) and is to be adopted by the other members by 1970. The Communities have yet to decide on a common rate for the TVA and a date by which this rate must be applied.

The Common Market treaty stresses the need to bring living standards in less-favored parts of the Communities up toward the levels of the more prosperous areas. The major problem areas are the more remote agricultural regions and areas largely dependent on industries which have fallen into decline. The major instruments for the Communities *regional policy* are the European Social Fund (discussed below), the European Investment Bank, and the social and economic redevelopment policies of the ECSC in areas producing coal, iron ore, and steel (cited above). With a capital of $1 billion, the European Investment Bank aids investment in the Communities underdeveloped regions and helps finance modernization and new economic activities of general Communities interest. By the end of October 1968 it had approved loans totaling $827 million for projects within the Communities, of which more than half were for projects in southern Italy.

In addition to assuring the free movement of workers, the Communities *social policy*, which aims at the upward harmonization of living and working conditions, is furthered by the European Social Fund. The Fund aids employment and the mobility of workers, helps finance vocational retraining and resettlement, and provides other aids.

Before the merger of the three Communities, the ECSC was responsible for the coal sector, Euratom for nuclear energy, and the Common Market for oil and natural gas. Now that the Communities have a common executive, progress toward a *common energy policy* may be facilitated. Other crucial areas requiring the attention of the Communities are the formation of a Community-wide *capital market;* agreement on a *commercial policy;* and policies on *company law, patents,* and *science and technology.*

After Economic Union

The customs union that is now complete and the ever-growing economic union which will demand so much of the Communities attention in the immediate future are viewed as steppingstones toward a politically united Europe. The Commission, in its statement of July 1, 1968, declared that "Europe must have institutions enabling it to become a politically organized continent, having not only its economic institutions . . . but also political institutions enabling it to act and become . . . the European Federation." Political union then is the ultimate objective of the European Communities. While no one foresees its early realization, the Communities leaders have by no means lost sight of their federal dream.

RELATIONS WITH THIRD COUNTRIES

Trade Liberalization

The Communities from the beginning have been committed to the most liberal trade and tariff policy compatible with internal cohesion. The Communities liberal trade orientation was evident in the Kennedy Round of trade negotiations. In these negotiations the six member nations were represented by the Commission. The Commission's able negotiator was Jean Rey, formerly a Belgian political leader, who became President of the Commission following the merger of the executives in July 1967. The historic agreement which resulted from the Kennedy Round was in no small measure due to the positive and coordinated approach of the Six. Duties were cut on goods in which world trade is estimated at $40 billion a year. A general reduction in duties of between 35 and 40 percent was achieved.

In the agricultural field the Communities have followed a more restrictive trade policy which has resulted in a number of more or less serious problems. The Communities and the United States are attempting through consultations to resolve these trade difficulties.

New Members

A number of European countries have sought membership in the Communities since the early 1960's. At present the United Kingdom, Denmark, Ireland, and Norway have applications for full membership before the Communities.

France has twice blocked progress toward U.K. membership—in 1963 and 1967—in effect blocking at the same time consideration of the other candidates. Unanimity of the Six is essential for admission of new members.

Associated States

The Rome treaties provide for association of third countries. Greece, Turkey, and the Yaoundé states (see below) have association agreements with the Communities, and a number of other countries are actively interested in association. The treaties do not prescribe any precise form for association. The possibilities range from a partial reduction in tariffs between the Communities and the associated state to a customs union looking to eventual full membership.

The Yaoundé Convention

In 1963 the Communities and 17 African states[3] and Madagascar signed the Yaoundé convention. The convention provided that the products of the Yaoundé states would enter the Common Market duty-free by July 1, 1968, and that the AOC (Associated Overseas Countries) states will gradually reduce tariffs on goods imported from the Six.

While this benefits the AOC states, others point out that the benefit is conferred only by discriminating against other countries, including developing countries competing with the AOC states, and restricts the AOC states in their choice of the most favorable supplier of needed imports. The Common Market also set up, in 1958, a European Development Fund to aid the AOC states. The resources of this fund, originally $581 million, were increased by an additional $730 million under the Yaoundé convention. The agreement expired on June 1, 1969, but its major provisions have been extended until June 30, 1970, in order to allow additional time to complete negotiations for its renewal.

Other Arrangements

Nigeria in 1966 signed an association agreement with the European Communities along the lines of the Yaoundé convention (but not involving financial aid). Similar agreements between the Communities and the East African Community countries (Kenya, Tanzania, and Uganda) were concluded in 1968. None of these agreements were fully ratified. All expired on June 1, 1969. Their renewal is under consideration.

Israel had, and Iran currently has, trade agreements with the EEC providing for most-favored-nation reductions of duties on particular goods. Lebanon has entered into a trade and technical assistance agreement. Tunisia and Morocco recently signed agreements with the Communities providing for special trade relations. Britain, since 1954, has maintained a loose working arrangement with the Communities regarding matters of coal and steel tariffs.

UNITED STATES POLICY

Every U.S. Administration in the postwar period has supported European unity and has looked to the institutions of the European Communities as the most promising means for achieving that unity. The United States continues to endorse the concept of a vigorous European community linked to America by an enduring community of interest.

President Nixon on his departure from Brussels on February 24, 1969, said: "My talks with President Rey and the Commission of the European

Communities have strengthened my convictions as to the high purpose and indispensability of European economic integration."

At his March 4 press conference following his return from his European tour, President Nixon had this to say on unity in Europe: ". . . the world will be a much safer place and, from our standpoint, a much healthier place economically, militarily, and politically, if there were a strong European community to be a balance, basically a balance between the United States and the Soviet Union, rather than to have this polarization of forces in one part of the world or another."

Secretary of State William P. Rogers, in a statement on March 27, 1969, before the Senate Foreign Relations Committee, said: "This administration's long-range sympathies remain with those Europeans who see their most hopeful future in an independent Europe increasingly united. It is neither appropriate nor feasible for us to chart a blueprint for European union. This is Europe's concern. But the United States is at one with those Europeans who see the best future of their continent in a progressive release of those great energies which cannot reach their full potential within traditional frontiers."

U.S. DIPLOMATIC REPRESENTATION

The political and economic importance of the Communities has grown significantly over the years, and they are now the world's largest trader and one of the fastest growing economic units of the world. The United States maintains close relations with the Communities—through its Mission to the European Communities in Brussels and through consultations with senior officials in Washington and Brussels.

The first United States Ambassador accredited to the Communities was named in 1952 to the Coal and Steel Community at Luxembourg. In 1958, following formation of the Common Market and Euratom, the American Ambassador moved from Luxembourg to Brussels and served as the accredited U.S. Representative to all three Communities.

The United States Mission to the European munities is located at 23 avenue des Arts, Brussels, Belgium.

COMMUNITIES REPRESENTATION IN THE UNITED STATES

The European Communities maintain a Liaison Office and an Information Office in Washington, D.C., at: 808 Farragut Building, 900-17th Street, N.W., Washington, D.C. 20006. (Telephone 296-5131 or 296-5145.)

The European Communities Information Office in New York is located at: 2207 Commerce Building, 155 East 44th Street, New York, New York 10017. (Telephone MU 2-0458.)

NOTES

[1] The European Communities are not an "international organization": They provide an institutional framework for welding the national economies of the member countries into a single unit with the objective of "establishing the foundations of an ever closer union among European peoples." However, in the belief that basic information about the European Communities will be of interest to users of *International Organizations,* the Editors are including this pamphlet in the series.

[2] Subsequently the British, together with the Danes, Swedes, Norwegians, Austrians, Swiss, and Portuguese, formed the European Free Trade Association (EFTA) which came into being in May 1960 following the ratification of the Stockholm convention by all seven member countries.

[3] Burundi, Cameroon, Central African Republic, Chad, Congo (Brazzaville), Congo (Kinshasa), Dahomey, Gabon, Ivory Coast, Mali, Mauritania, Niger, Rwanda, Senegal, Somalia, Togo, and Upper Volta.

Headquarters of the Commission of the European Communities at Brussels, Belgium.

The Central Treaty Organization

U.S. Department of State

CENTO like its counterpart organizations SEATO (the Southeast Asia Treaty Organization) and NATO (the North Atlantic Treaty Organization) was established for purposes of mutual defense. Much of their work is now in the areas of economic and social development and it is on these topics rather than on the military aspects that these organizations produce publications available to libraries.

ORIGIN

The Central Treaty Organization (CENTO) began, as did its regional sister alliances the North Atlantic Treaty Organization (NATO) in 1949 and the Southeast Asia Treaty Organization (SEATO) in 1954, as a response of free peoples to the threat from communism. The establishment of the alliance demonstrated the determination of the Middle Eastern members, forming what has been known as the "northern tier," to preserve their independence by resisting Communist aggression or subversive penetration and by working together for stability. In addition to their membership in CENTO, Turkey belongs to NATO and Pakistan is a member of SEATO.

CENTO's existence dates from February 24, 1955, when Turkey and Iraq, consistent with articles of the U.N. Charter dealing with regional arrangements and collective security, signed the Pact of Mutual Cooperation (the Baghdad Pact). The Pact was open to accession by any other states "actively concerned with security and peace in this region." The United Kingdom joined the alliance on April 5, Pakistan on September 23, and Iran on November 3, 1955. After the revolution in Iraq overthrowing the Hashemite regime on July 14, 1958, that country took no further part in the work of the Pact and formally withdrew on March 24, 1959. The headquarters was transferred from Baghdad to Ankara in August 1958, and the new name, Central Treaty Organization, was adopted on August 19, 1959.

Although the formation of the Pact of Mutual Cooperation in 1955 was stimulated by the security concerns of the post-World War II period, the roots of cooperation among the countries of the region actually reach considerably further back. The states of the Turco-Iranian plateau had recognized a certain community of interests in the Saadabad Pact which was concluded by Turkey, Iran, Iraq, and Afghanistan in 1937. And in 1954 Pakistan and Turkey had signed an agreement for friendly cooperation as a result of their desire for closer relations.

CENTO, however, has broadened and deepened collaboration among the regional member states, within its own framework as well as in other ways. Drawing upon their experience in CENTO, Iran, Pakistan, and Turkey formed an organization in 1964 known as Regional Cooperation for Development (RCD) to promote the economic development of the area.

The U.S. Role

Although the United States had encouraged the formation of the Pact, it did not itself become a formal member, accepting instead an invitation to participate in Council meetings in the role of an observer. The United States did become, however, a formal participant in the Organization's committees, and since the early years of the alliance has supported and taken an active part in all its work.

When the Ministerial Council met in London on July 28 and 29, 1958, shortly after the Iraqi revolution, Iran, Pakistan, Turkey, the United Kingdom, and the United States signed a declaration which reaffirmed the determination of the mem-

SOURCE: U.S. Department of State. *THE CENTRAL TREATY ORGANIZATION.* Washington, Government Printing Office, 1970 (International Organizations Series. No. 1)

ber states to continue the alliance and which stated that the United States "in the interest of world peace, and pursuant to existing Congressional authorization, agrees to cooperate with the nations making this Declaration for their security and defense, and will promptly enter into agreements designed to give effect to this cooperation."

Subsequently, the United States signed identical bilateral executive agreements with Iran, Pakistan, and Turkey on March 5, 1959. These agreements were executed pursuant to authority created by the Mutual Security Act of 1954 and the Joint Resolution of the Congress in 1957 to Promote Peace and Stability in the Middle East (the Eisenhower Doctrine). The agreements provided that in case of aggression against any of the three countries, the United States, in accordance with the U.S. Constitution, would take such appropriate action, including the use of armed forces, as may be mutually agreed upon and as envisaged in the Joint Resolution. The United States reaffirmed that it would continue to furnish the three countries such military and economic assistance as may be mutually agreed upon.

The agreements provide that the security arrangements would be called into effect only in the event of Communist aggression as envisaged by the Congressional measures under which the agreements were developed. Secretary of State Christian A. Herter's opening statement at the Pact's 1959 Ministerial Council meeting in Washington, D.C., made clear that United States support of the organization was designed to resist Communist aggression.

ORGANIZATION

The Council

The Council is the highest body of the Central Treaty Organization. It provides a forum for continuous consultation on political and economic issues as well as military matters affecting the mutual interests of the member states.

The Council meets at the Ministerial level and at the Deputy level. Ministerial meetings have usually been held annually, with each CENTO capital in turn acting as host and providing the chairman. Each country is normally represented by its Foreign Minister. The Council, which makes all decisions on the basis of unanimity, reviews the work accomplished through subordinate bodies of the Organization, approves future programs, and exchanges views on international issues of common interest.

Continuing consultation and detailed direction are accomplished by regular meetings of the Council at the Deputy level. Each CENTO country's Ambassador to Turkey serves as a Deputy on the Council. Turkey is represented by an official of ambassadorial rank from the Turkish Foreign Ministry. The Council of Deputies usually meets once a fortnight in Ankara and is chaired by CENTO's Secretary General, Turgut Menemencioglu.

While the United States attends Council meetings as an observer, it participates fully in the discussions. The Secretary of State heads the U.S. delegation at the Ministerial meetings, and the U.S. Ambassador to Turkey attends those at the Deputy level.

Four major committees are responsible to the Council: the Military Committee, the Economic Committee, the Counter-Subversion Committee, and the Liaison Committee. These committees meet once a year in a CENTO capital and serve to keep the Council in close touch with the work CENTO does in specialized fields. They review and guide the work of subordinate bodies and prepare reports of their activities for the Council. The United States is a full member of all four committees of the Council.

The Military Committee

CENTO's military work lies mainly in coordination of existing military resources of its members. The Military Committee makes recommendations to the Council with a view to strengthening the military security of member countries and insuring their effective cooperation in defense matters. At the annual meetings of the Committee each country has usually been represented by its Chief of Staff.

Like the Council, the Military Committee is represented by a group of Deputies permanently stationed at Ankara and available for decisions at any time. This group of five military officers (Permanent Military Deputies Group—PMDG) carries out the decisions of the Military Committee and supervises a Combined Military Planning Staff (CMPS) stationed with the CENTO Secretariat at Ankara. The CMPS, a small staff of experienced military officers drawn from the five participating countries, prepares and coordinates plans and combined training exercises.

The Economic Committee

This Committee is responsible to the Council for CENTO's regional economic development program. Member states are represented at the annual meetings by ministers or other top-ranking officials. Activities undertaken at the Committee's direction range from railroad construction to seminars on mineral development and practical training in marketing fruits and vegetables.

The Economic Committee is assisted by an Economic Experts Group, which meets annually at CENTO headquarters to review in technical detail the year's work of all subcommittees; and by an Economic Steering Group, which meets regularly in Ankara to provide continuing guidance for the economic activities, especially in the intervals between the annual meetings of the Economic Committee and the Economic Experts Group.

Subcommittees are entrusted with implementing CENTO's economic program in certain fields. There are, for instance, subcommittees on communications, agriculture, and health. There are also a number of "working parties" in such specialized areas as mining, agricultural marketing, cholera, development of ranges, narcotics control, and agricultural statistics. One of the working parties supervises the CENTO Multilateral Technical Cooperation Fund, a special arrangement under which Iran, Pakistan, and Turkey offer technical training at their national facilities to selected trainees from the other two regional countries. The result is a sharing within the region of skills and experience available in one regional country but not in another.

The Council for Scientific Education and Research evaluates and approves for the Economic Committee those regional scientific and research activities recommended by a Scientific Coordinating Board. The Board administers CENTO's scientific program which is financed through a Multilateral Science Fund.

Counter-Subversion Committee

This Committee advises the Council on how best to meet and counter Communist efforts to weaken the CENTO regional governments through subversion.

The Liaison Committee

The Liaison Committee supplements the work of the Counter-Subversion Committee by facilitating the exchange of information among the CENTO countries on questions relating to the security of the region.

The Secretariat

The Secretariat is CENTO's permanent administrative and operational agency. It is located in Ankara and is headed by a Secretary General who is responsible to the Council for the conduct of all Secretariat operations. The Secretary General also serves as Chairman of the Council of Deputies. A high-ranking Turkish civilian official is currently filling the post; previously the position was held by similarly high-ranking government officials from Iran and Pakistan. The Secretary General is appointed by the Council. The term of office is normally 3 years, but may be extended.

The Secretariat administers the programs determined by the various bodies of the alliance. It provides services for the meetings of the Council, the major Committees, and the subordinate bodies; advises the Council on technical matters; maintains liaison with the NATO and SEATO Secretariats; and promotes public knowledge and understanding of CENTO and its activities. In this work the Secretary General directs a staff drawn from the five participating countries, which bear equal shares of the Secretariat's expenses. English is CENTO's working language.

WORK OF THE ALLIANCE

Cooperating for Defense

The military work of CENTO lies principally in the fields of planning, coordination, and training. The Combined Military Planning Staff, under the direction of the Permanent Military Deputies Group, performs this work since a unified command structure has not been established. U.S. and

U.K. military assistance to the regional members has been provided for the most part on a bilateral basis.

Some aspects of the CMP's planning are tested in the regular series of war games and combined military exercises that constitute the CENTO training program. Annual regional air defense exercises test the readiness and capacities of installations and equipment, and offer personnel an opportunity to work together under simulated wartime conditions. This element of actual experience in carrying out a complex military operation with forces drawn from different countries is an important part of the annual maritime exercise, known by its code name MIDLINK, which is staged off the coast of Iran.

Other annual exercises for which the Combined Military Planning Staff is responsible include air search and rescue, and small arms competitions. NATO officers are invited to observe these testing and training maneuvers from time to time, and CENTO representatives attend some NATO exercises.

Another duty of the Planning Staff is to draw up standardization agreements on military procedures and terminology. Standardized procedures make it possible, for example, for ships of the different CENTO navies to operate together as a single unit. Similarly, if ground forces are to have close air support by planes of another country, both want to be very certain that visual, radio, and other communications are mutually understood. Many such standardization agreements have been drawn up and approved, covering everything from mapping specifications to combat communications. The CMPS also is charged with assuring that the CENTO standardization agreements are compatible with NATO specifications, and maintains constant liaison with NATO for this purpose.

Regular conferences, stemming from CMPS responsibilities for coordination, are held on technical military subjects directly related to potential CENTO combined operations. Senior officers from the five participating countries gather to discuss such topics as air defense coordination, naval planning, communications, mapping, and military medicine. The exchanges serve to keep officers up to date on current practices in each of the countries concerned, and sometimes point up the need for new standardization agreements.

A related activity is the CENTO Professional Military Development Program, under which groups of selected officers study more generalized military subjects of professional interest. Initiated

and carried on by the United States as part of its contribution to CENTO, seminars have been held on the following topics: Military Civic Action Programs; Procedures, Methods, and Techniques of Planning within National Military Establishments; Programming within National Military Establishments; Search and Rescue; Air Support of Ground Forces; and Training of Army Officers and Non-Commissioned Officers. The proceedings and papers presented at these seminars are published for circulation among officers in the CENTO countries.

Over the years a considerable number of officers from the CENTO countries have worked together in the alliance's military activities. All have acquired valuable knowledge and experience thereby, and such cooperation has resulted in better understanding and close friendships among scores of officers of the five countries.

Cooperating for Economic Development

CENTO's regional economic development program has been the subject of increasing interest and emphasis. Benefits from completed major projects are beginning to be felt, and new cooperative endeavors are being undertaken.

CENTO economic projects are implemented in many ways. A major construction project may require advanced technical equipment not readily available in the region—from bulldozers and harbor cranes to complicated electronic gear. On projects such as building roads and railroads and developing harbors the United States and the United Kingdom have provided needed equipment, either through loans to the regional governments or by supplying the equipment directly. For more complex projects like the CENTO Microwave System or High-Frequency Radio Link, design, engineering, and installation have been done by U.S. or U.K. contractors.

In all cases the regional governments have contributed a major share of the effort in furnishing facilities, land, engineering services, construction materials, labor, and other essential ingredients. Details are worked out in bilateral agreements between the regional government and the Western partner concerned. Other projects are implemented by agreements among the regional governments only, or by an individual regional government alone, CENTO having served chiefly as a catalyst.

U.S. aid during the early years of CENTO was mostly in grants for specific projects such as a total of about $20 million for the Microwave System. Later U.S. financing for major capital projects was through long-term loans. Recently, grants to finance technical and scientific conferences, grants to finance training workshops, and the services of experts have been provided with emphasis on the fields of agriculture, health, and education.

The United Kingdom has contributed an annual sum, raised in 1966 from 850,000 pounds sterling to £1 million, for financing certain CENTO economic development activities. About half of this amount has been for supplies, equipment, and engineering services for projects such as roadbuilding and the High-Frequency Radio Link. The other half has been earmarked for technical assistance such as providing advisers, teachers, and fellowships for advanced training in the United Kingdom.

Communications

The great need for better communications in an integrated pattern throughout the CENTO region led to early emphasis on telecommunications, roads, railways, ports, and a modern airway system. At the time of CENTO's inception, no railways or telegraph lines crossed common boundaries to link the regional members. Only a few vehicles attempted to travel the one hazardous mountain road between Iran and Turkey, or the desert track crossing the Iran-Pakistan border. Telephone and telegraph traffic among the three countries had to be routed through Europe, usually via London. Aircraft were almost helpless in bad weather due to lack of ground controls.

The CENTO High-Frequency Radio Link connects Dacca, Rawalpindi, Karachi, Tehran, Ankara, and Istanbul directly with London, and thereby with the outside world in general, by shortwave radio telephone and teleprinter circuits. There is also a link between Tehran and Khorramshahr in southern Iran.

A major United States-supported joint capital project is the construction of a Turkish-Iranian rail link, scheduled for completion in 1969. Such a link between the two national rail systems has long been a dream of the leaders of both countries. To complete this link it is necessary to connect the railheads in Mus, Turkey, and in Sharif-khaneh, Iran. The distance between them is only about 285 miles, but the route has to cross some of the most rugged terrain of that part of the world. When this rail link is completed it will stimulate economic development of previously isolated areas in both countries. It will promote trade between the two countries and give Iran an alternative to its present rail route to Europe which passes through the Soviet Union.

The nearly completed CENTO Airway System will provide the three countries of the CENTO region with a fully controlled air route meeting international standards, including radar-equipped air traffic control centers at Ankara, Tehran, and Karachi.

Other major communications projects which have been undertaken as a result of CENTO planning include construction or improvement of all-weather roads linking the three countries and development of the cargo-handling capacities of Turkish ports.

While much remains to be done, the regional countries of CENTO today are being linked as never before in history by improved communications.

Agriculture

More than three-quarters of the populations of Iran, Pakistan, and Turkey depend upon agriculture for their livelihood. Many of the agricultural problems faced by each country are similar. CENTO has made a concentrated effort to help solve these problems and to increase food production. While emphasis has been placed on spreading knowledge of modern farming and veterinary techniques, attention has also been given to the managerial, financing, and marketing aspects of agricultural production.

Numerous technical experts have been provided by the United States and the United Kingdom on a temporary basis for various agricultural projects. More than a score of conferences and seminars on specific problems have been held, and equipment has been provided to universities and other institutions concerned with agricultural and livestock-raising problems. CENTO's Agricultural Machinery and Soil Conservation Training Center provides training for 20 to 30 students from the three regional countries each year. The Center is financed by the United Kingdom, Iran, Turkey, and Pakistan.

Health

The CENTO regional economic development program has also laid stress on cooperation in the field of health:

- Malaria eradication programs have been coordinated in the three regional countries.
- An Emergency Working Party on Cholera was formed in 1966, and its recommendations led to a number of steps to stop the spread of cholera. Iran and Pakistan provided special training in anti-cholera techniques to a team of Turkish doctors; the United States provided the services of a Regional Cholera Coordinator; and a stockpile of anti-cholera material has been built up.
- Hospital administration, the training of nurses and other medical personnel, nutrition, and sanitation are among other public health topics on which CENTO conferences and seminars have been held.
- Family planning is a relatively new field of interest and concern for CENTO, and considerable progress is anticipated.

U.S. Technical Assistance

As a United States contribution to CENTO's economic program, a small, effective technical assistance program has been developed under the supervision of the Office of the United States Economic Coordinator for CENTO in Ankara, Turkey. The program was designed to foster regional cooperation for economic development by supporting technical activities related to problems common to at least two (and normally all three) of the CENTO regional countries. U.S. support is primarily given to regional conferences, symposia, traveling seminars, workshops, and short and medium-term expert advisory services and consultant contracts. Almost all major fields of economic development have been covered by these activities with concentration in the areas of agriculture, health and nutrition, education, minerals, and industrial development. Technical experts, planners, and administrators in each of these fields have been brought together from all CENTO countries to consult on mutual problems and to take advantage of each other's experience.

THE BROAD VIEW

The Central Treaty Organization is part of the web of friendly ties and cooperation that exists among Iran, Pakistan, Turkey, the United Kingdom, and the United States. It is an example of international cooperation which has put down roots.

Constructed on a foundation of common interest and goals, it complements and builds upon a wide range of active bilateral relationships. The alliance has lived through years of important changes both in the Middle East and in the world at large. It still meets a need of countries gathered together in support of their common defense and welfare.

CENTO has not only provided a security umbrella, but also has been helping to encourage economic and social development among the peoples of Iran, Pakistan, and Turkey. The promotion of a regional cooperative spirit among them has been a basic CENTO contribution toward their development of new sources of strength.

Further published information on CENTO may be requested directly from the Central Treaty Organization, Public Relations Division, Ankara, Turkey.

The proceedings and recommendations of many CENTO economic conferences and symposia are available in published form and may be requested from the United States Economic Coordinator for Cento, American Embassy, Ankara, Turkey.